JURY

SAM BARZILAY
—
United Photo Industries

ANTONIO DE LUCA
—
Self Publish, Be Happy

MARYANNE GOLON
—
The Washington Post

WHITNEY JOHNSON
—
The New Yorker

JODY QUON
—
New York

CASEY TIERNEY
—
Real Simple

PLATES

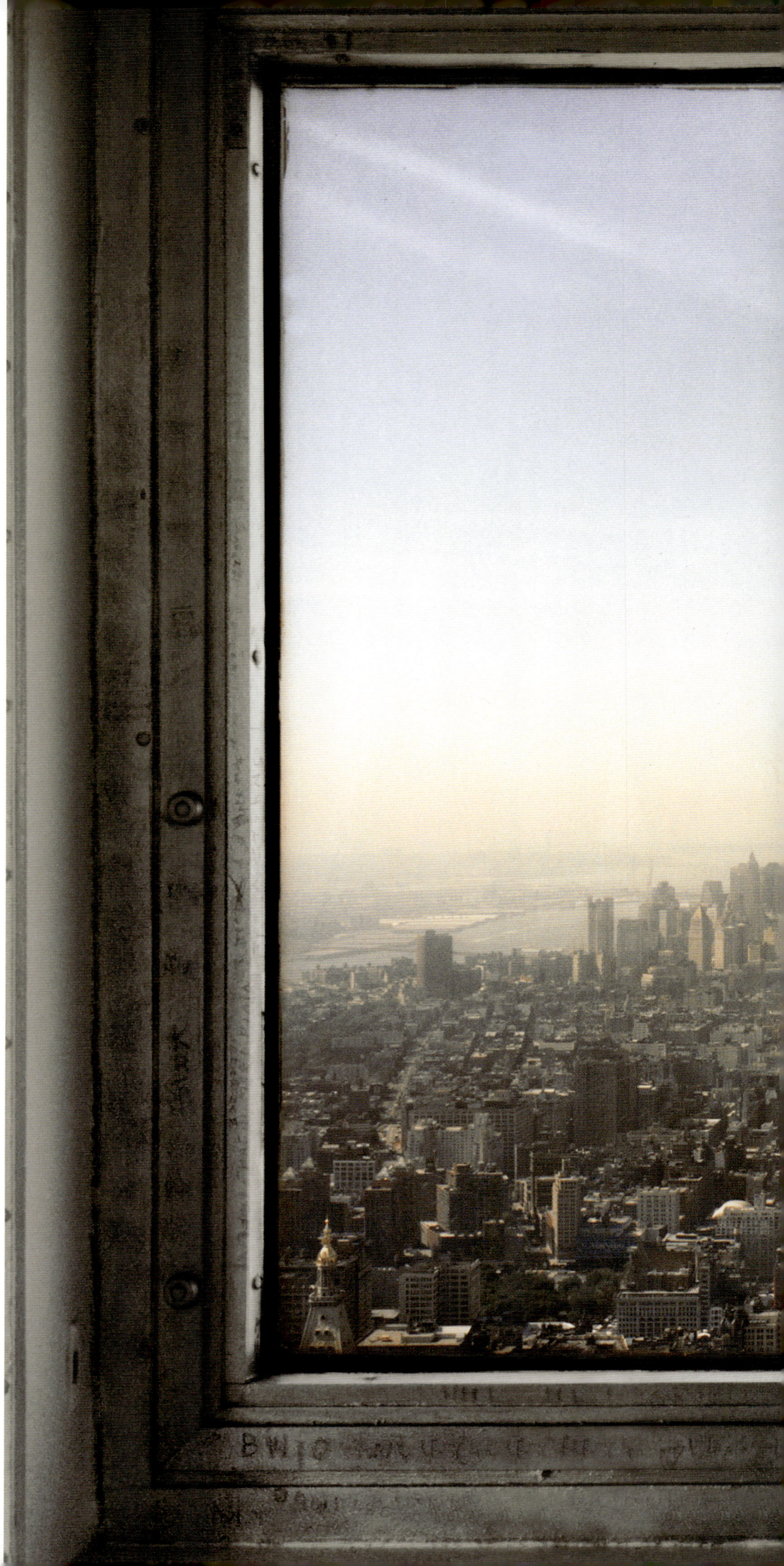

DAVID ALLEE

001

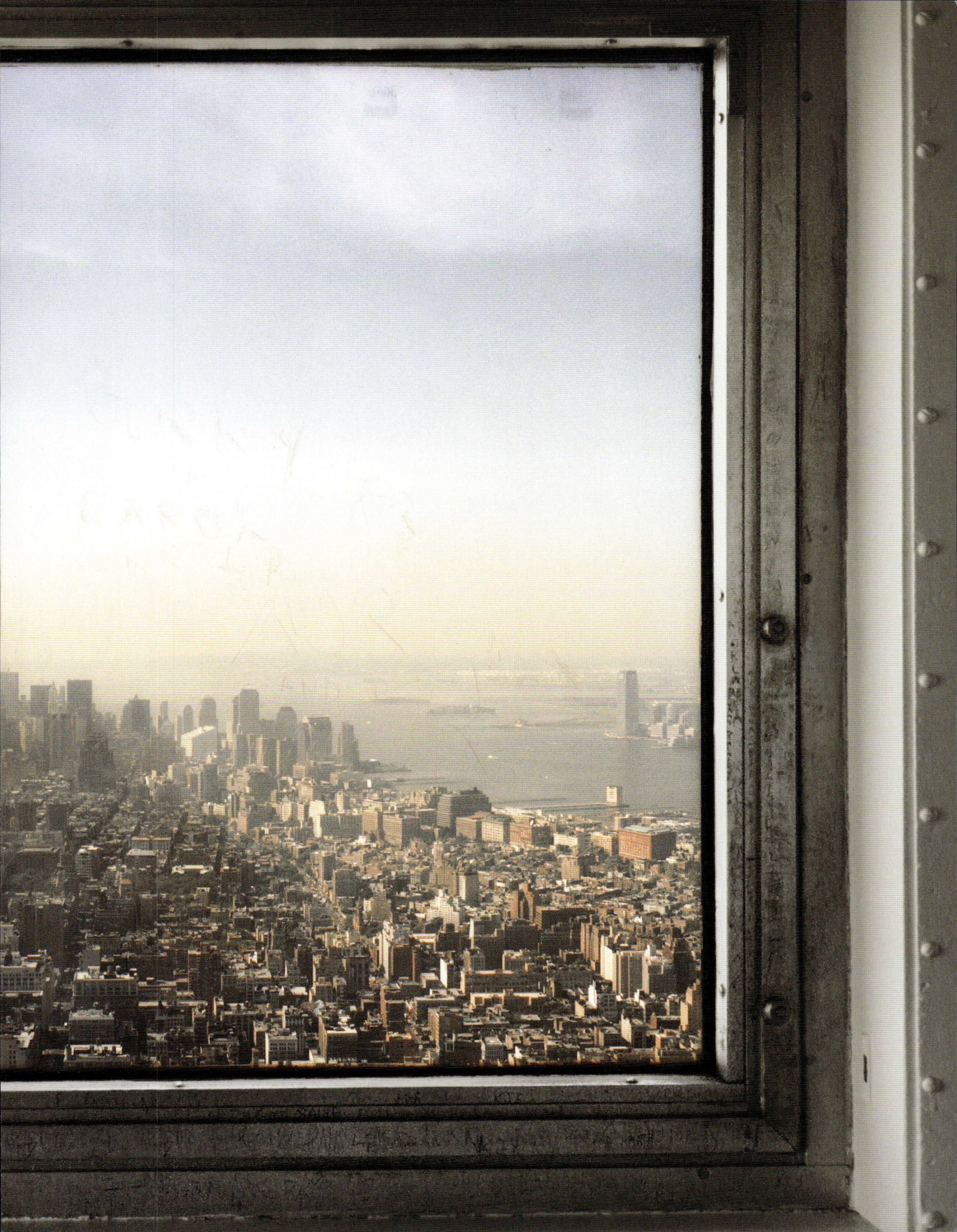

CHRISTOPHER ANDERSON

002

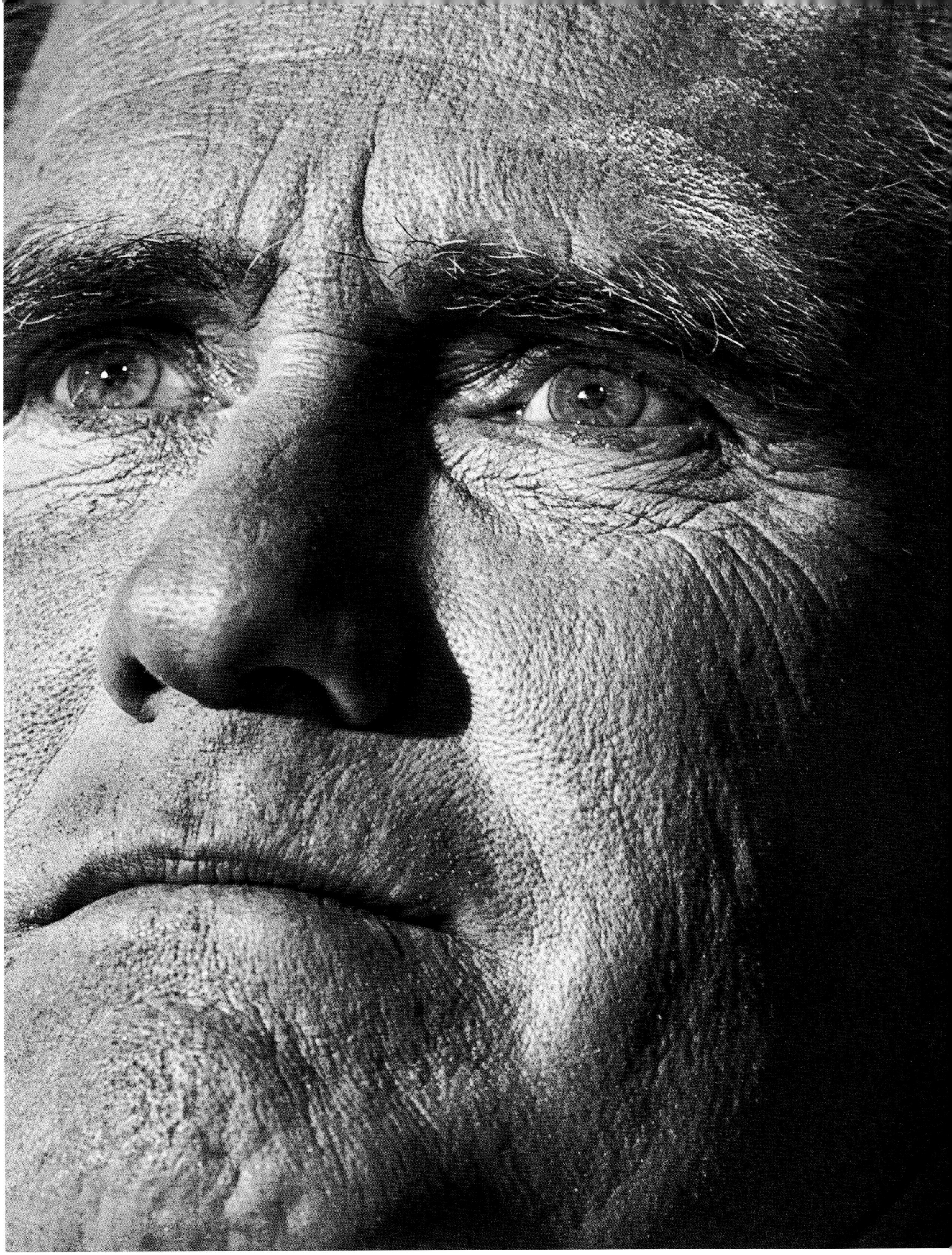

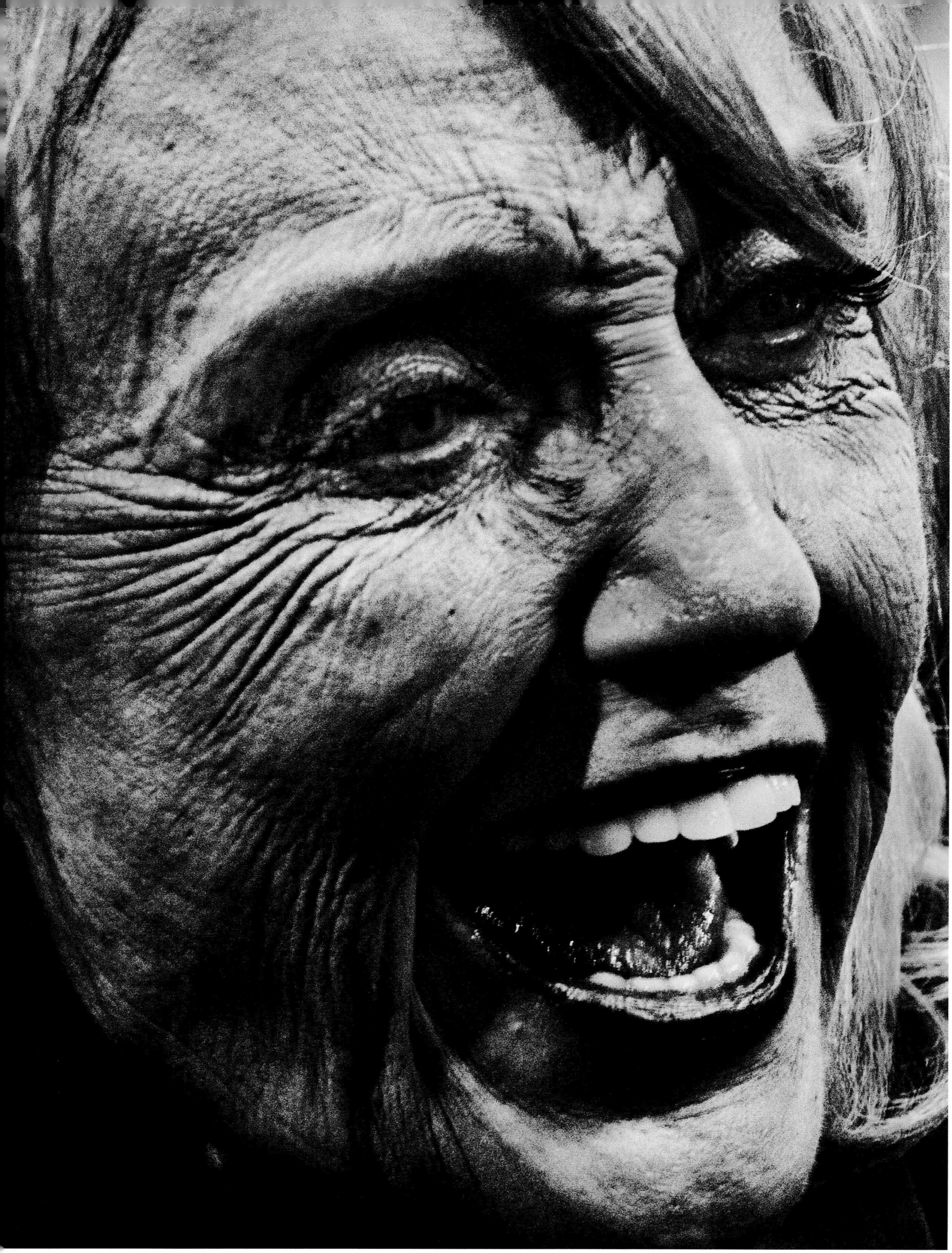

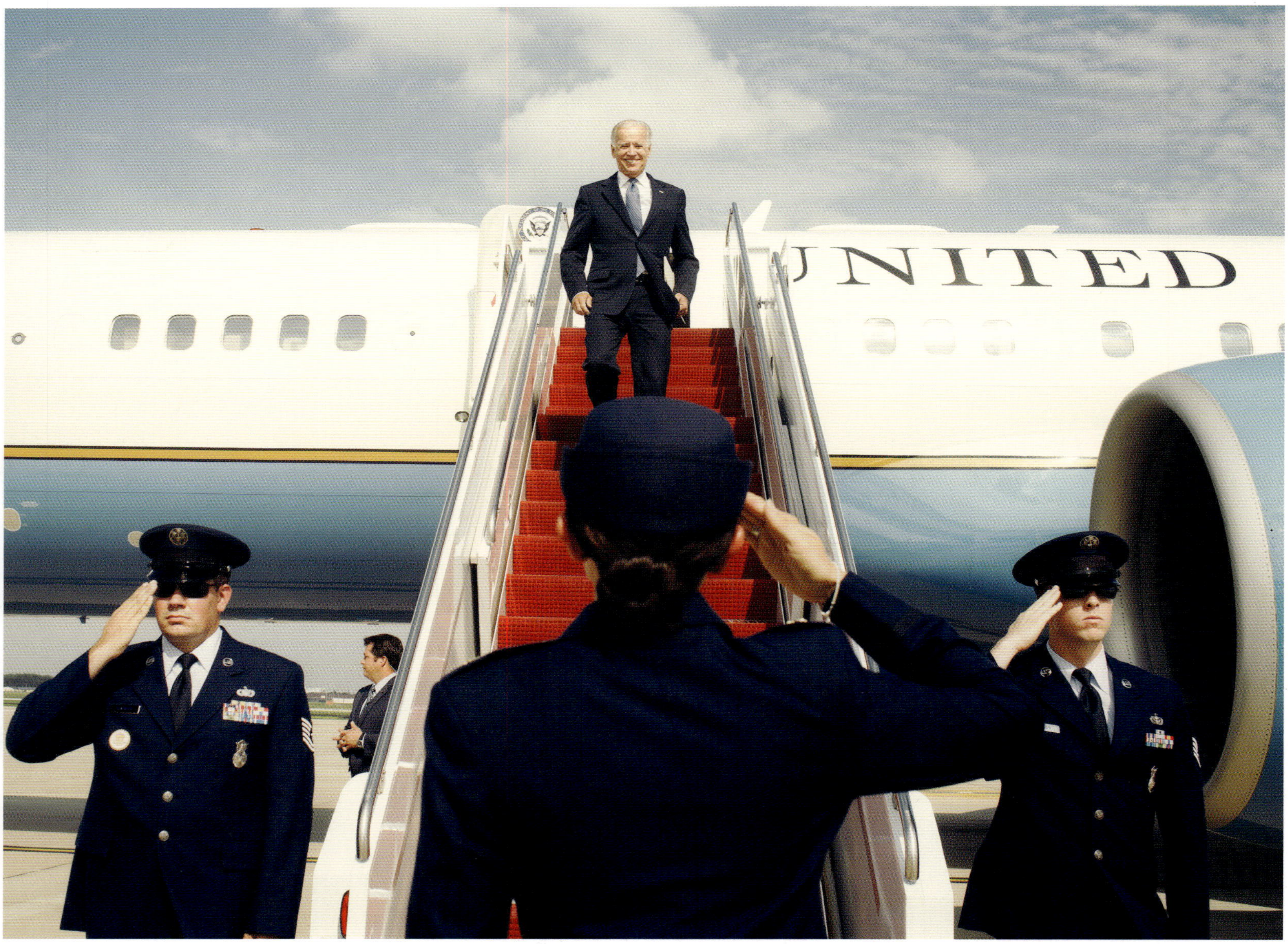
UNITED

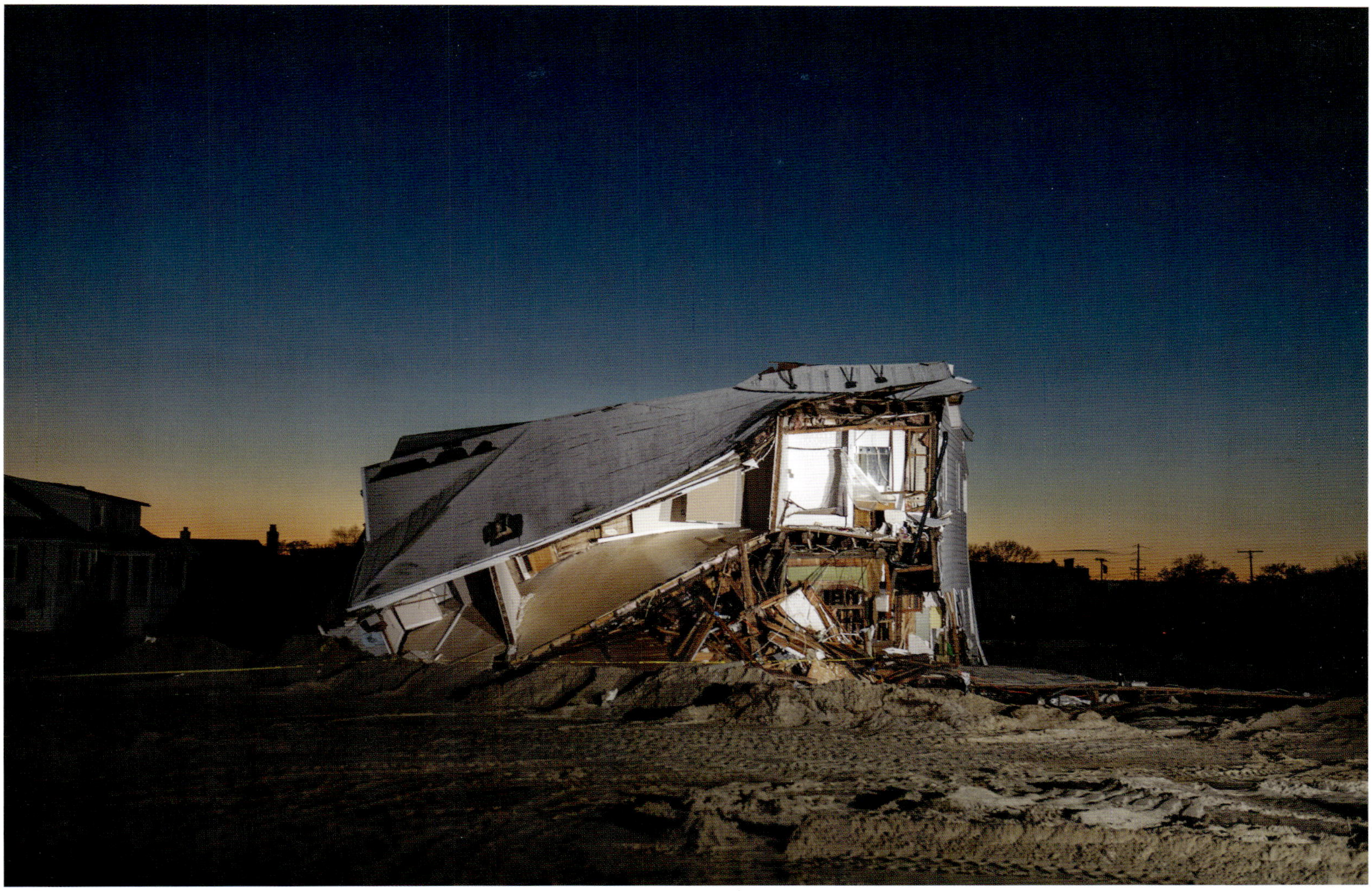

JASON ANDREW

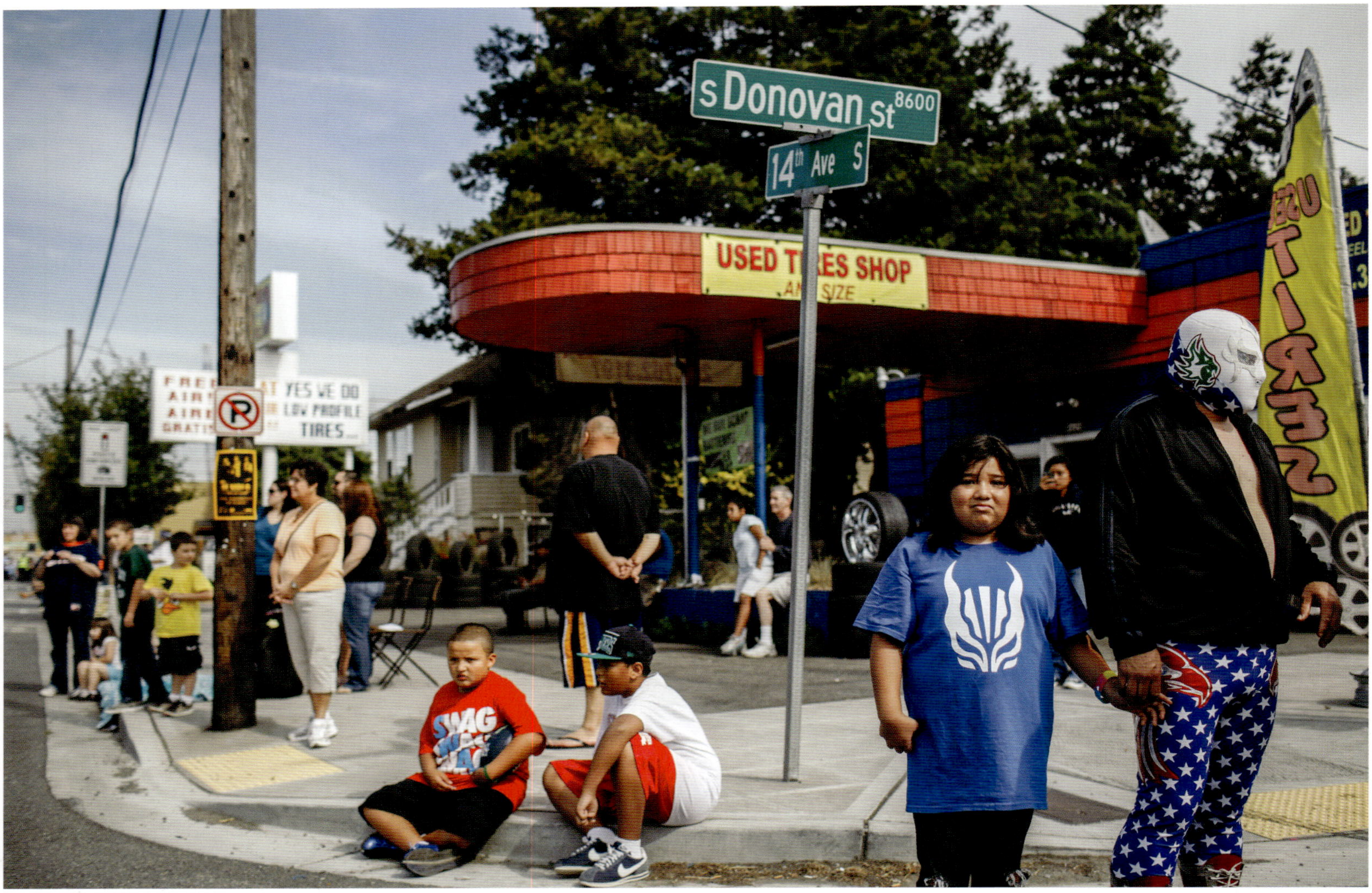

NICK ADAMS

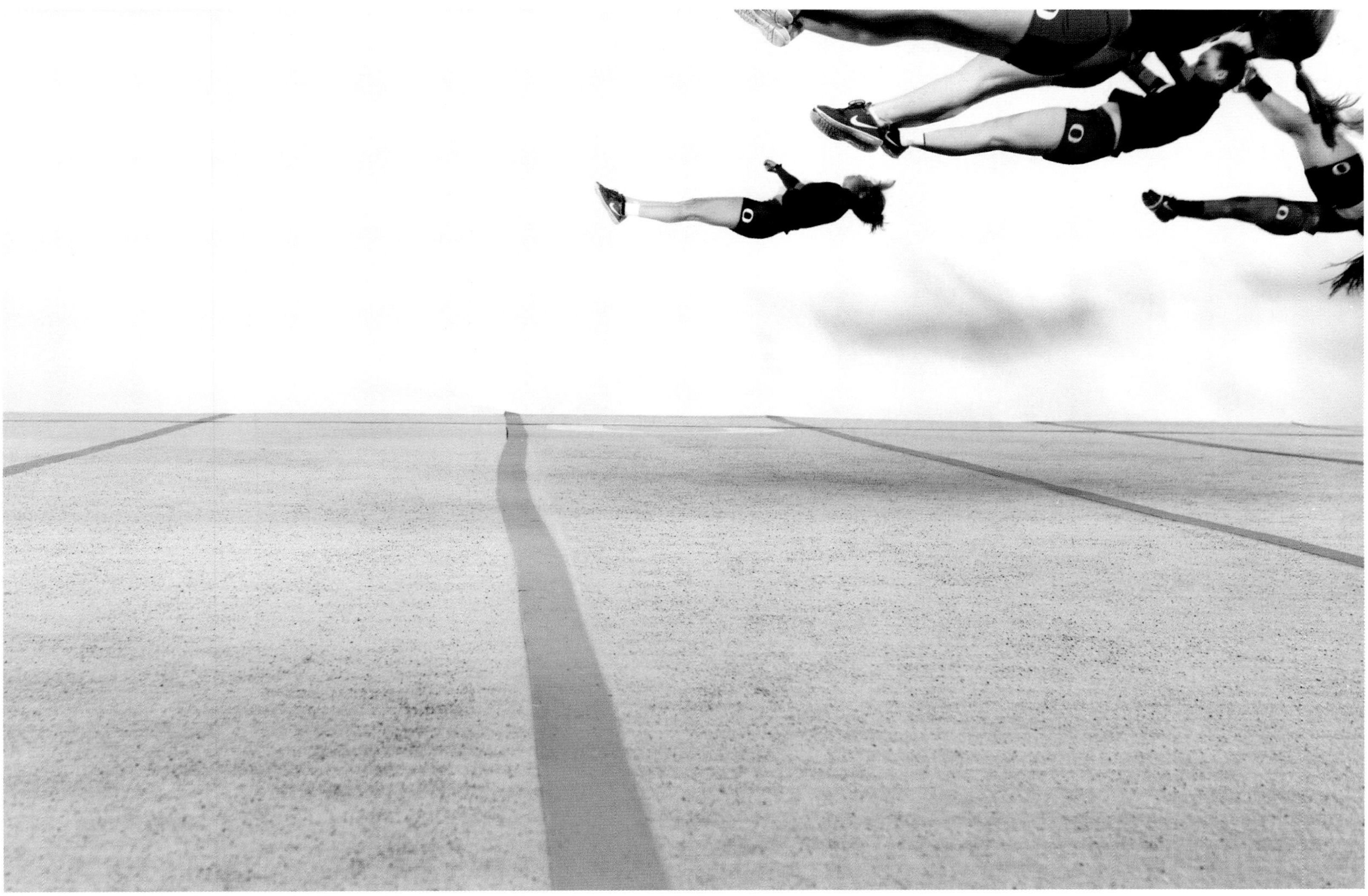

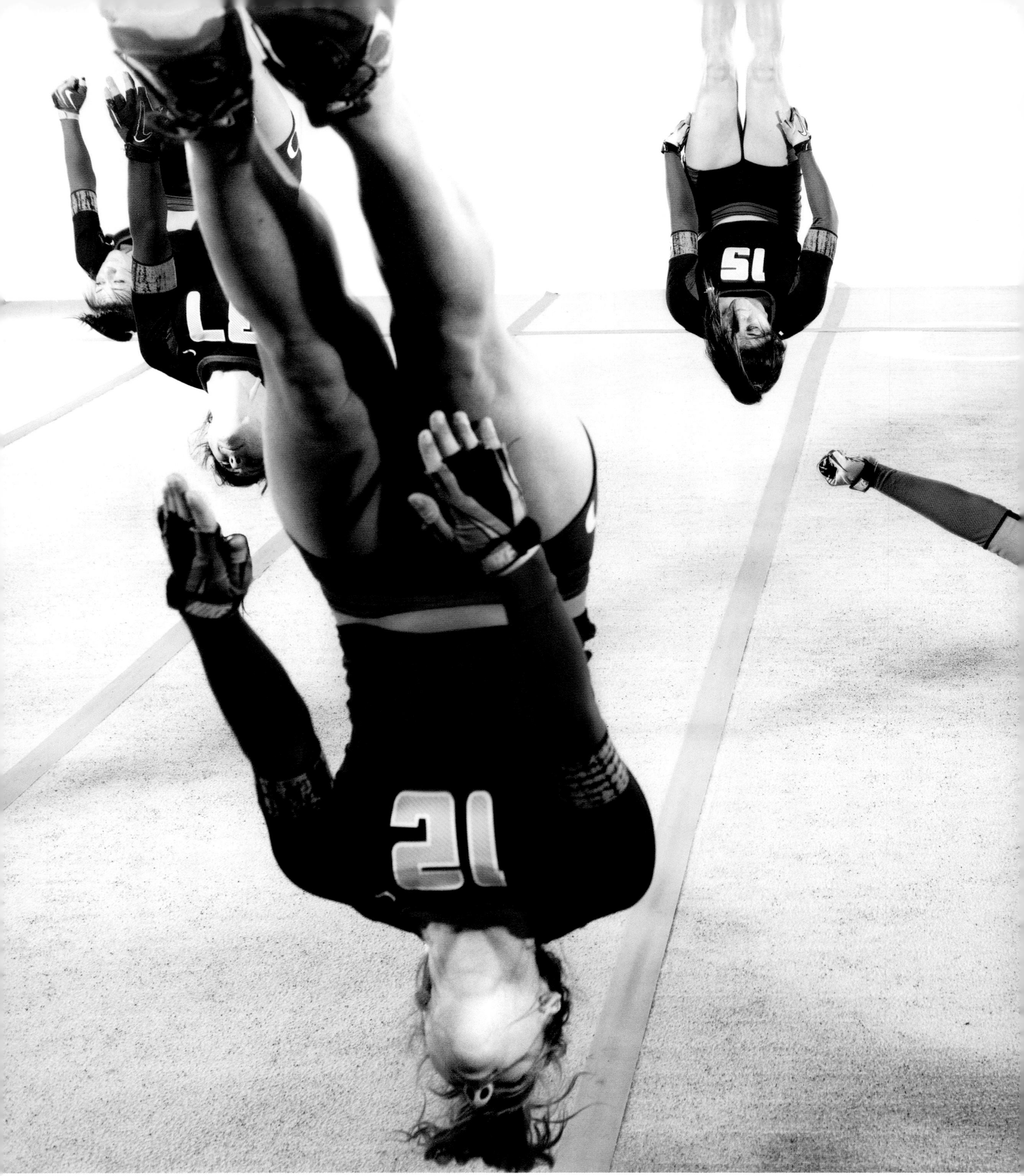

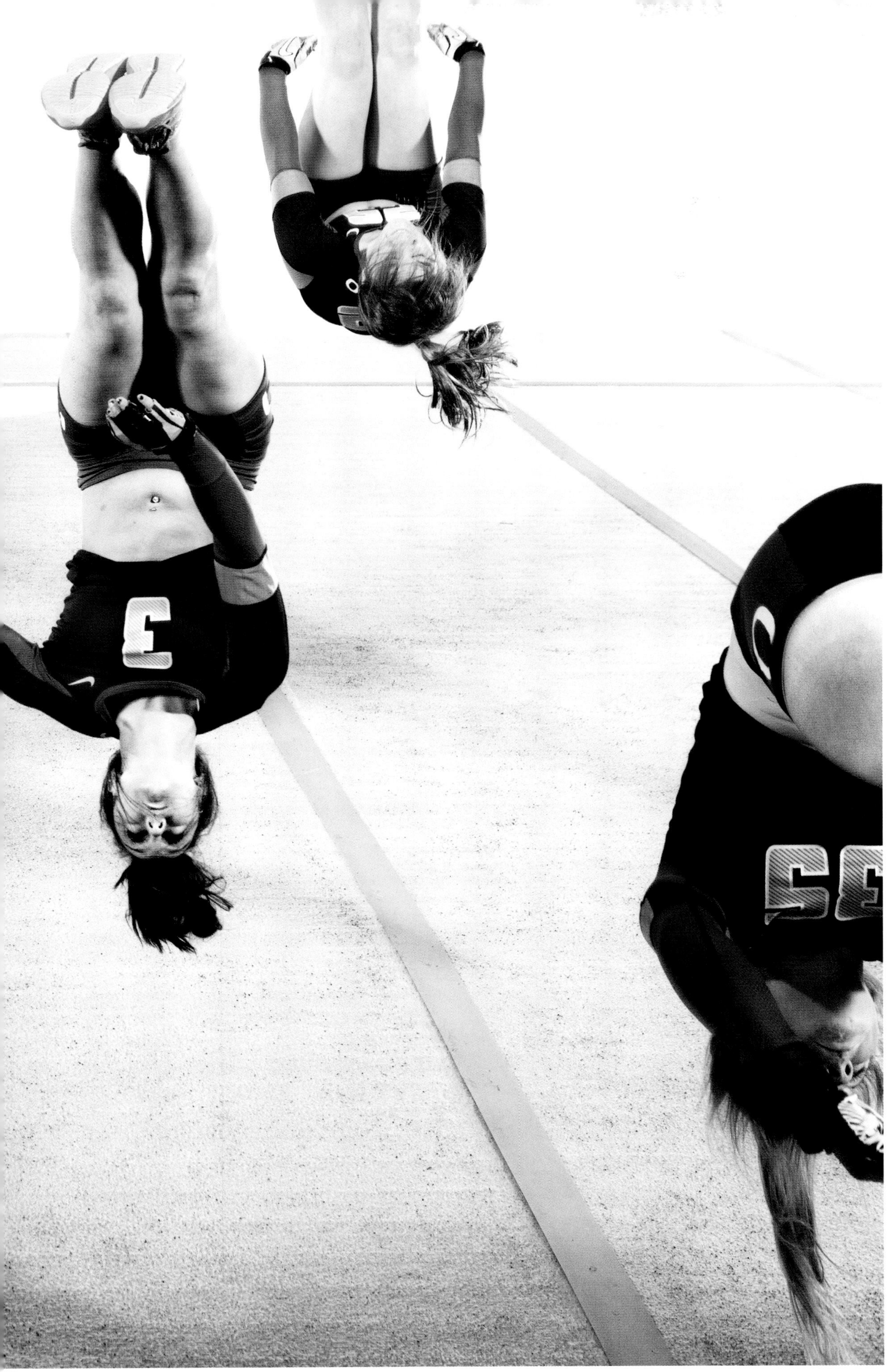

HOLLY ANDRES

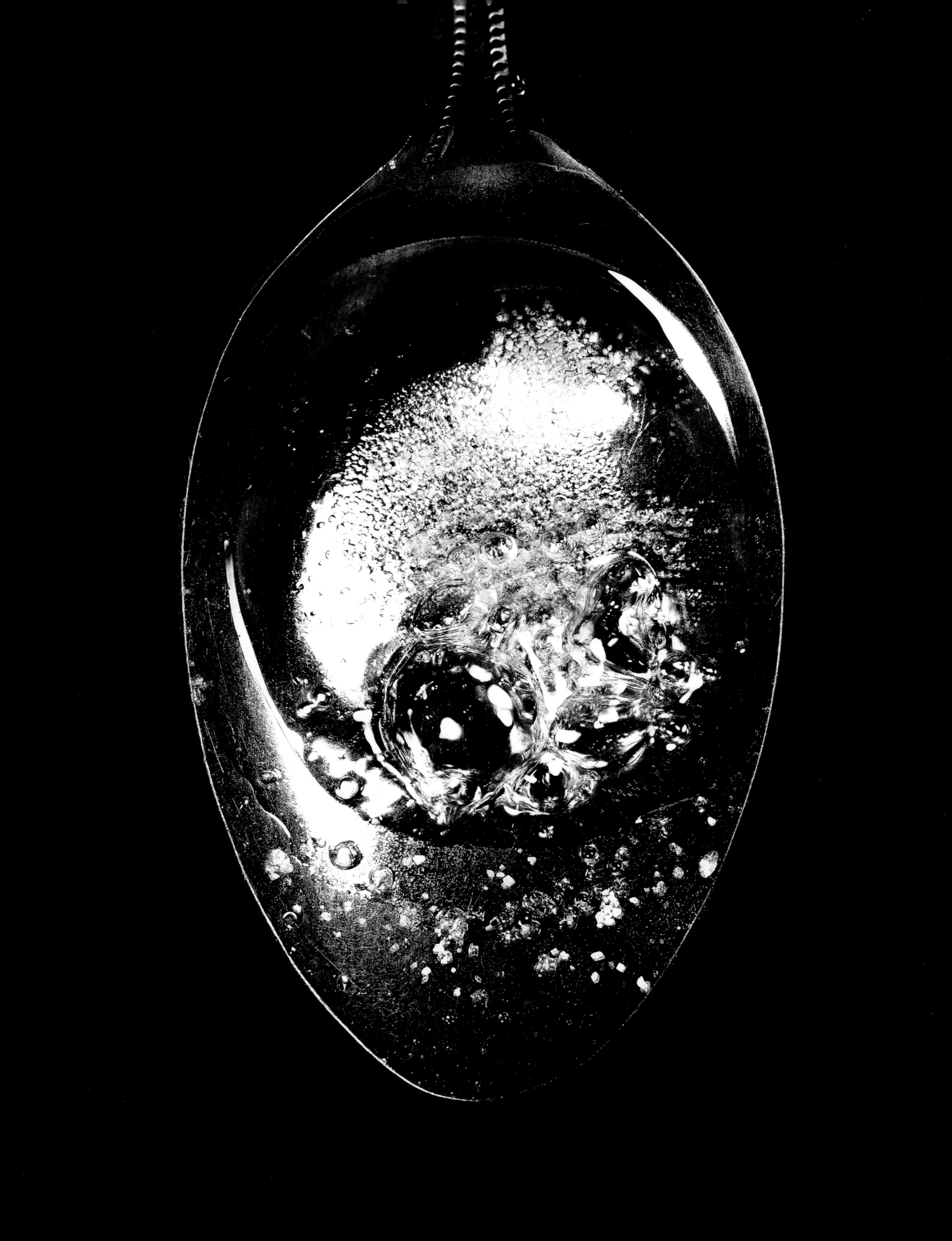

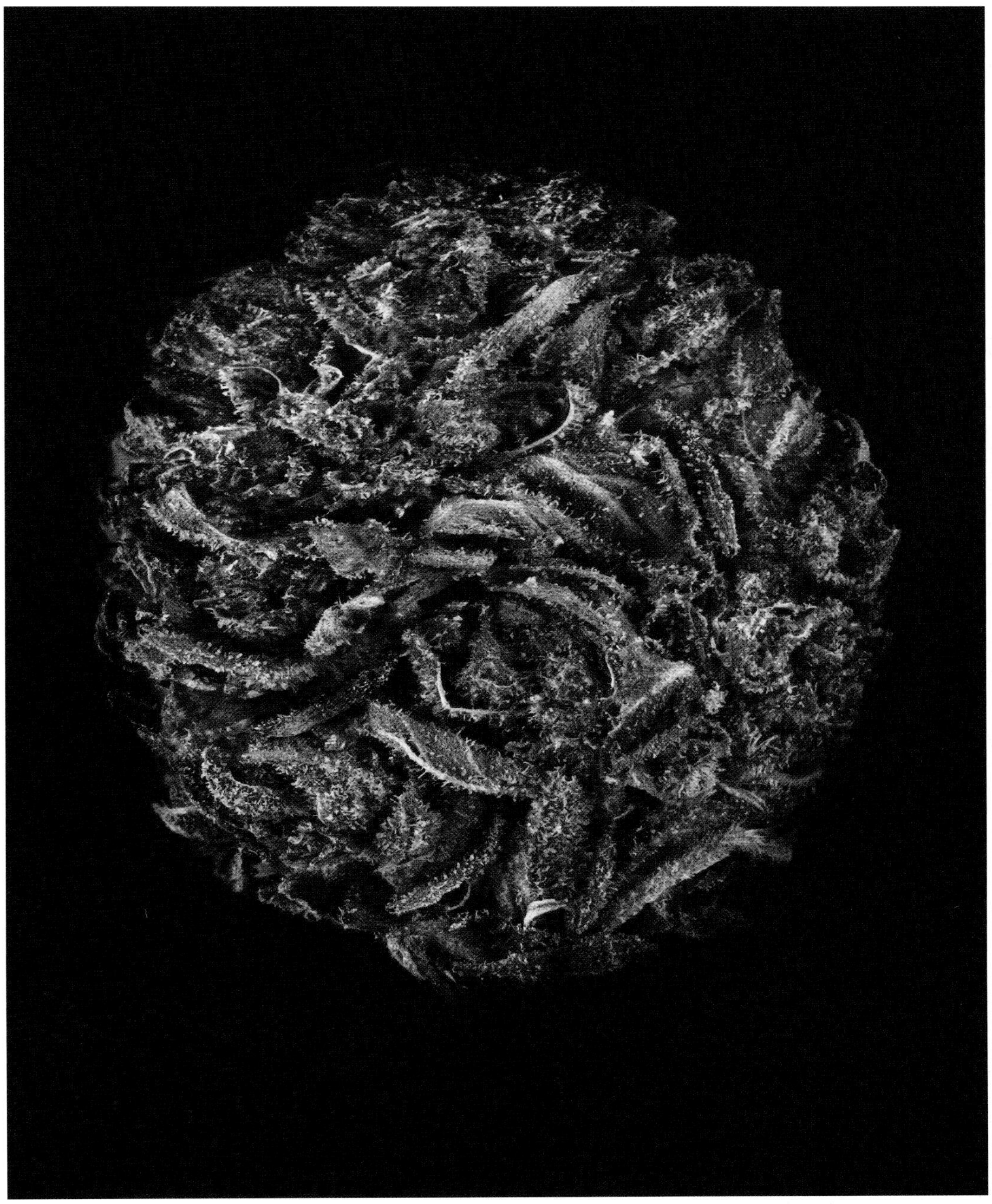

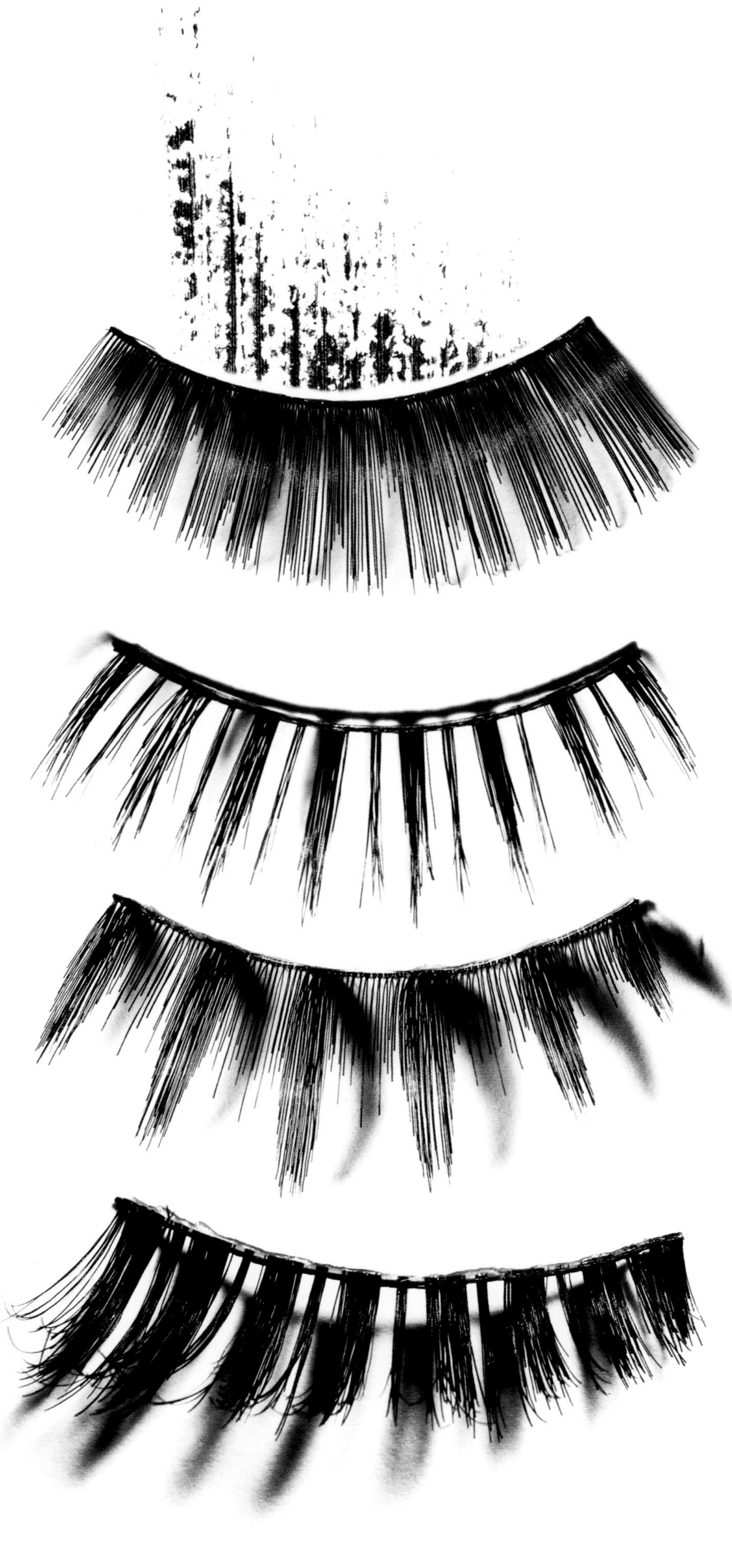

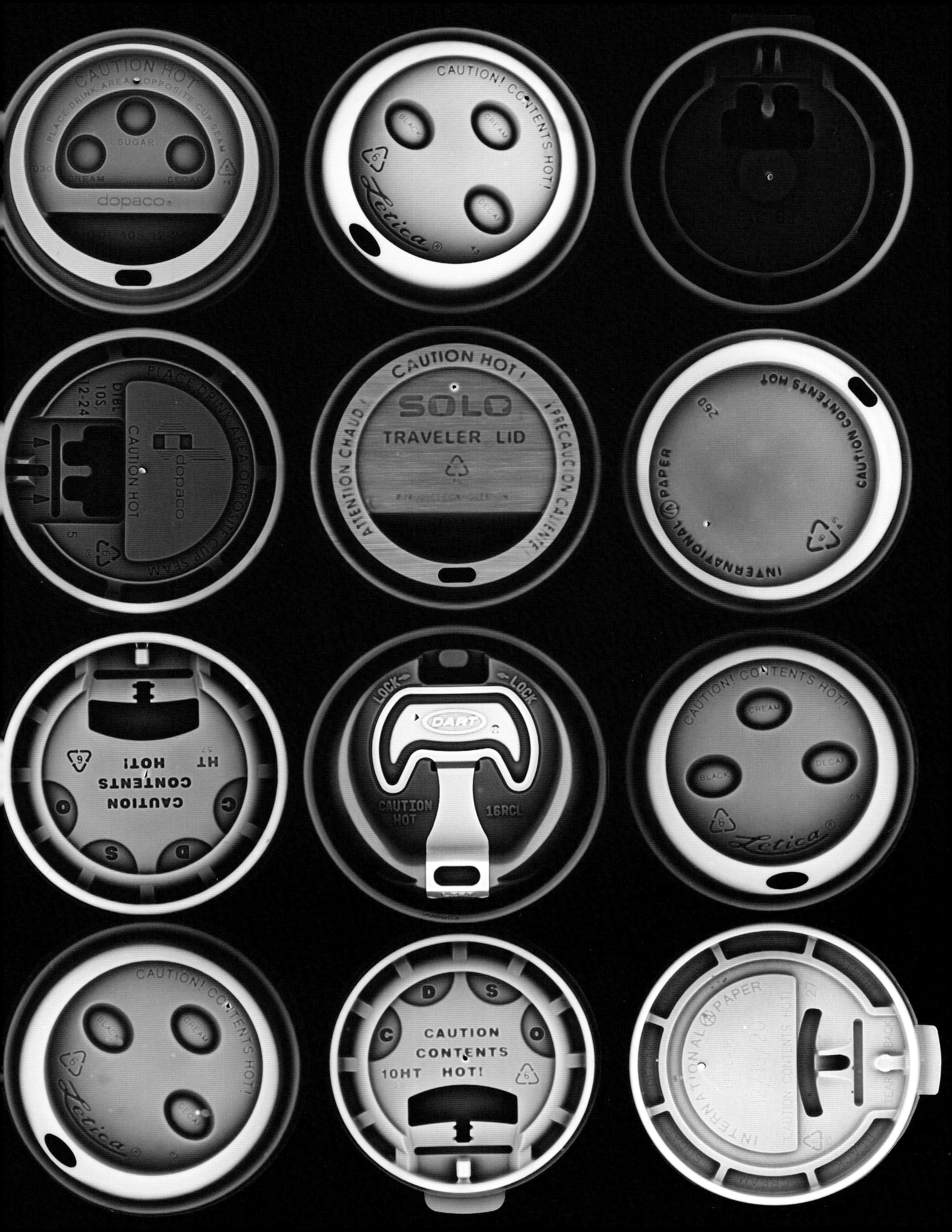

CAUTION HOT
PLACE DRINK AREA OPPOSITE CUP SEAM
SUGAR
CREAM
DECAF
dopaco
CAUTION! CONTENTS HOT!
BLACK
CREAM
DECAF
Lotica
CAUTION HOT
dopaco
CAUTION HOT !
SOLO
TRAVELER LID
ATTENTION CHAUD !
PRECAUCION CALIENTE
CAUTION CONTENTS HOT
INTERNATIONAL PAPER
CAUTION CONTENTS HOT!
LOCK
LOCK
DART
CAUTION HOT
16RCL
CAUTION! CONTENTS HOT!
CREAM
BLACK
DECAF
Lotica
CAUTION! CONTENTS HOT!
BLACK
CREAM
DECAF
Lotica
D
S
C
O
CAUTION CONTENTS
10HT HOT!
INTERNATIONAL PAPER

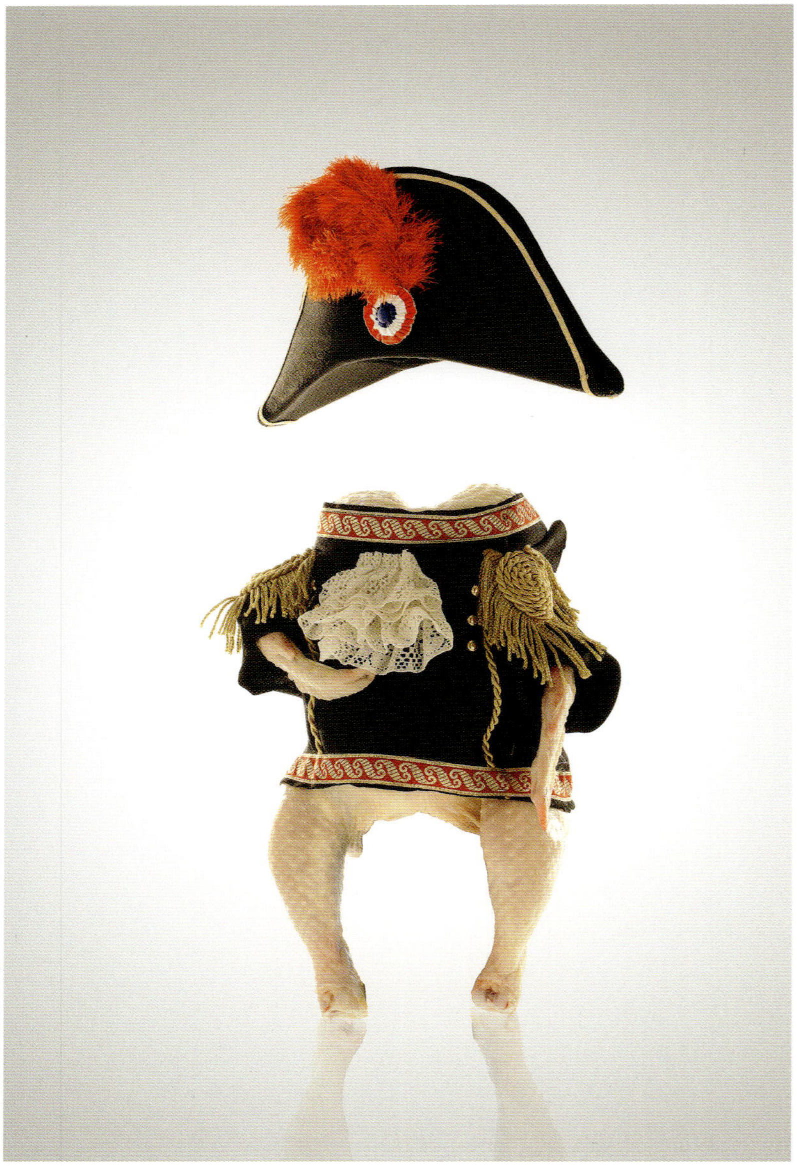

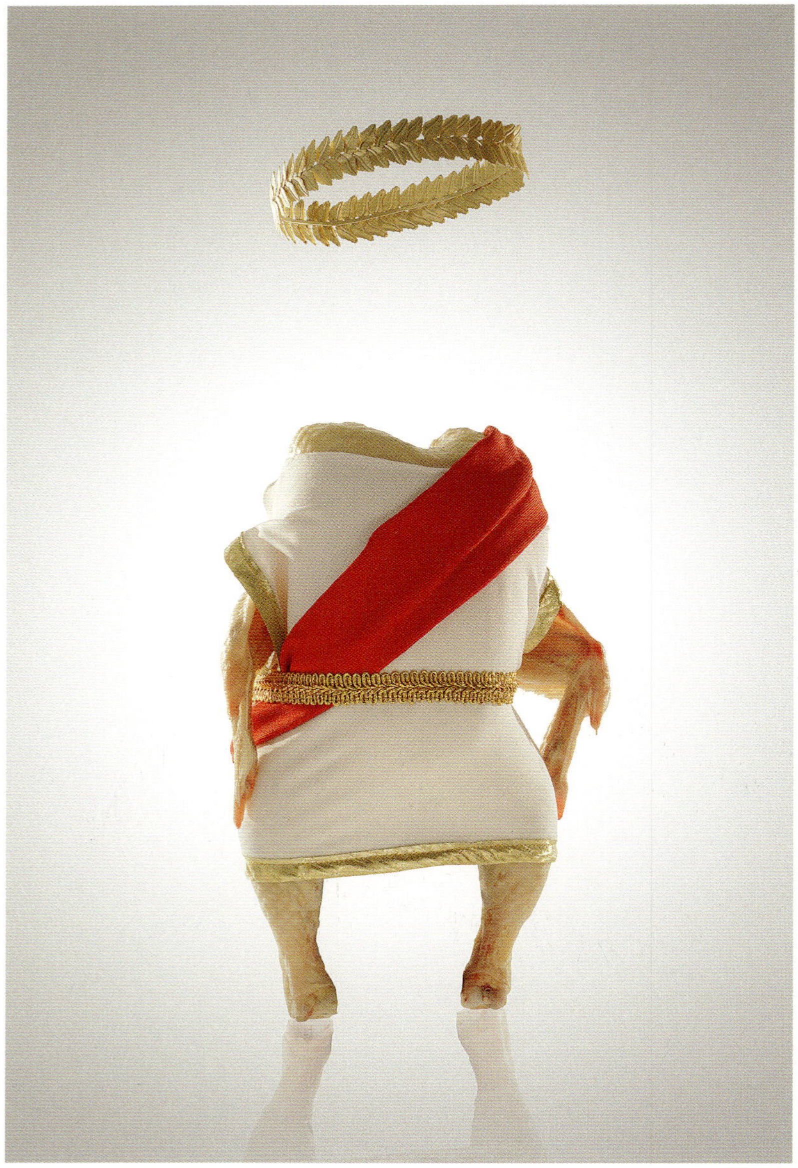

TIMOTHY ARCHIBALD

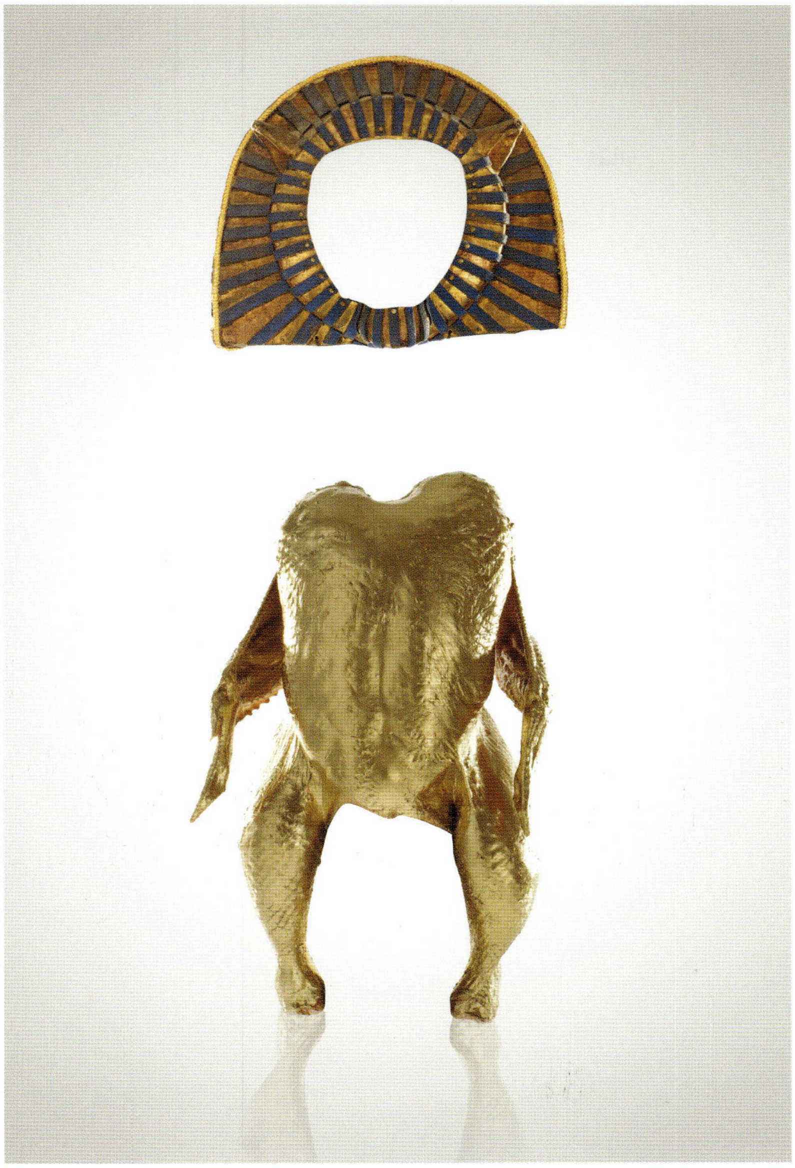
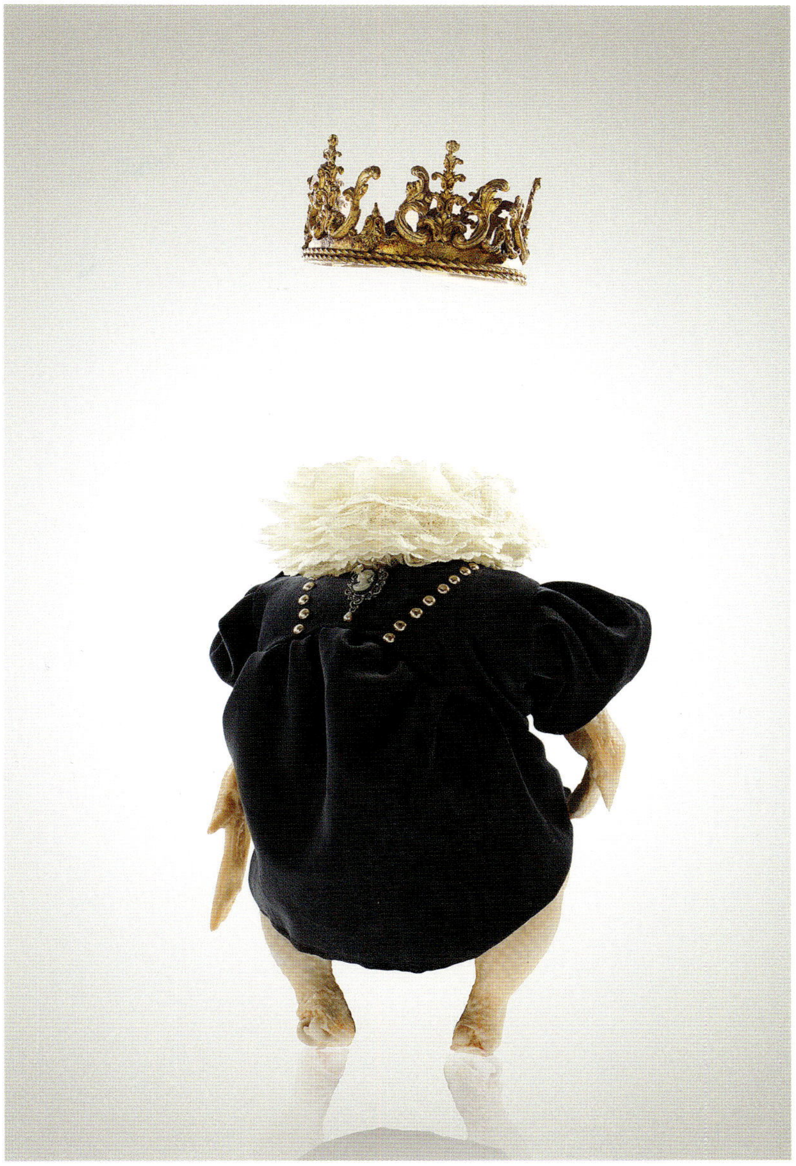

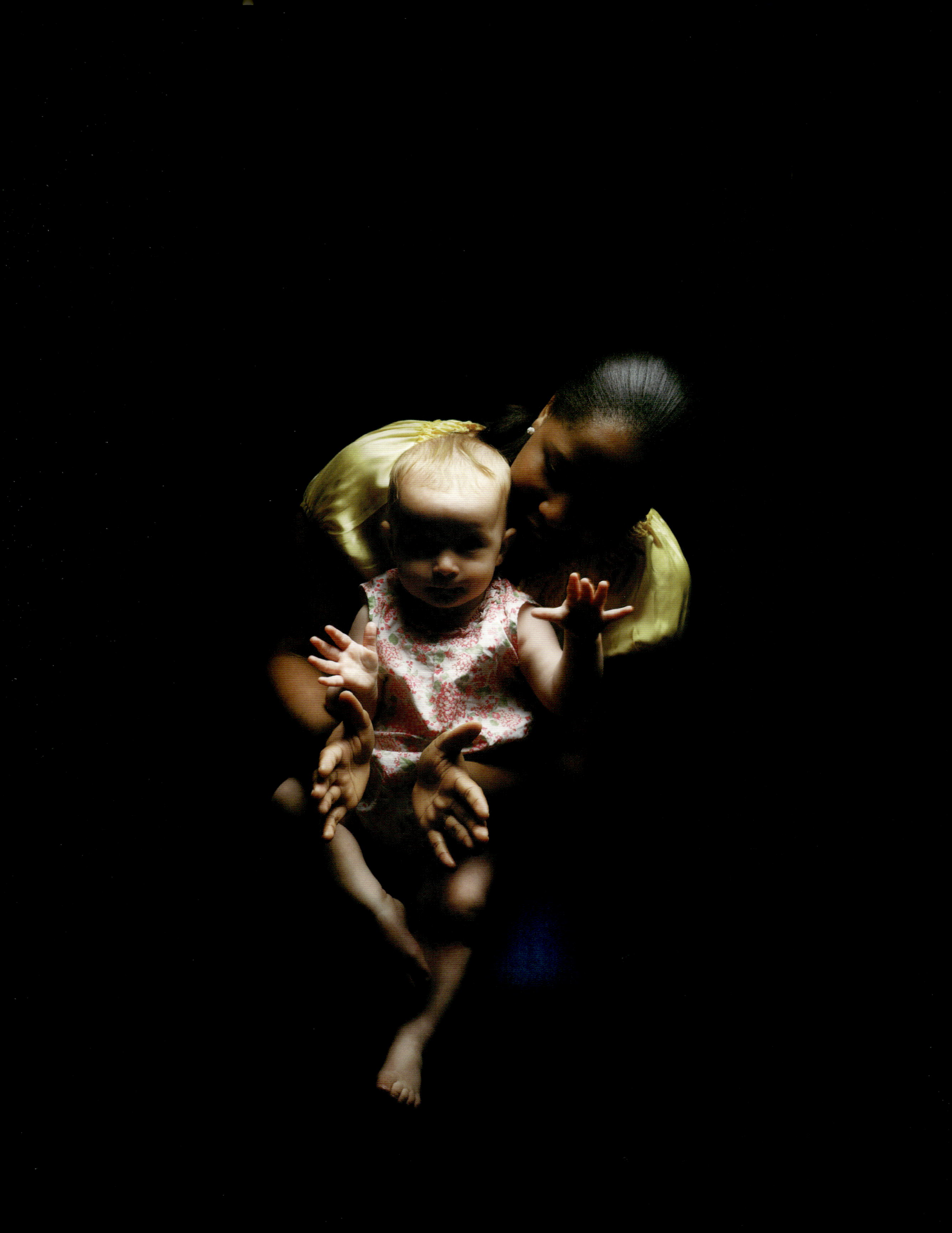

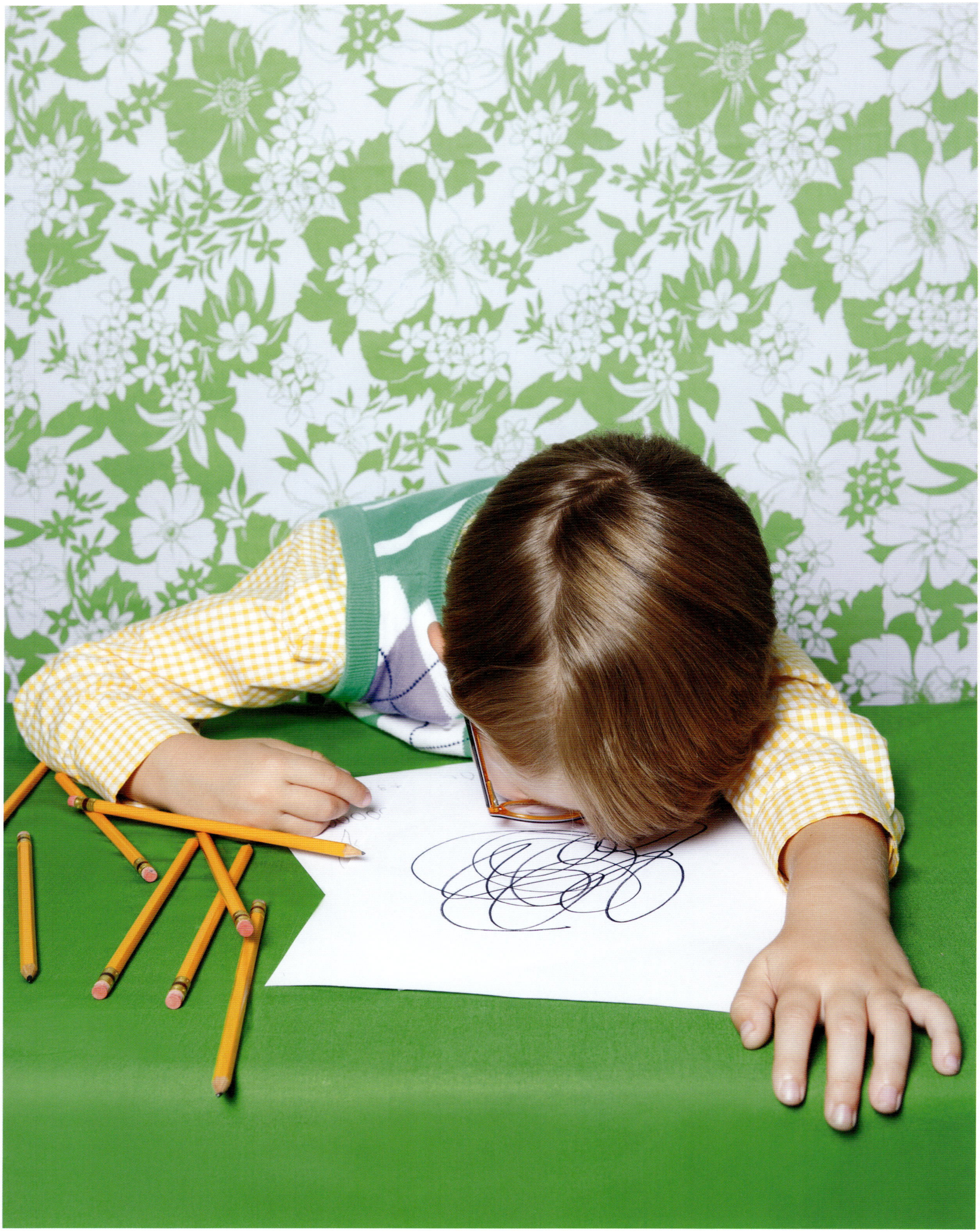

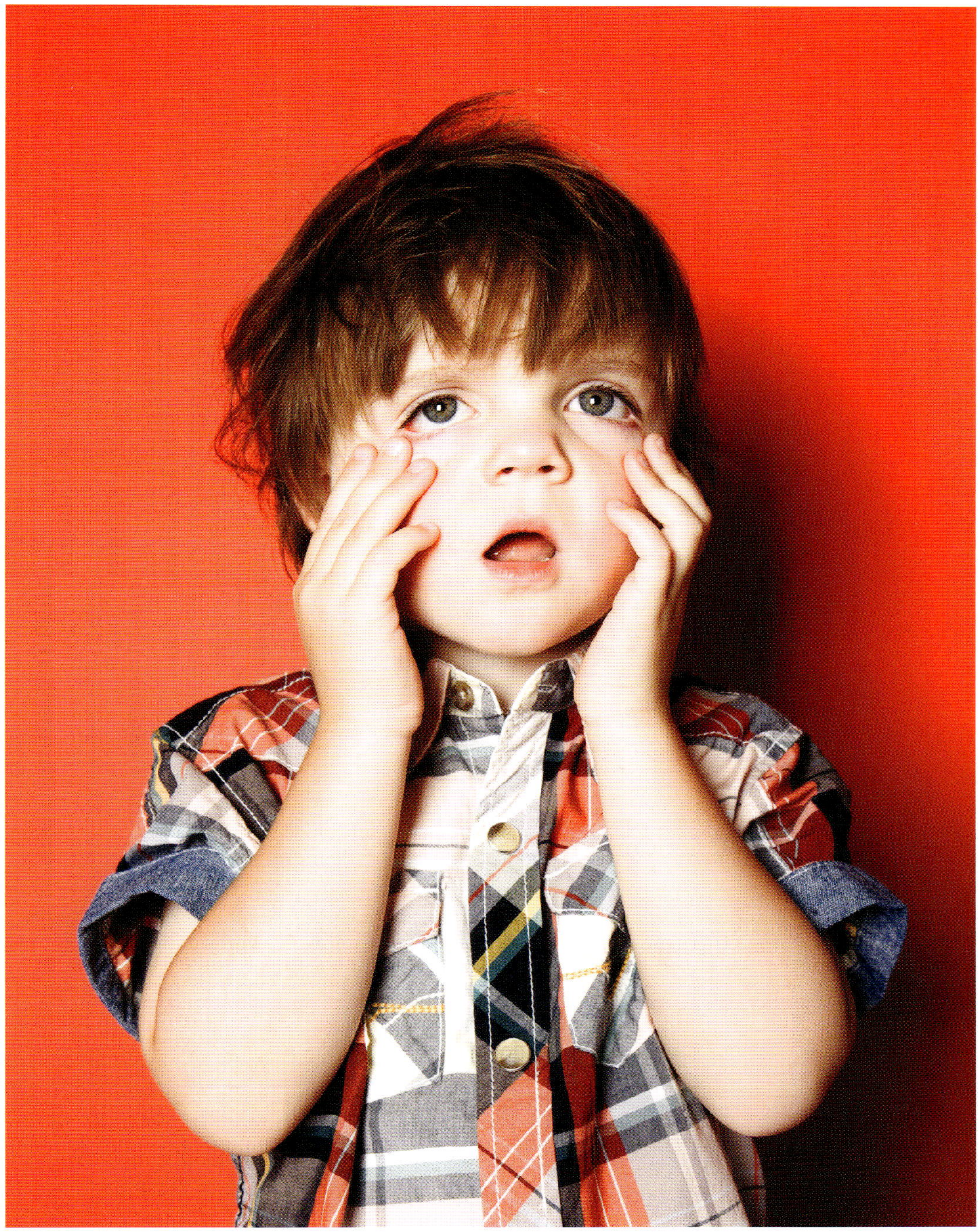

MEIKO TAKECHI ARQUILLOS

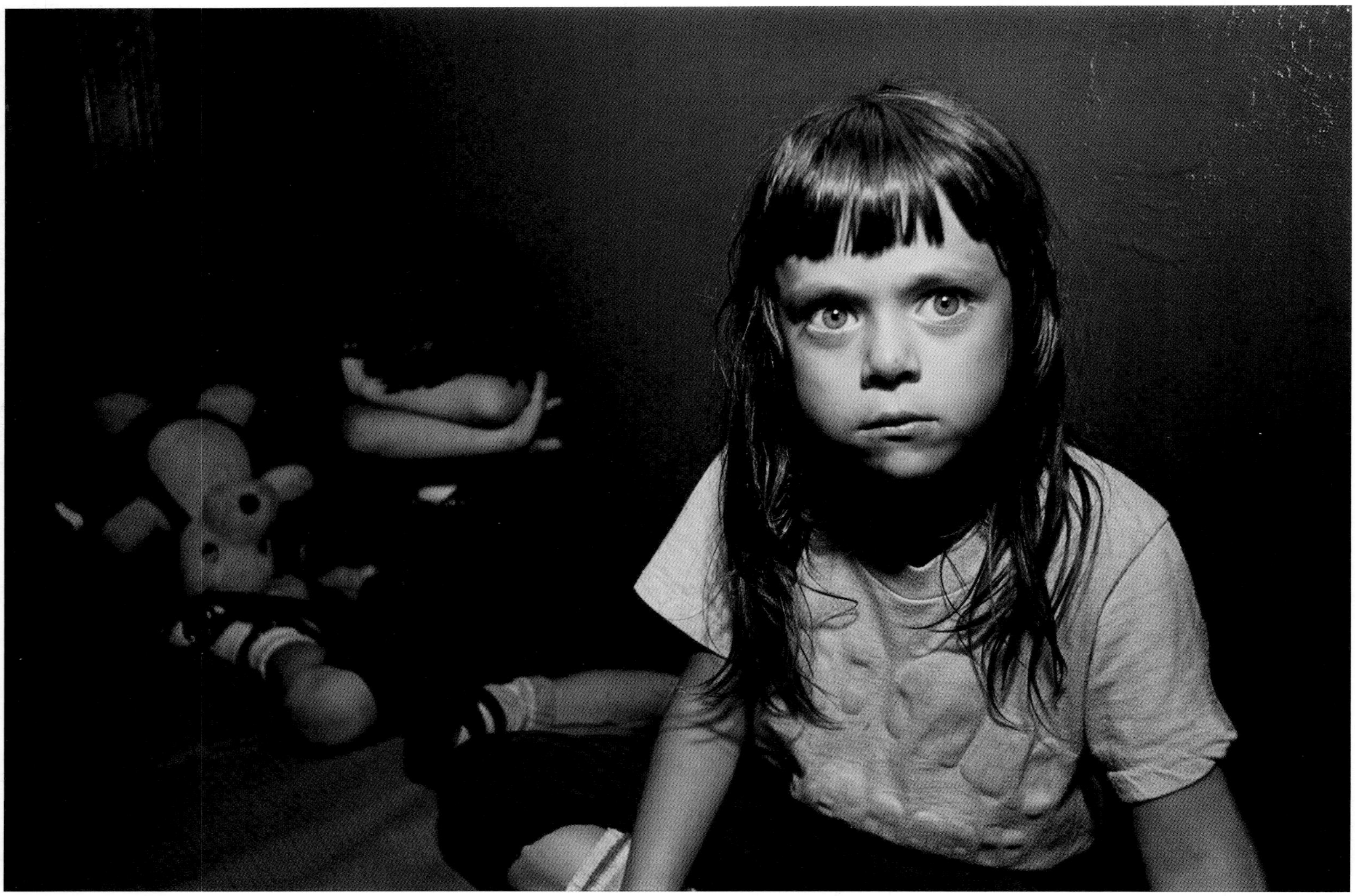

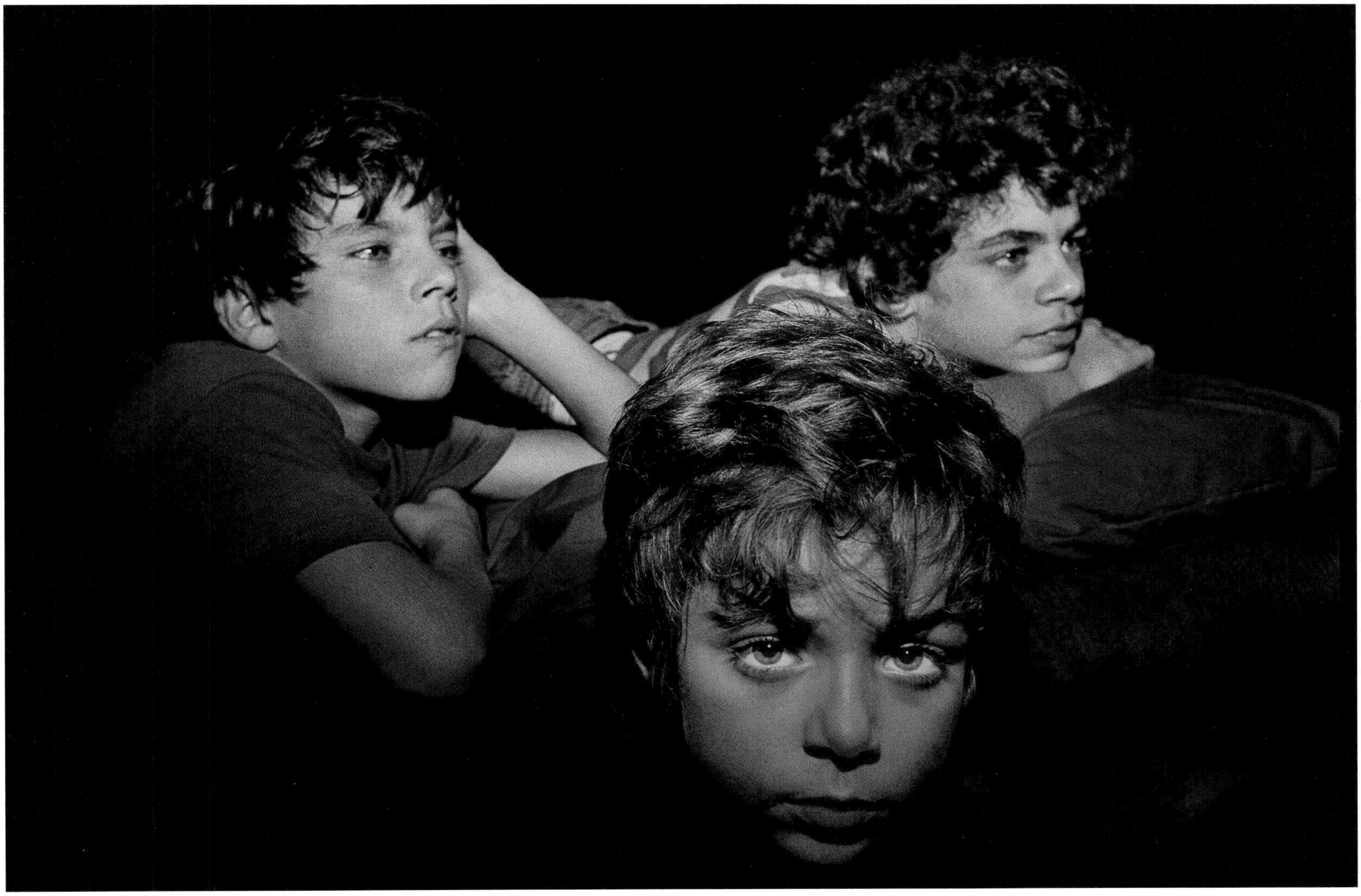

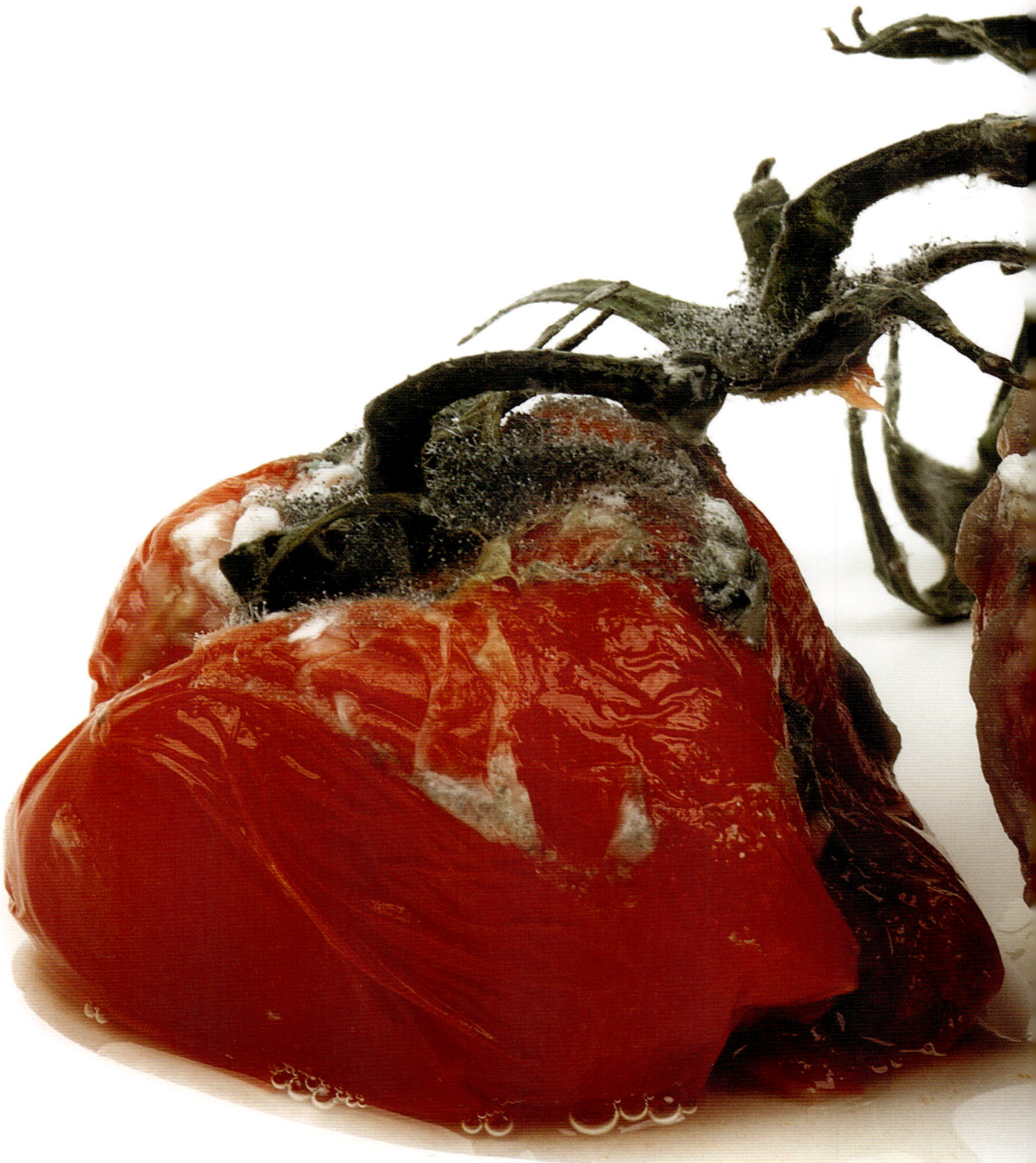

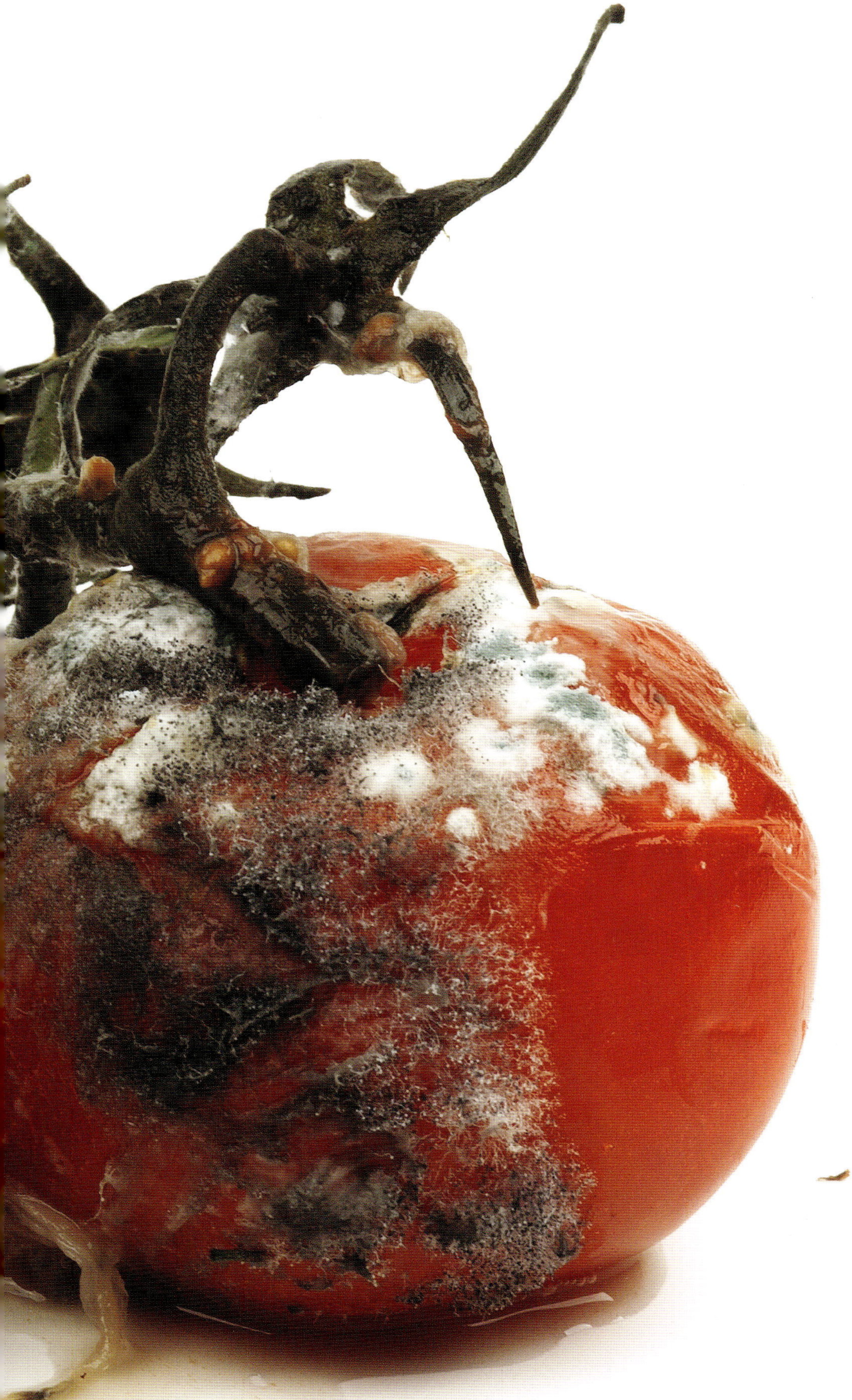

JOE BUGLEWICZ

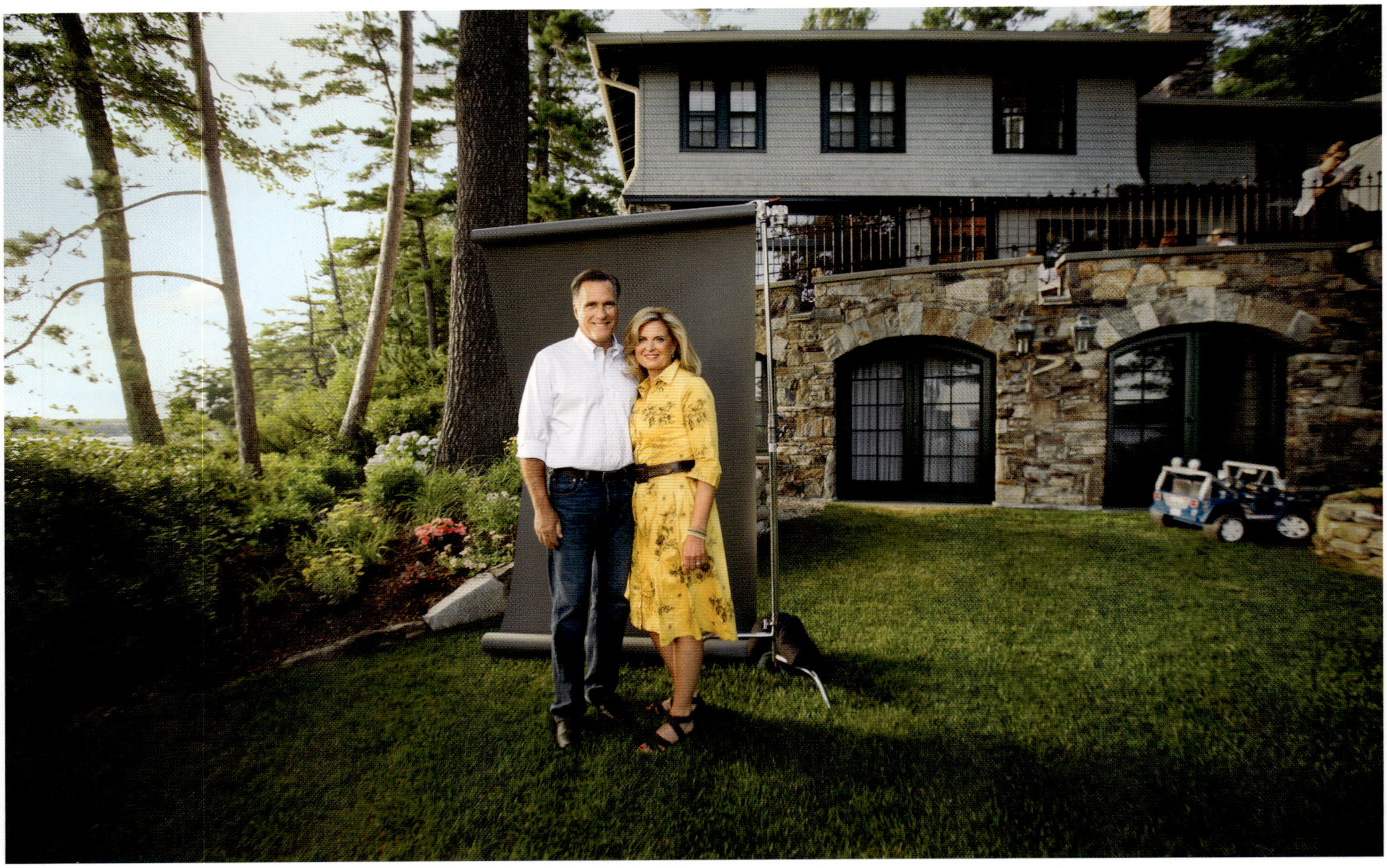

BEN BAKER

CLAIRE BENOIST

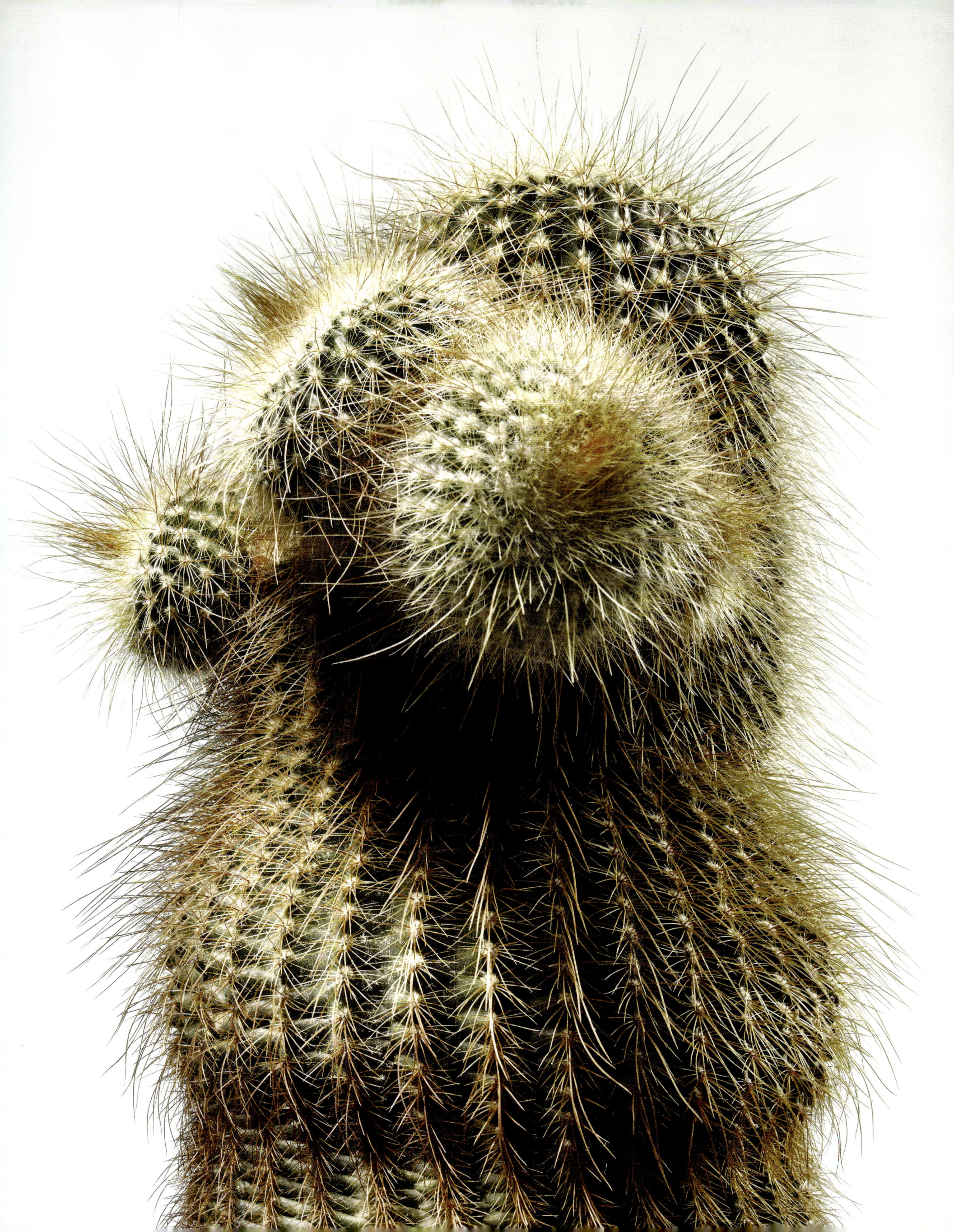

RICHARD BARNES

022

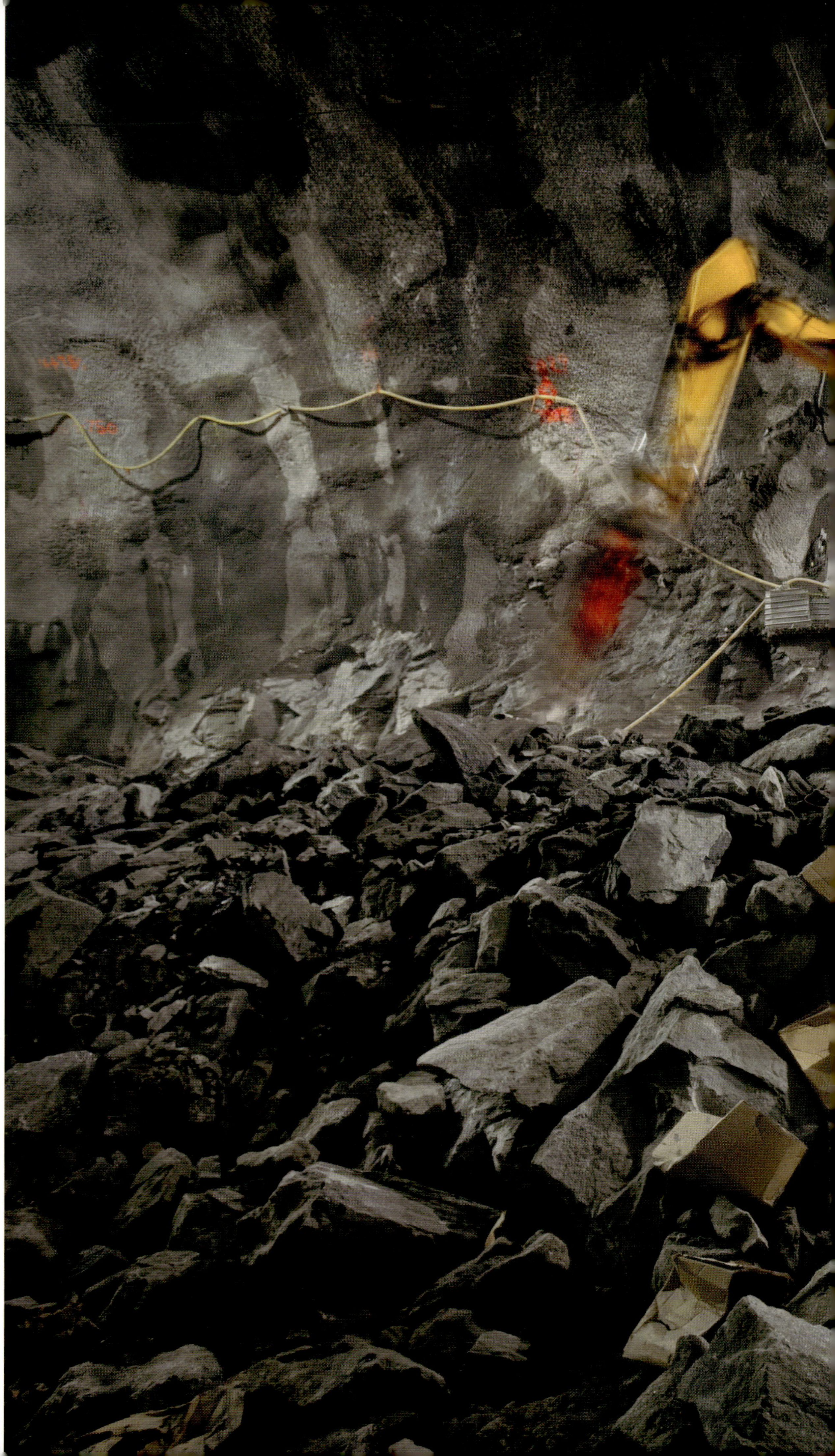

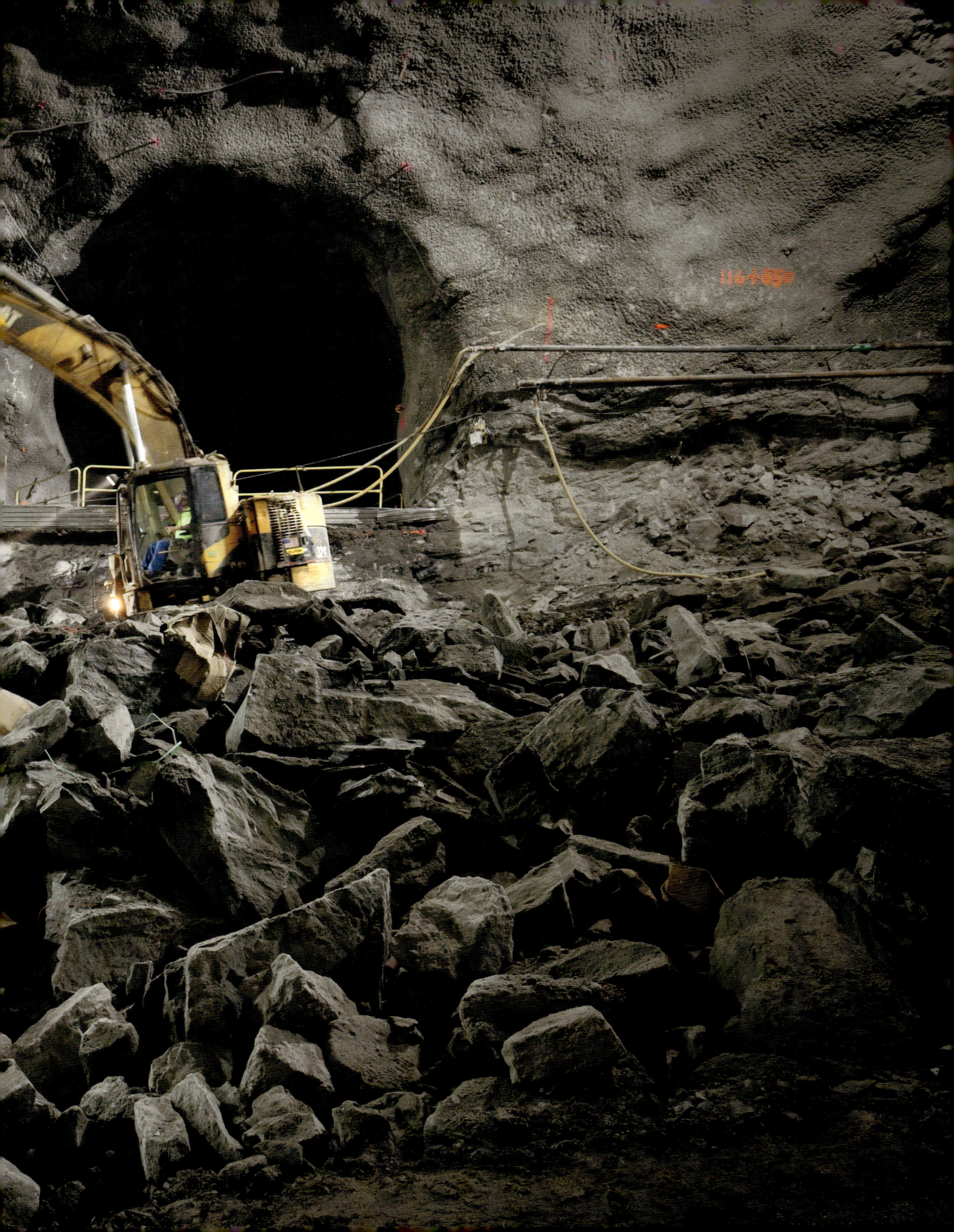

RICHARD BARNES

023

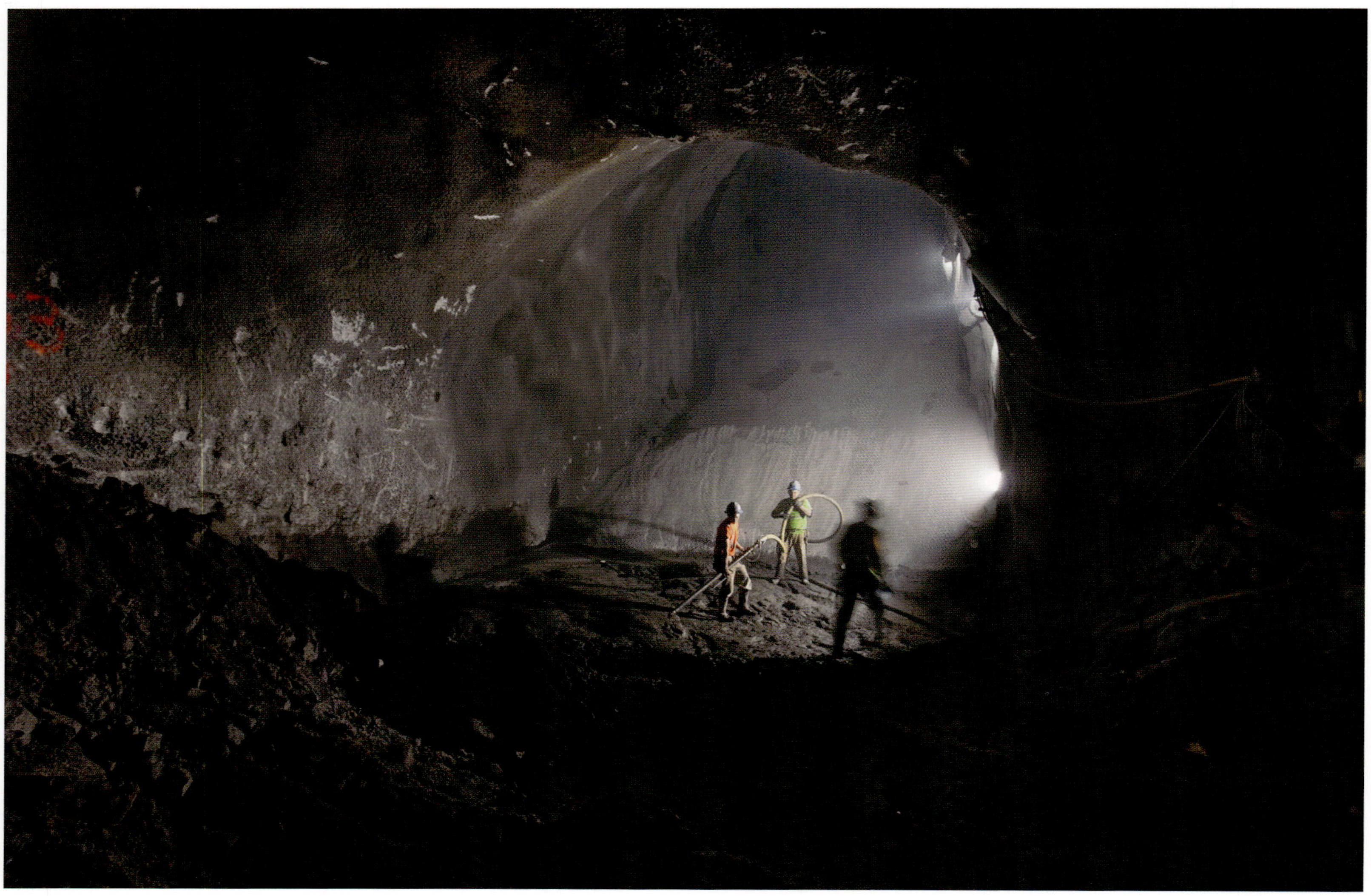

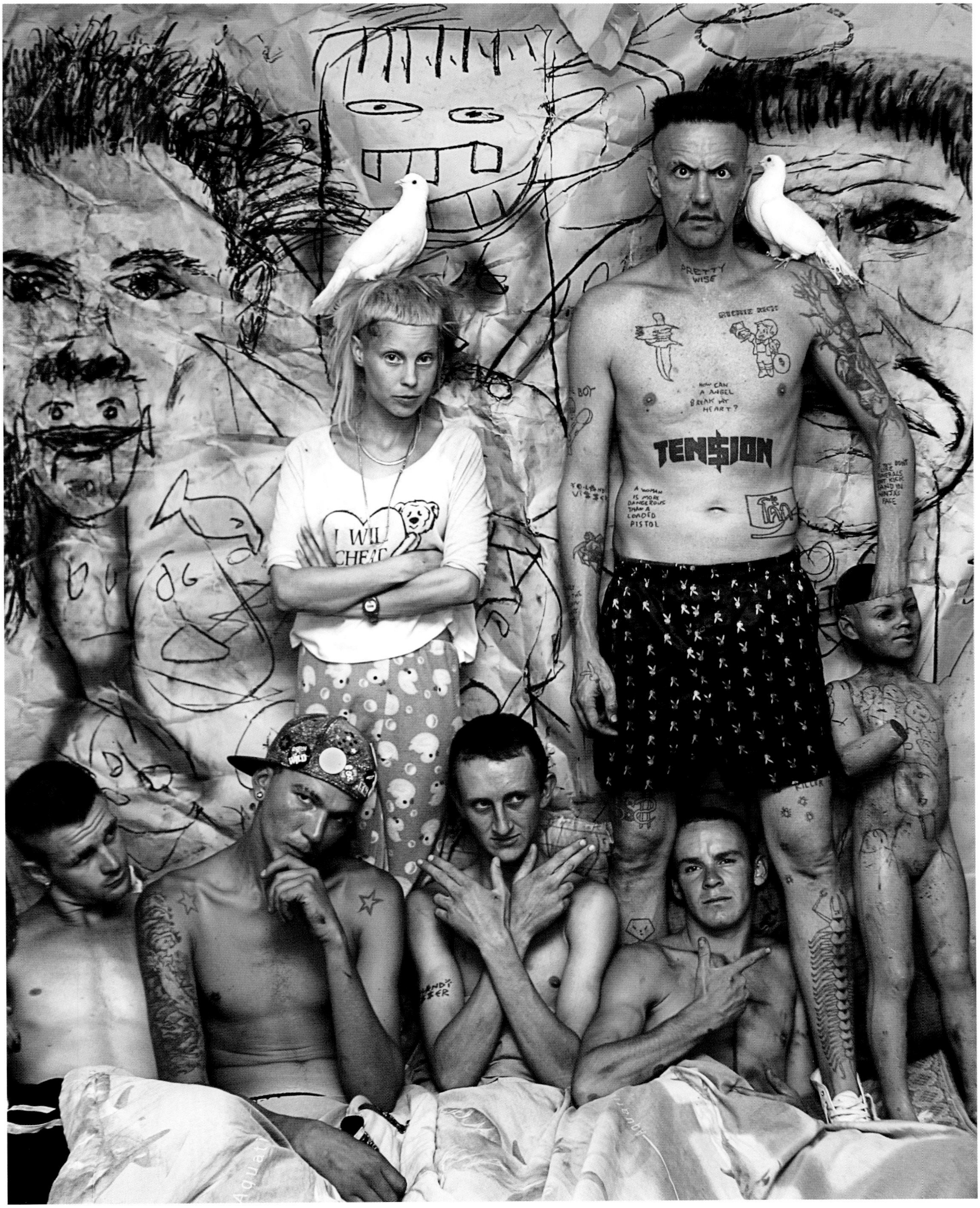

ROGER BALLEN

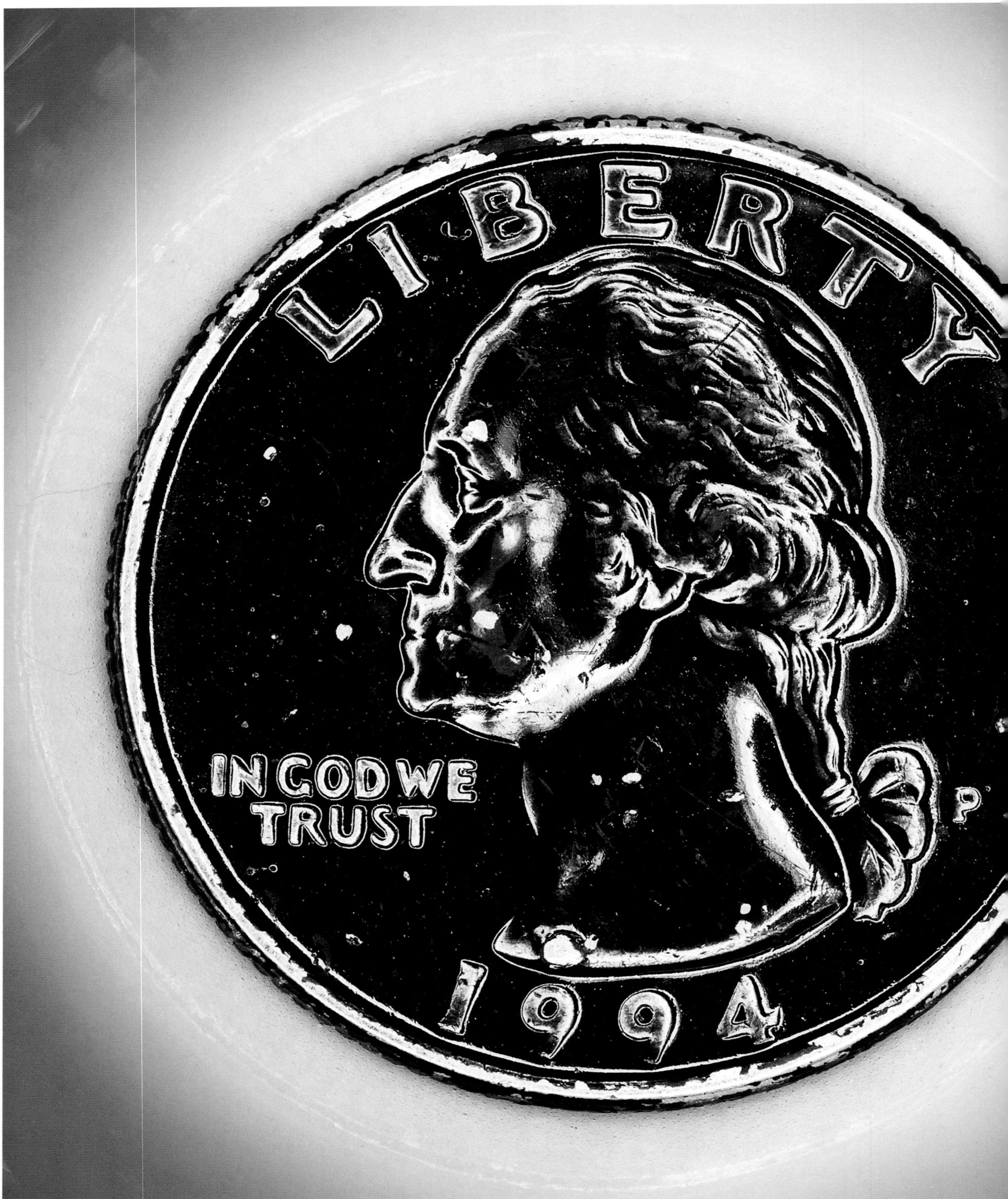
LIBERTY
IN GOD WE
TRUST
P
1994

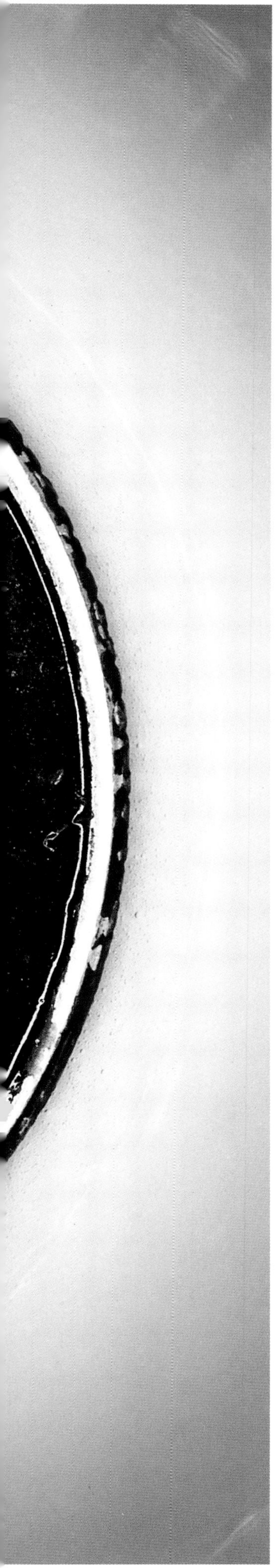

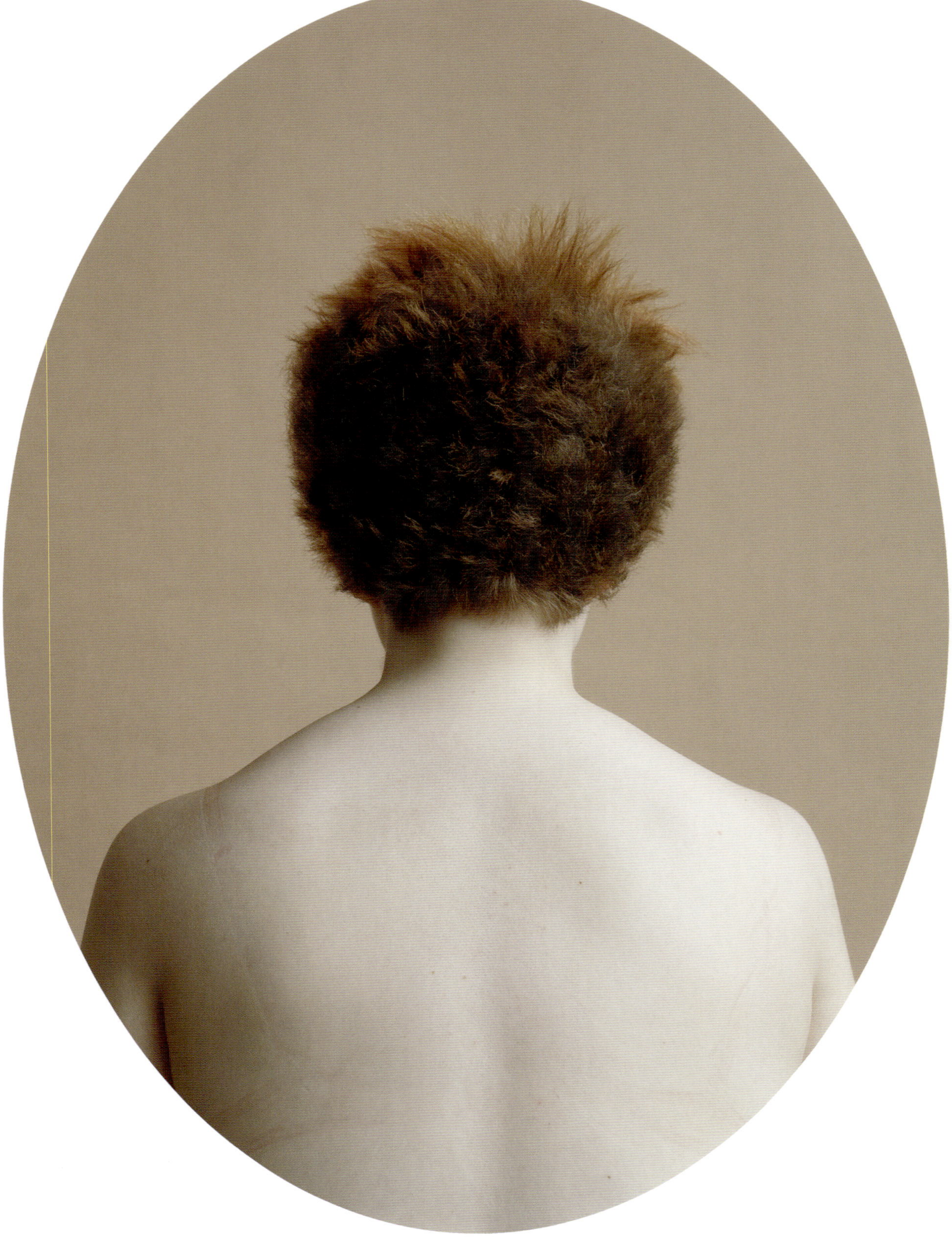

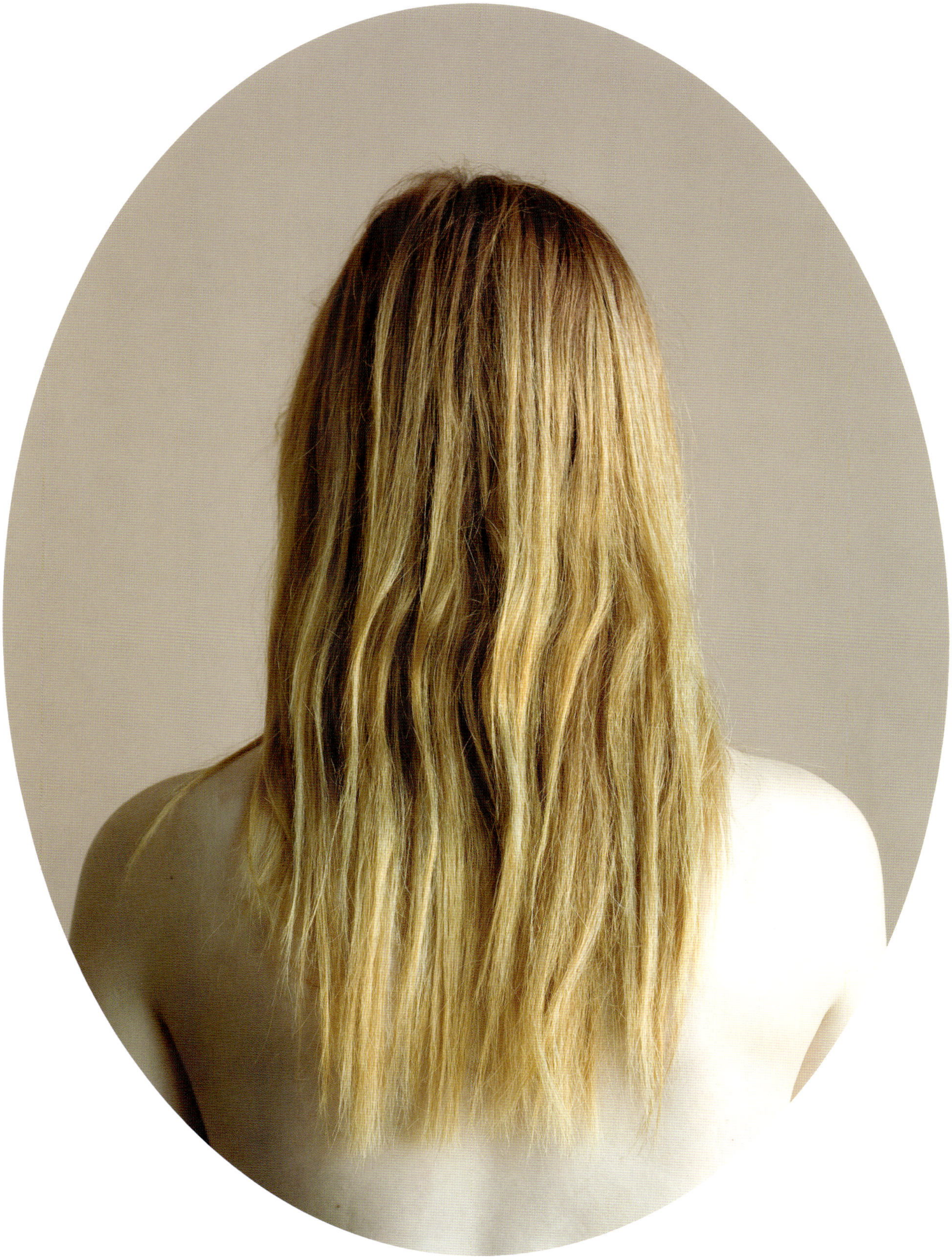

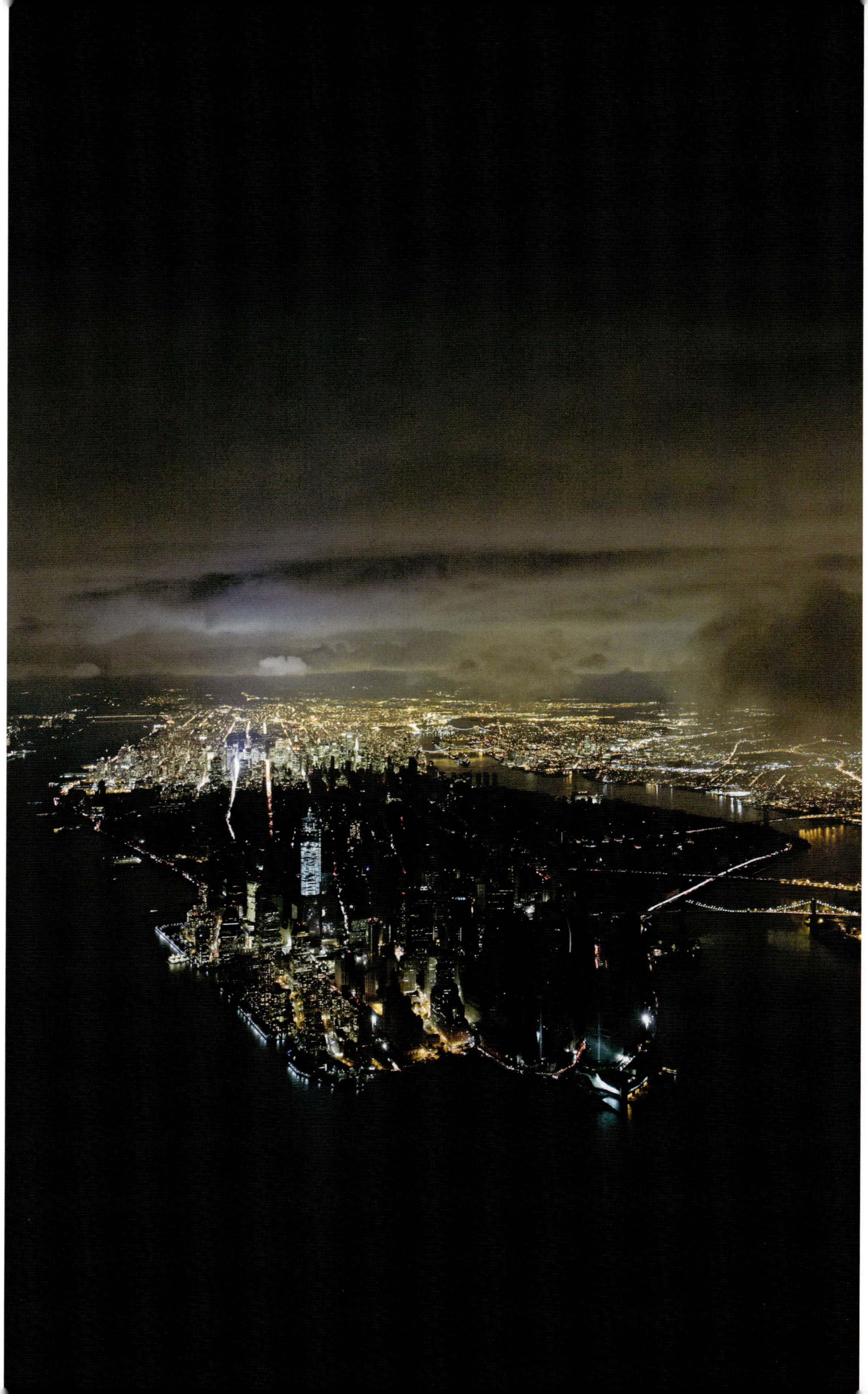

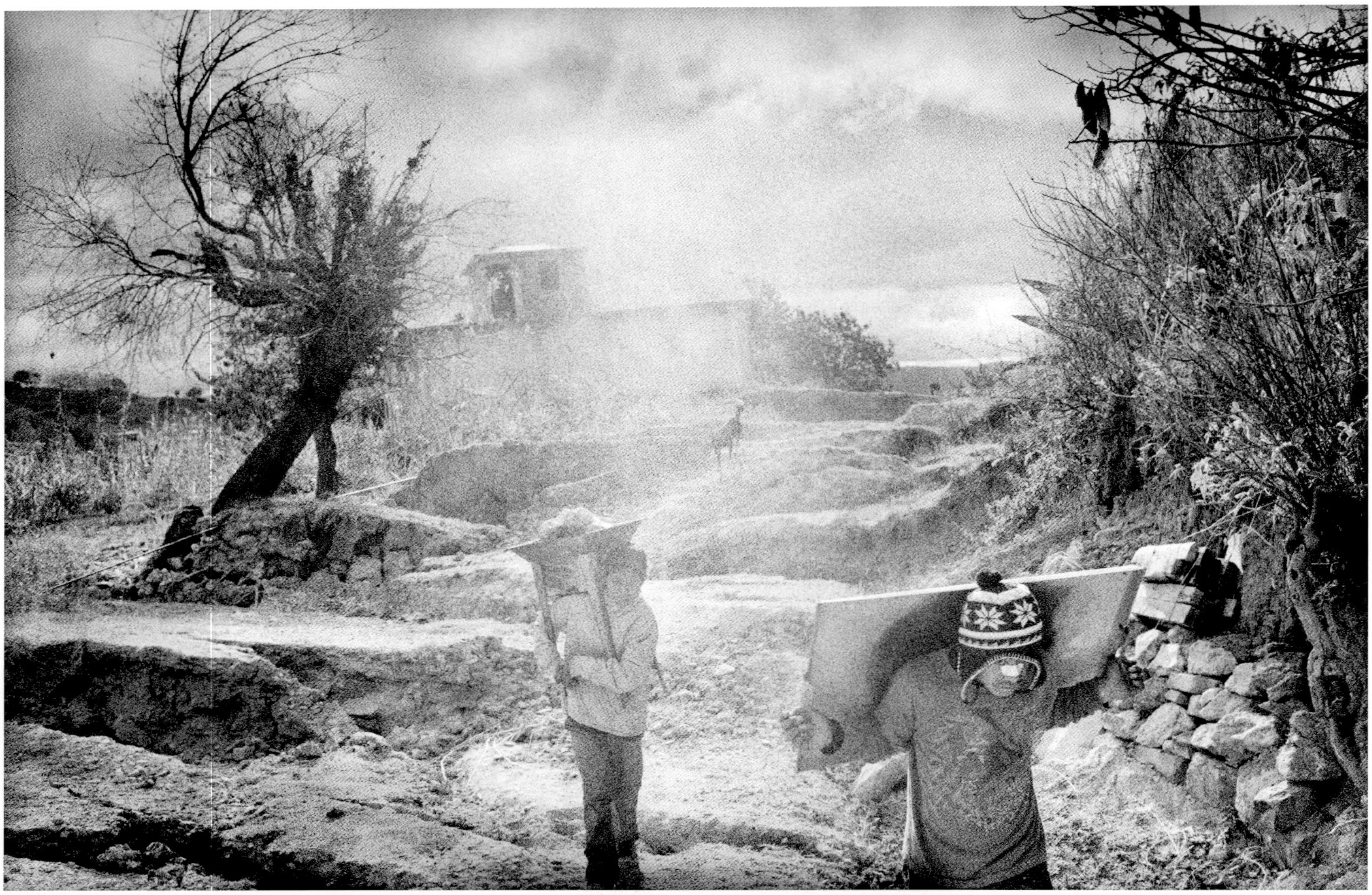

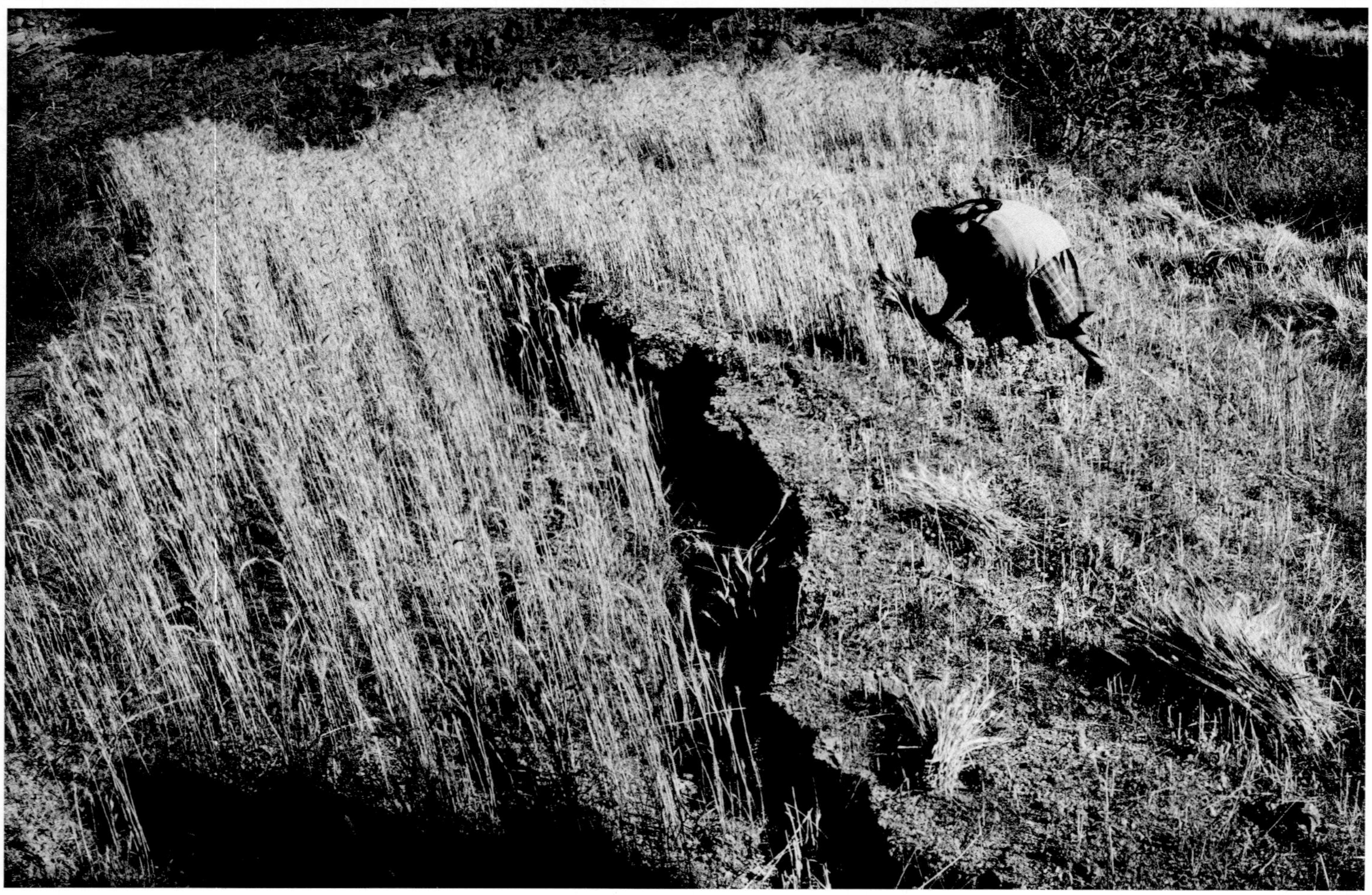

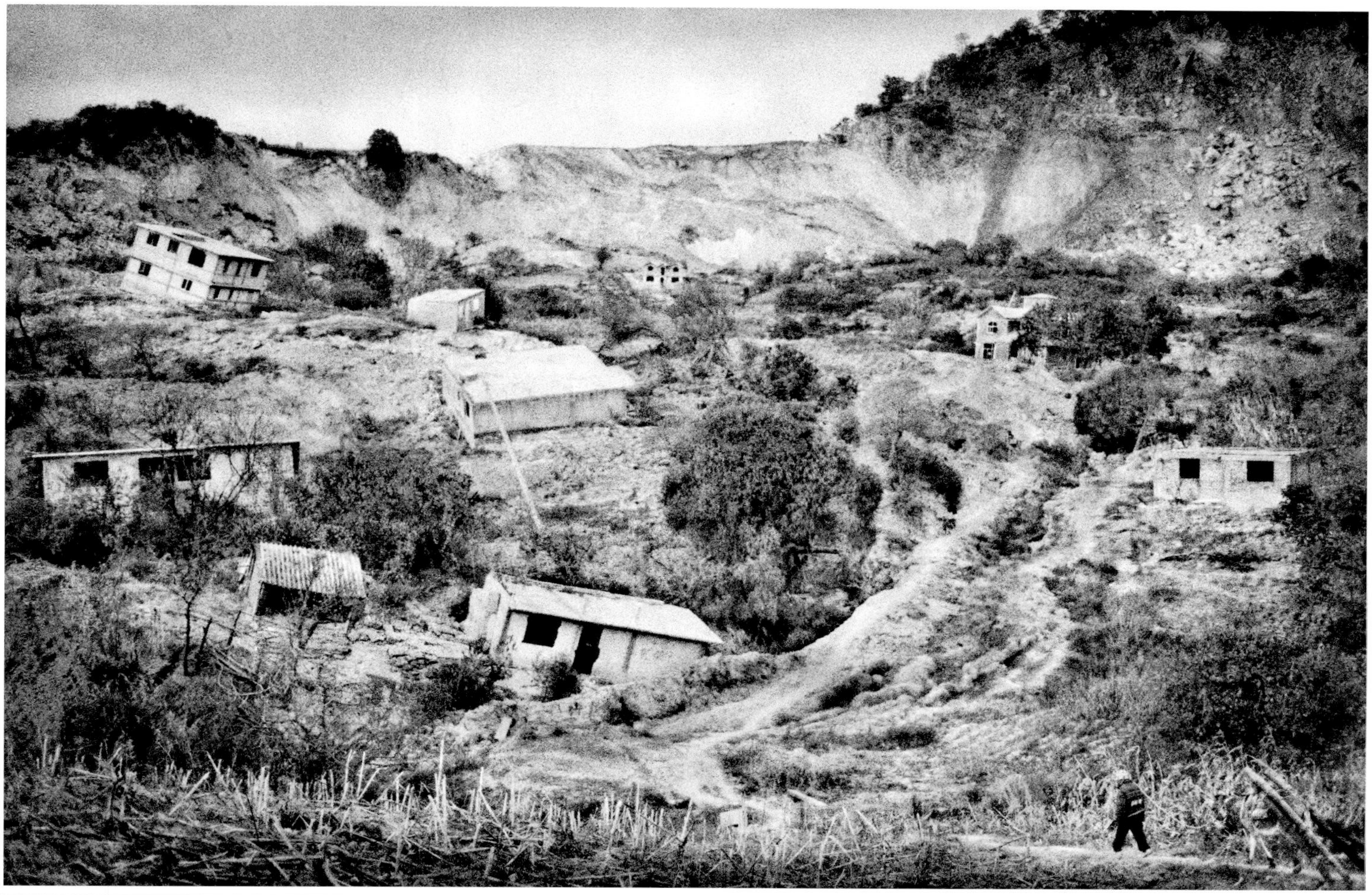

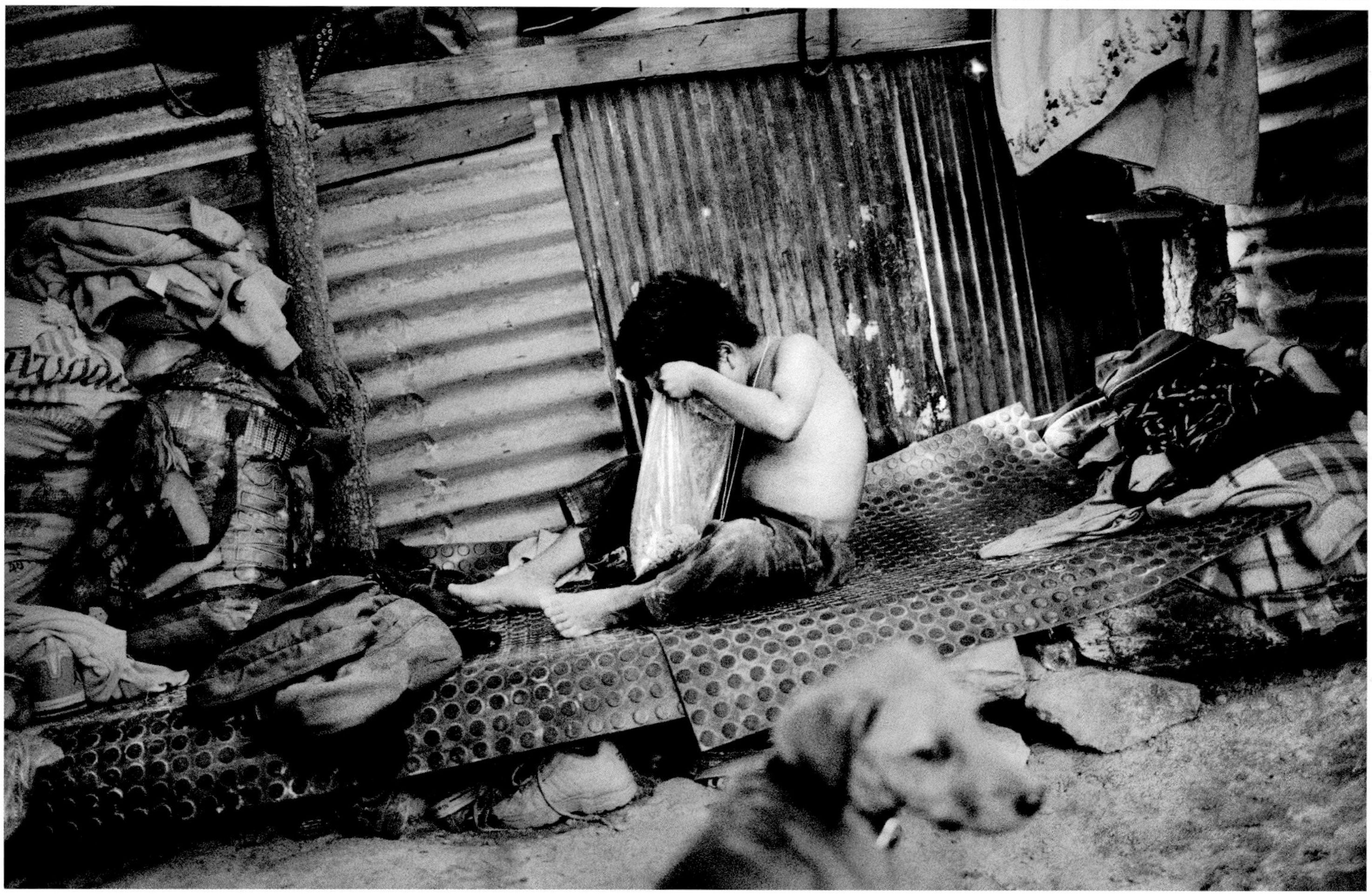

MATT BLACK

029 / 030 / 031 / 032

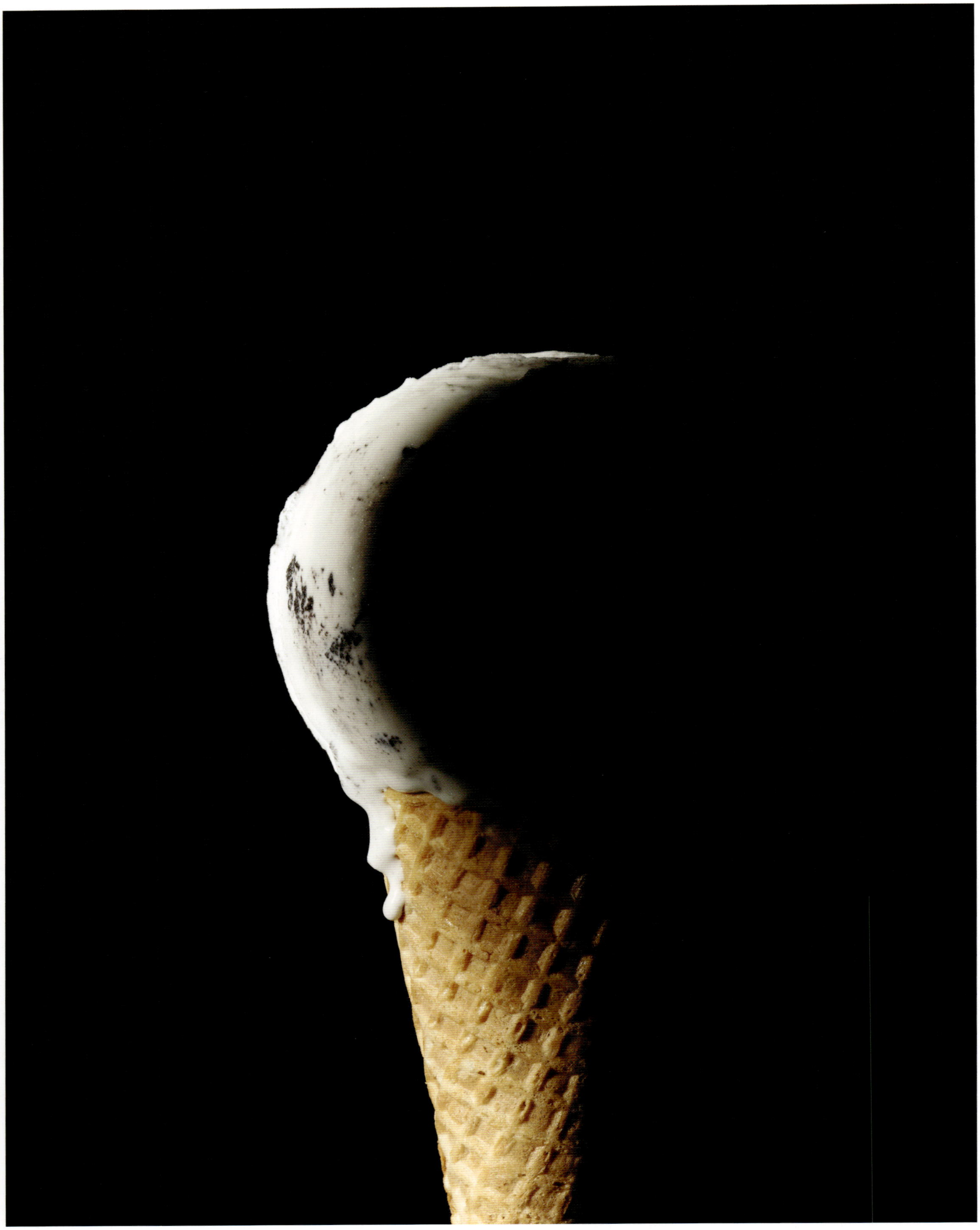

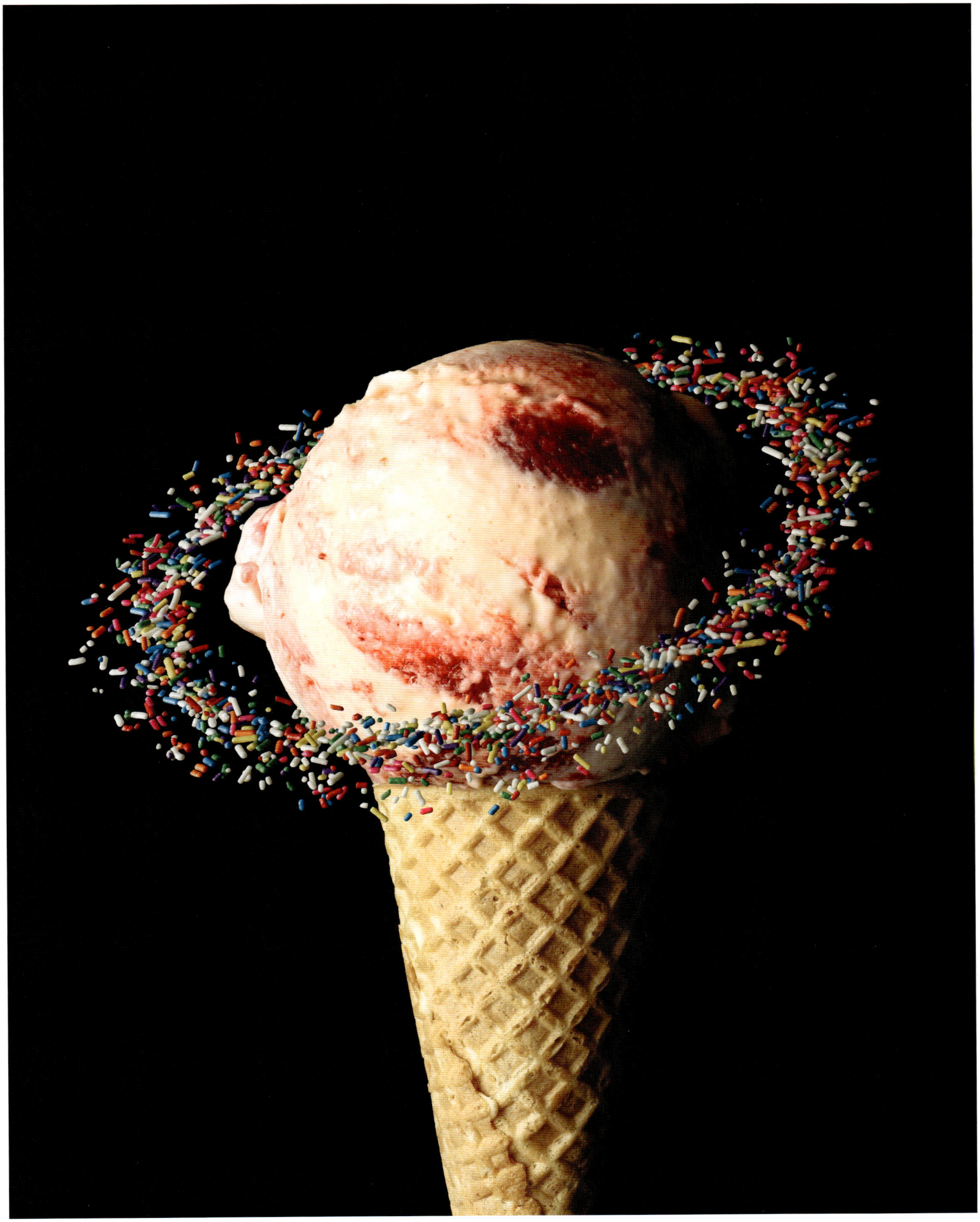

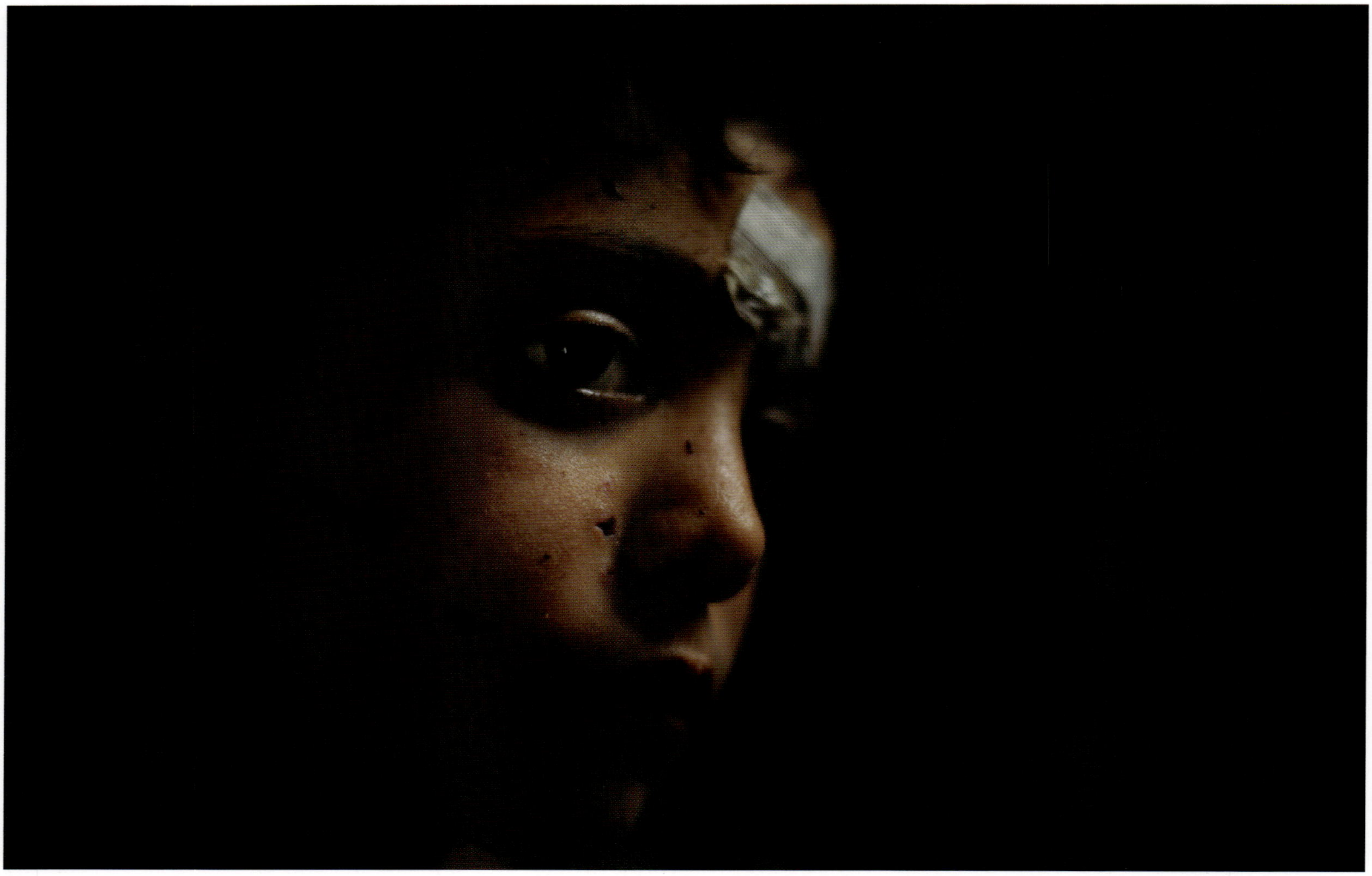

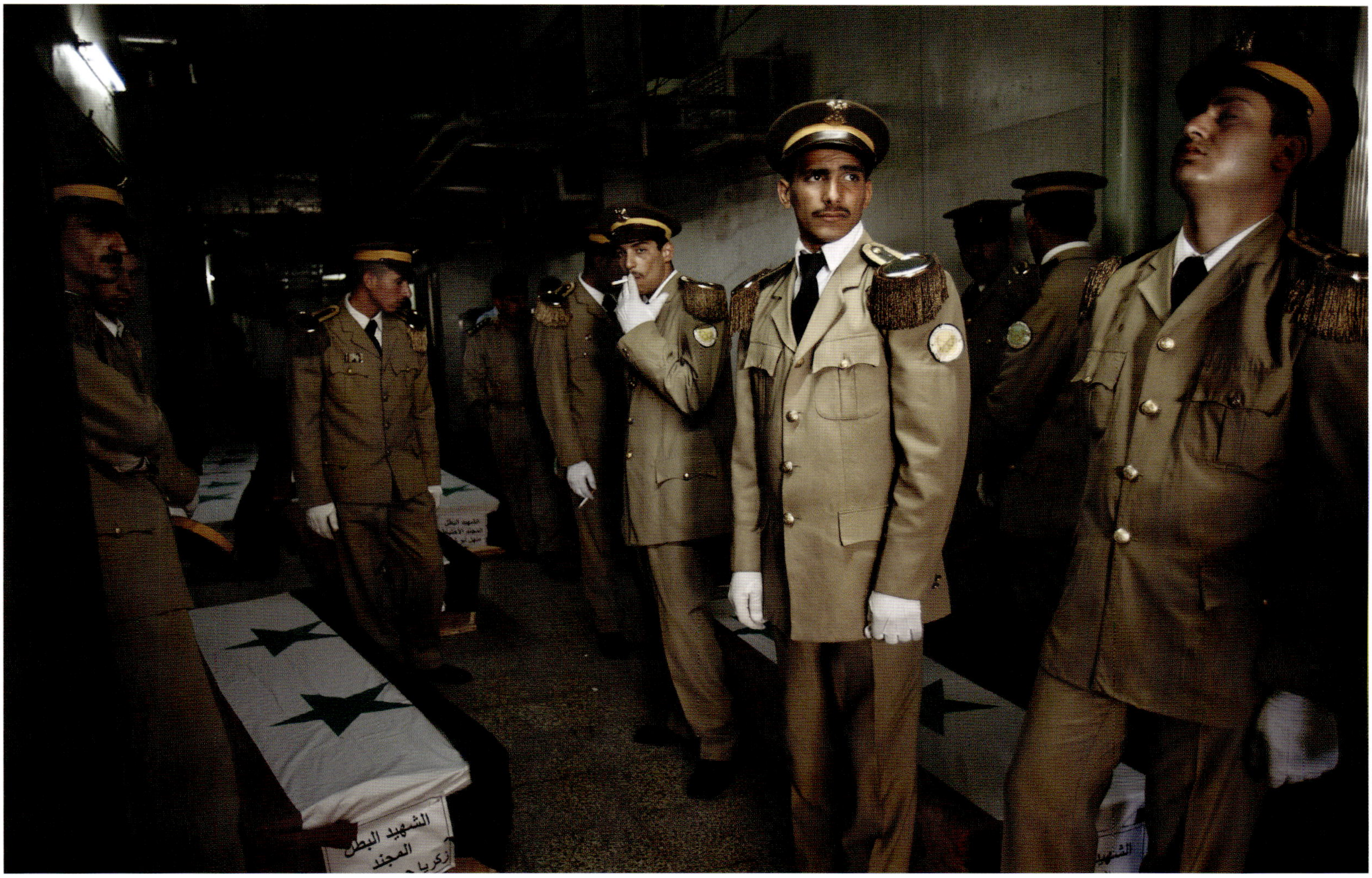
الشهيد البطل
المجند

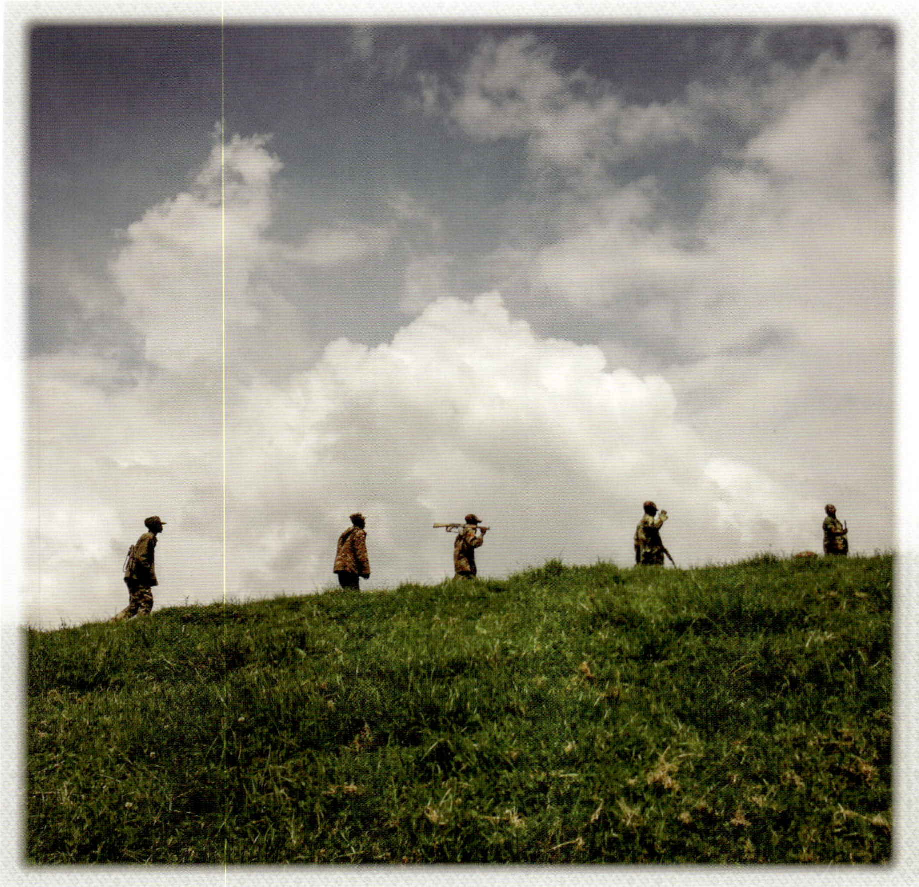

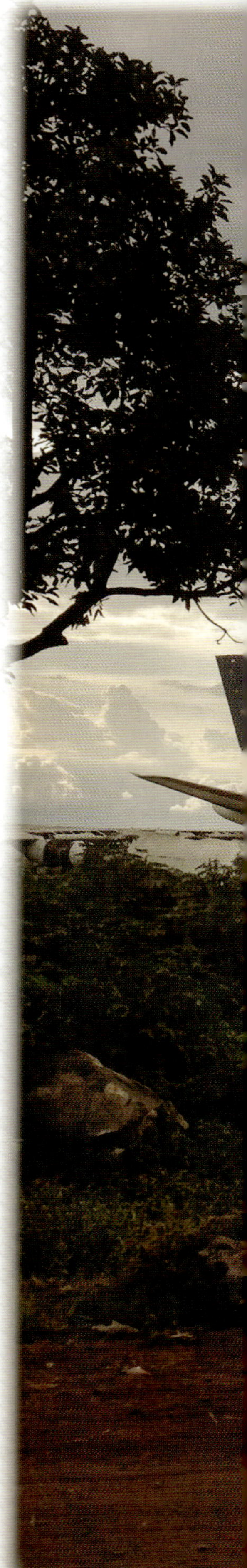

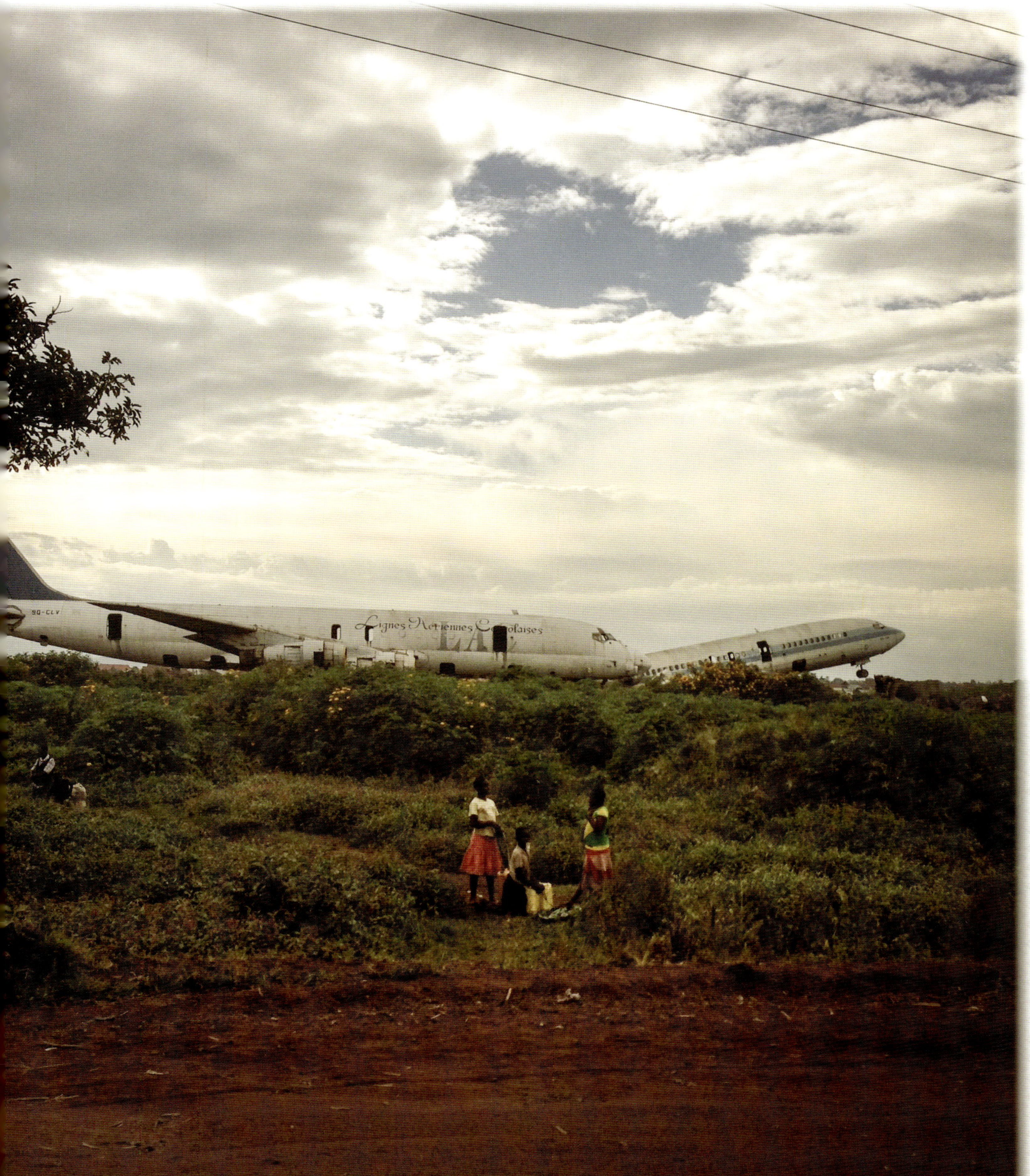
9Q-CLV

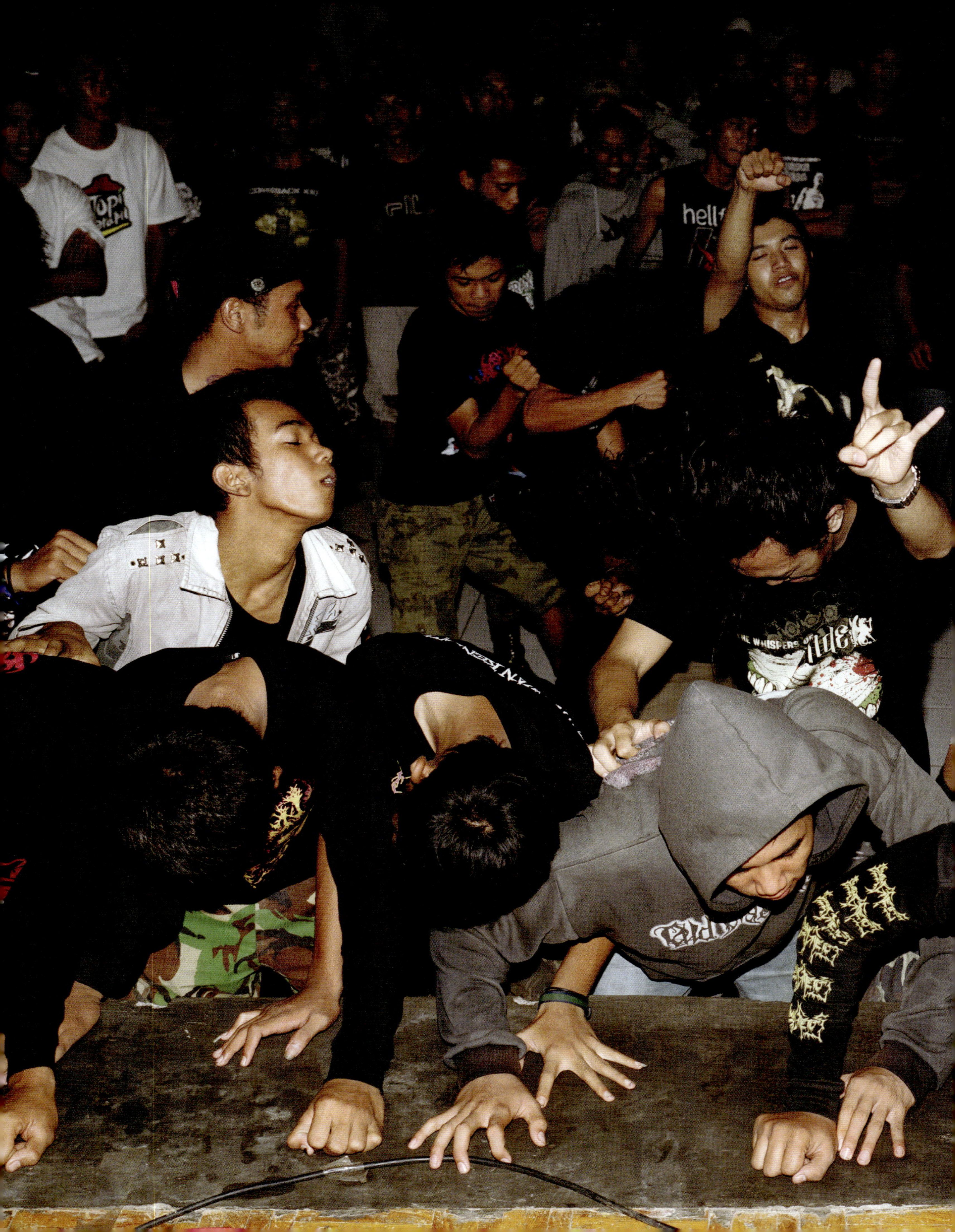

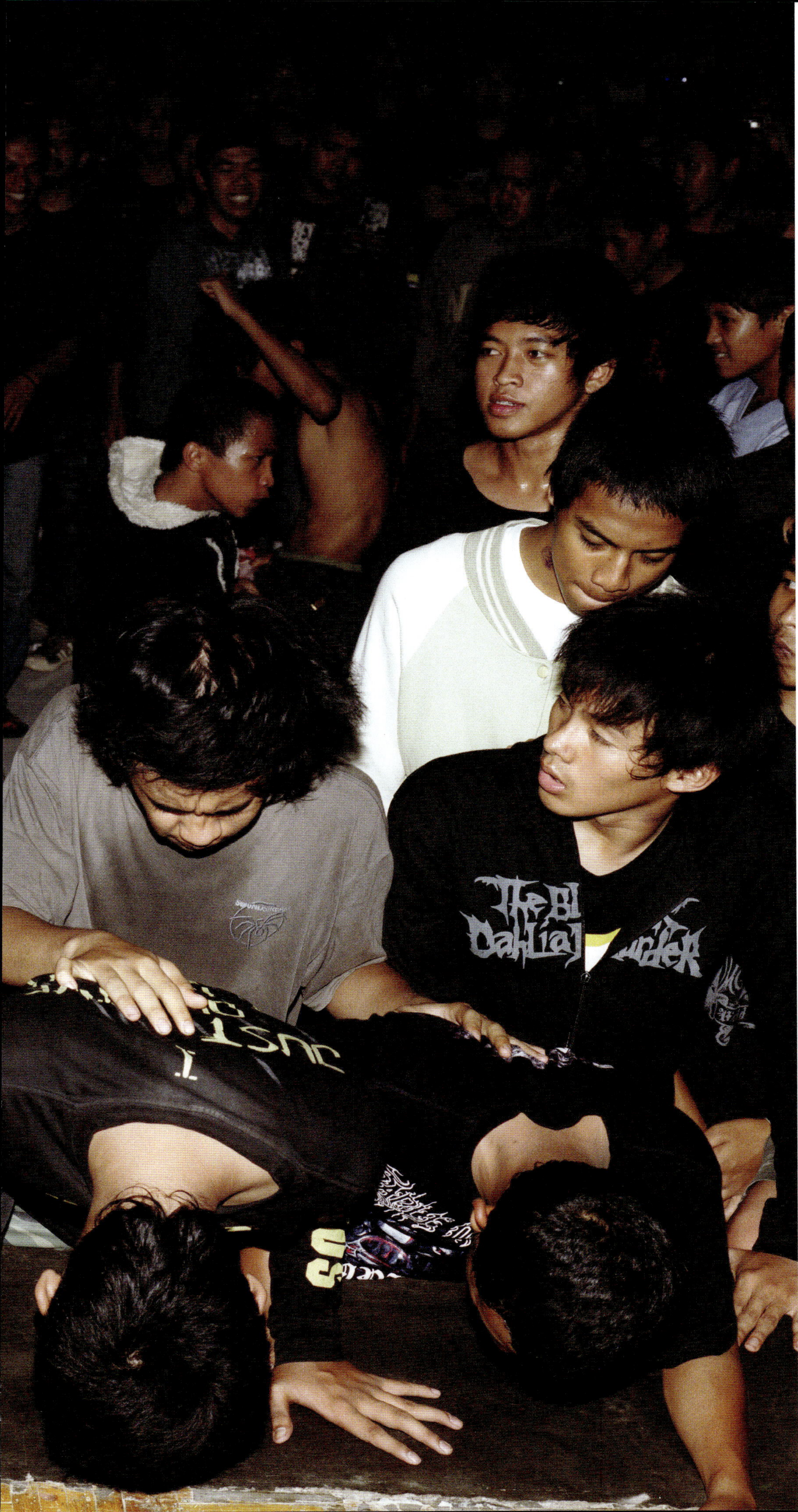

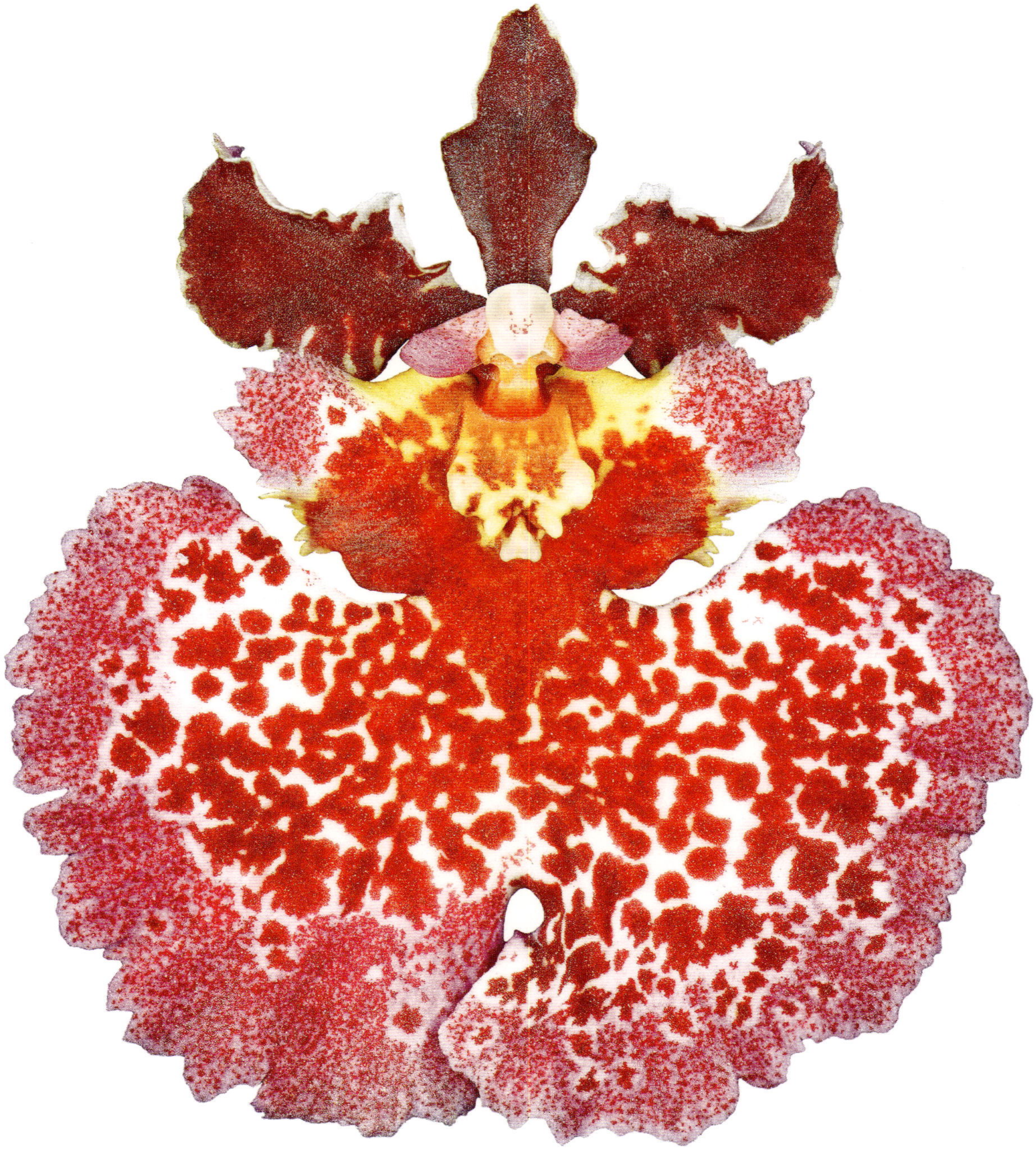

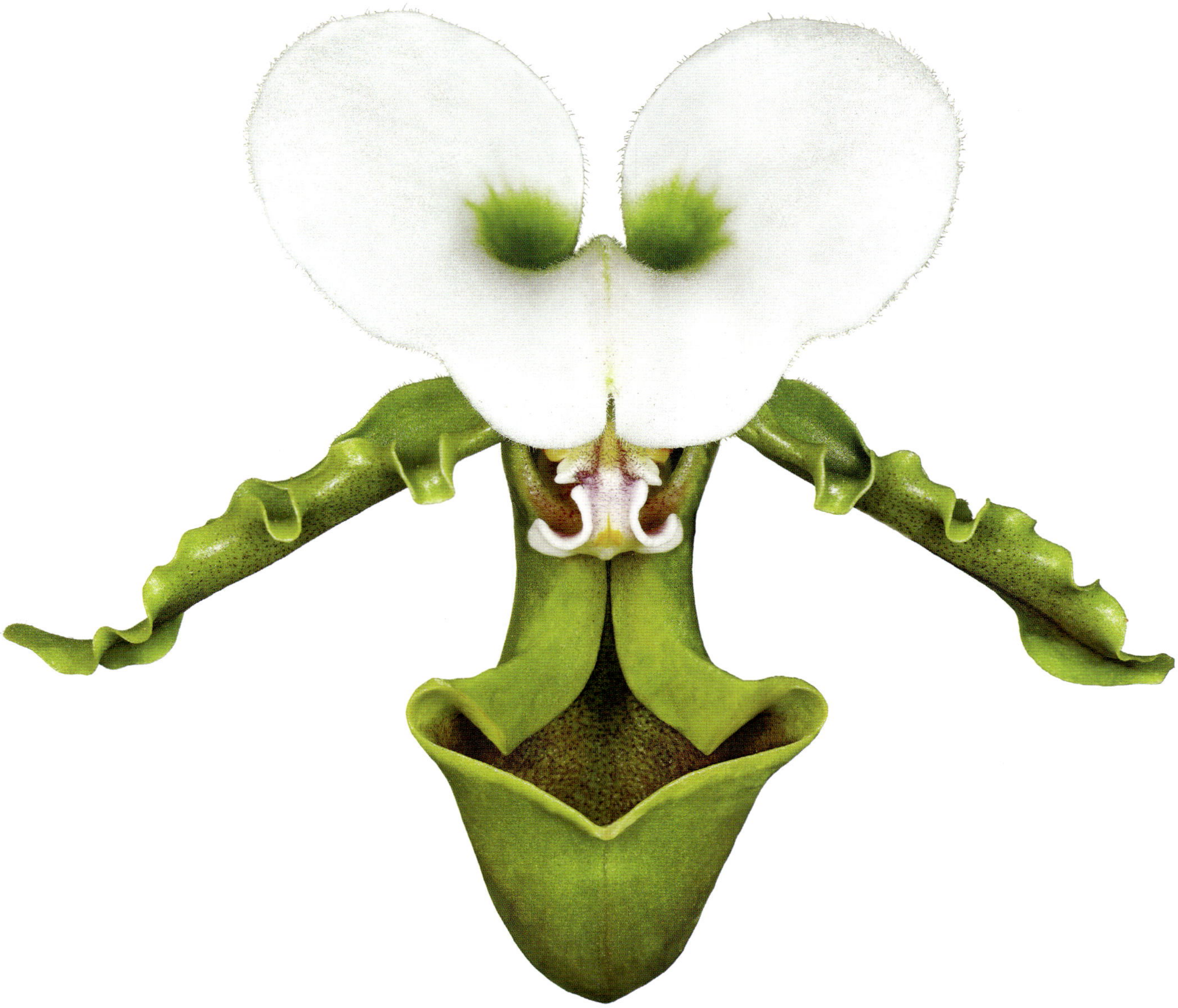

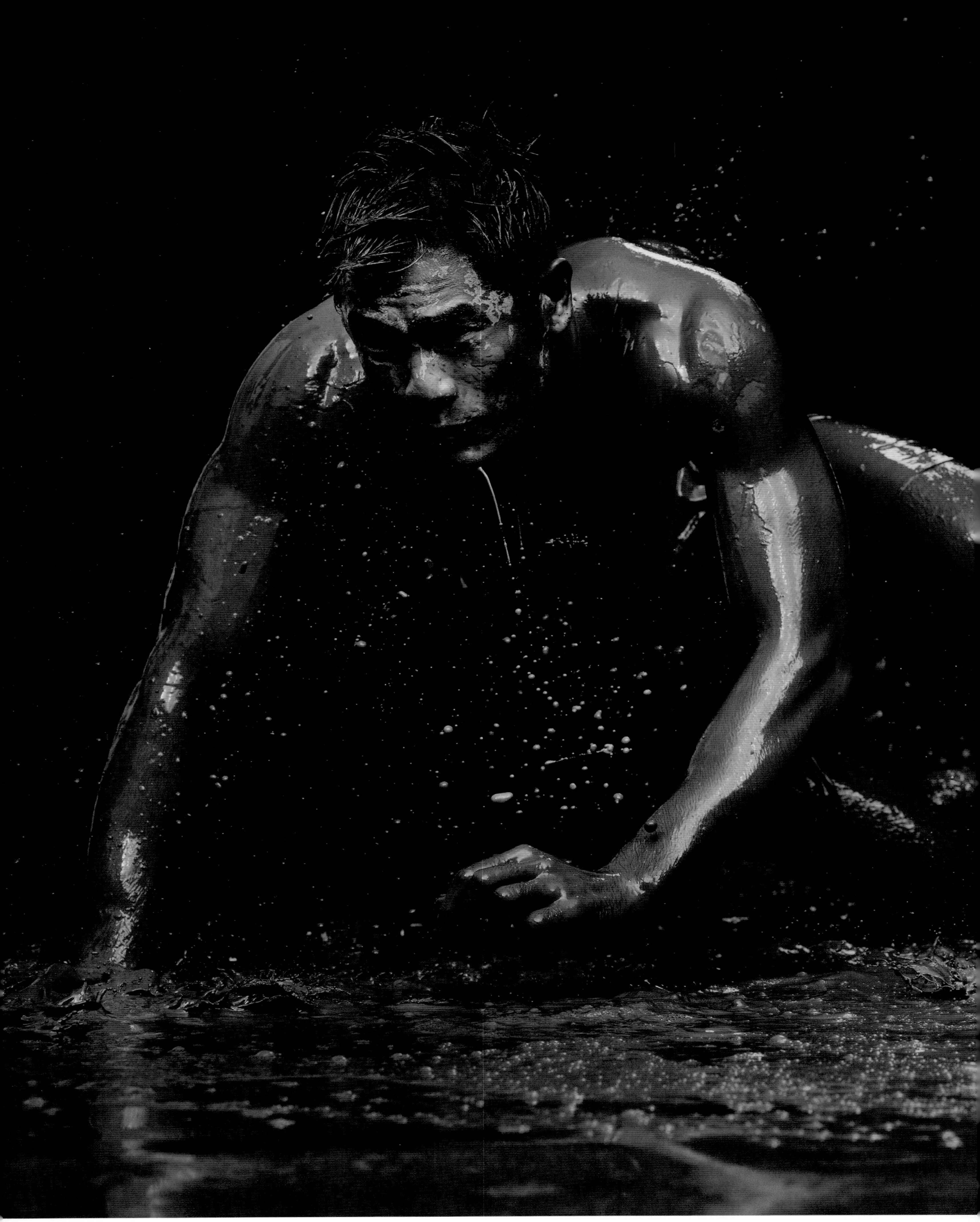

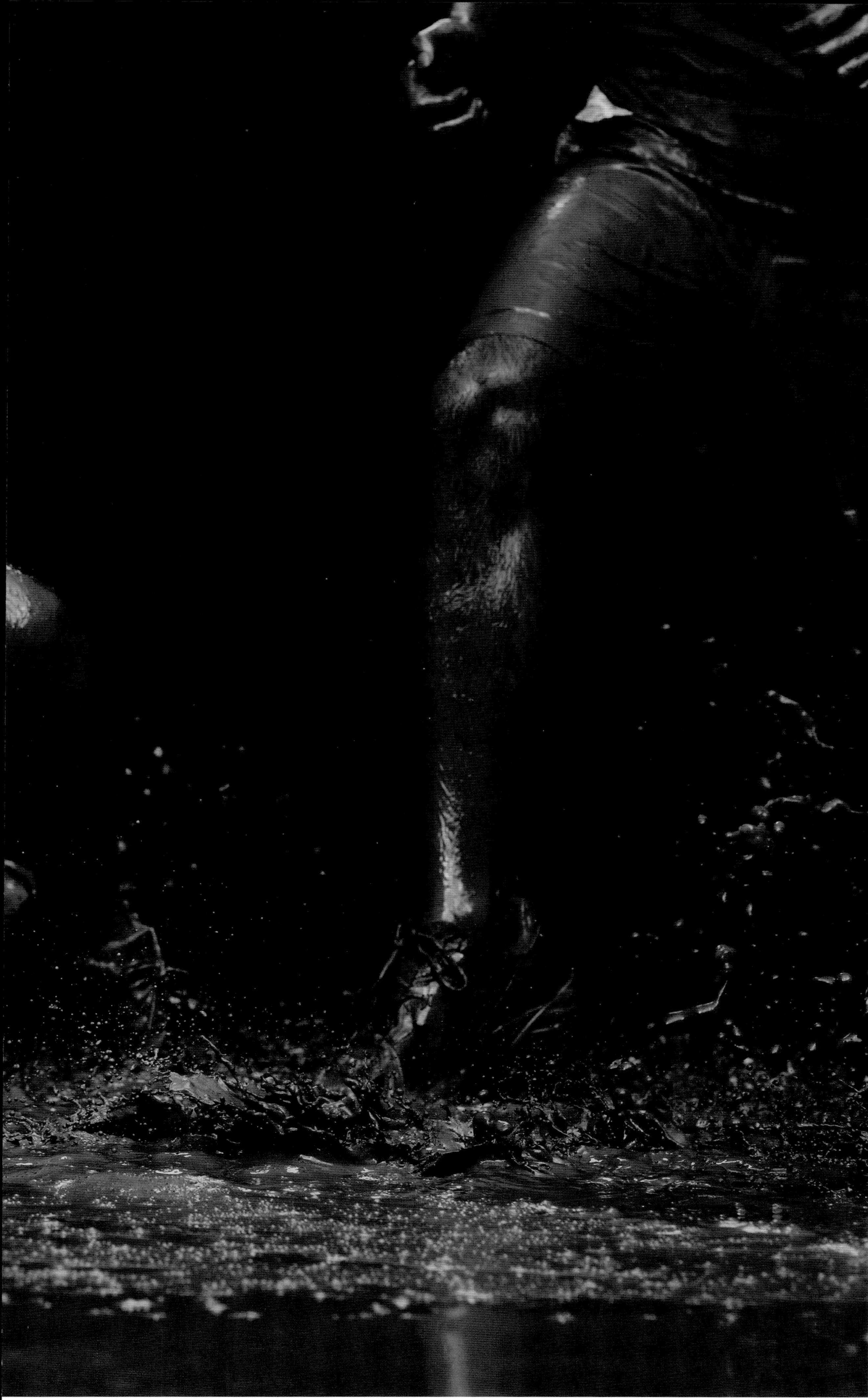

JAMIE CHUNG

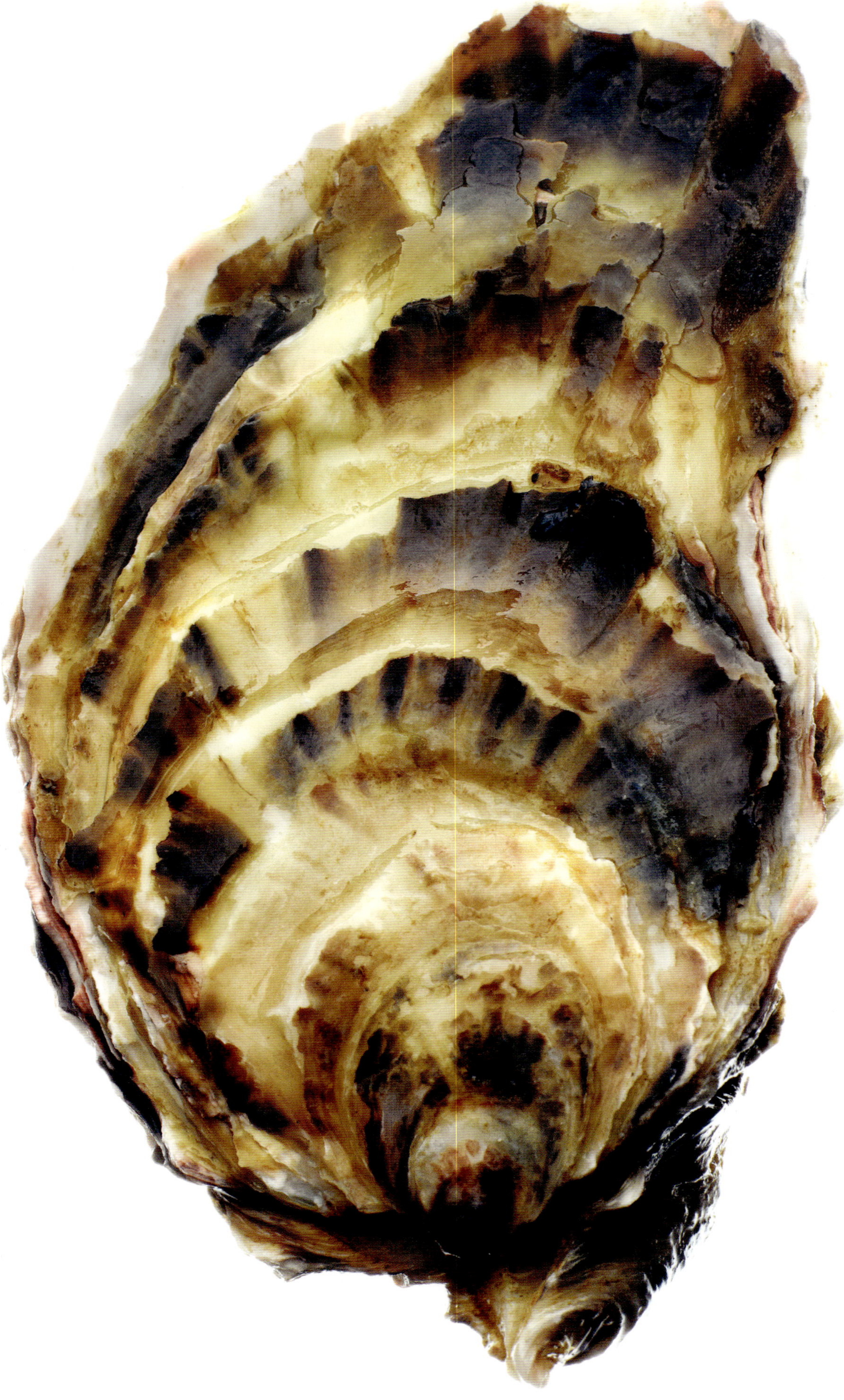

JAMIE CHUNG

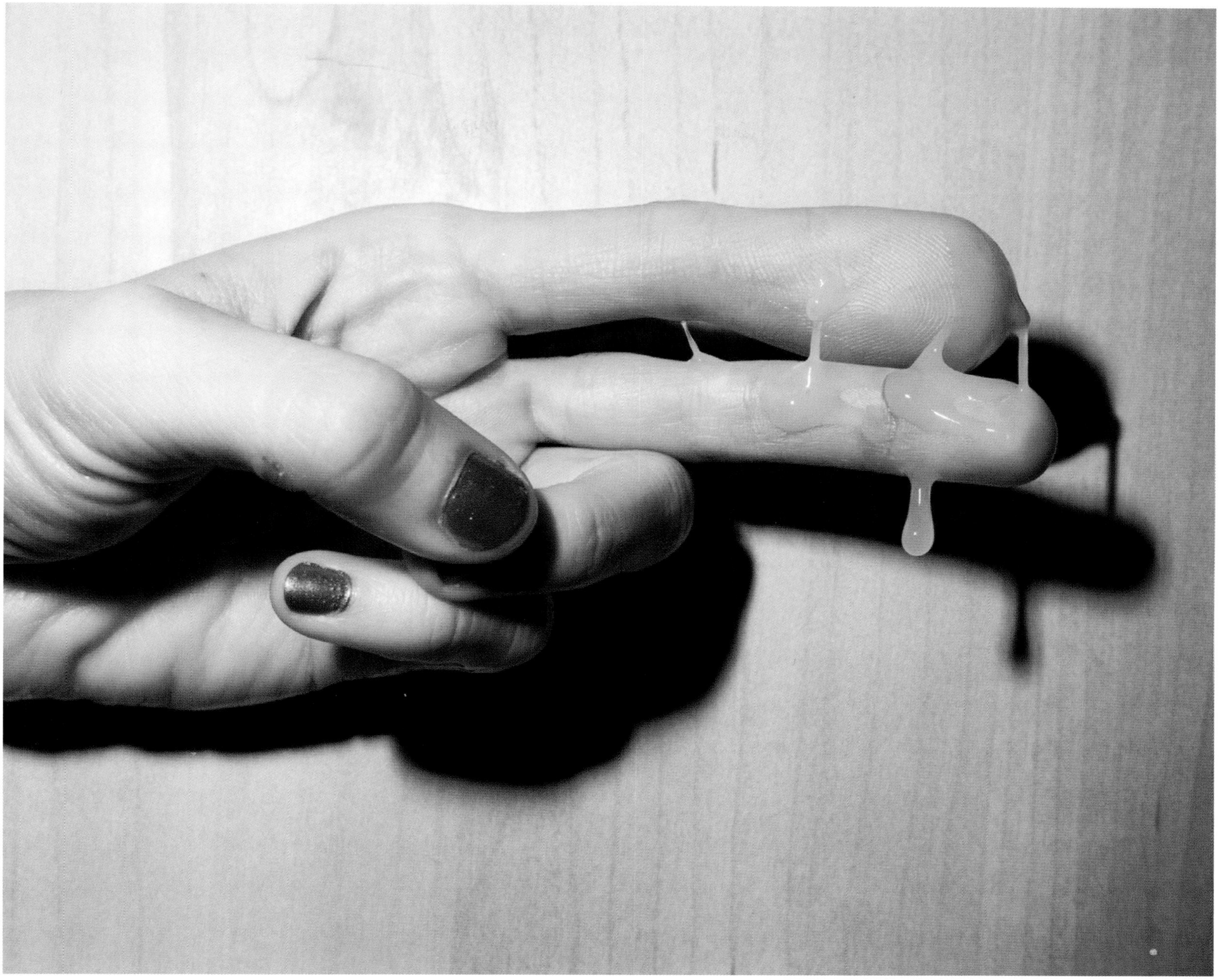

ASGER CARLSEN

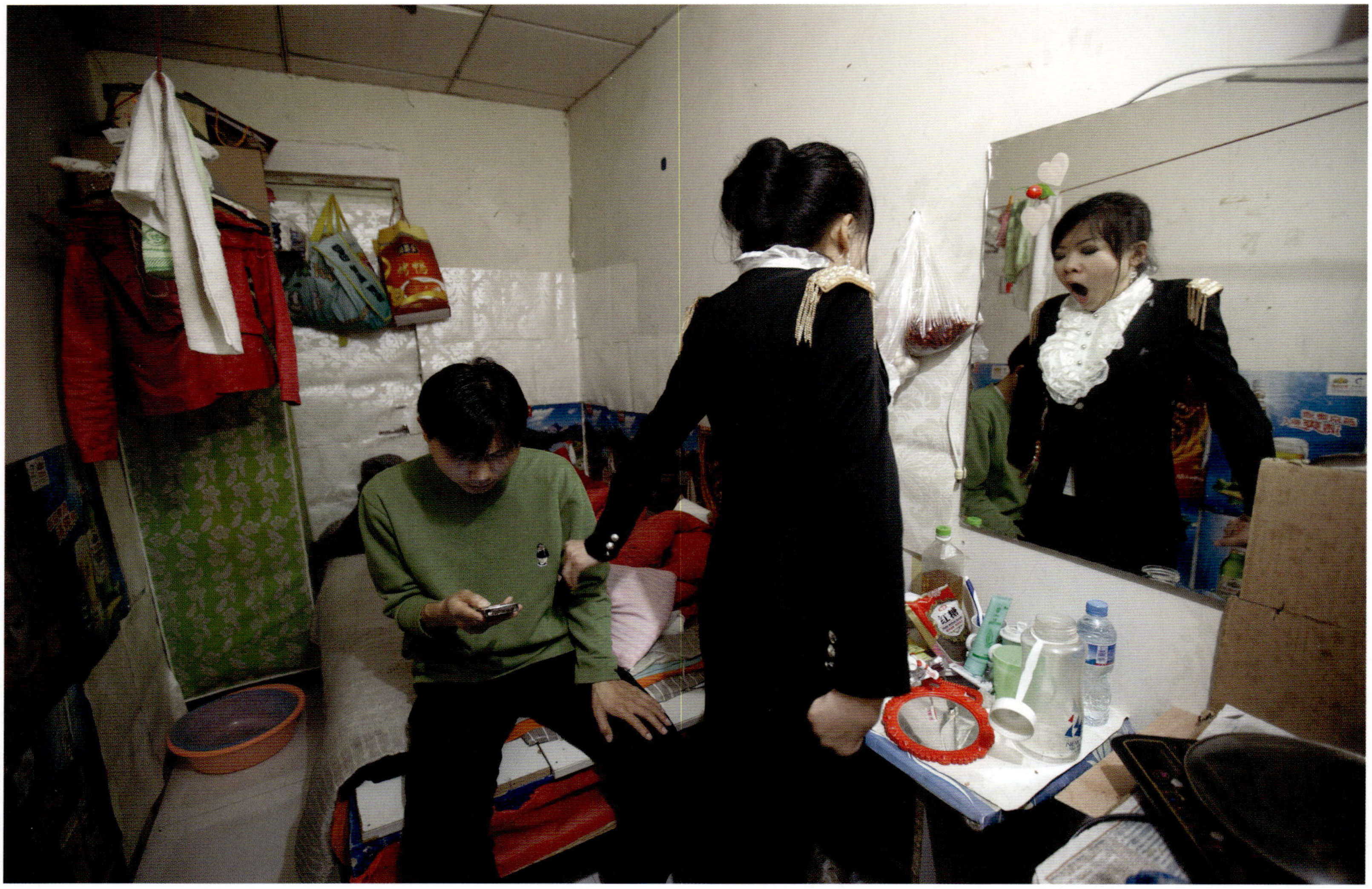

SIM CHI YIN

045 / 046

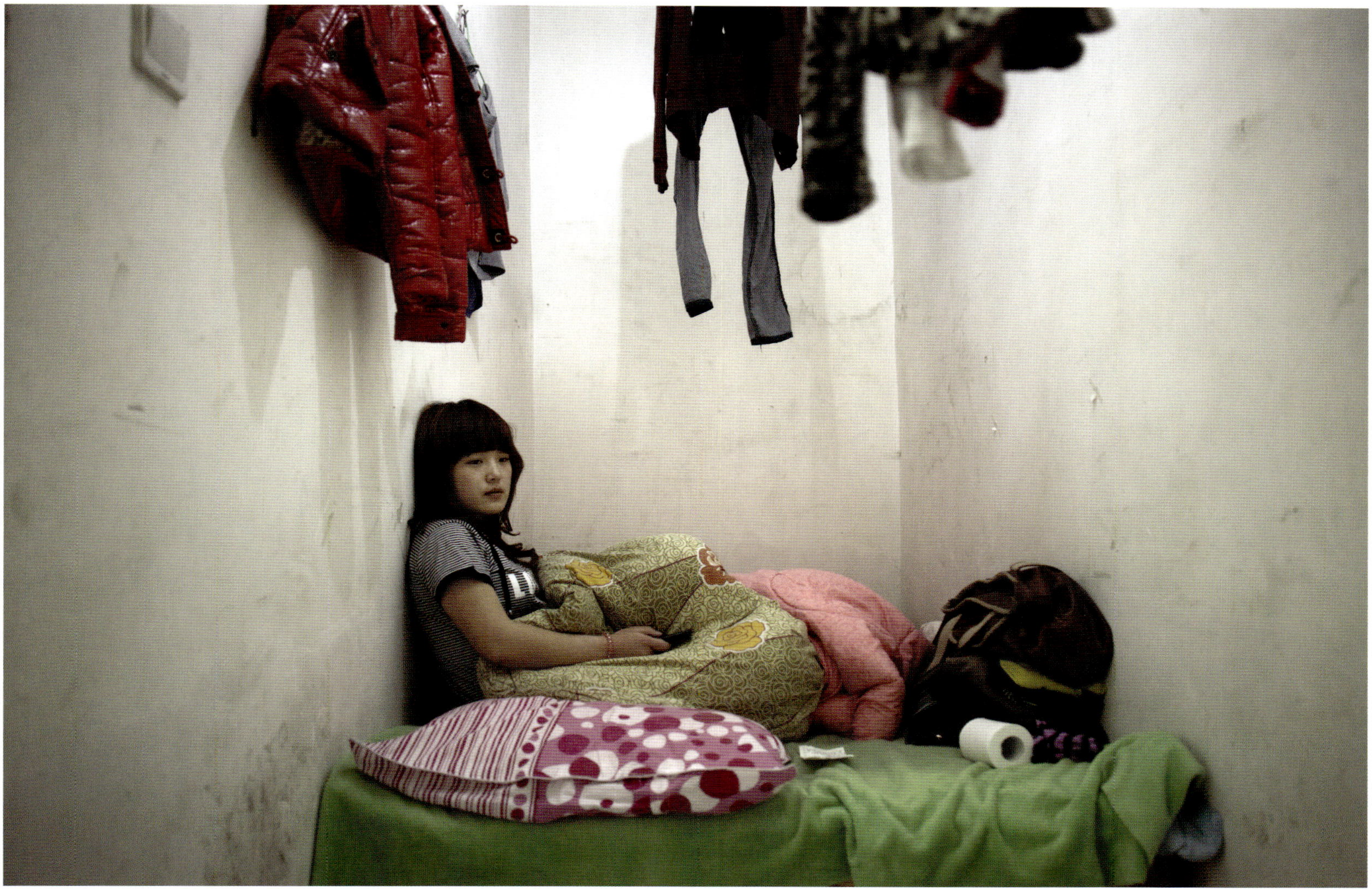

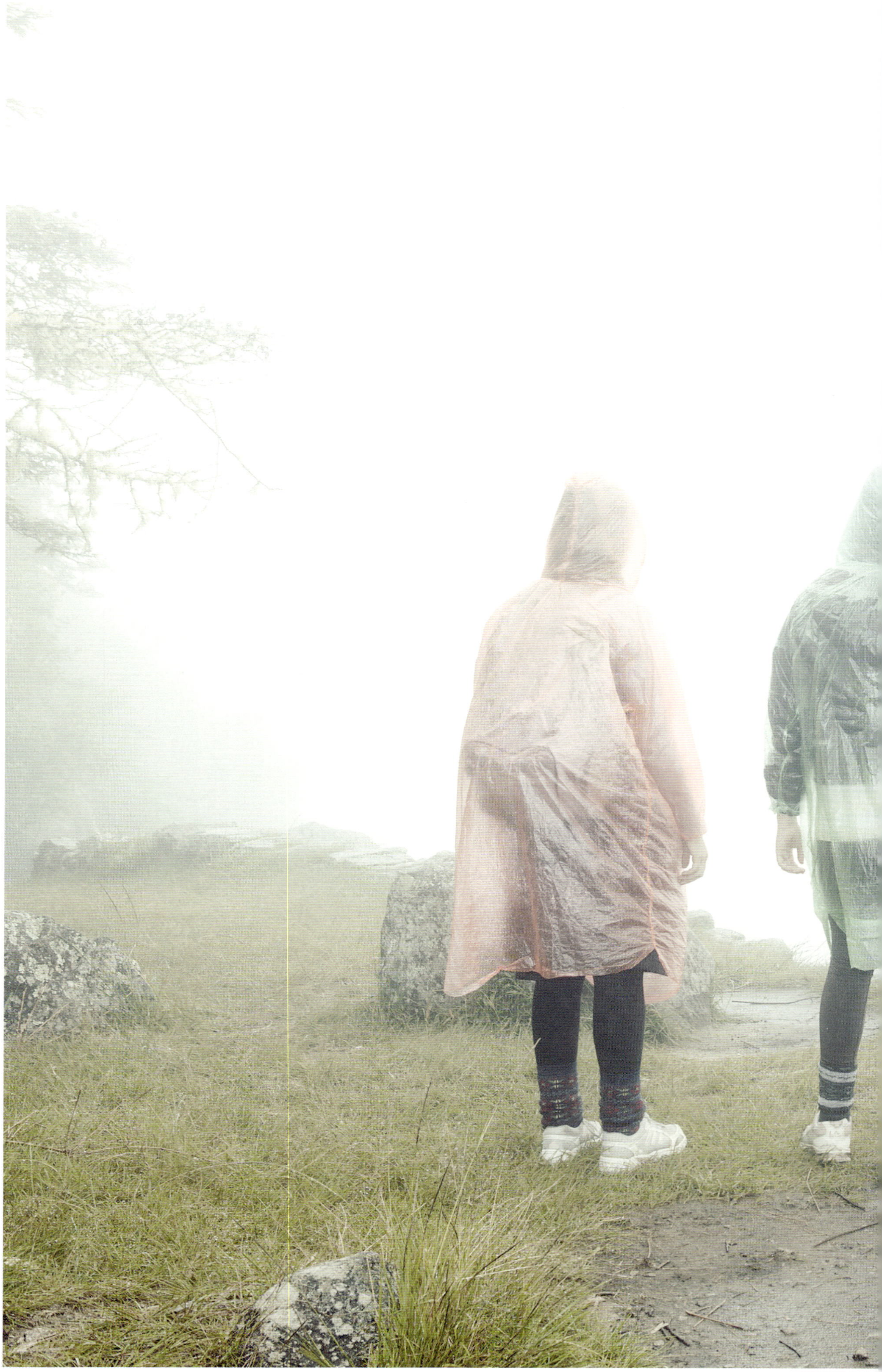

JOAO CANZIANI

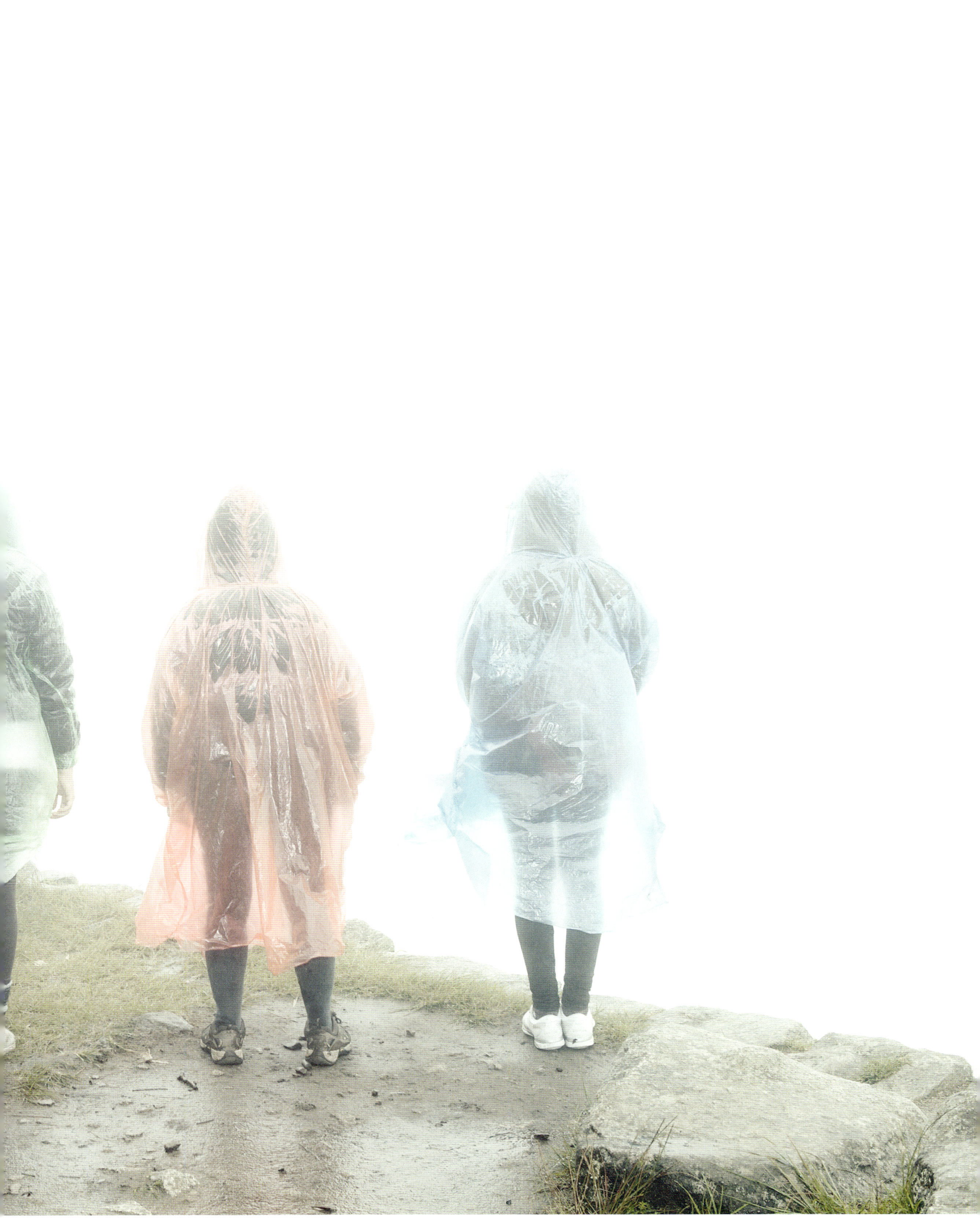

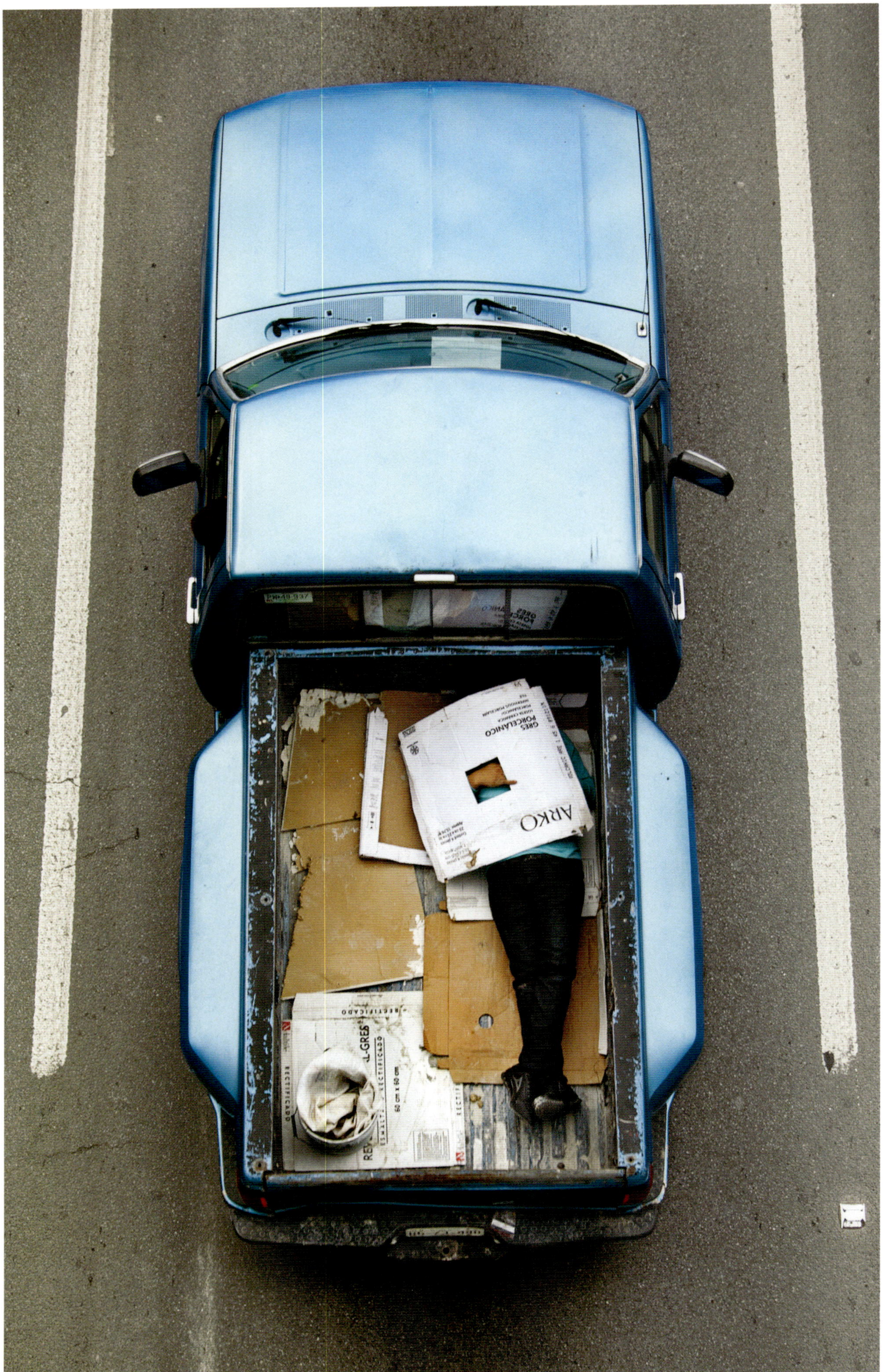

ALEJANDRO
CARTAGENA

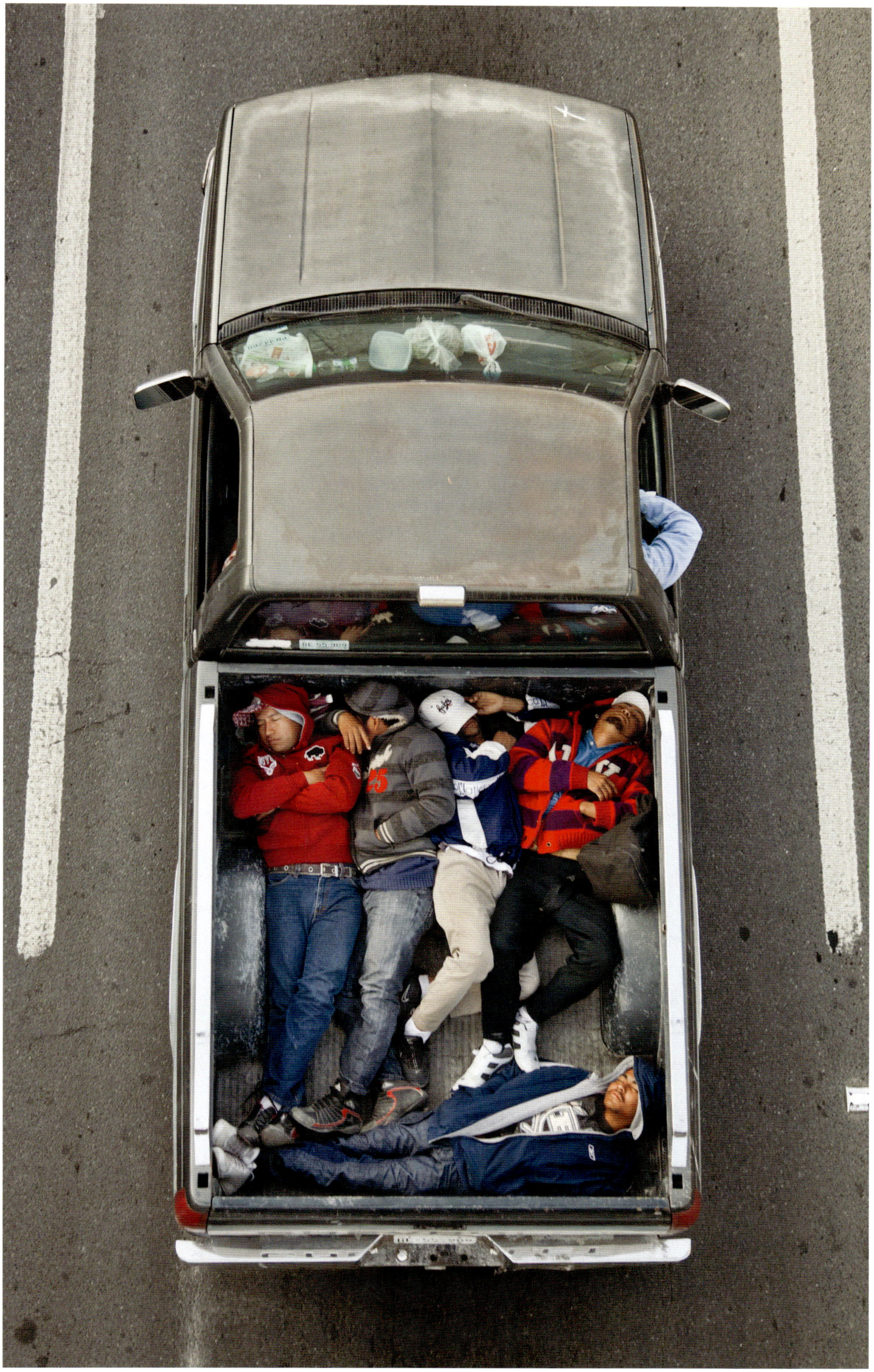

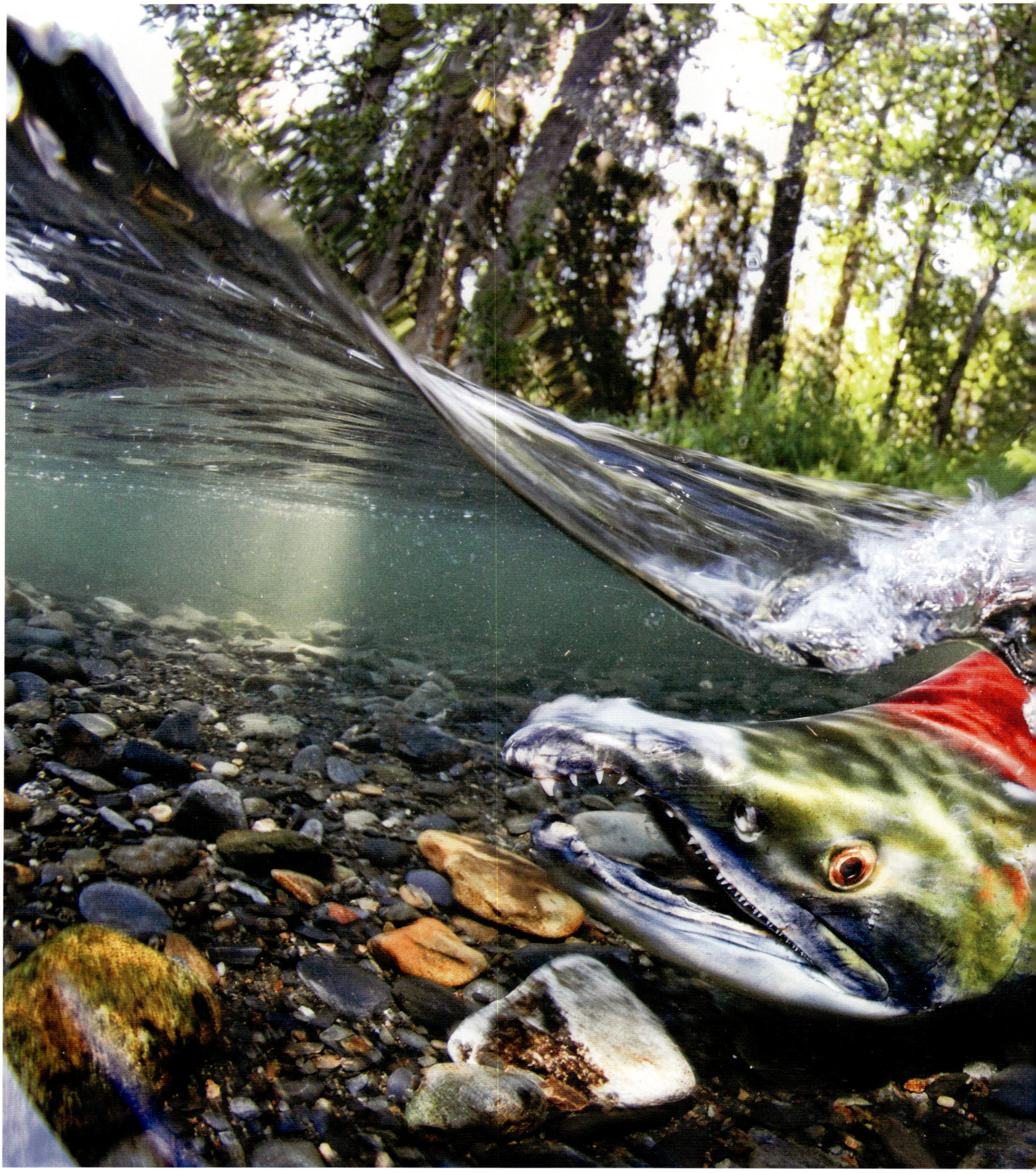

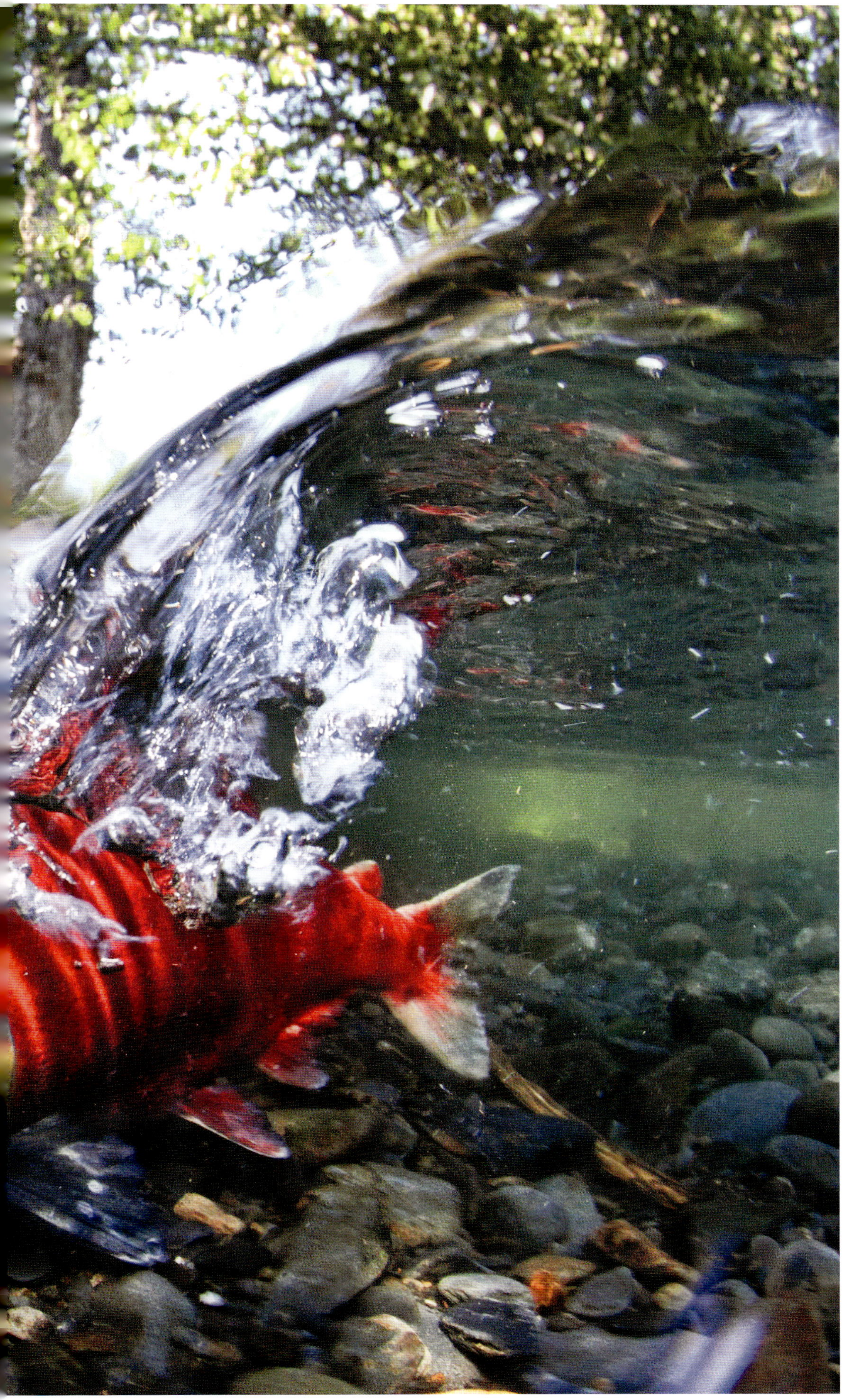

SETH CASTEEL

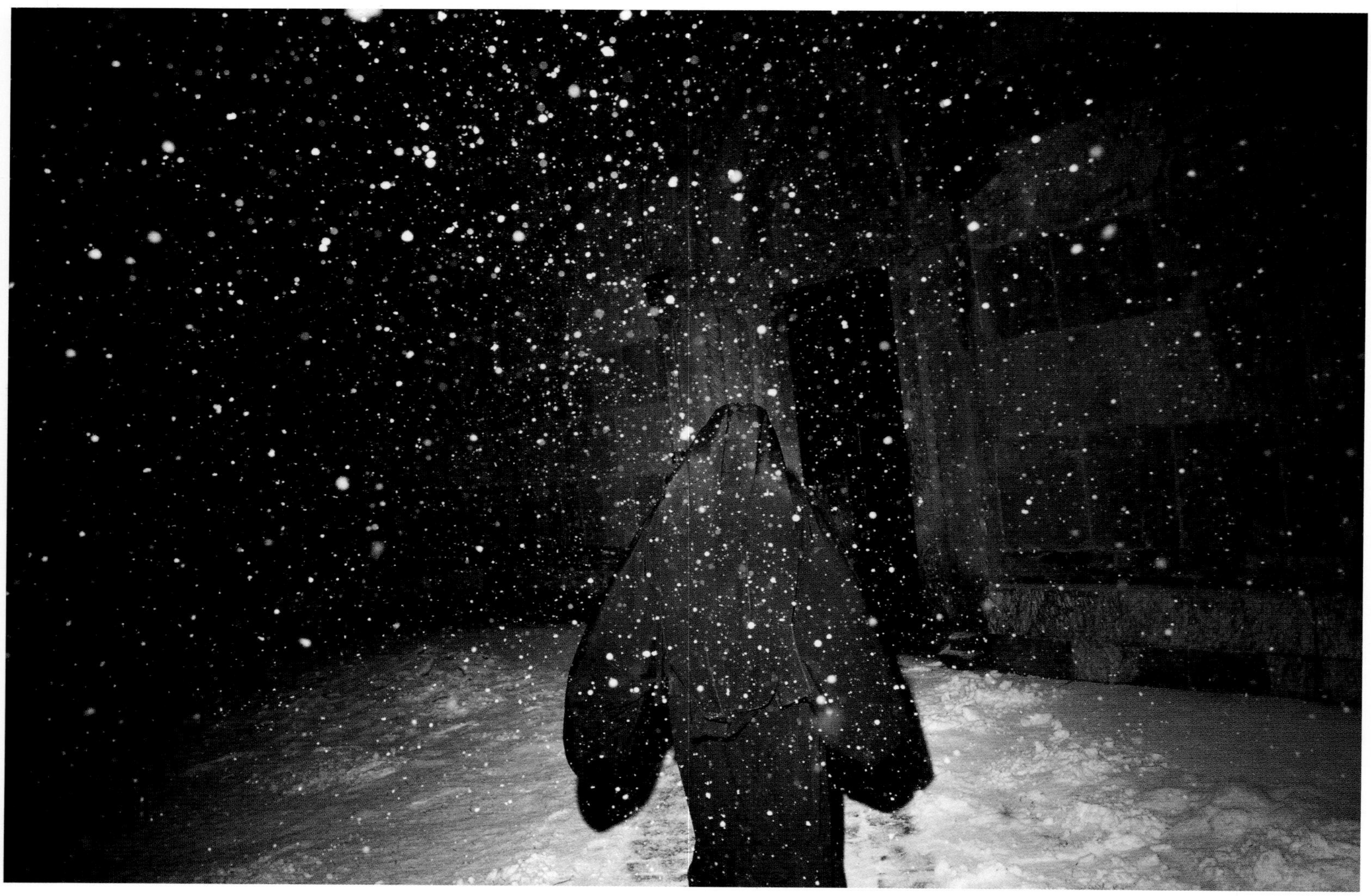

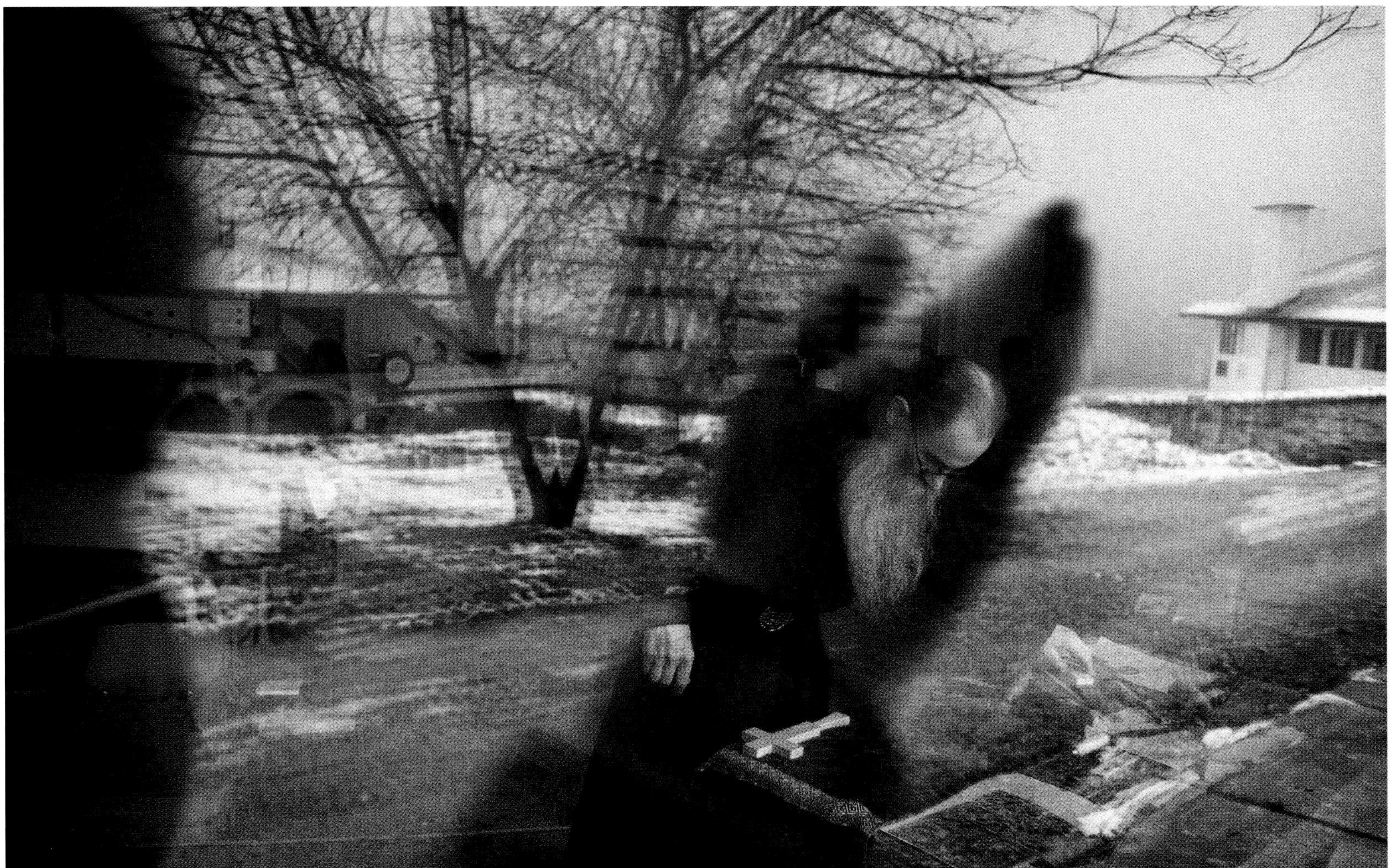

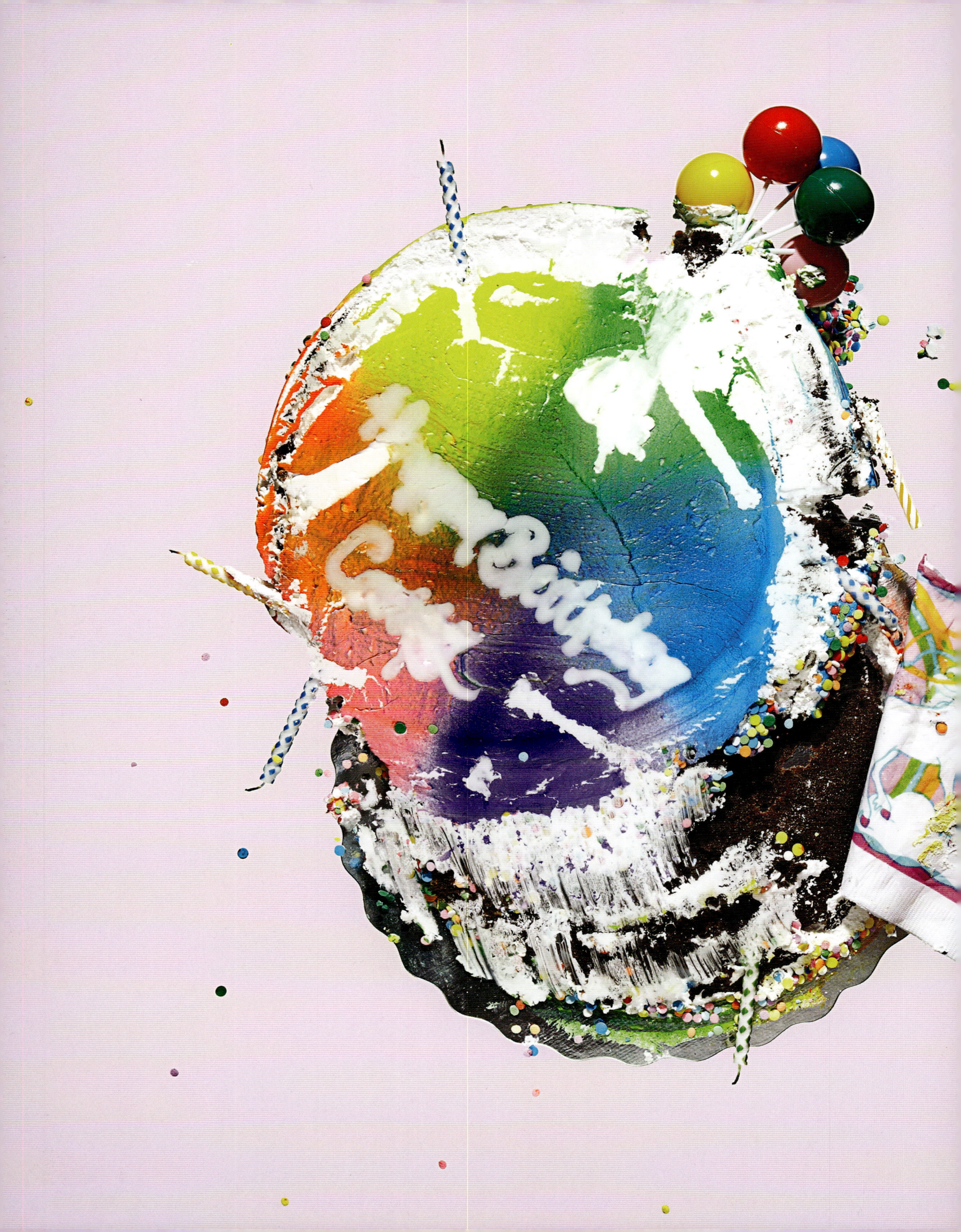

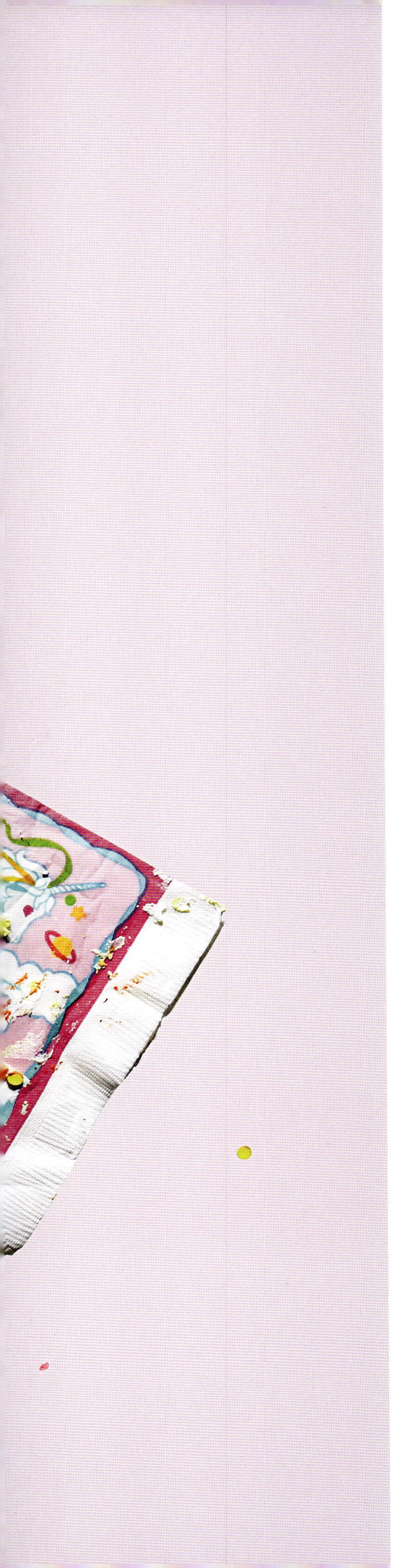

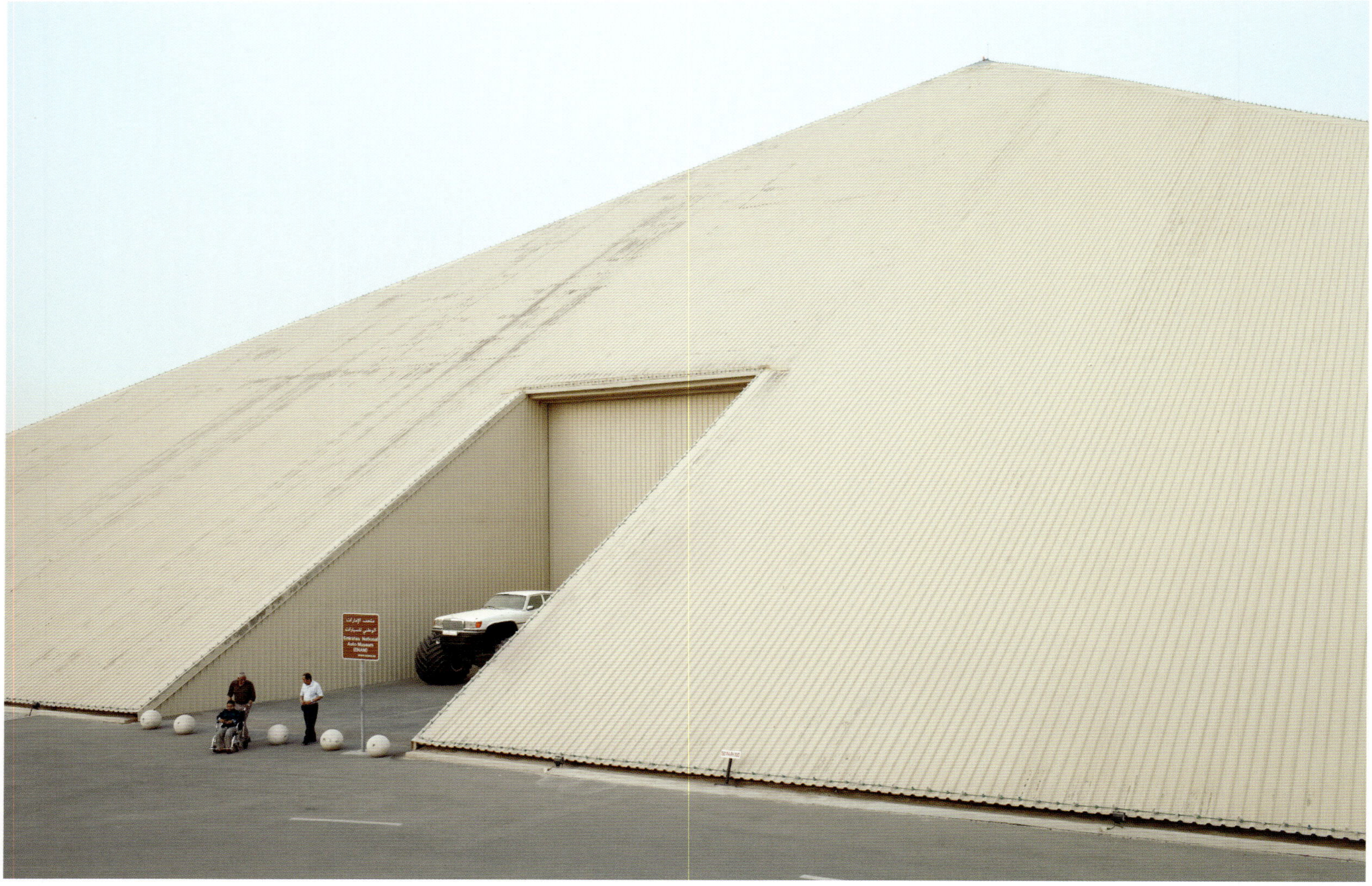

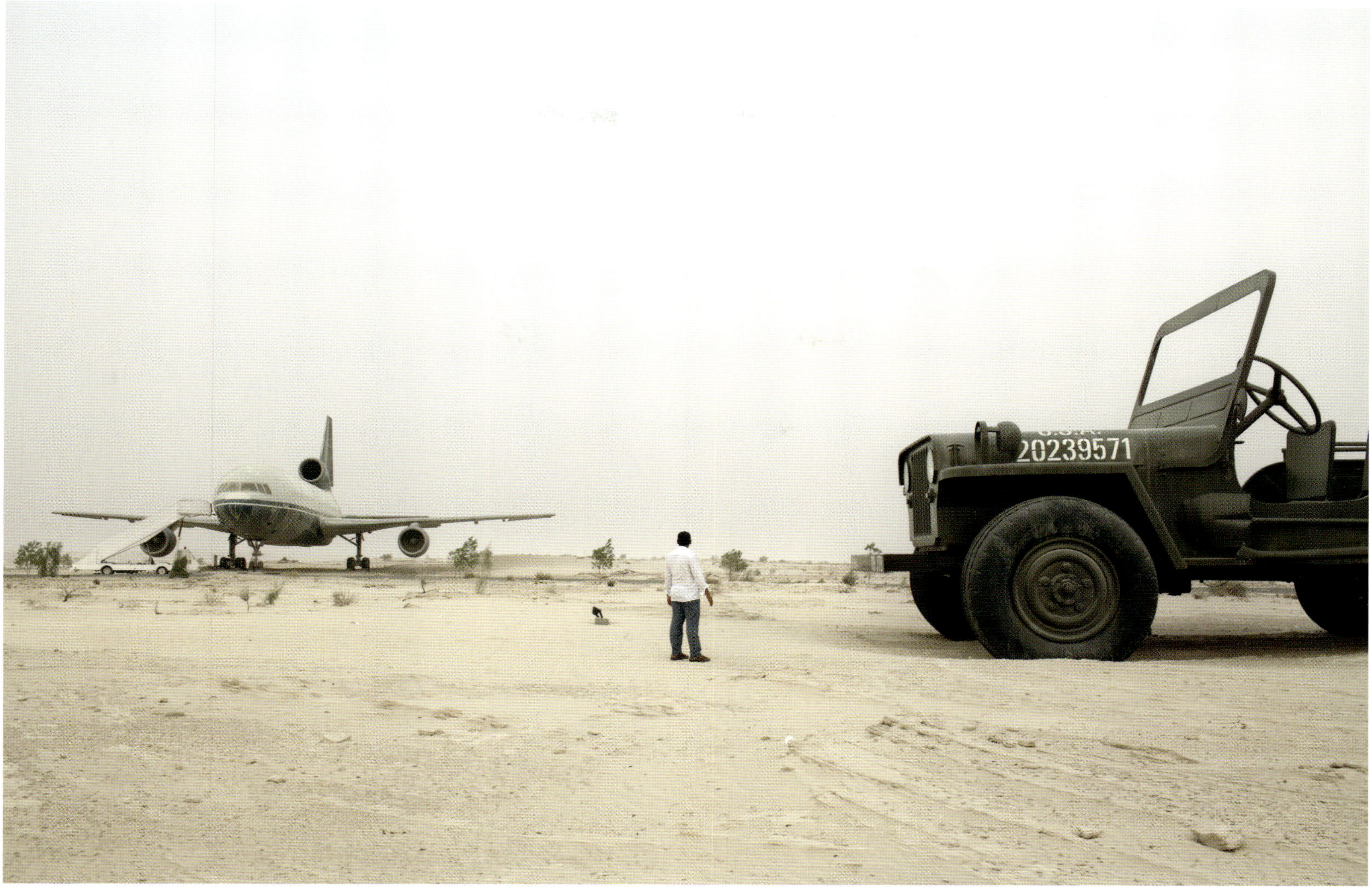
20239571

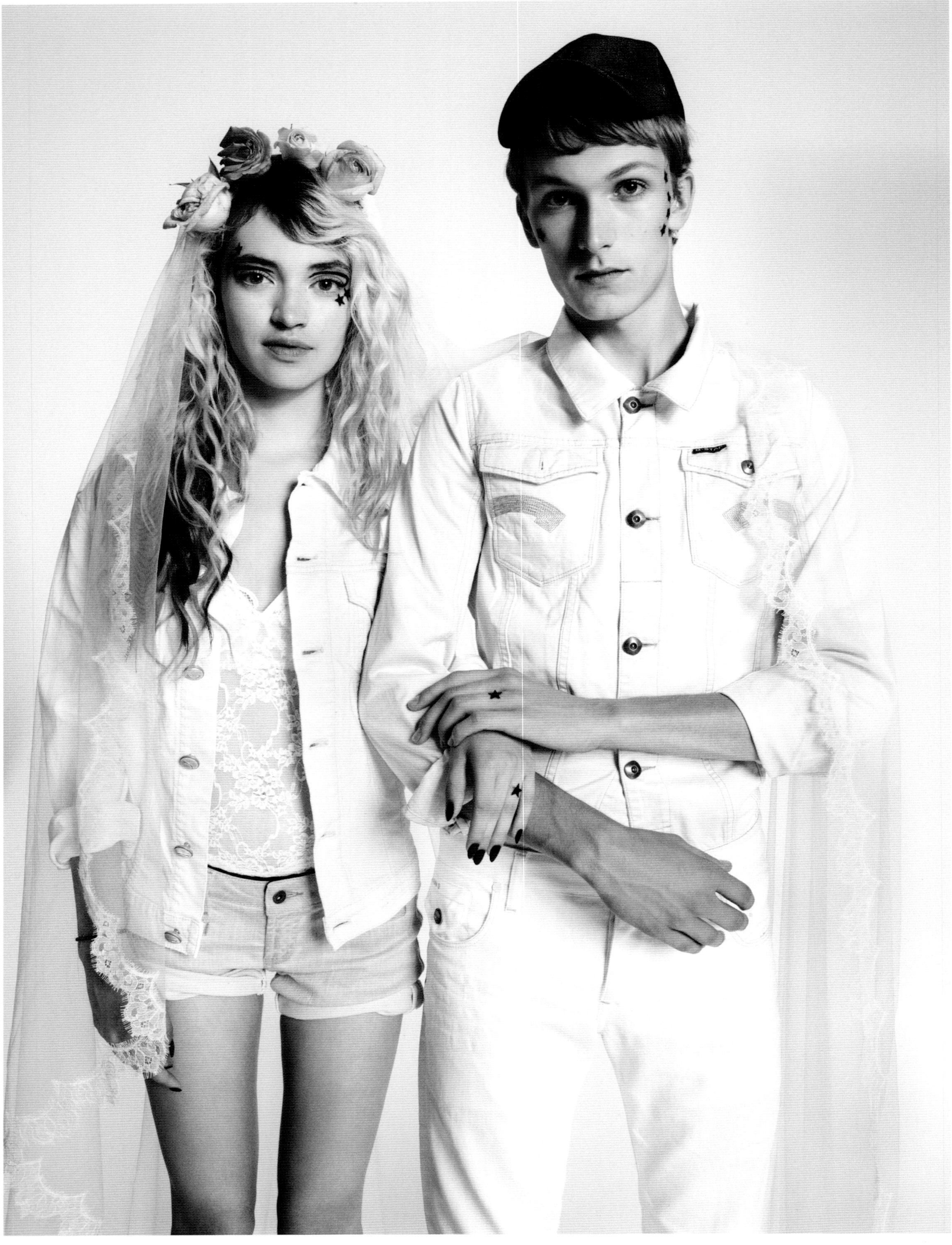

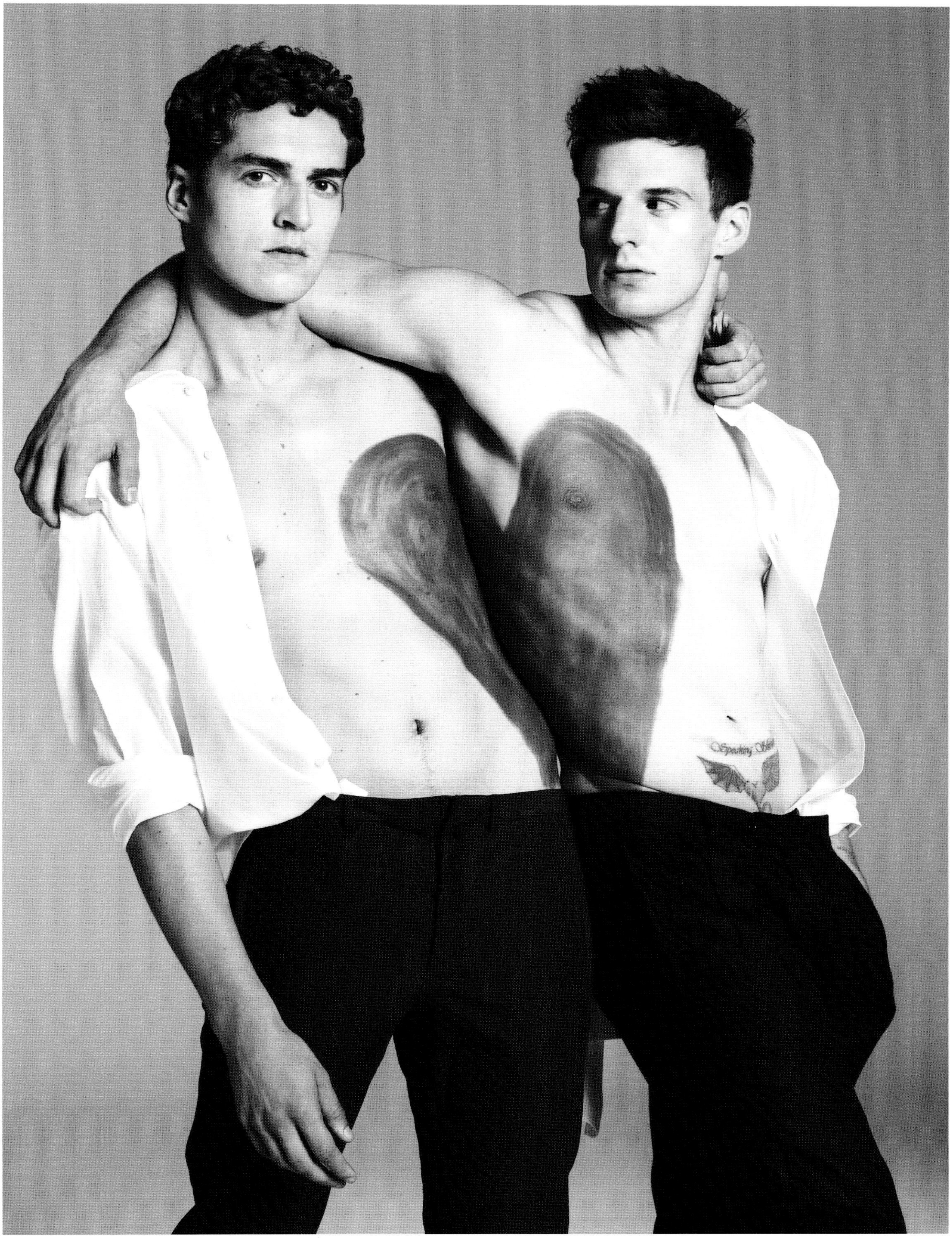

CHRIS CRAYMER

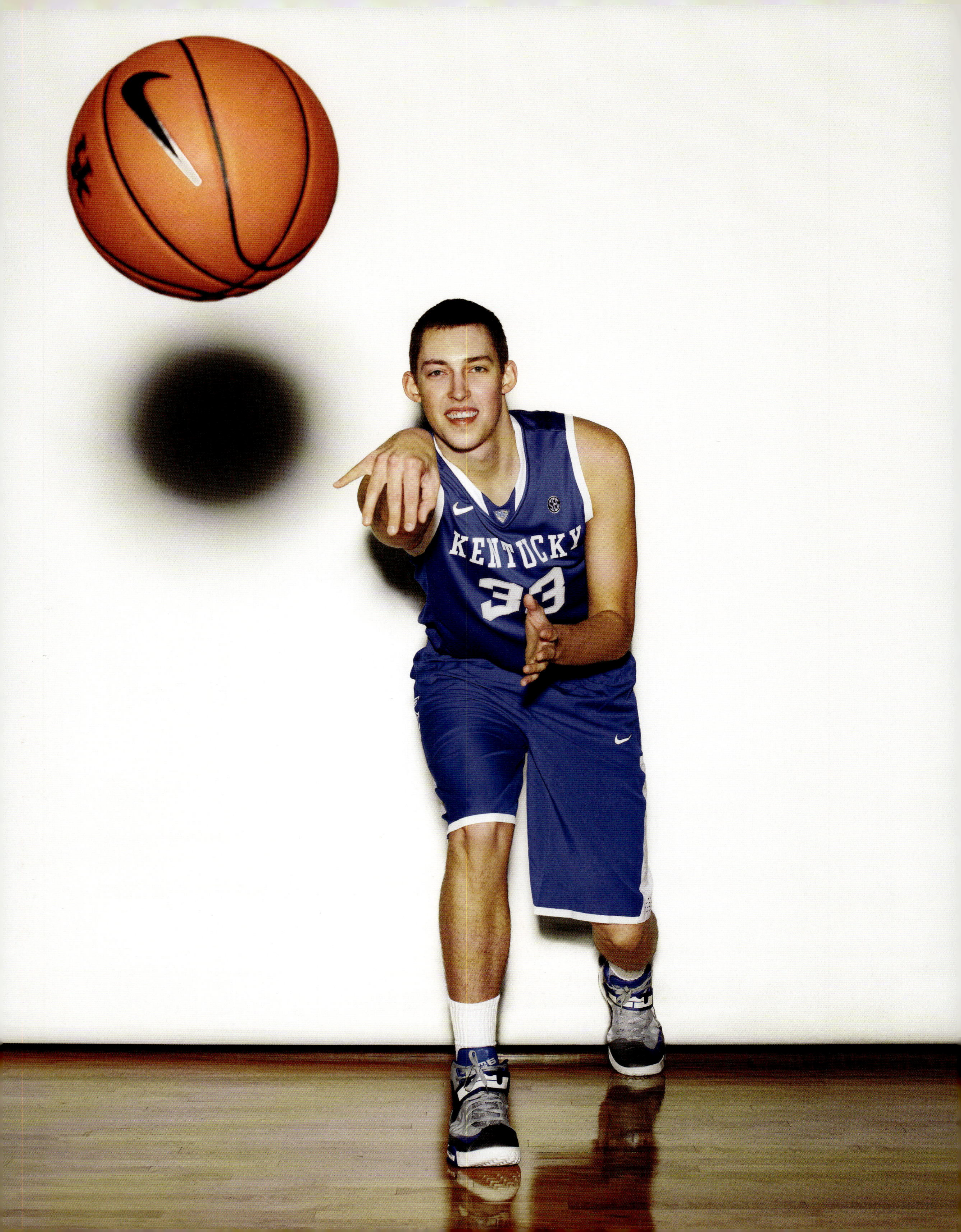
KENTUCKY
33

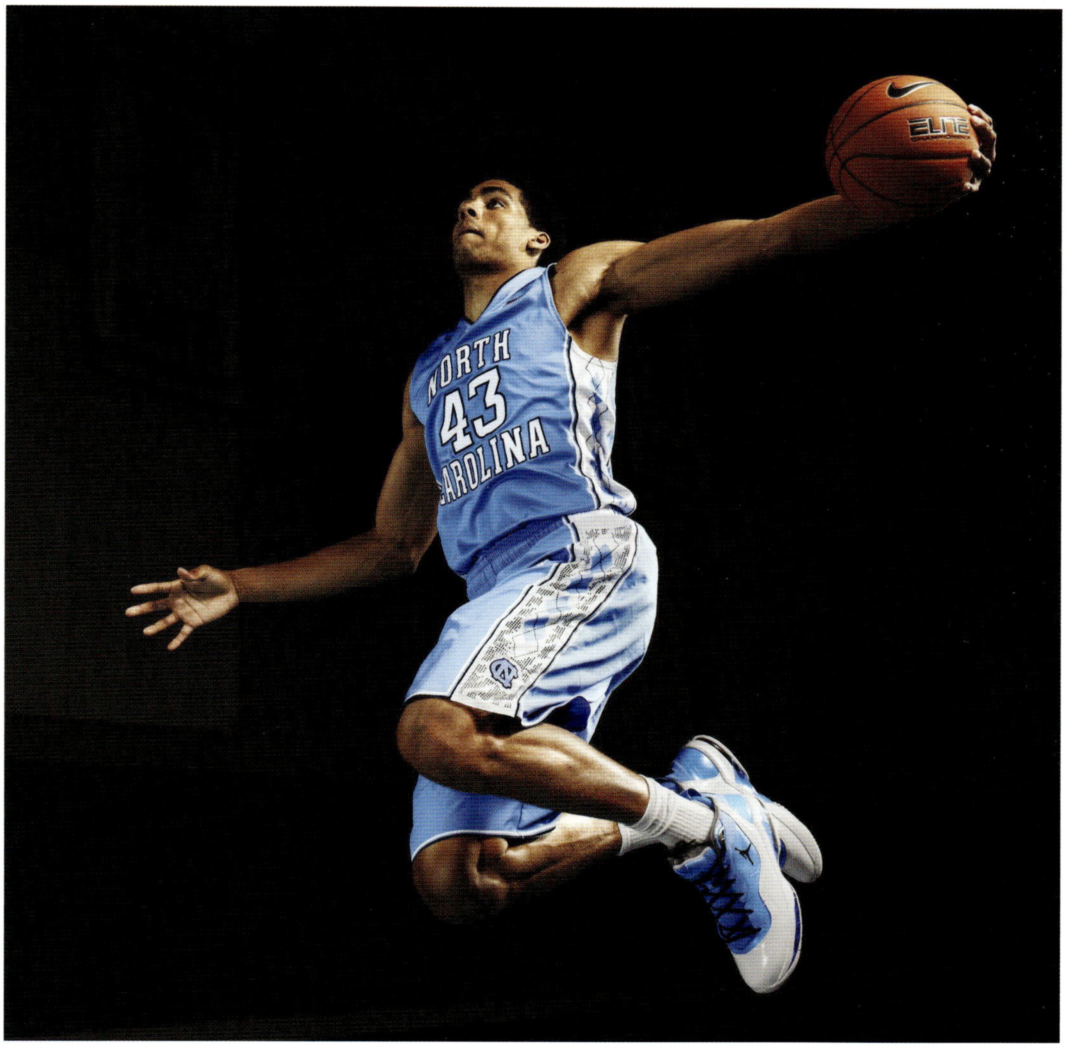
NORTH
43
CAROLINA

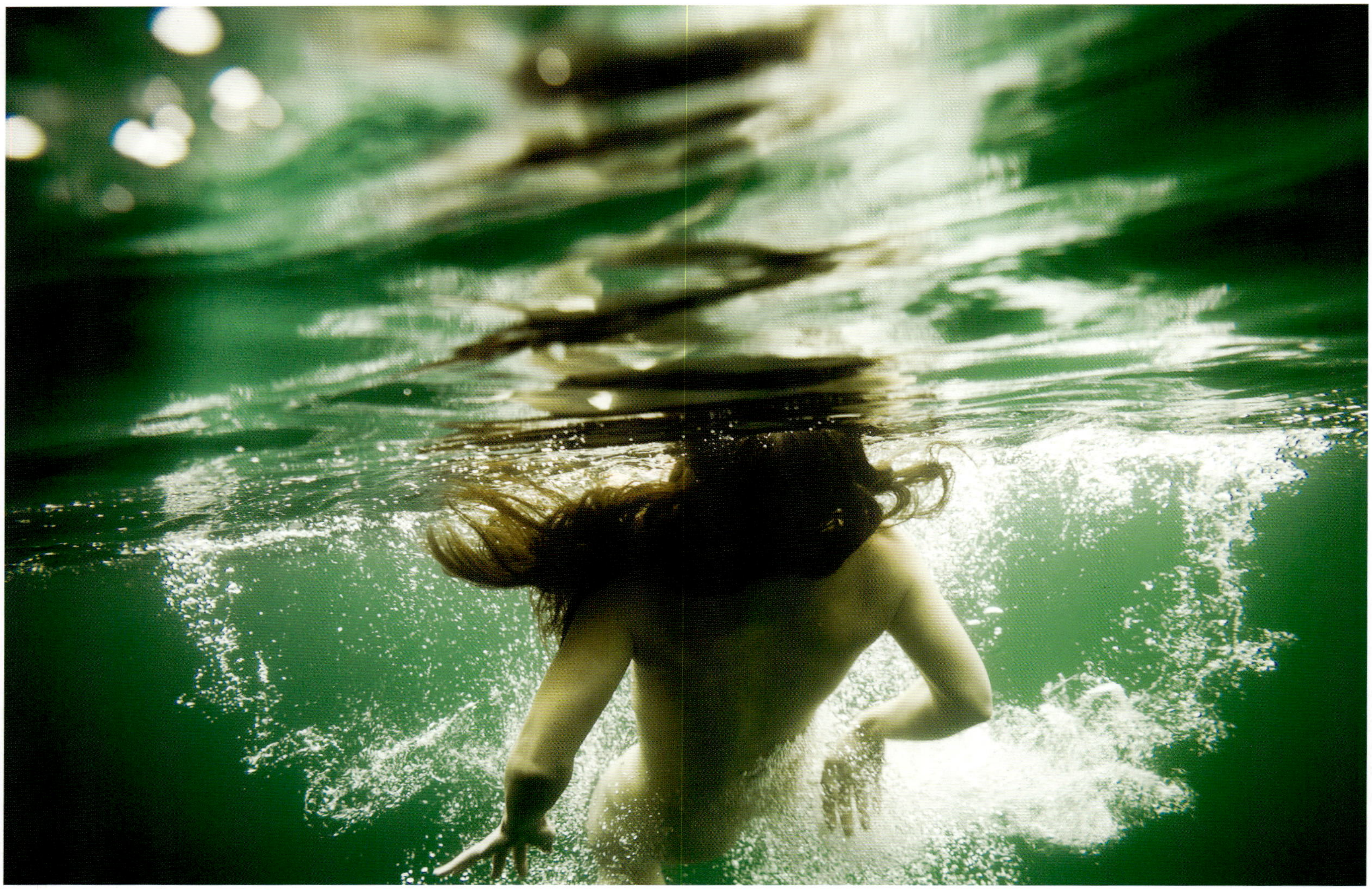

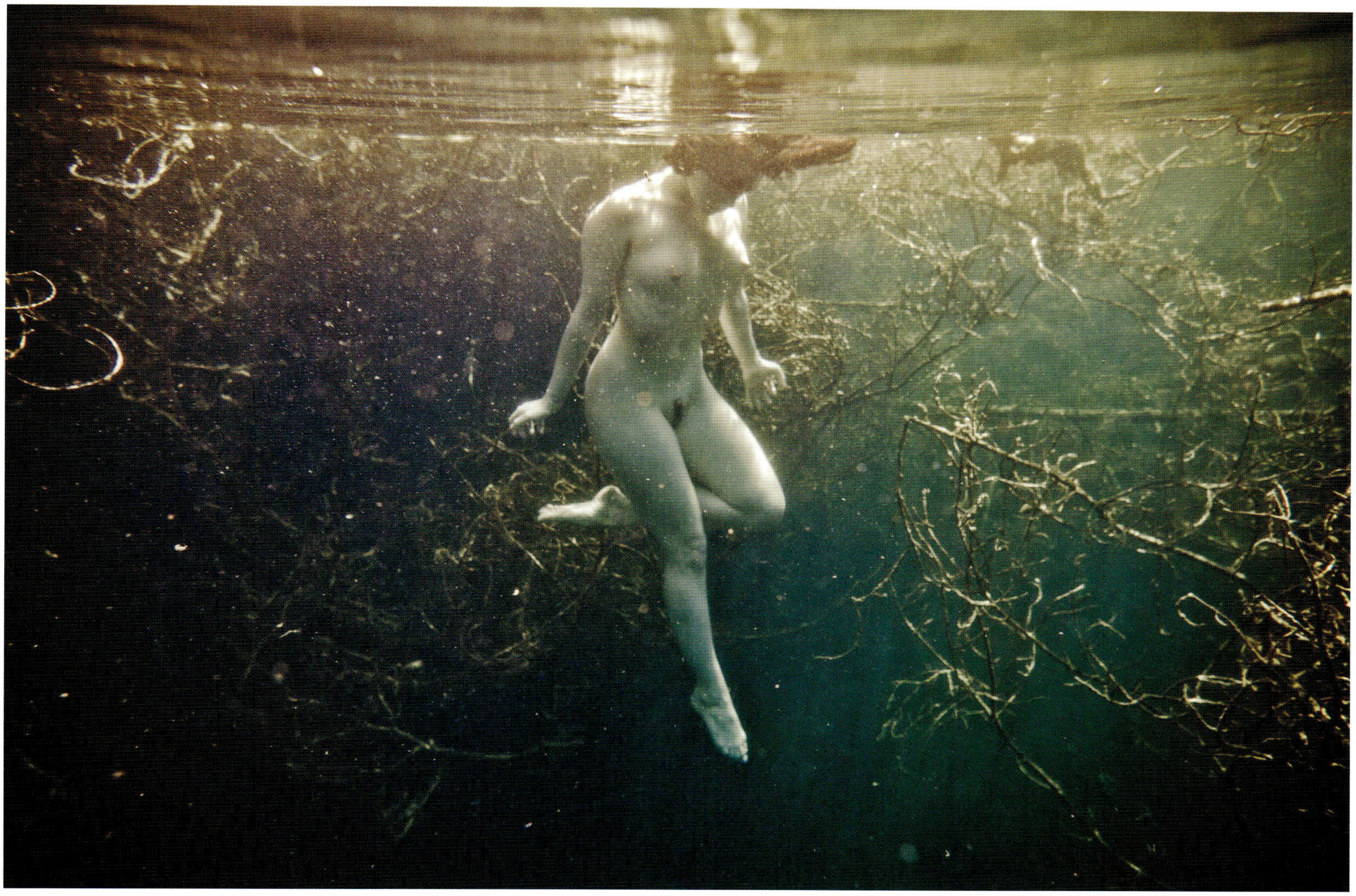

NEIL CRAVER

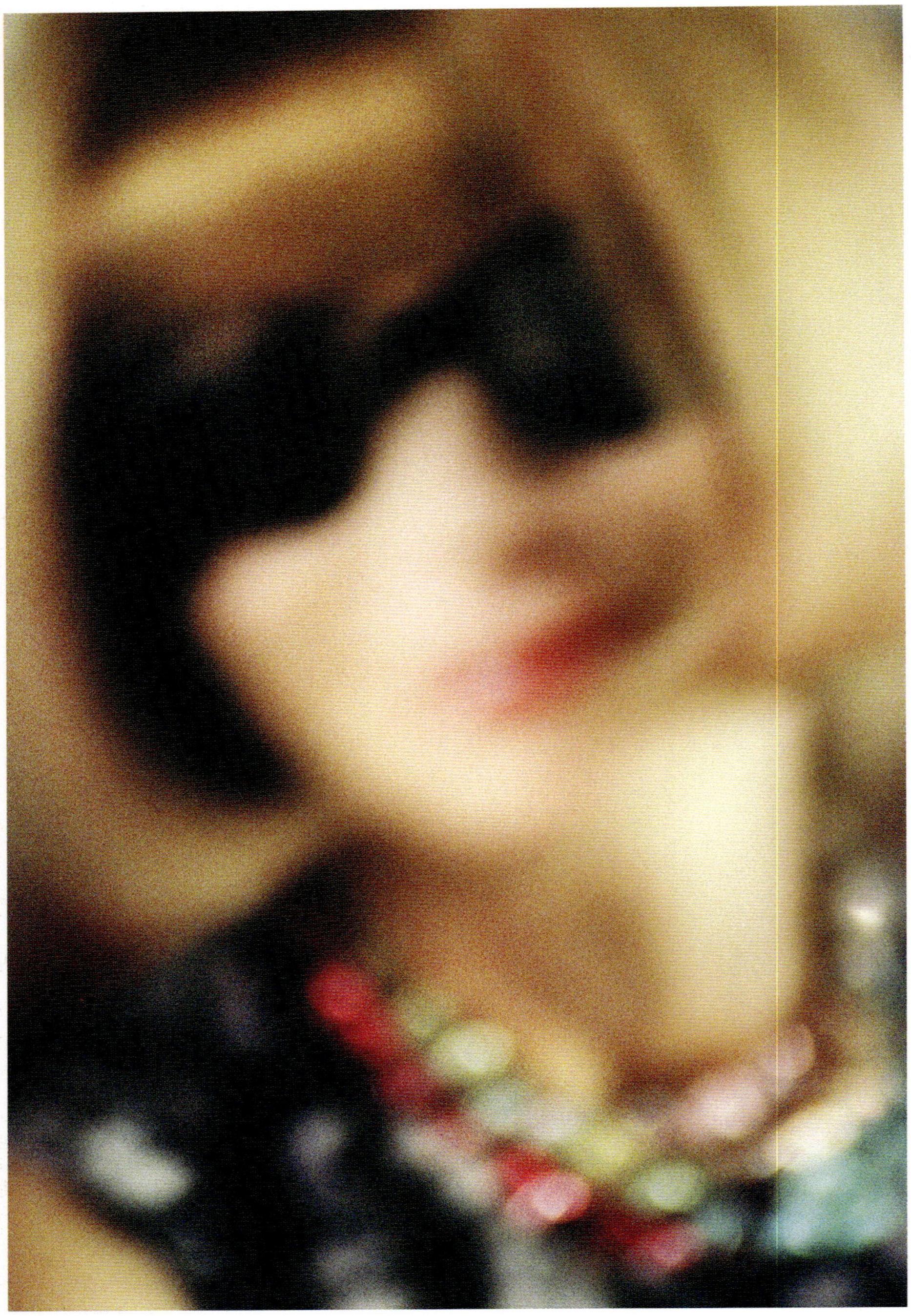

PARI DUKOVIC

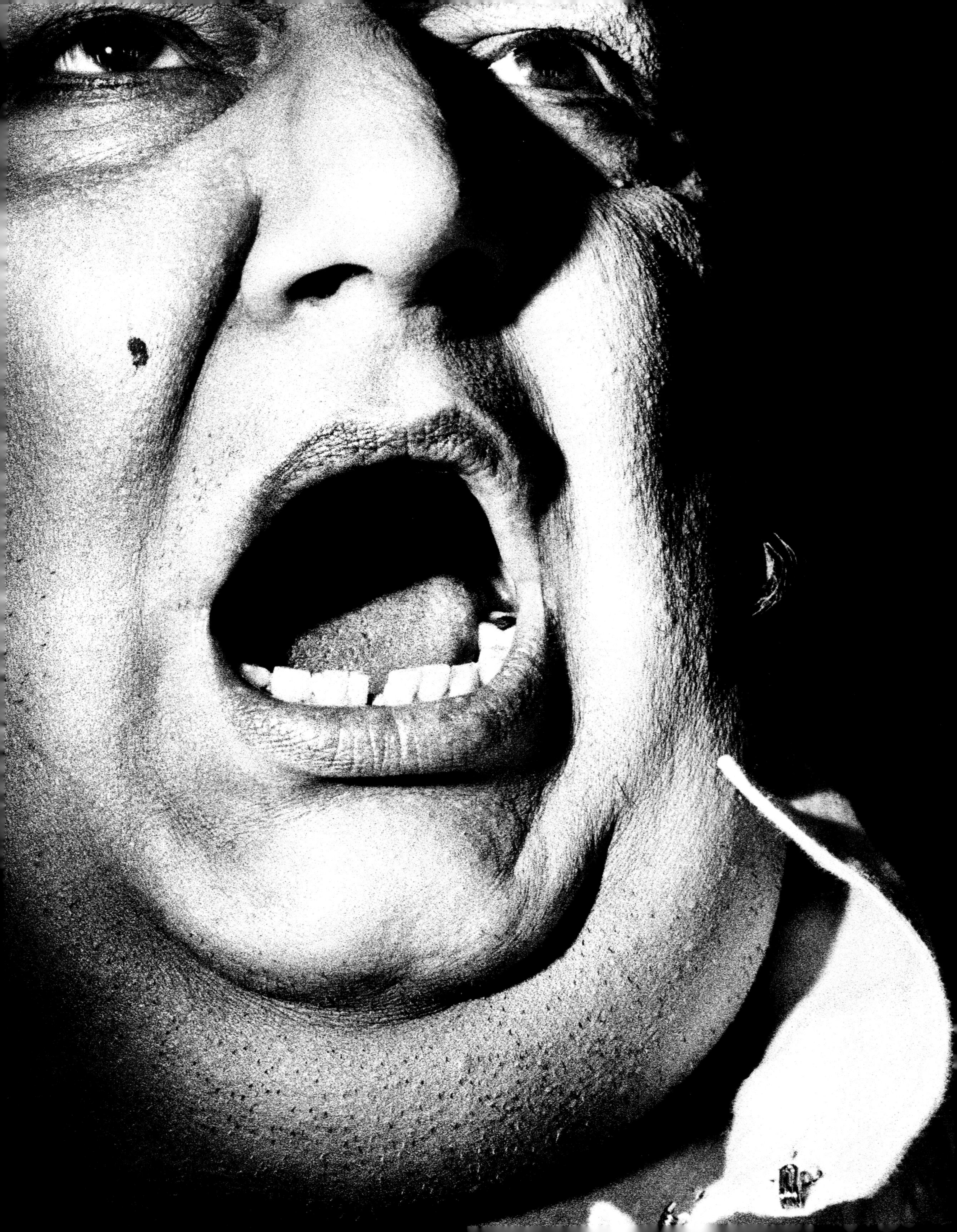

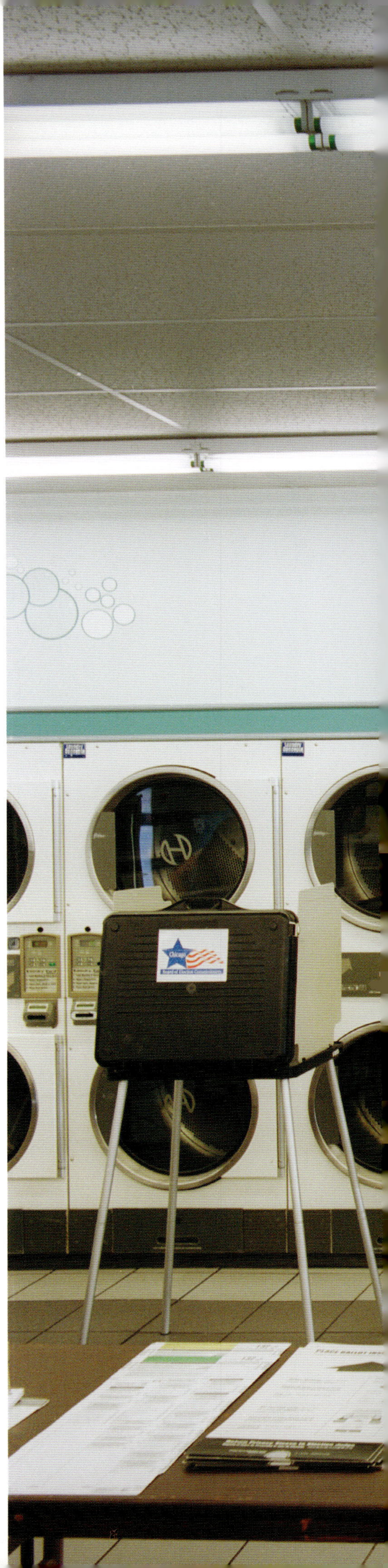

RYAN DONNELL

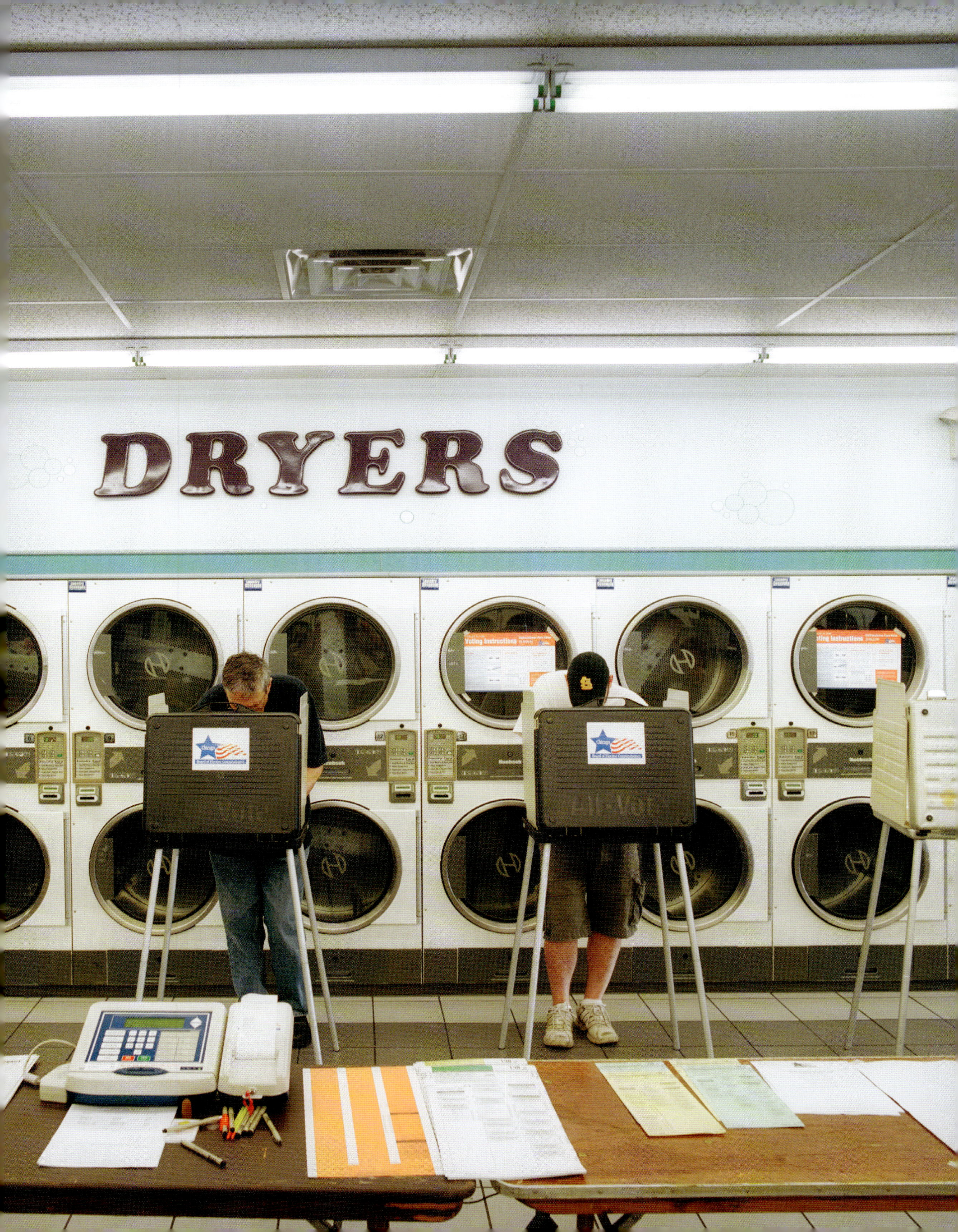
DRYERS
Voting Instructions
All-Vote

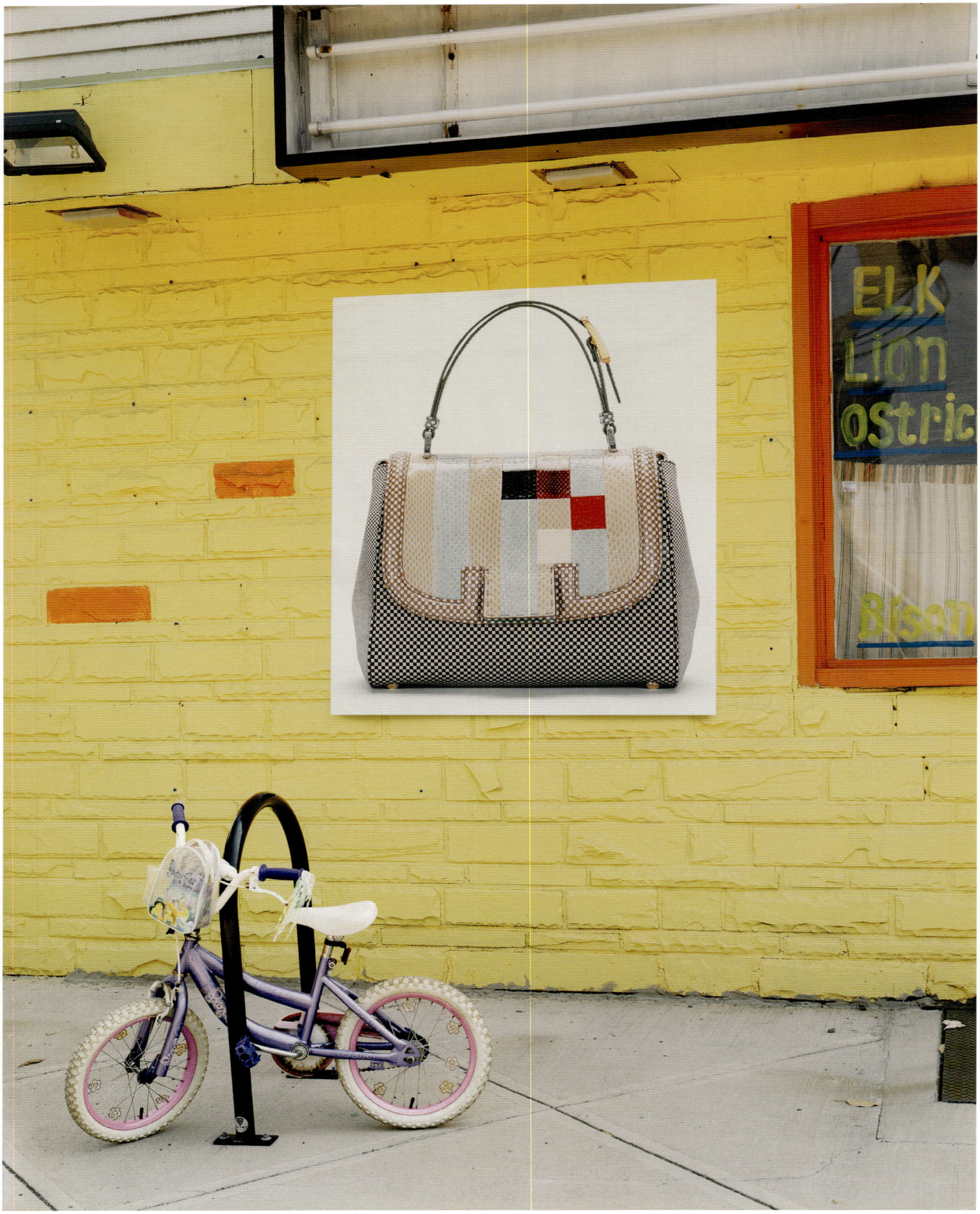

TIM DAVIS

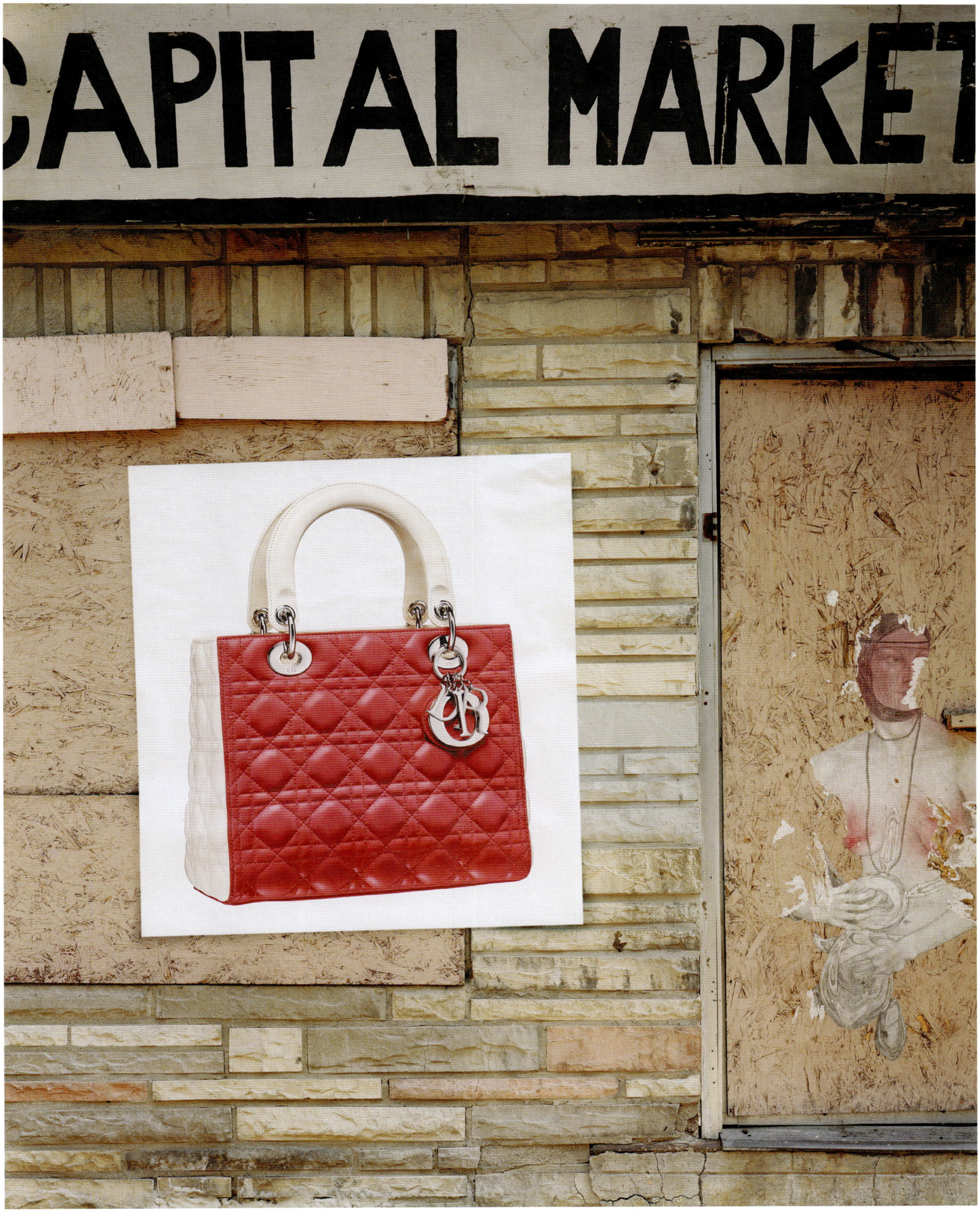
CAPITAL MARKET

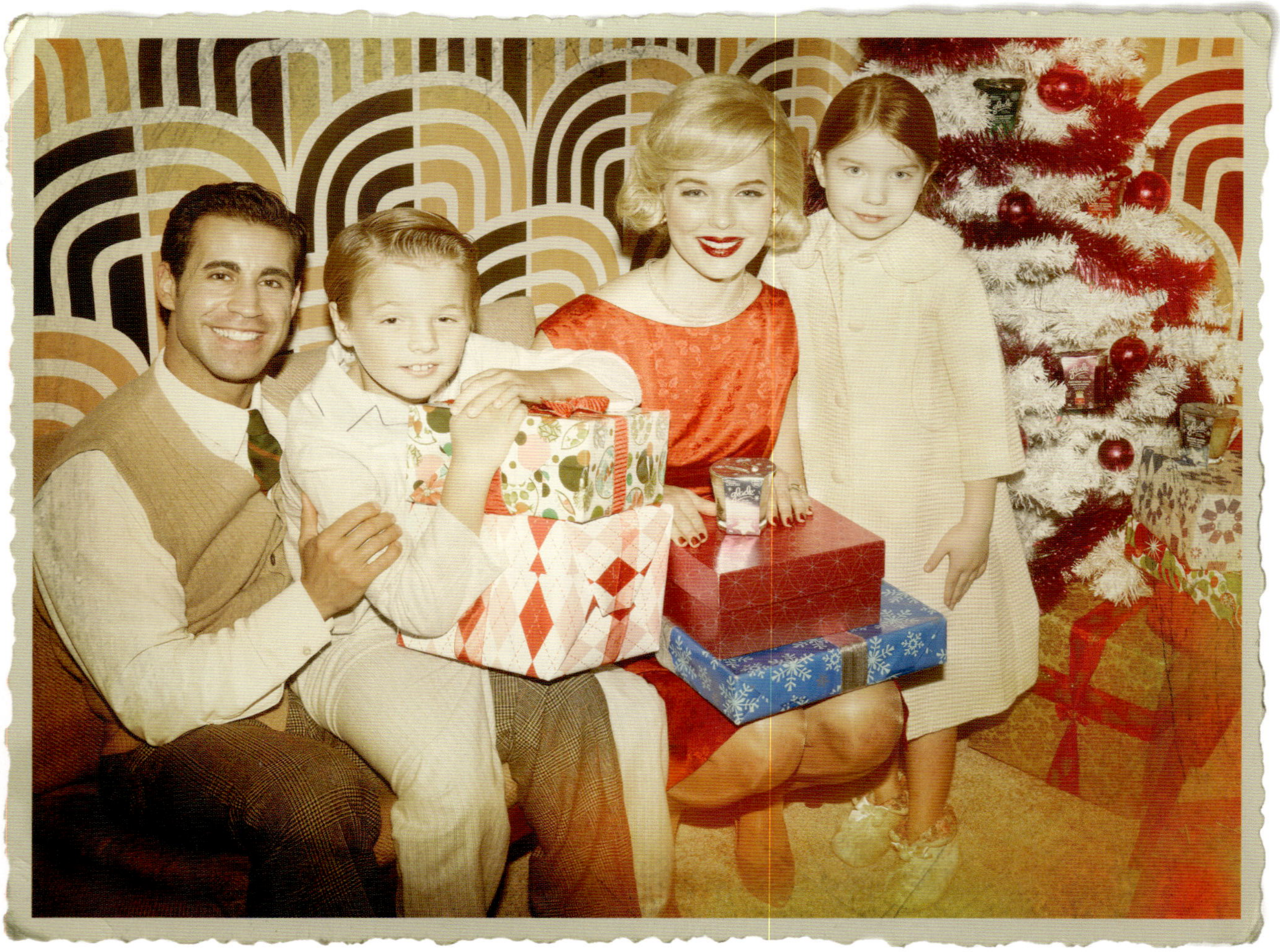

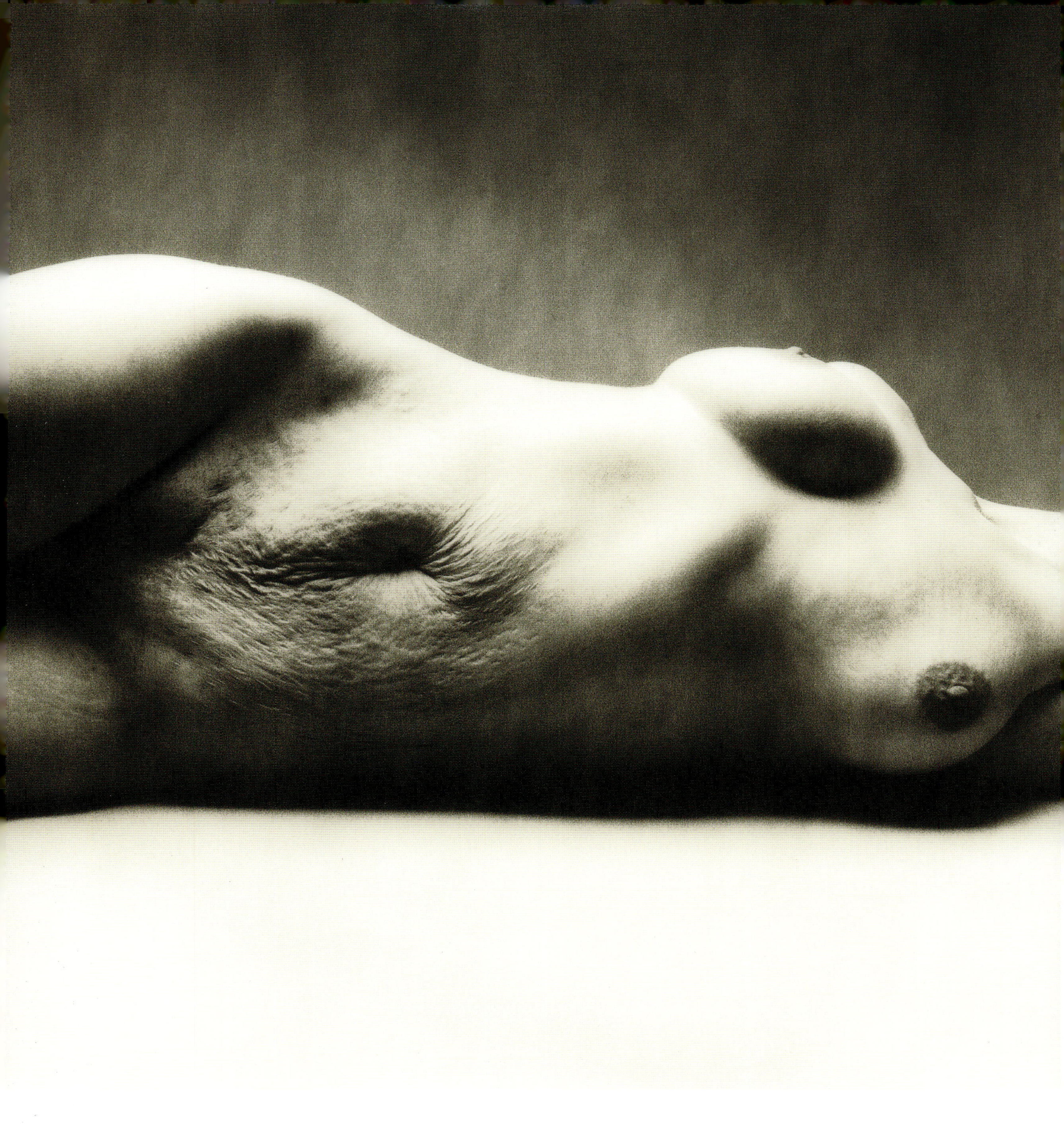

SAMAN DEILAMANI

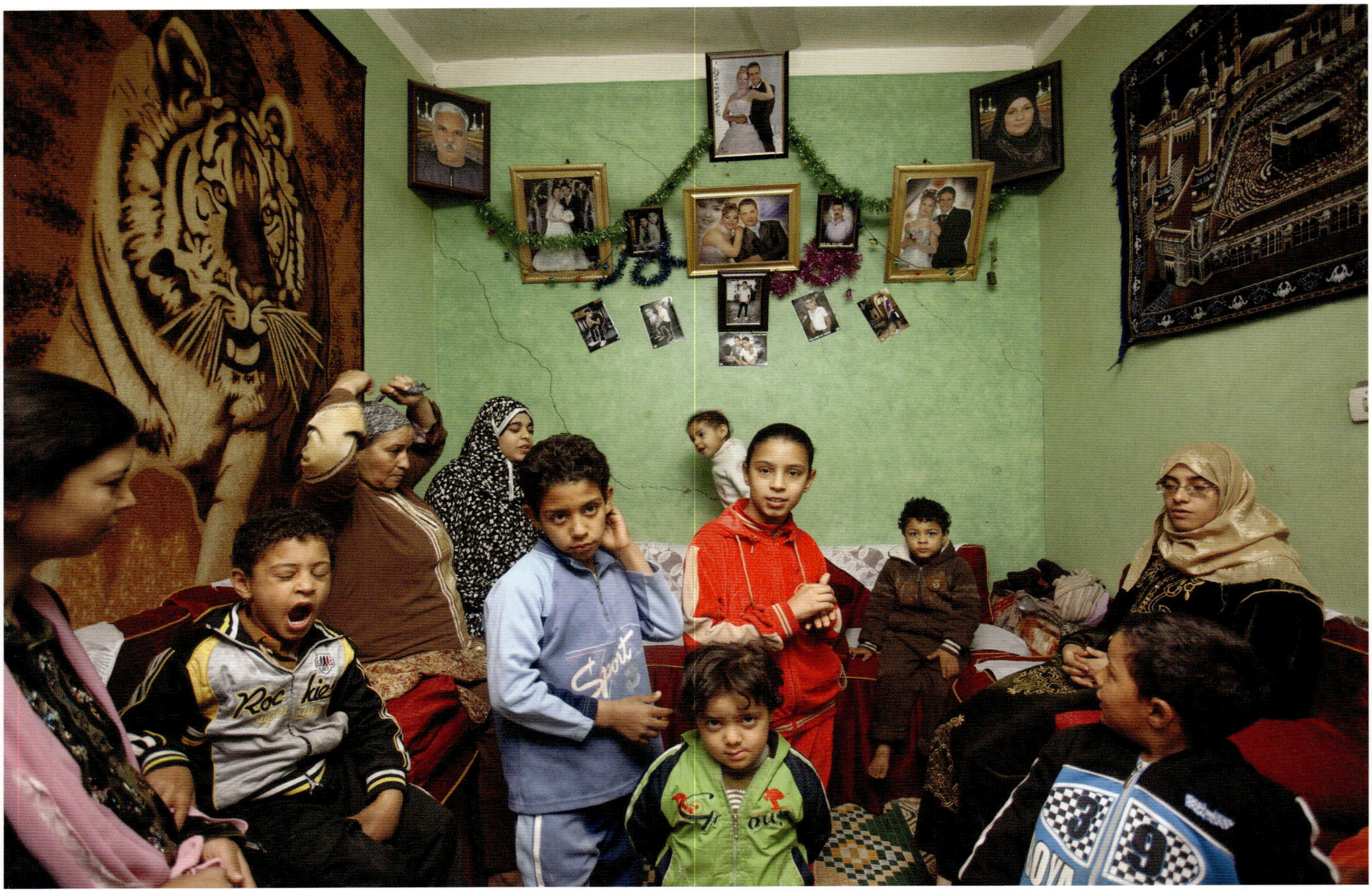

BIEKE DEPOORTER

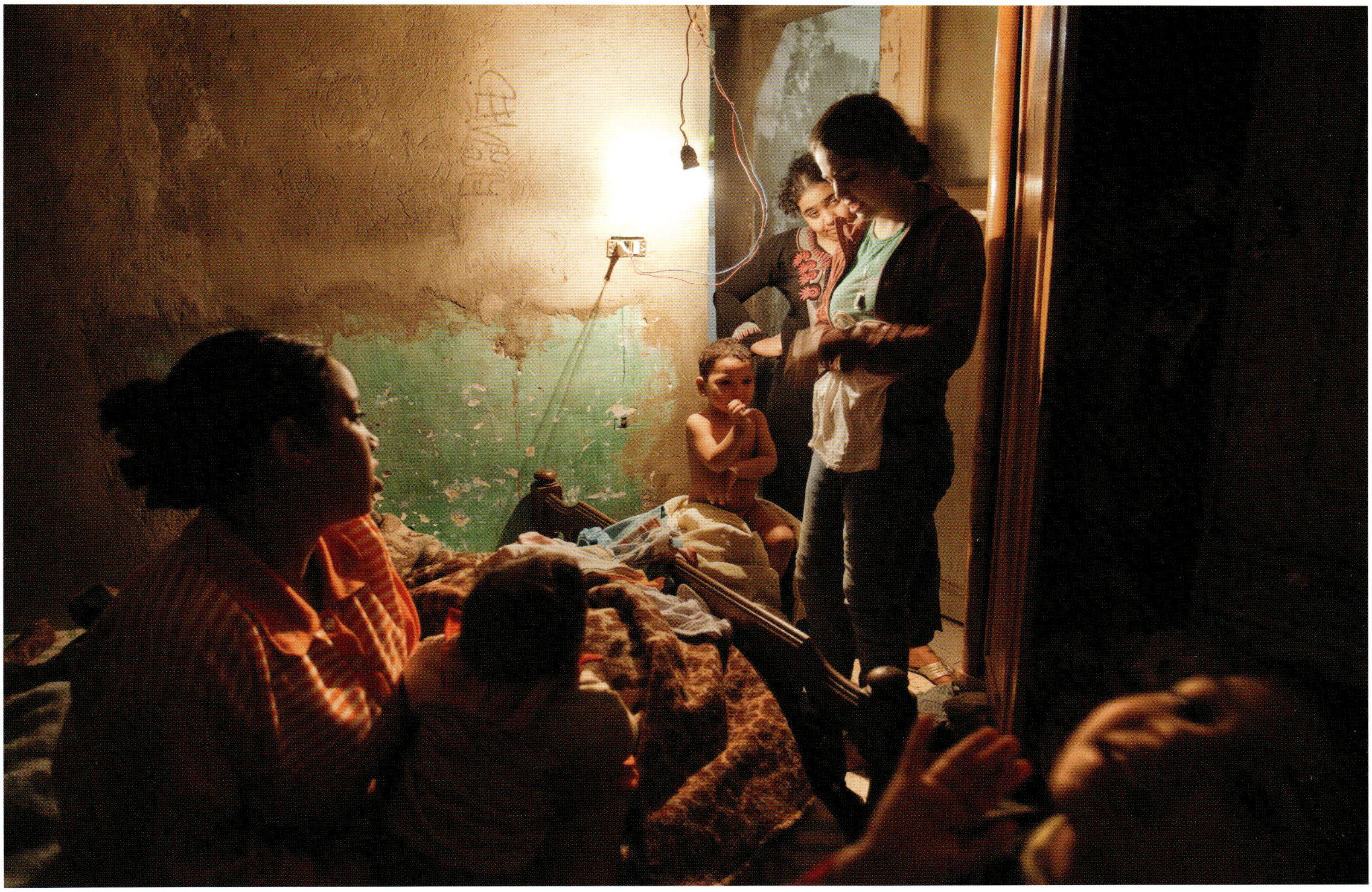

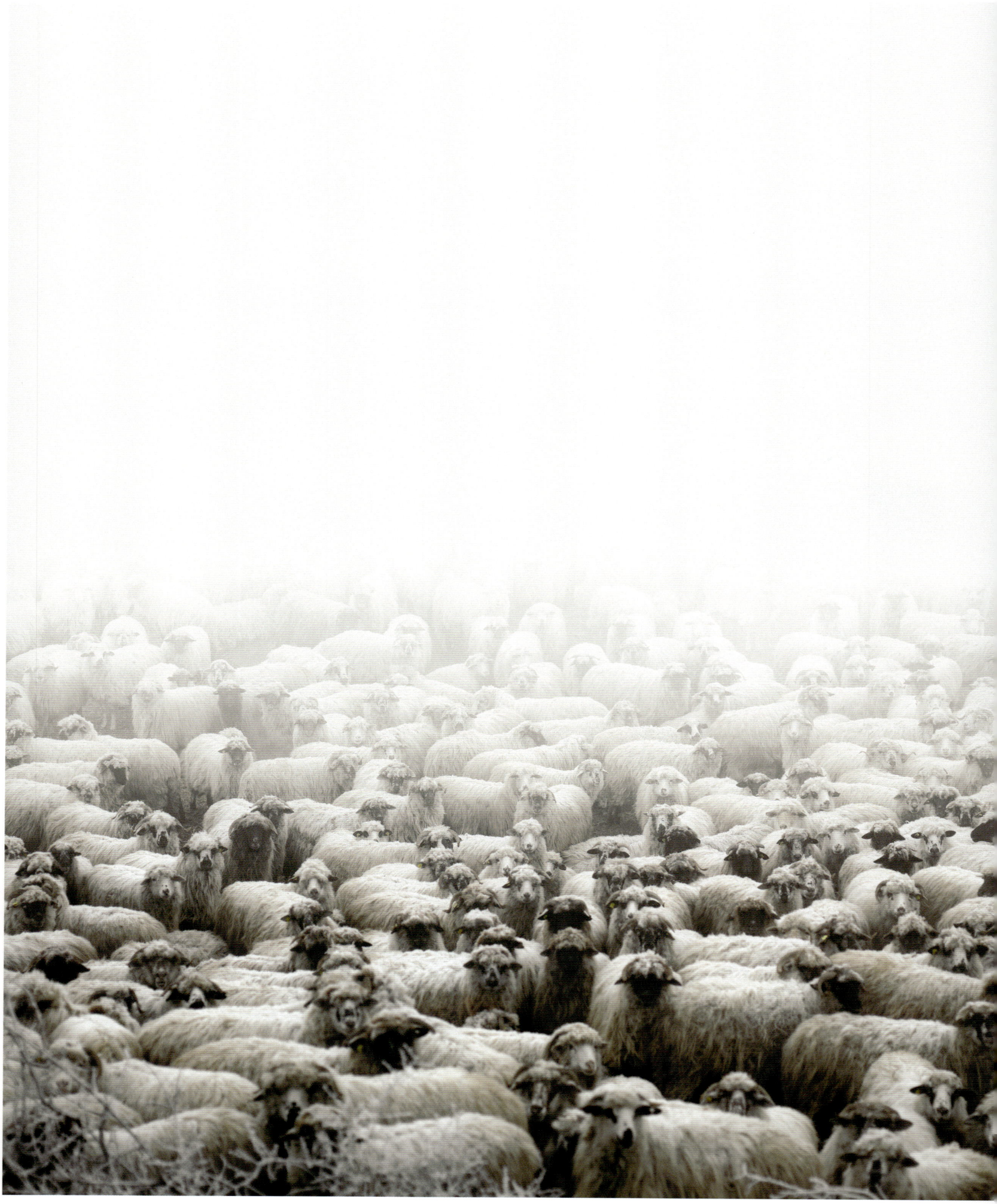

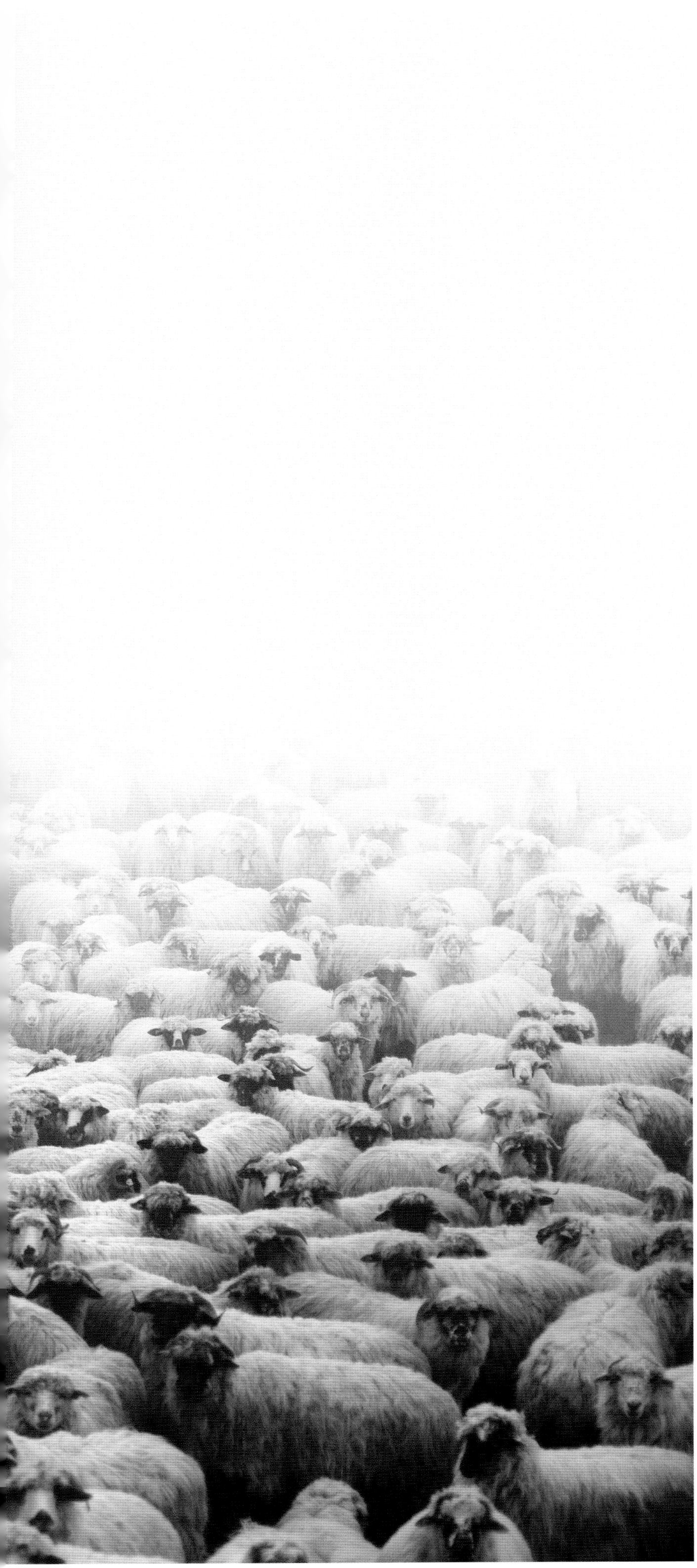

TAMAS DEZSO

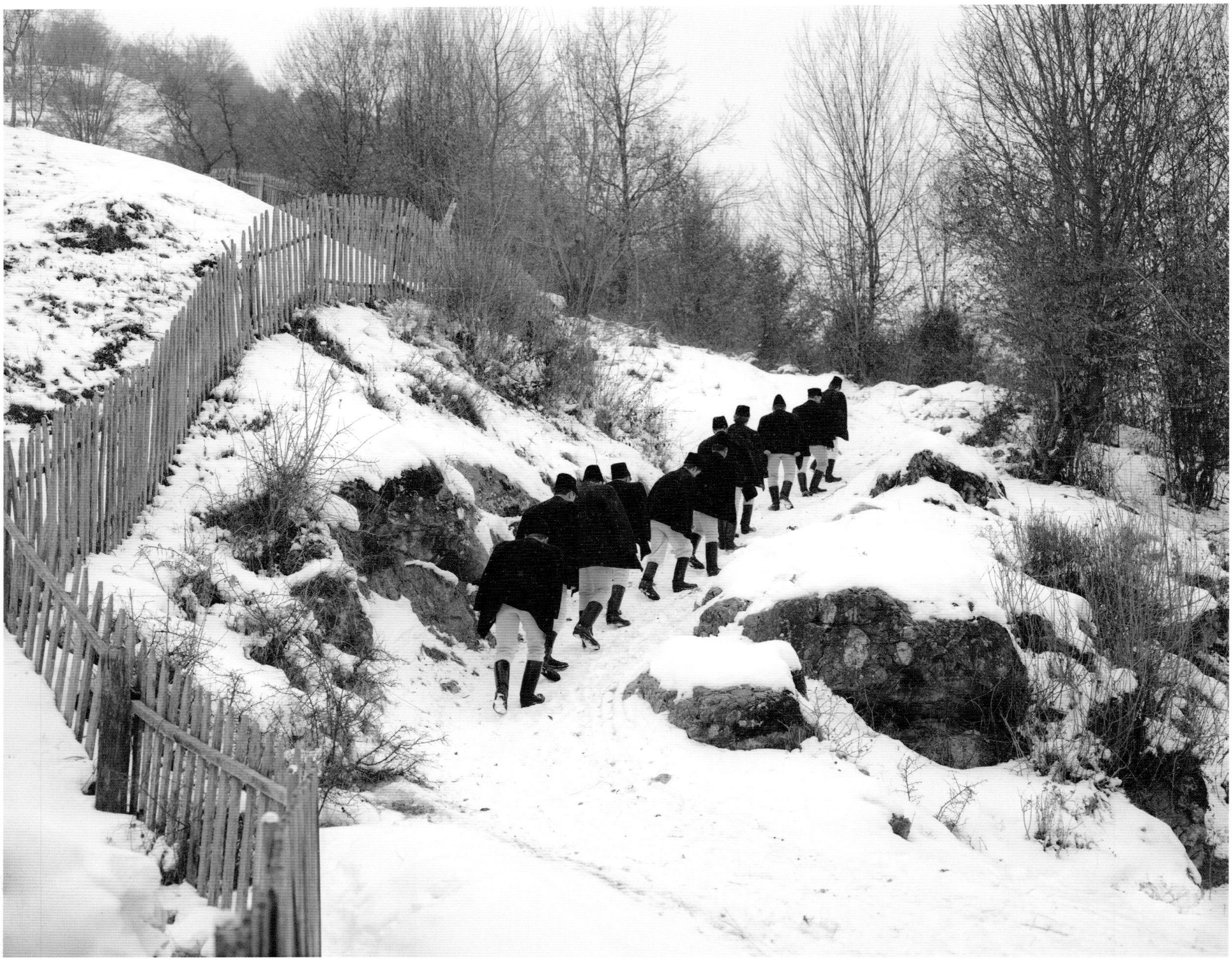

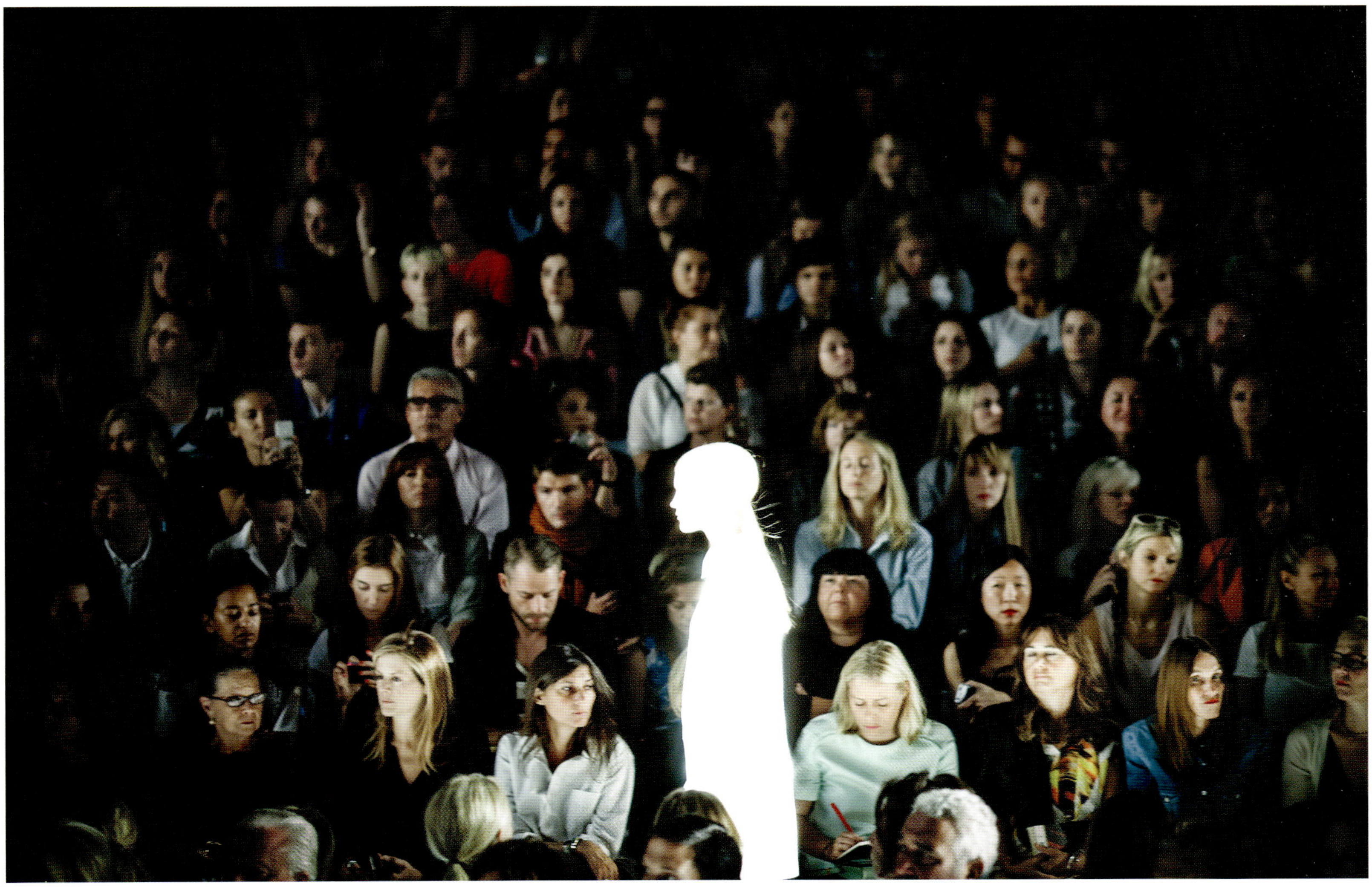

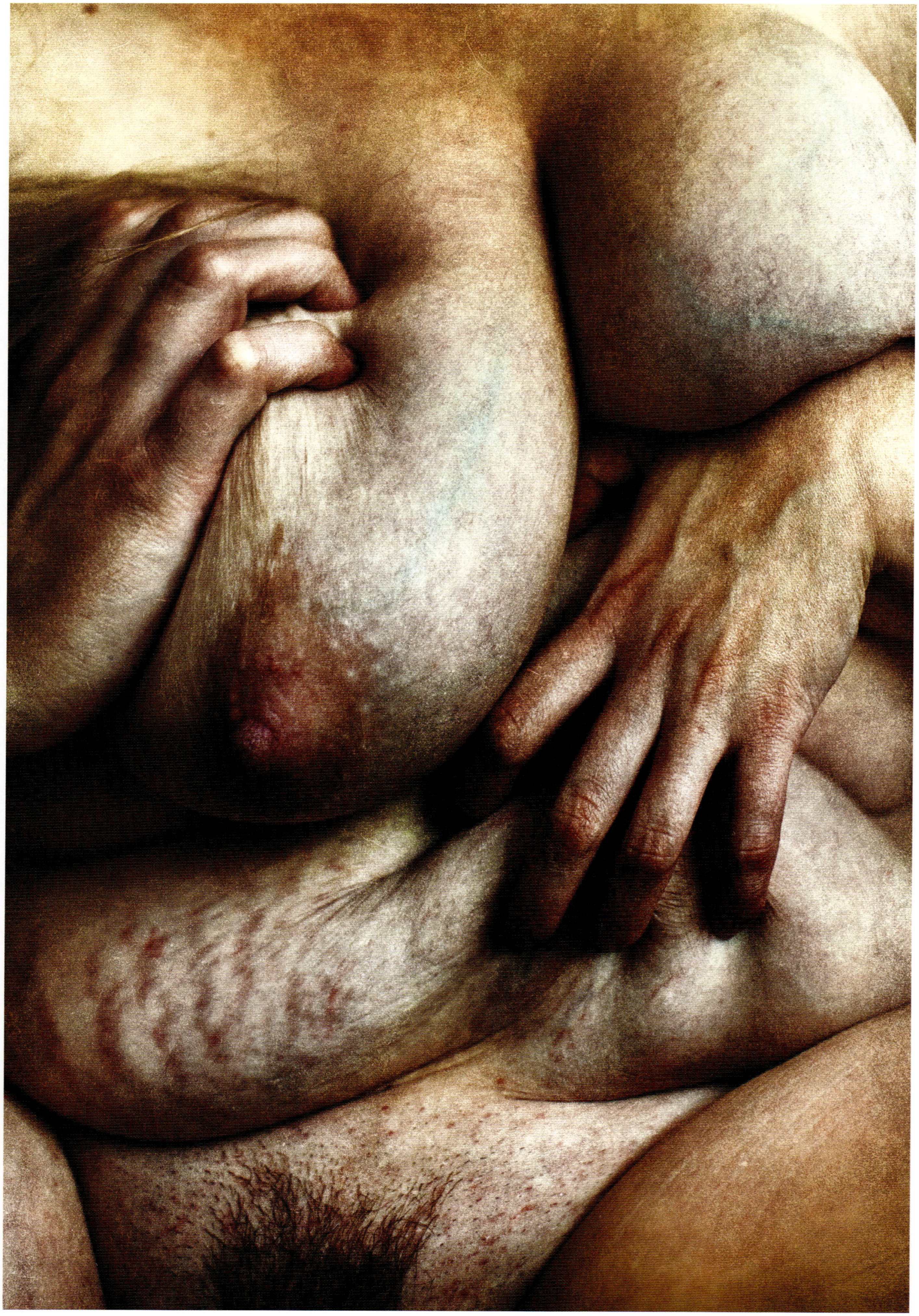

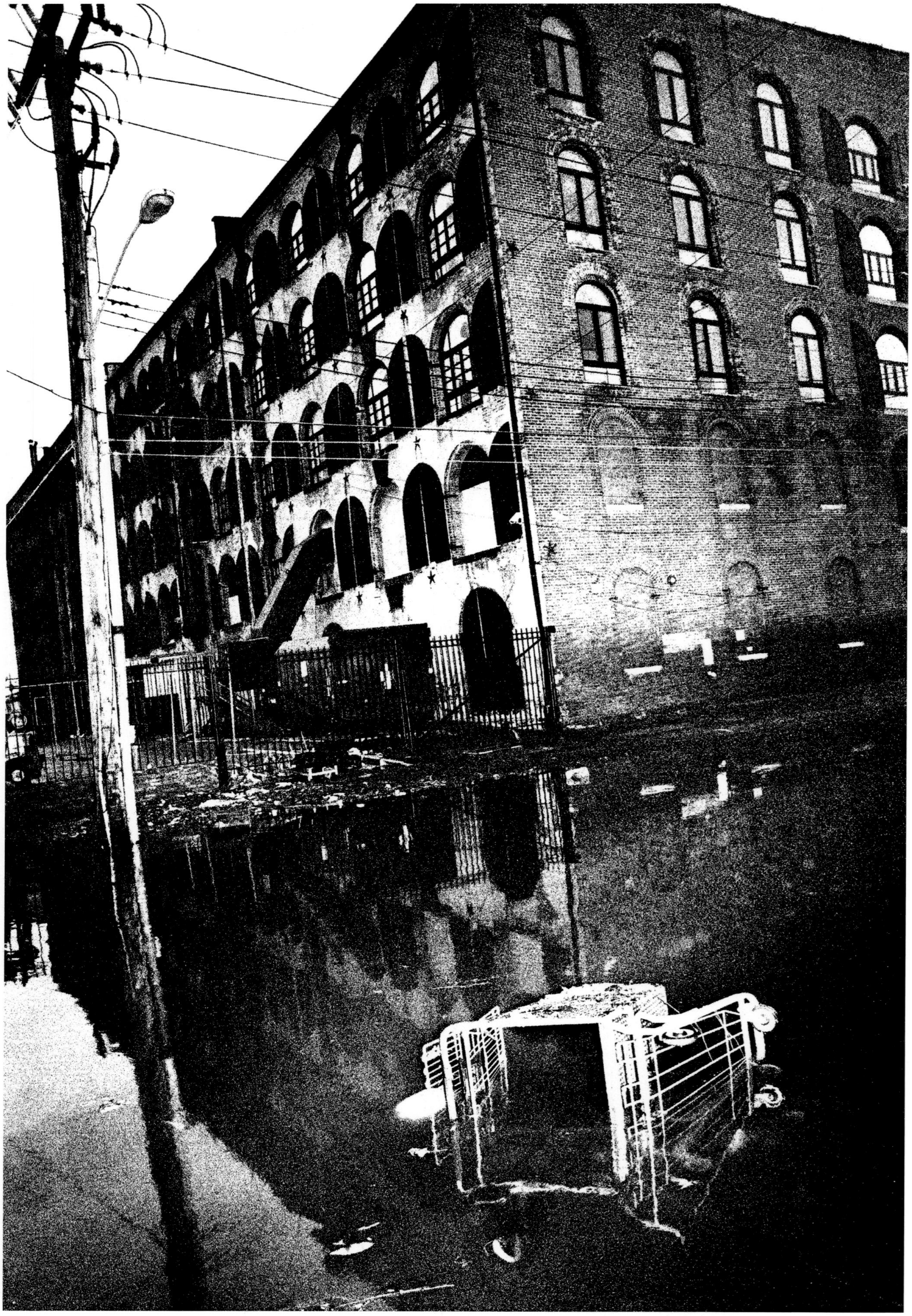

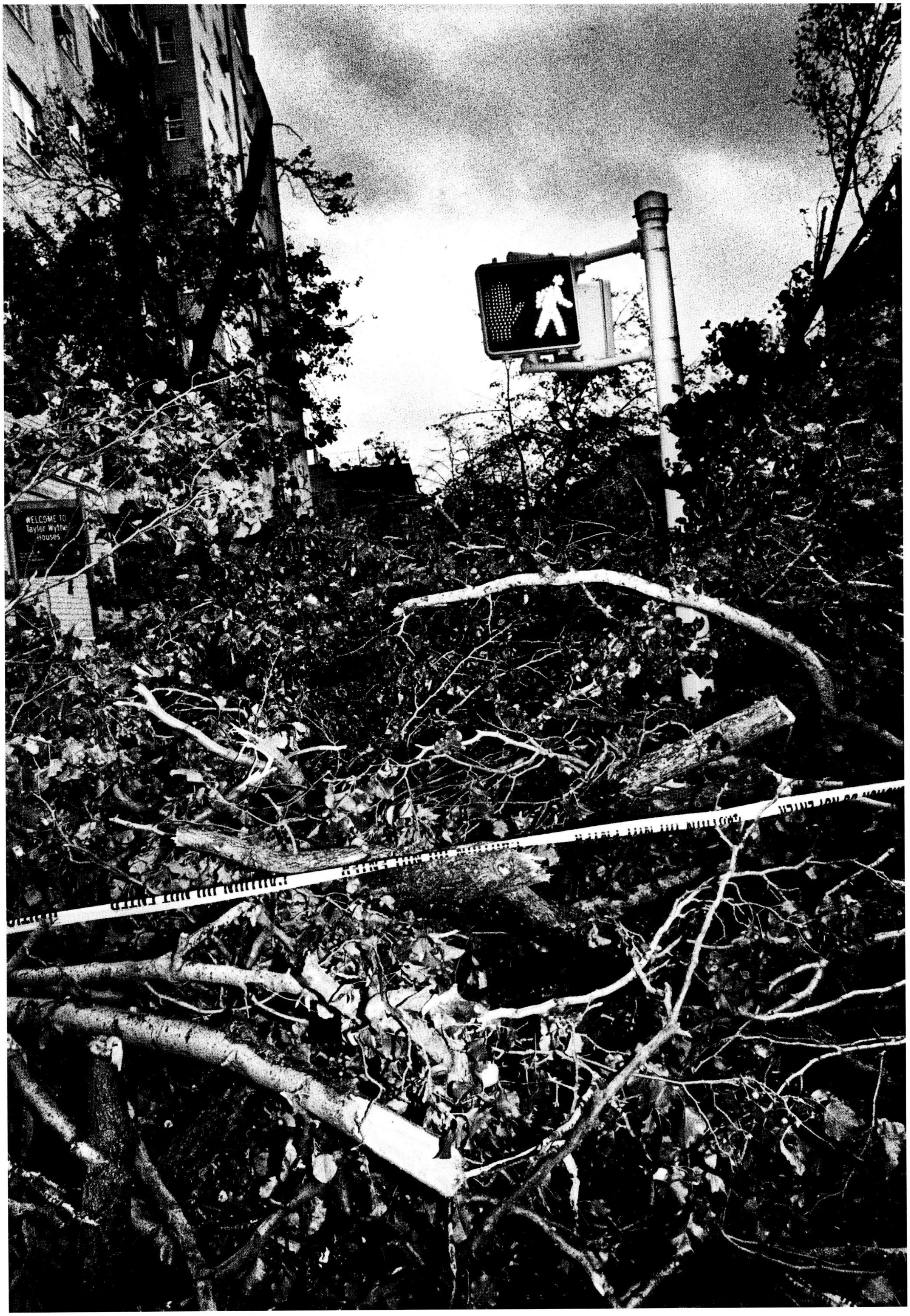

PARI DUKOVIC

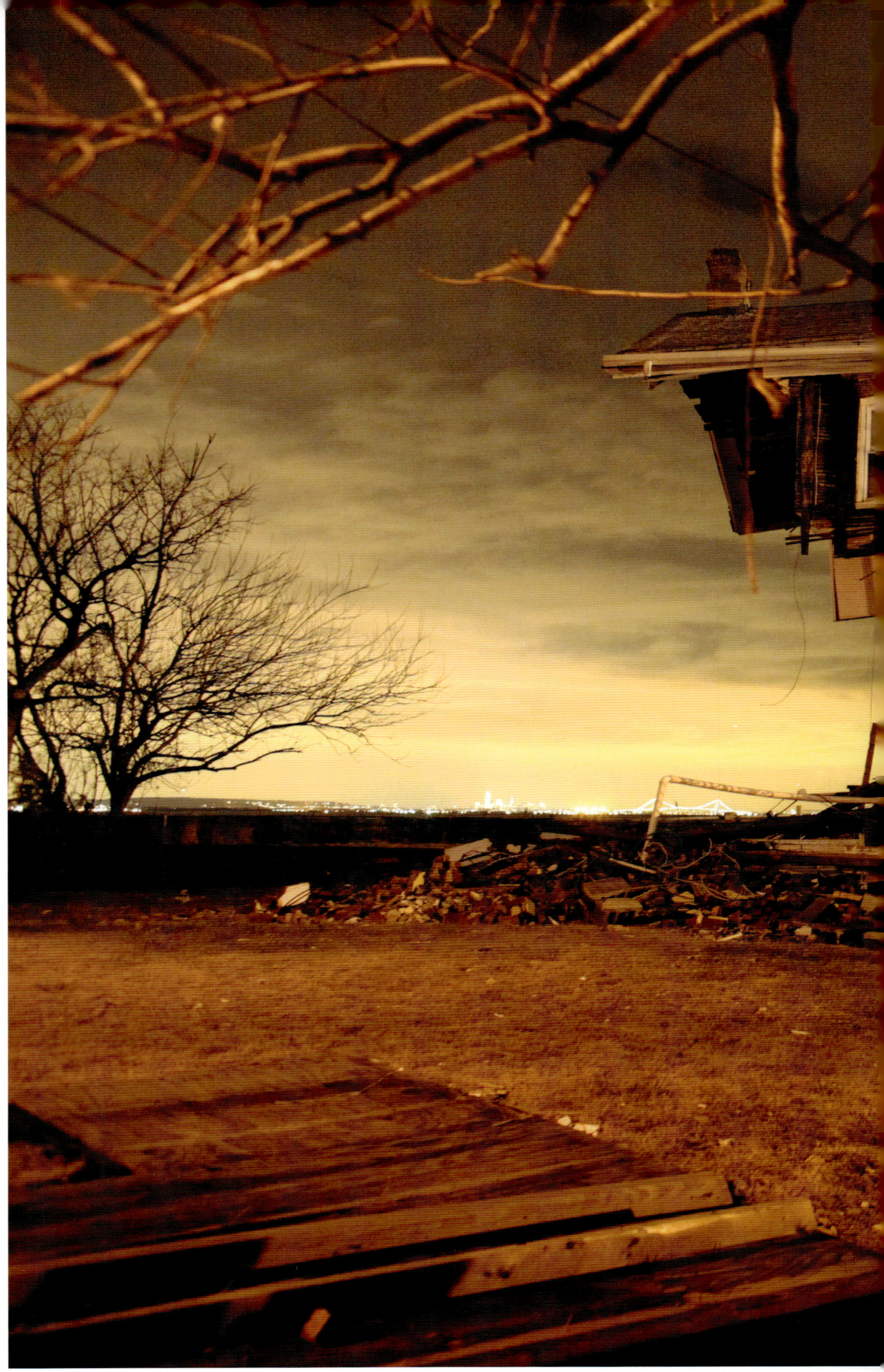

ARISTIDE
ECONOMOPOULOS

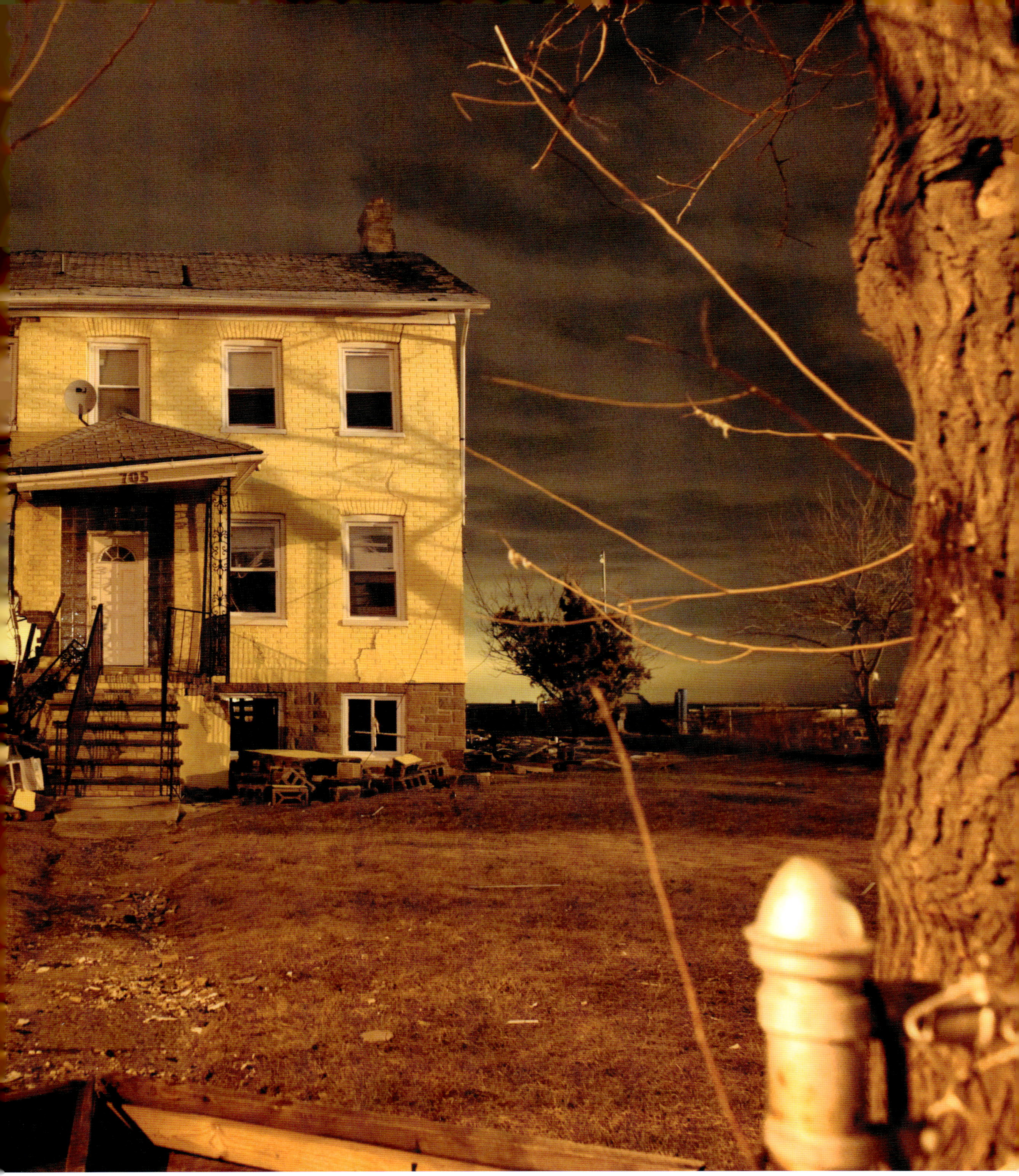

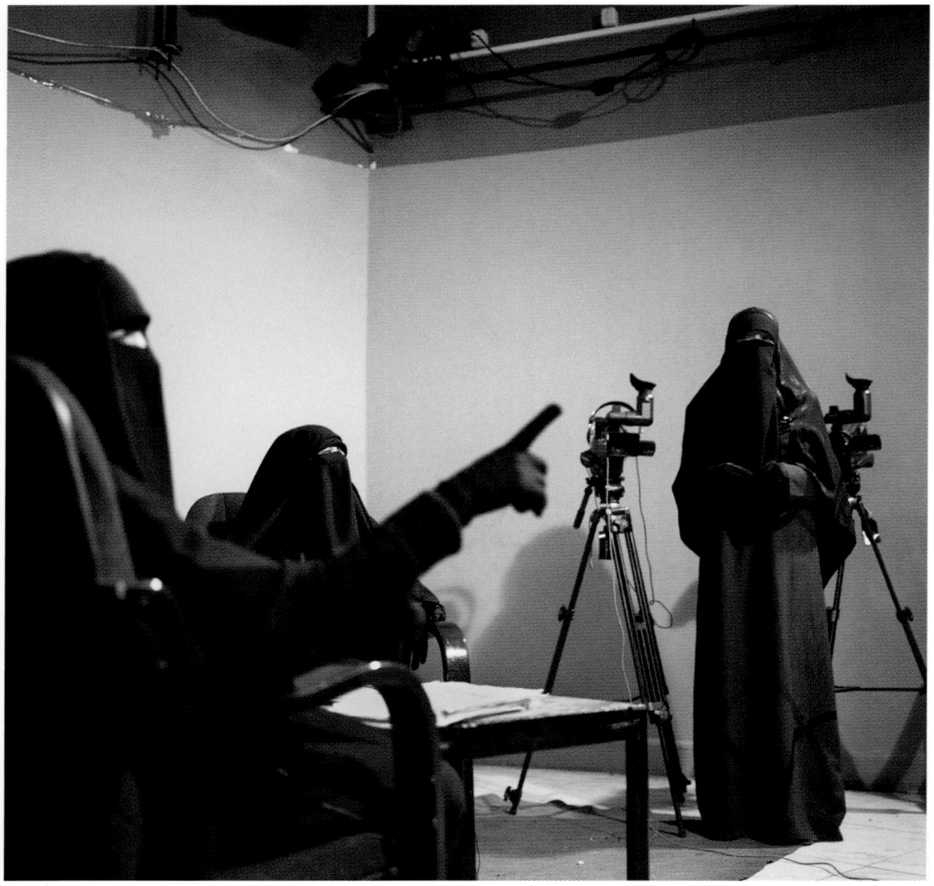

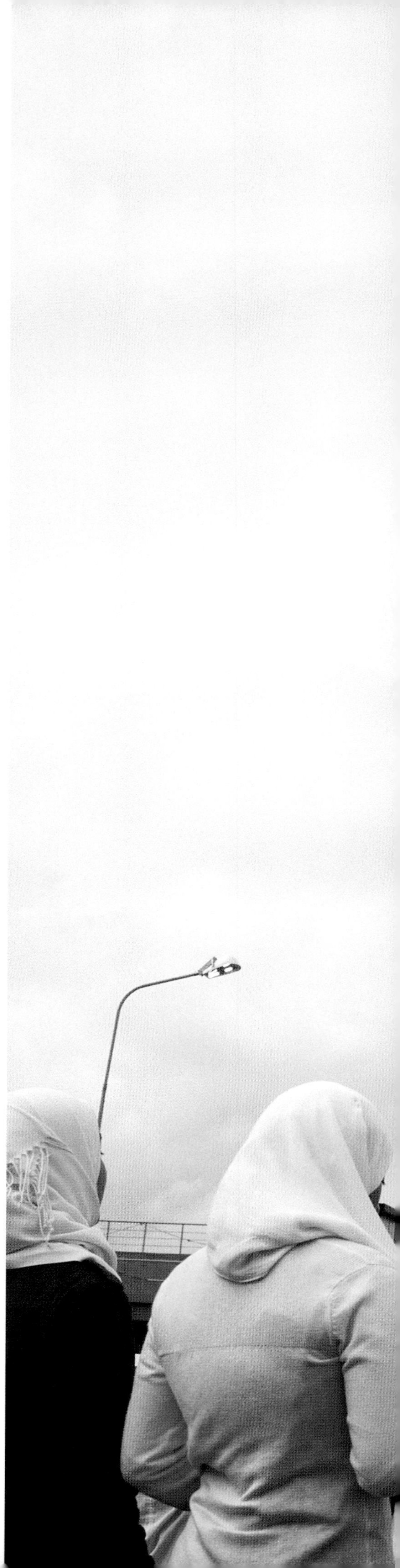

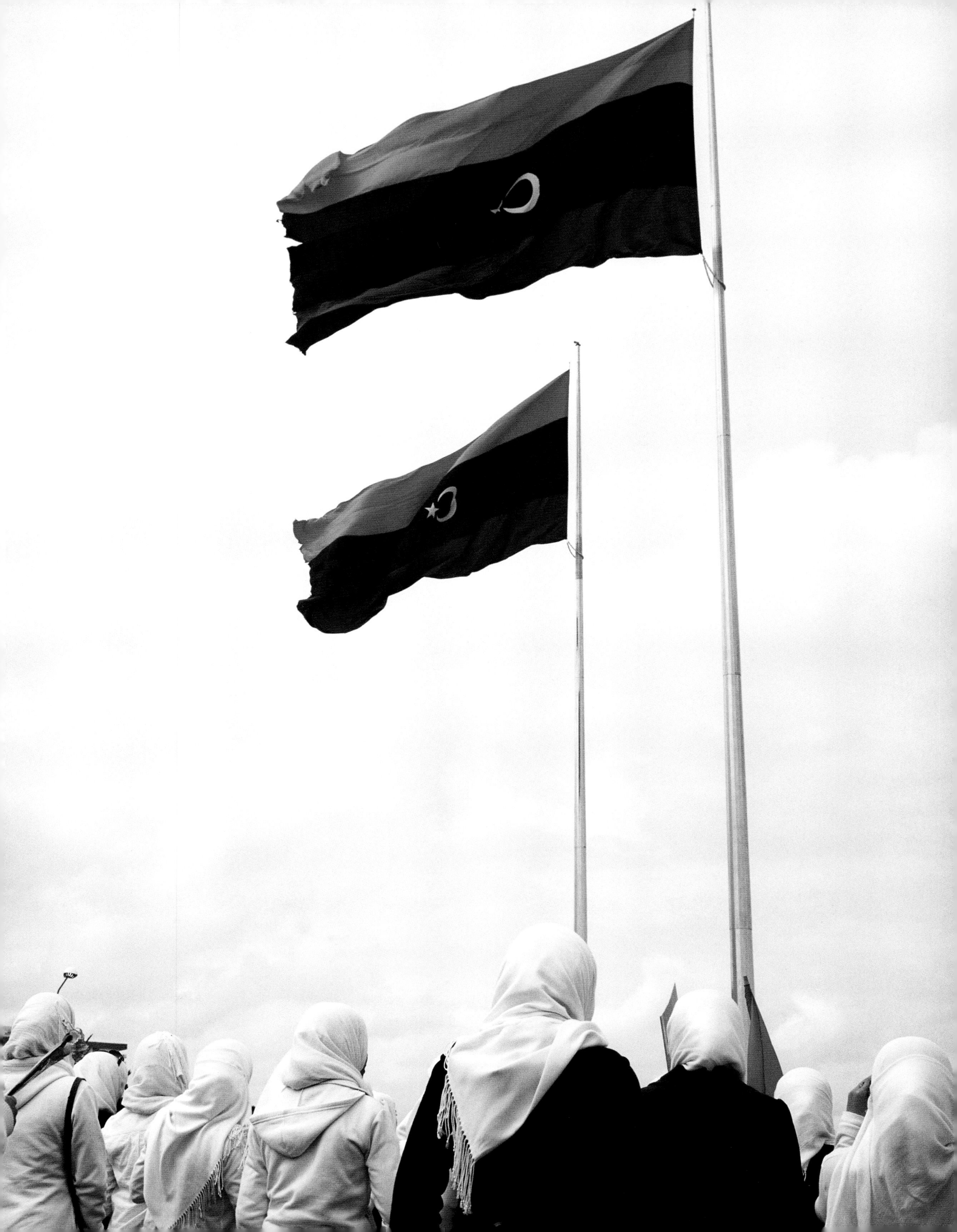

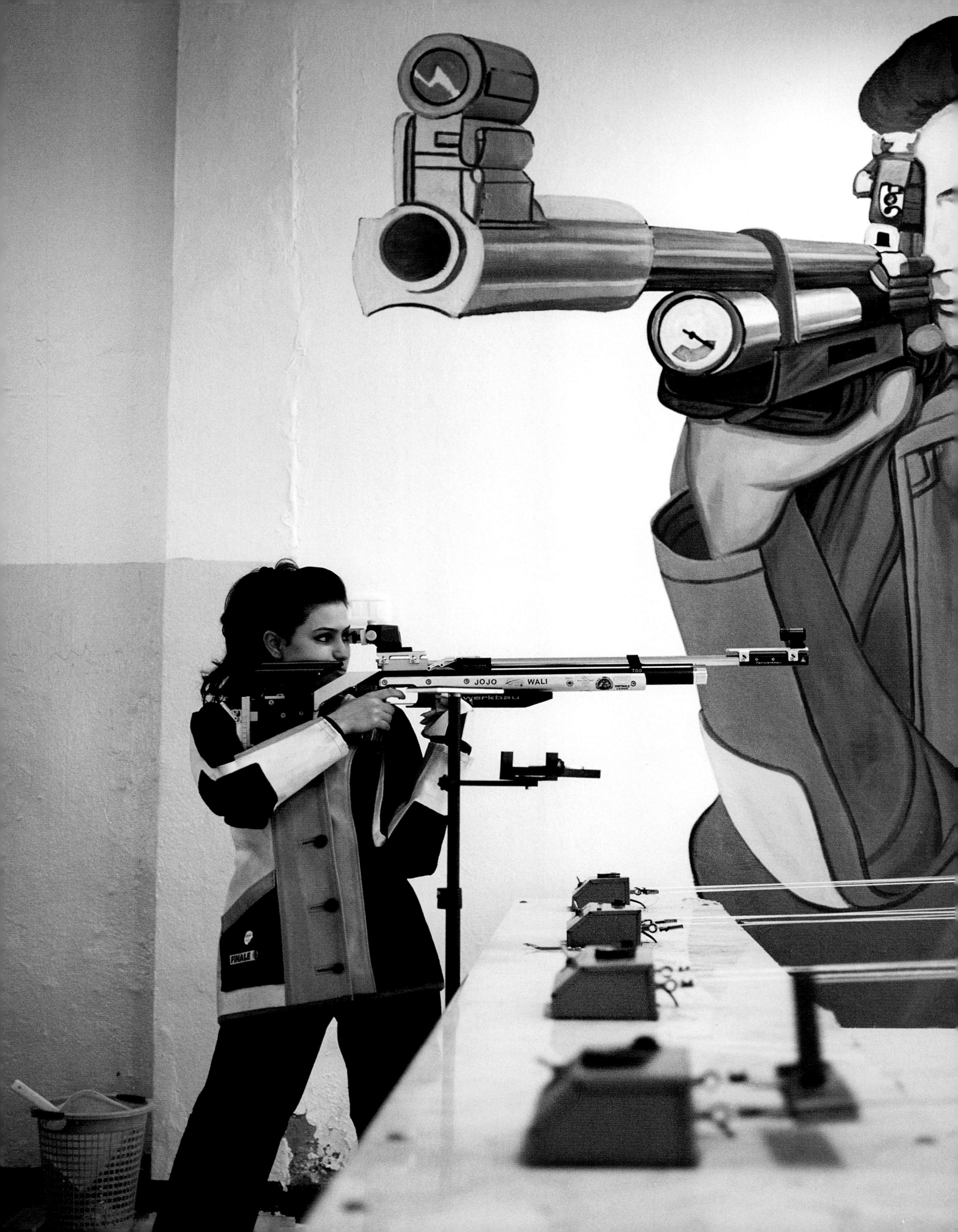
JOJO
WALI
werkbau
FINALE

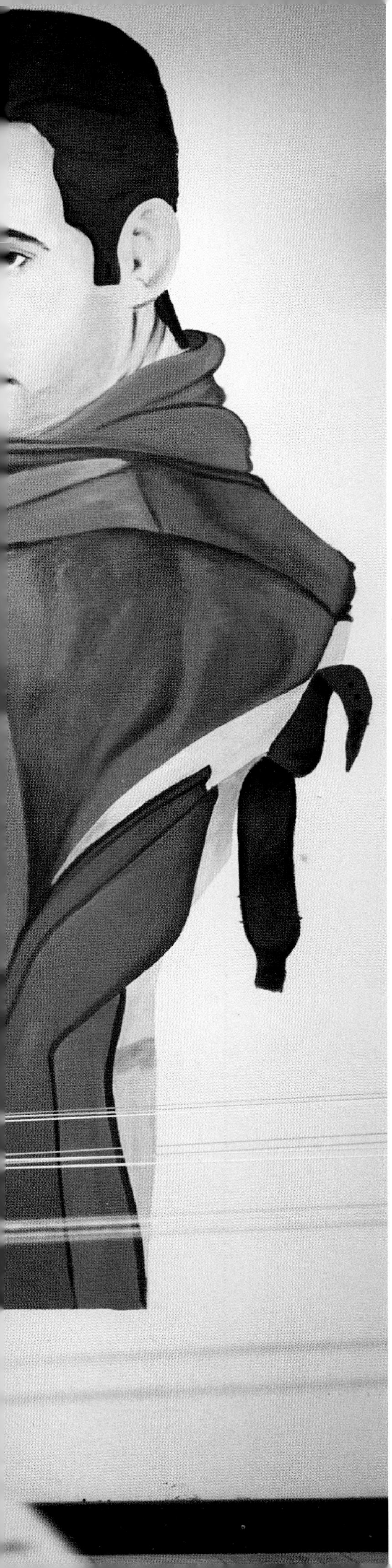

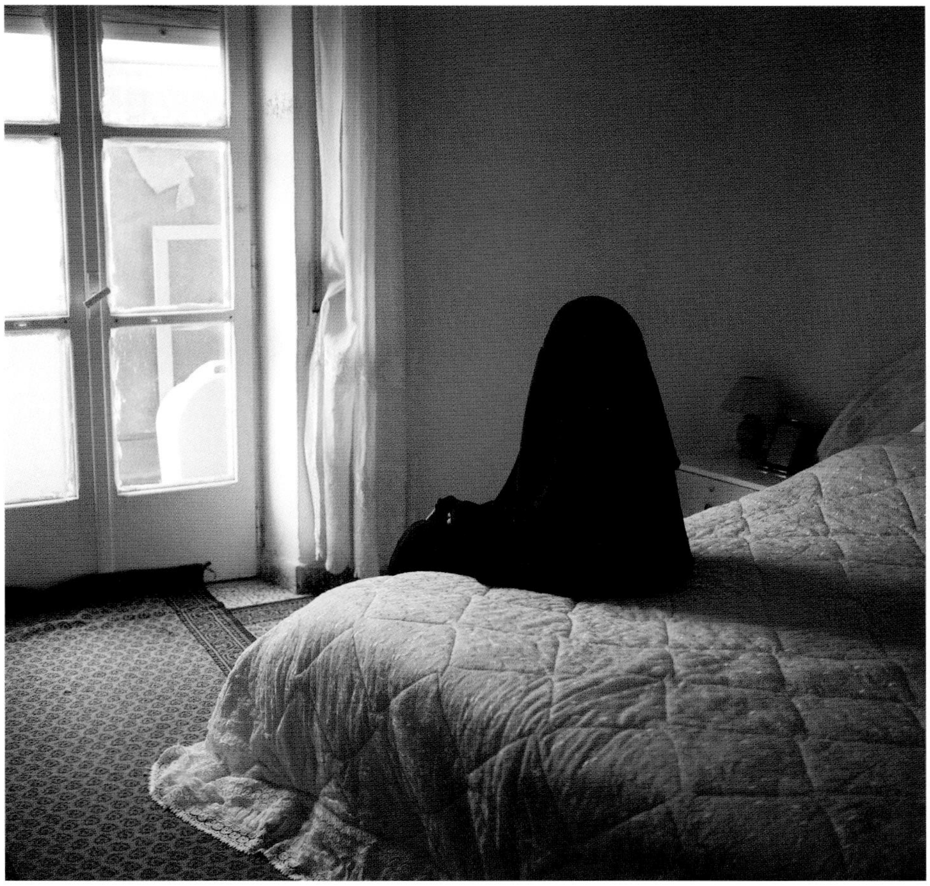

SARAH ELLIOTT

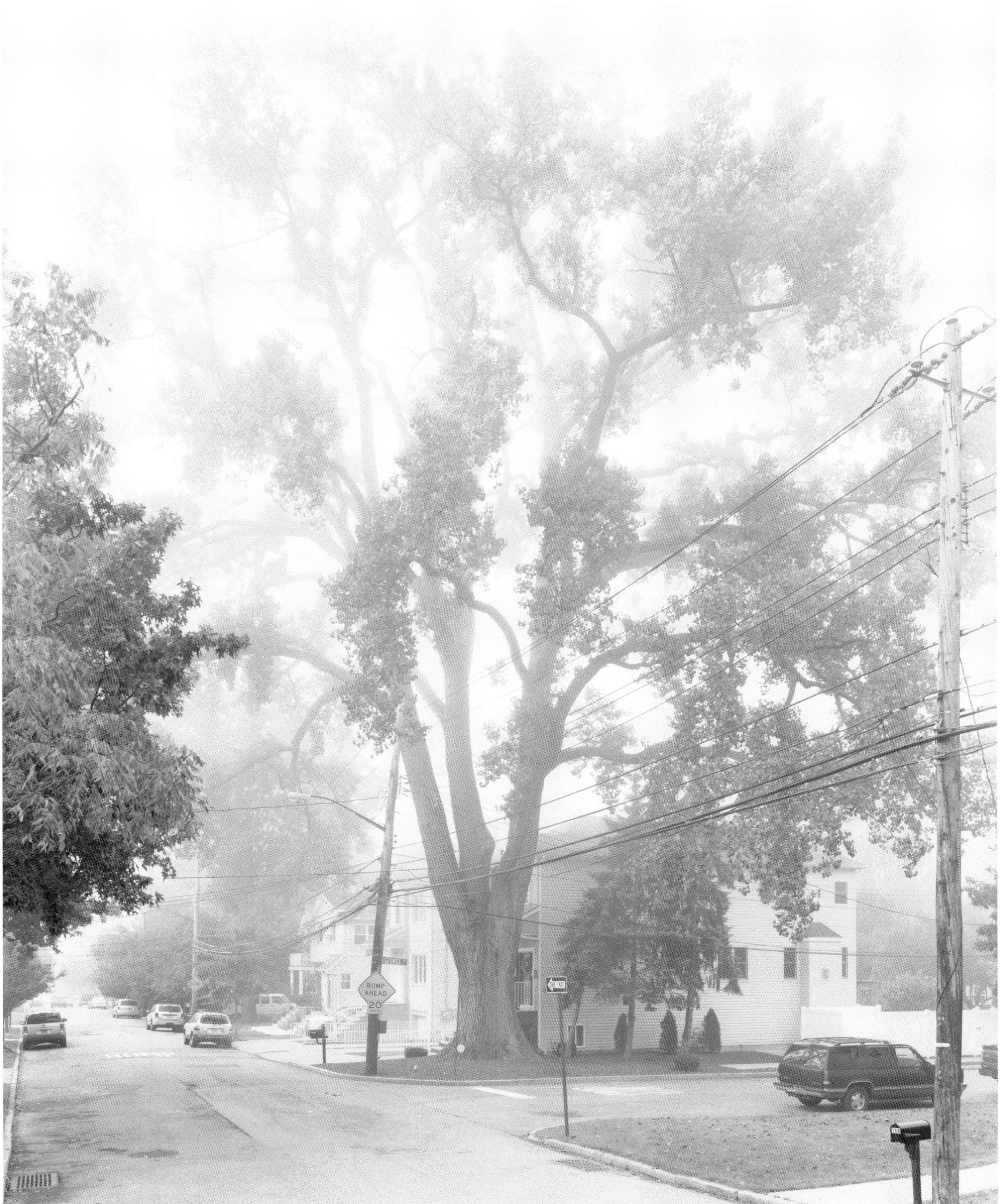
BUMP AHEAD
20
ONE WAY

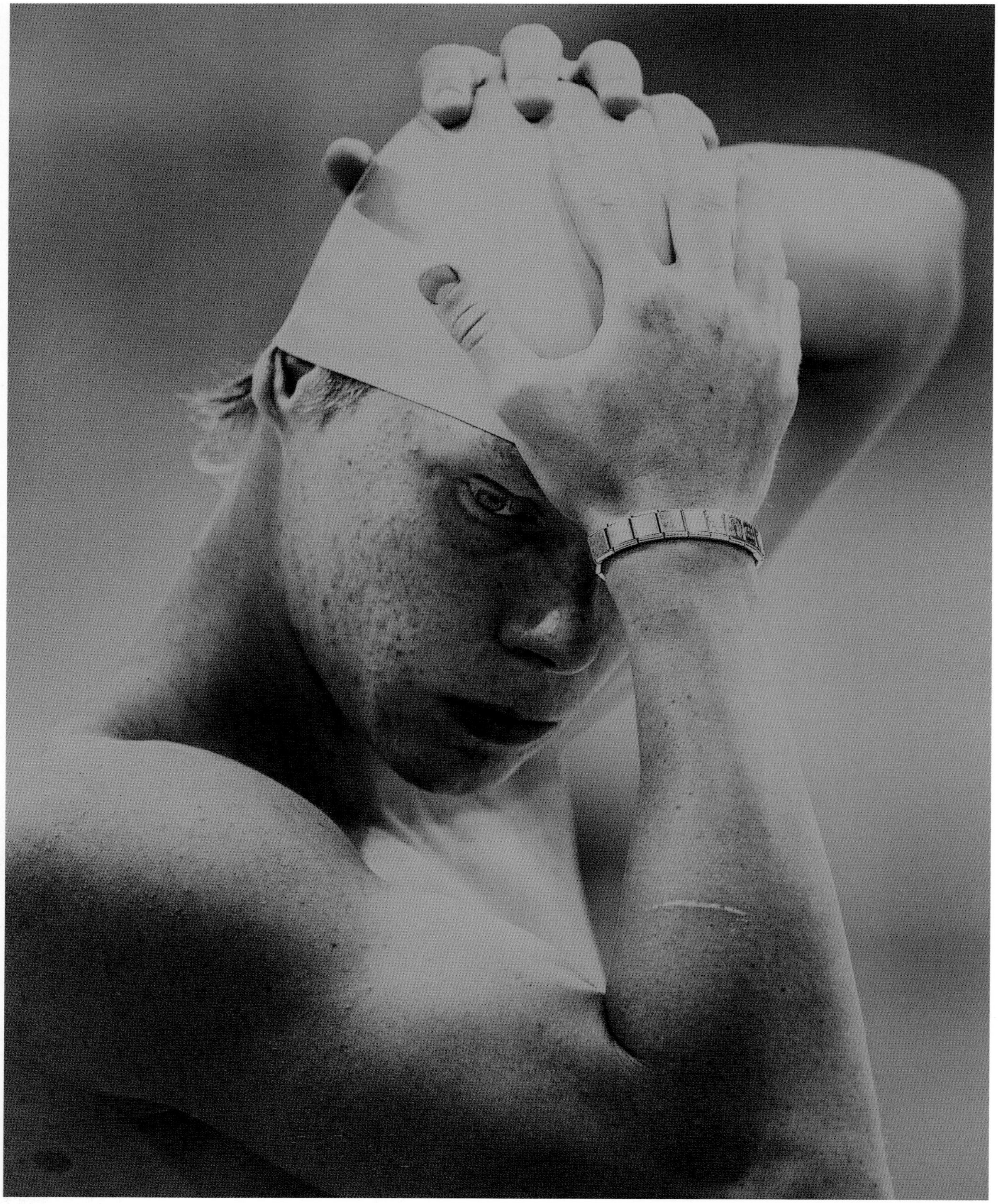

JASON EVANS

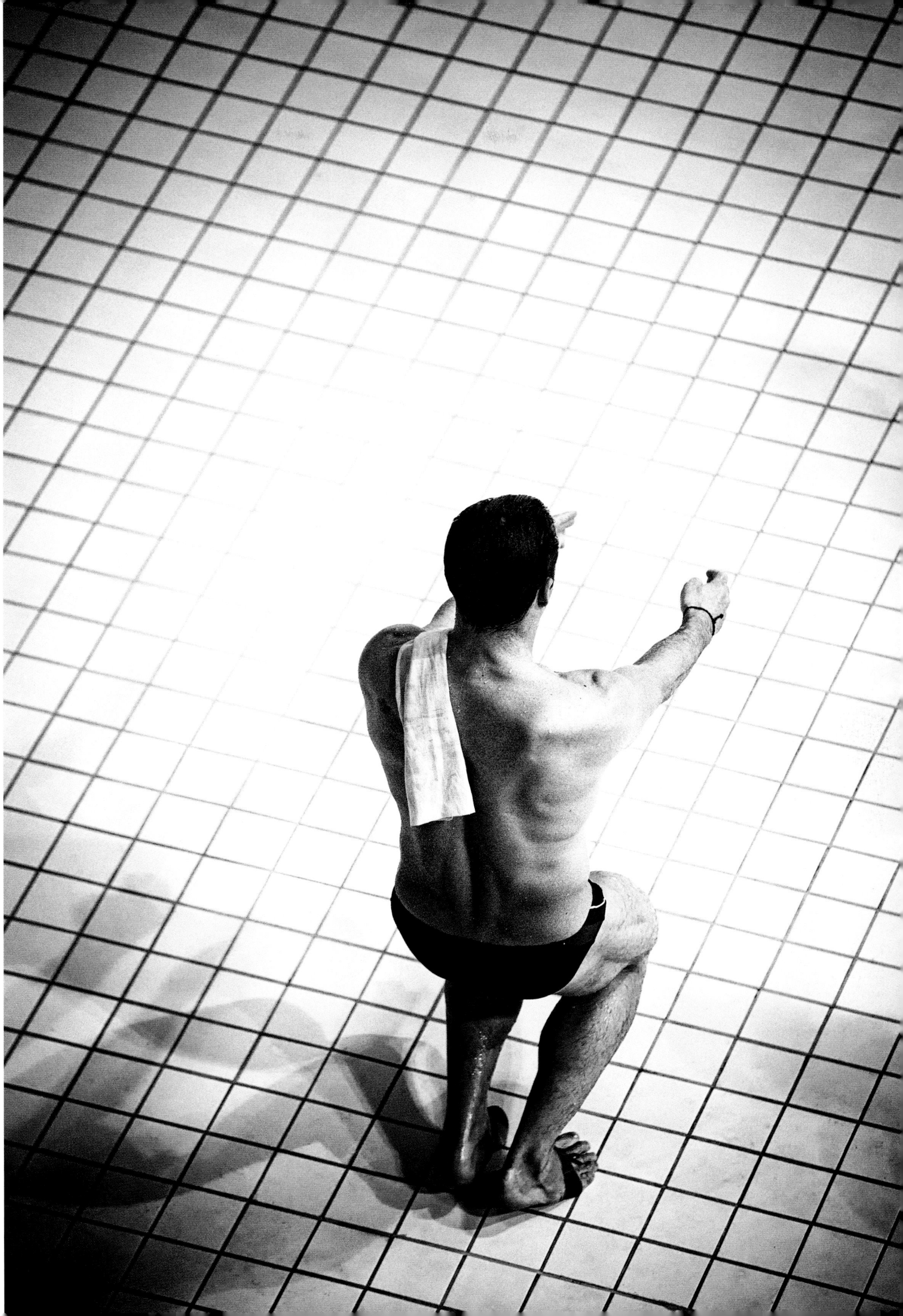

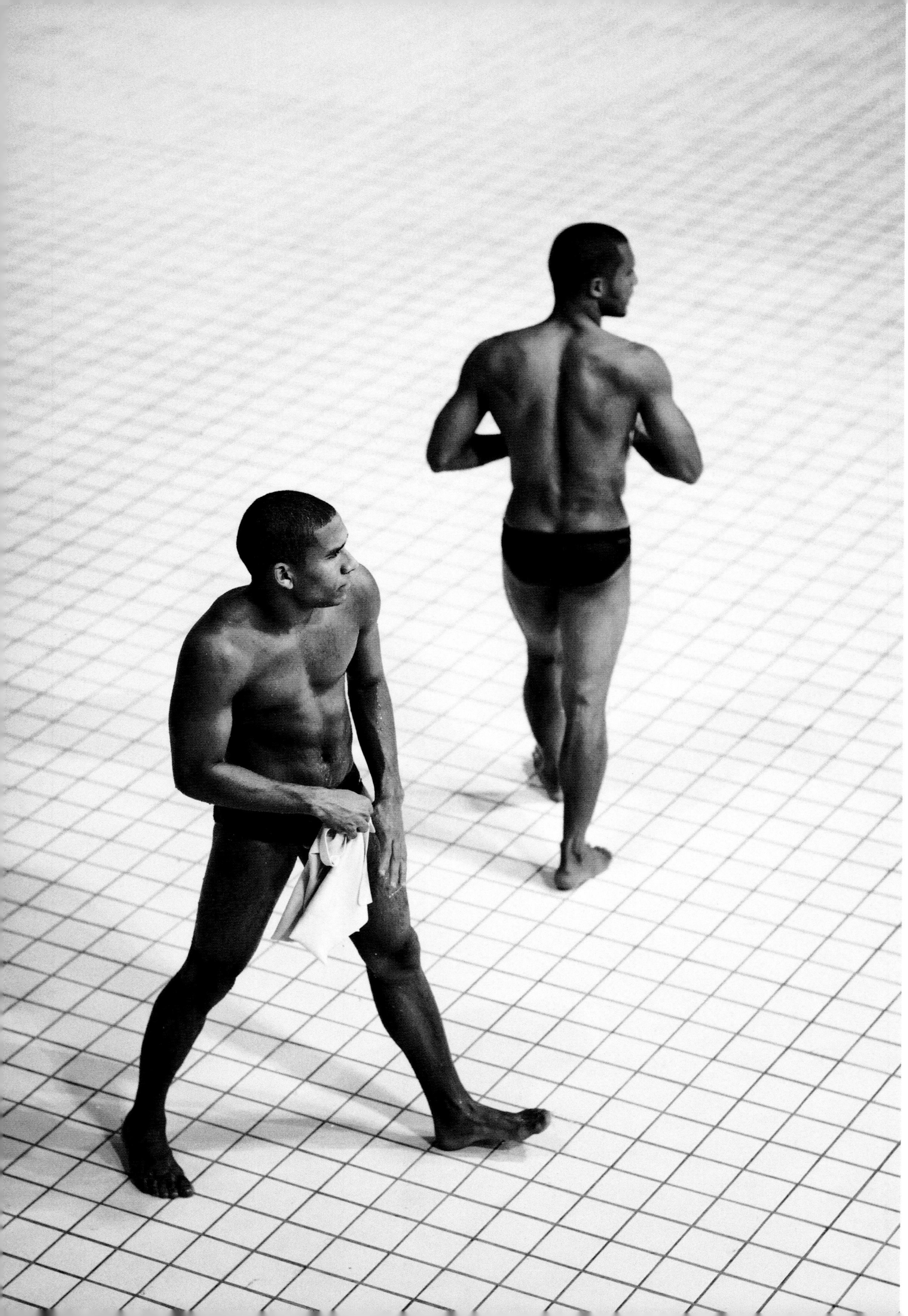

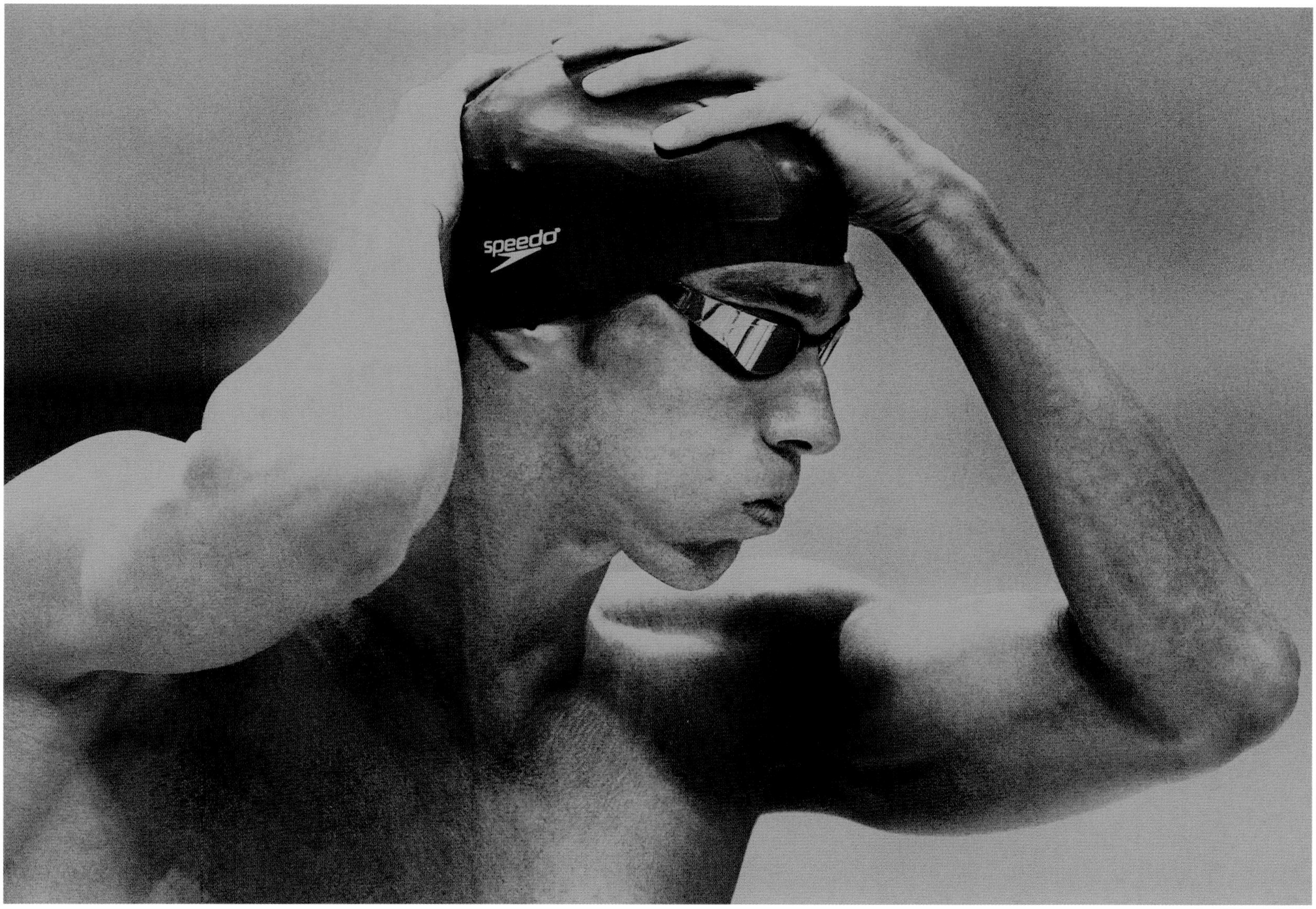

JASON EVANS

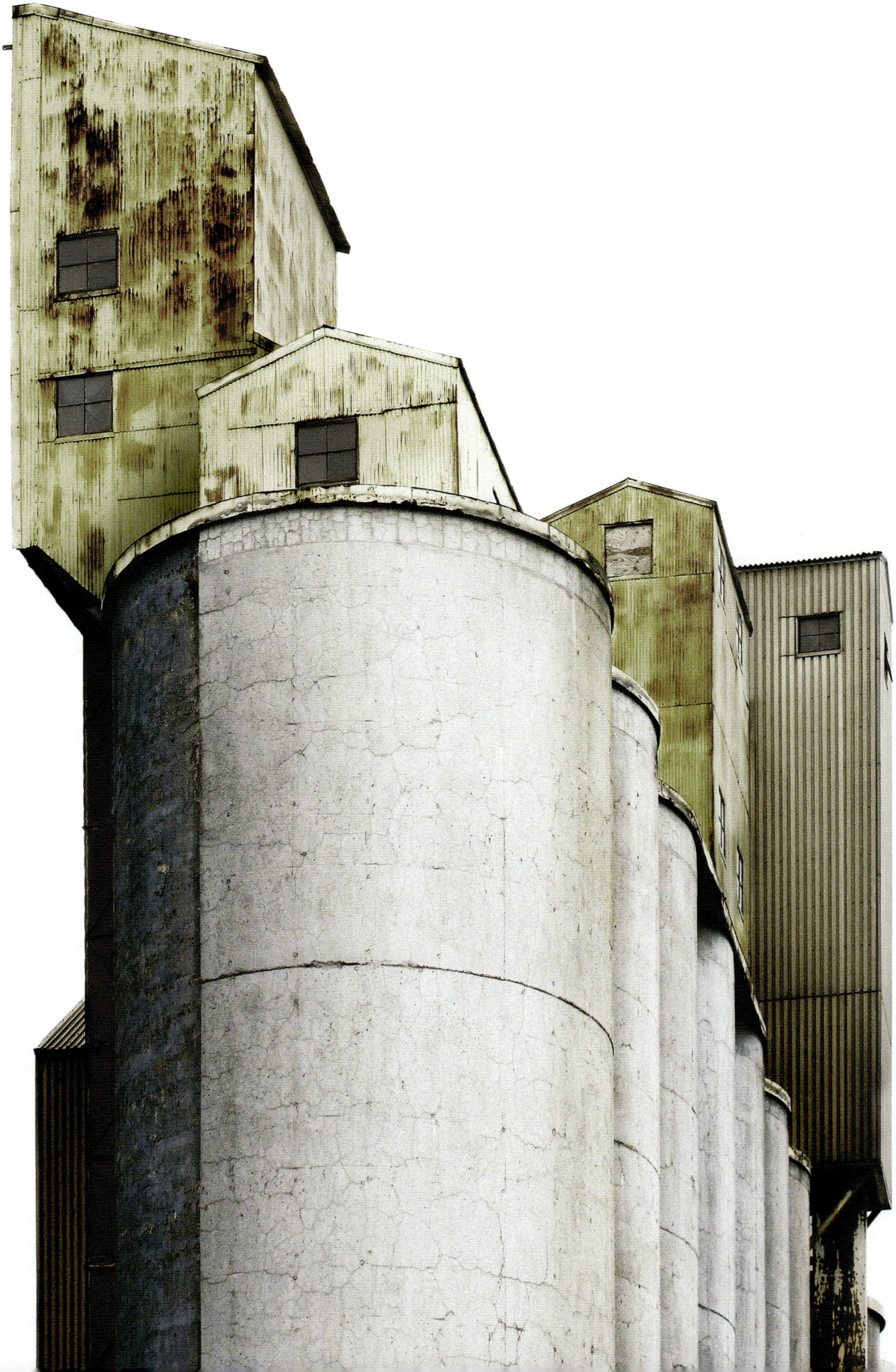

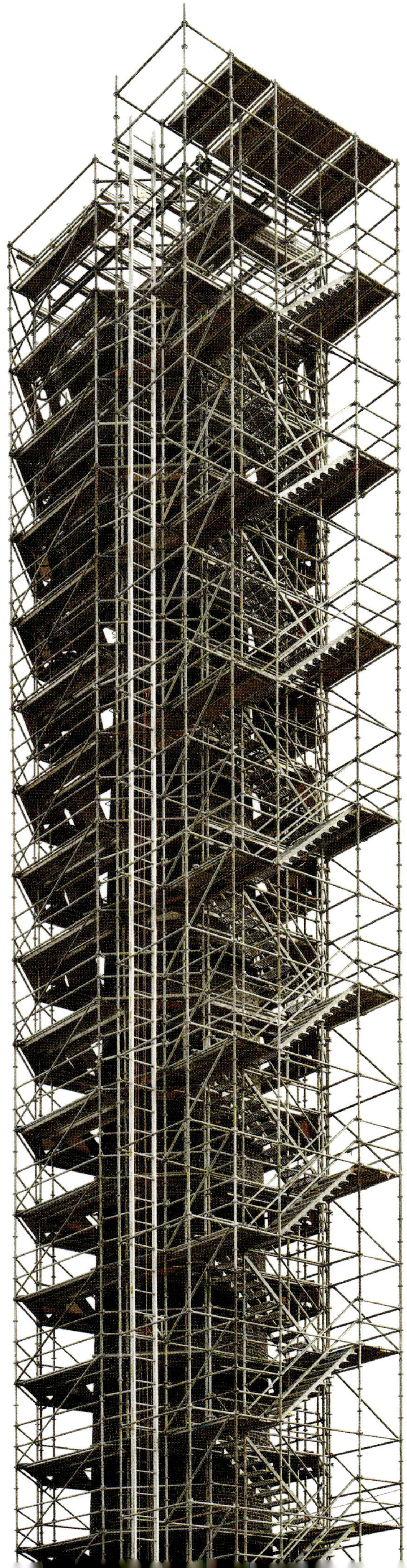

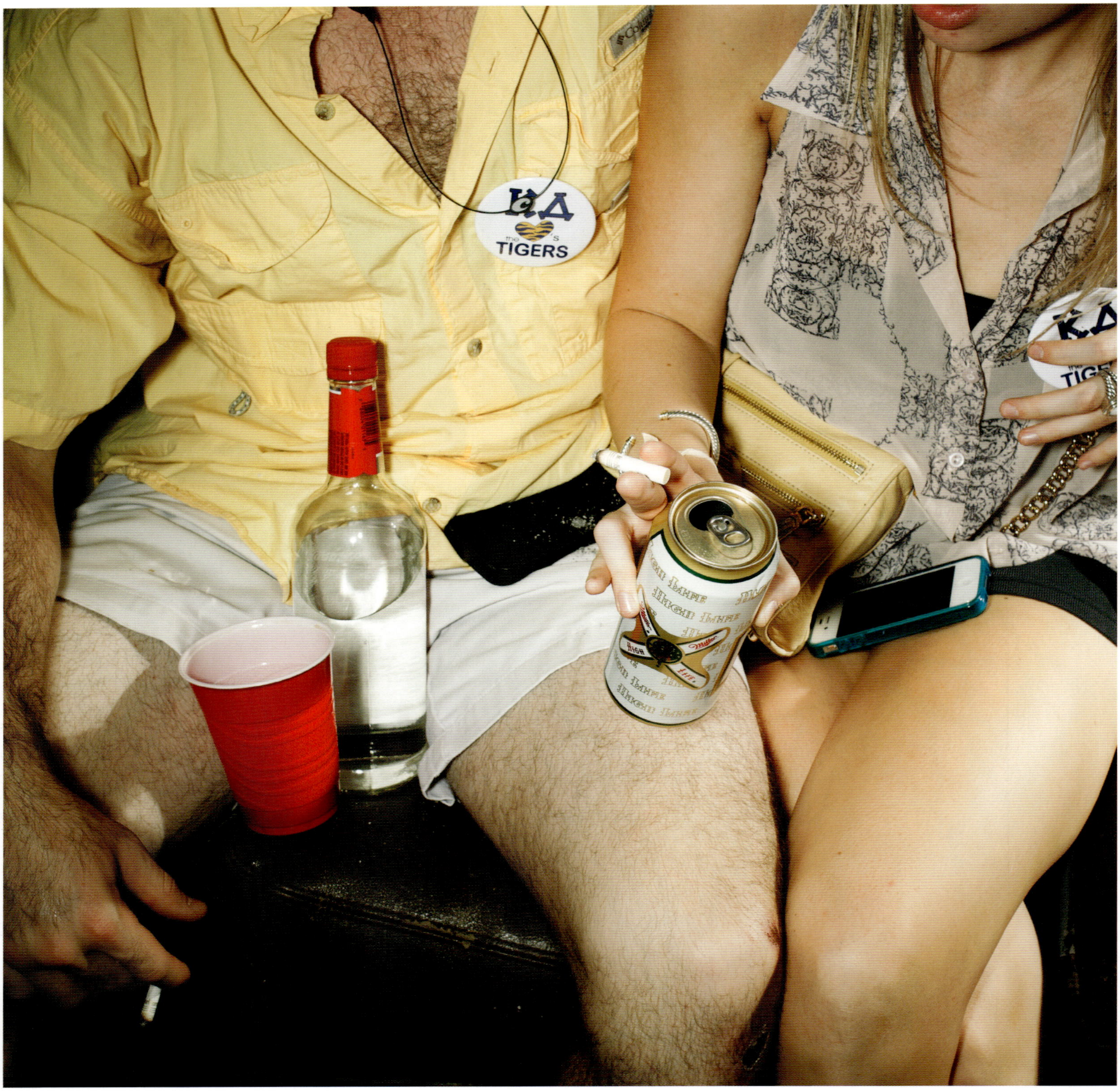
ΚΔ
TIGERS

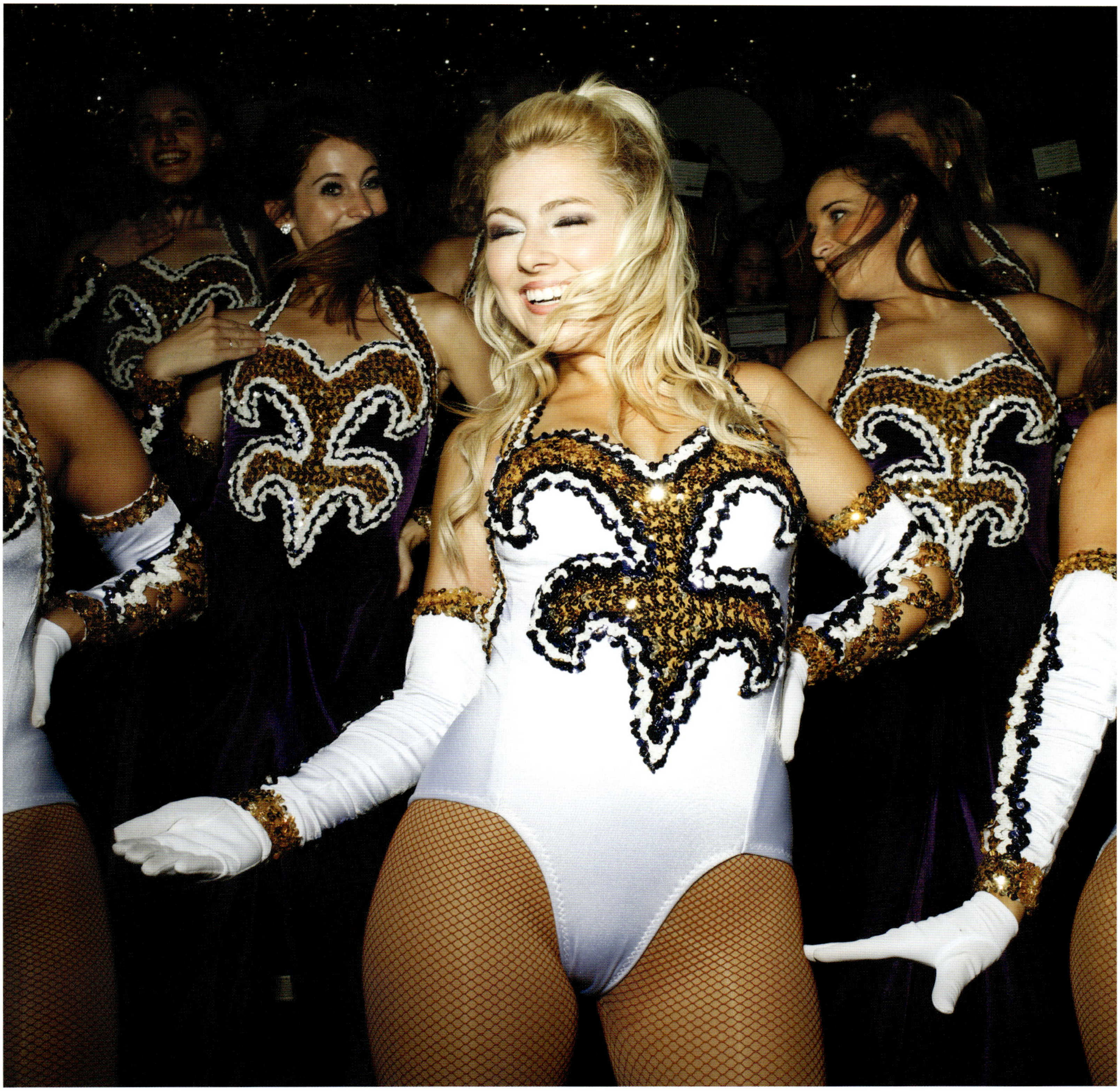

BRIAN FINKE

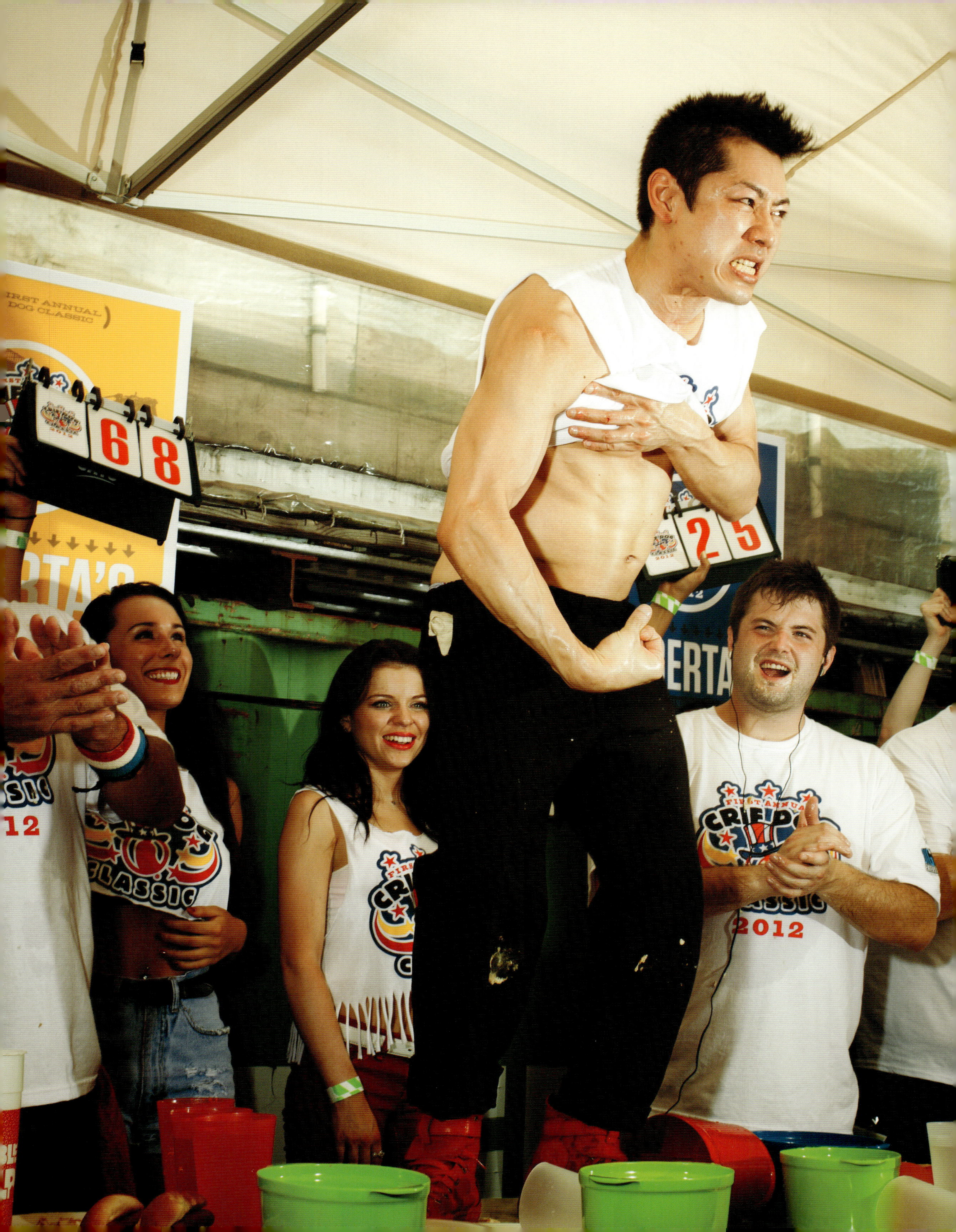
68
25
CLASSIC
2012

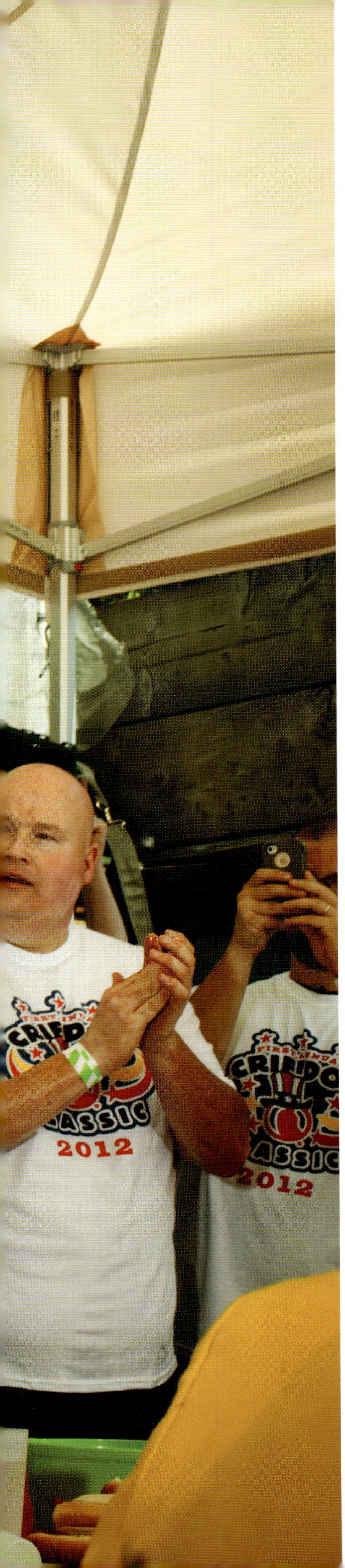
2012
2012

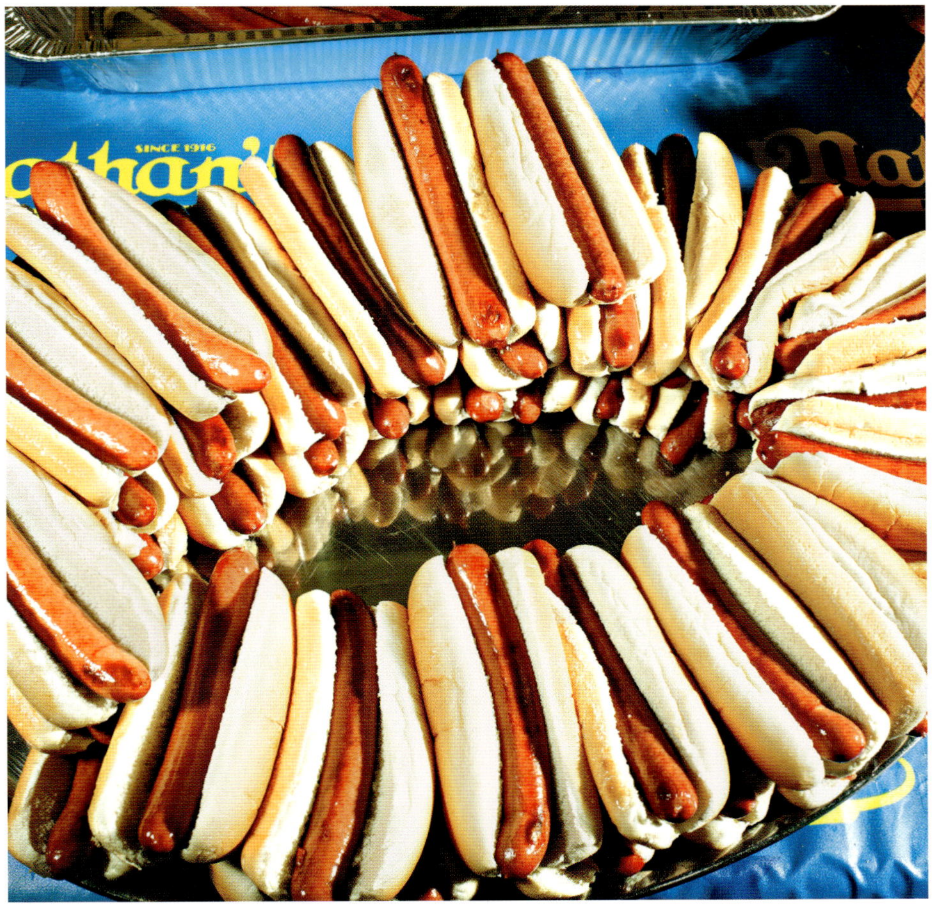
SINCE 1916

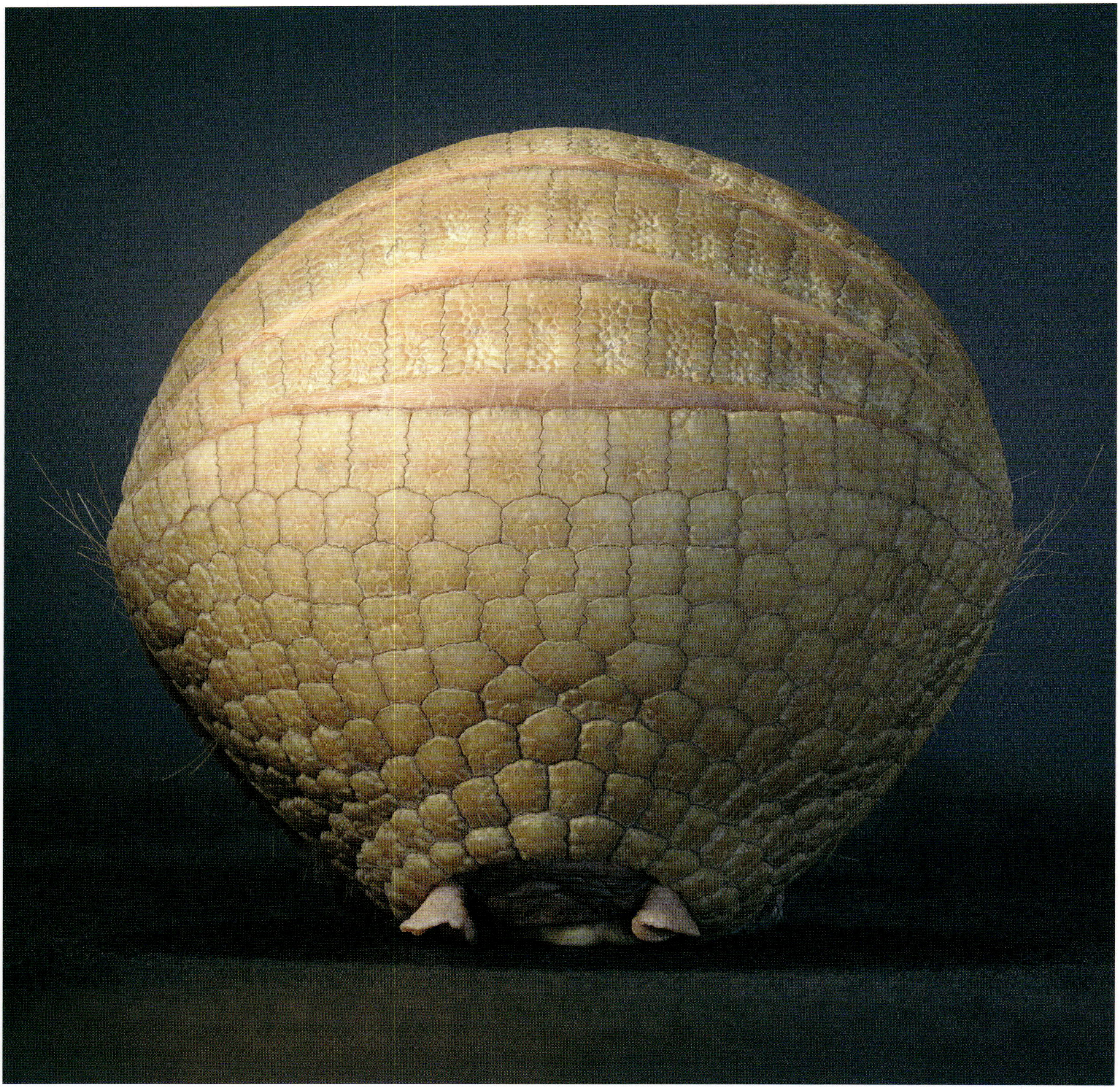

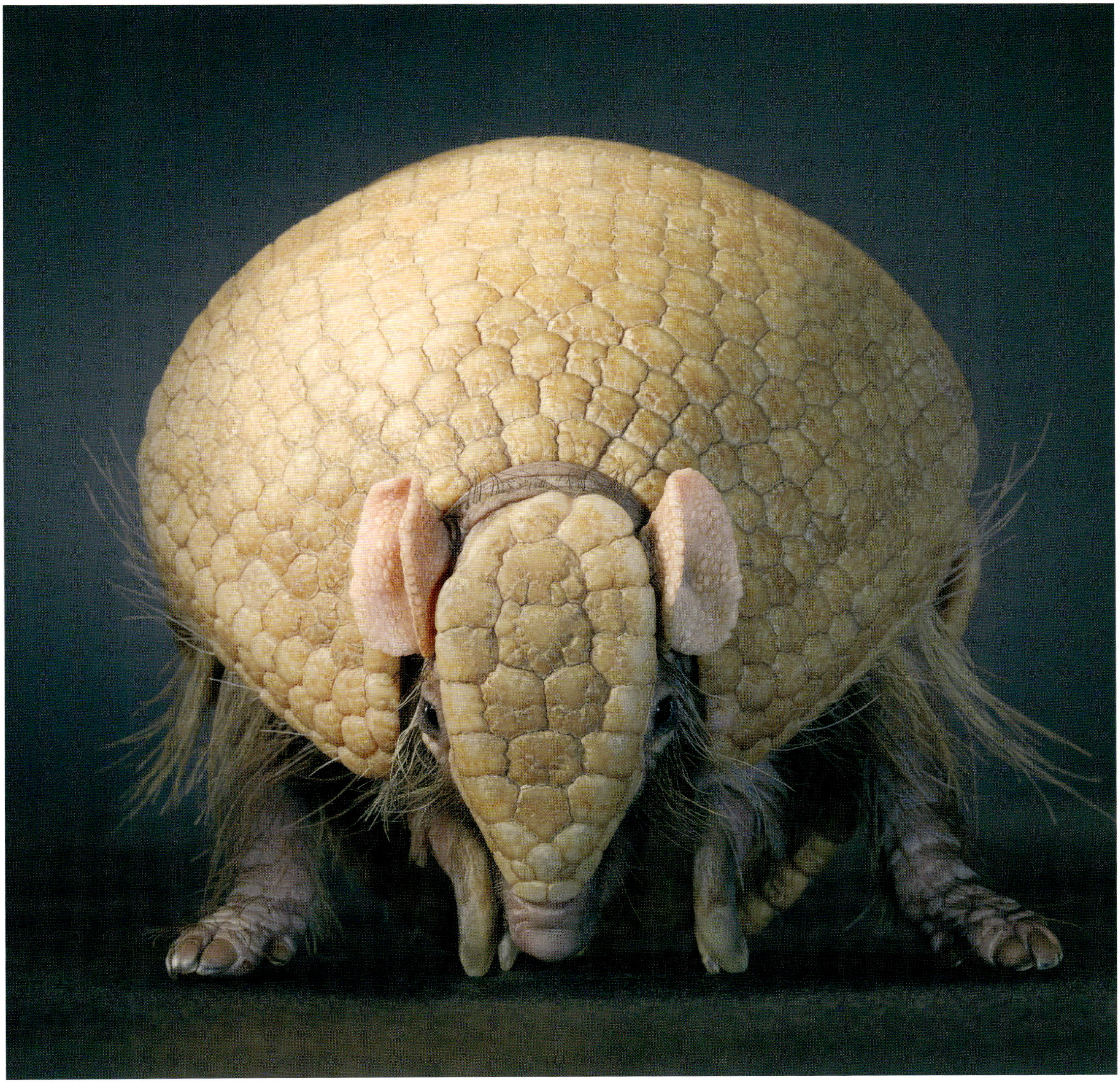

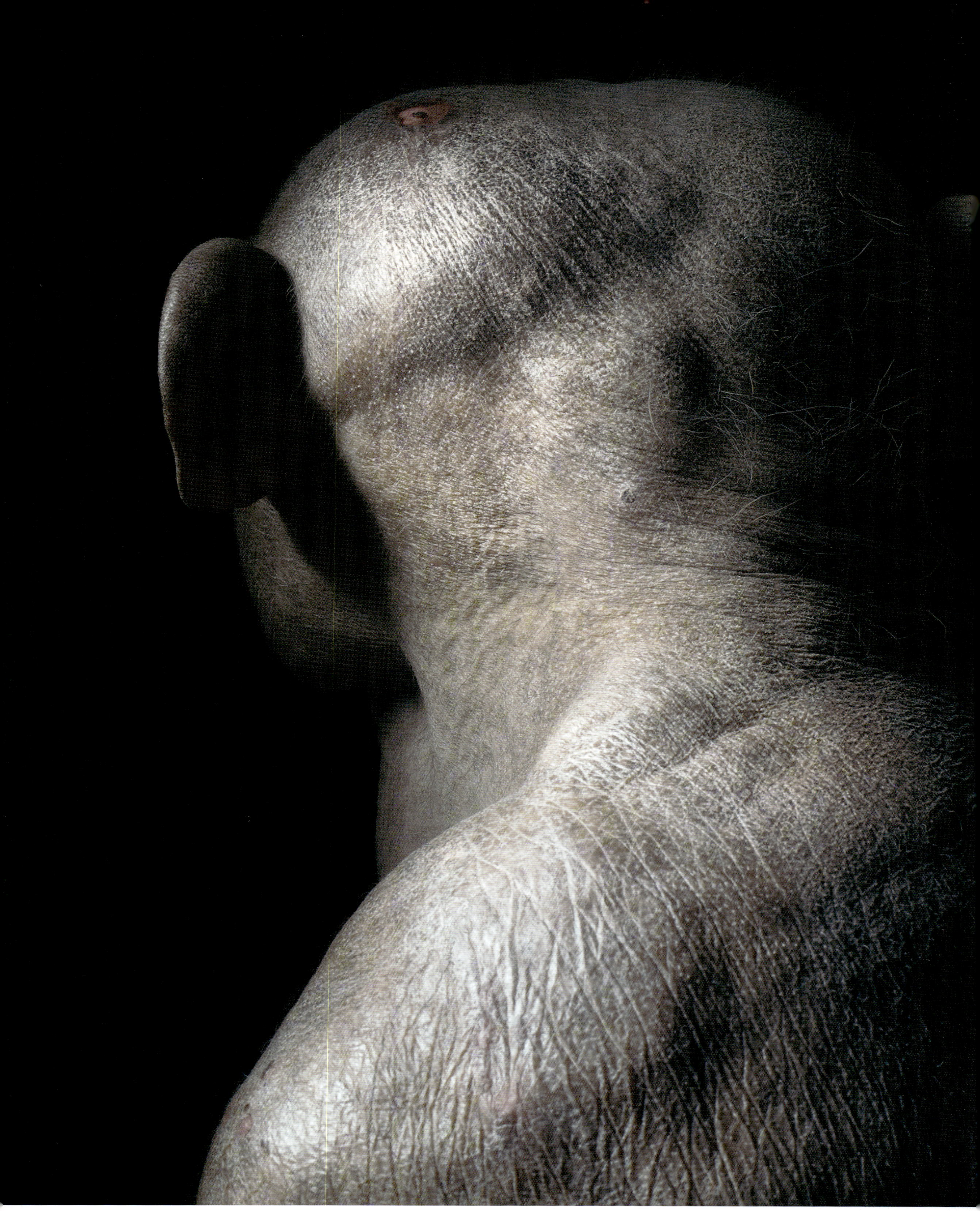

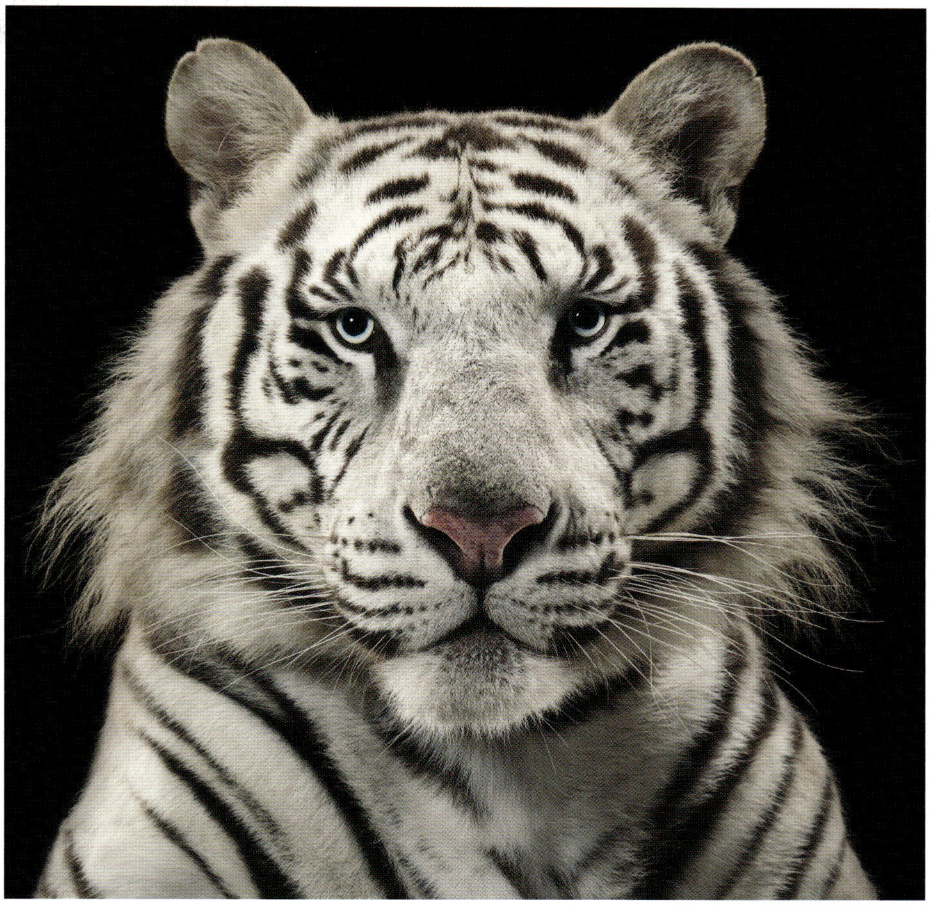

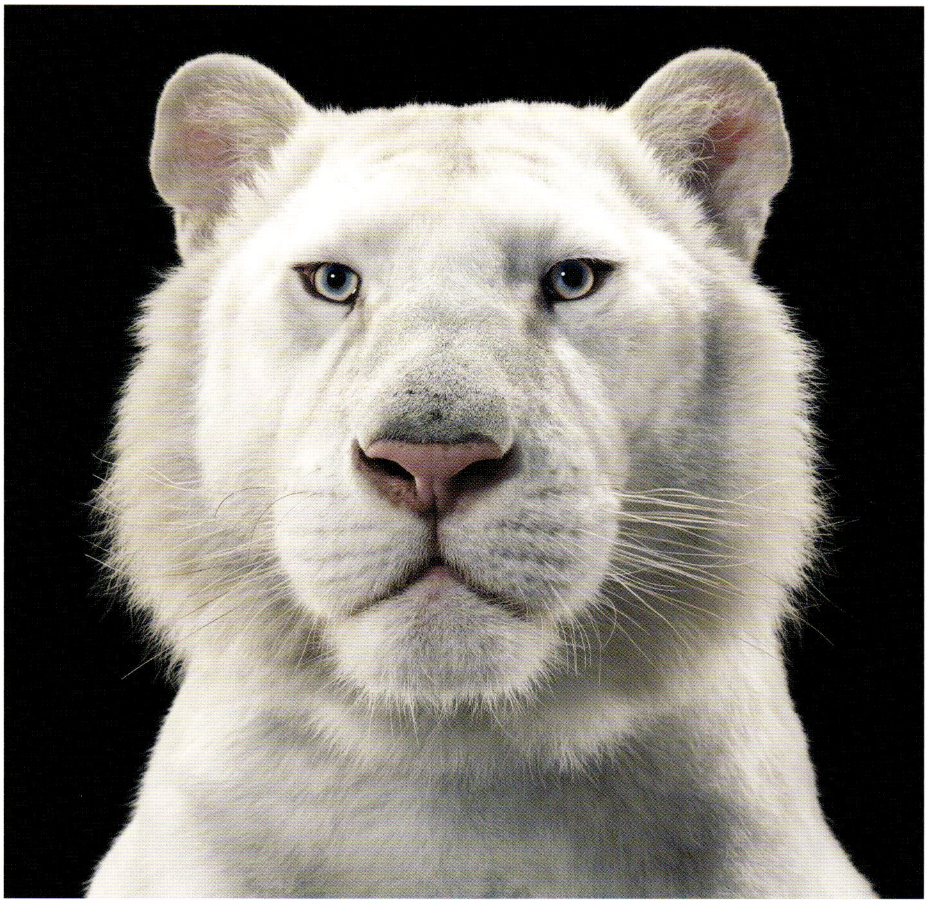

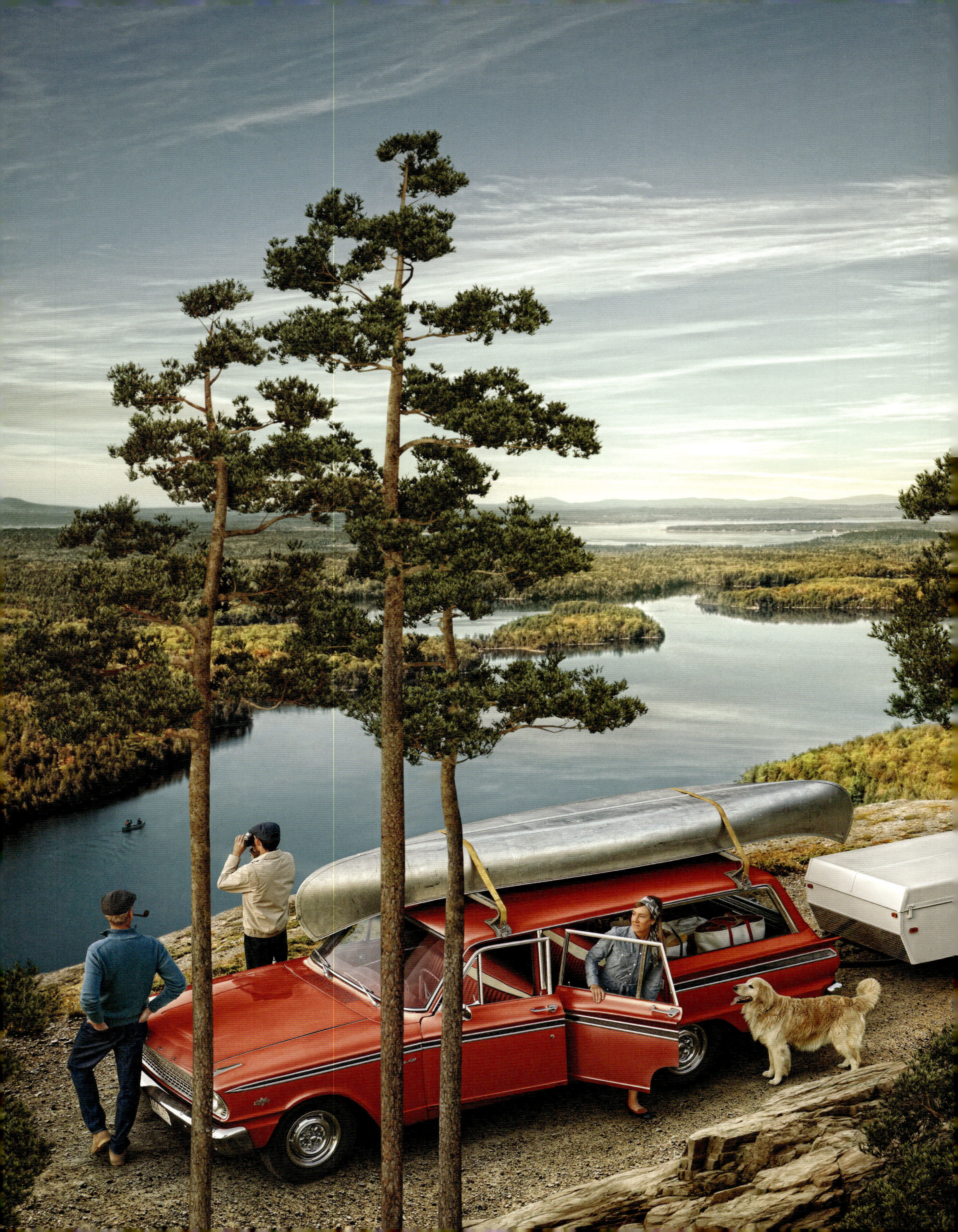

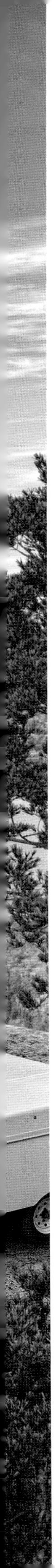

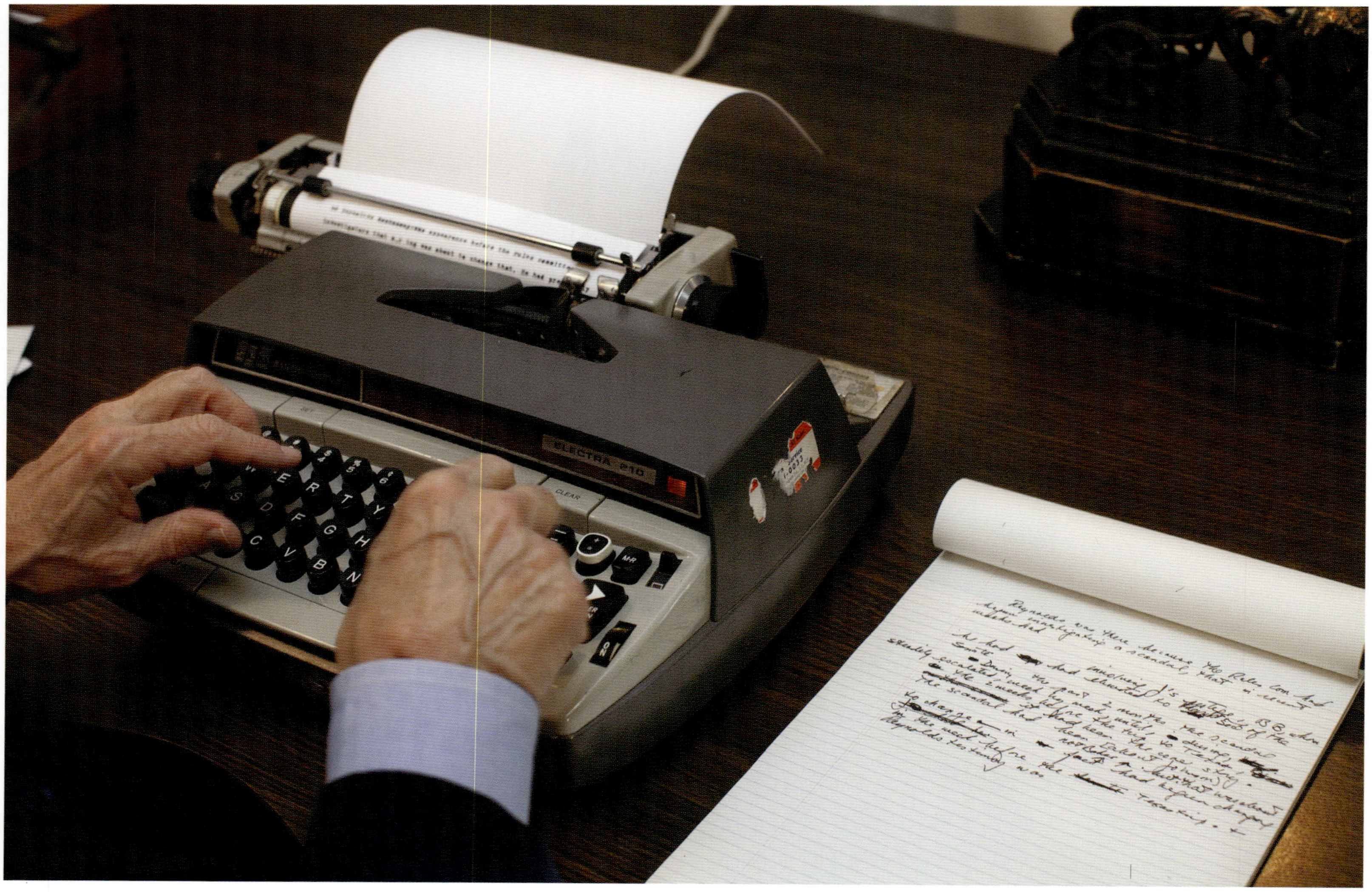

MARTINE FOUGERON

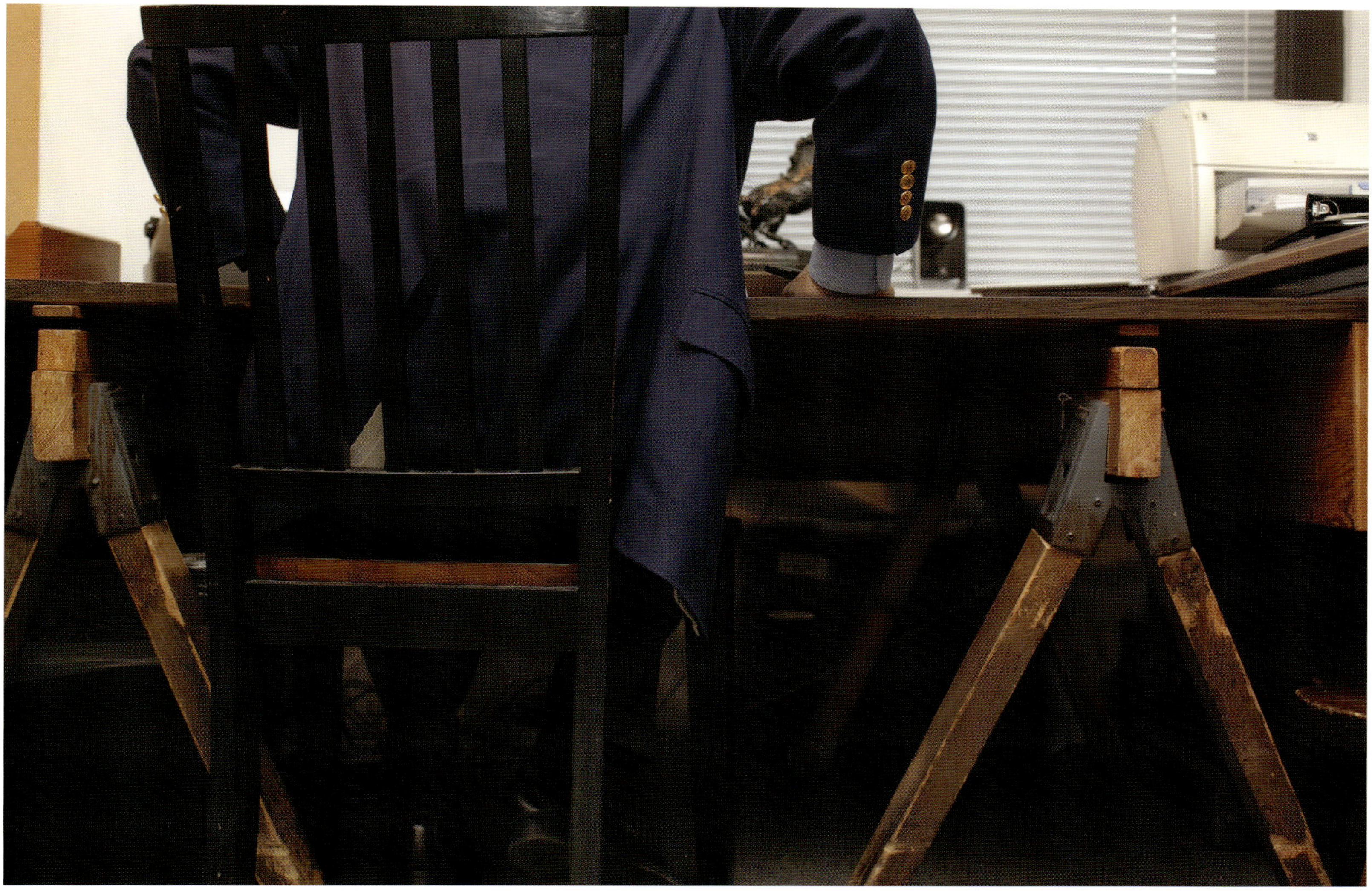

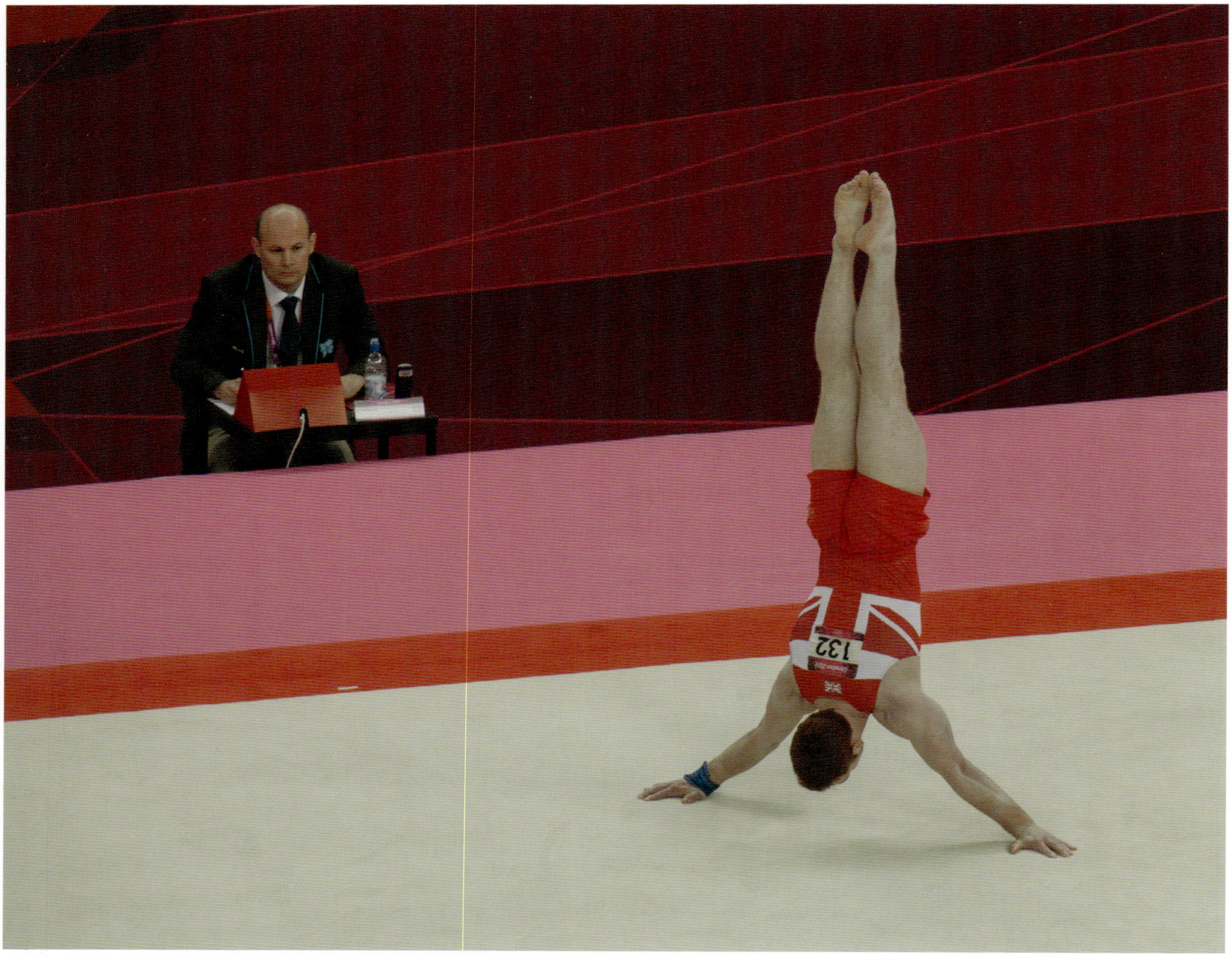

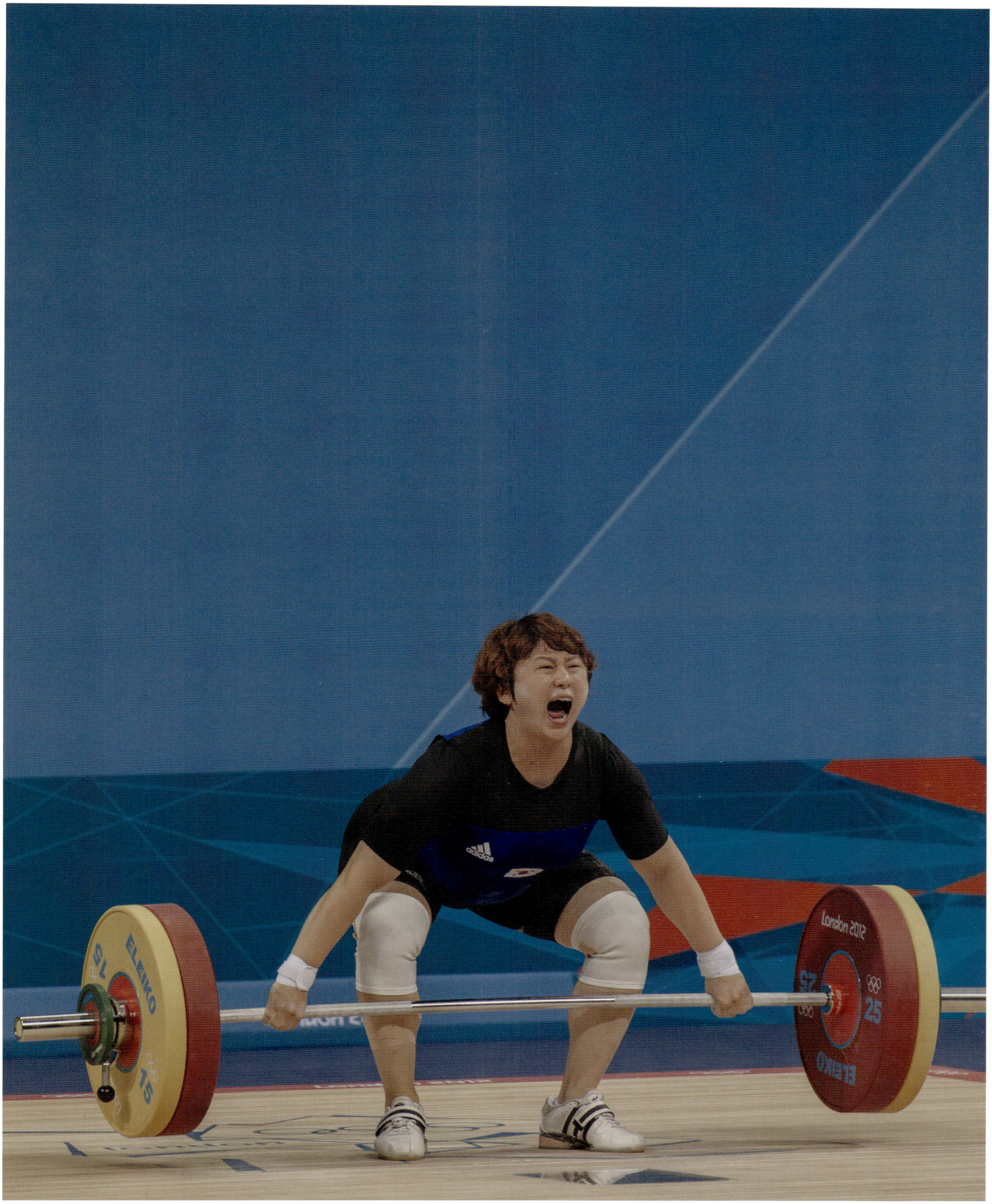
ELEKO
15
London 2012
25
adidas

JULIA FULLERTON-BATTEN

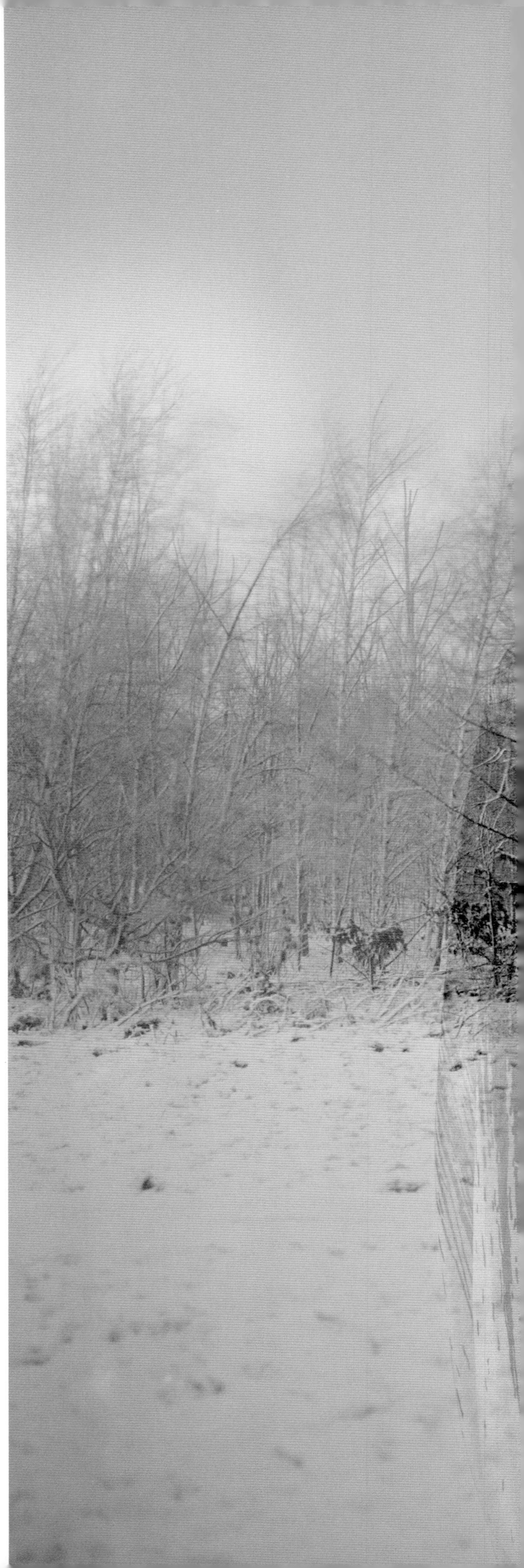

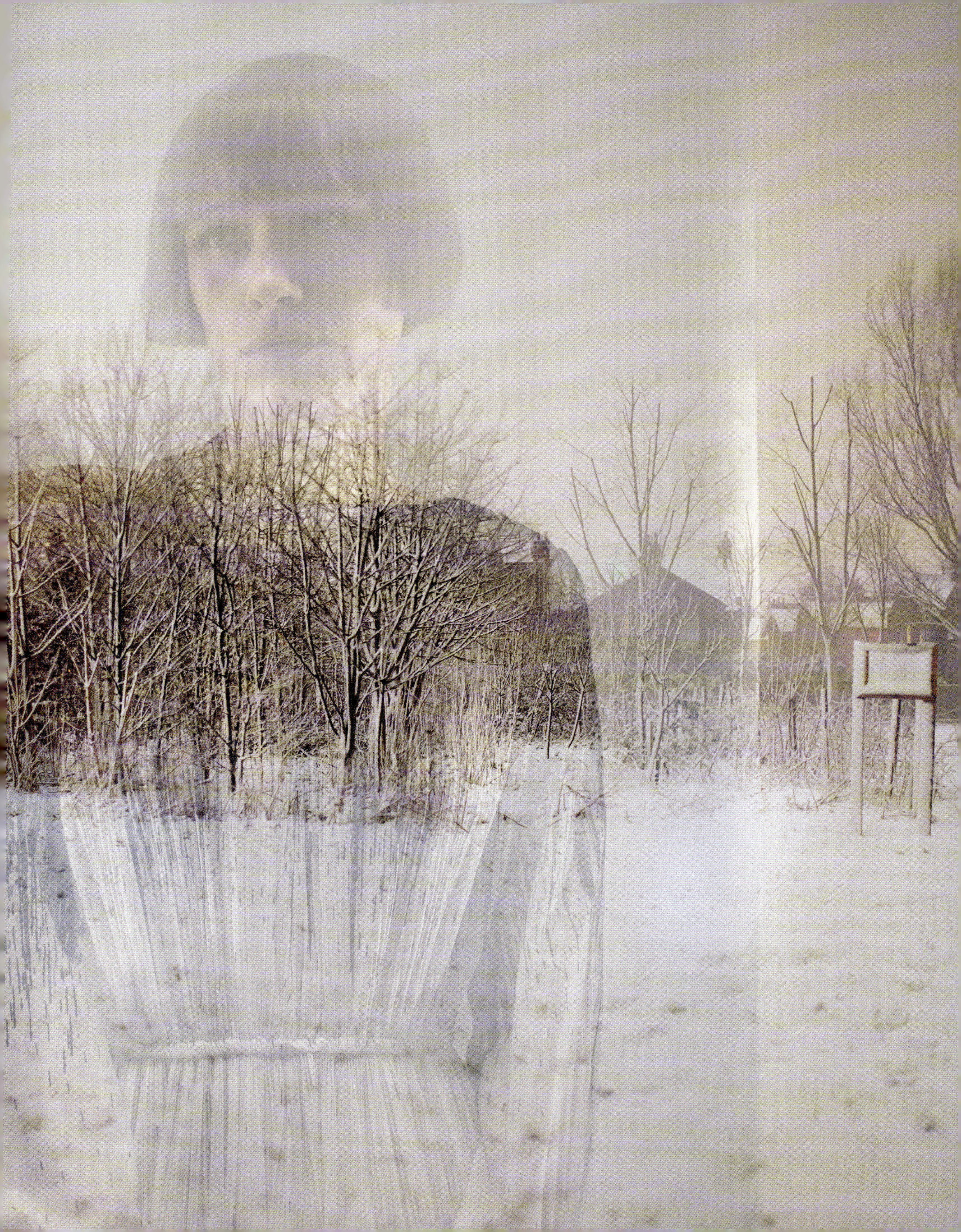

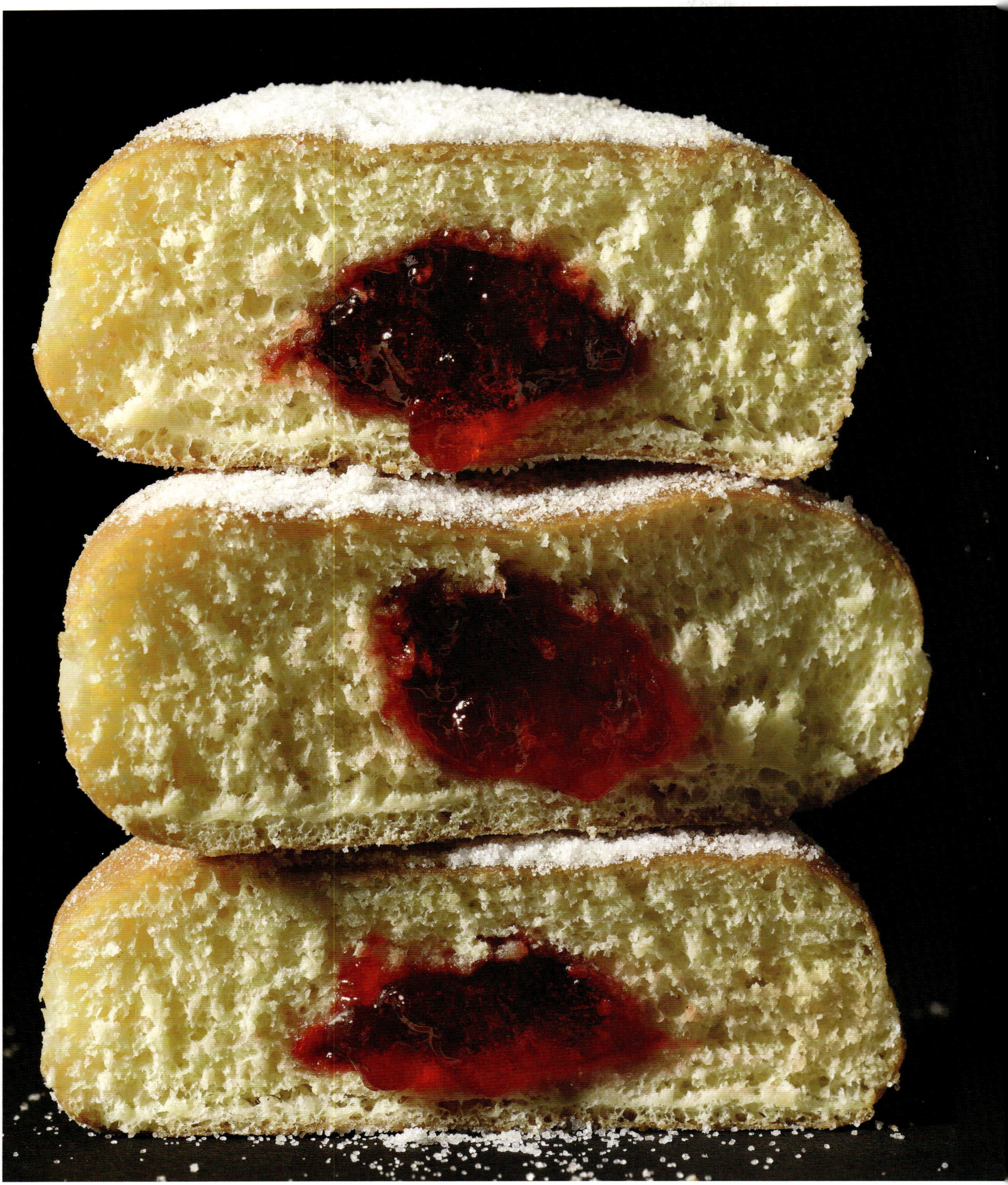

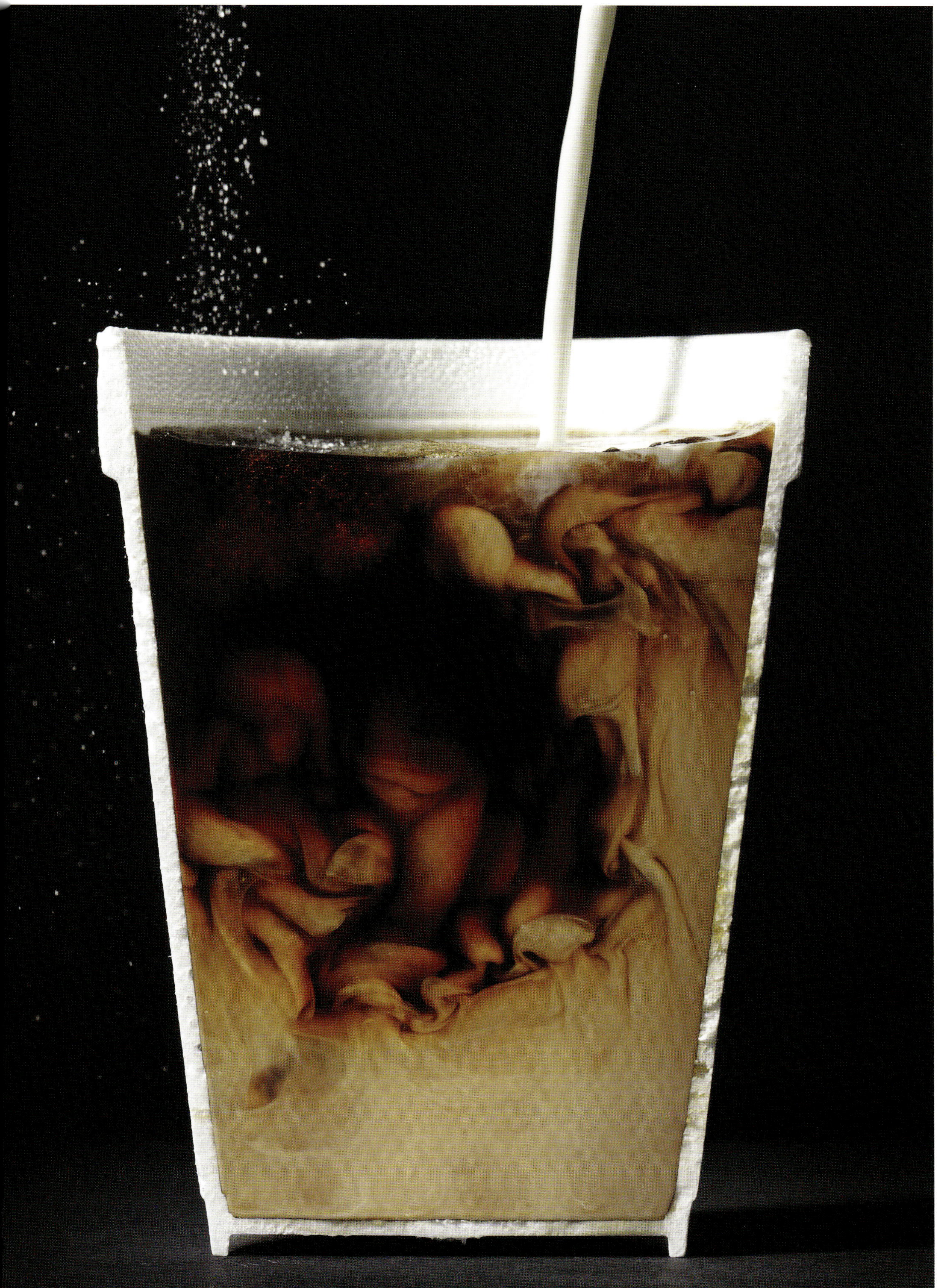

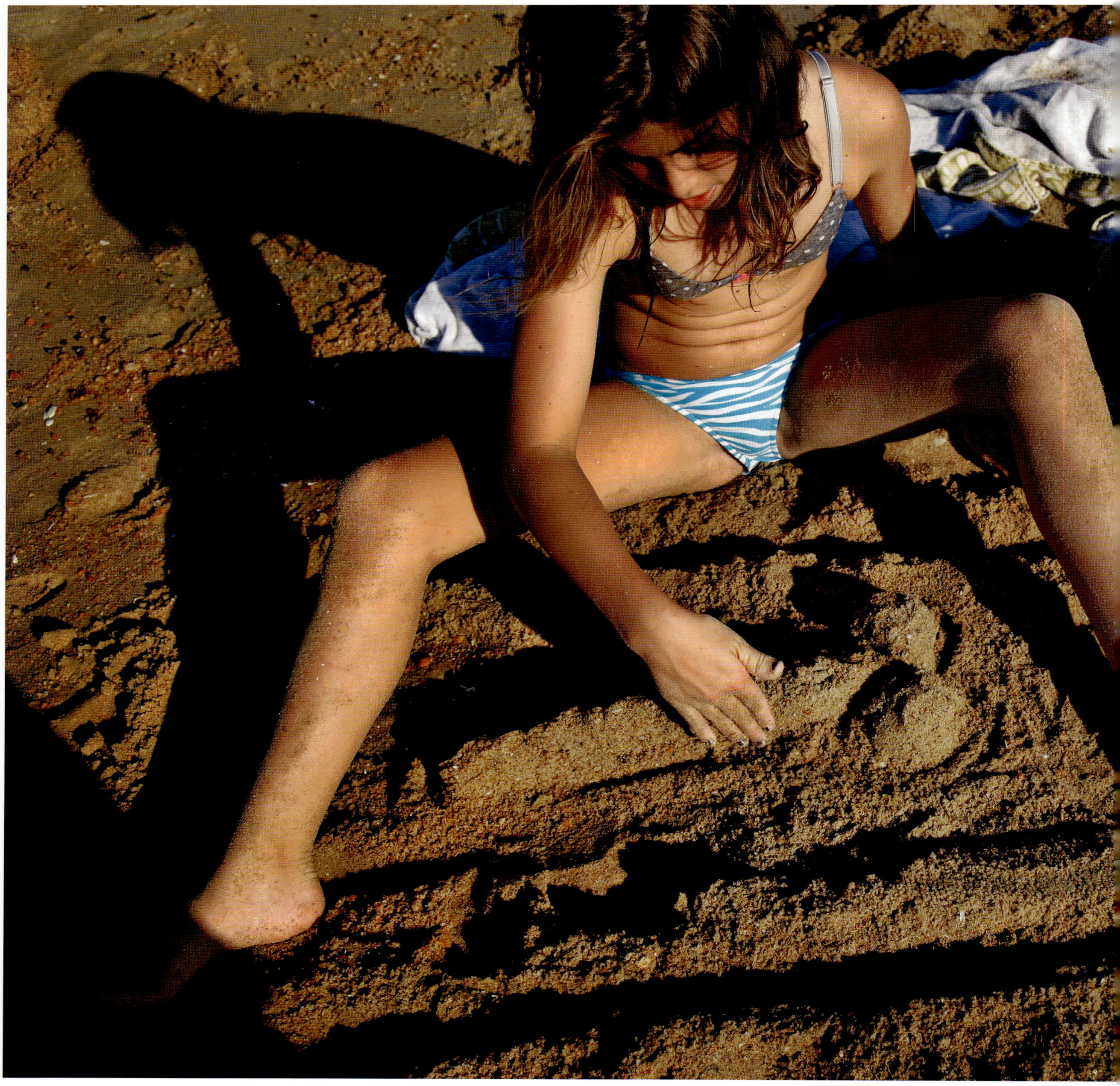

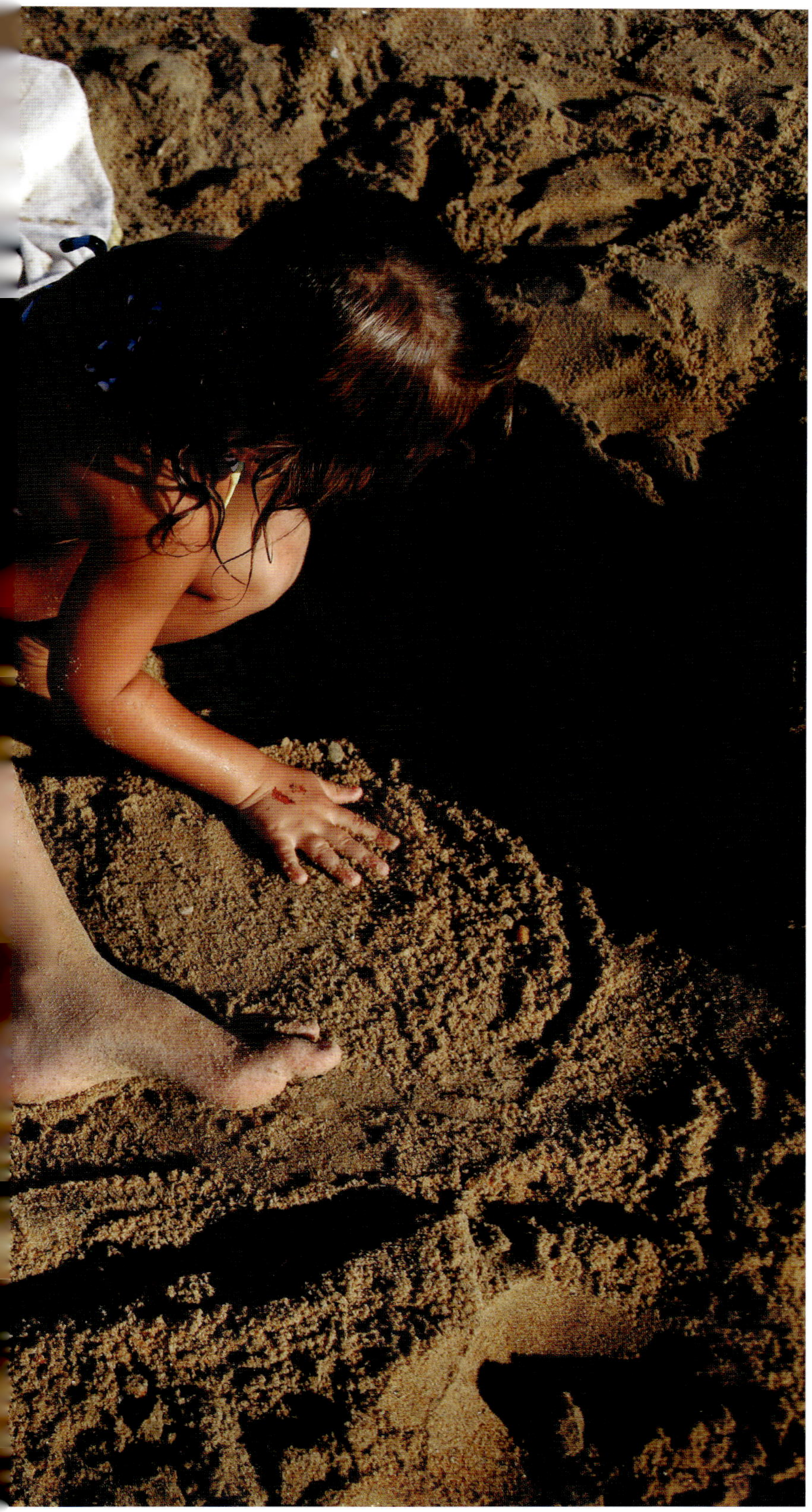

PRESTON GANNAWAY

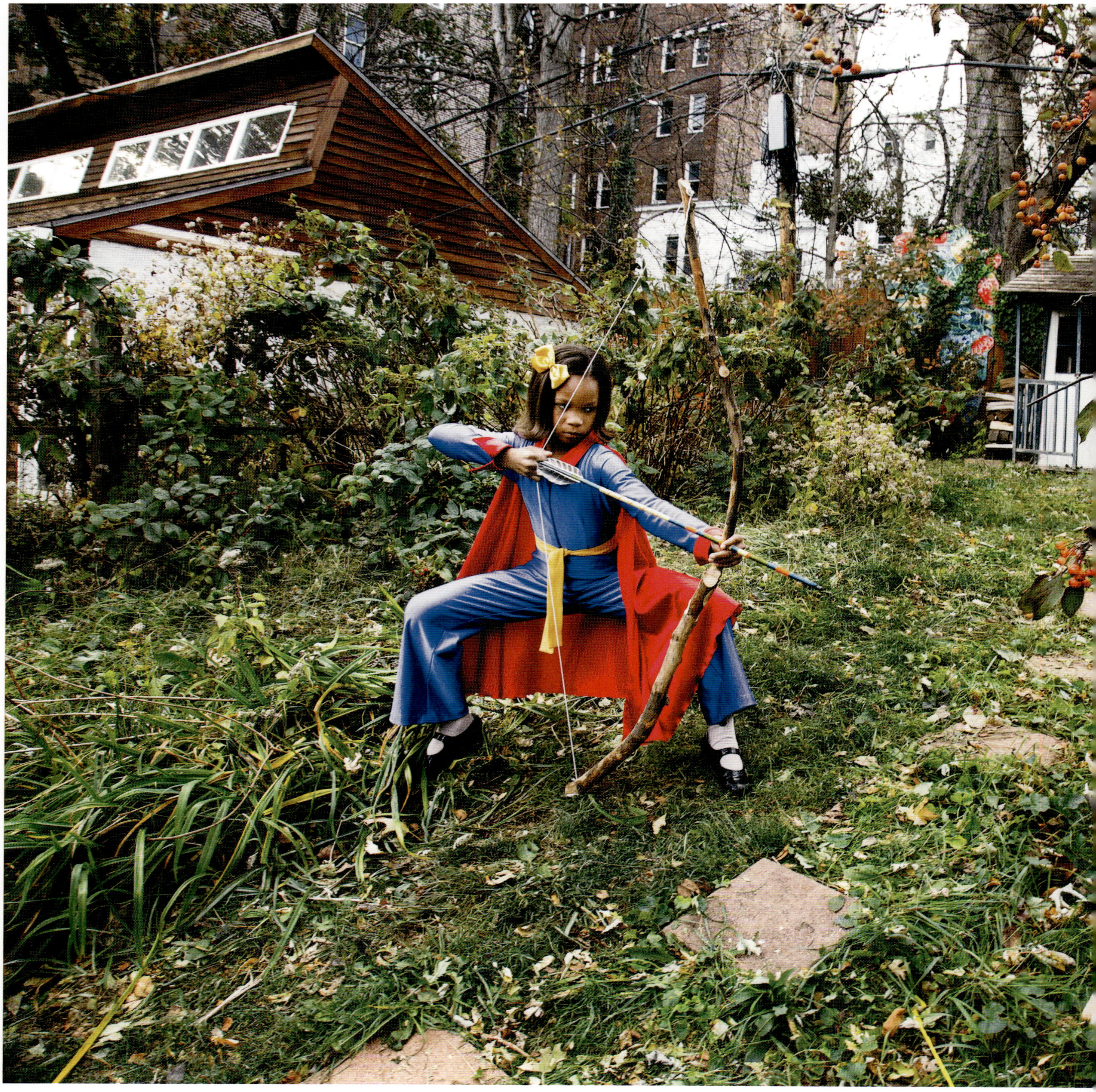

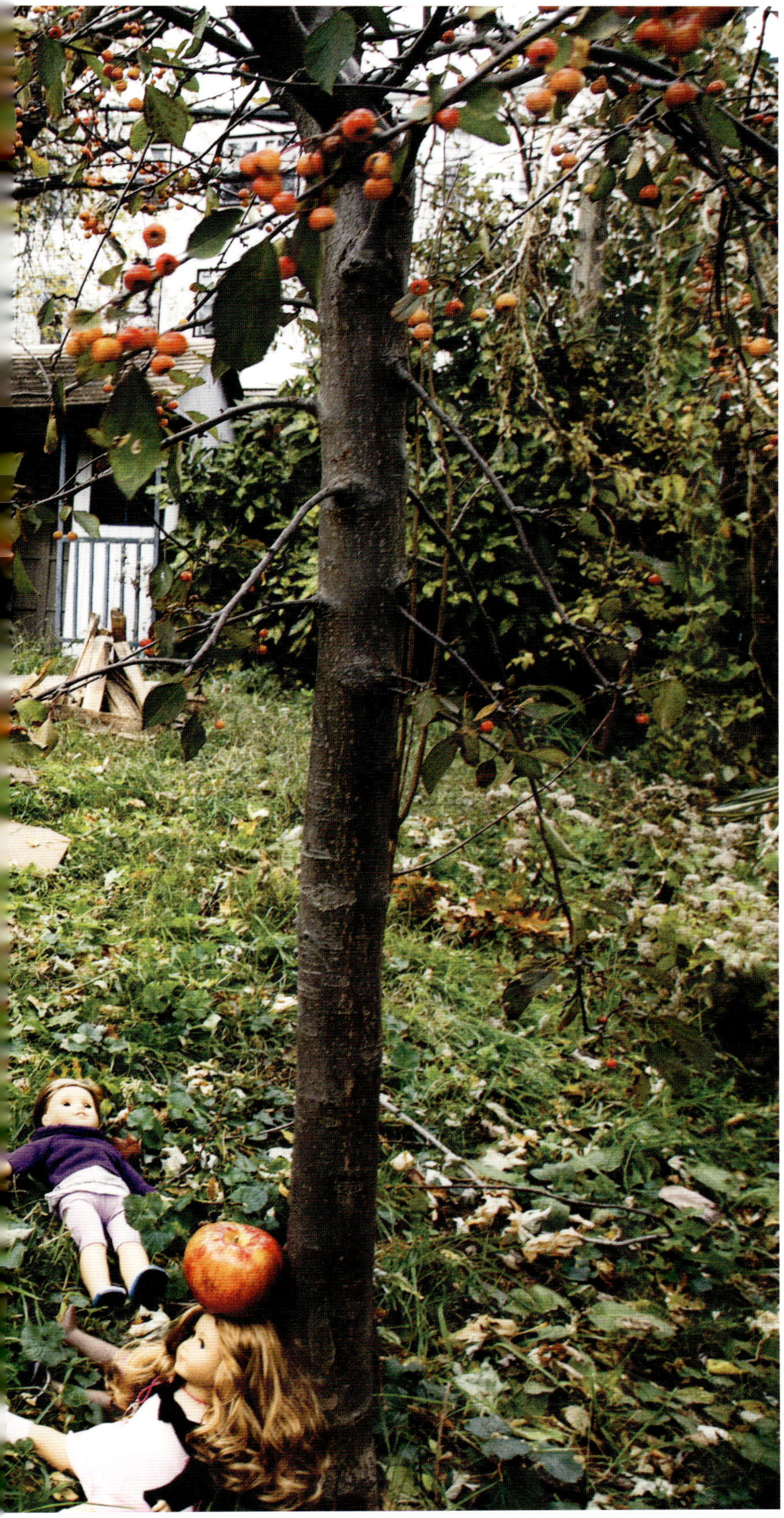

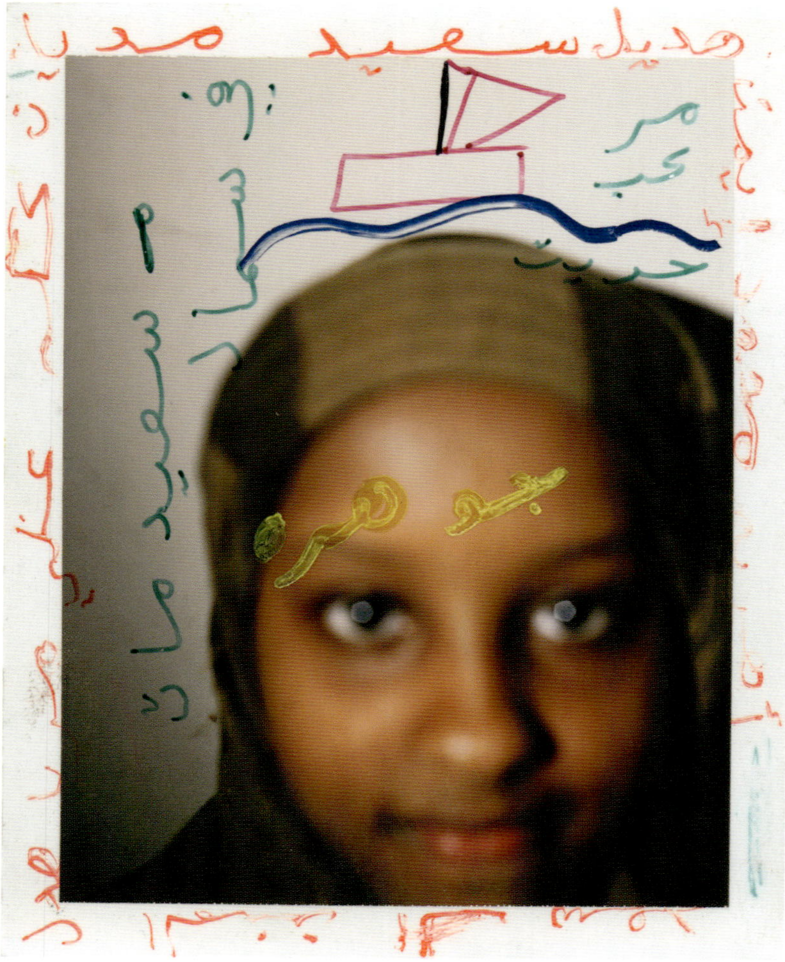

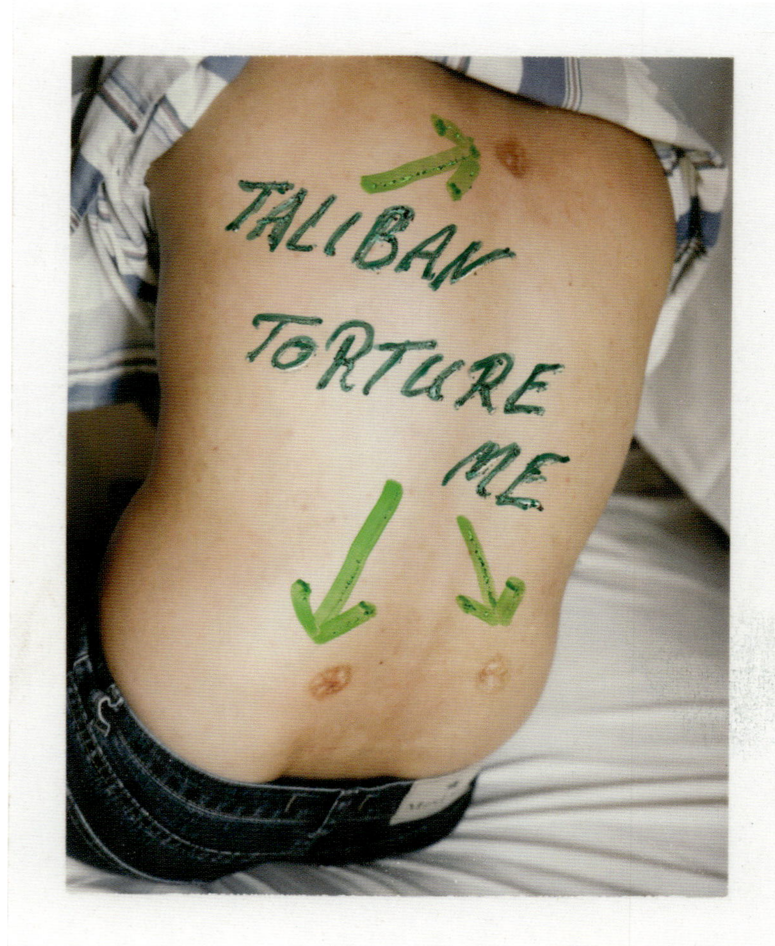
TALIBAN
TORTURE
ME

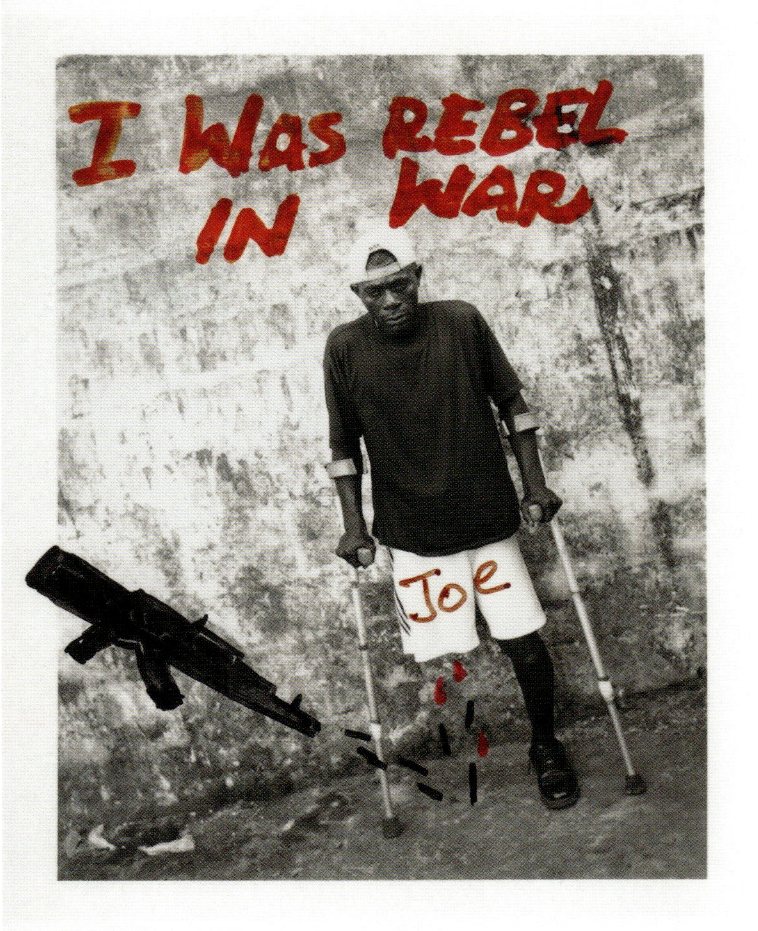
I WAS REBEL IN WAR
JOE

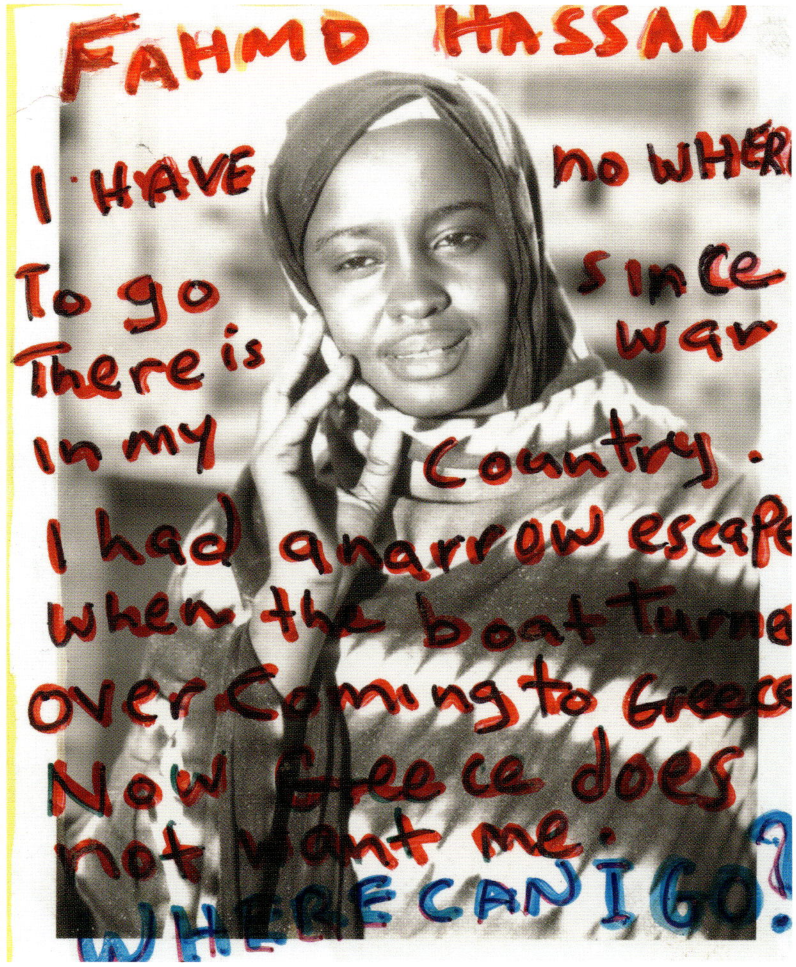
FAHMD HASSAN
I HAVE no WHERE
To go since war
There is
in my Country.
I had a narrow escape
when the boat turned
over Coming to Greece
Now Greece does
not want me.
WHERE CAN I GO?

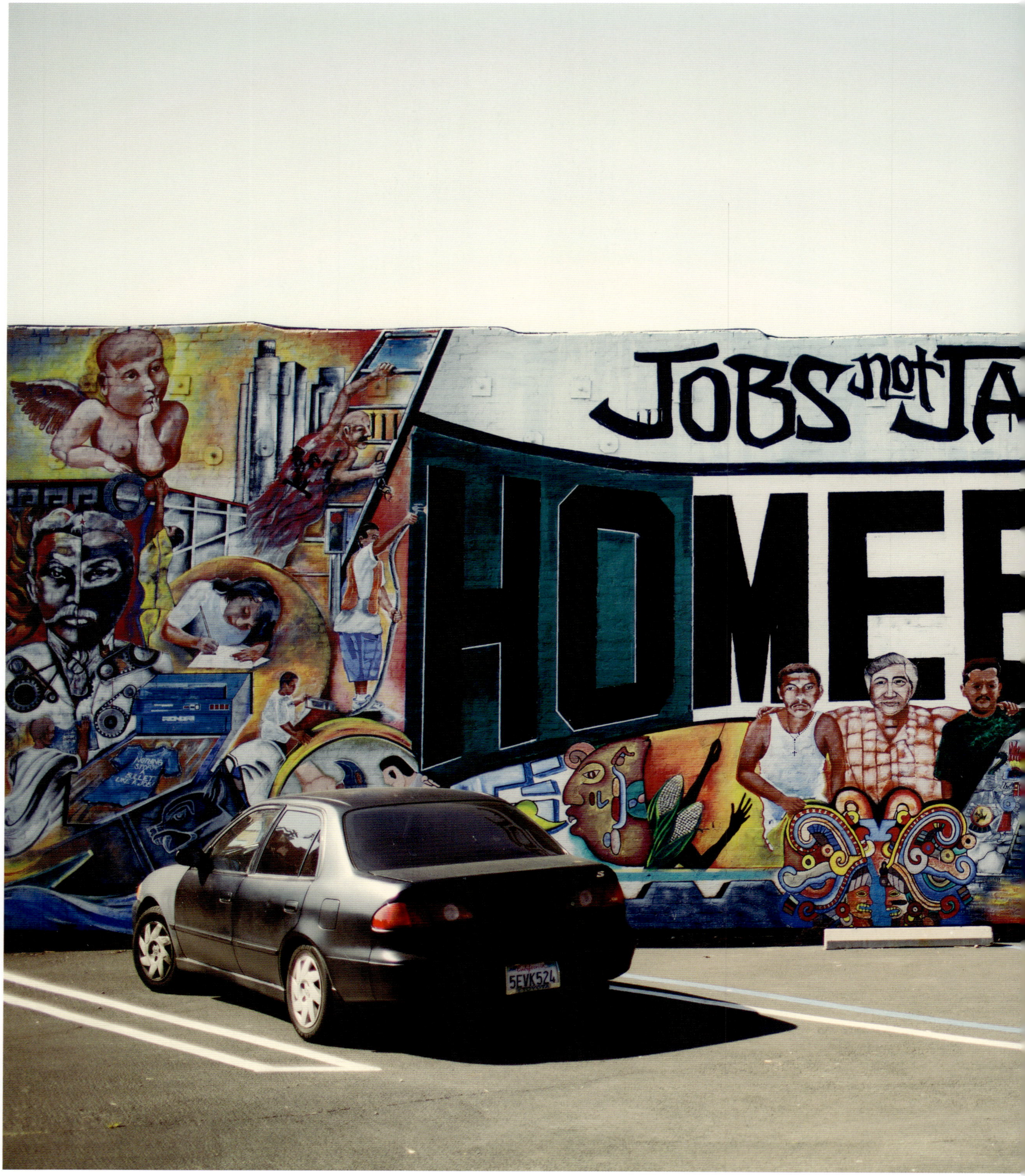
JOBS not
HOME
5EVK524

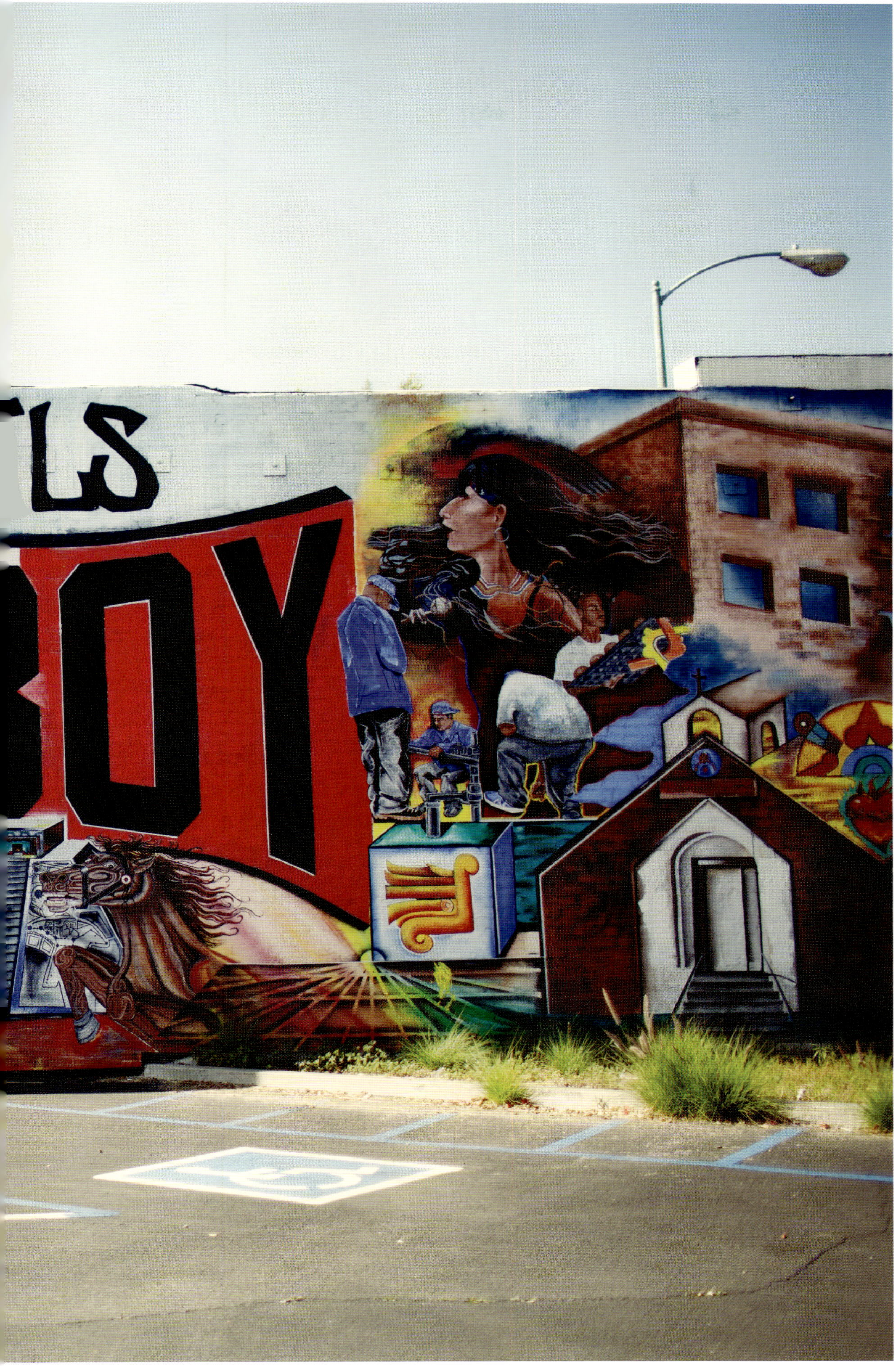

MELISSA GOLDEN

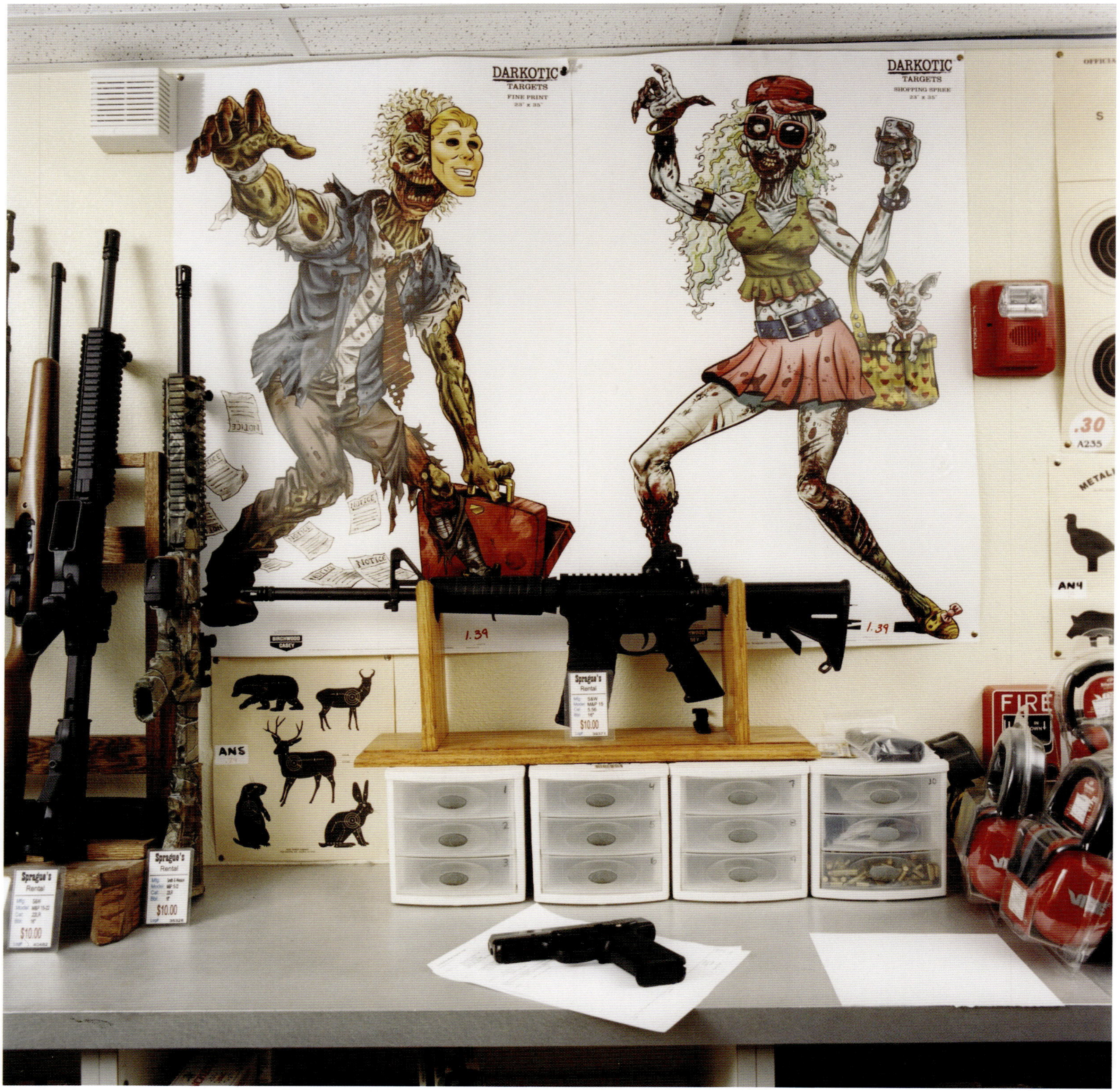
DARKOTIC
TARGETS
FINE PRINT
DARKOTIC
TARGETS
SHOPPING SPREE
1.39
1.39
Sprague's
Rental
$10.00
.30
A235
FIRE

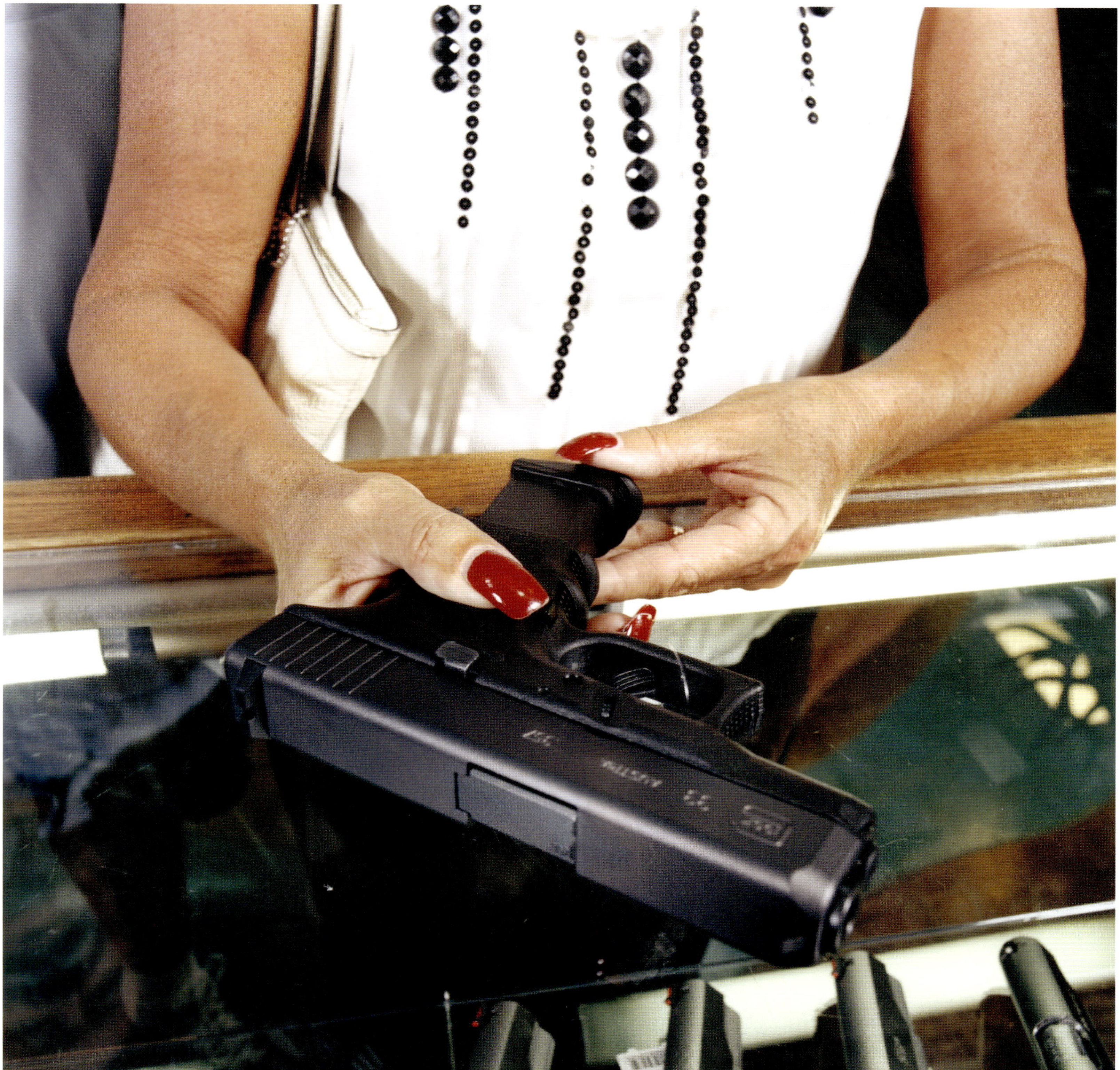

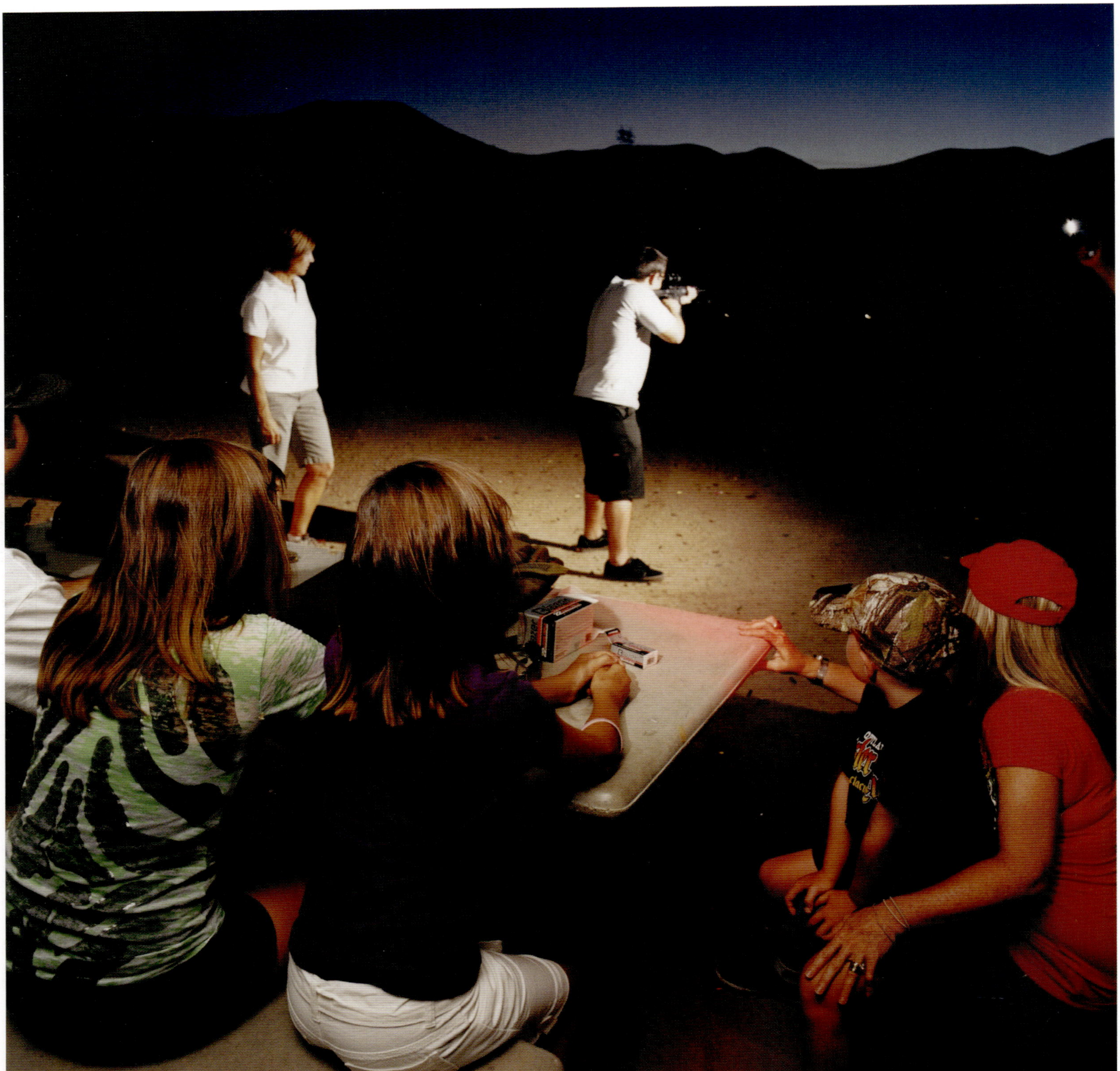

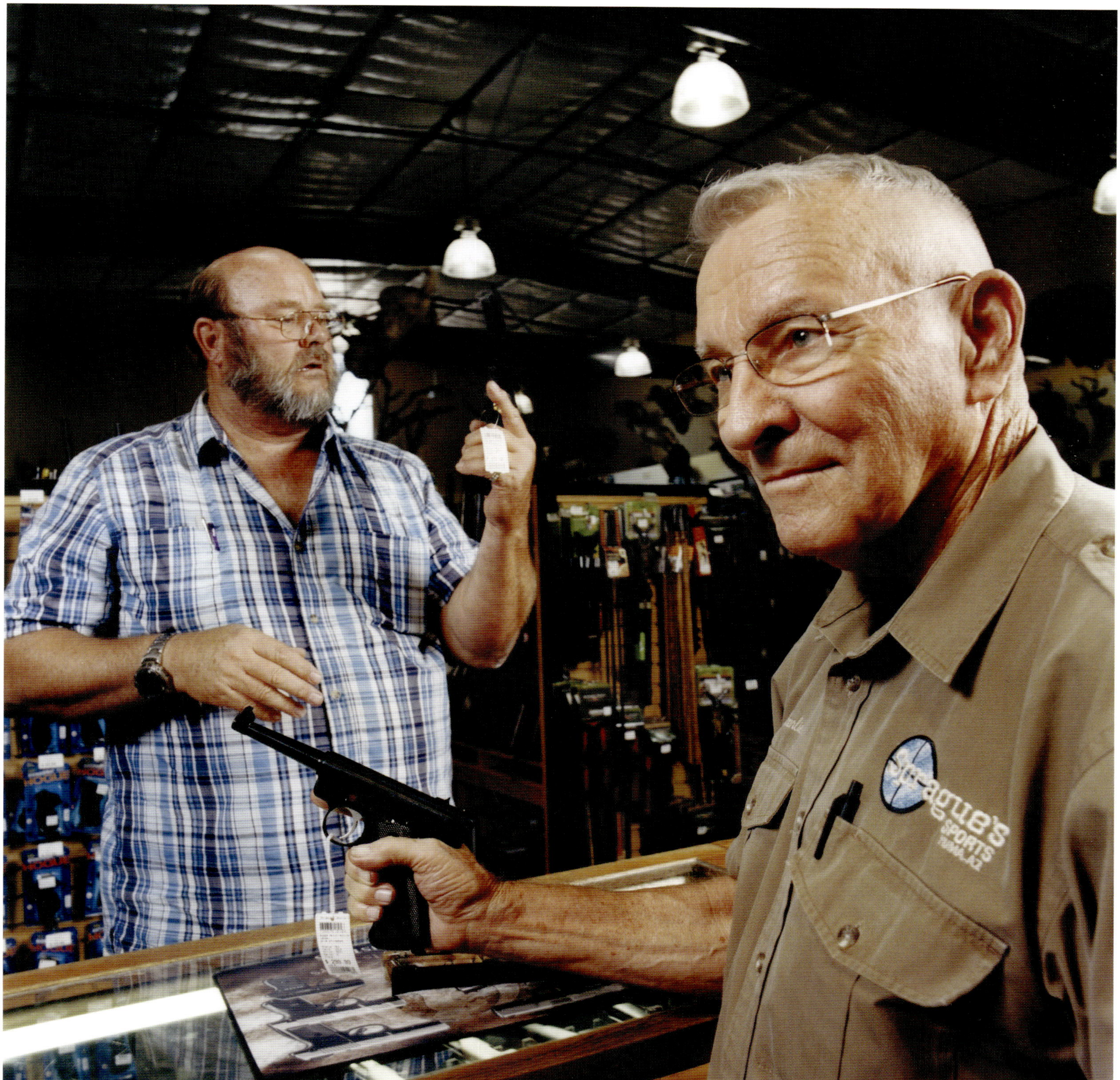

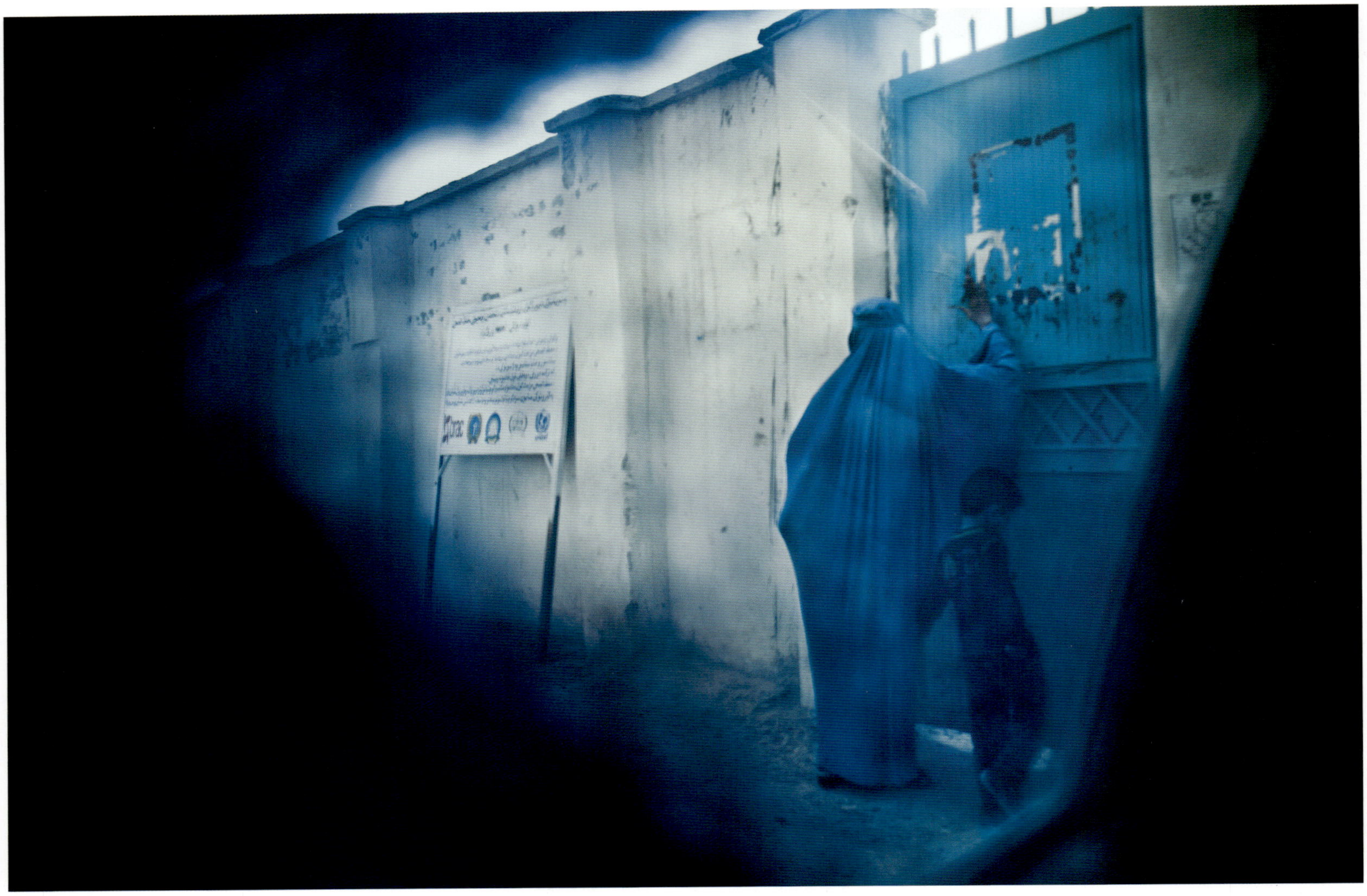

TONI GREAVES

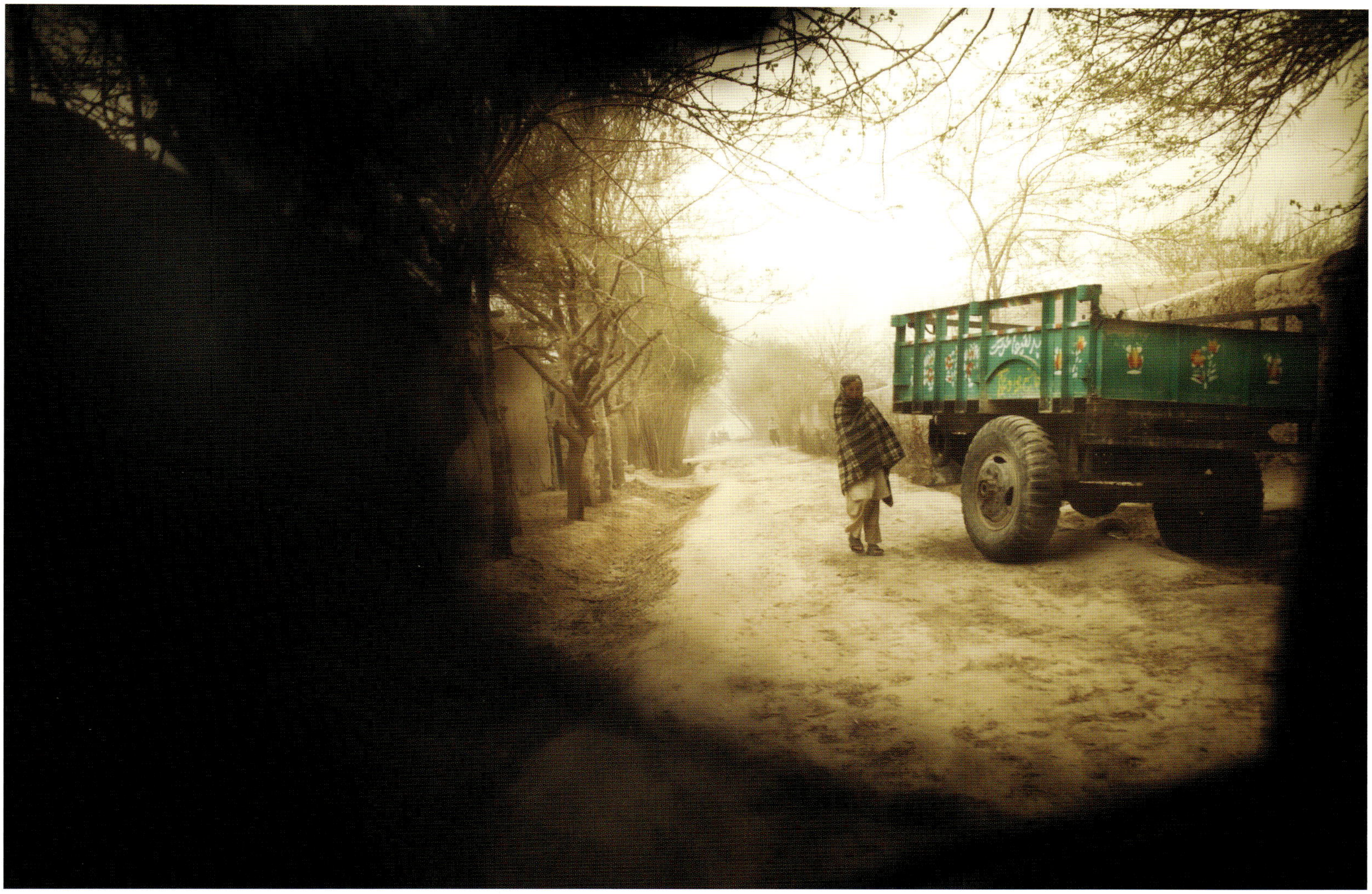

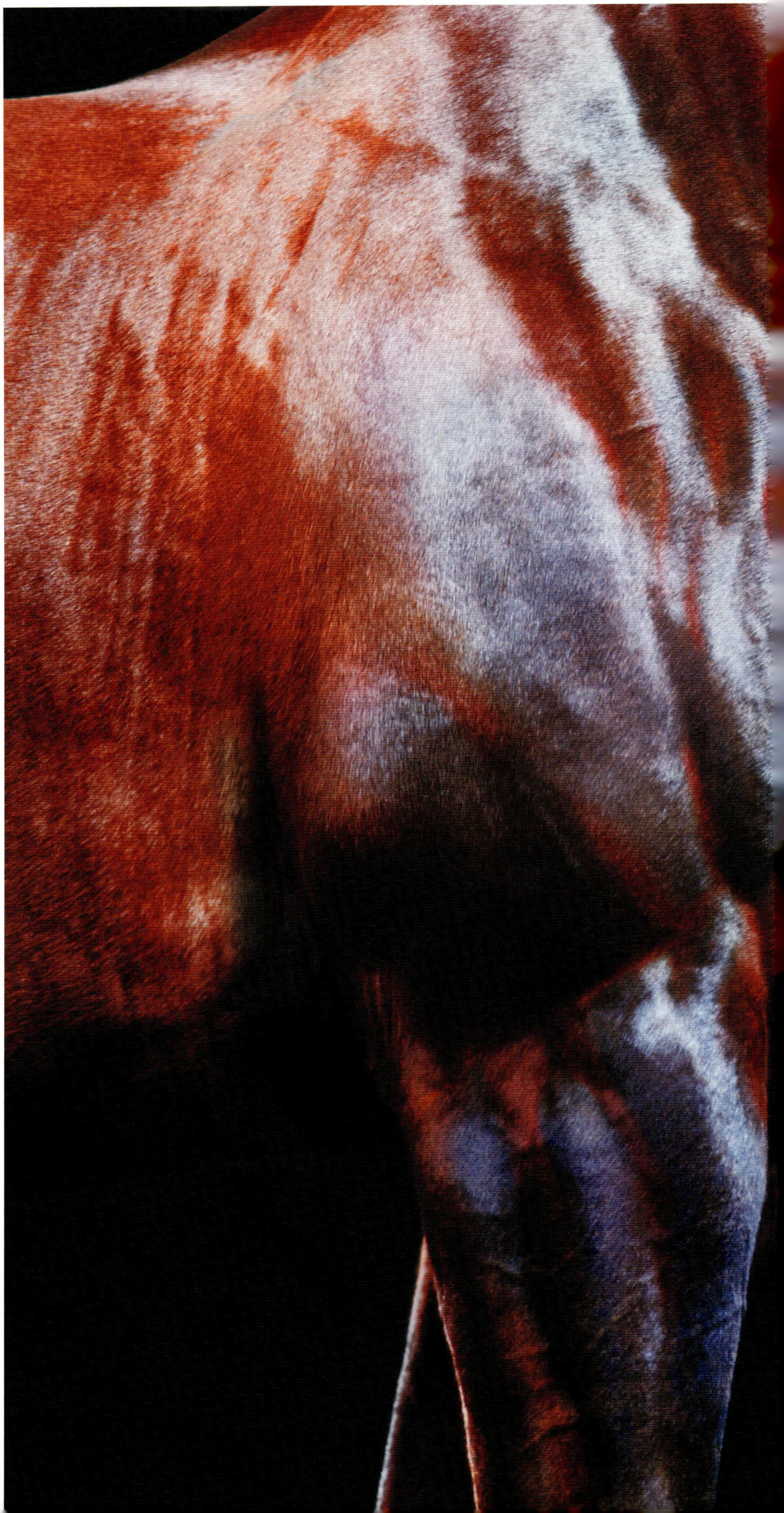

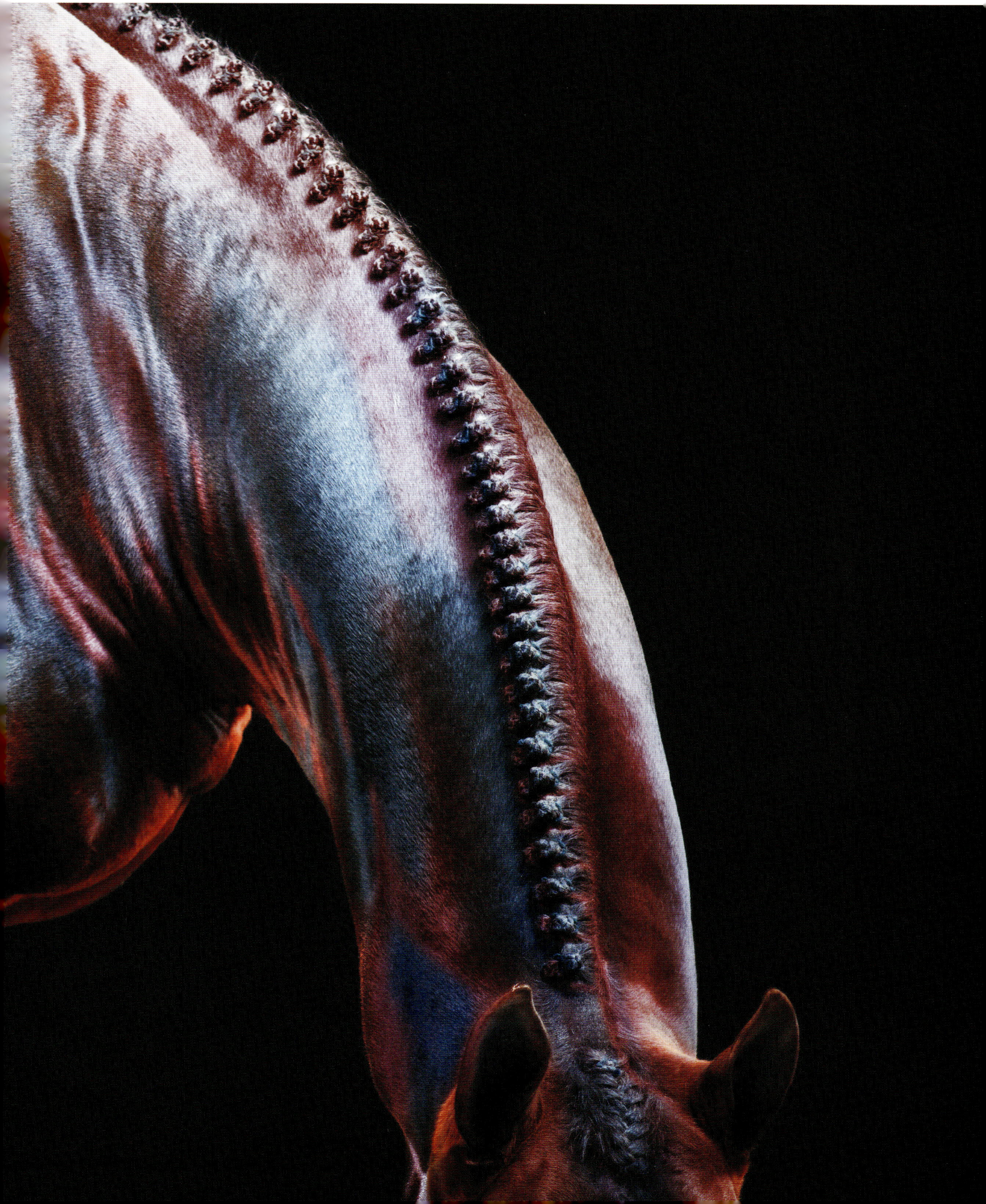

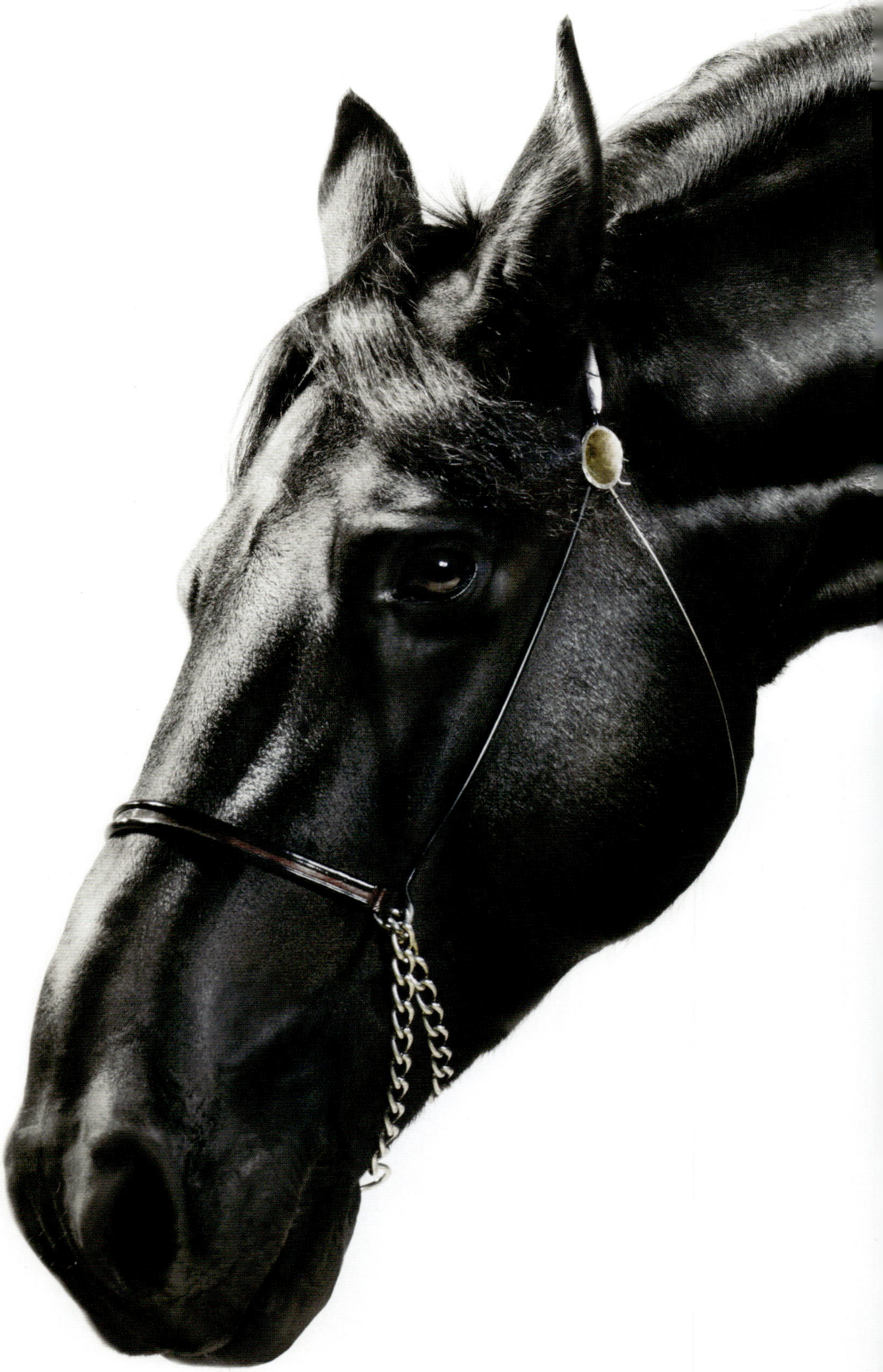

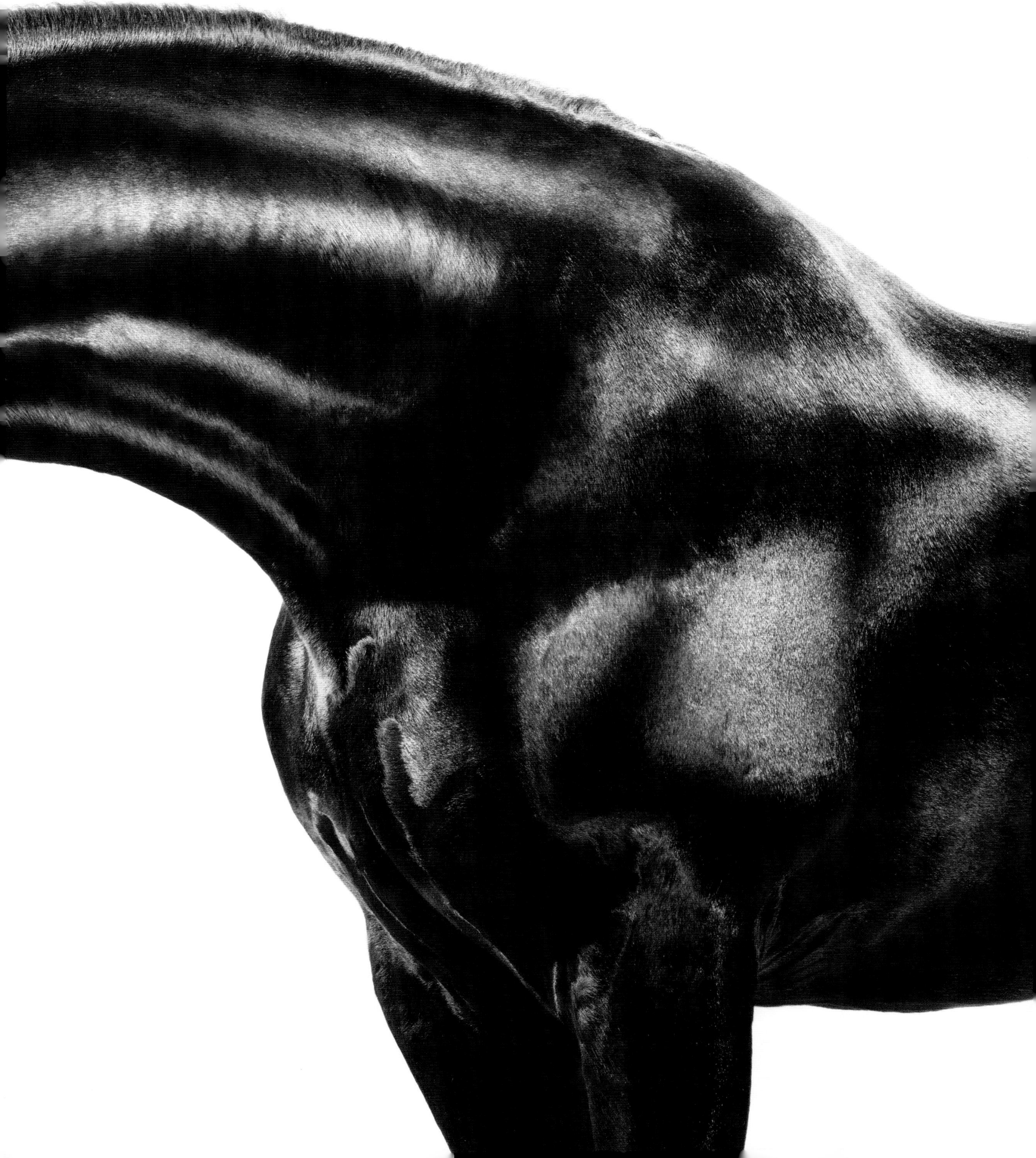

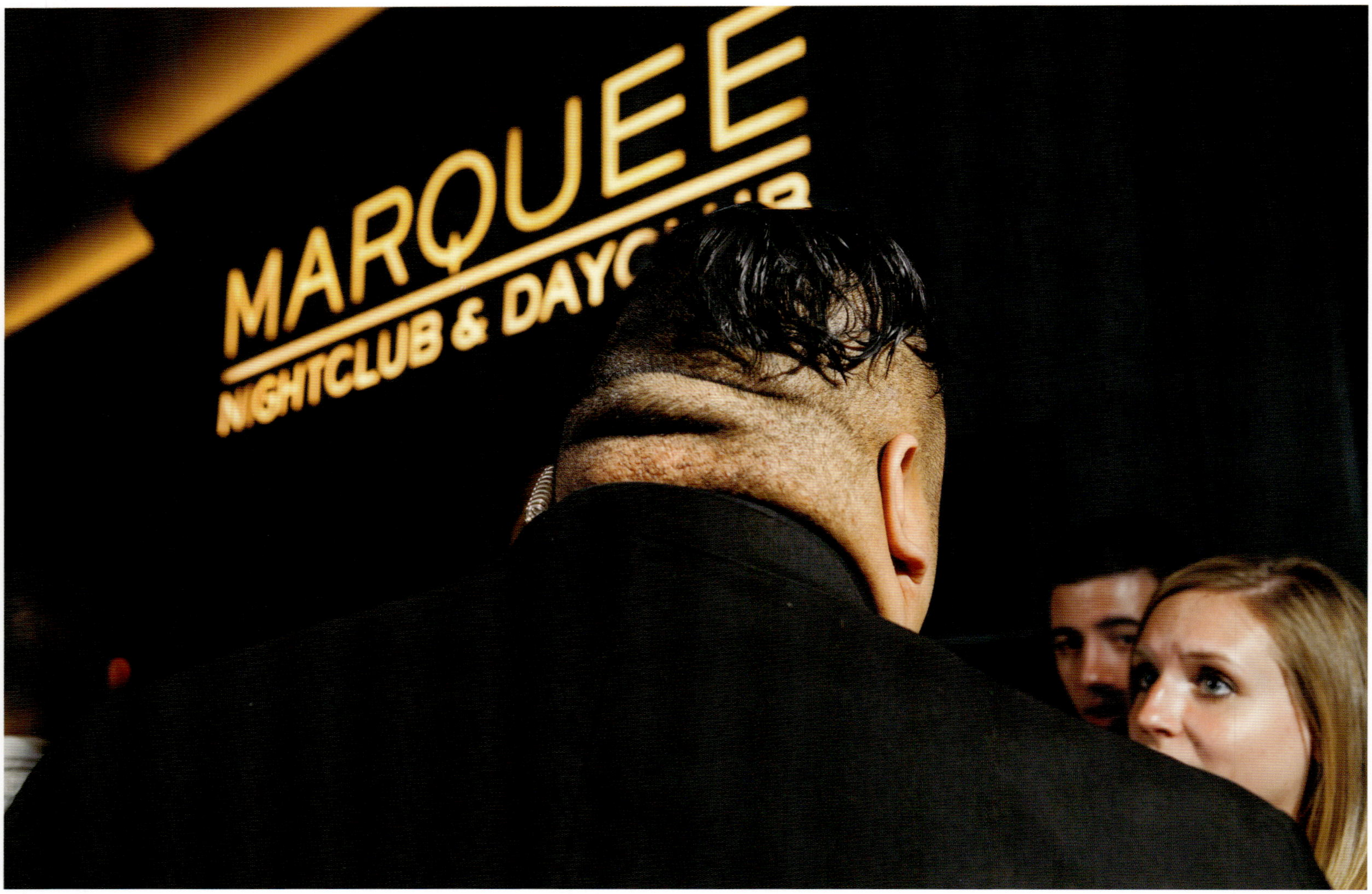
MARQUEE
NIGHTCLUB & DAYC

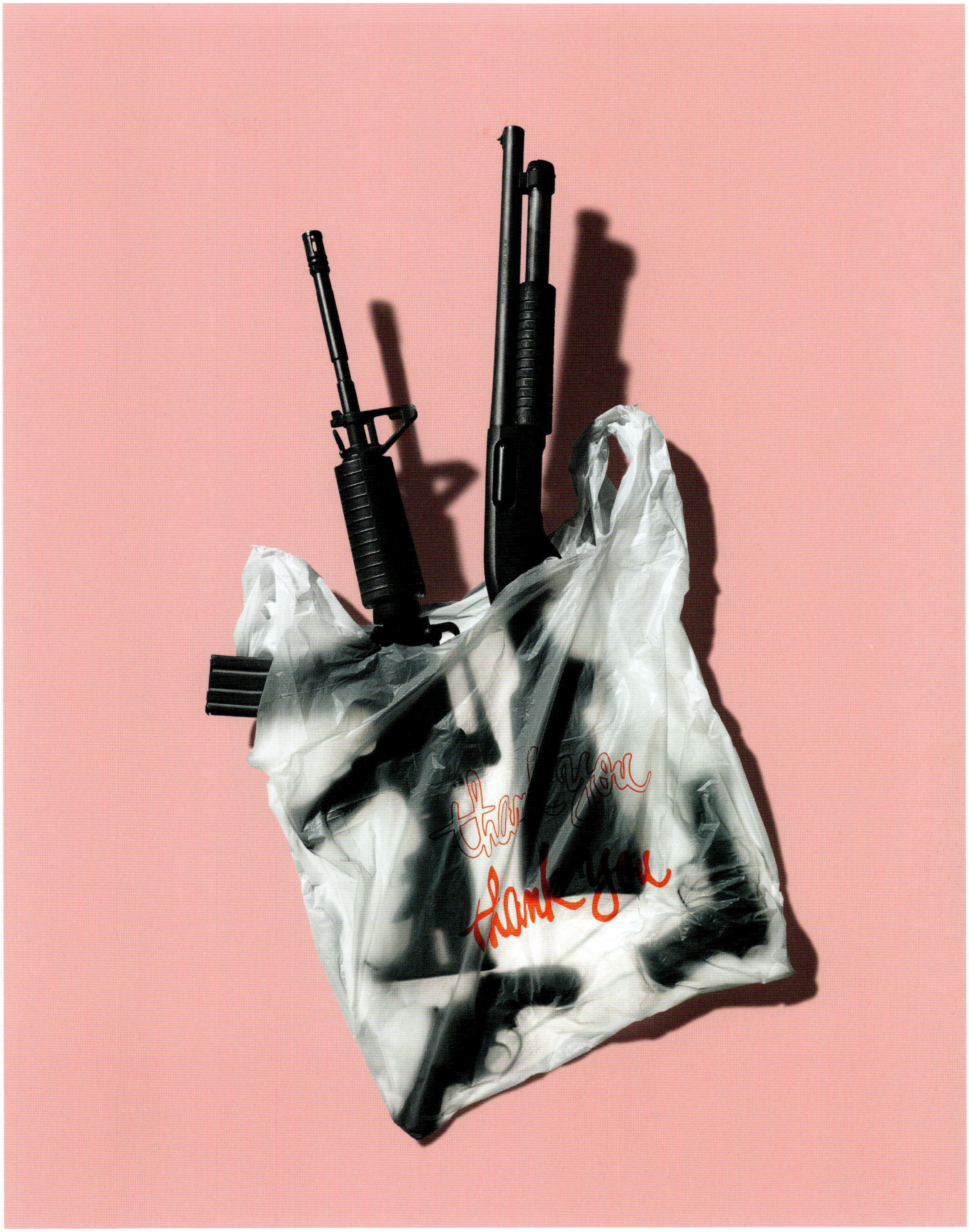

CHRISTOPHER GRIFFITH

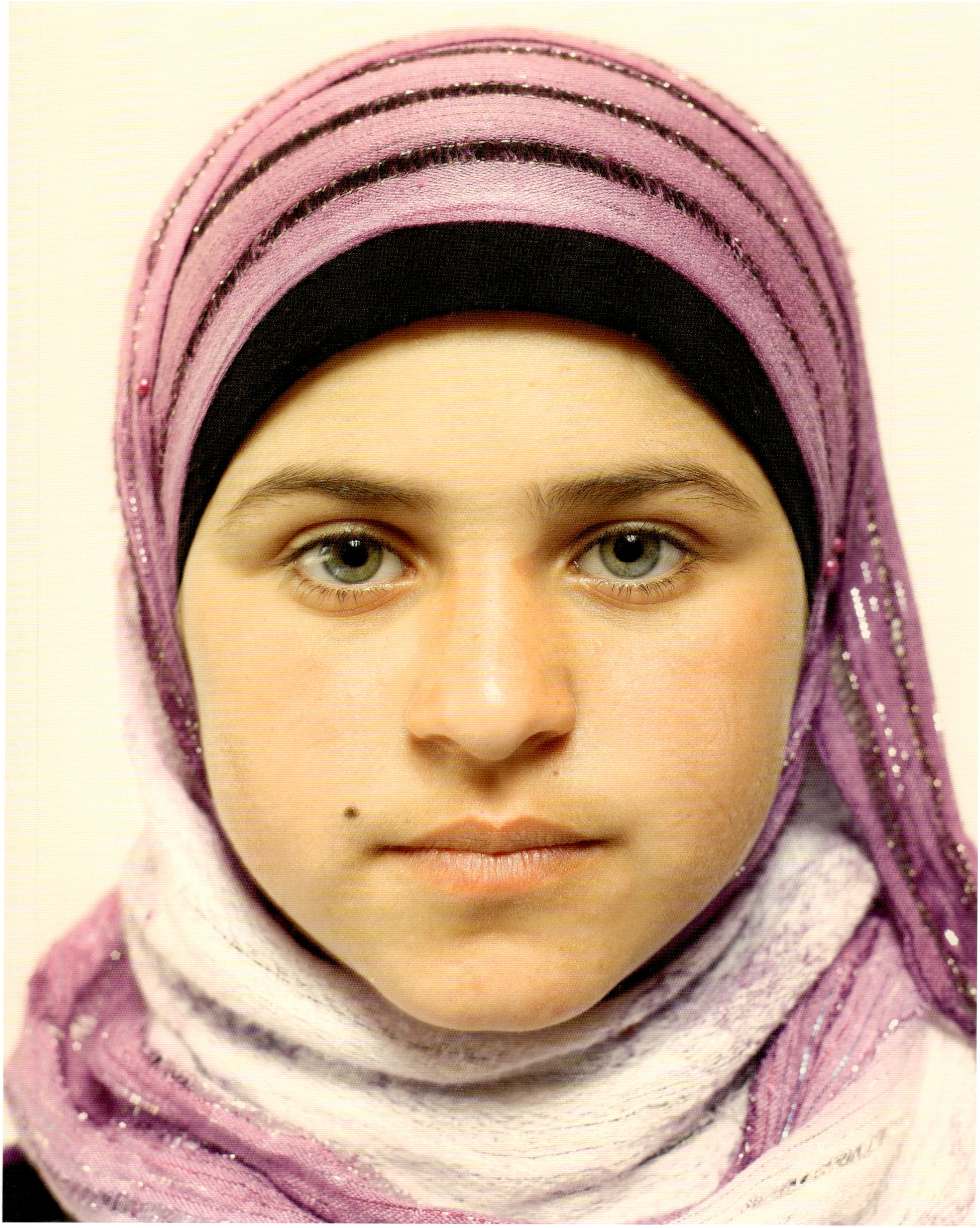

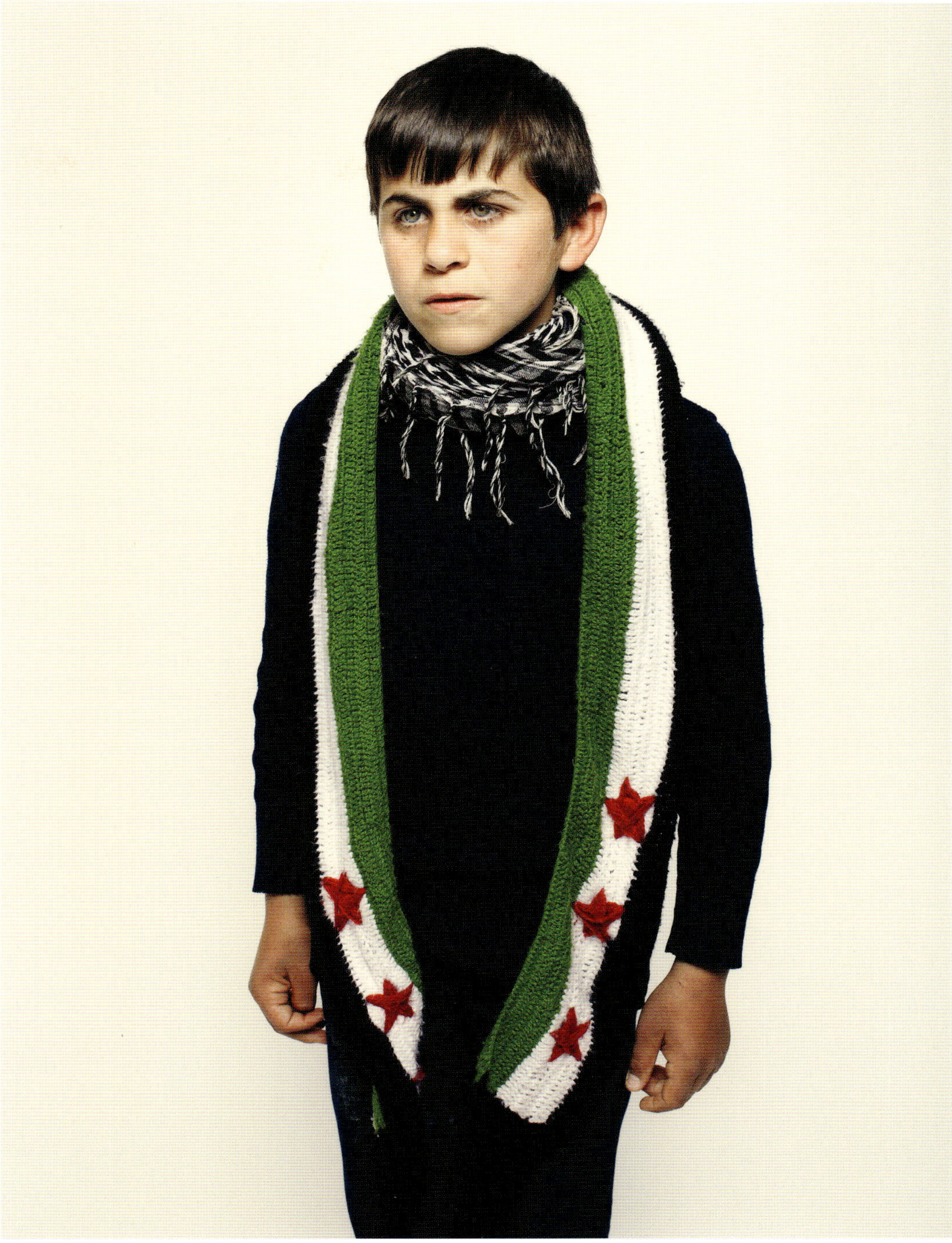

PETER HAPAK

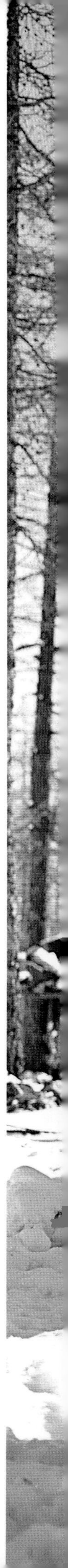

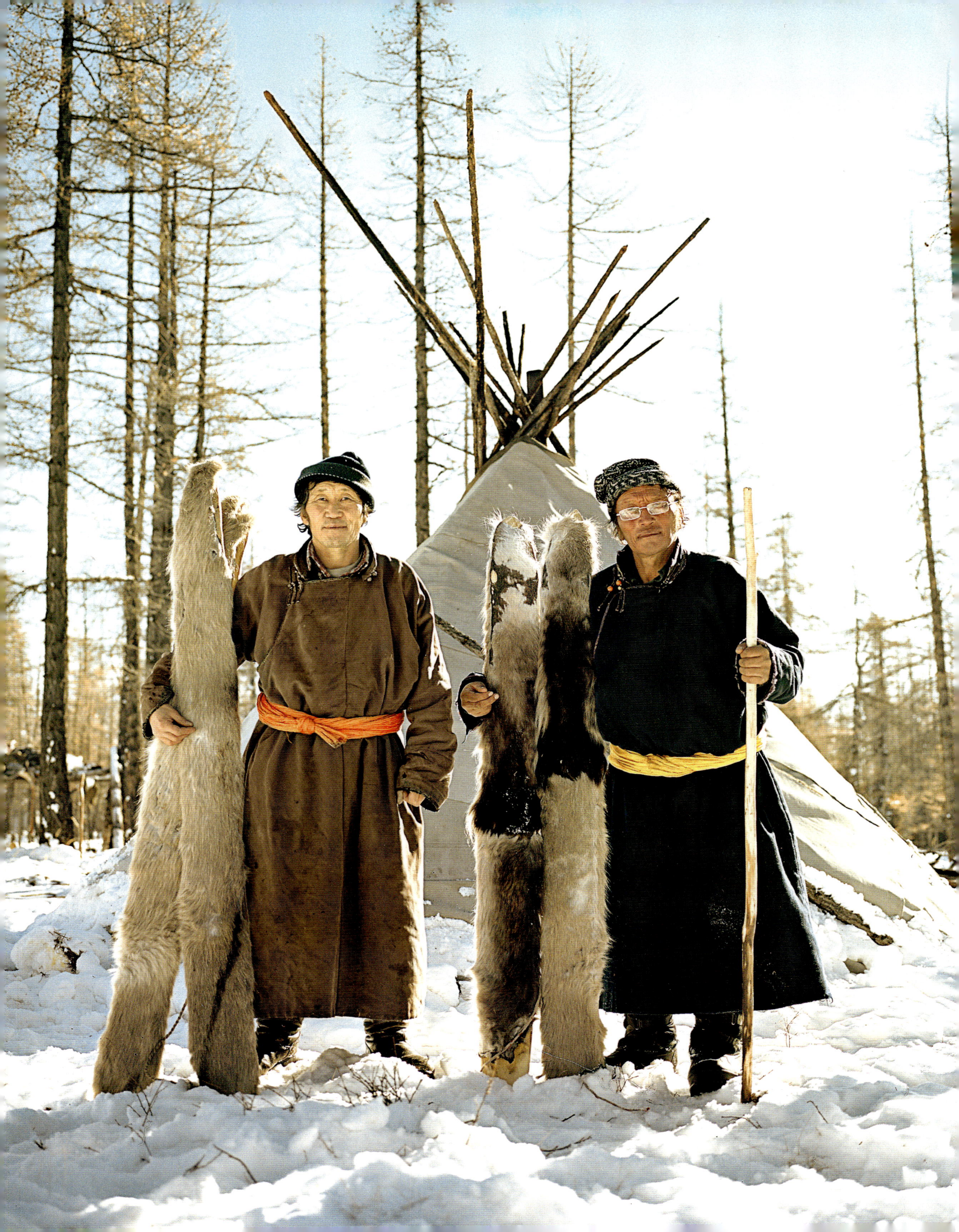

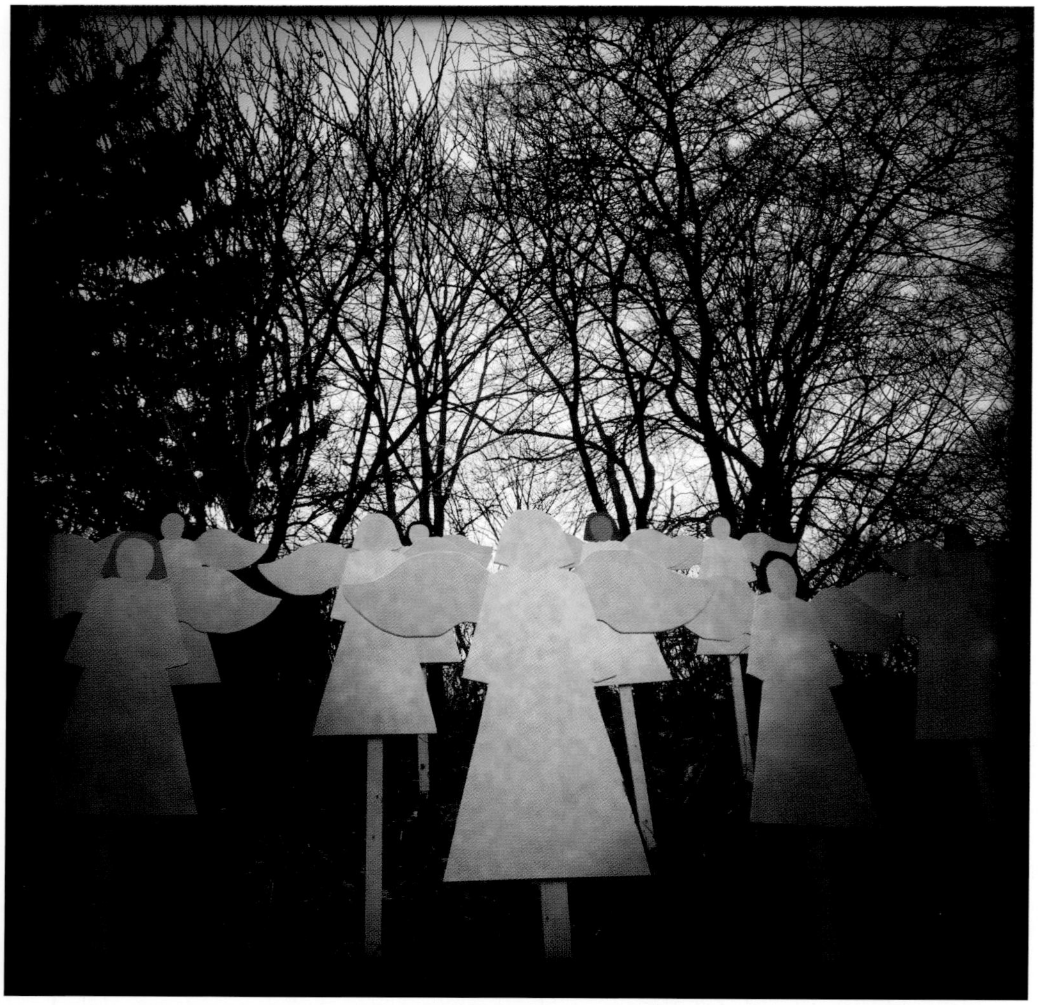

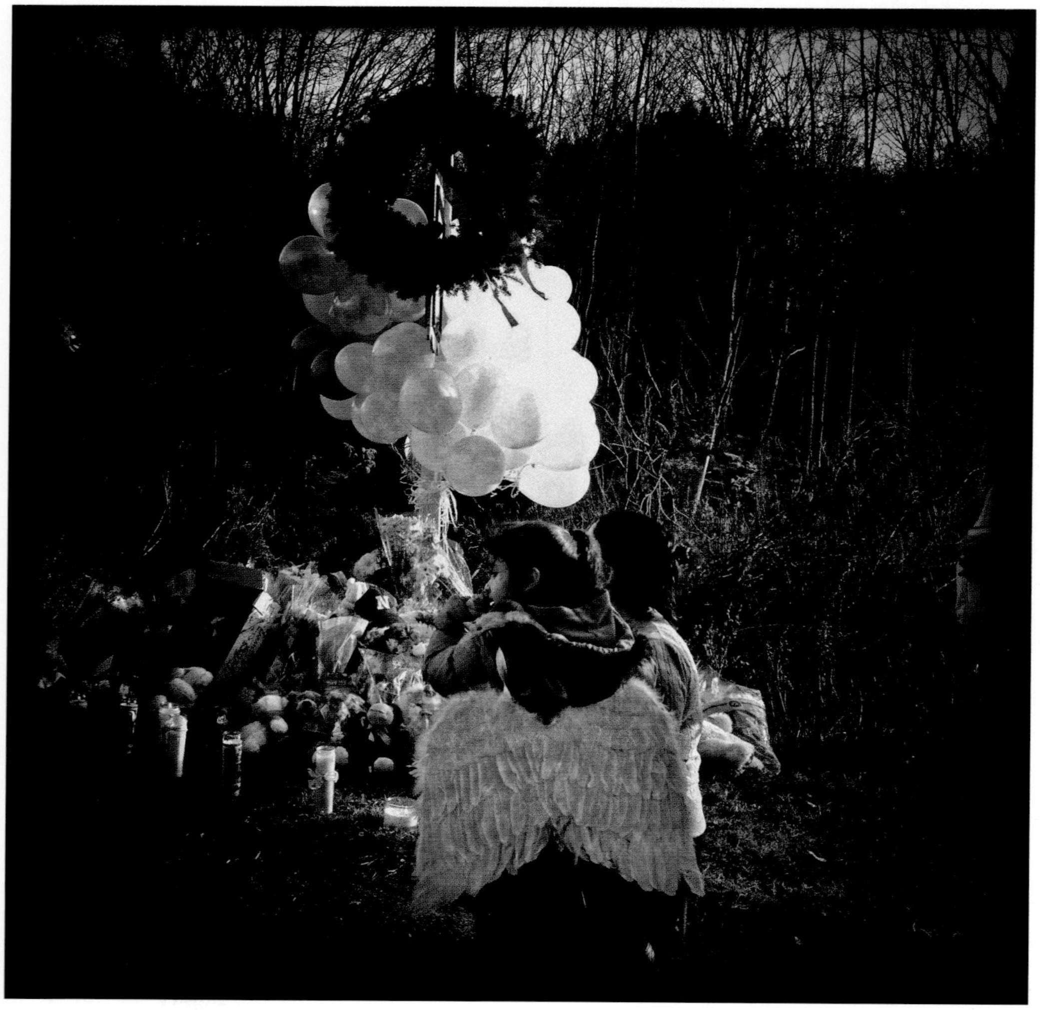

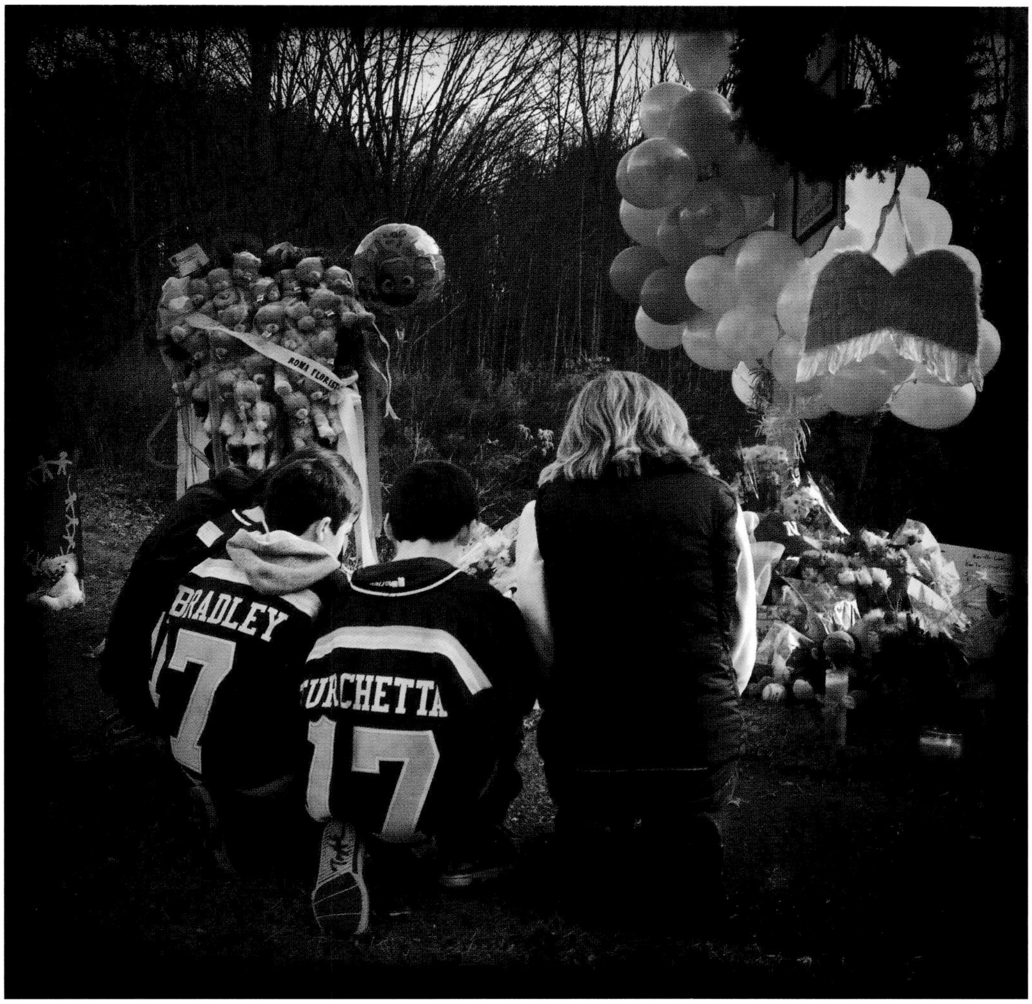

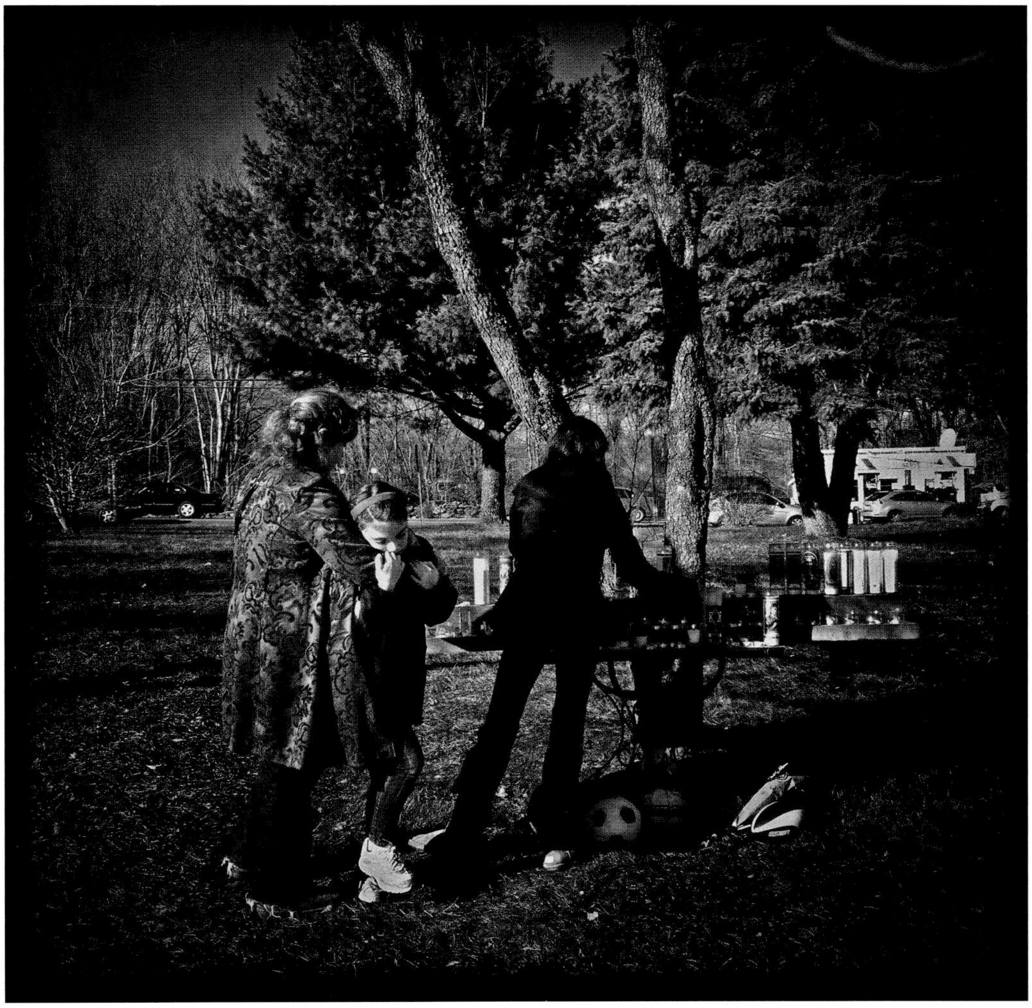

RON HAVIV

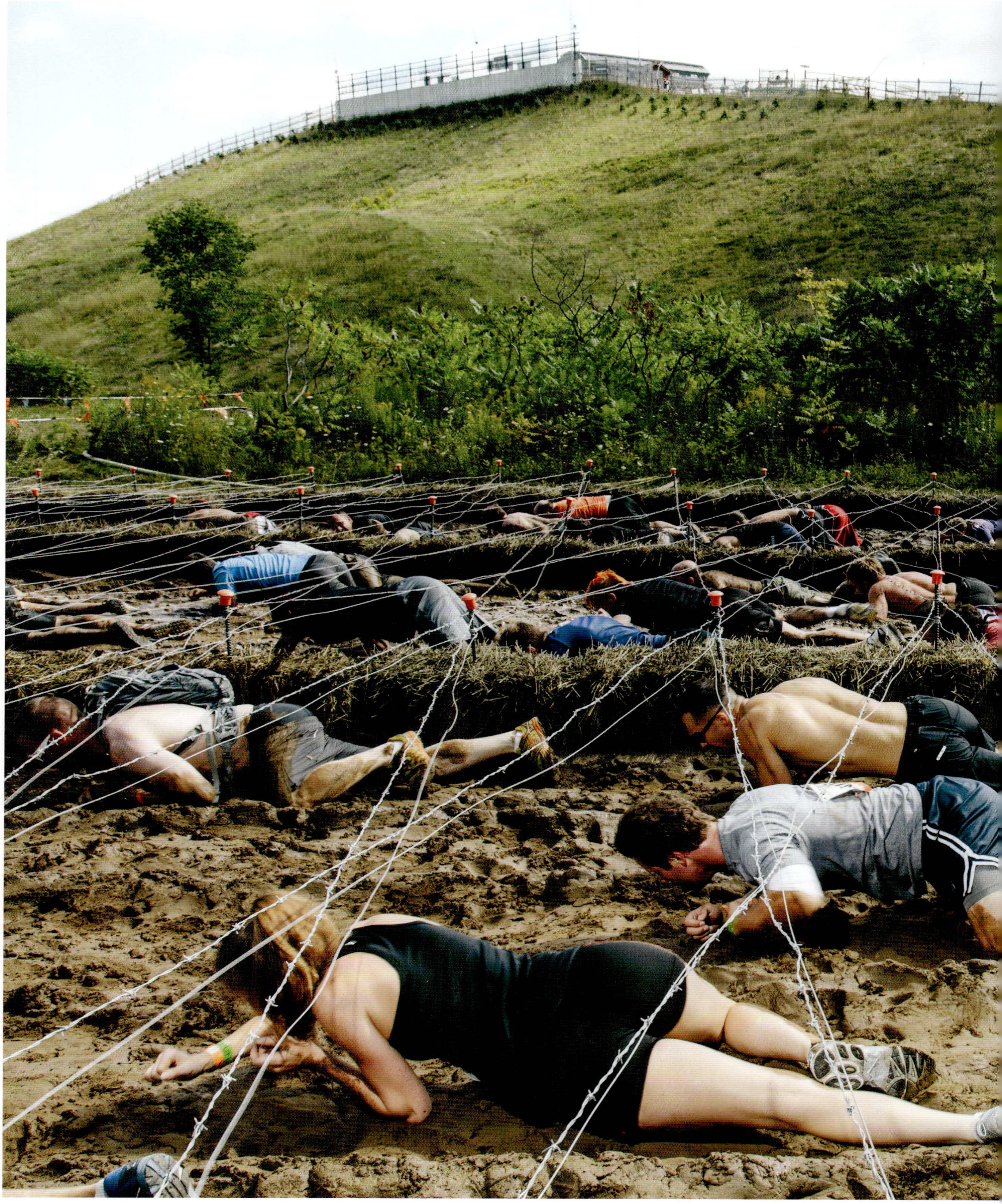

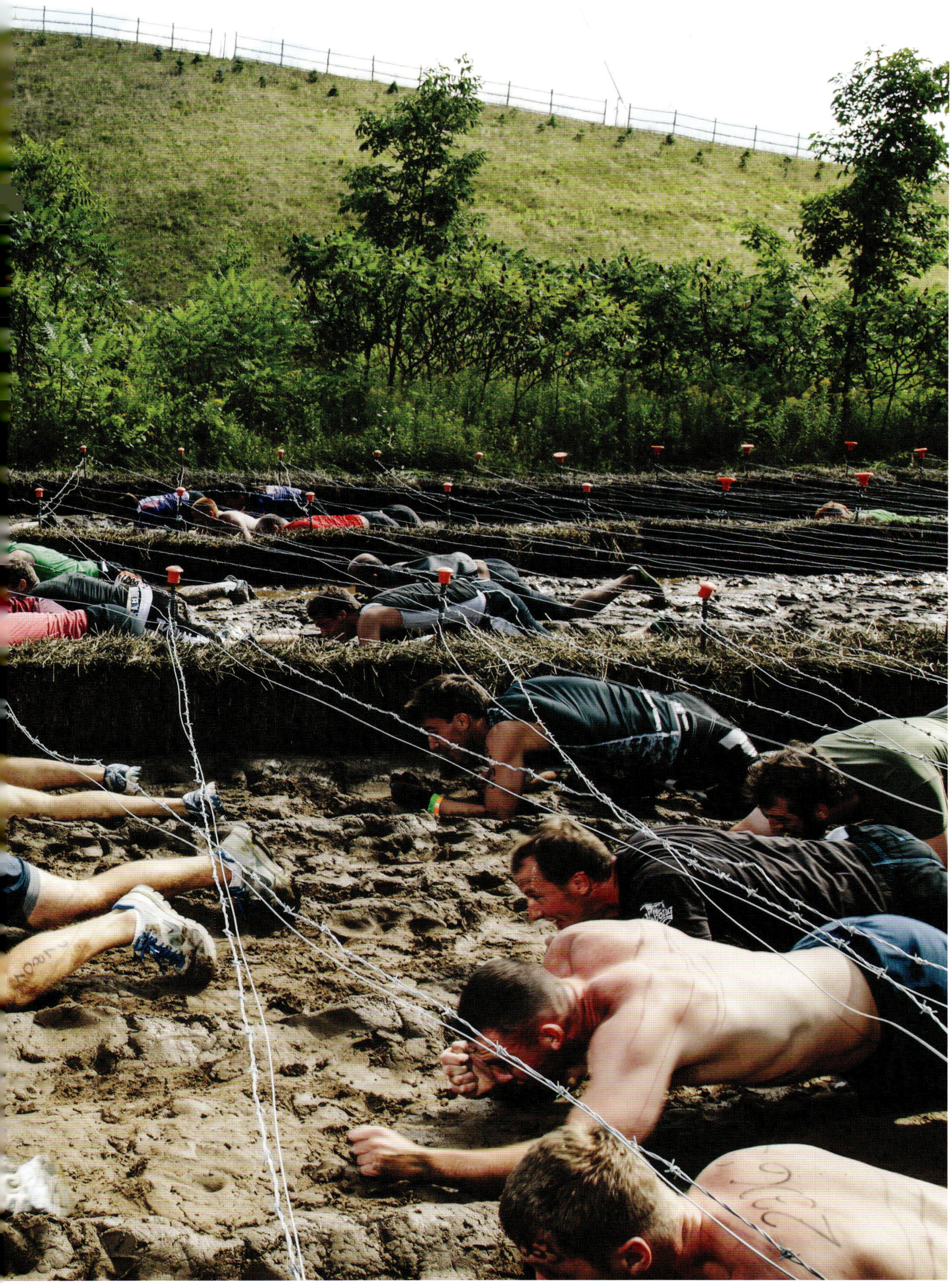

ANDREW
HETHERINGTON

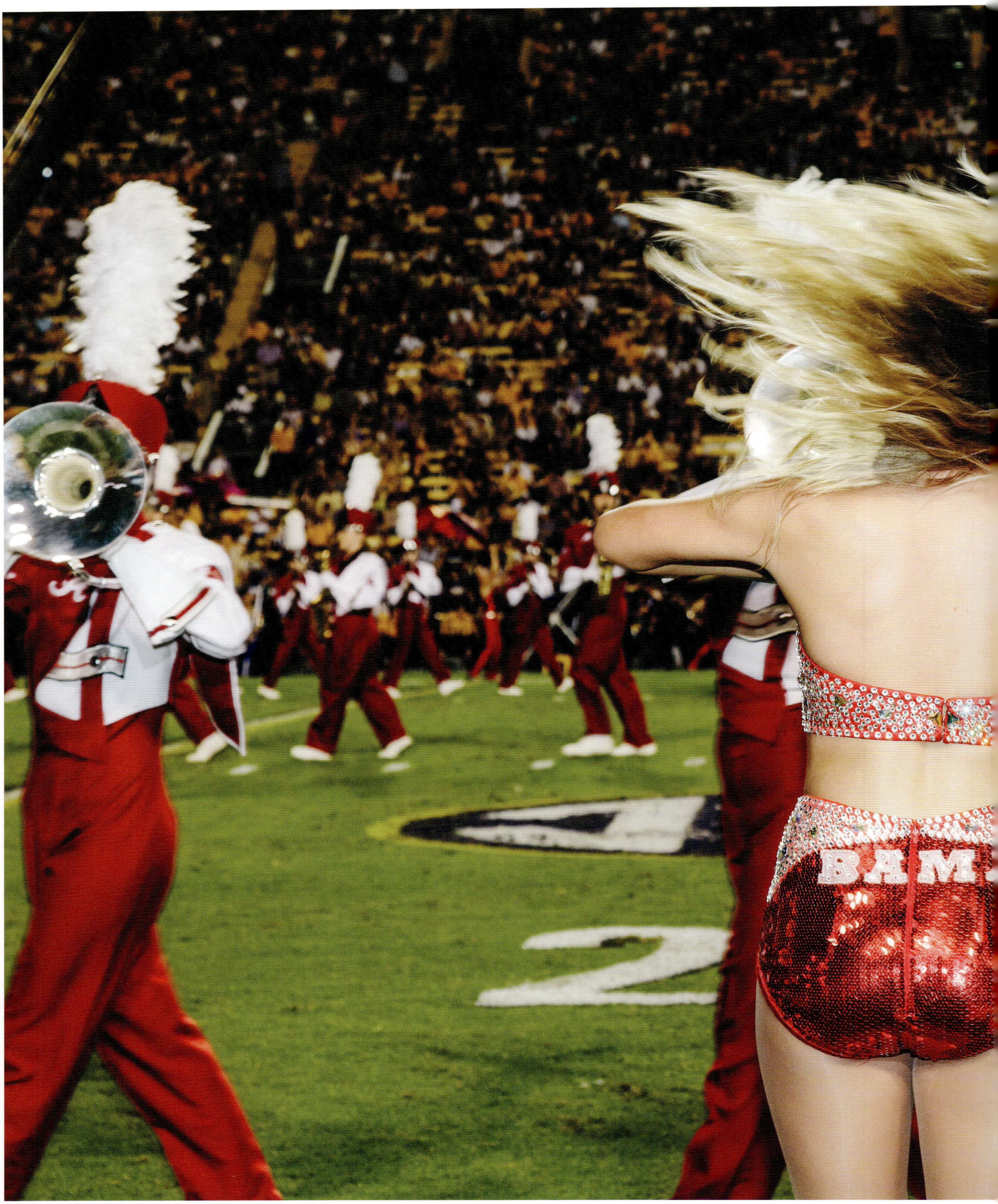
BAM

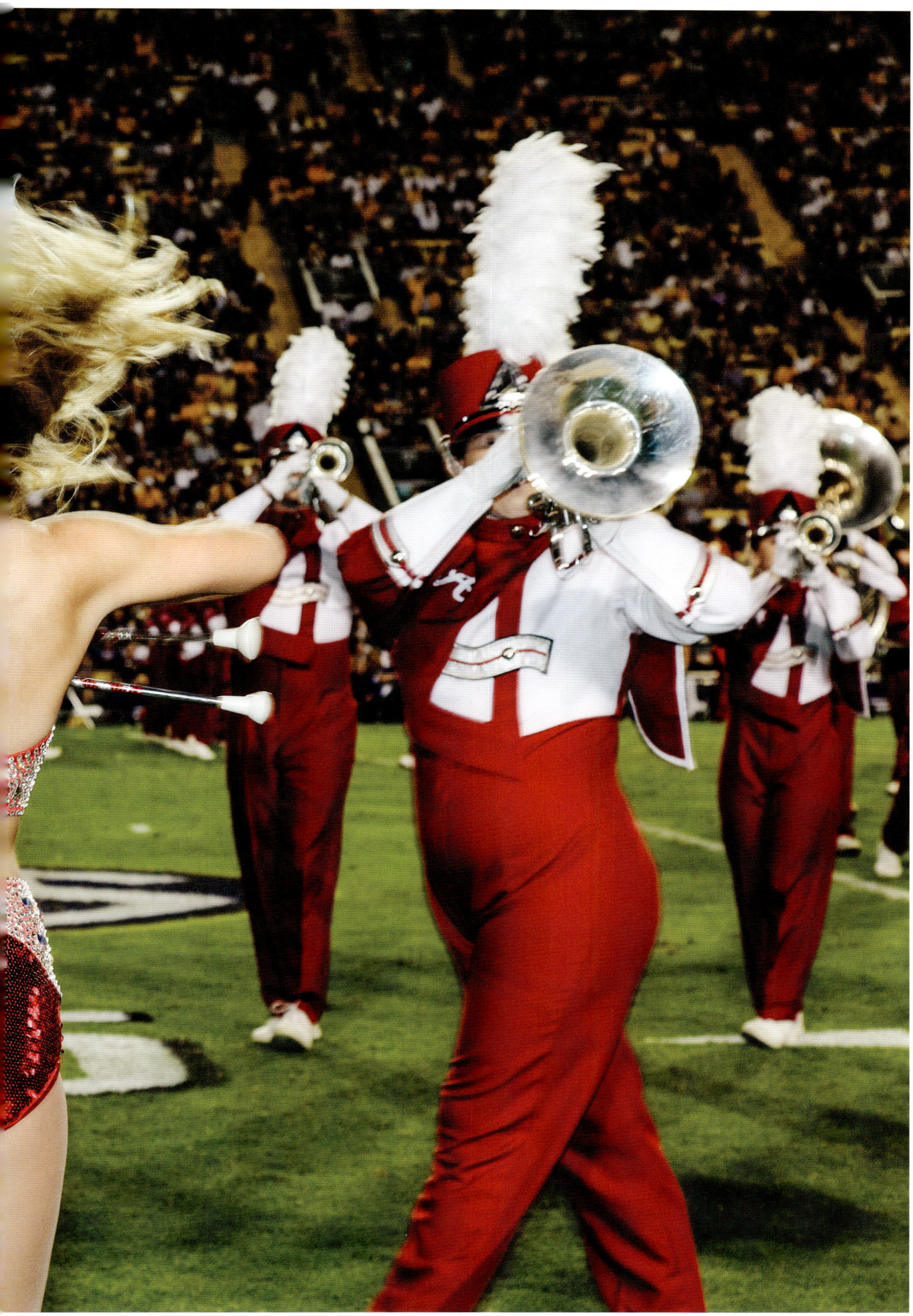

ANDREW
HETHERINGTON

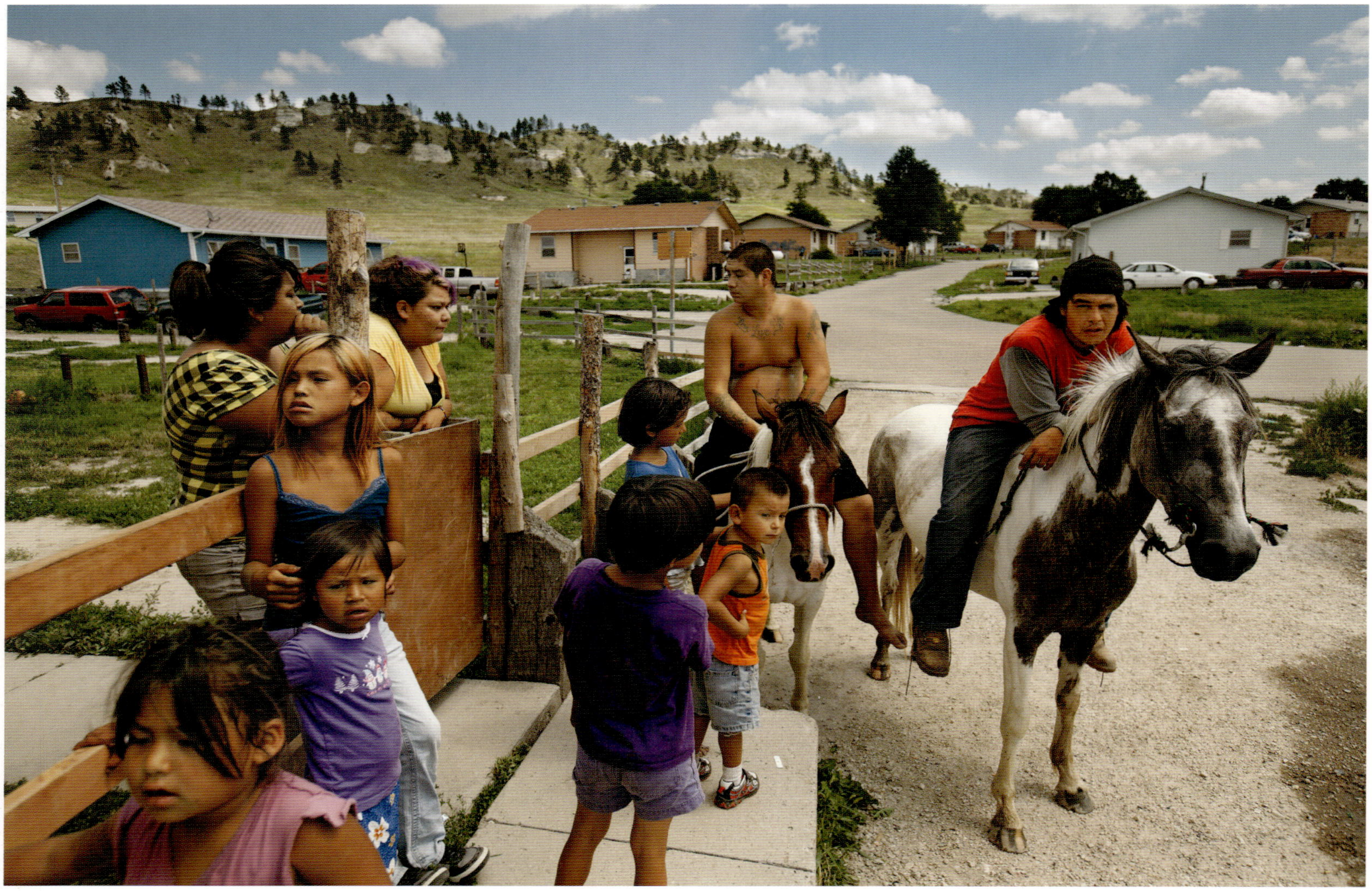

AARON HUEY

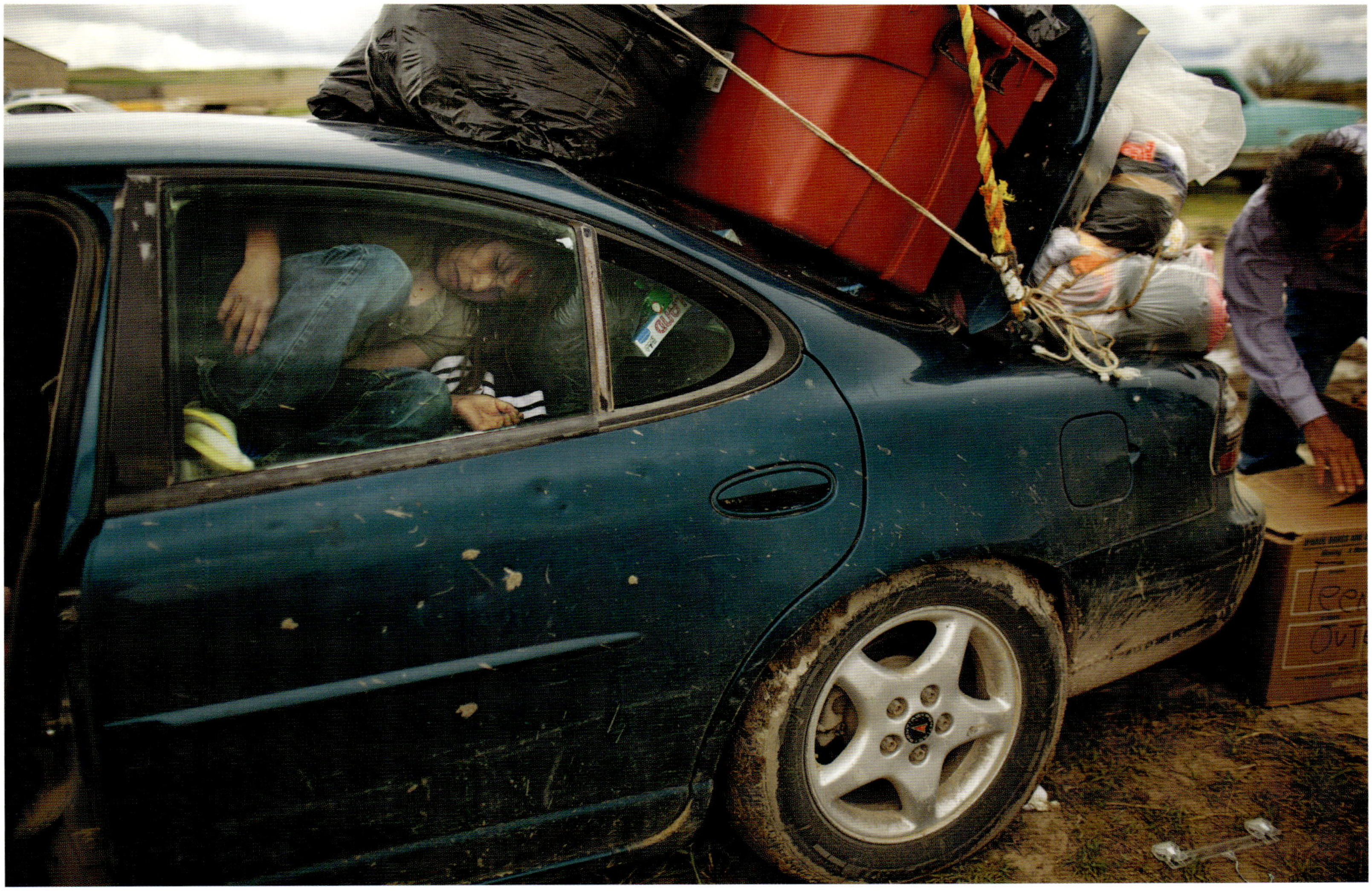

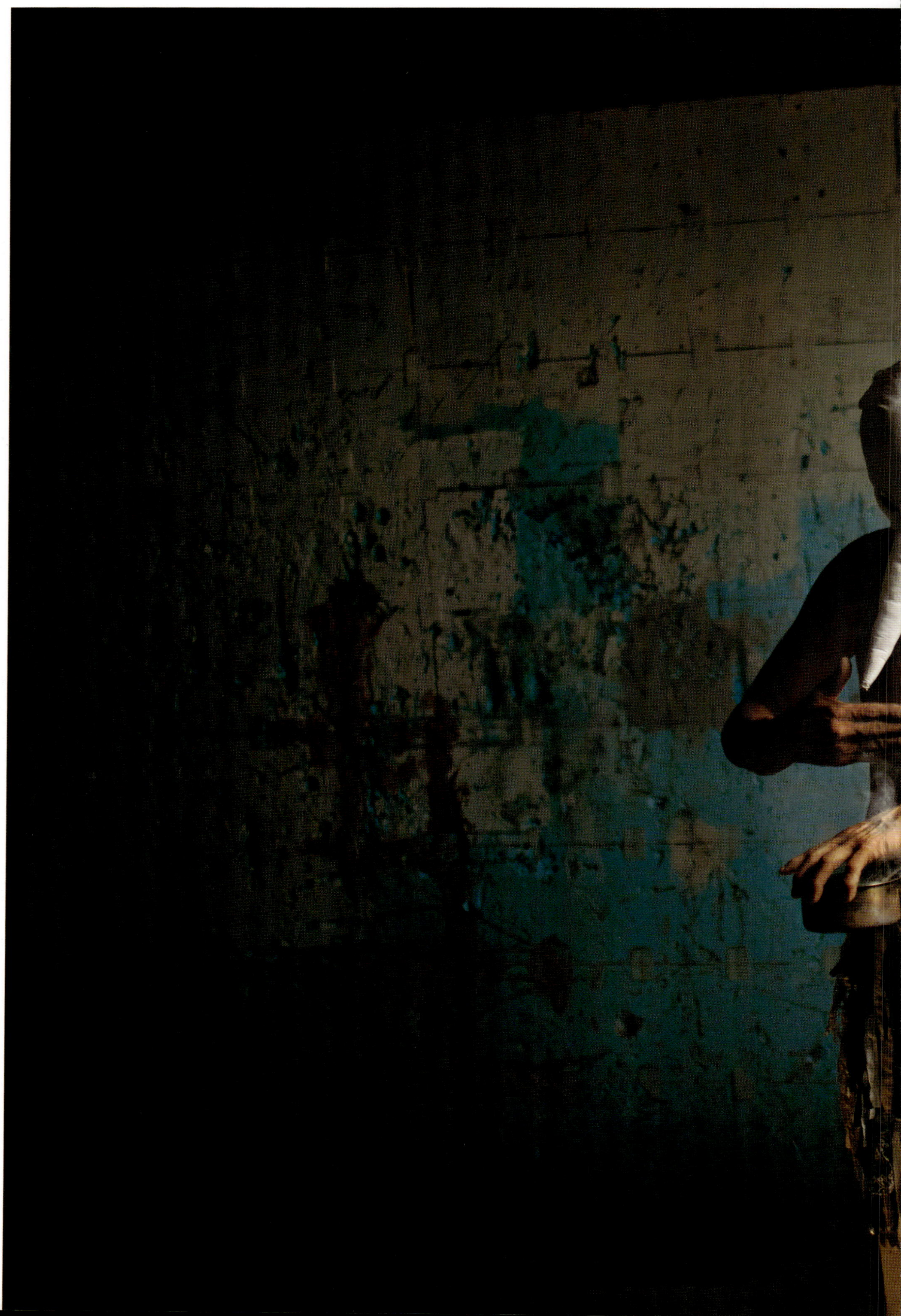

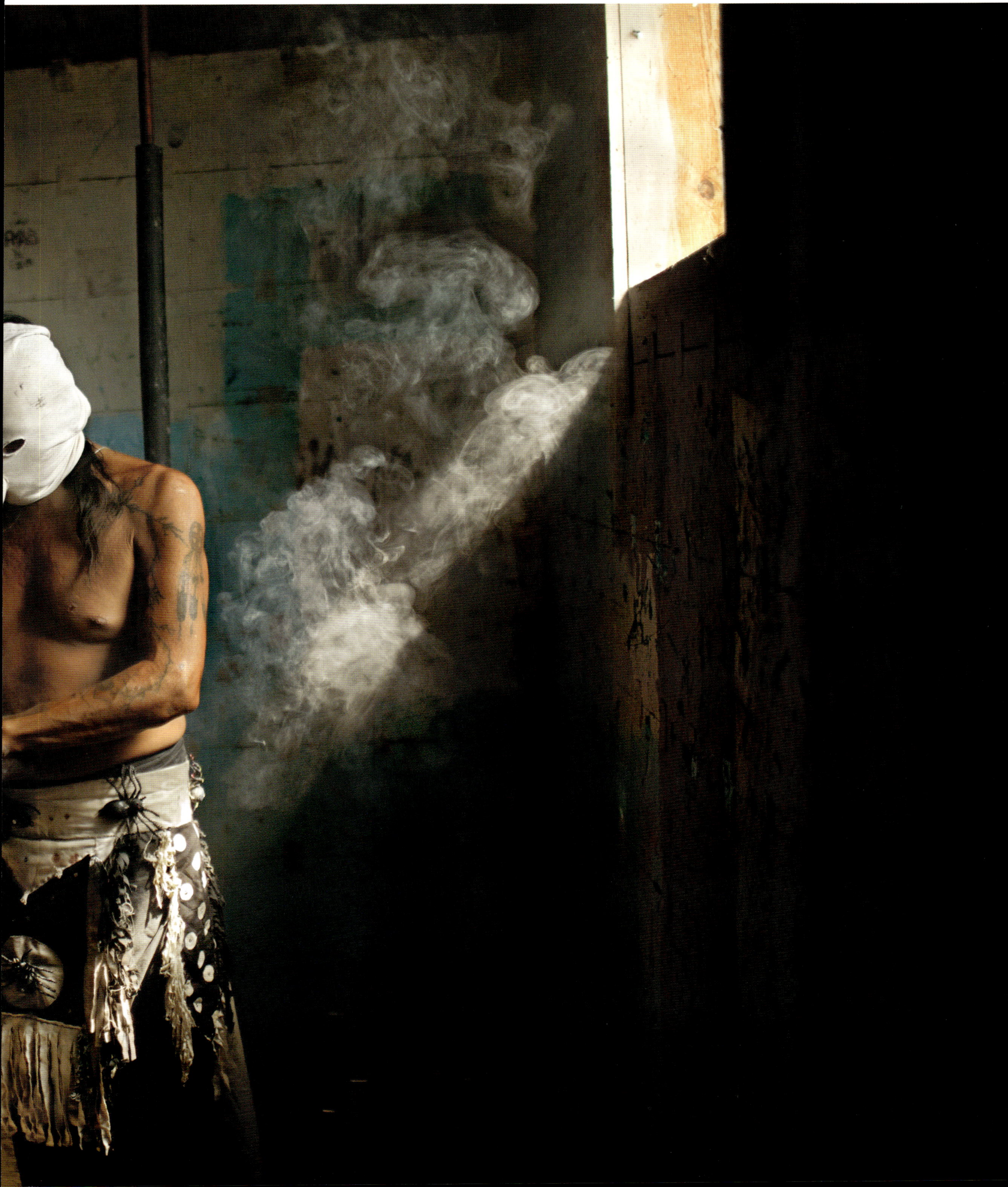

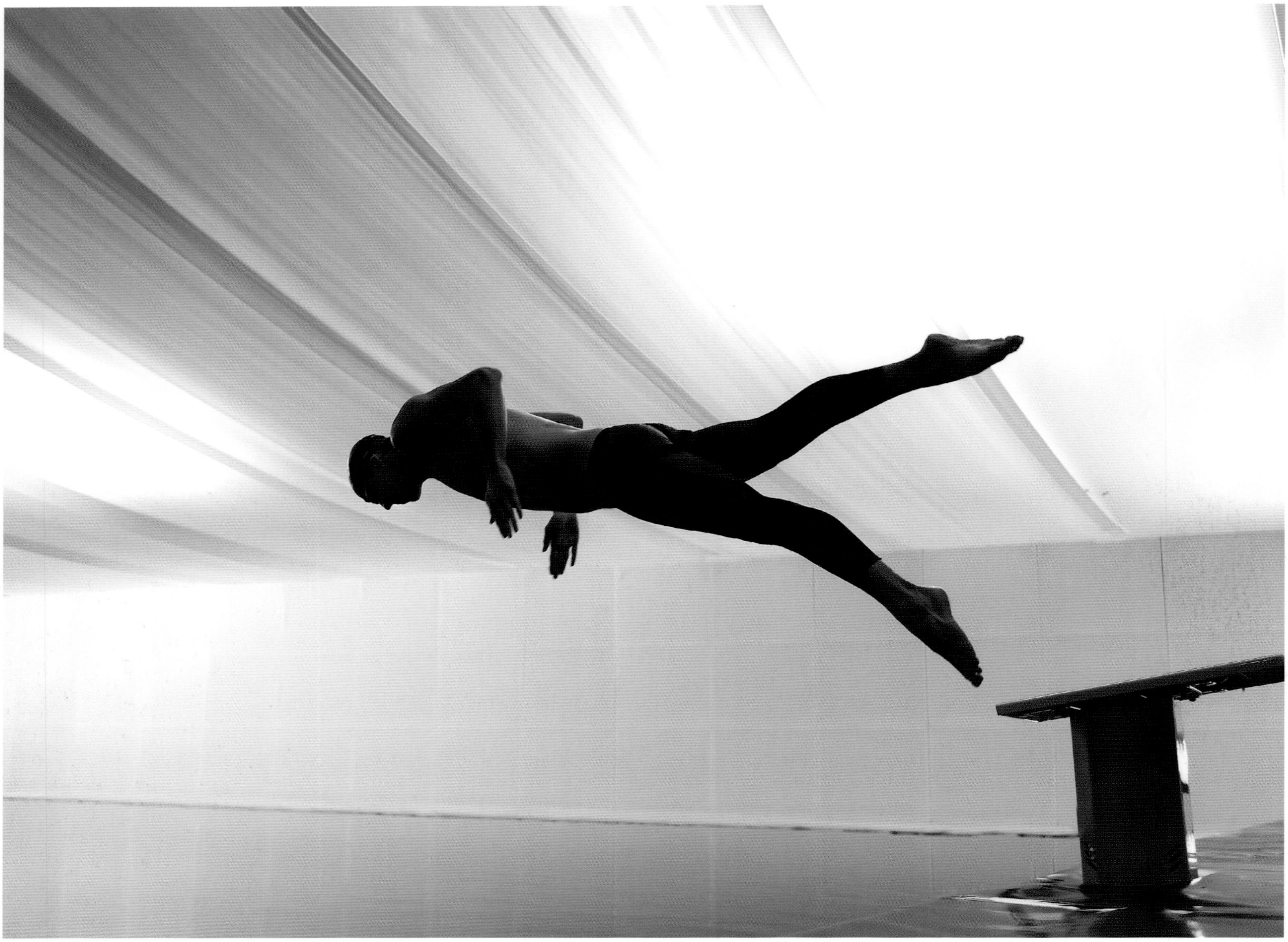

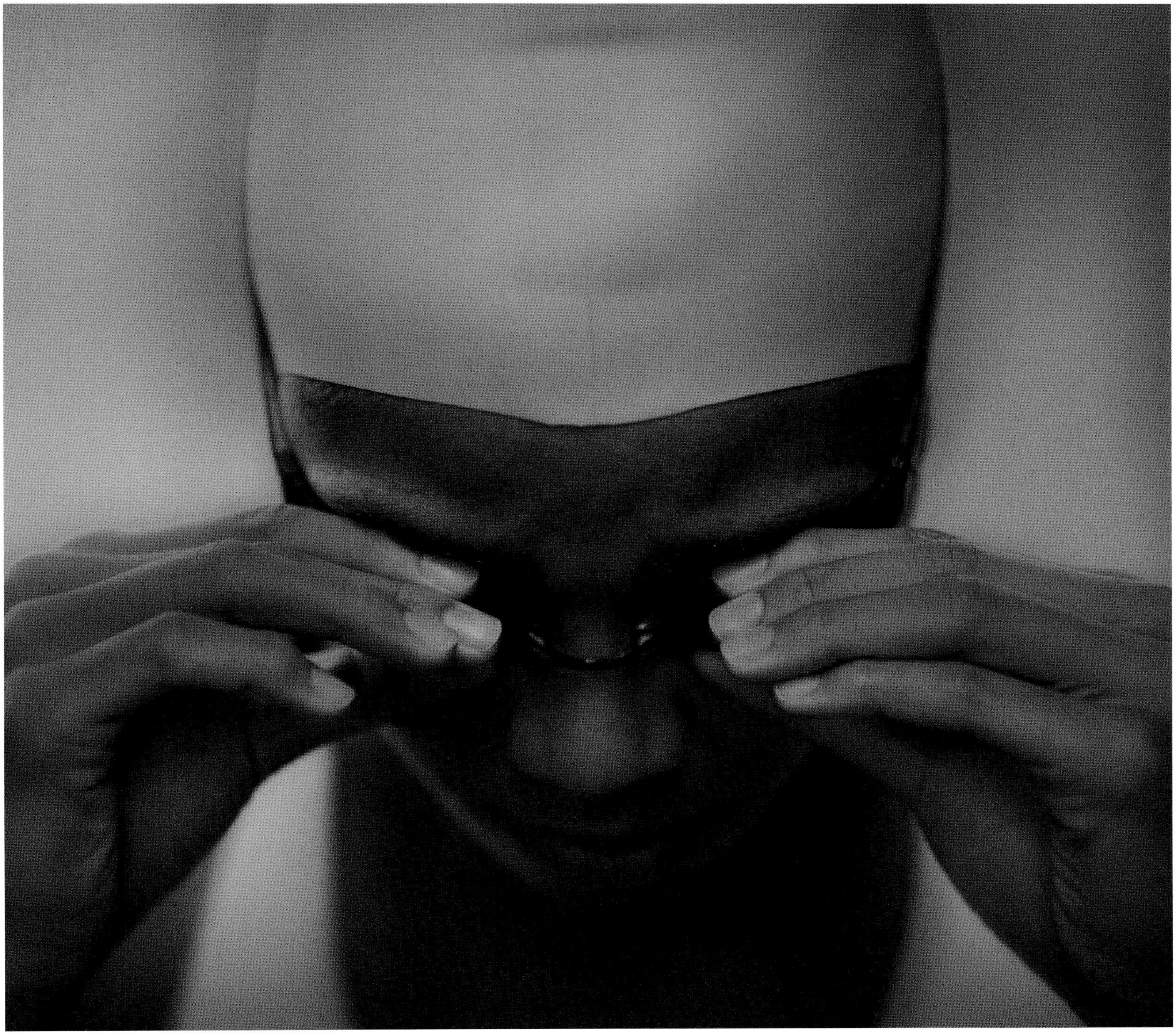

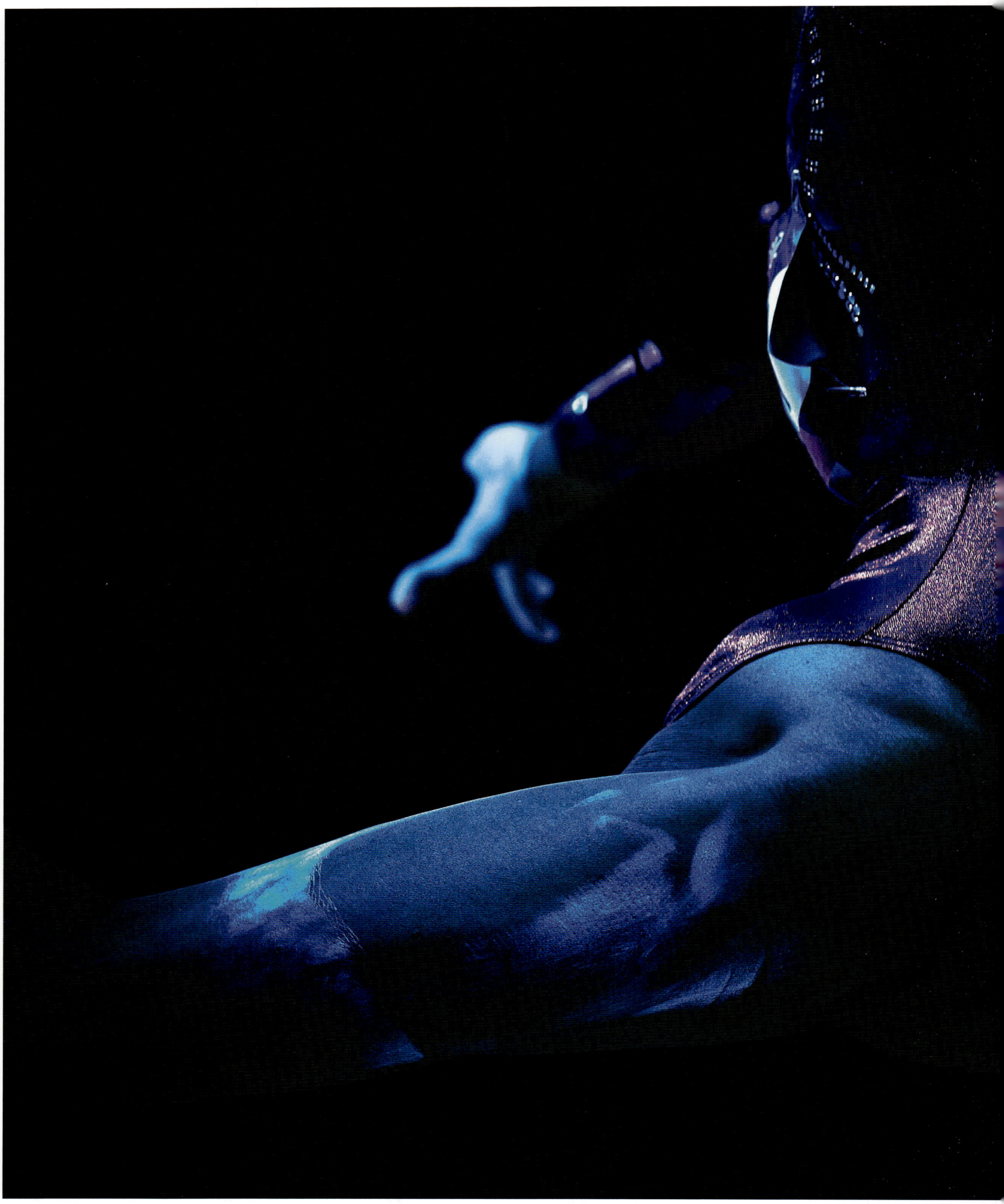

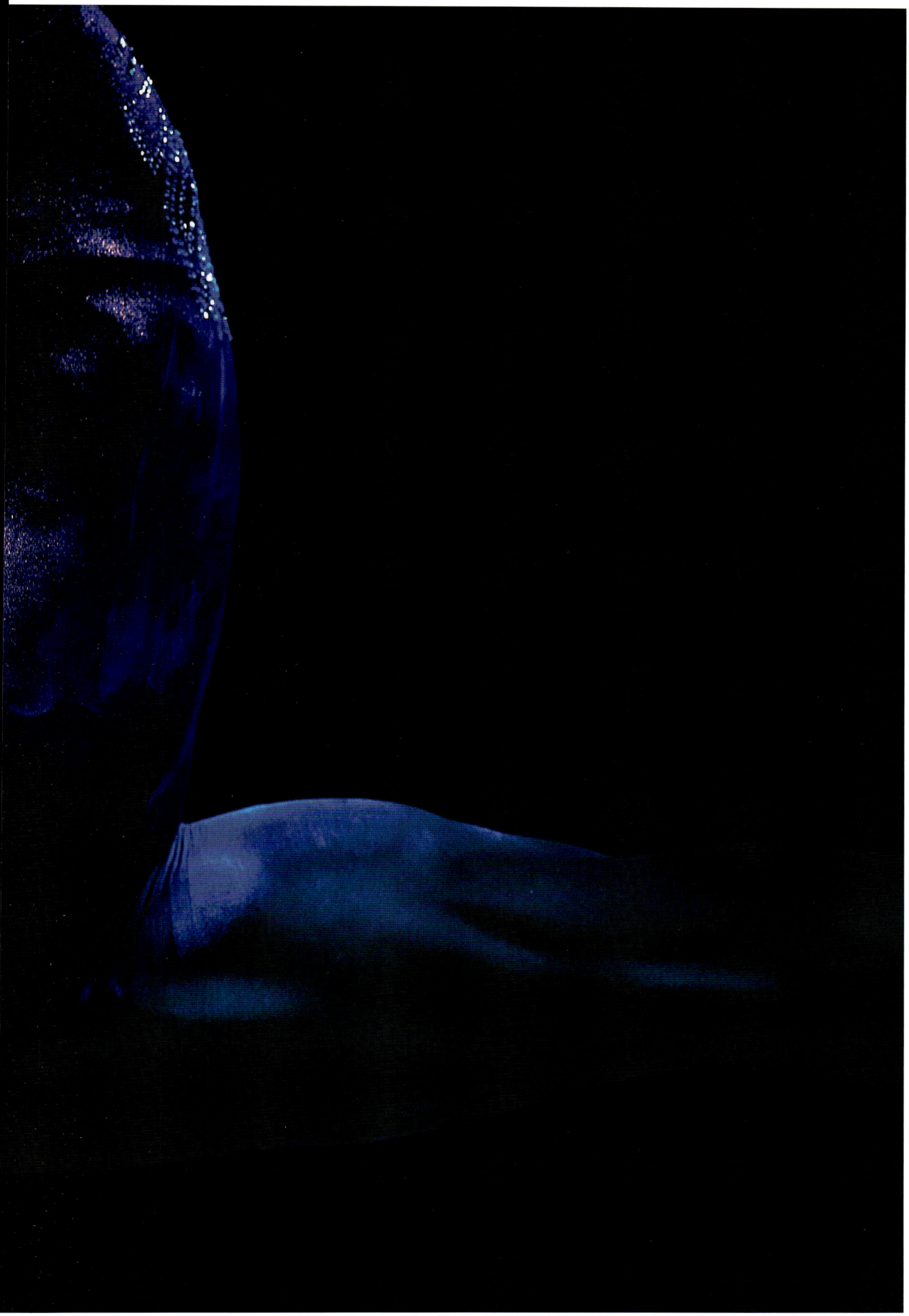

JOHN HUET

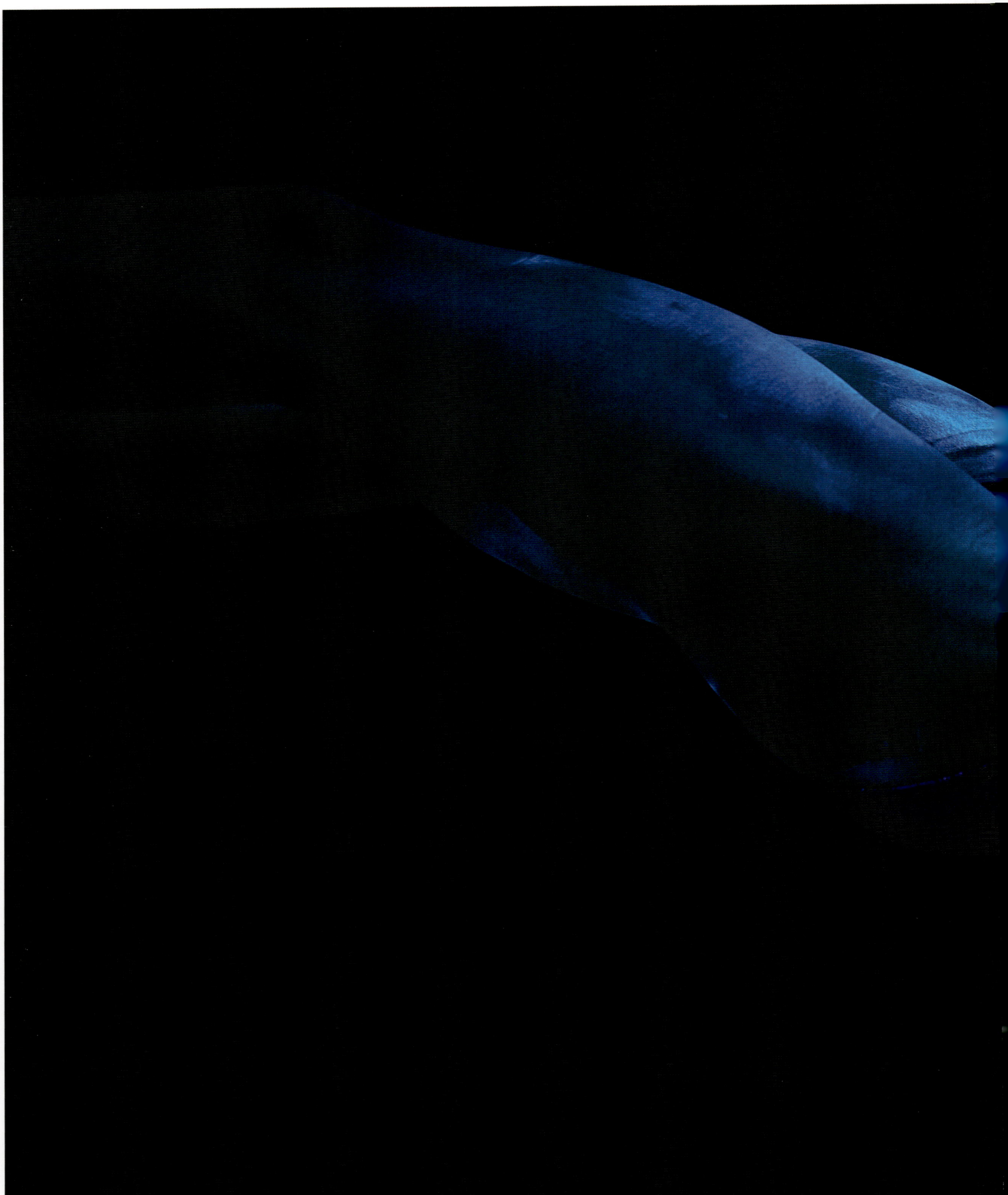

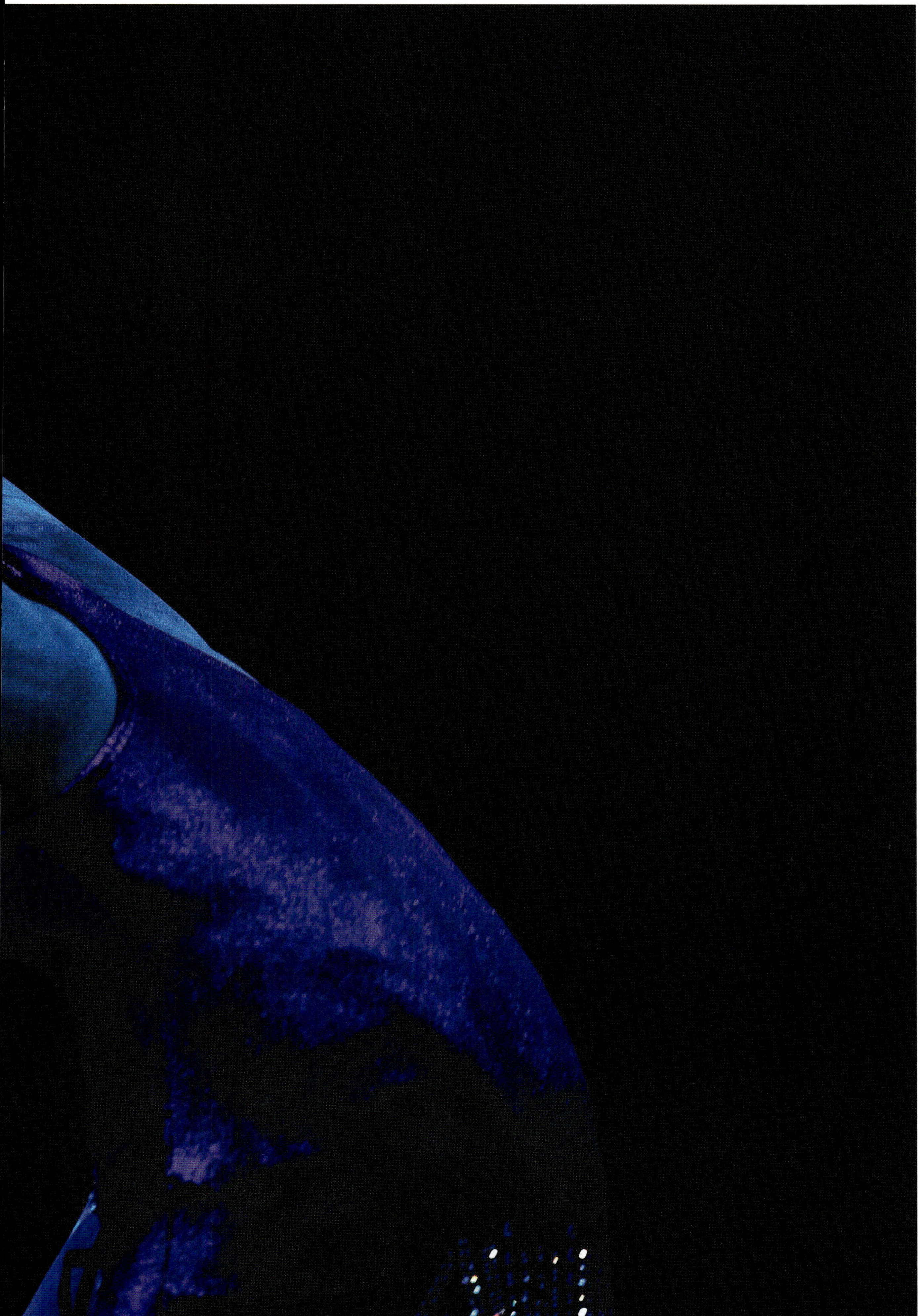

JOHN HUET

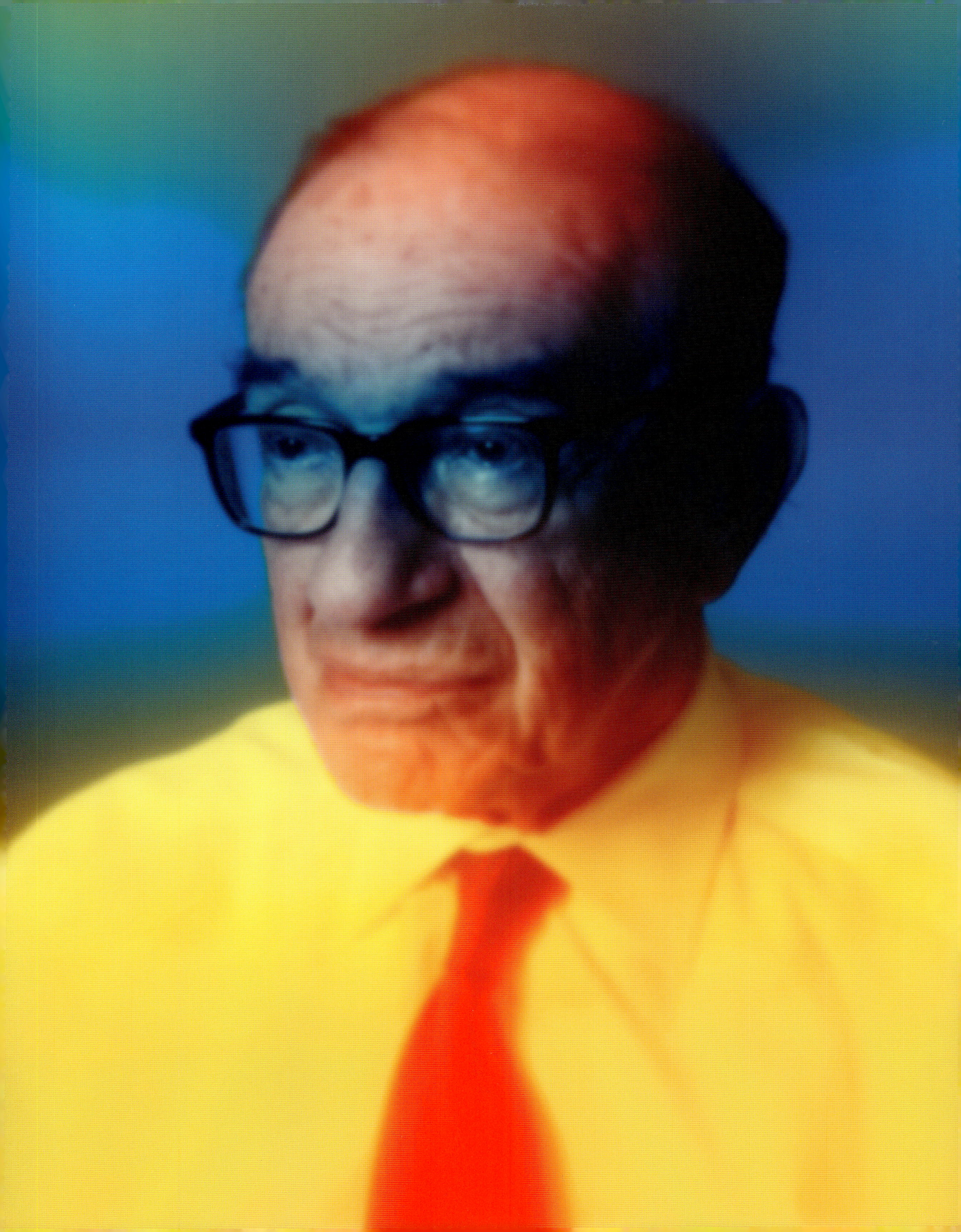

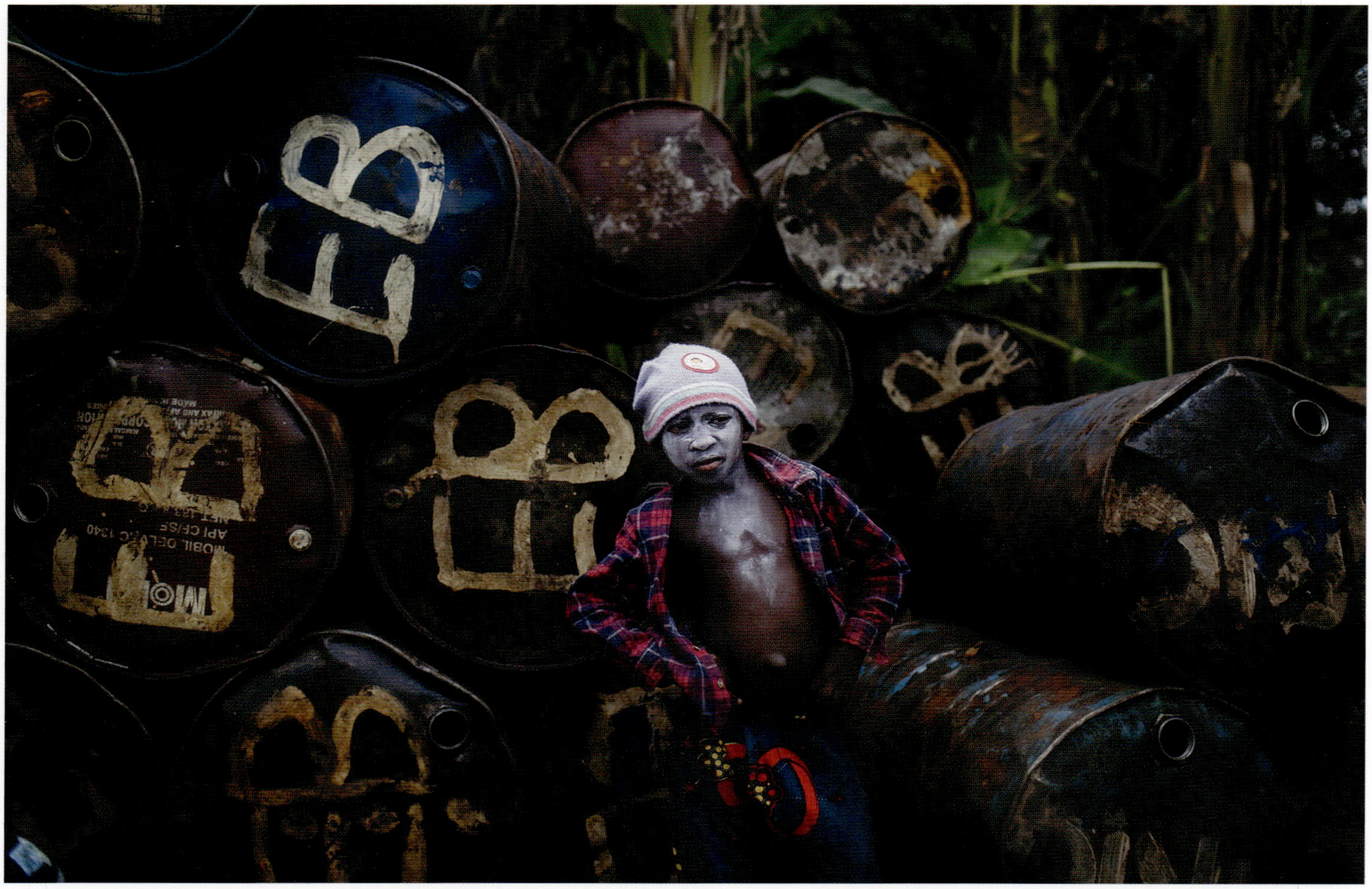

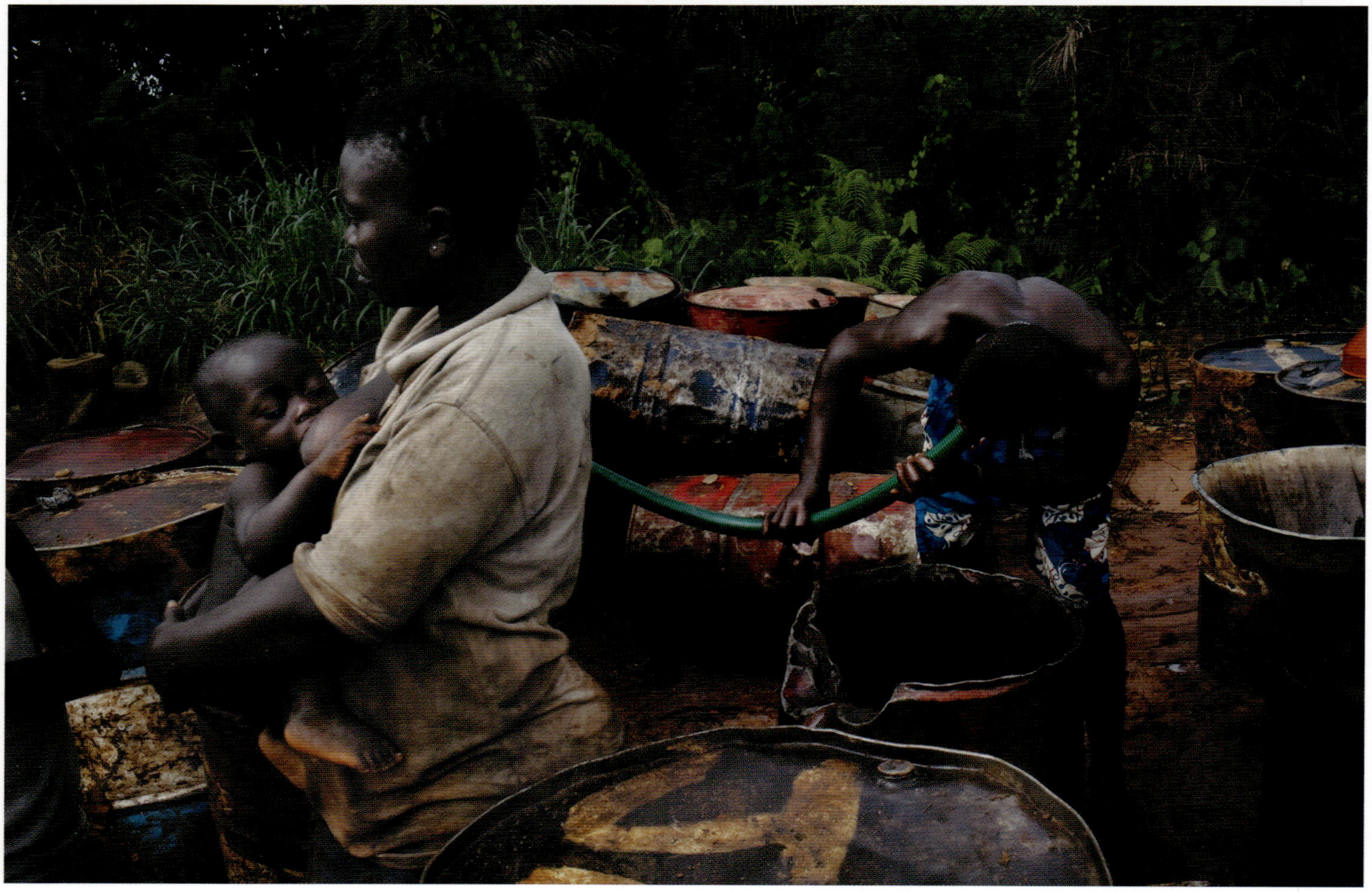

SAMUEL JAMES

139 / 140 / 141 / 142

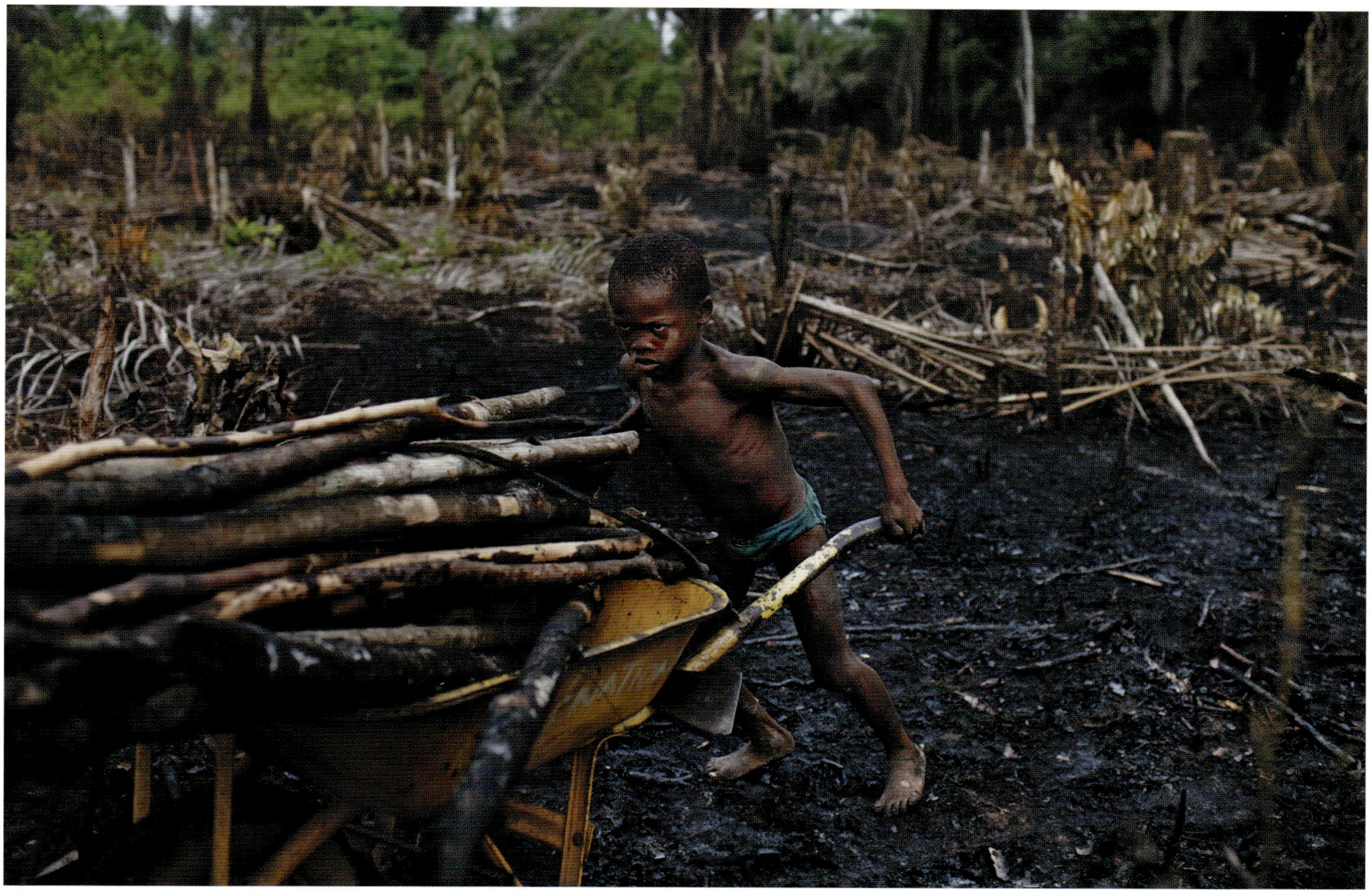

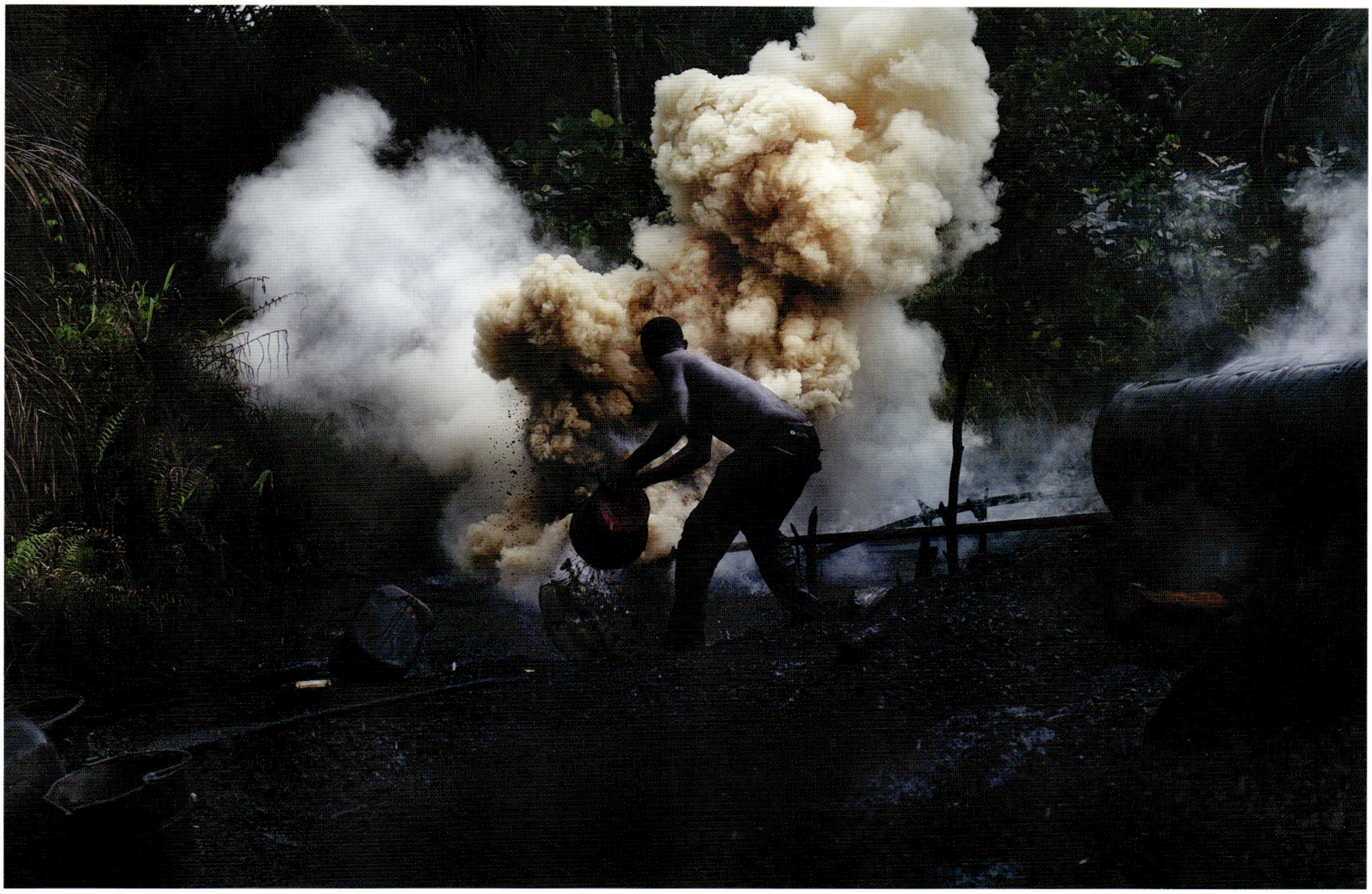

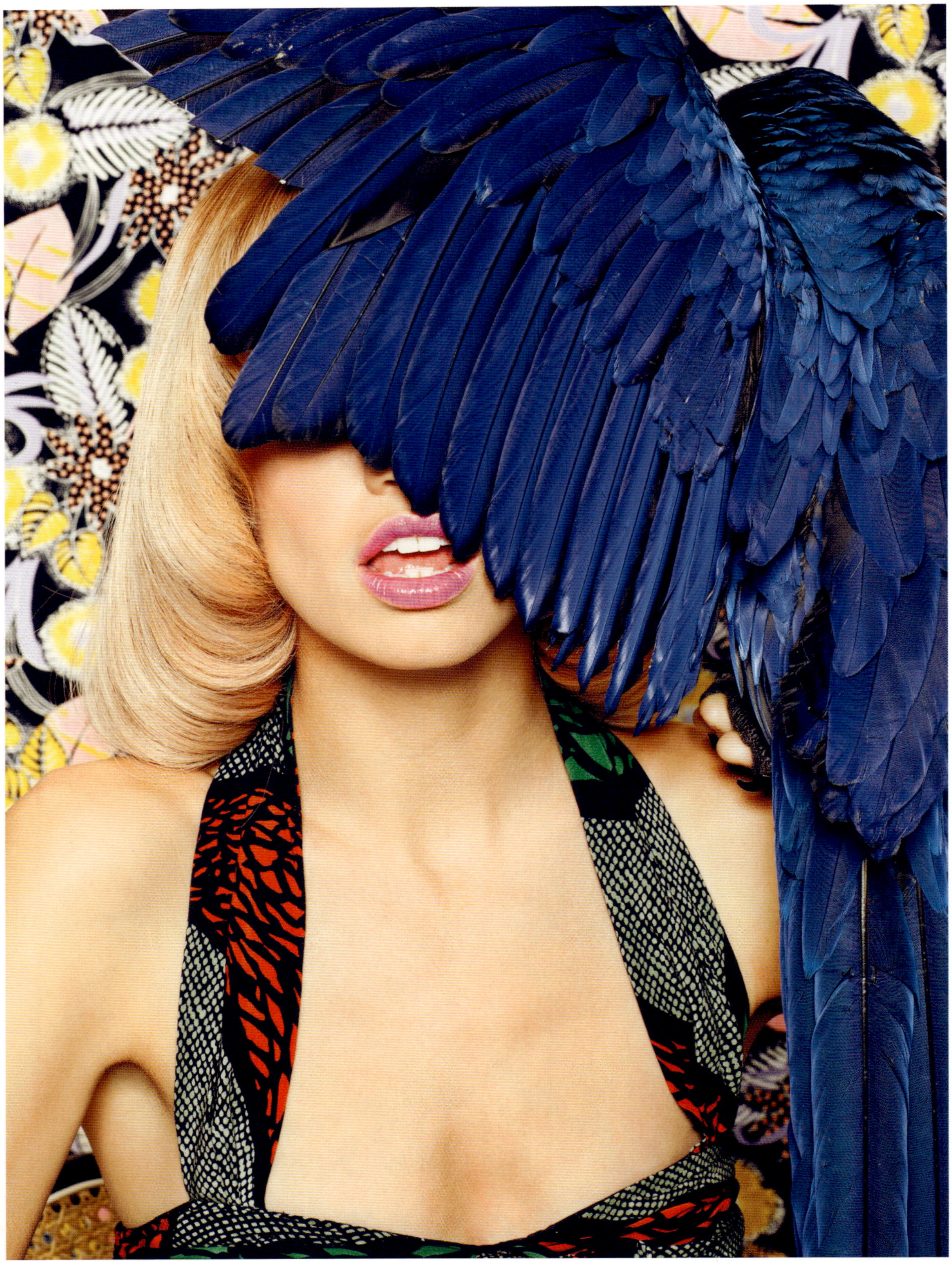

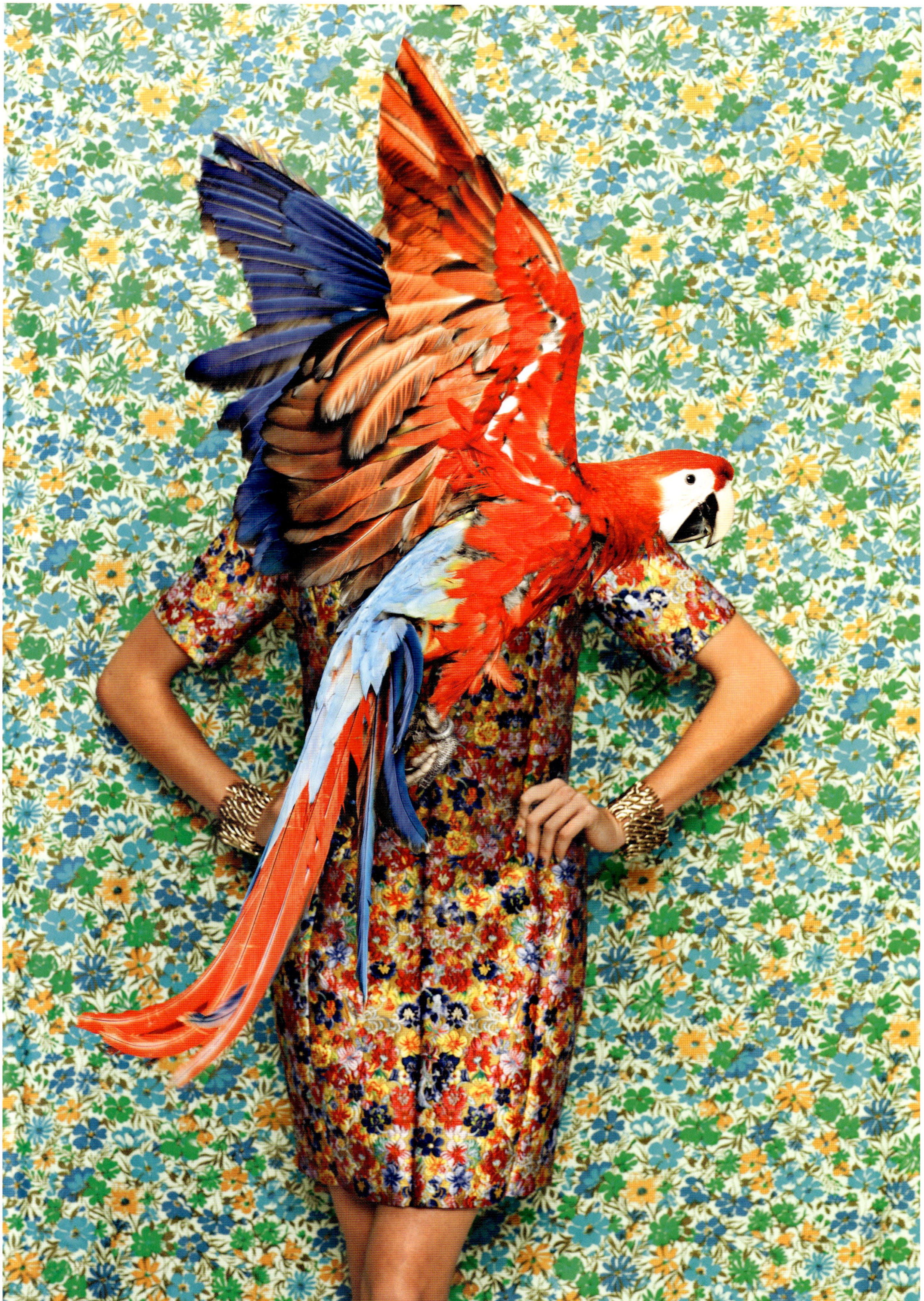

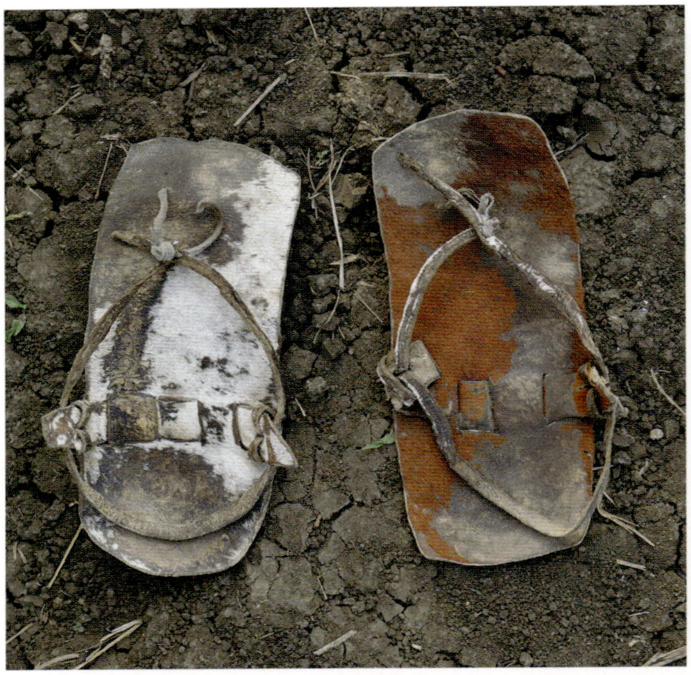
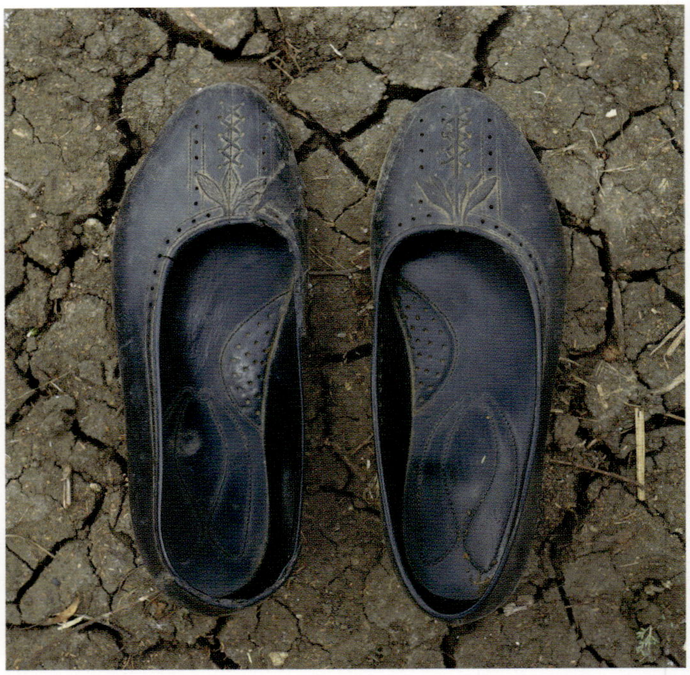
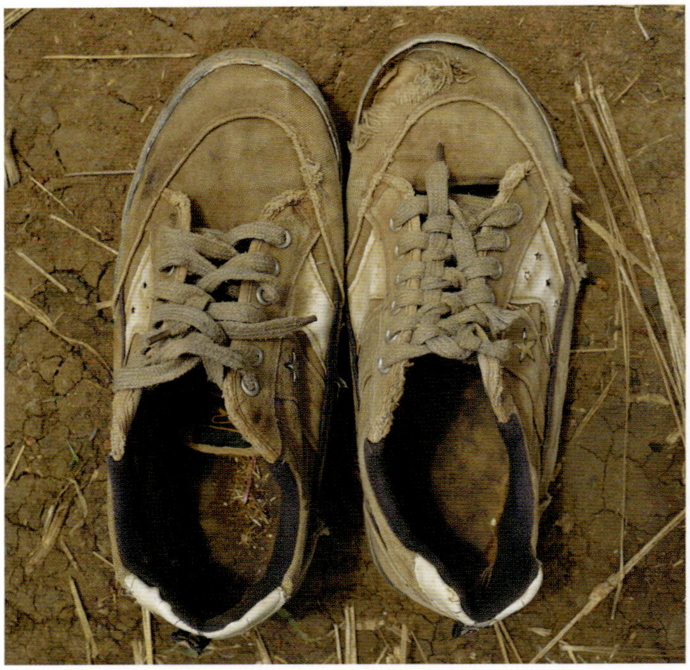
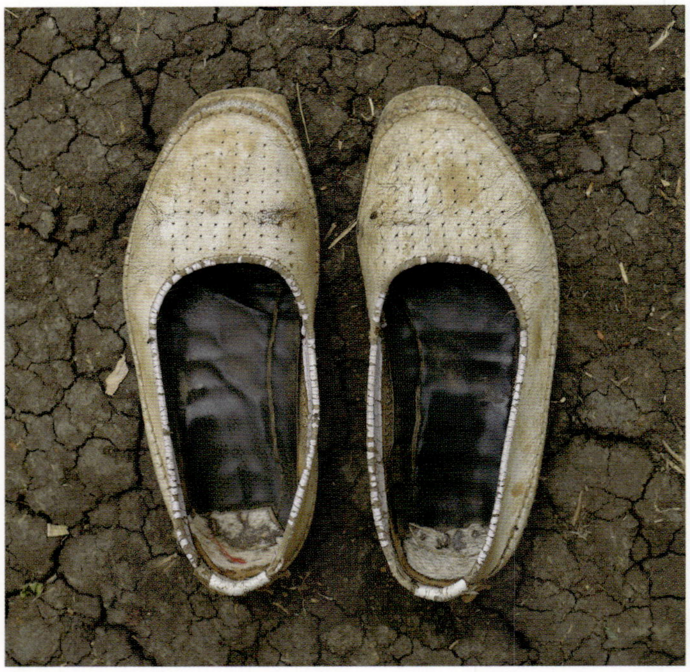
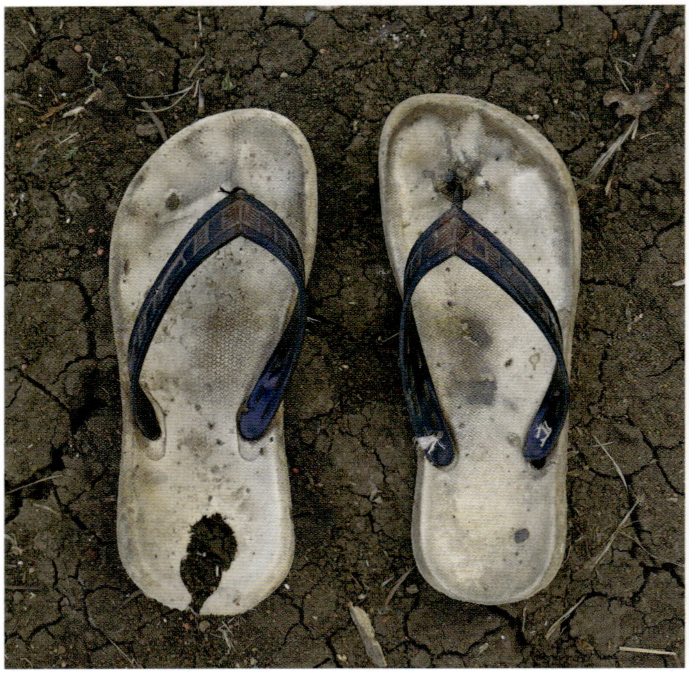
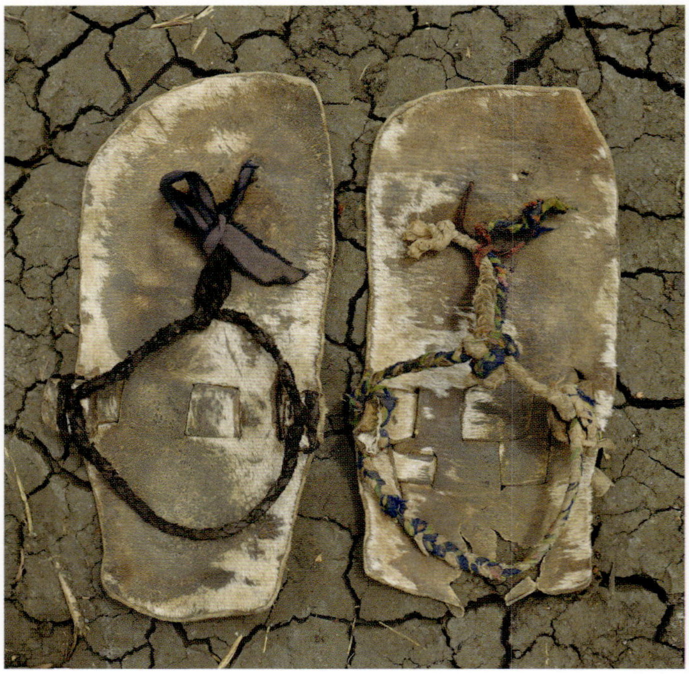

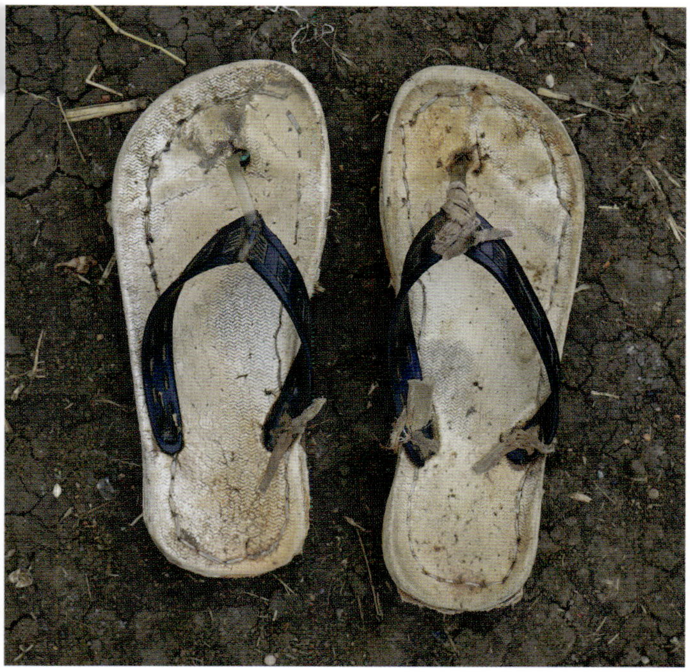

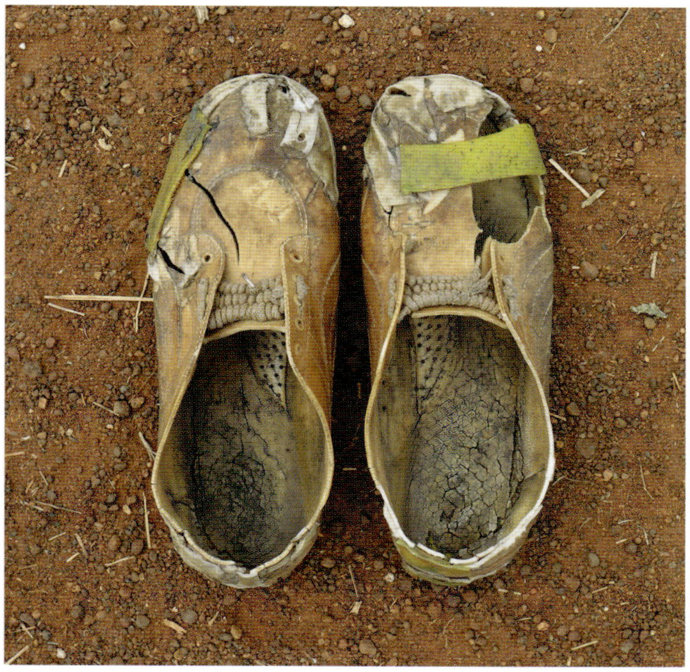

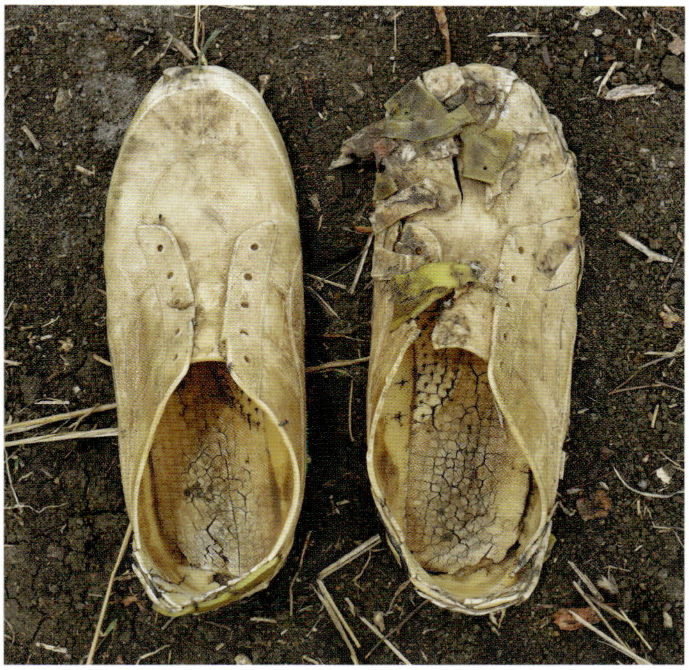

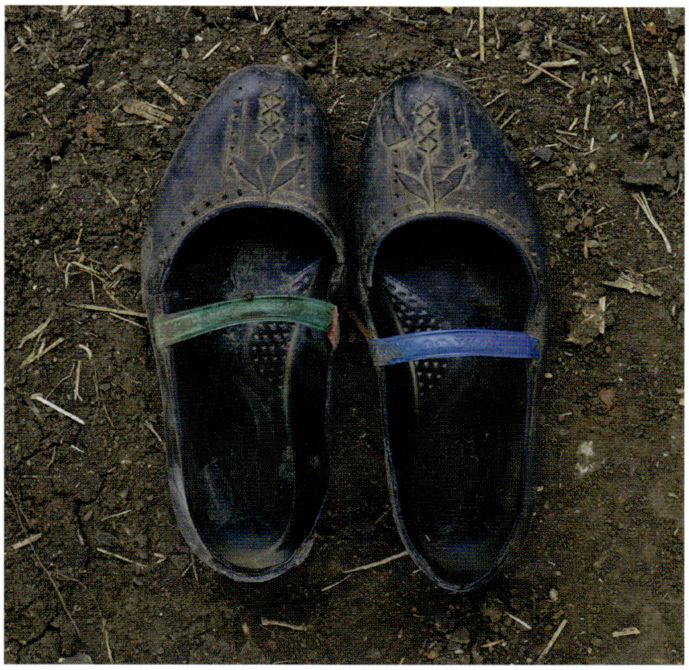

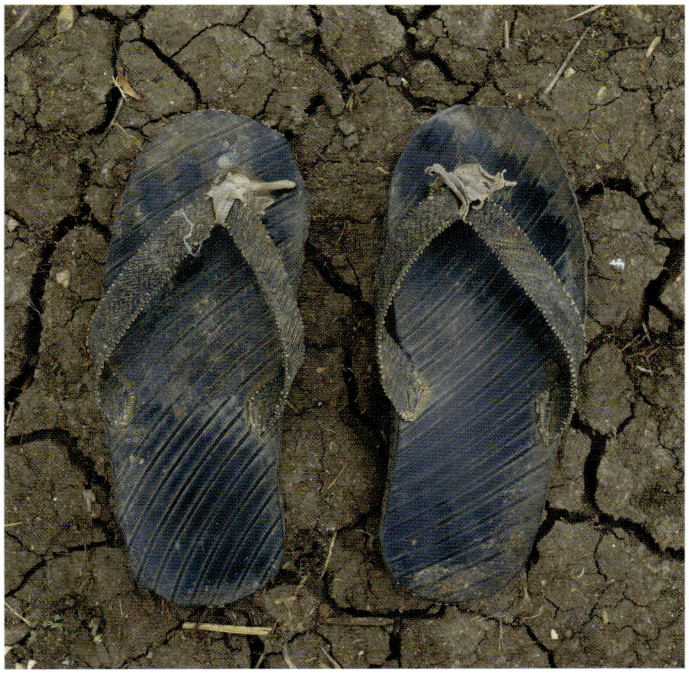

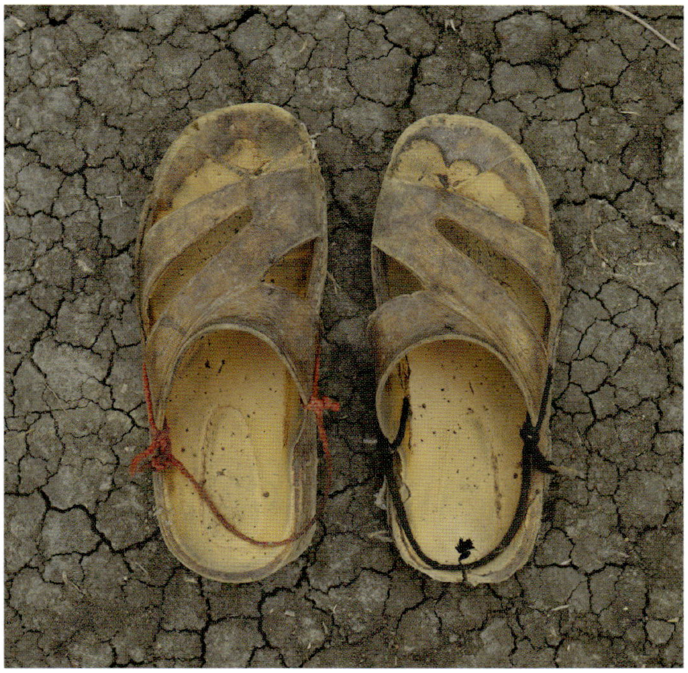

SHANNON
JENSEN

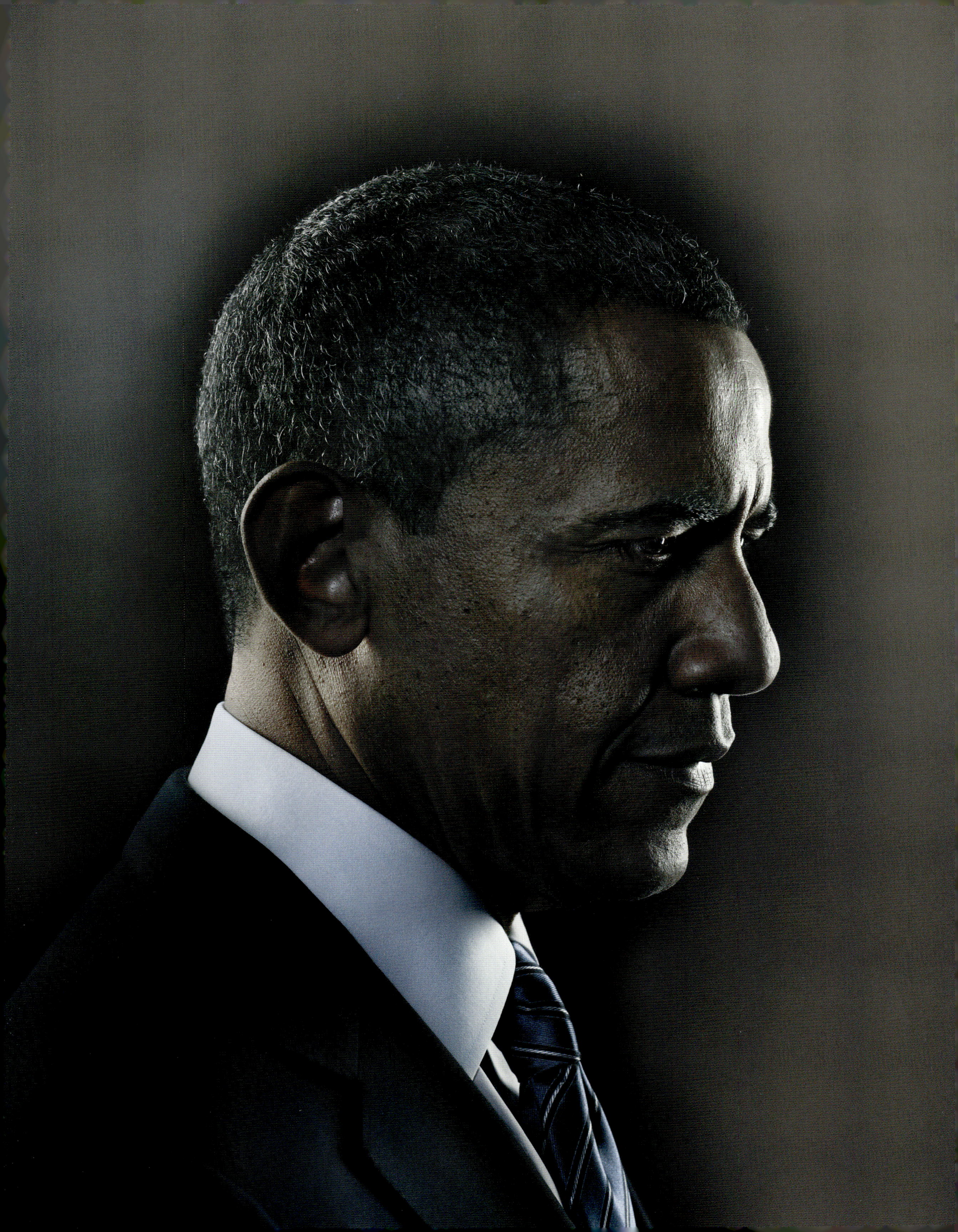

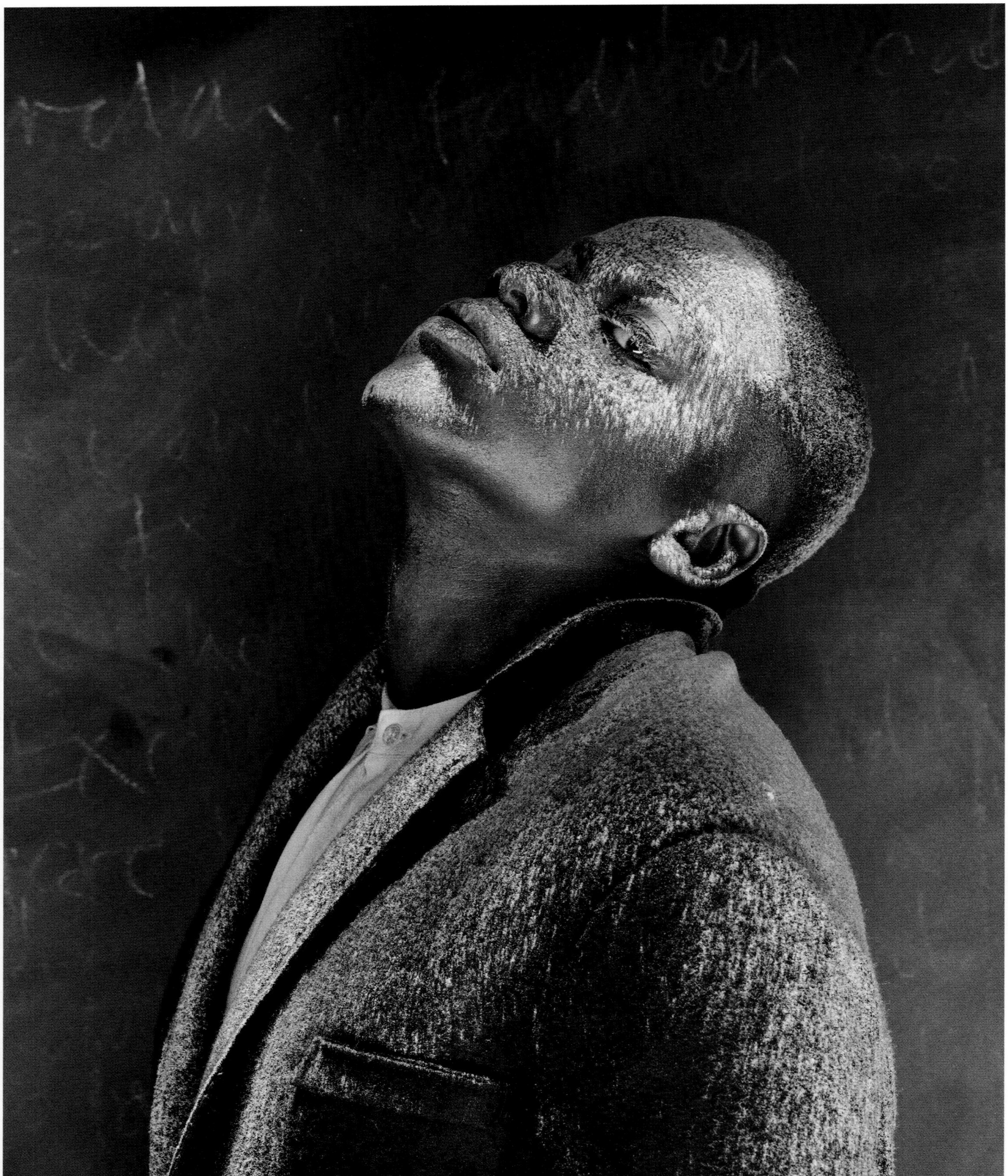

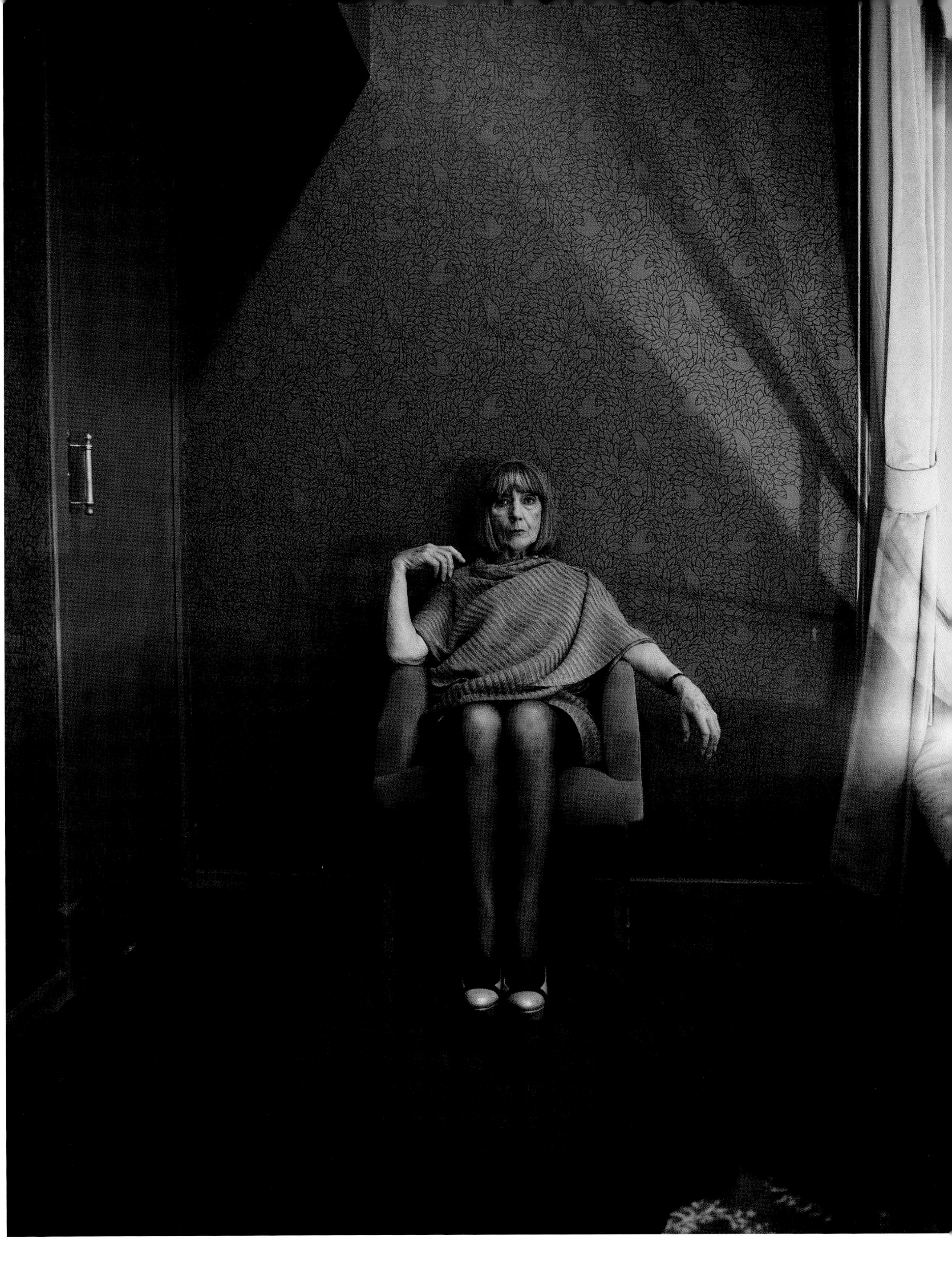

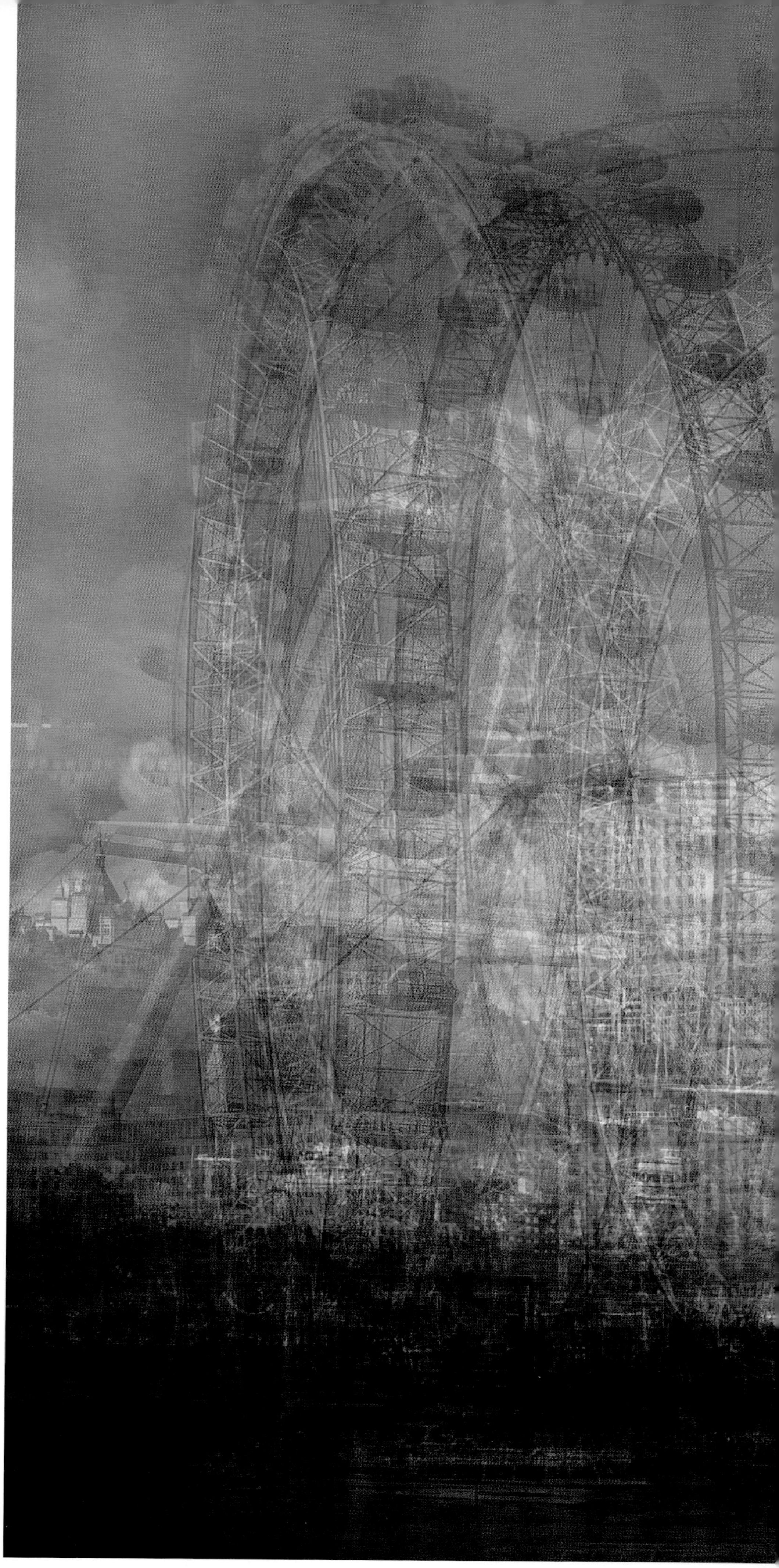

IDRIS KHAN

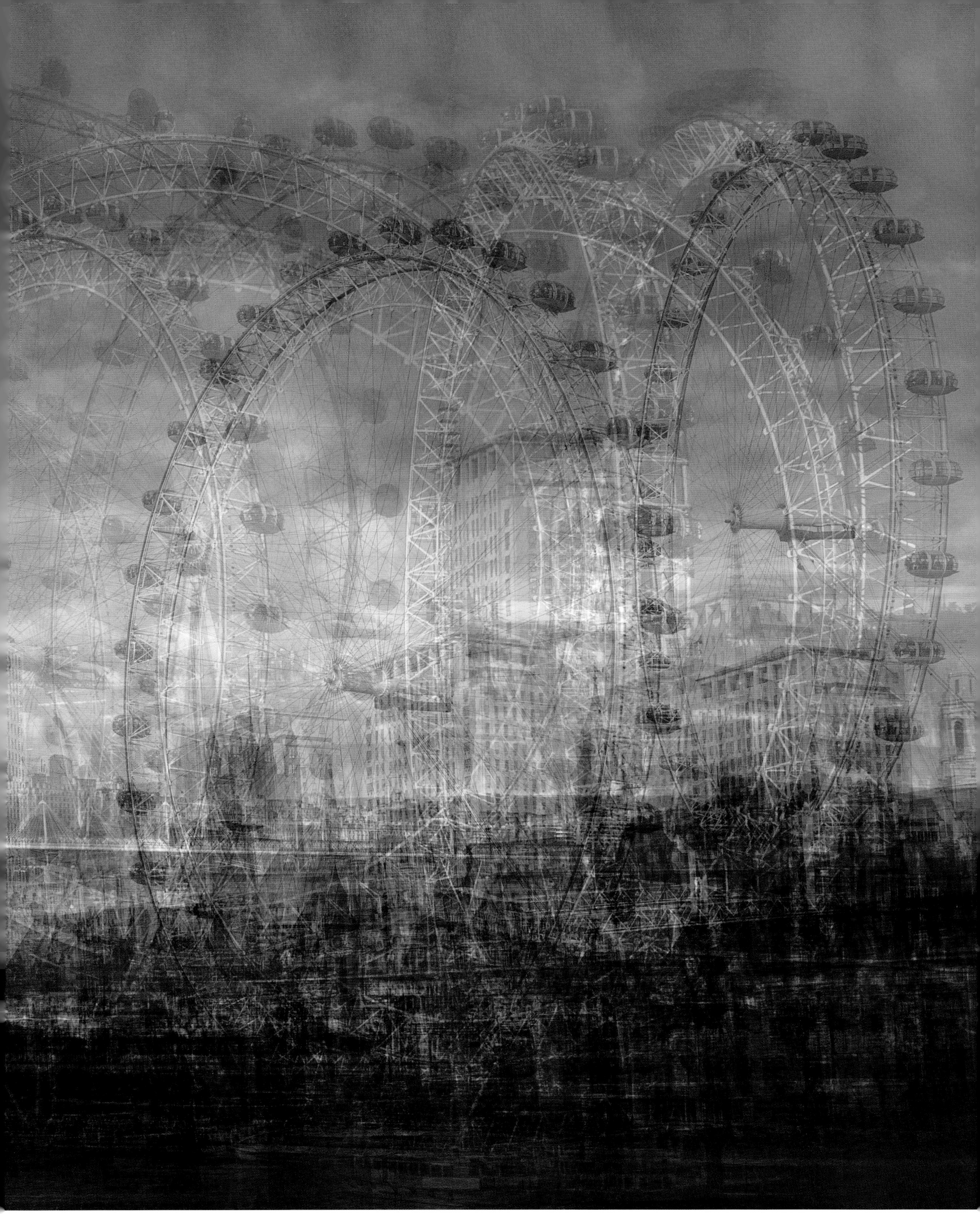

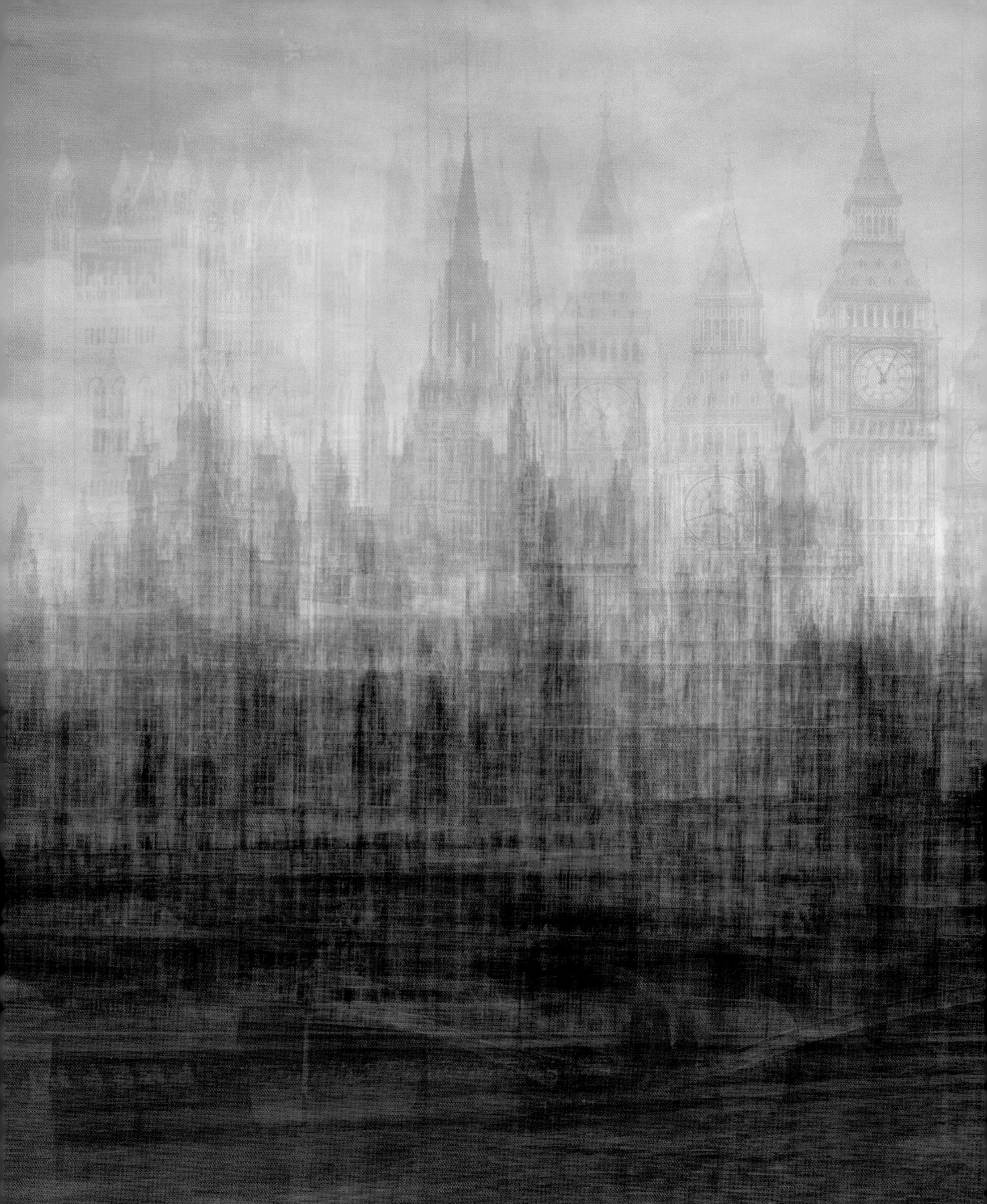

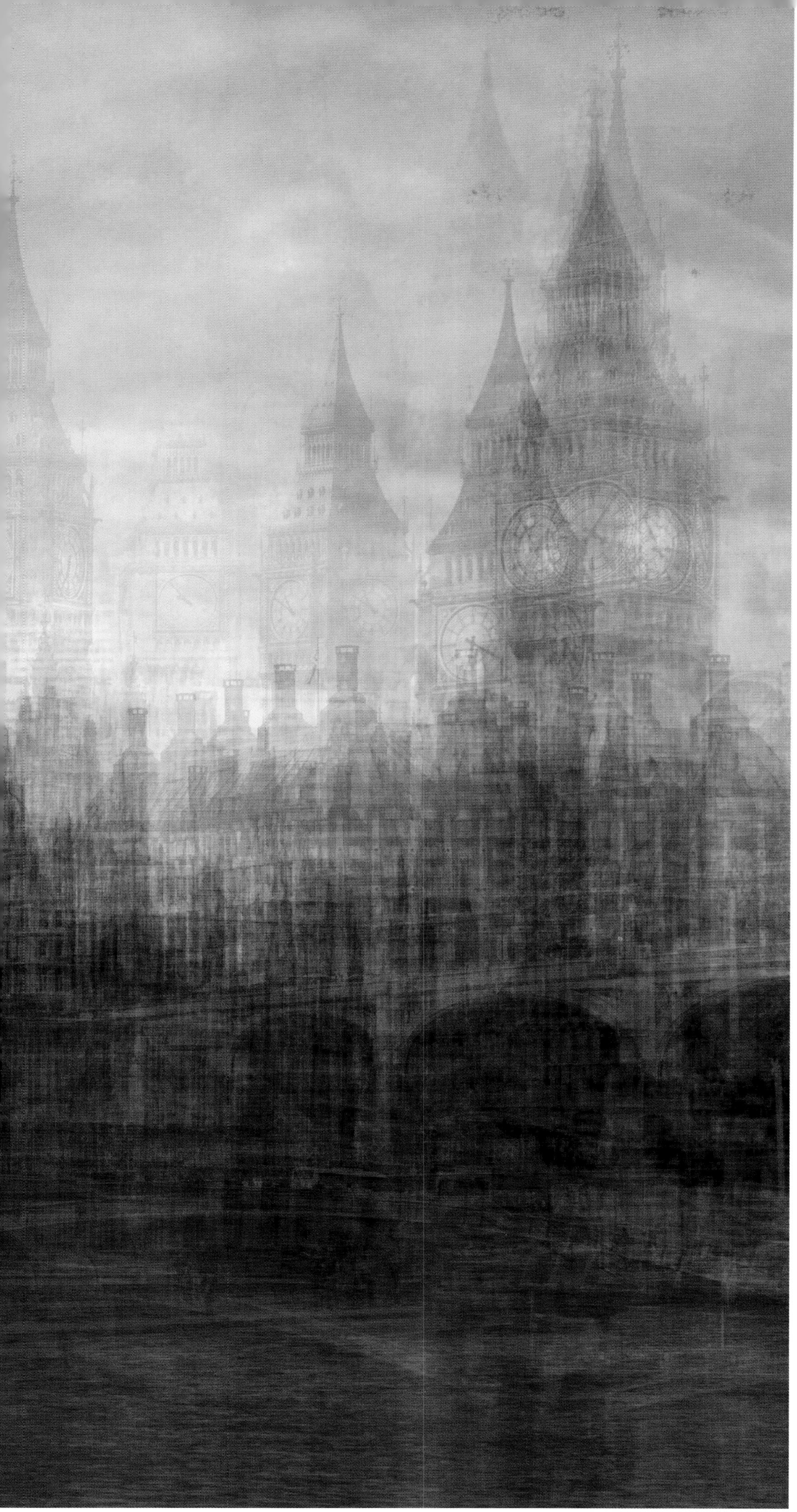

IDRIS KHAN

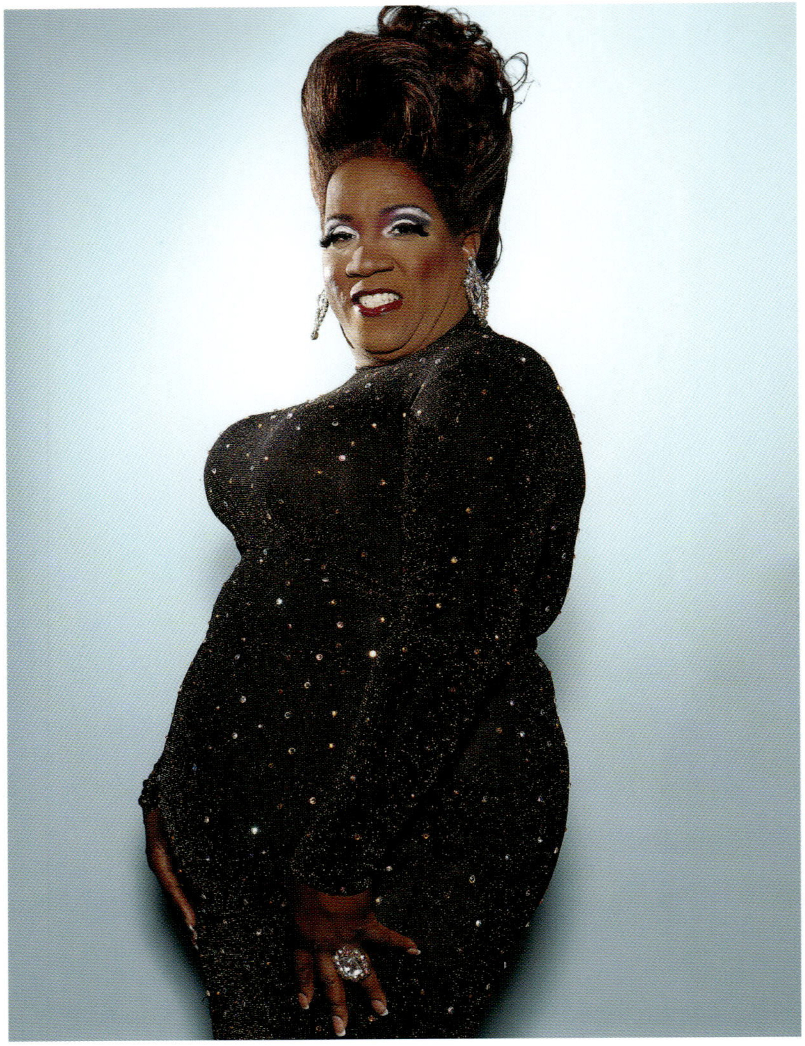

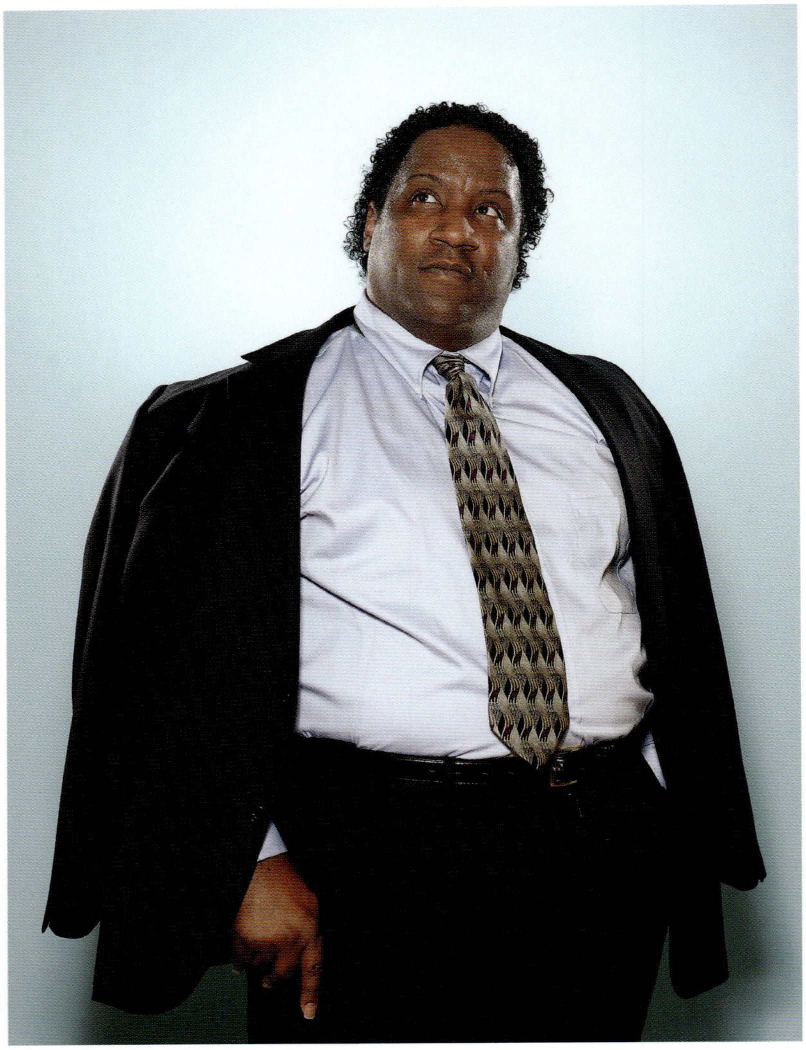

ELI MEIR KAPLAN

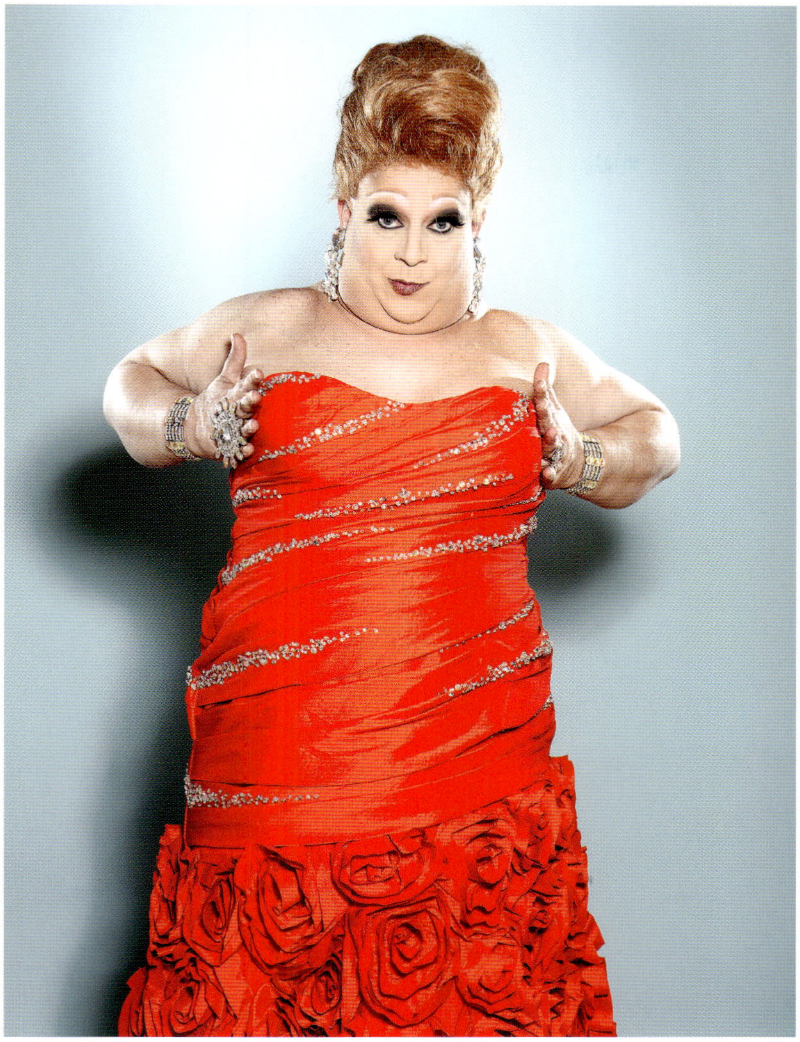

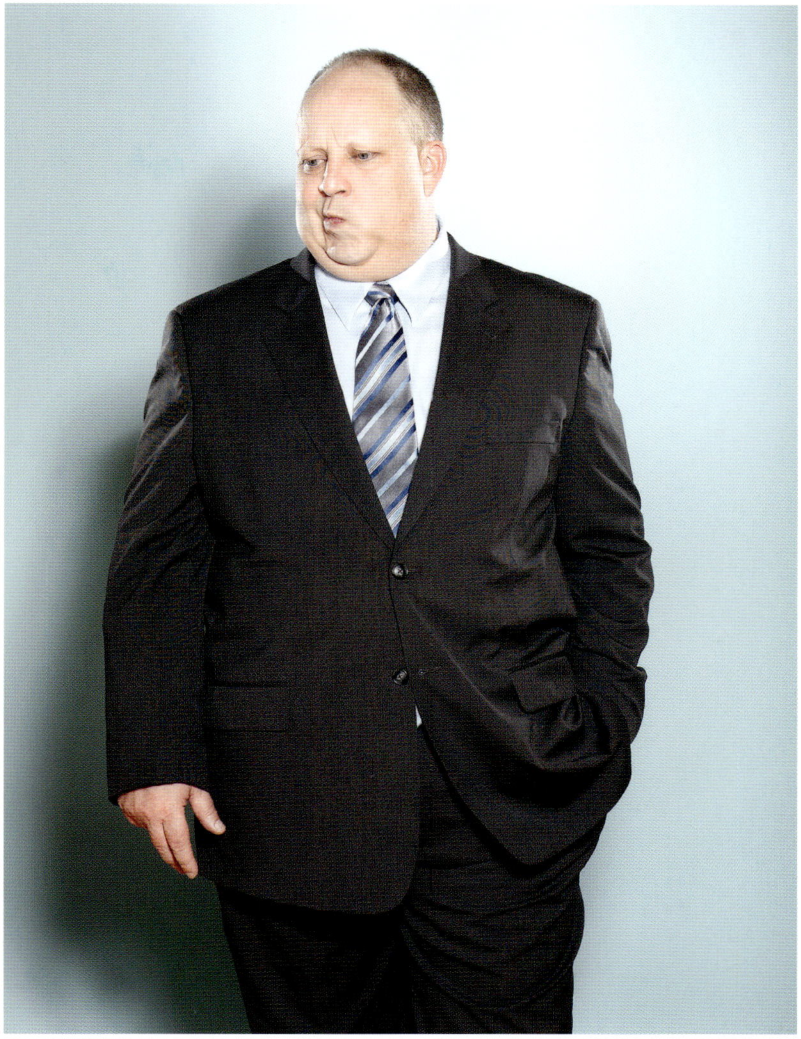

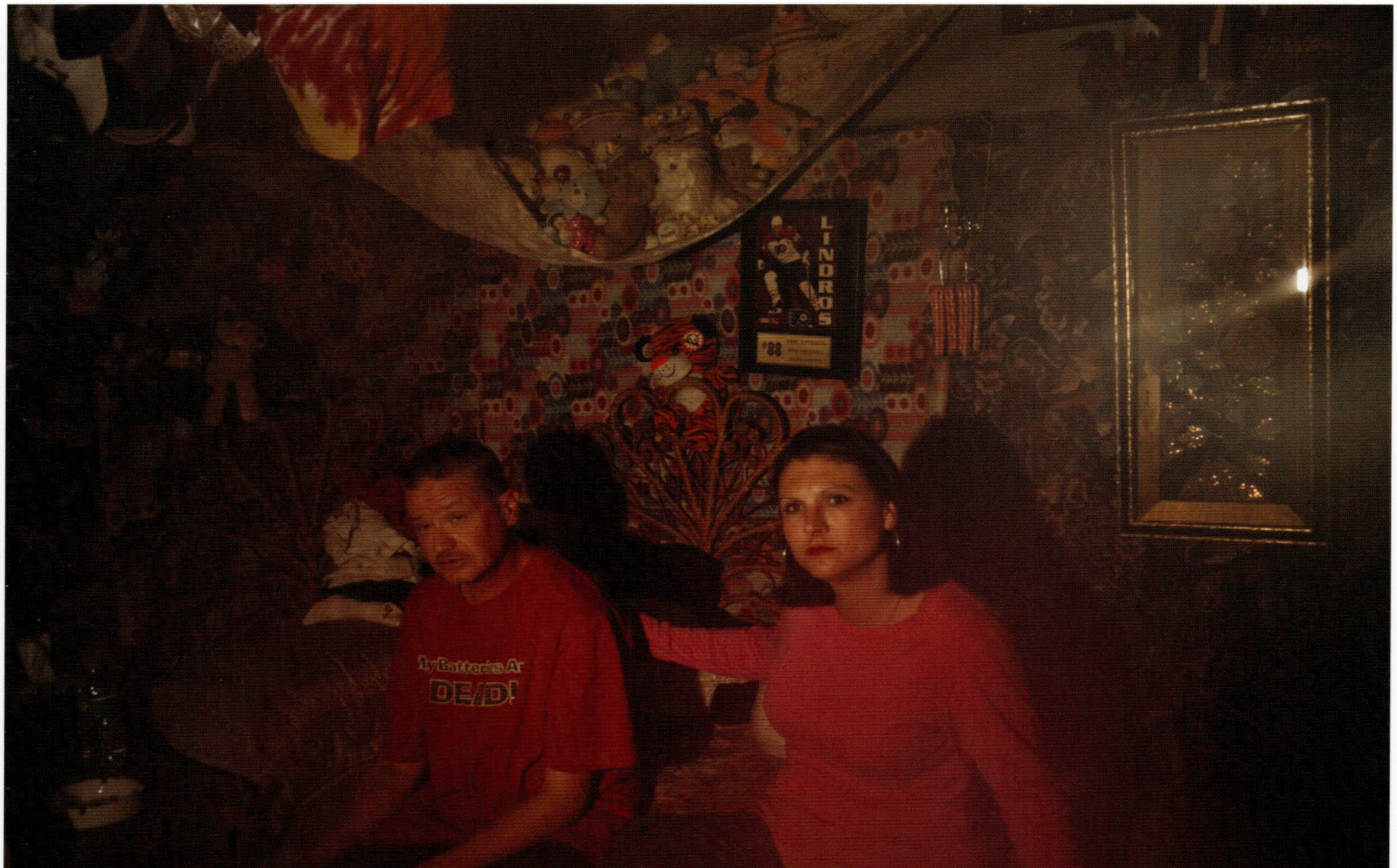
LINDROS
#88
DEAD!

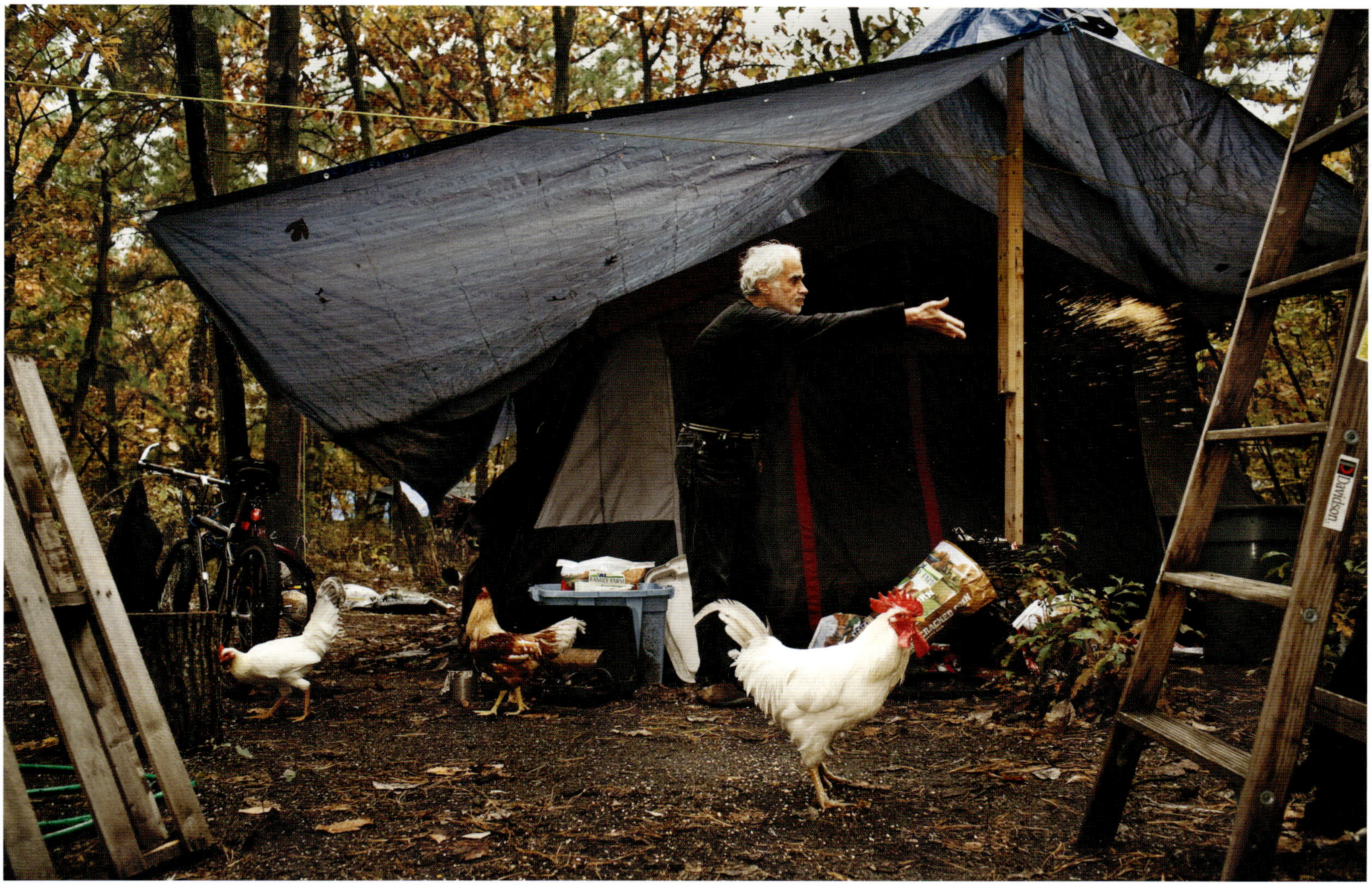
Davidson

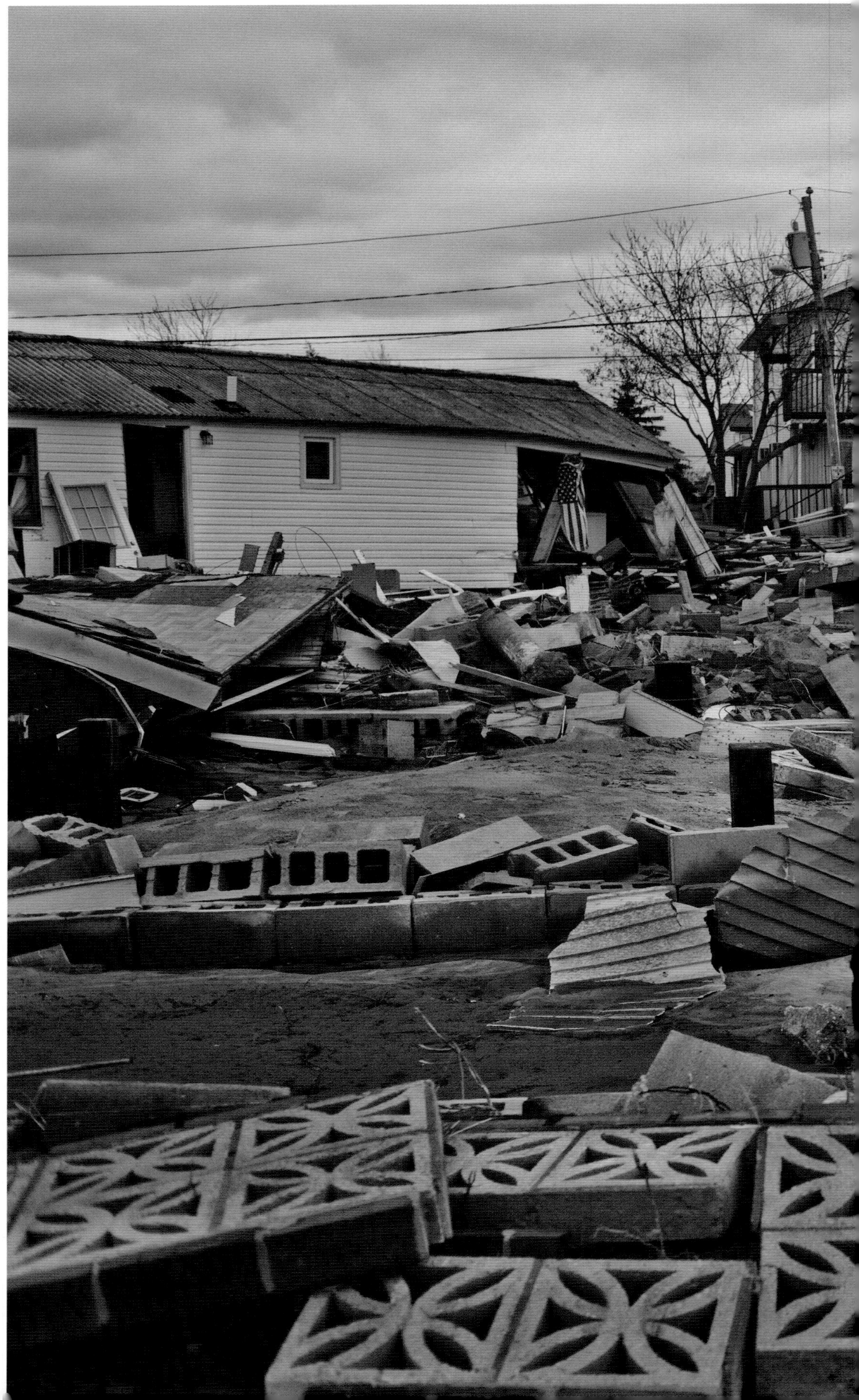

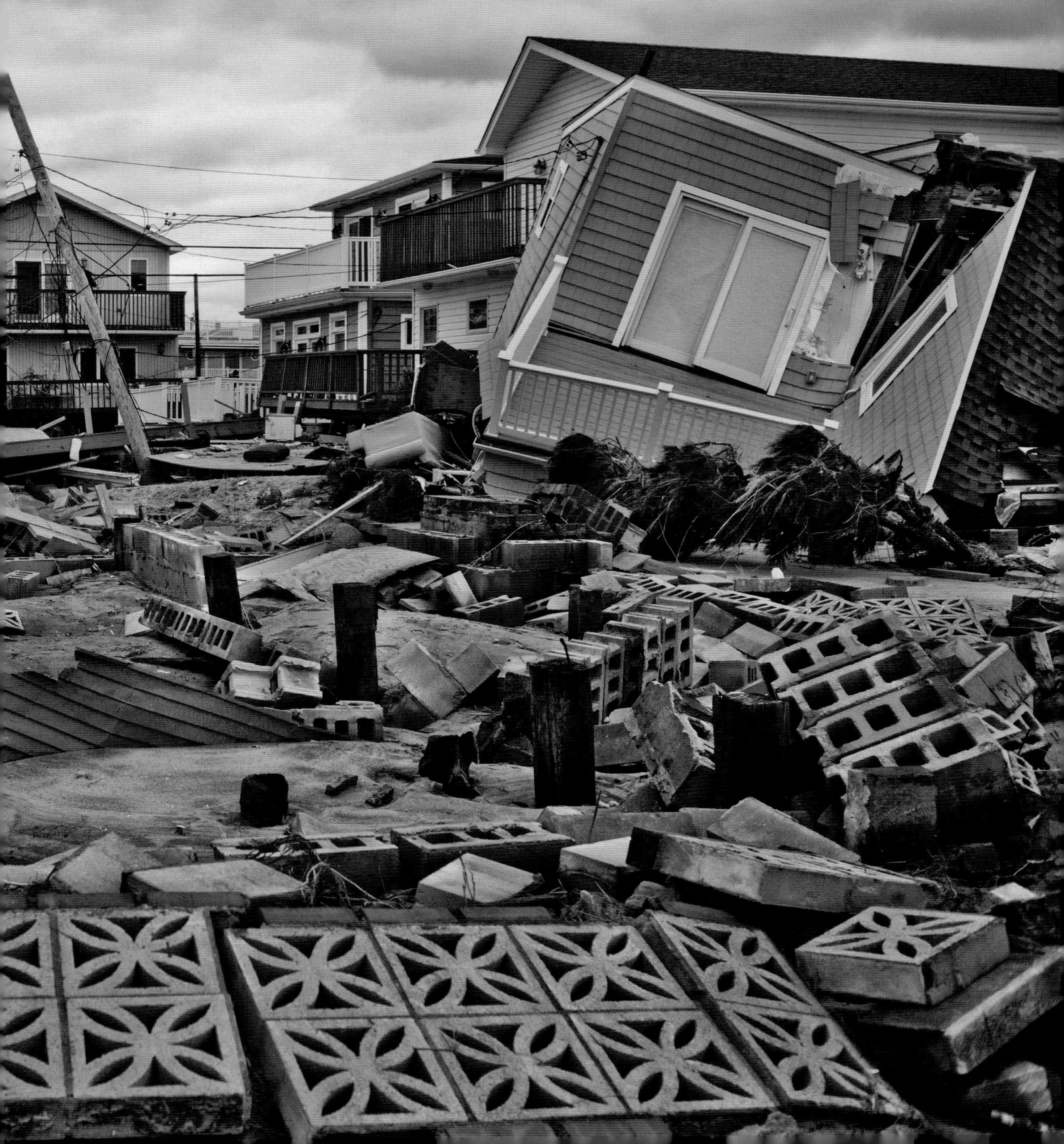

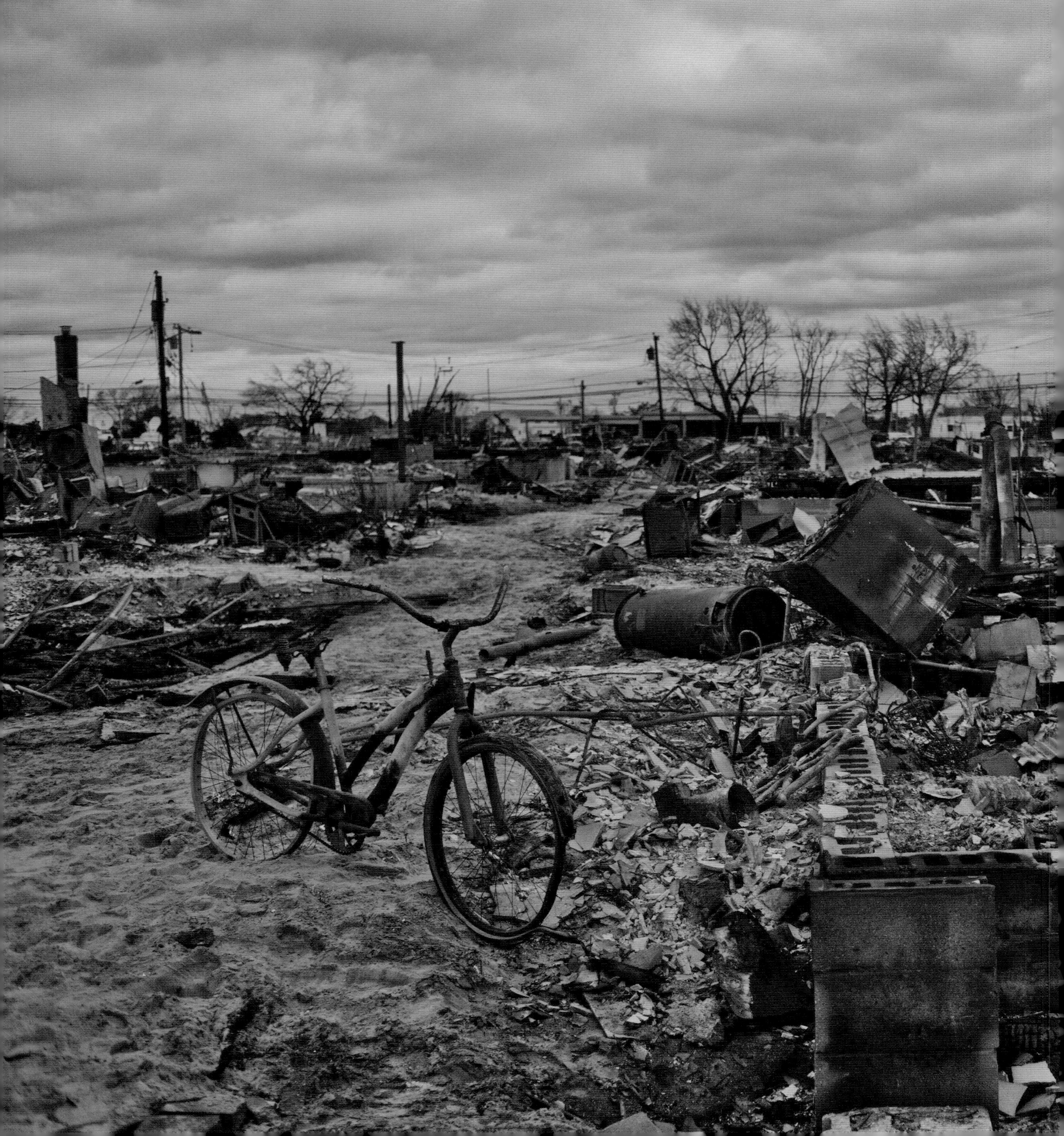

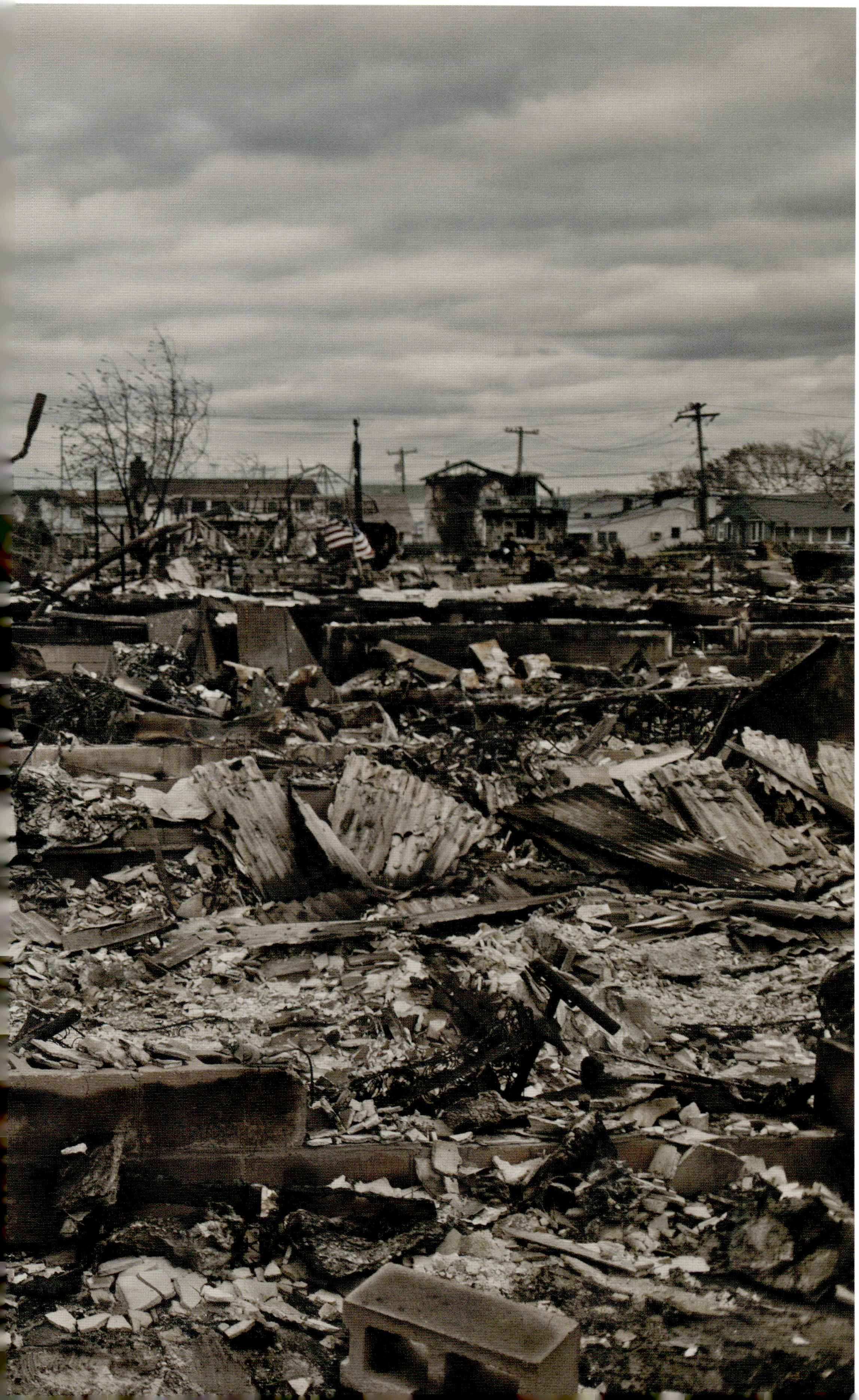

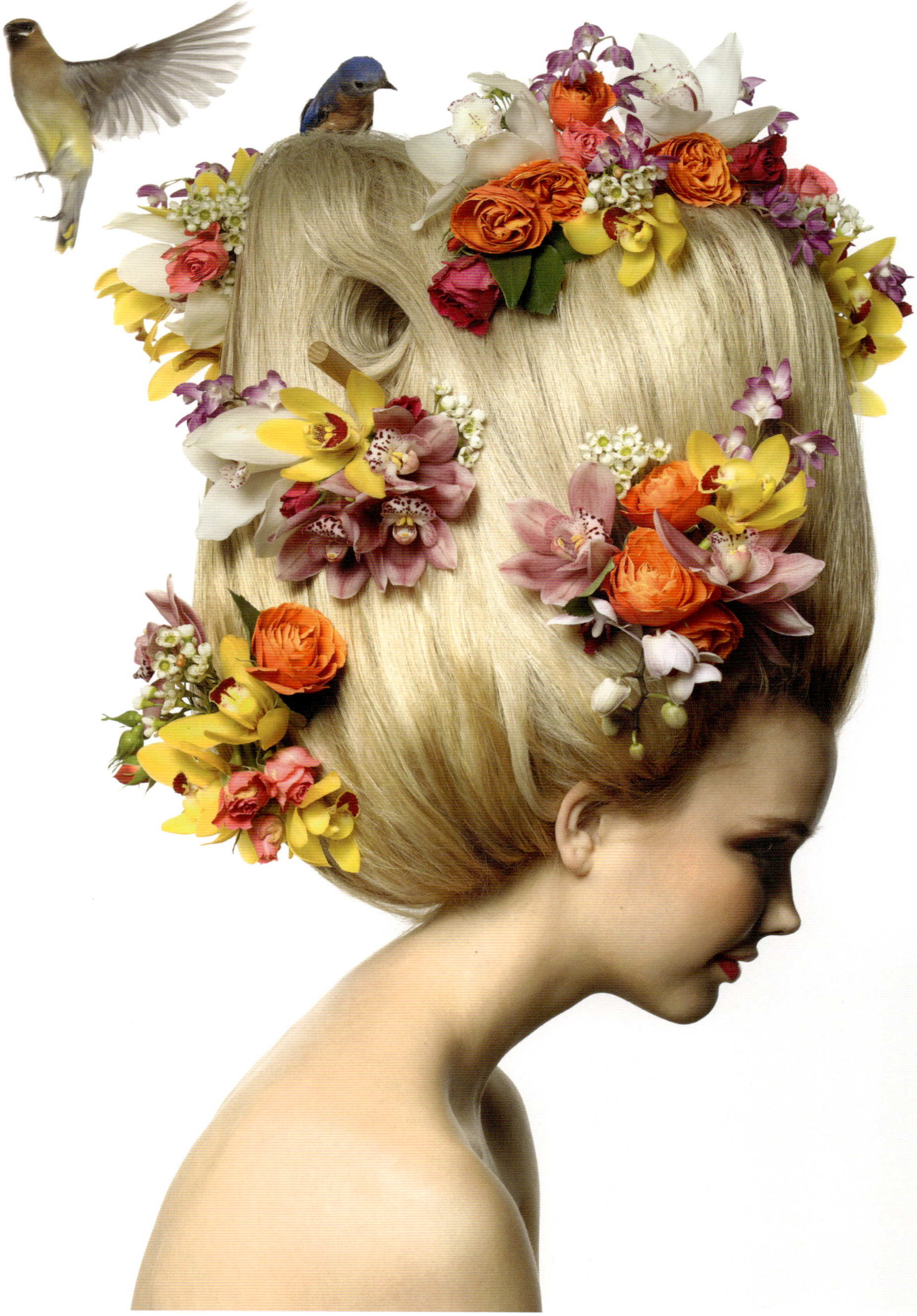

GEOF KERN

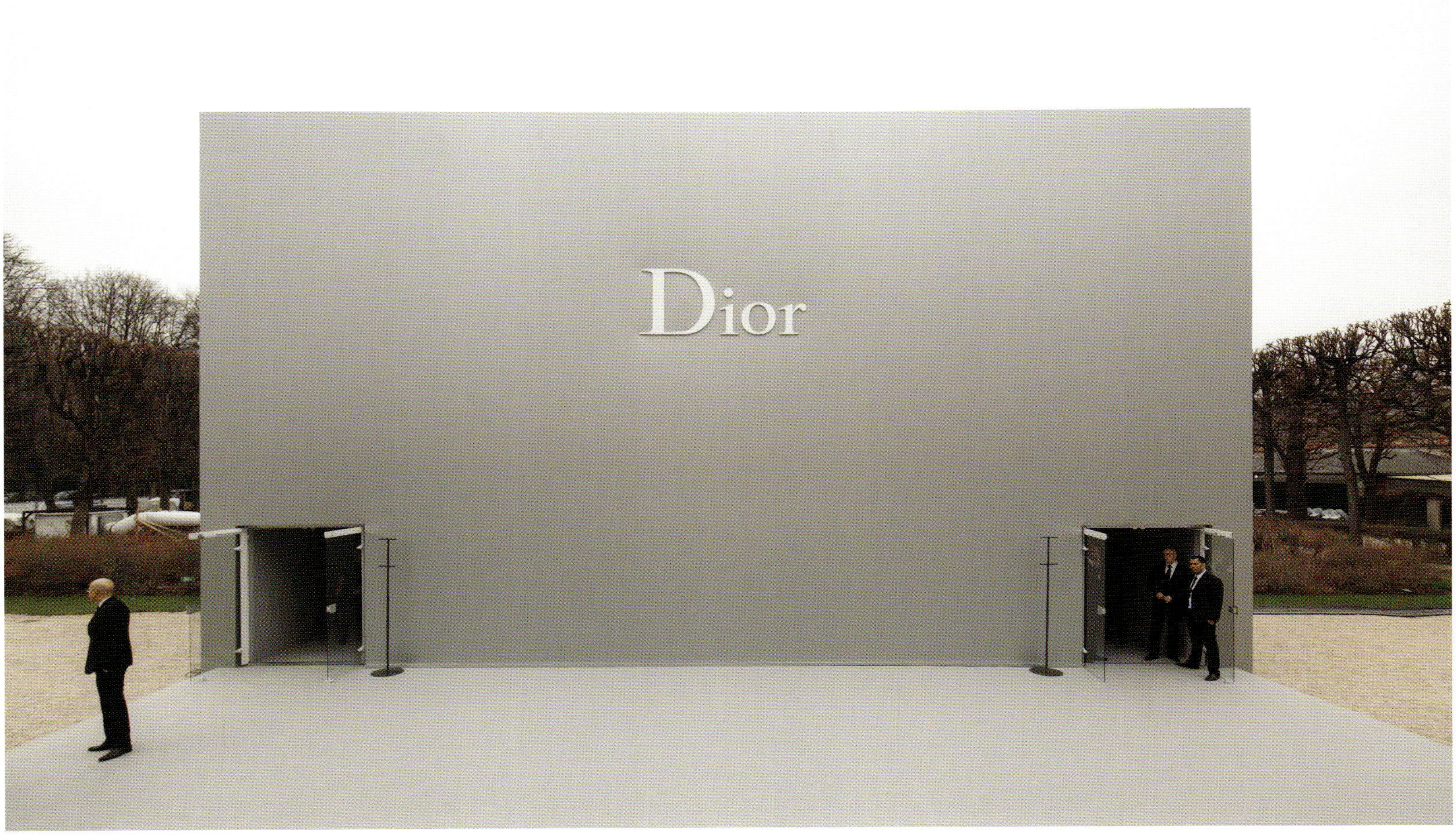
Dior

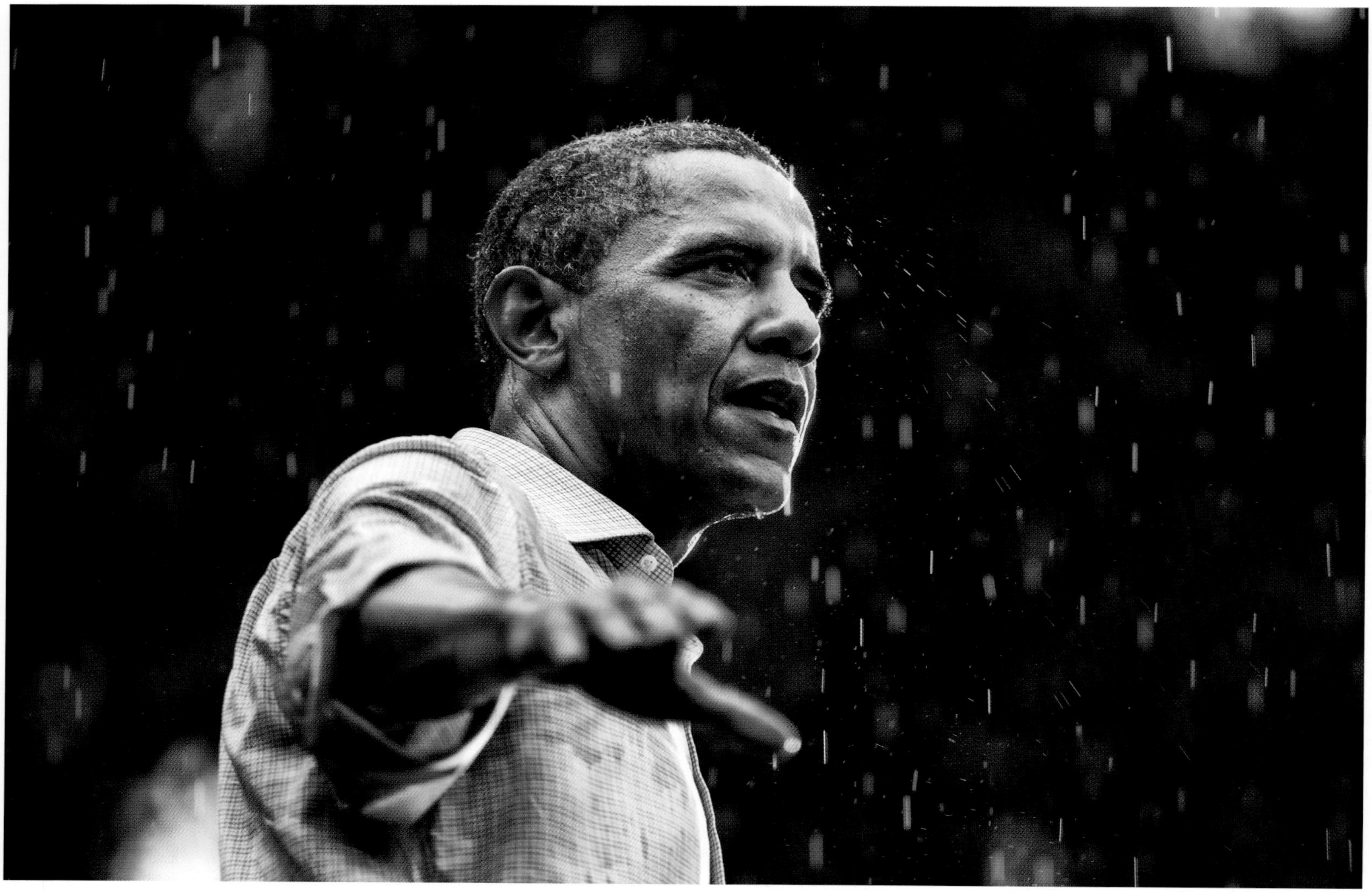

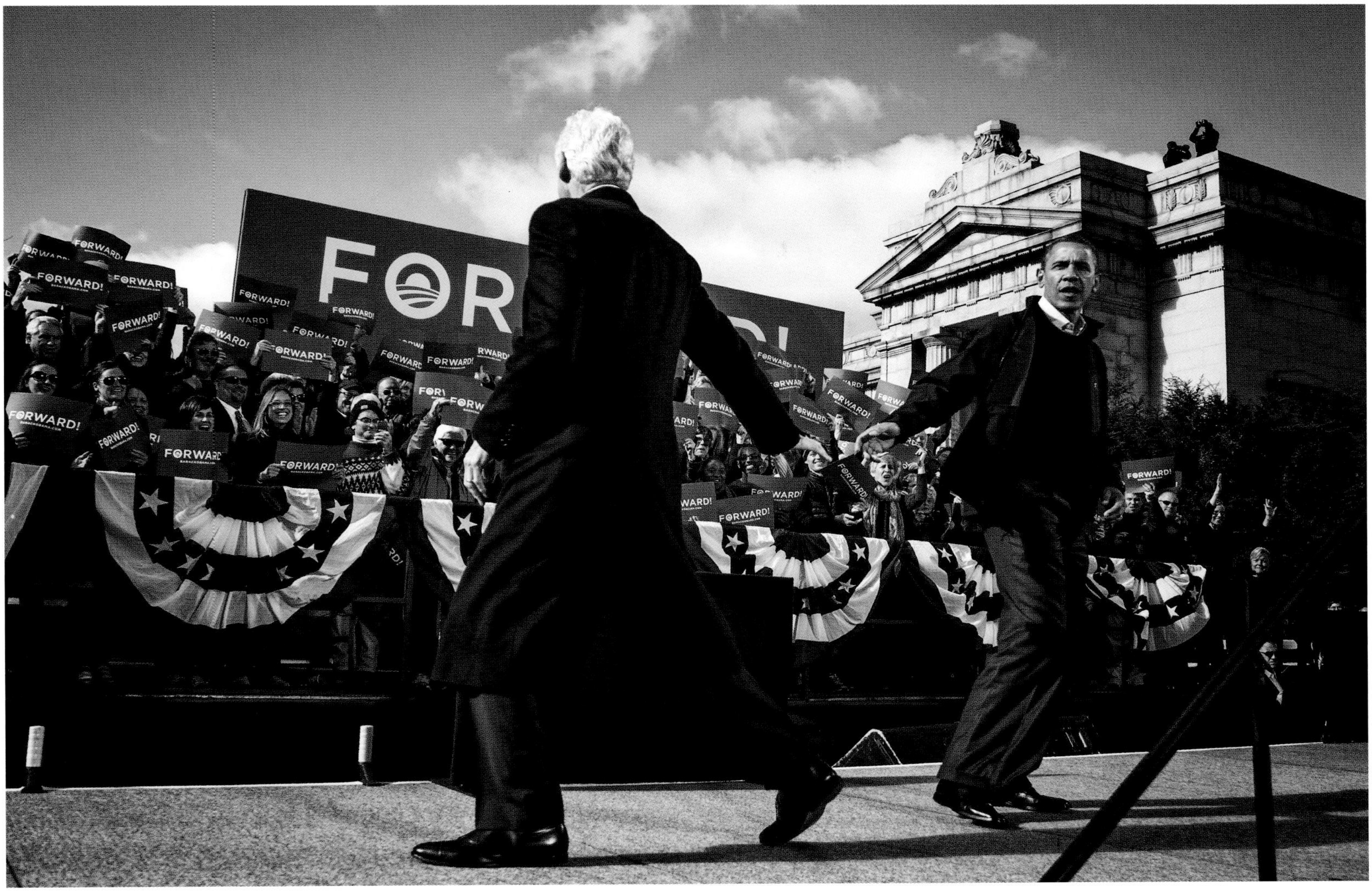

BROOKS KRAFT

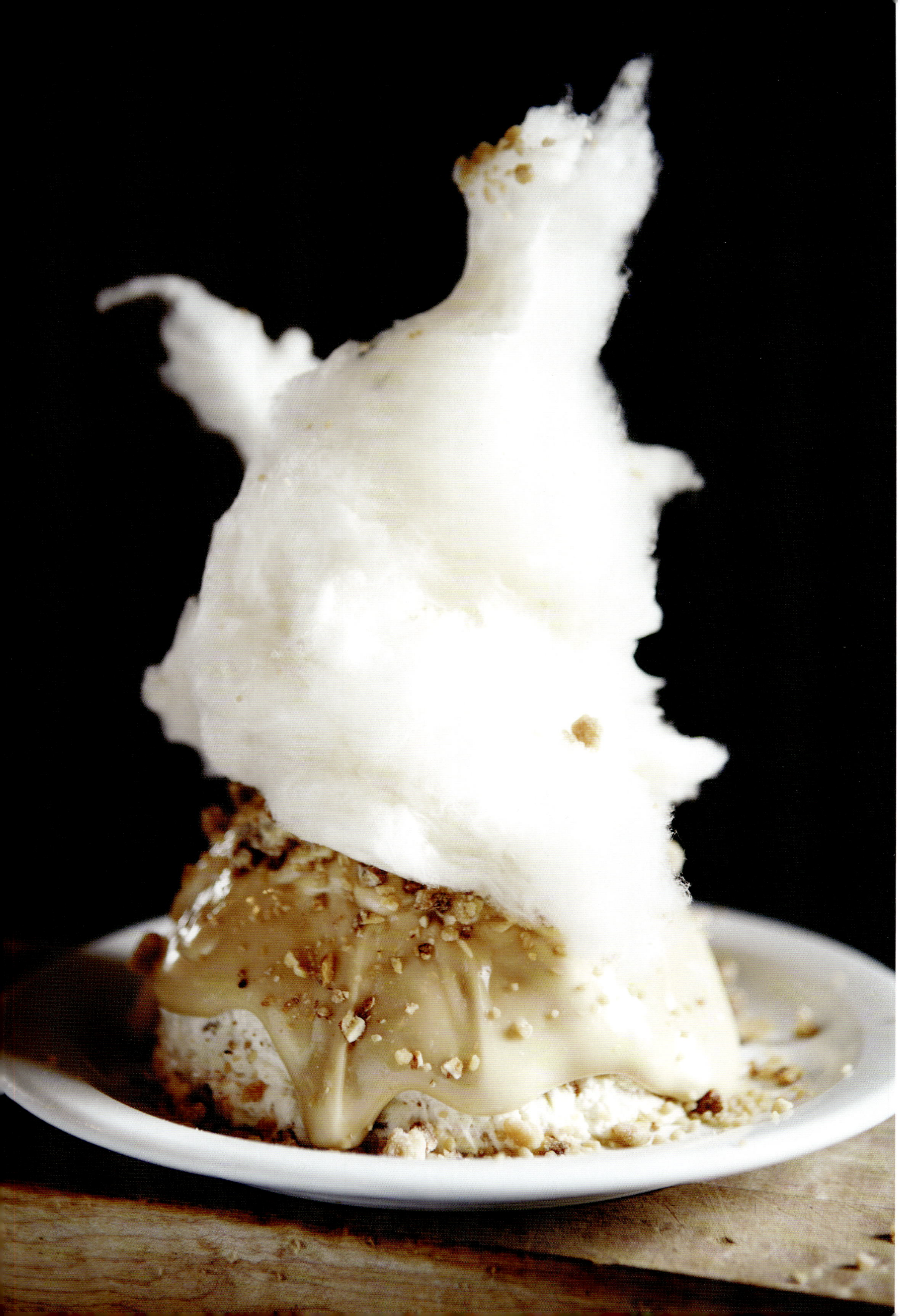

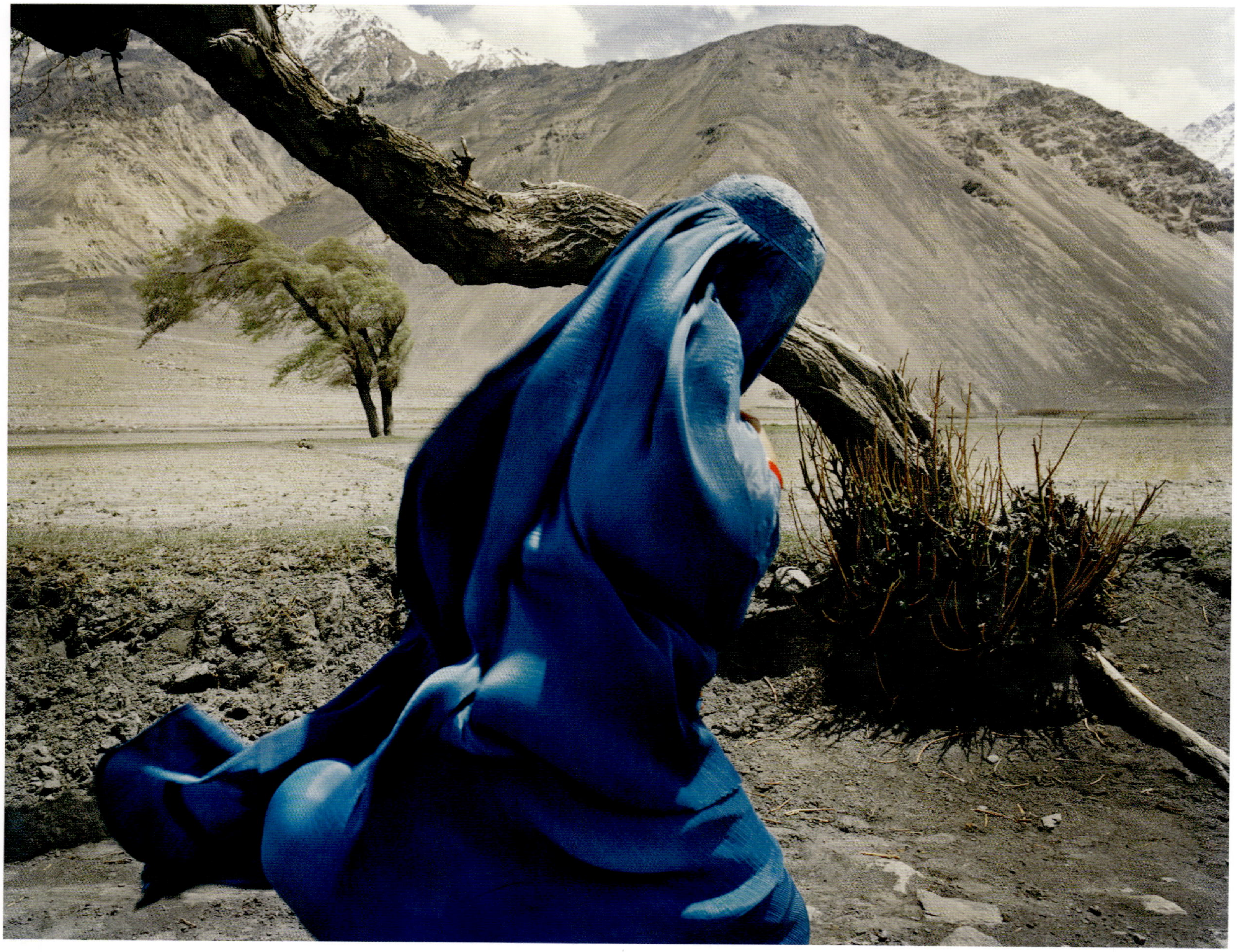

FREDERIC LAGRANGE

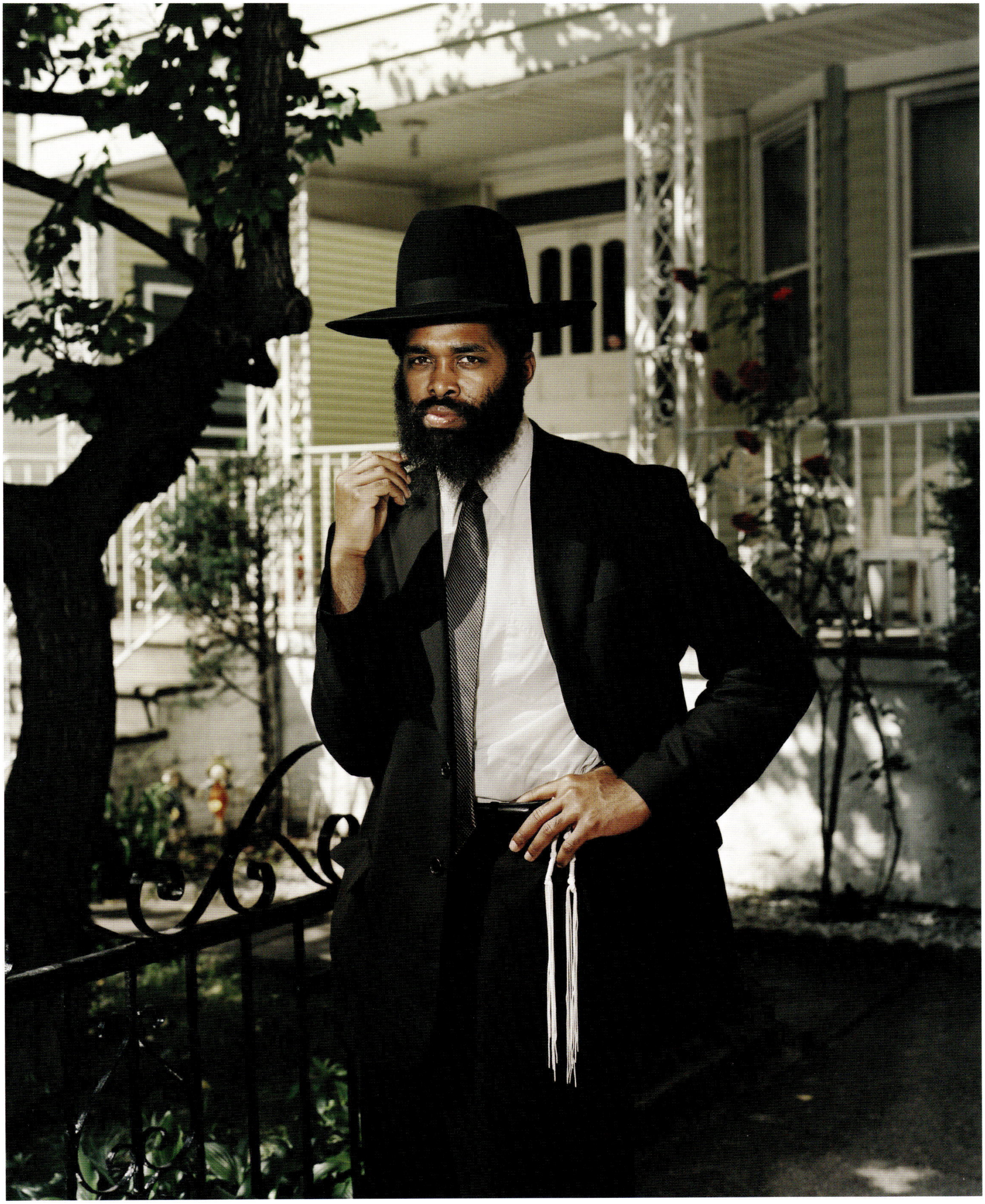

DAVE LAURIDSEN

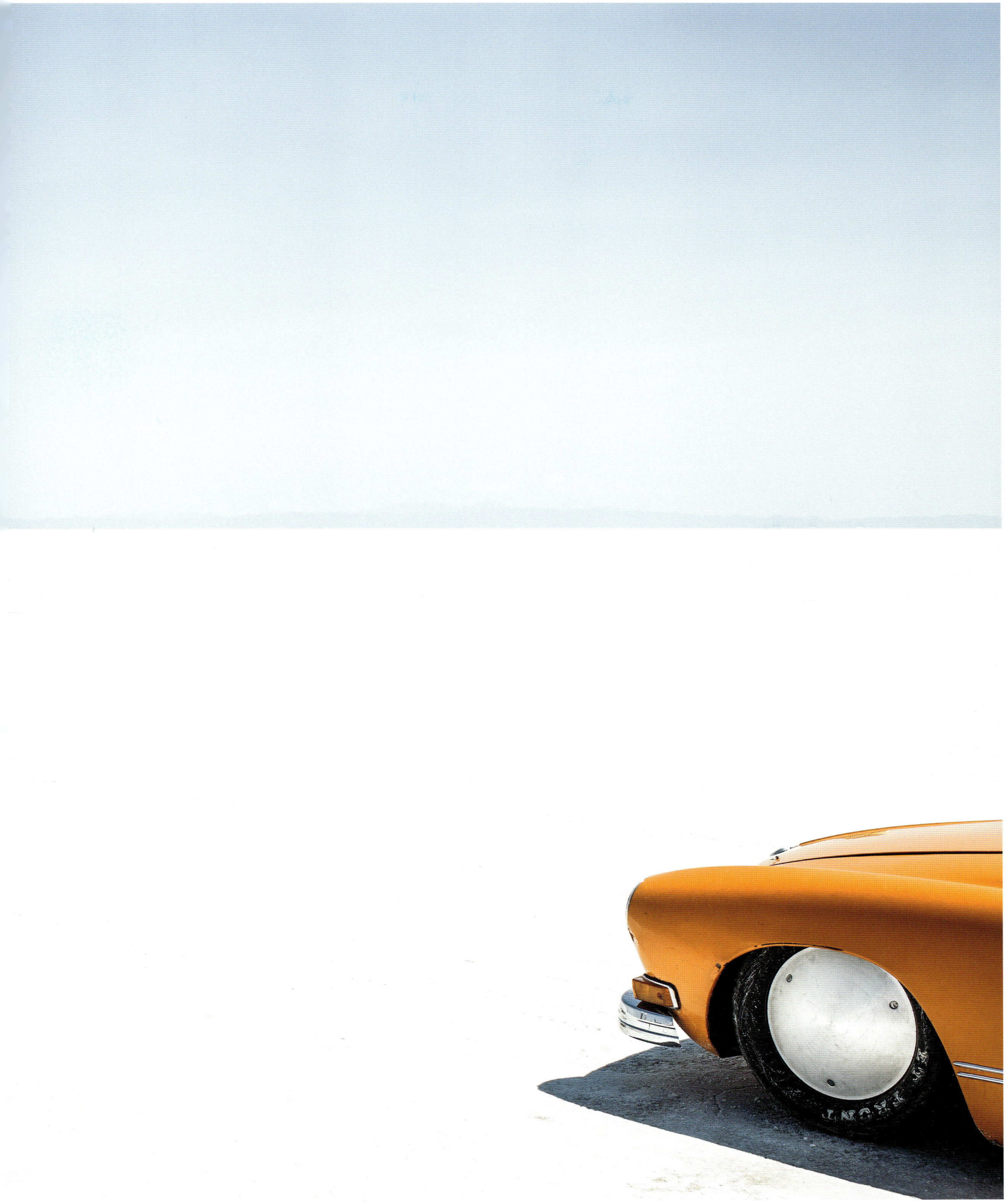

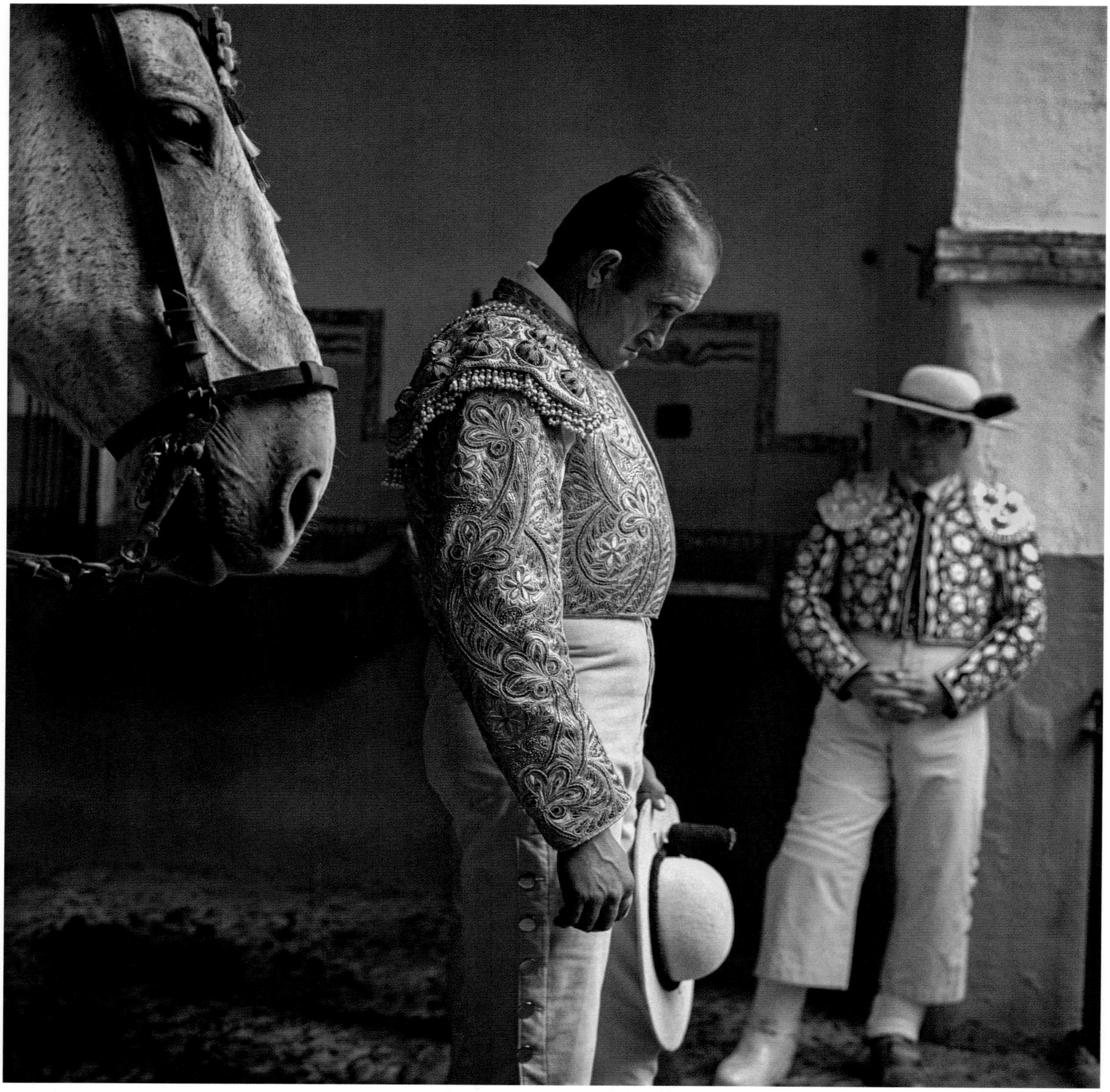

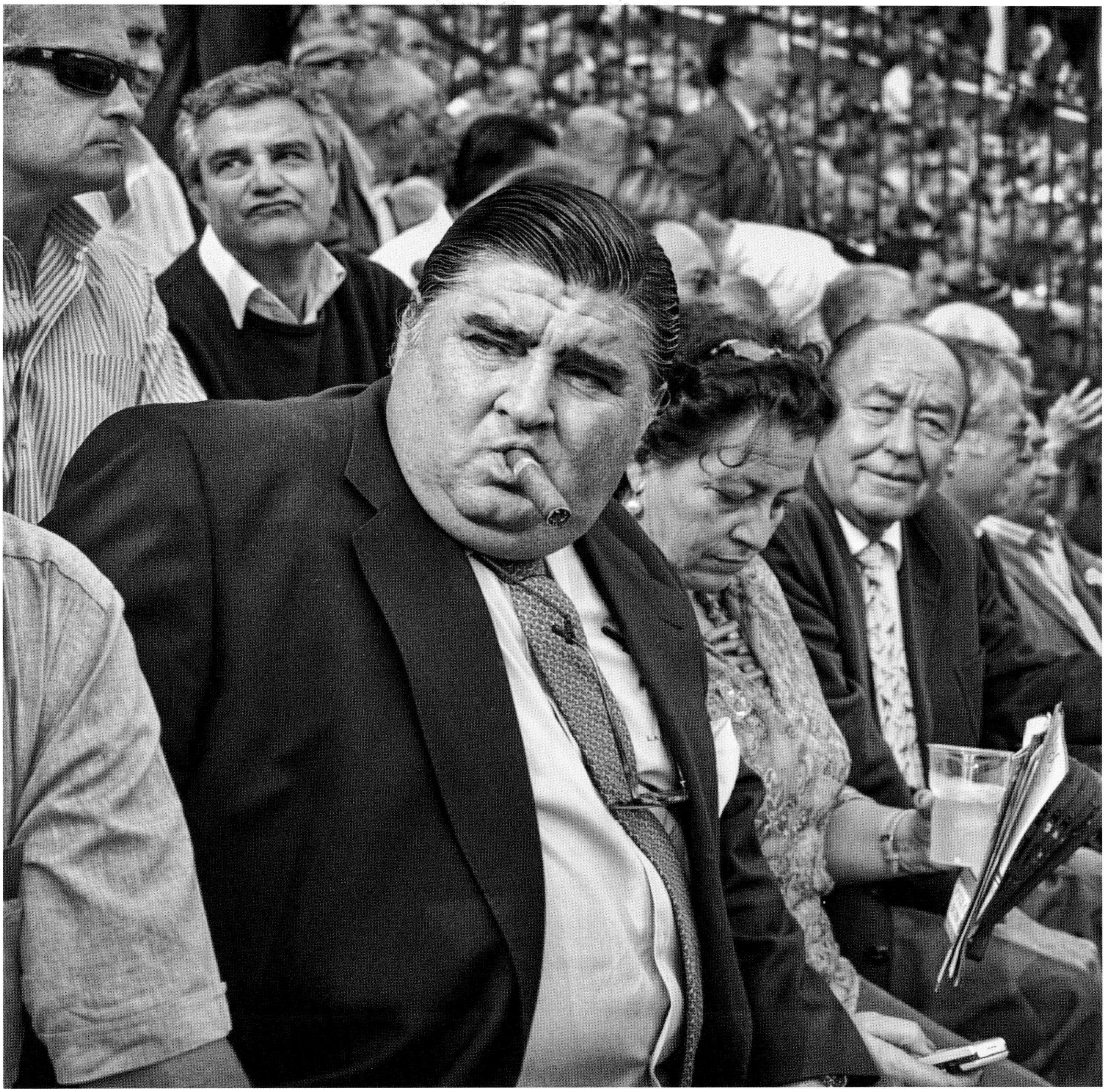

AITOR LARA

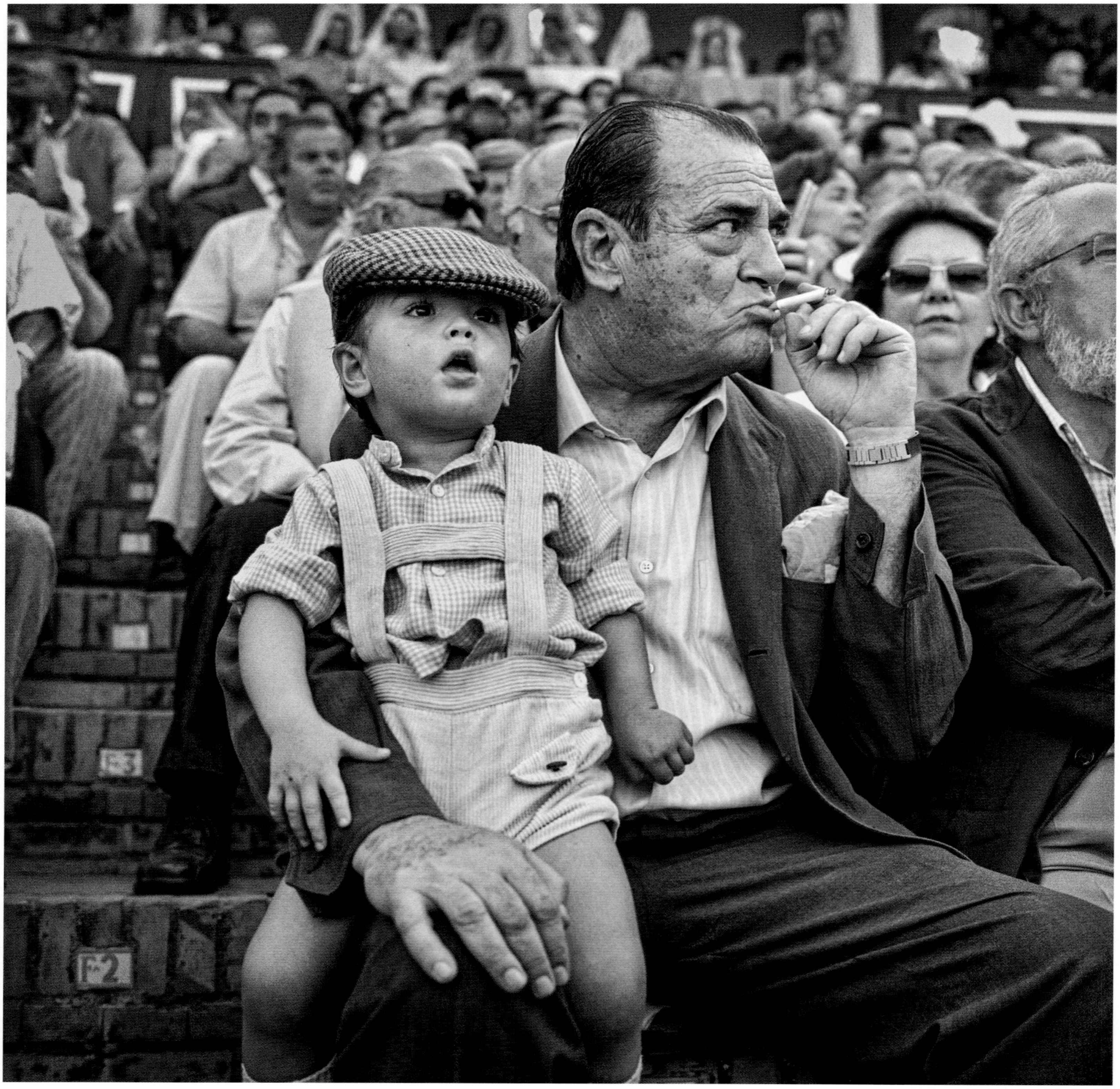

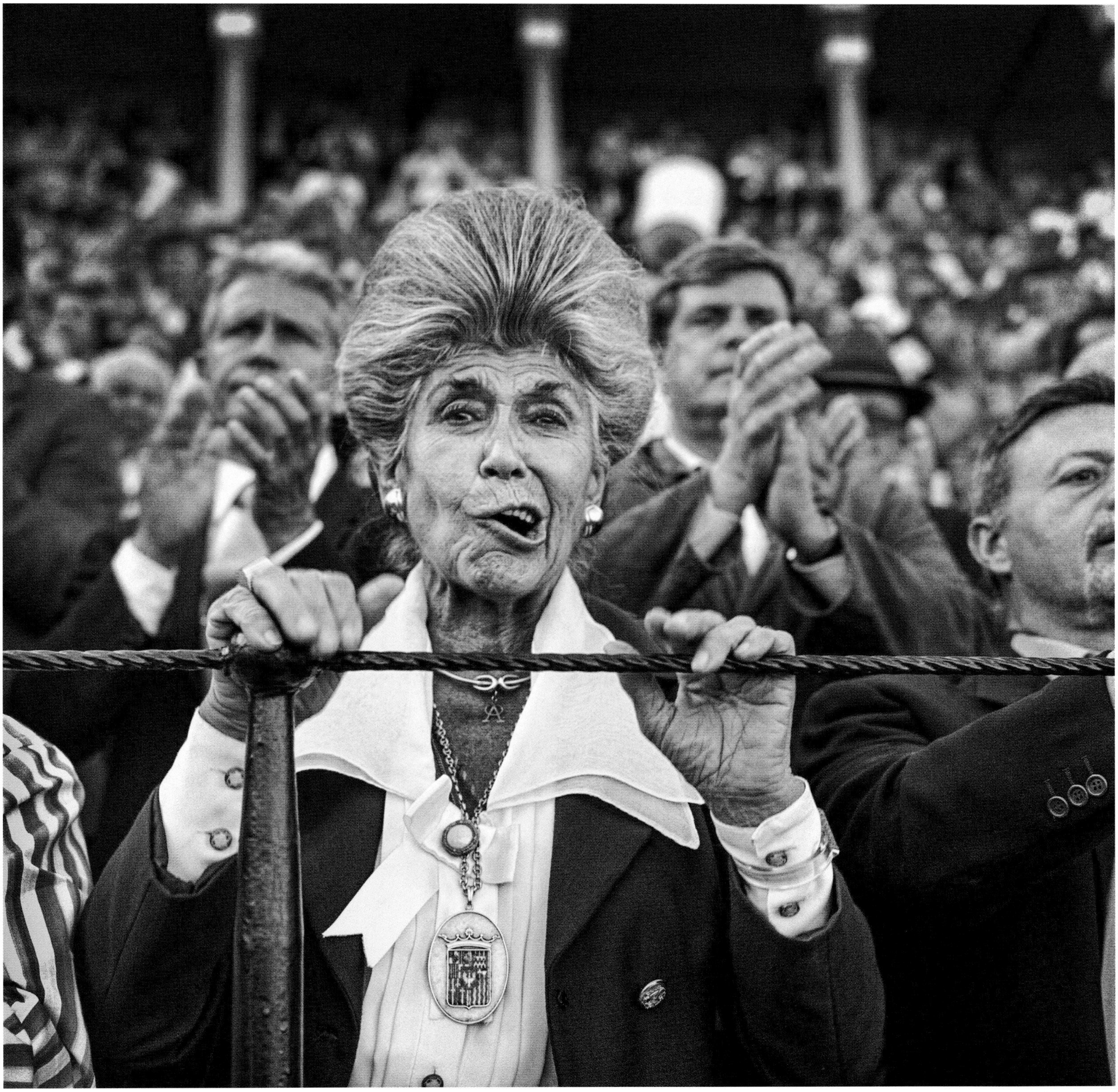

AITOR LARA

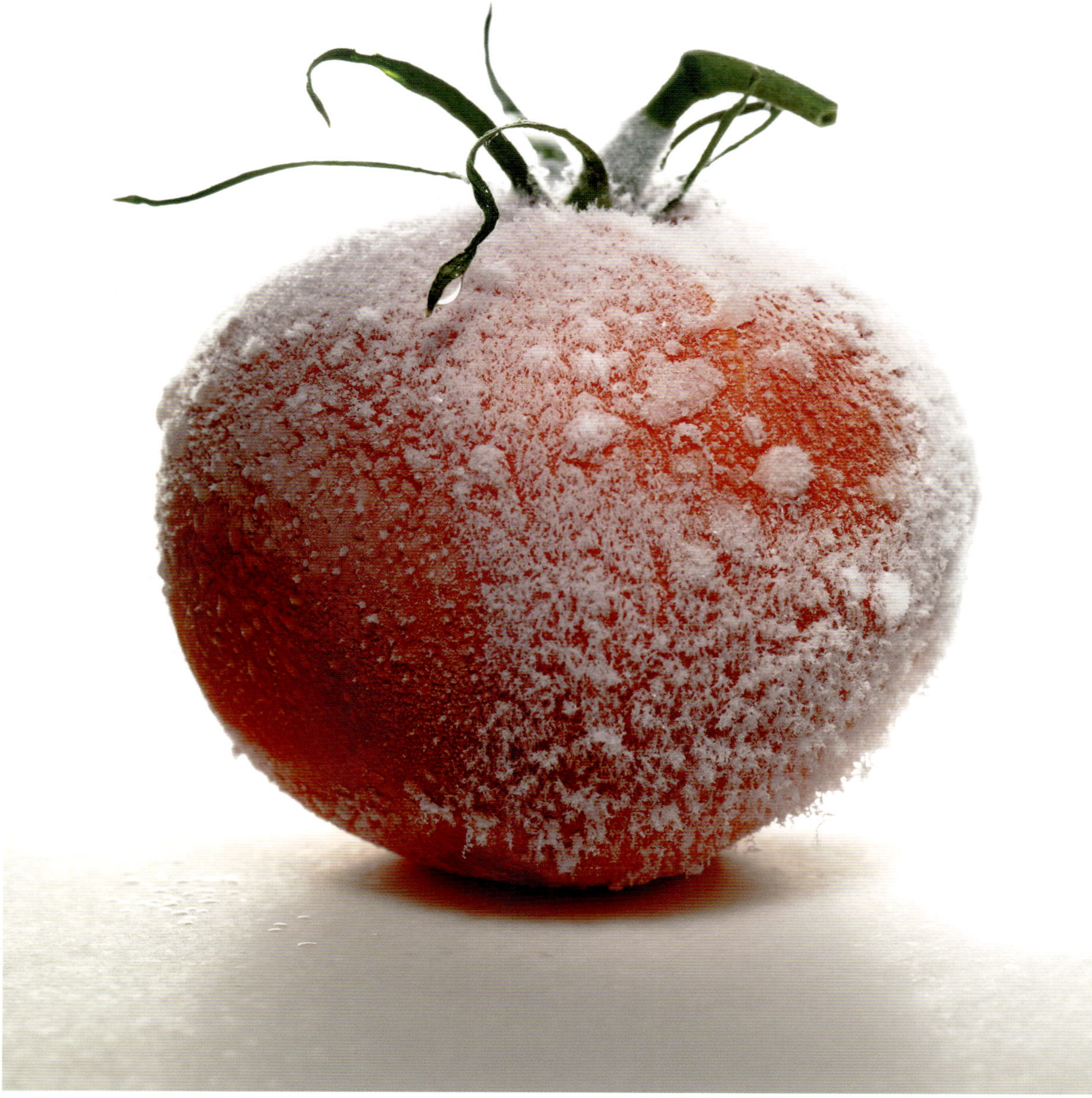

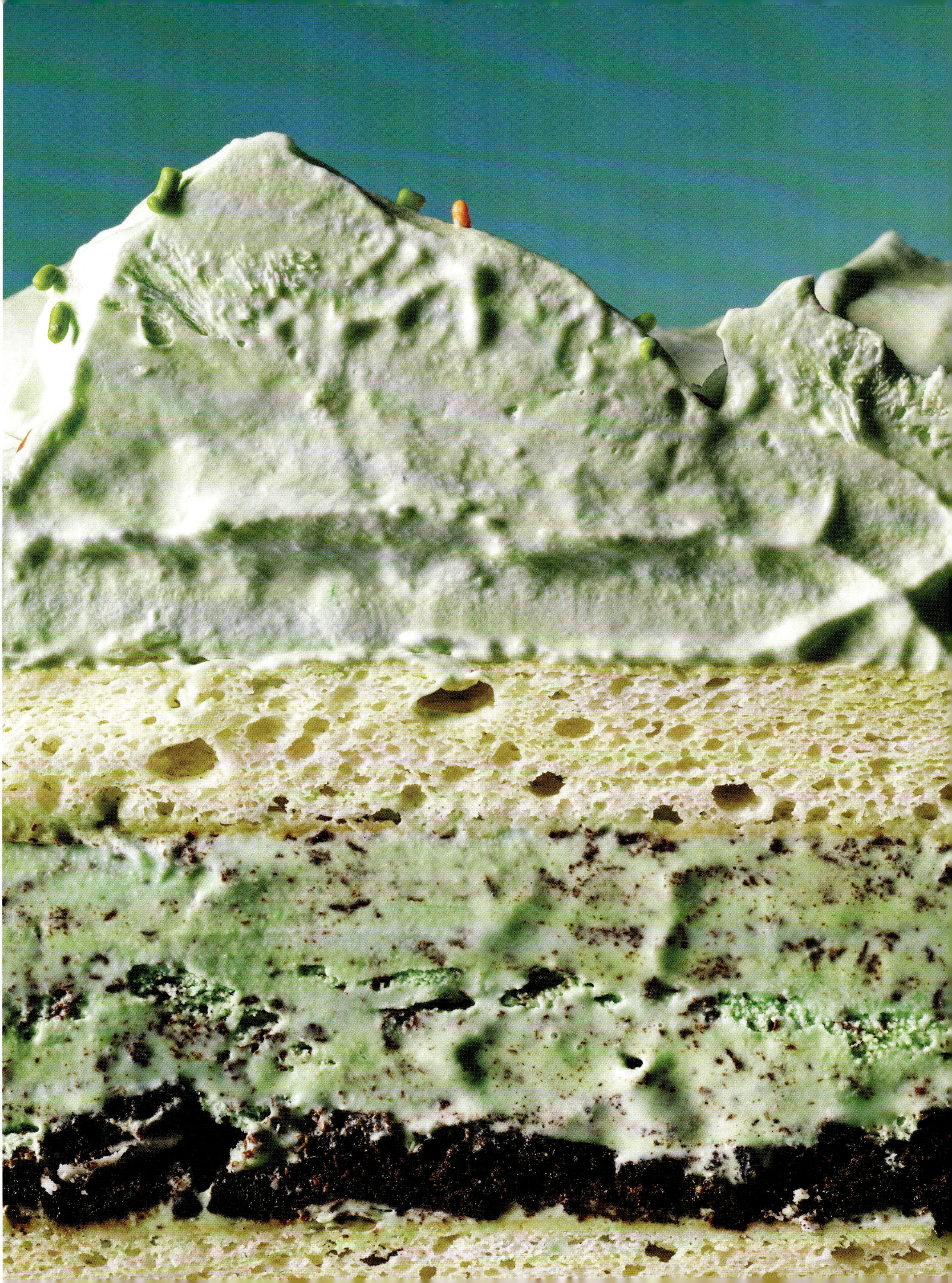

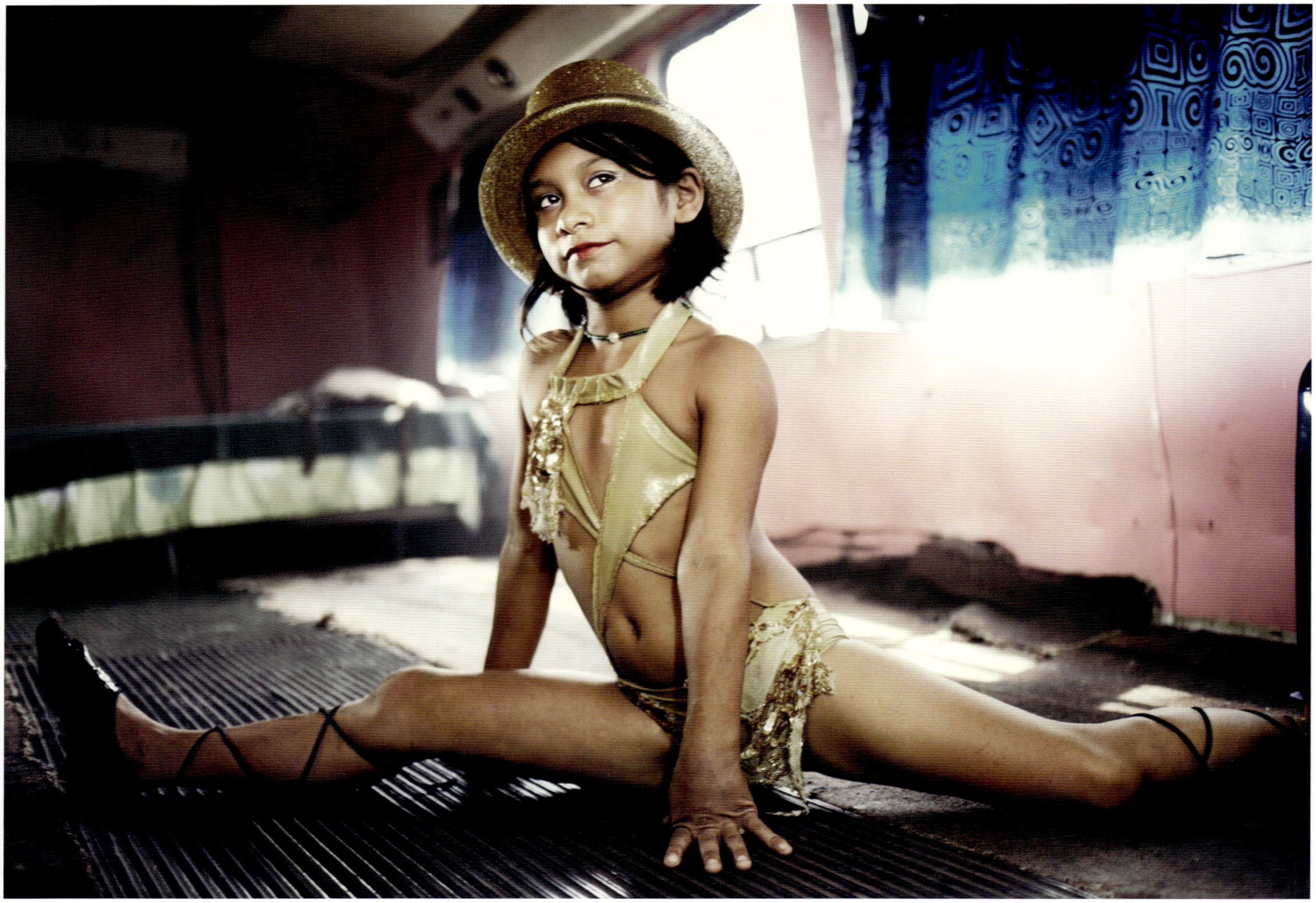

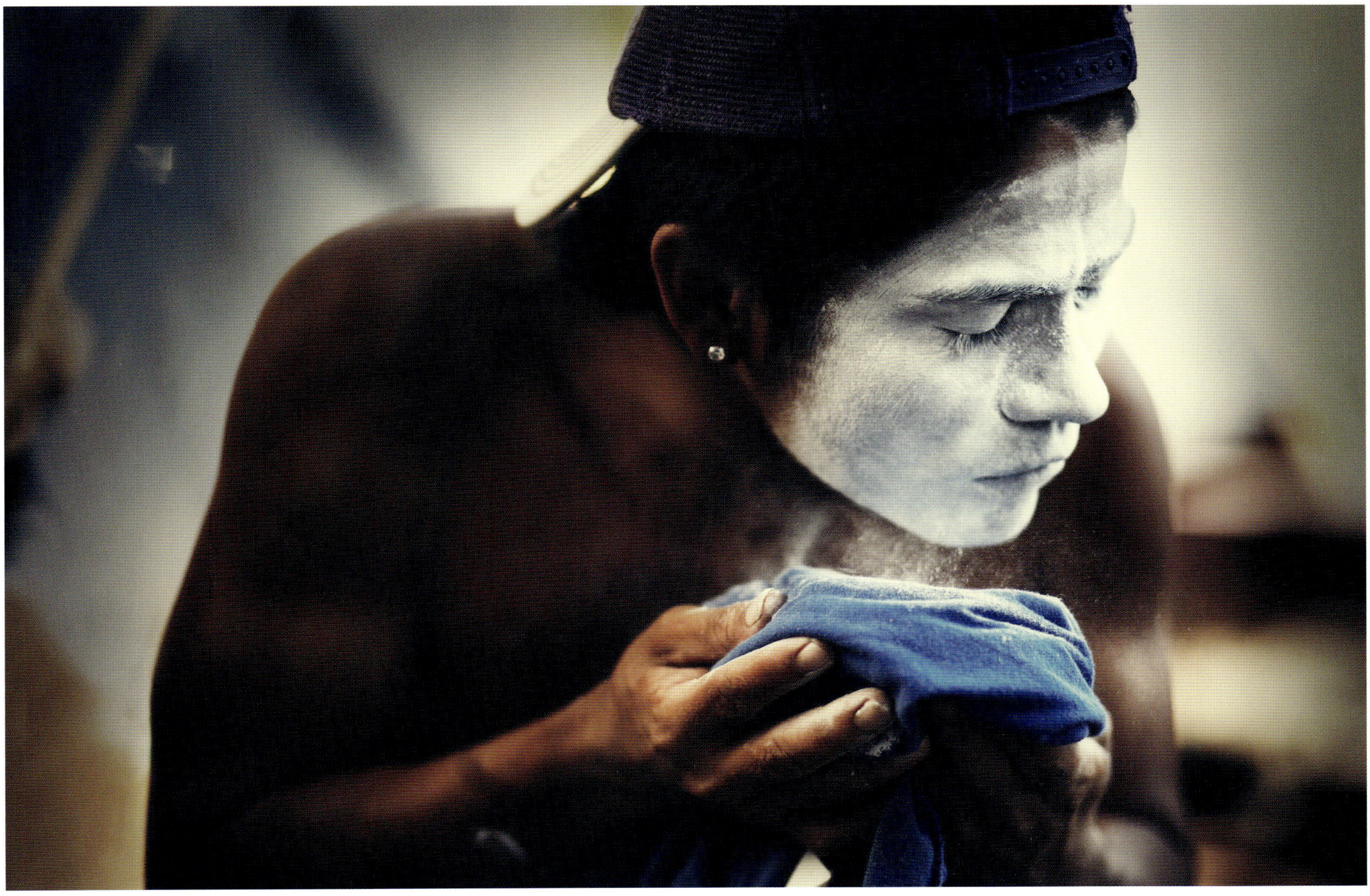

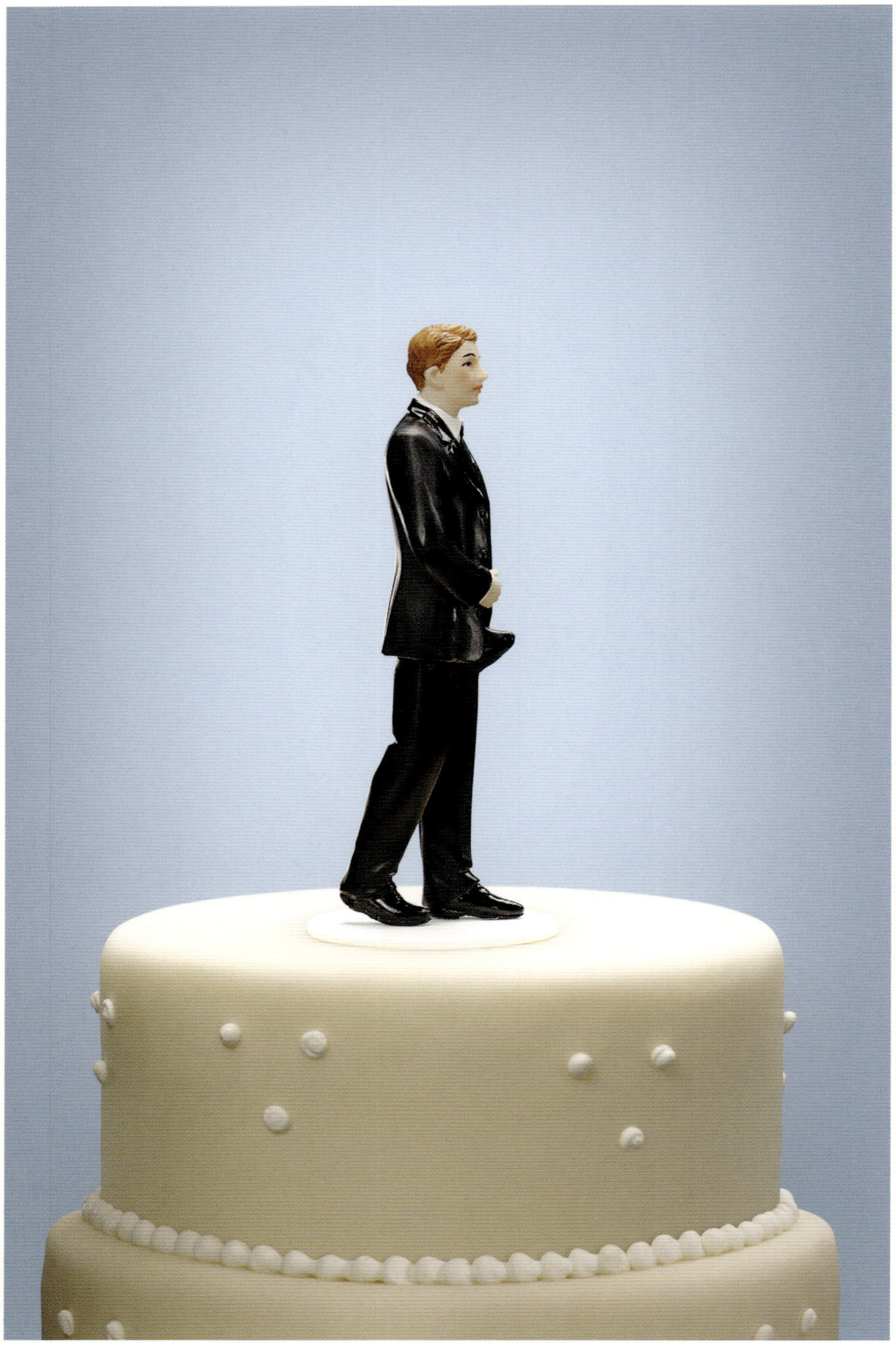

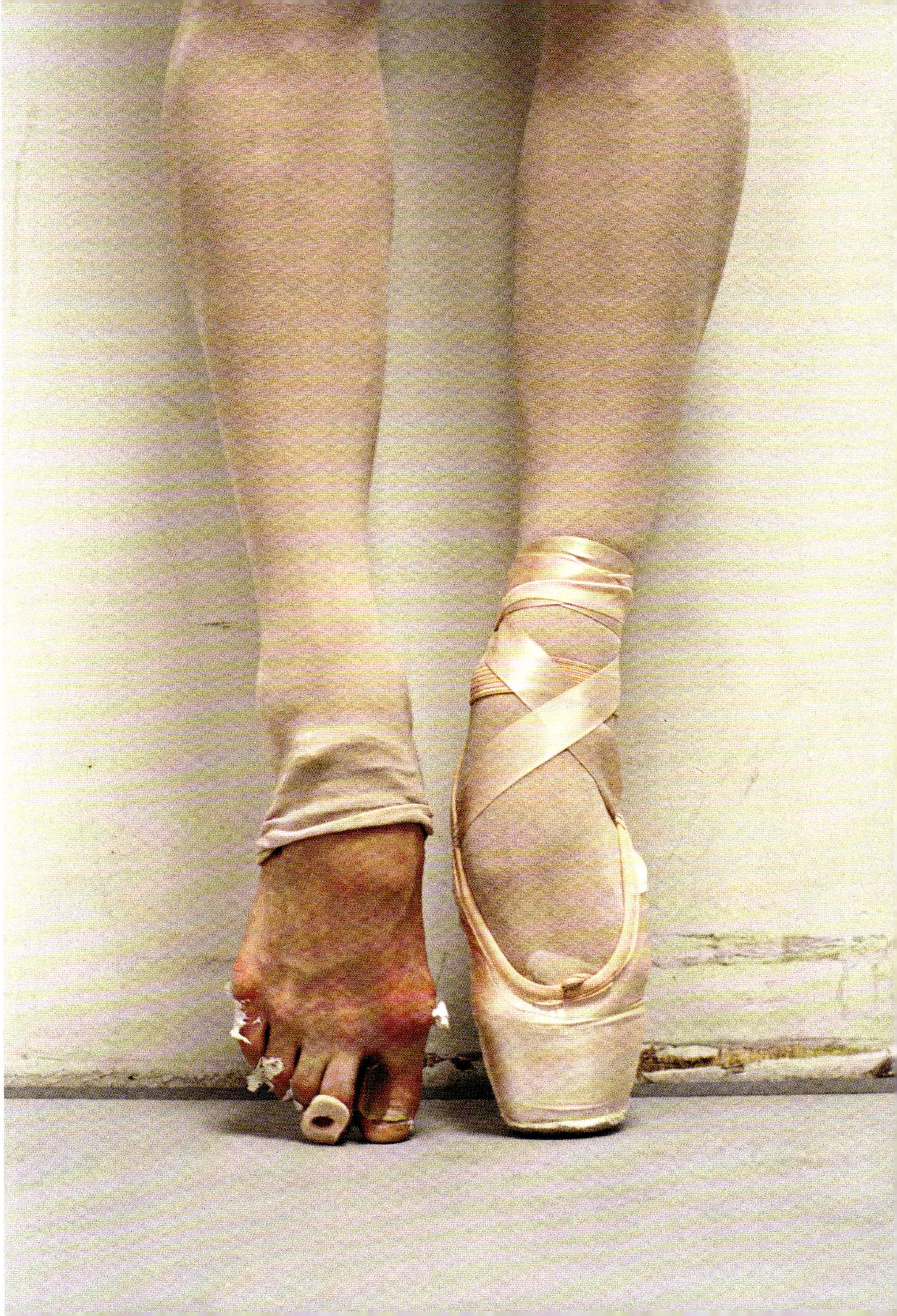

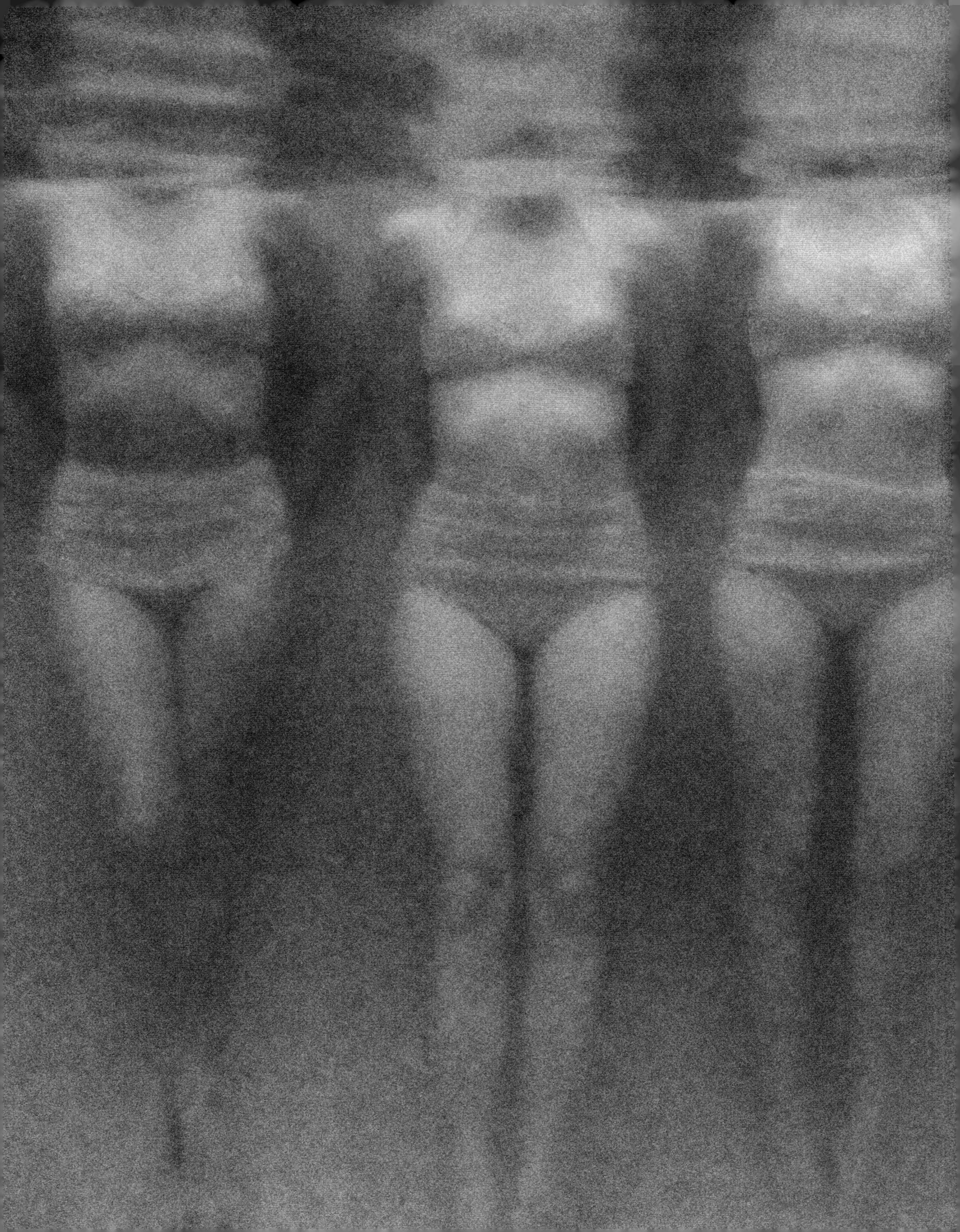

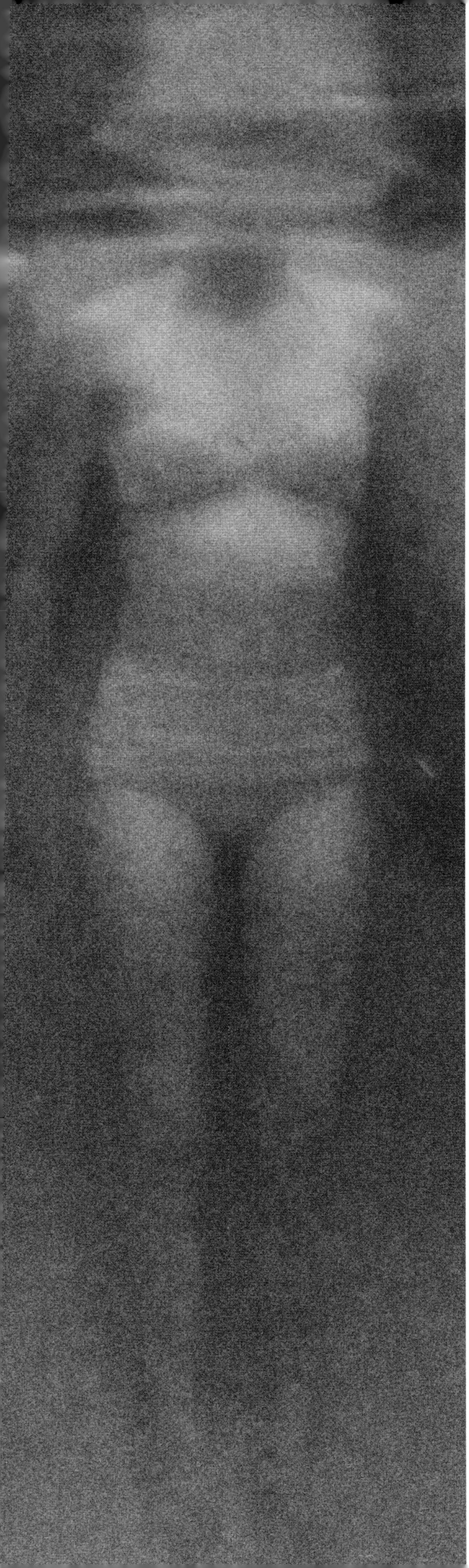

TAMAR LEVINE

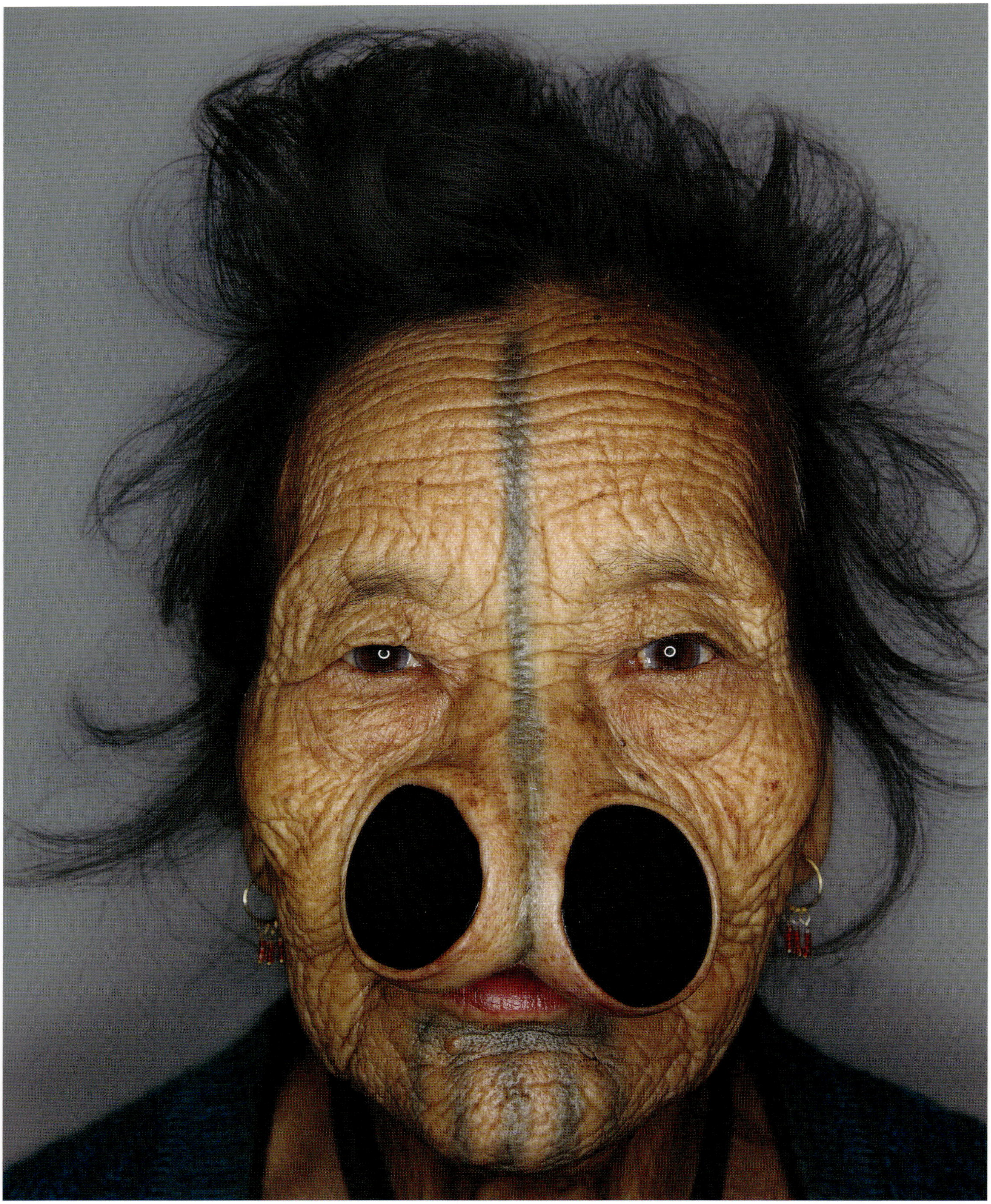

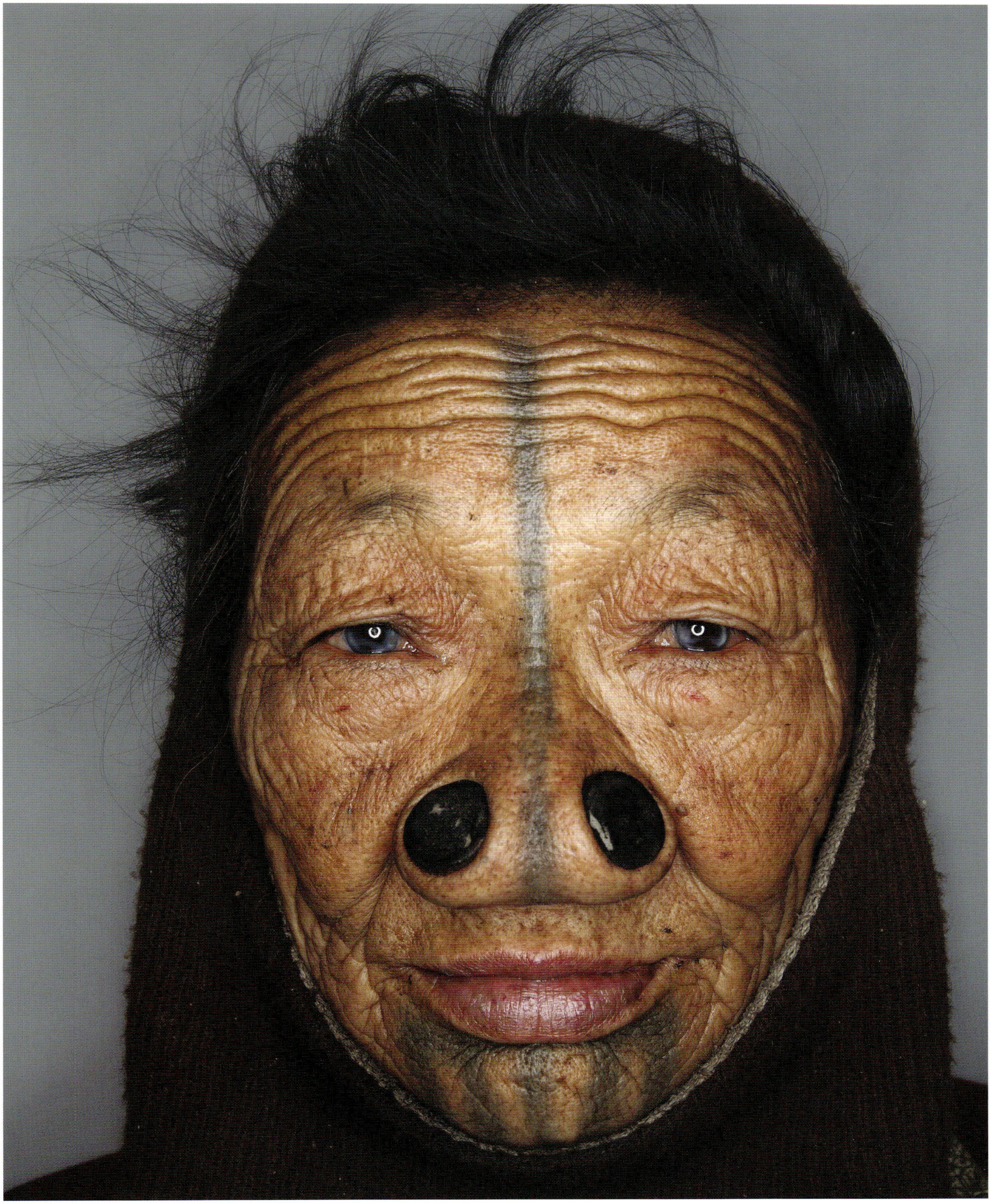

BRENT LEWIN

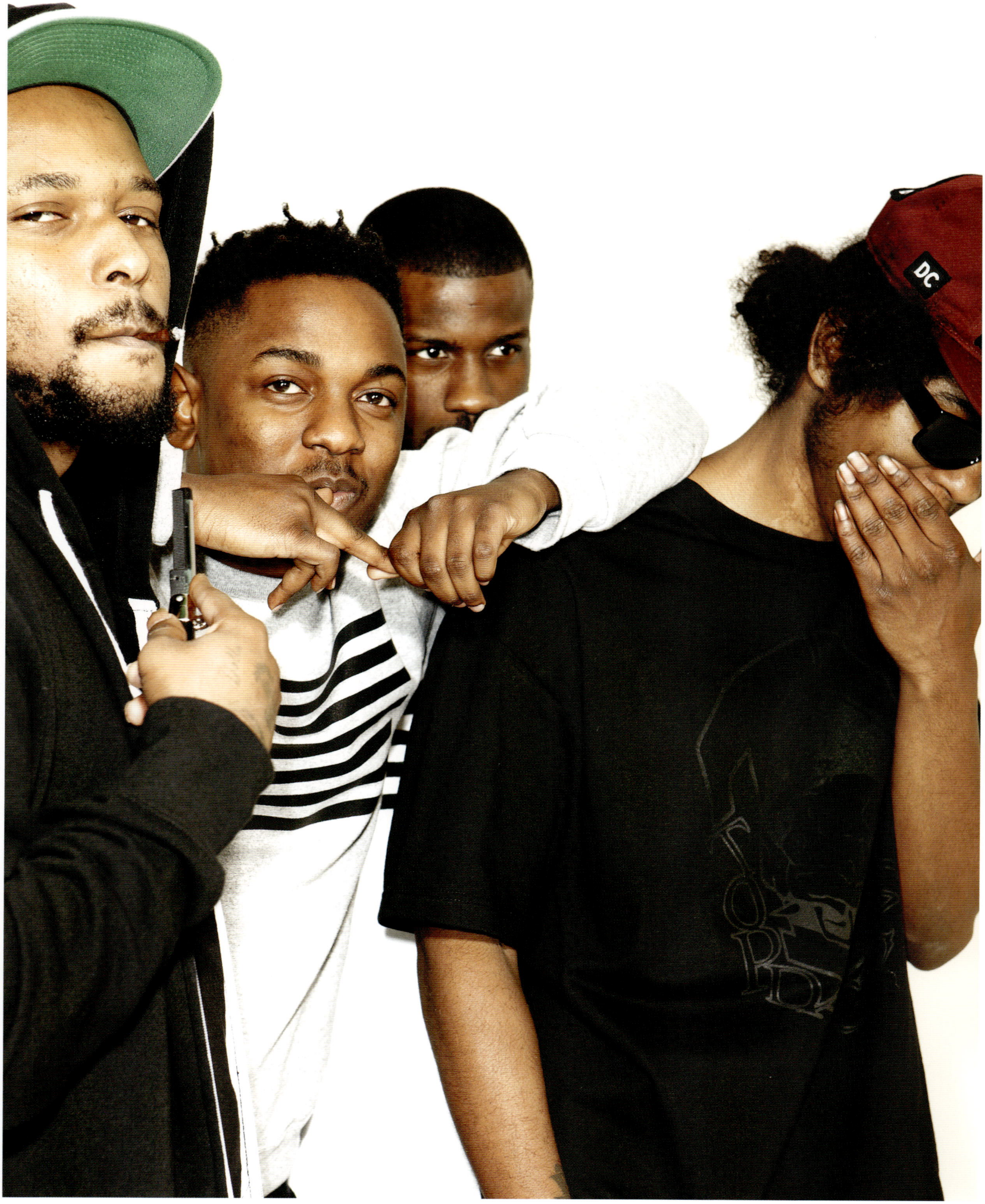
DC

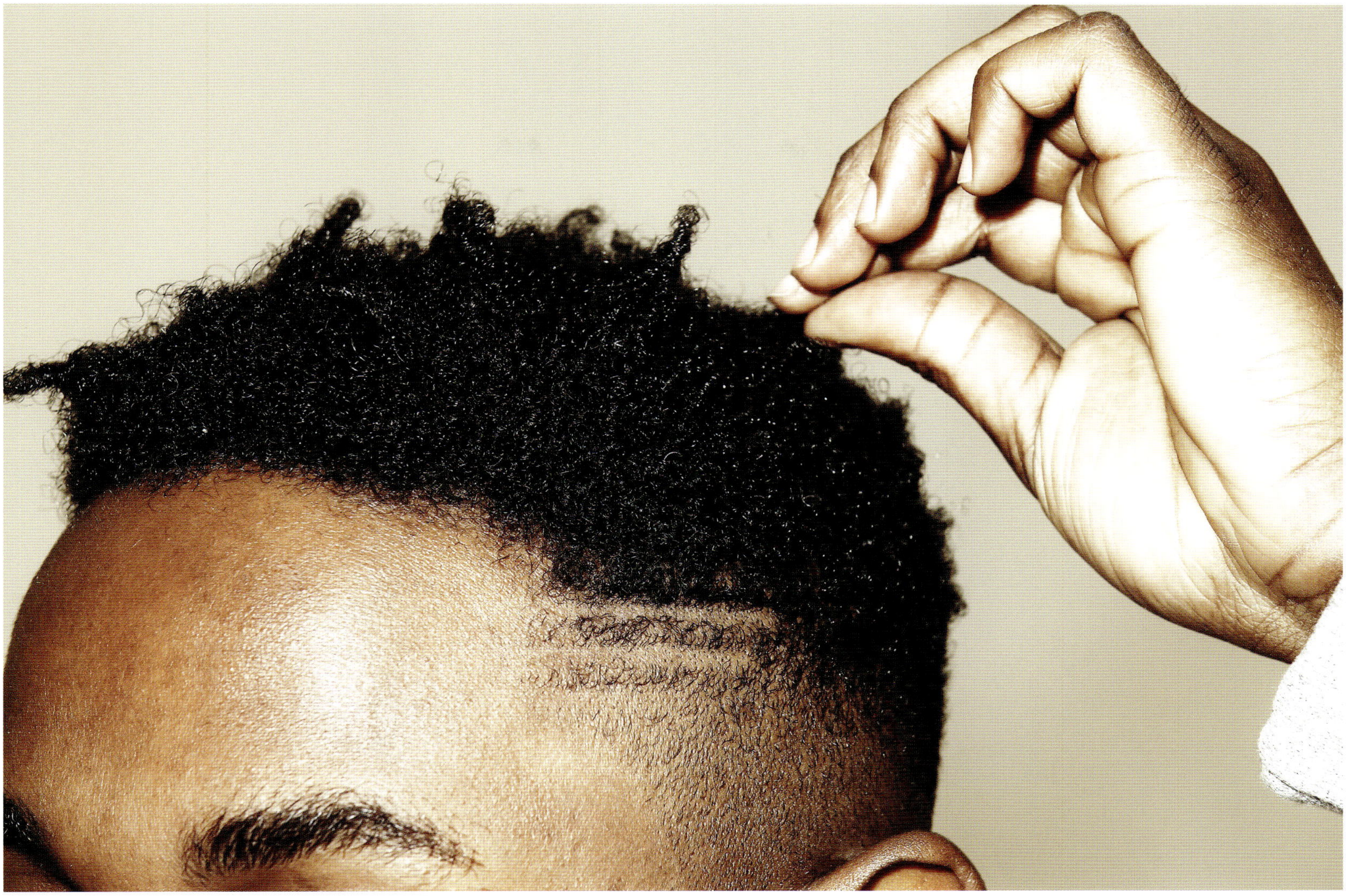

TURE LILLEGRAVEN

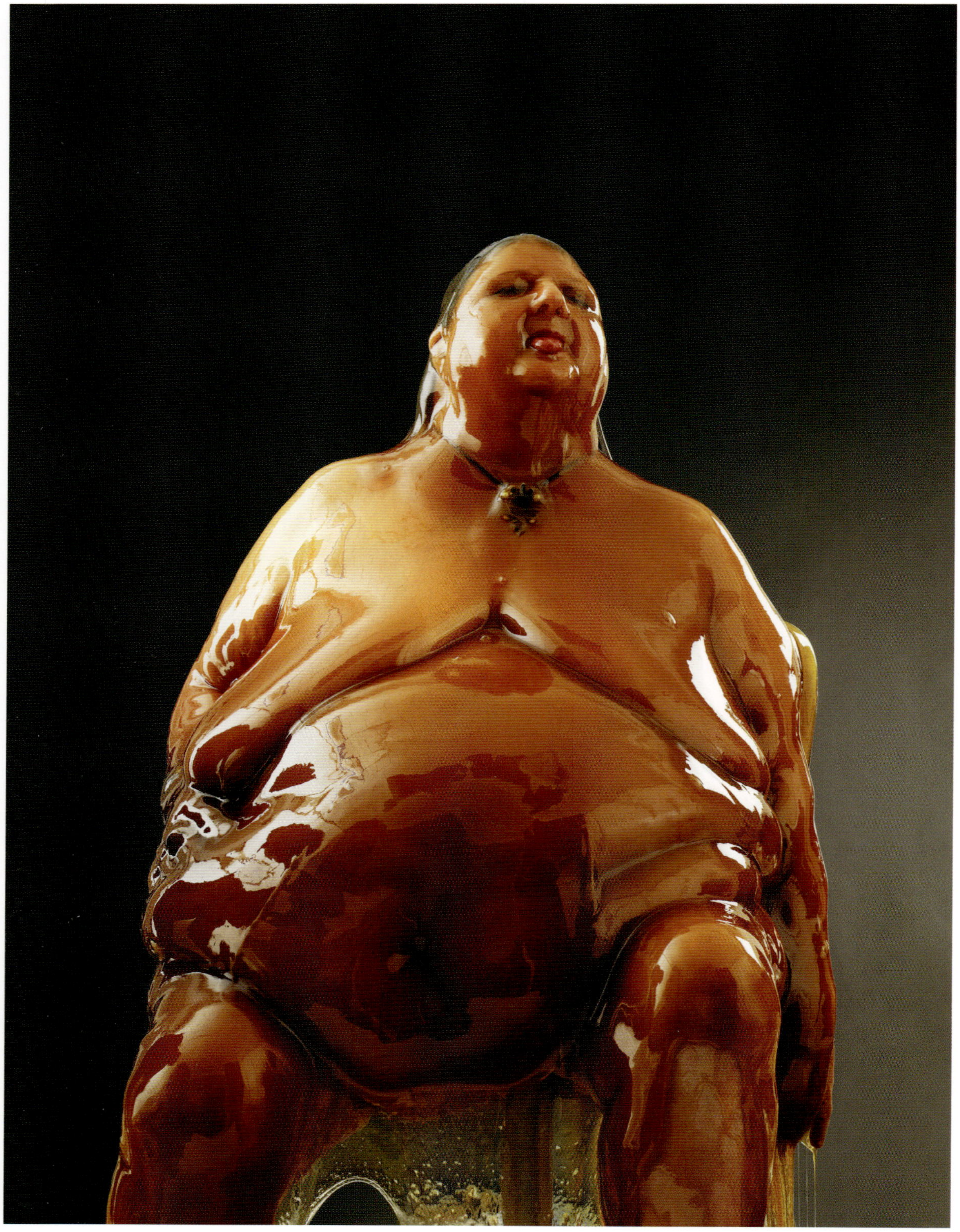

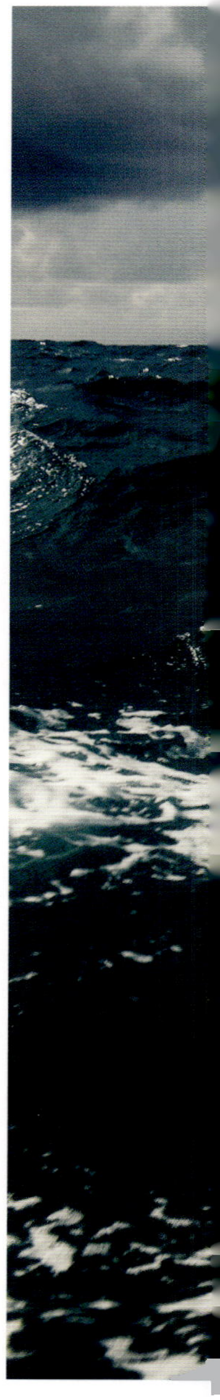

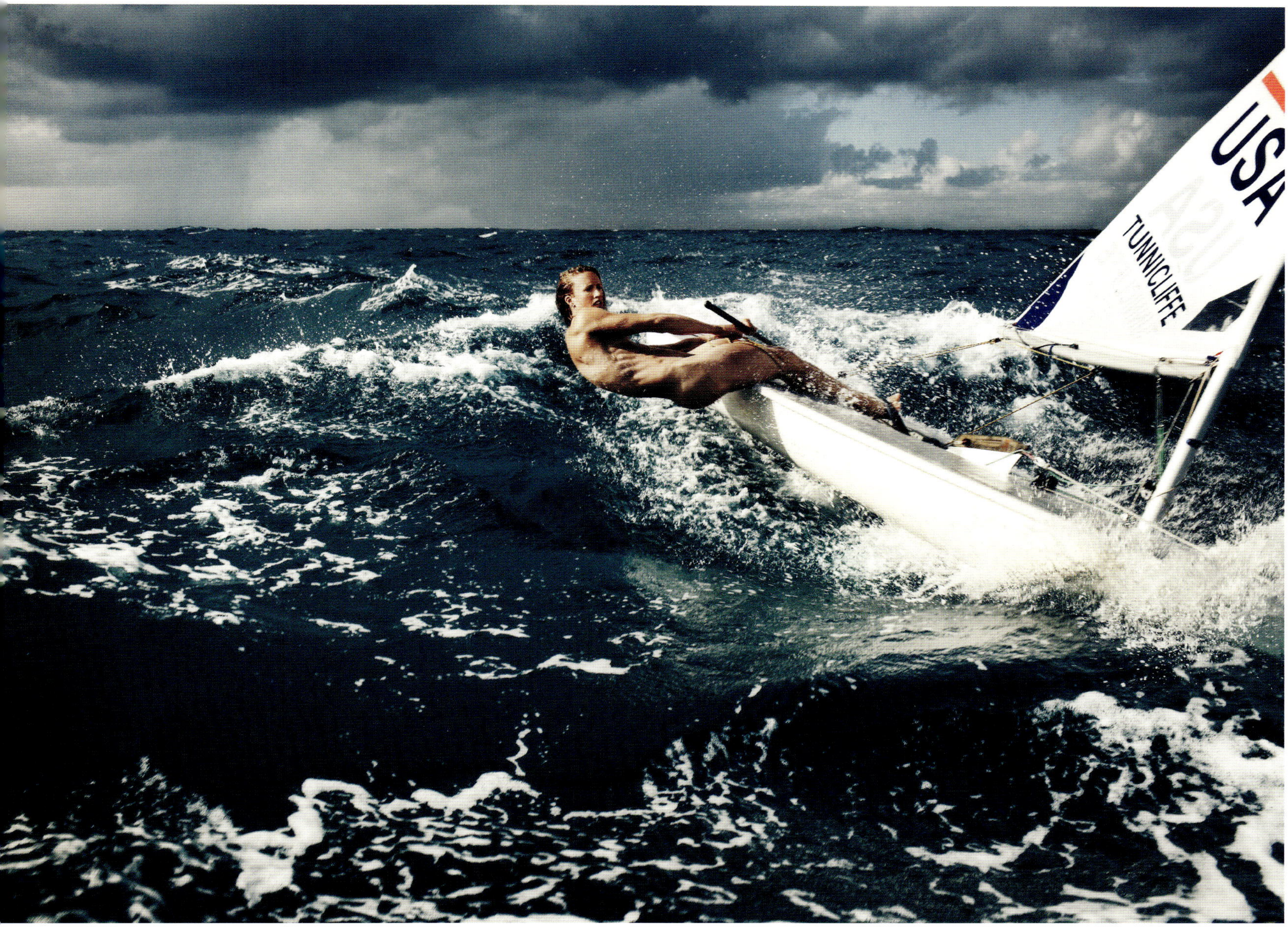

STEVEN LIPPMAN

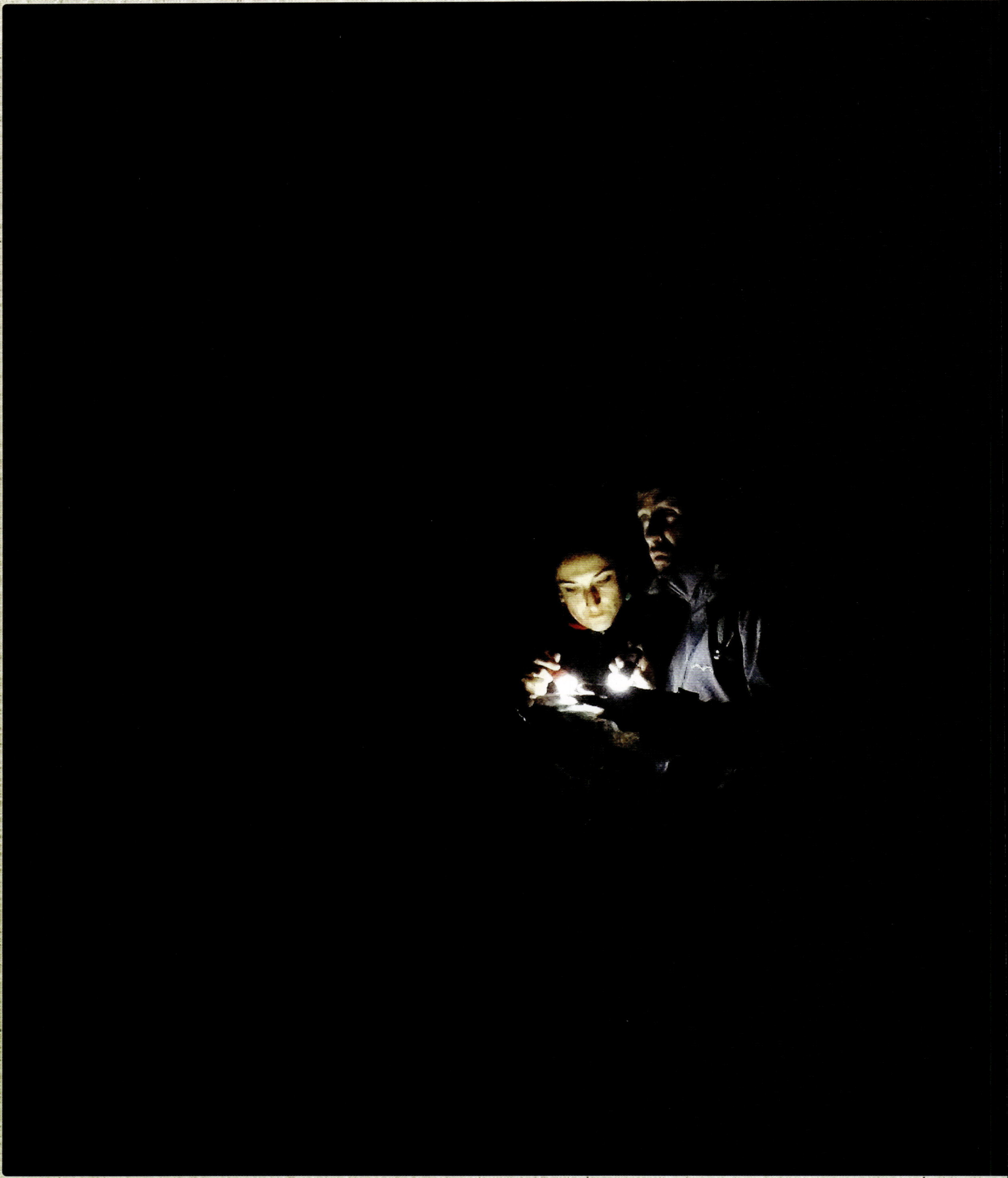

BENJAMIN LOWY

182 / 183 / 184

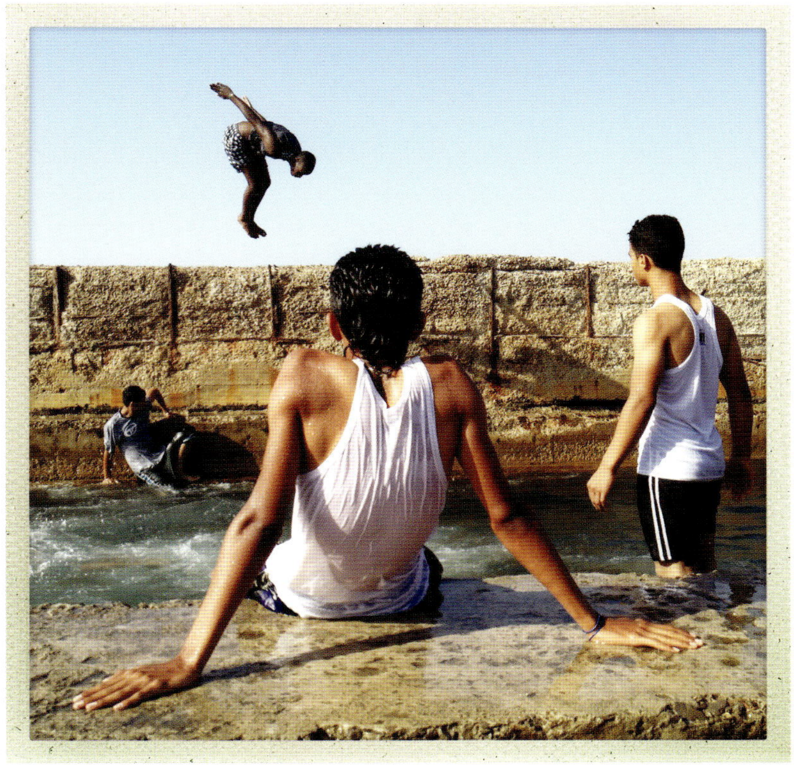

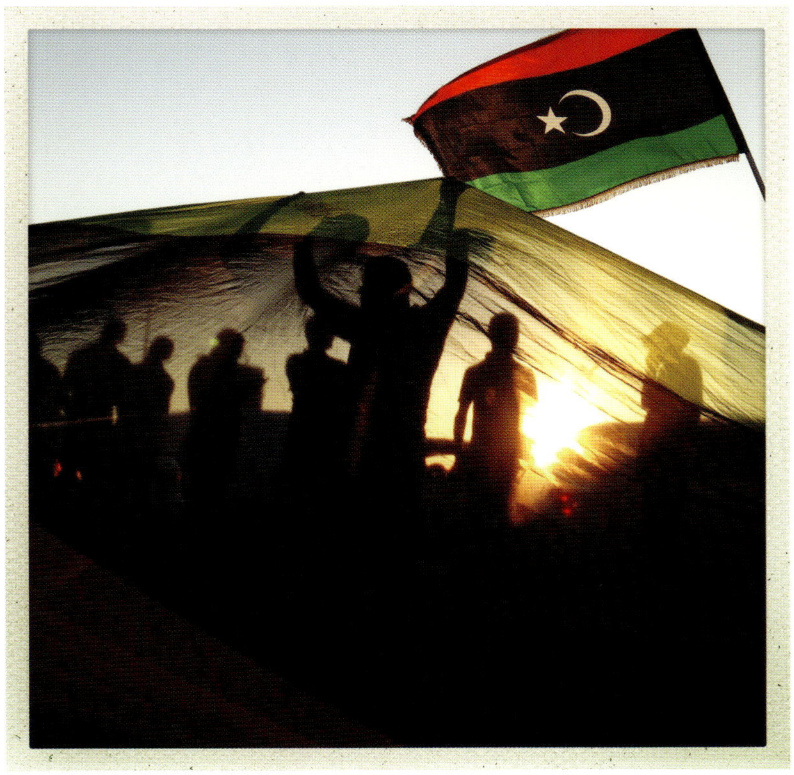

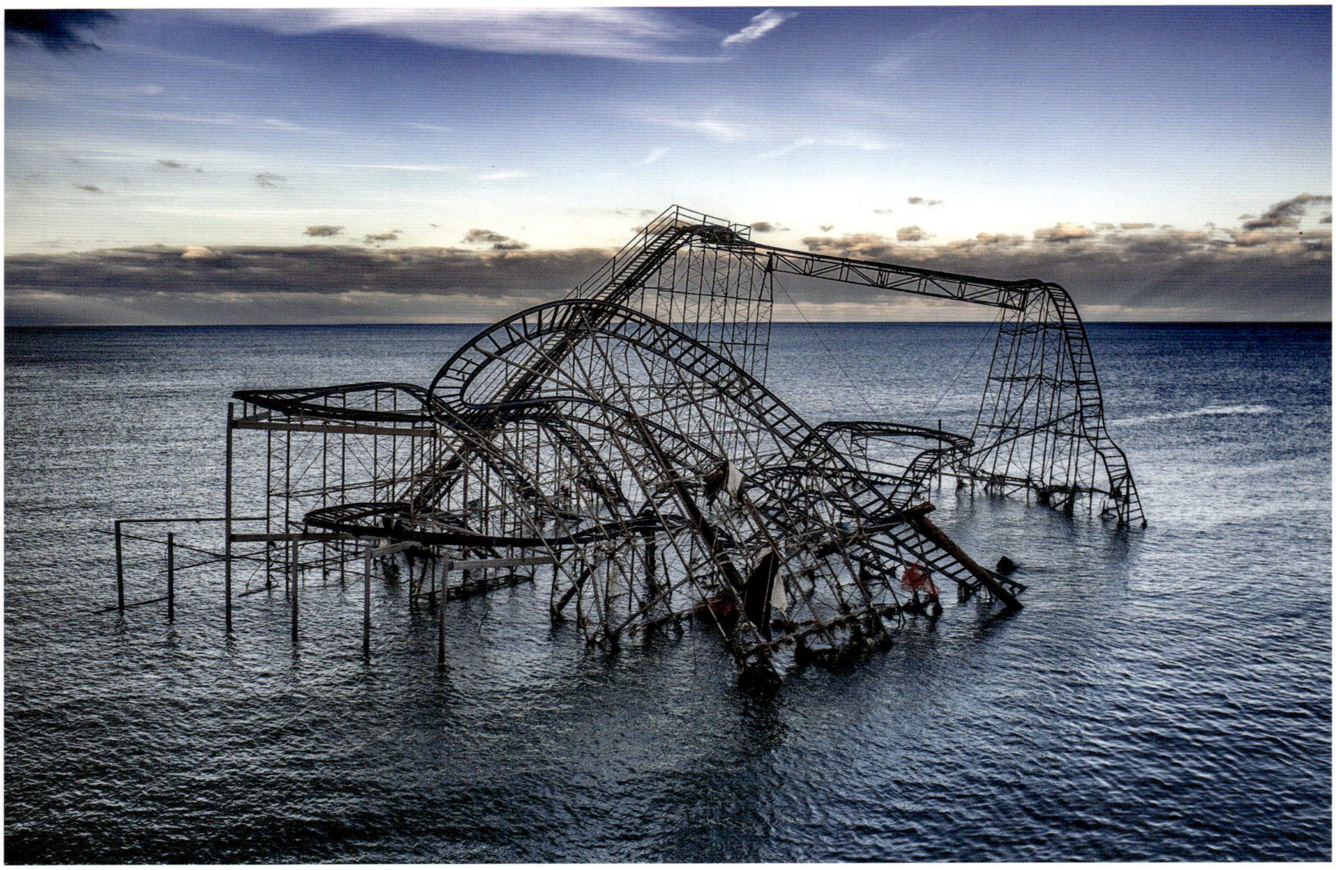

BENJAMIN LOWY

185 / 186

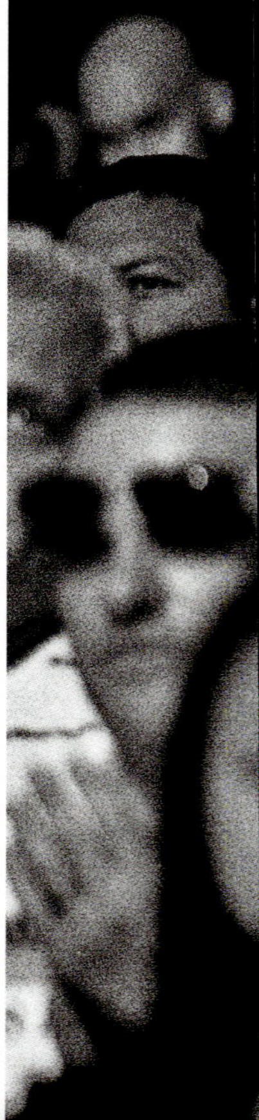

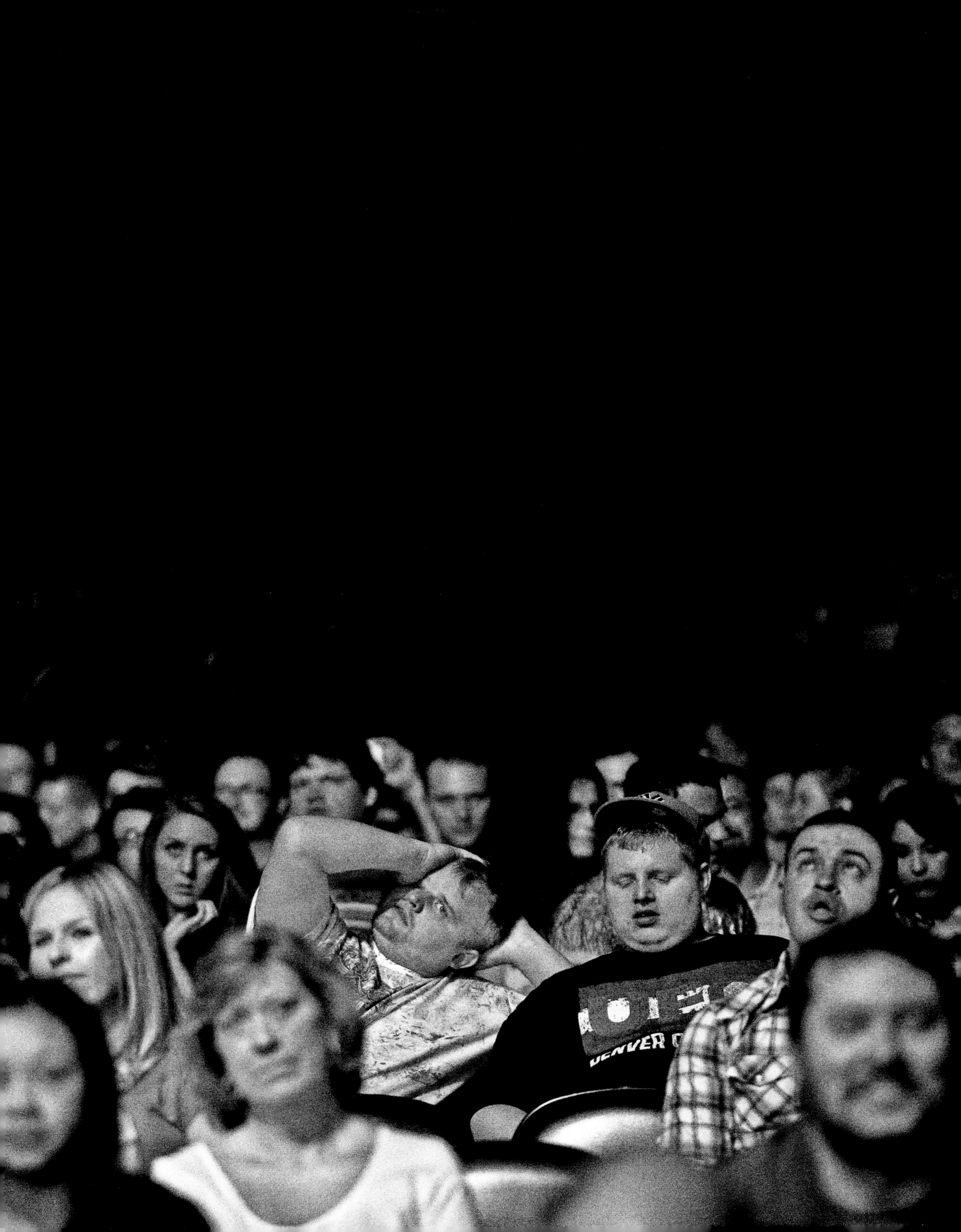

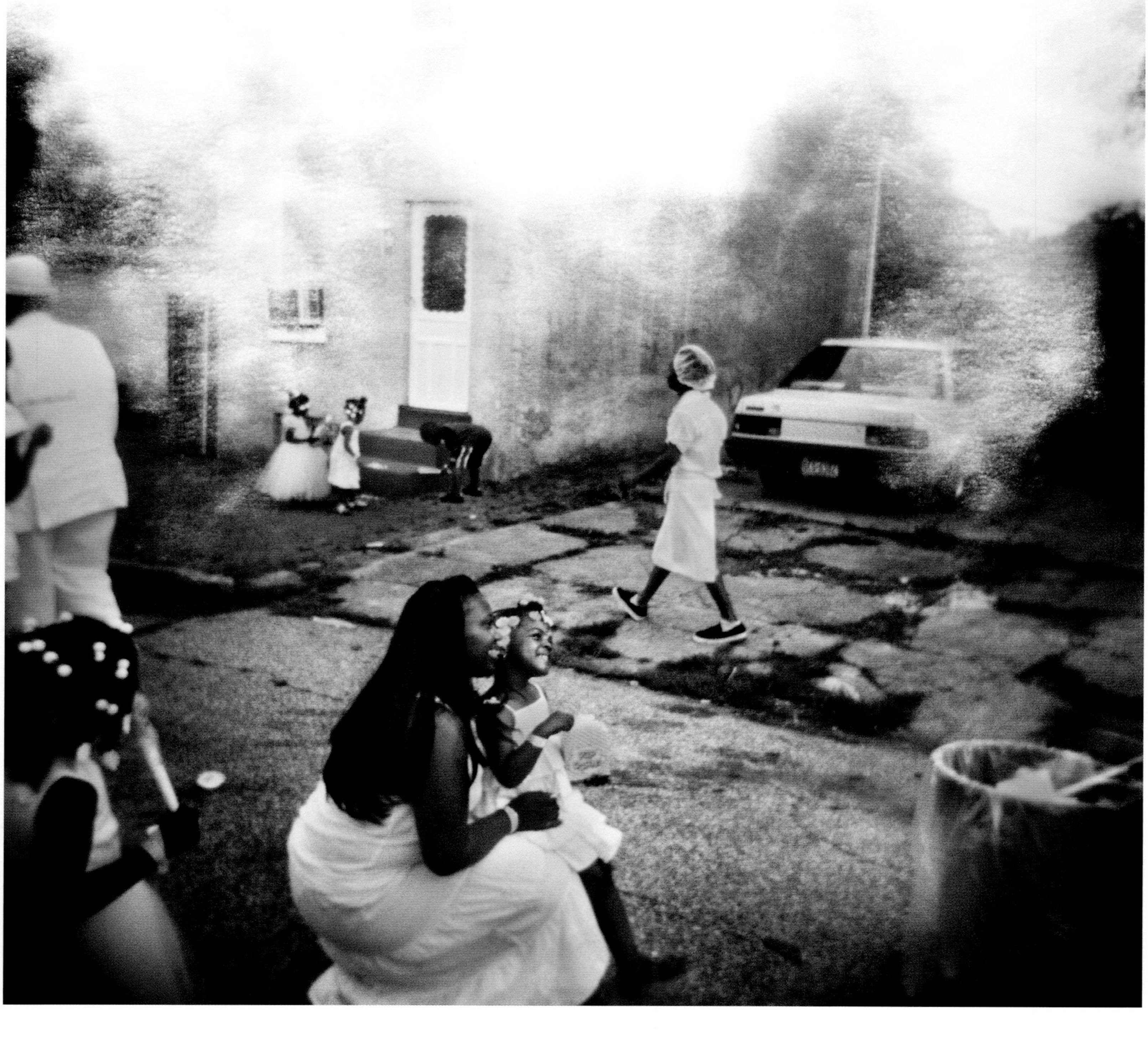

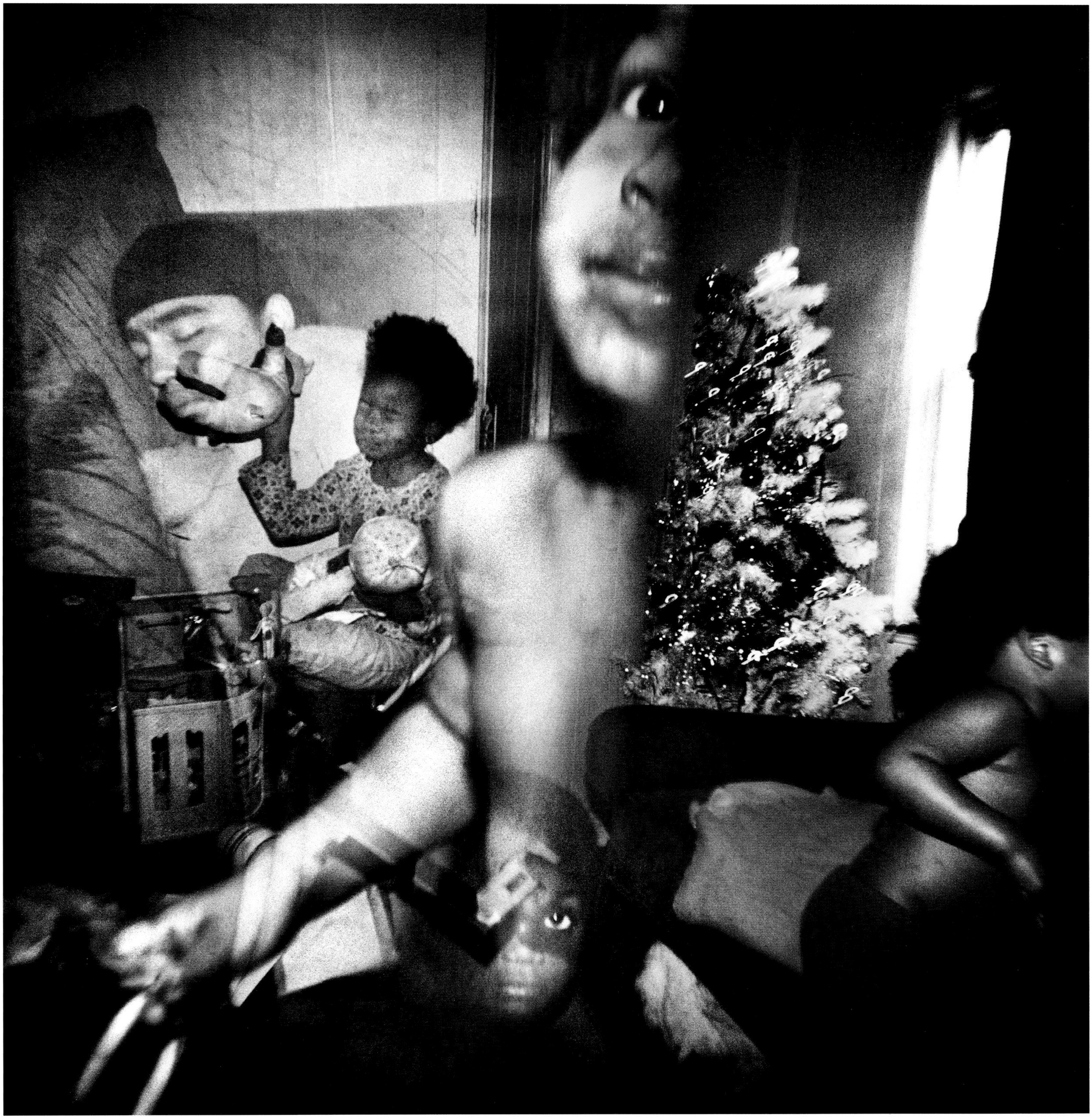

JUSTIN MAXON

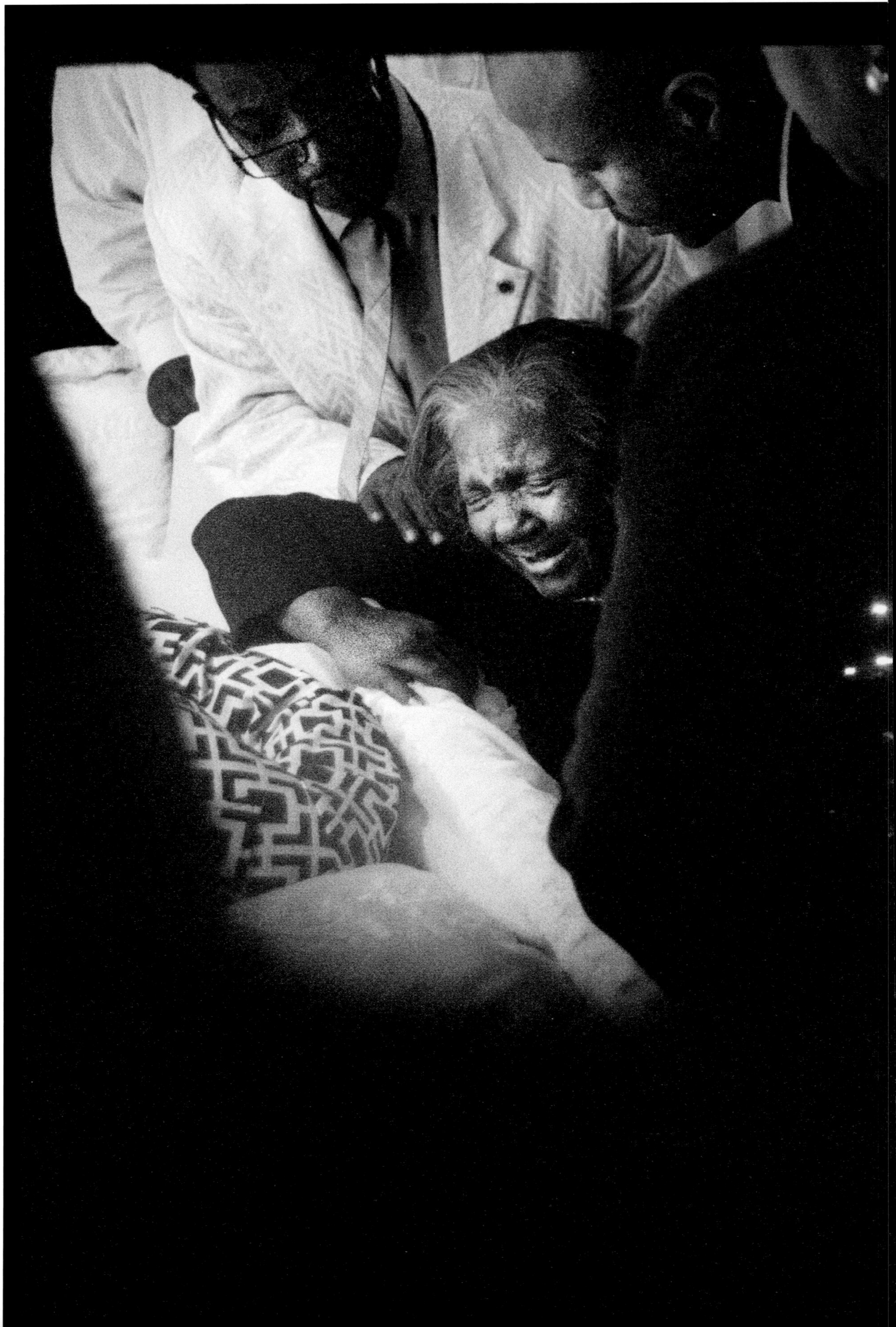

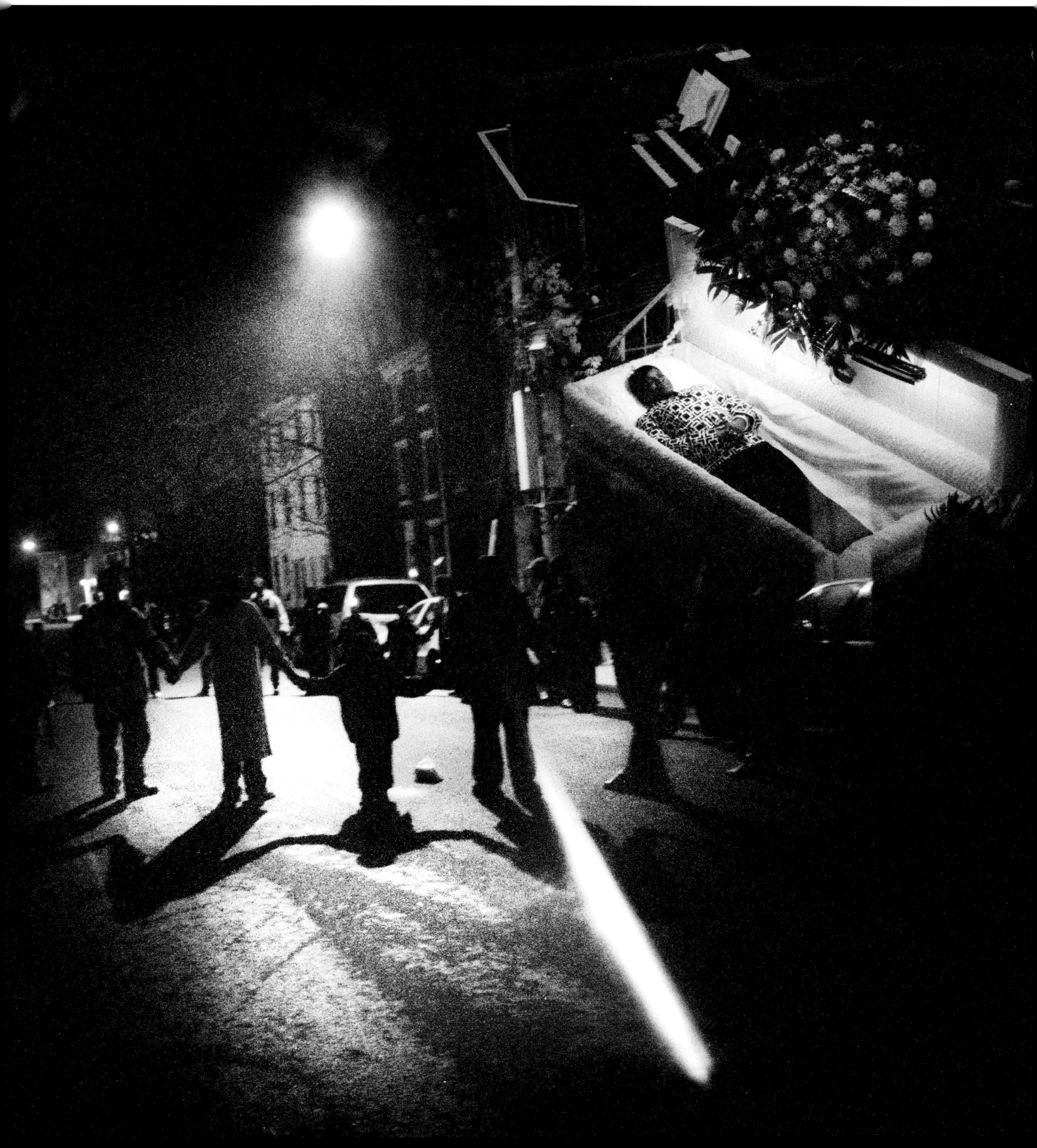

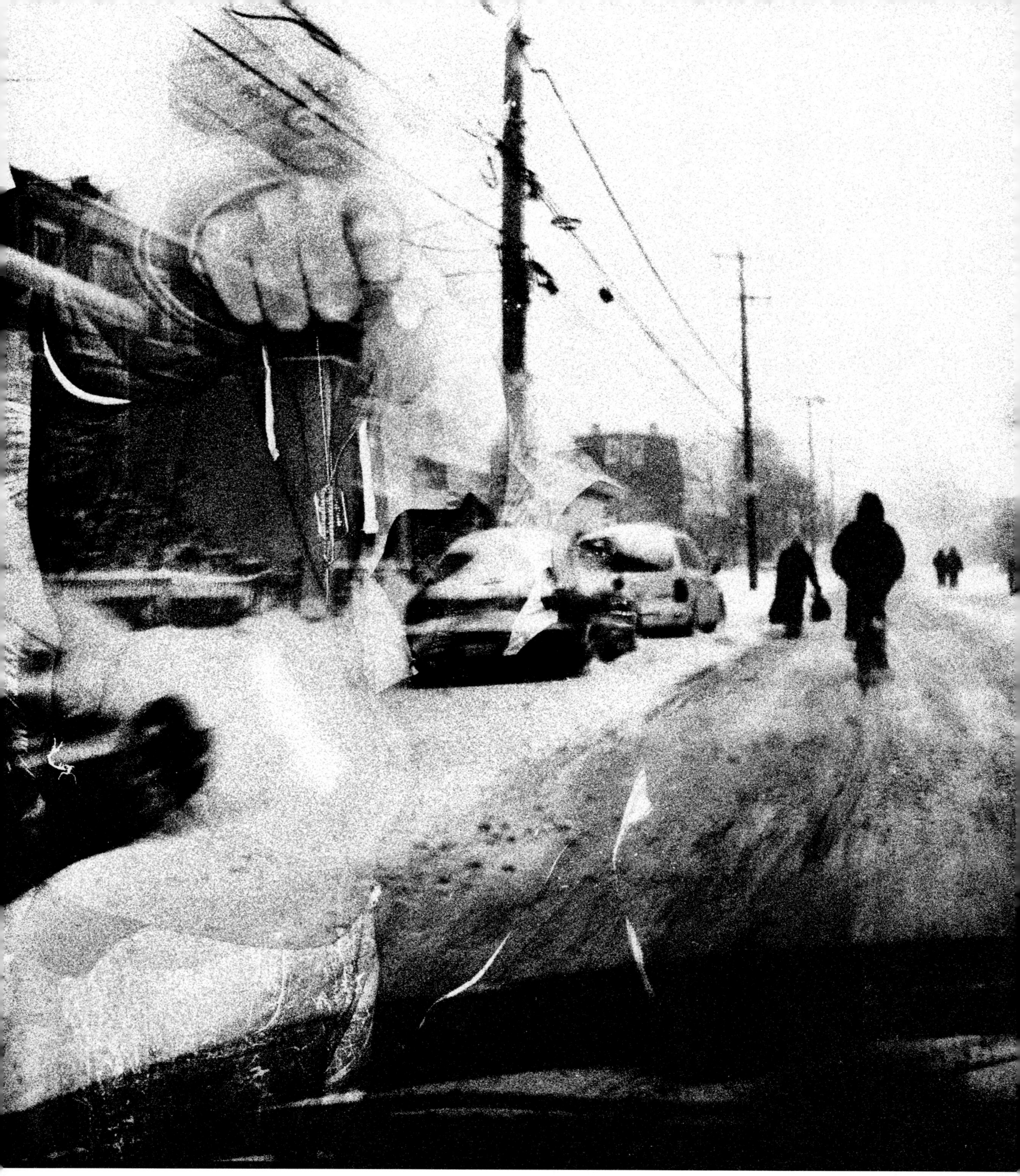

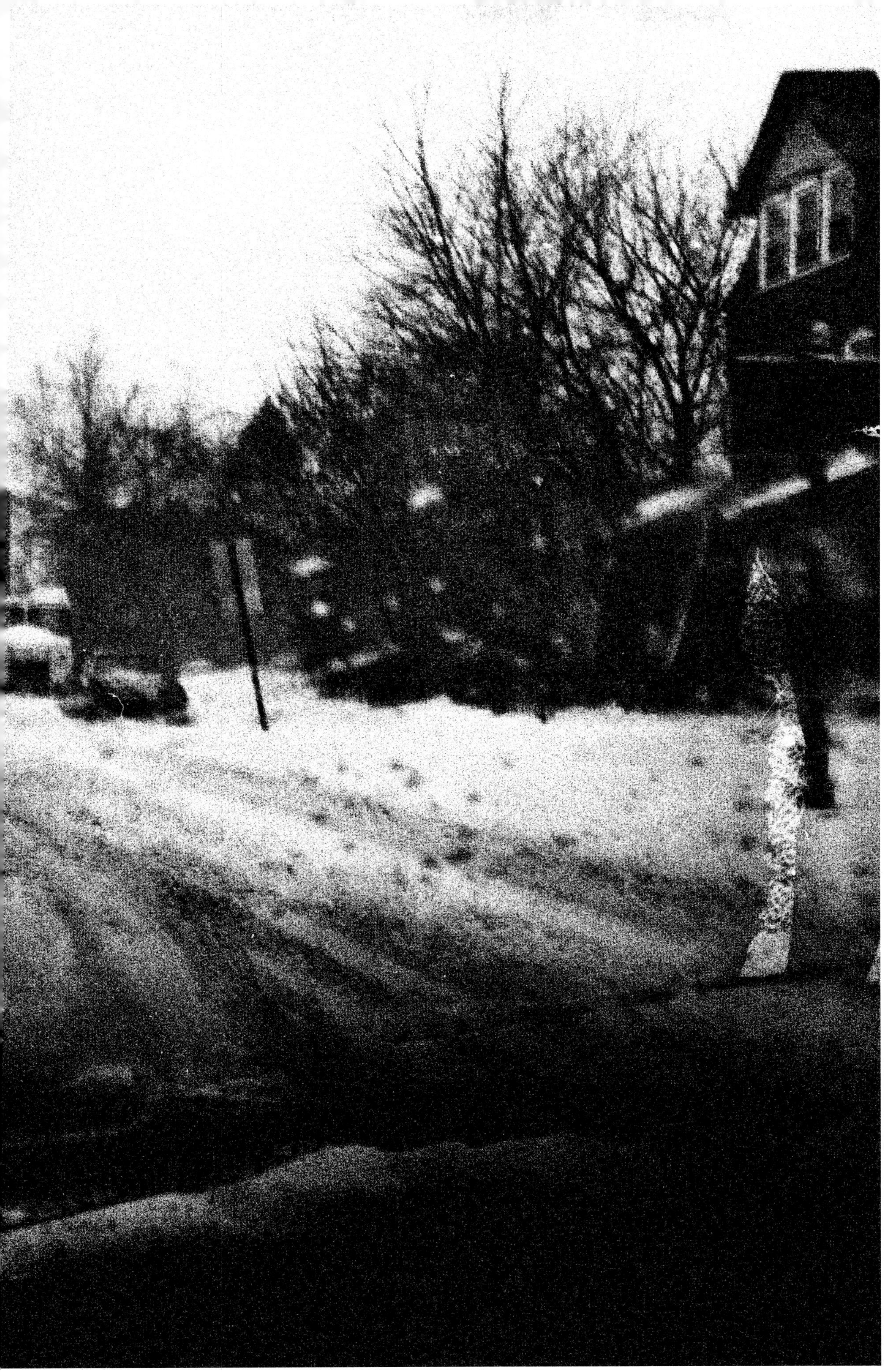

JUSTIN MAXON

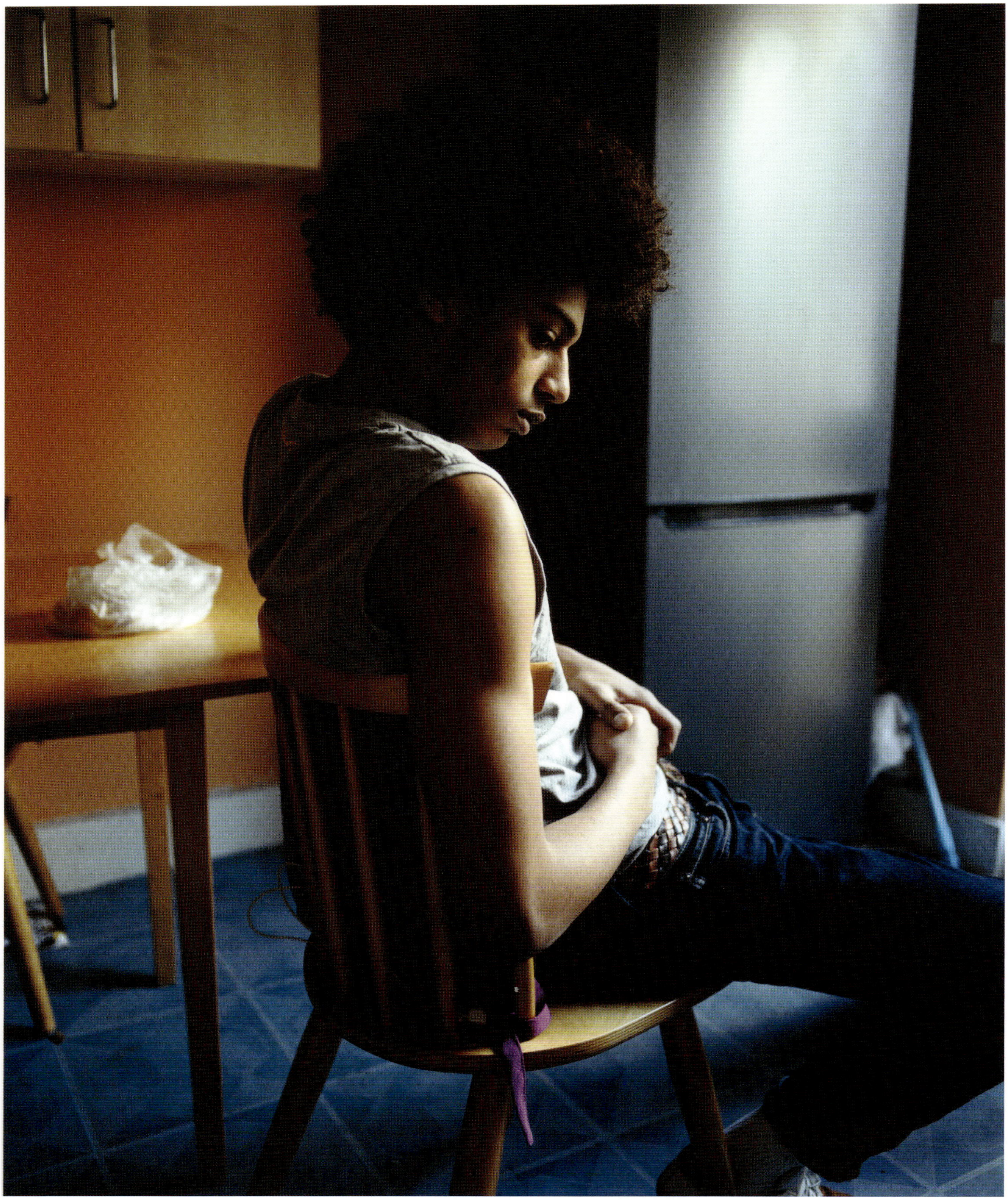

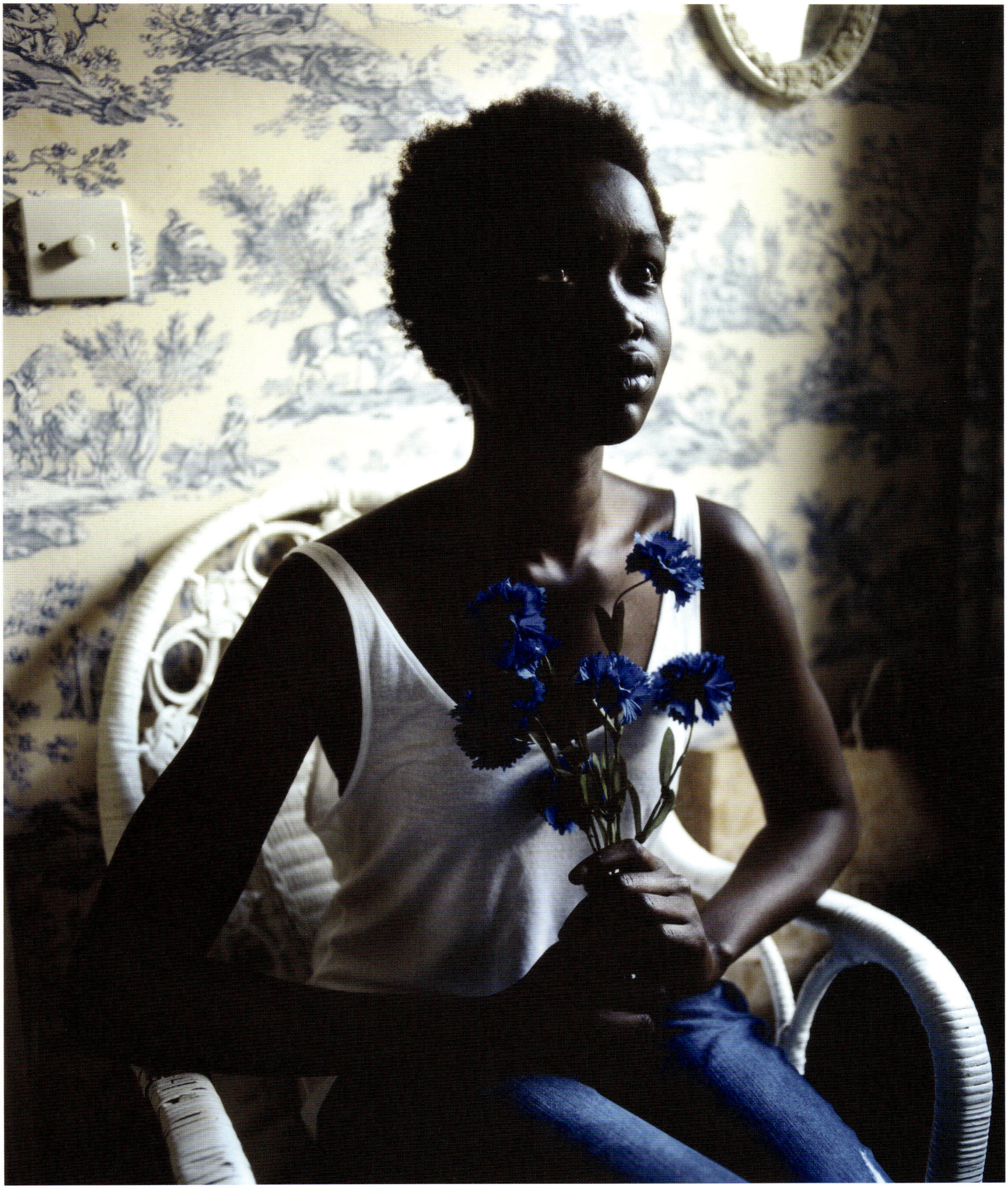

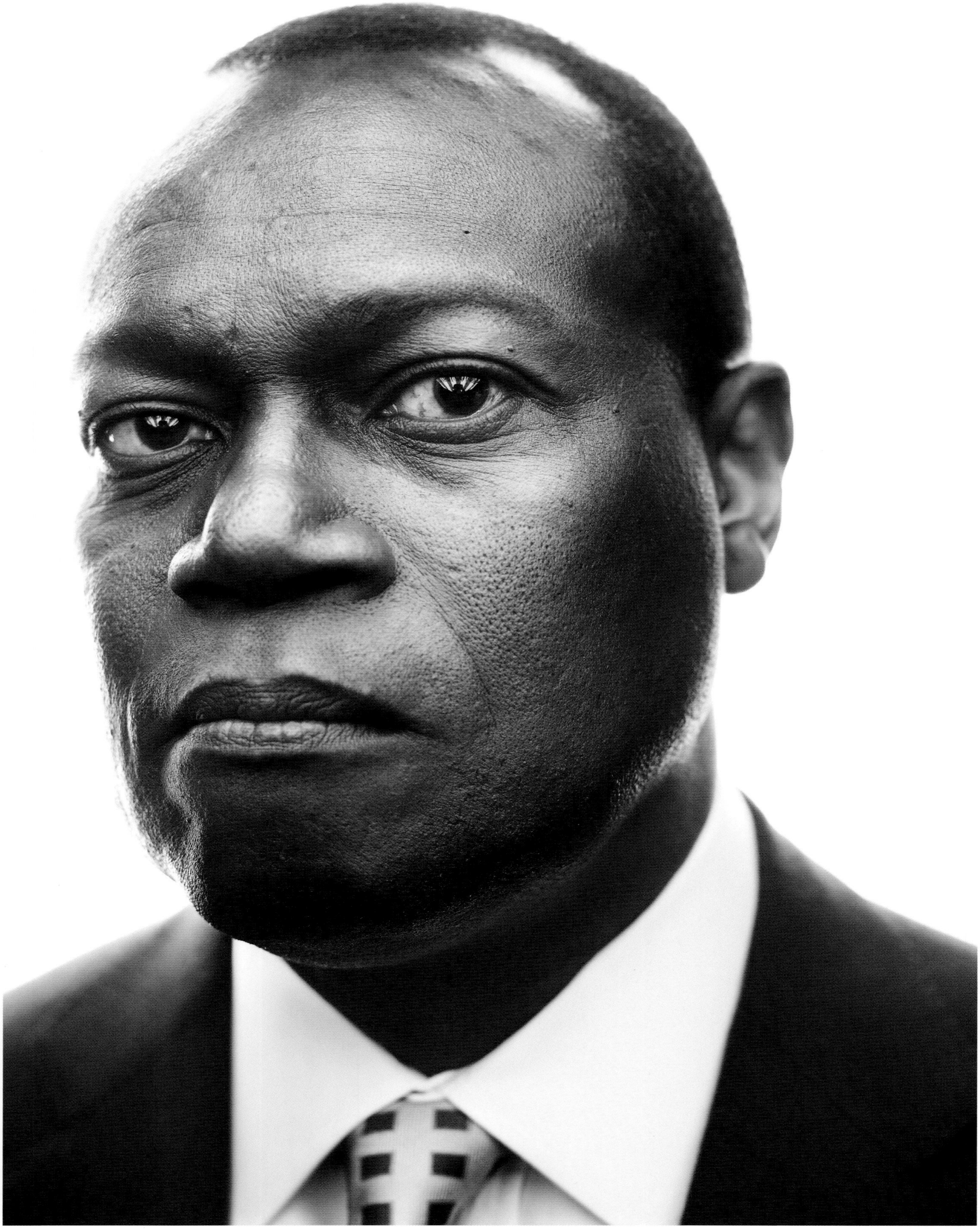

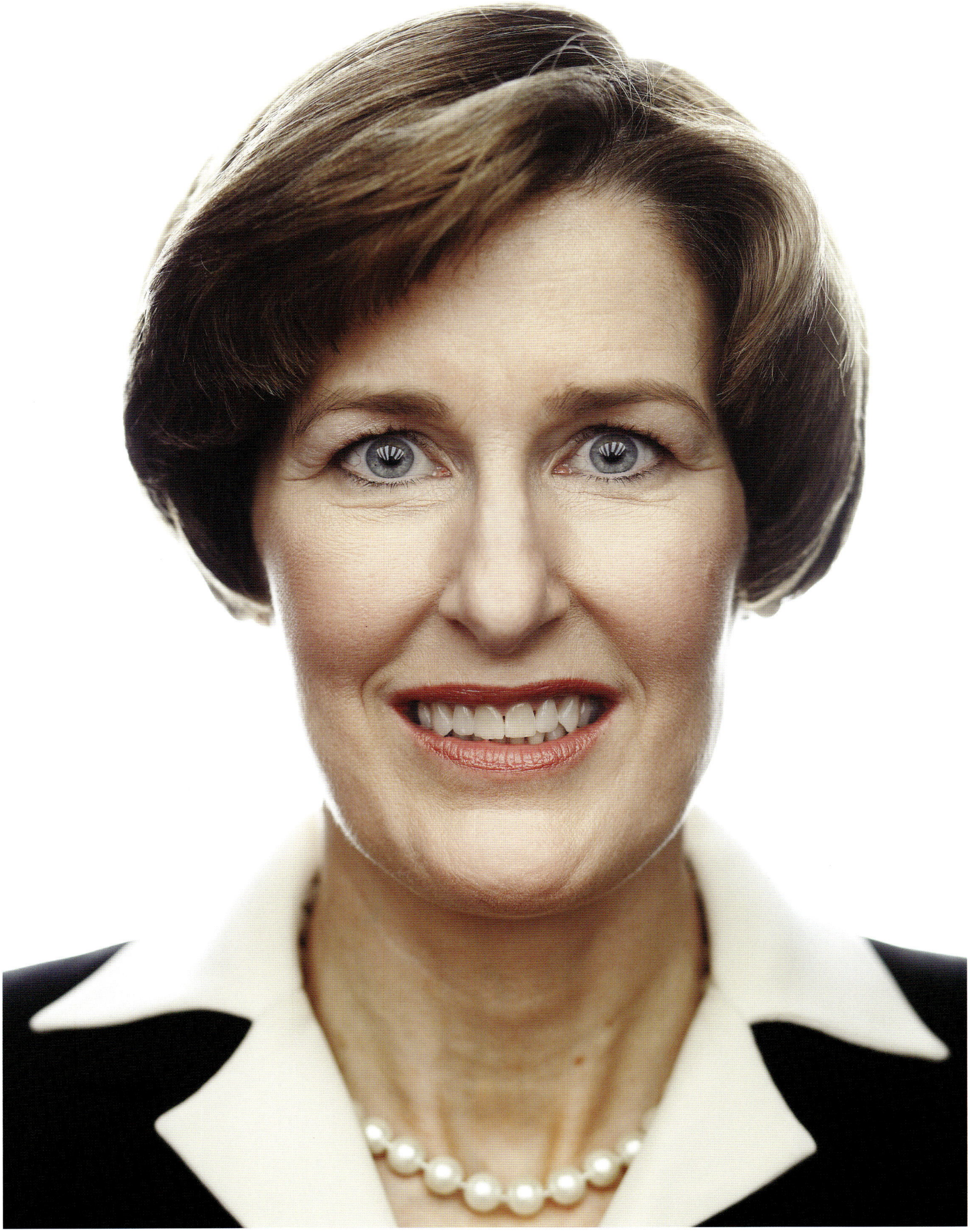

MIKE MCGREGOR

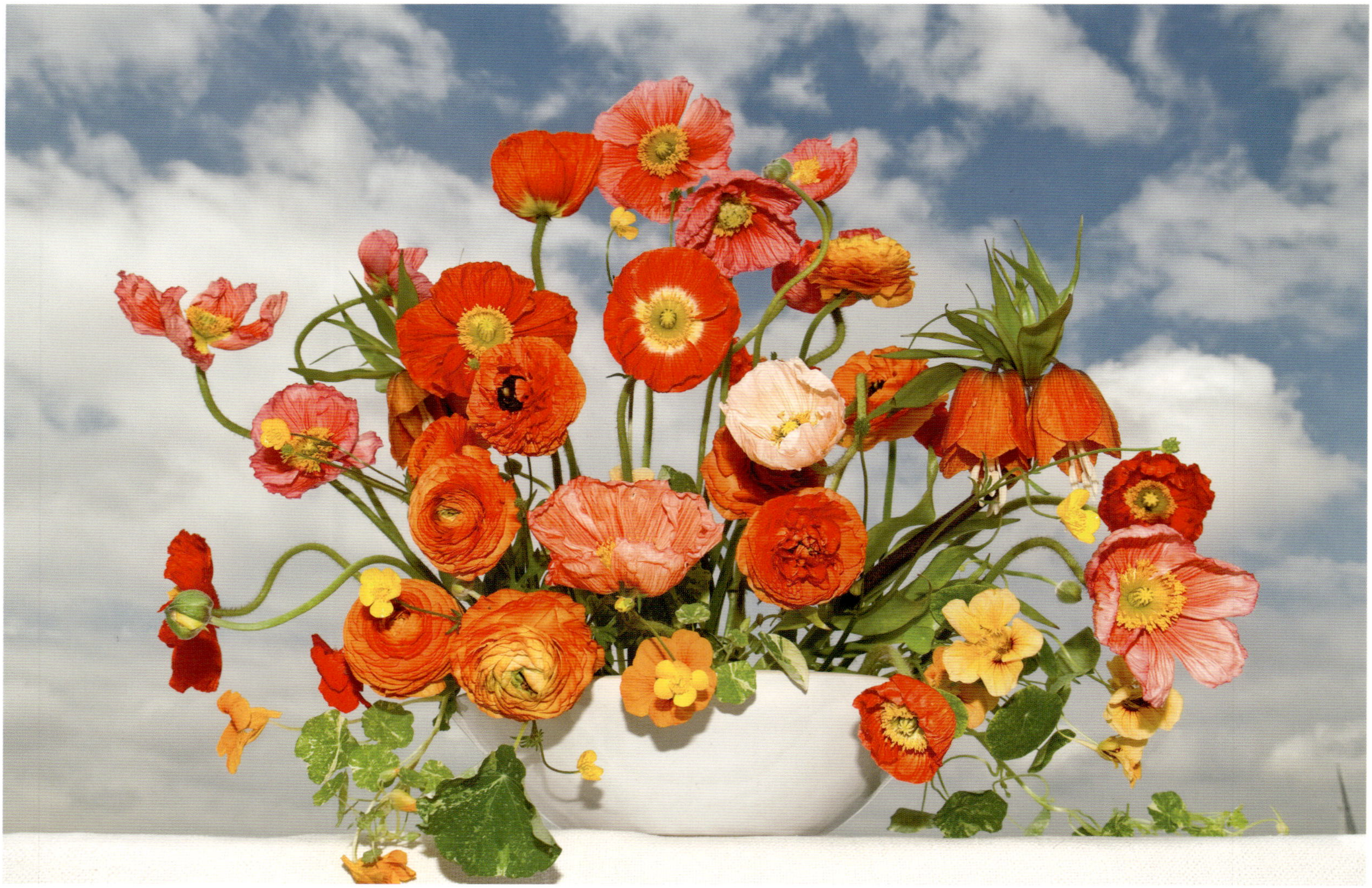

TONY MENDOZA

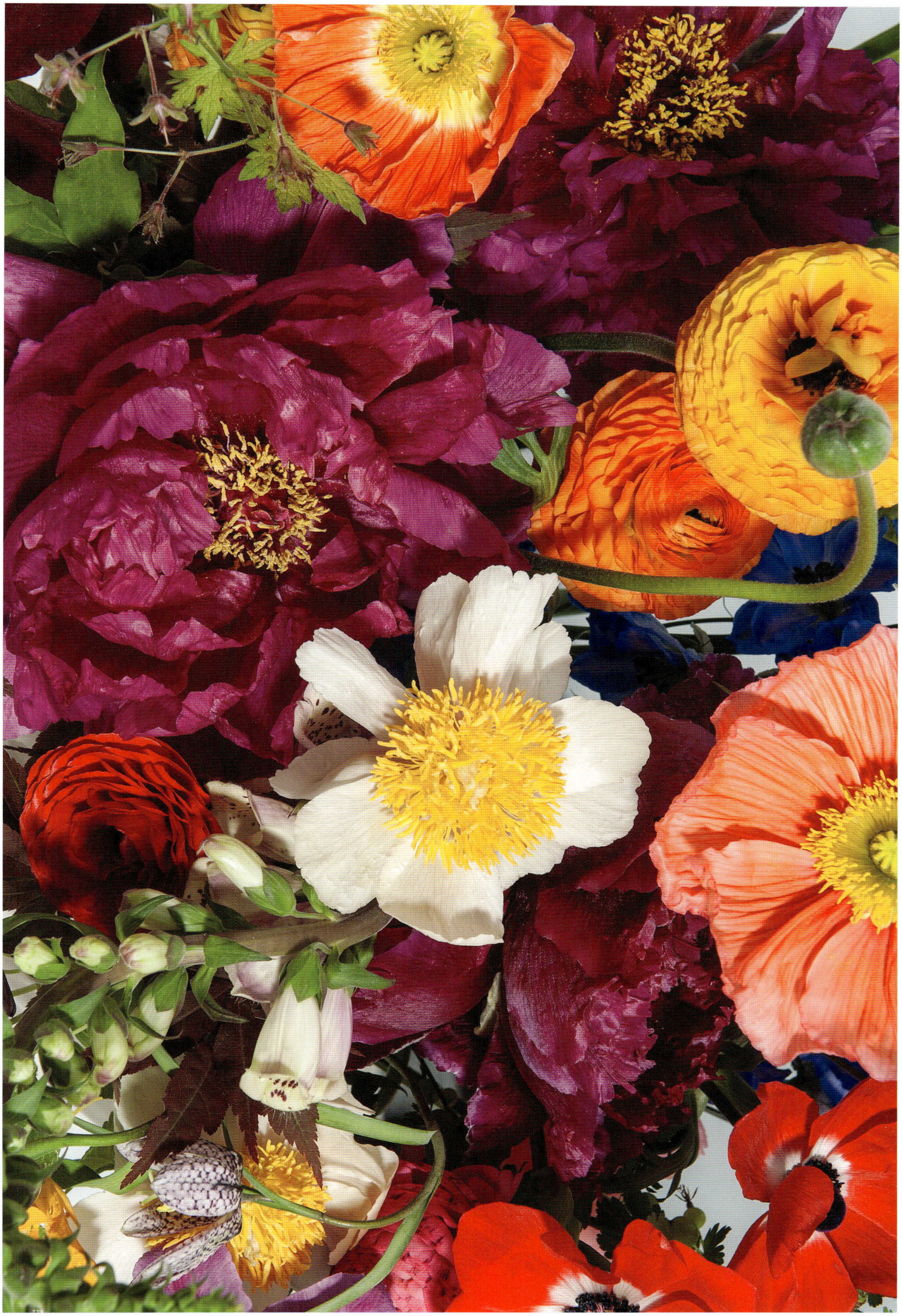

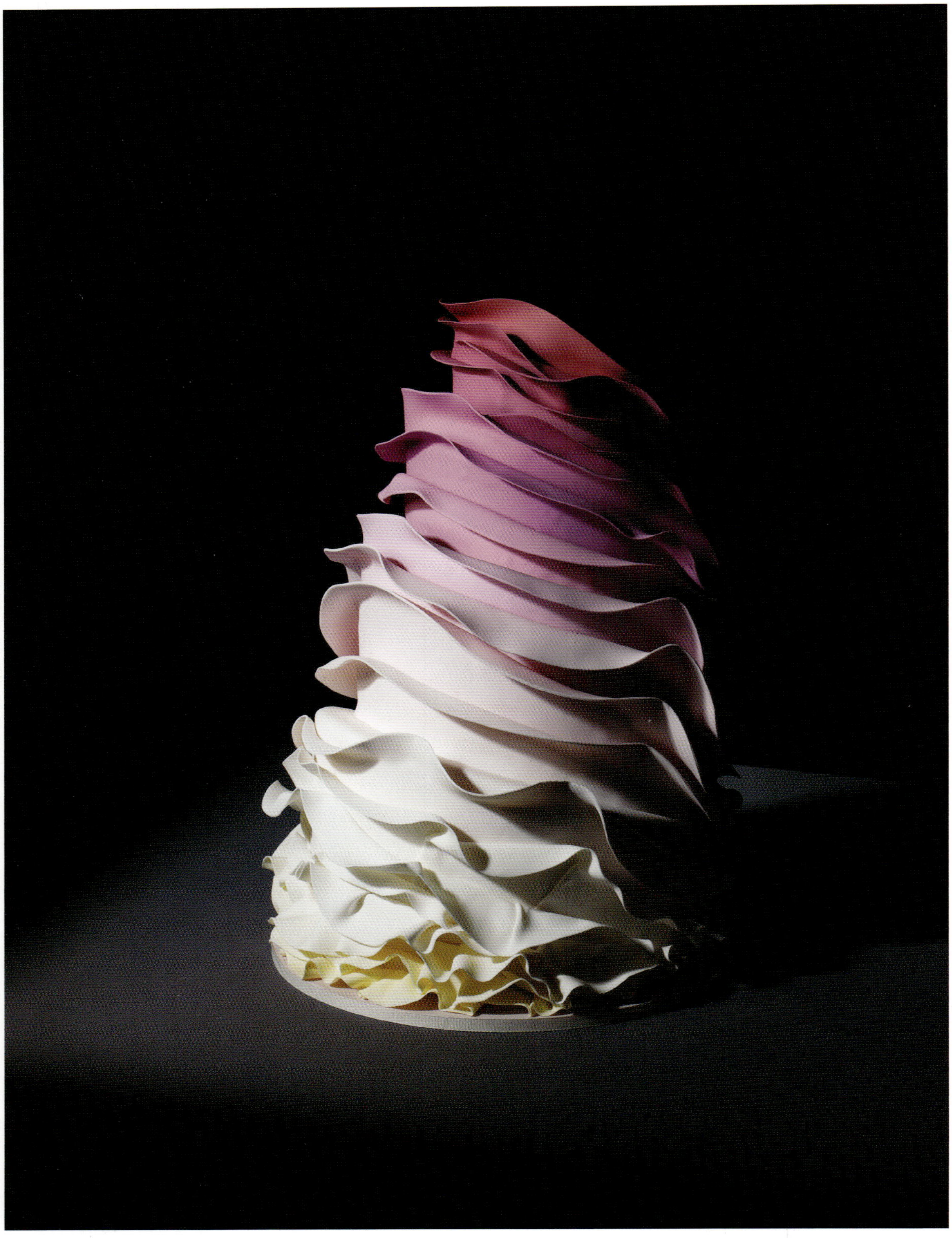

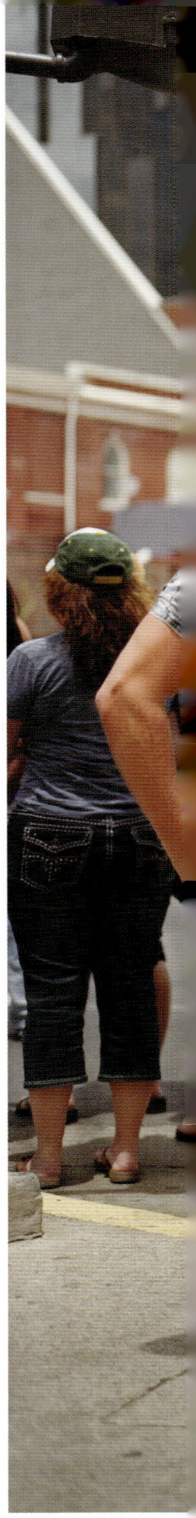

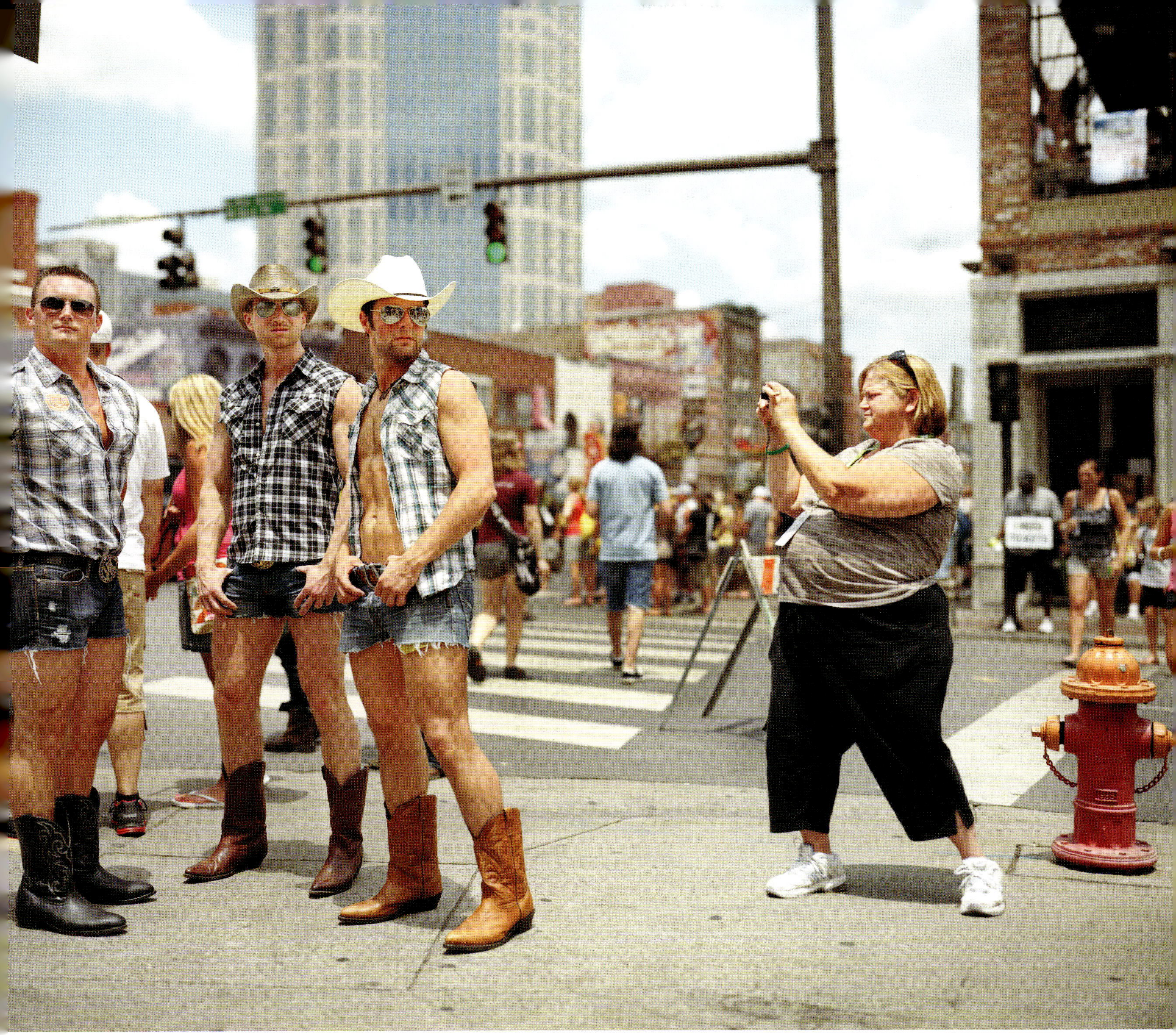

GREG MILLER

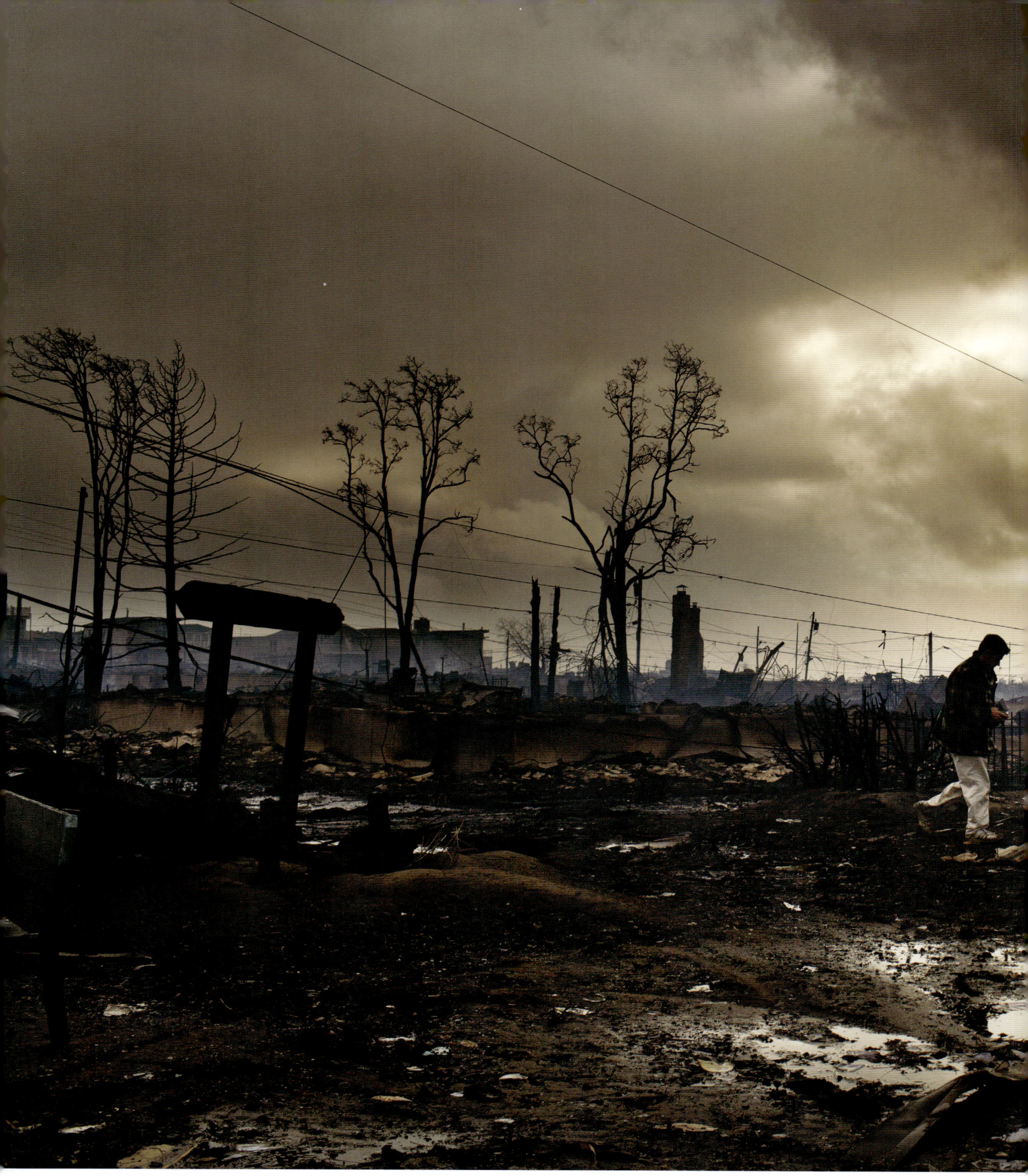

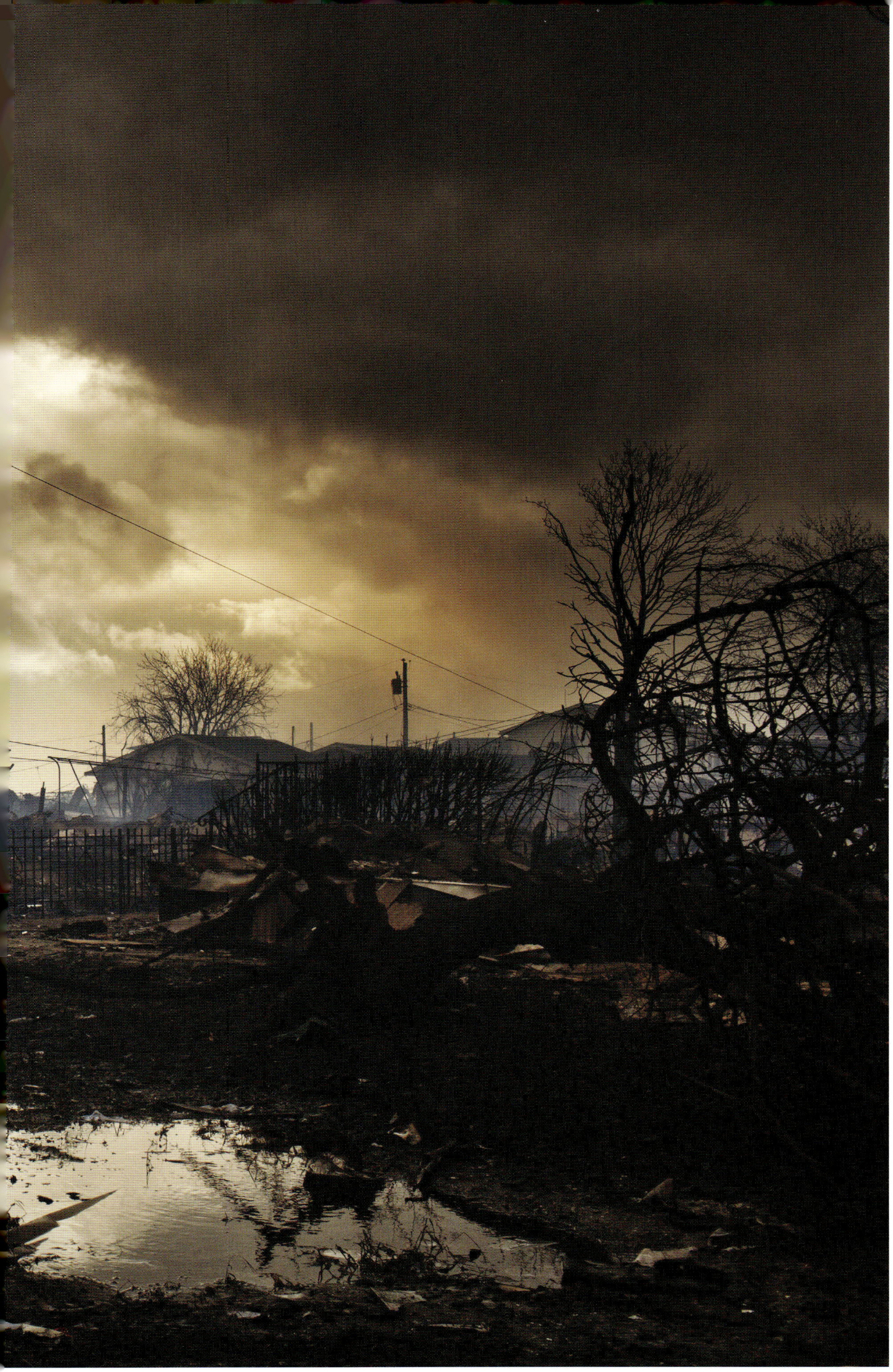

PHILIP MONTGOMERY

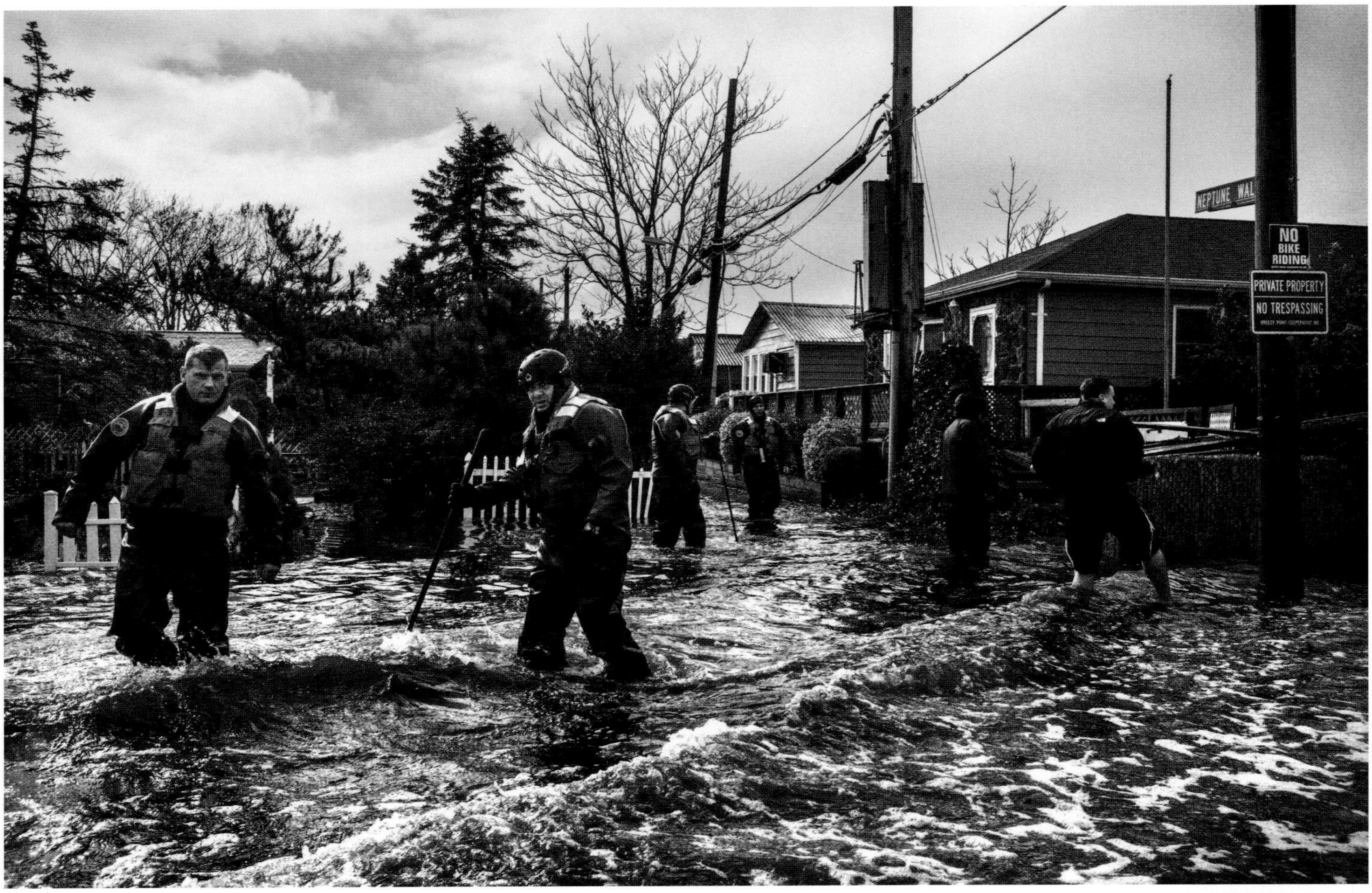

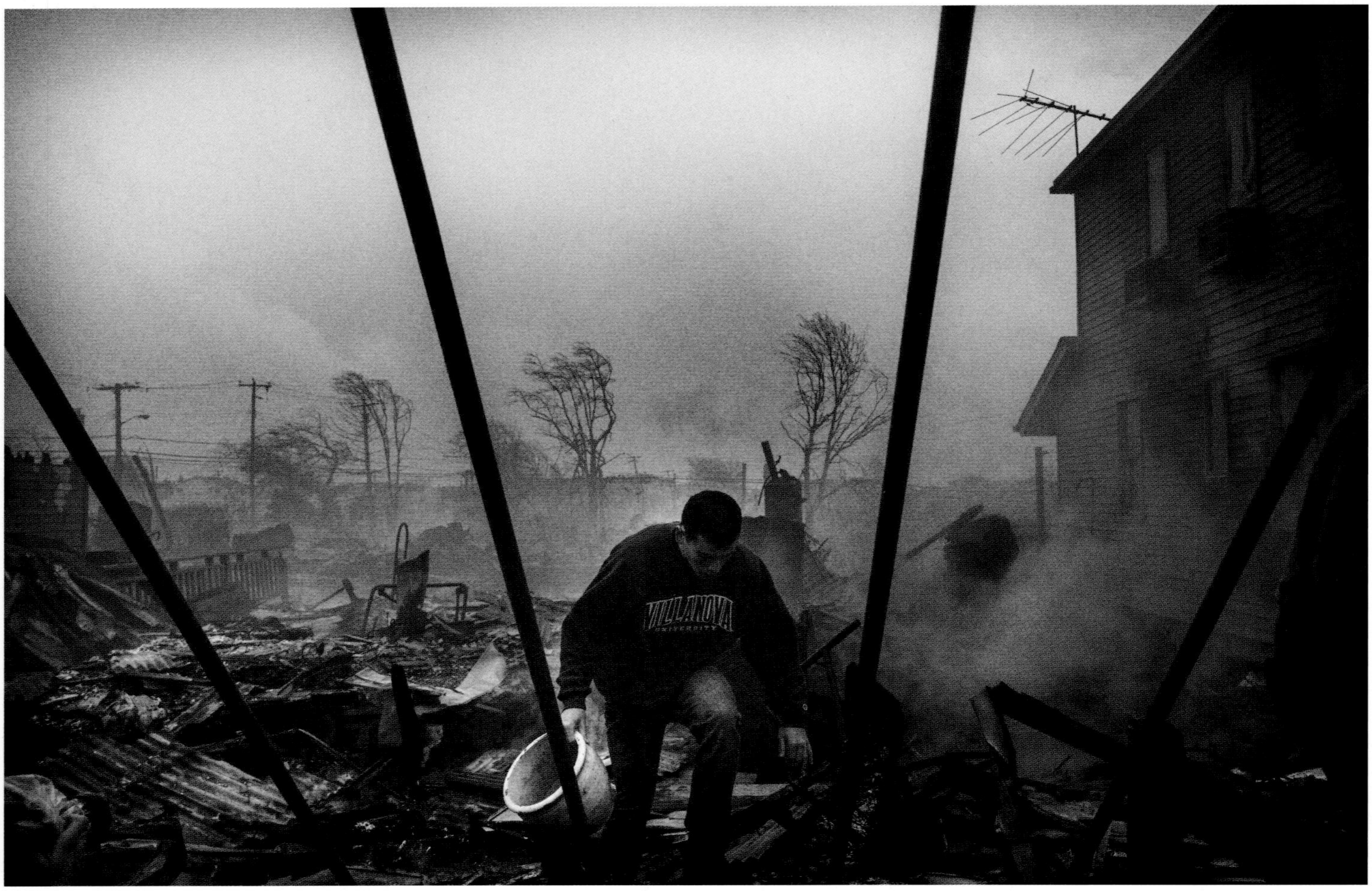

PHILIP MONTGOMERY

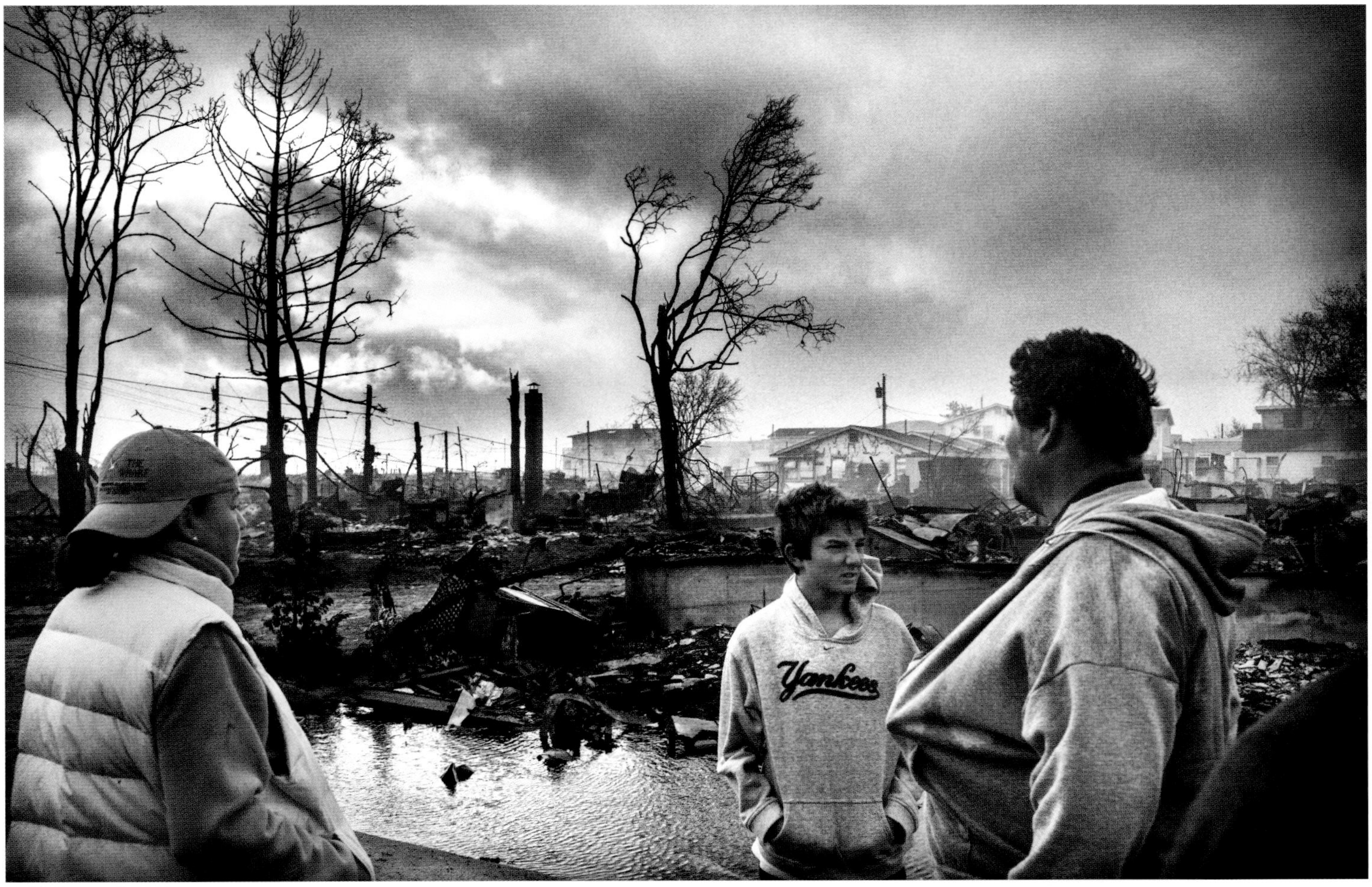
Yankees

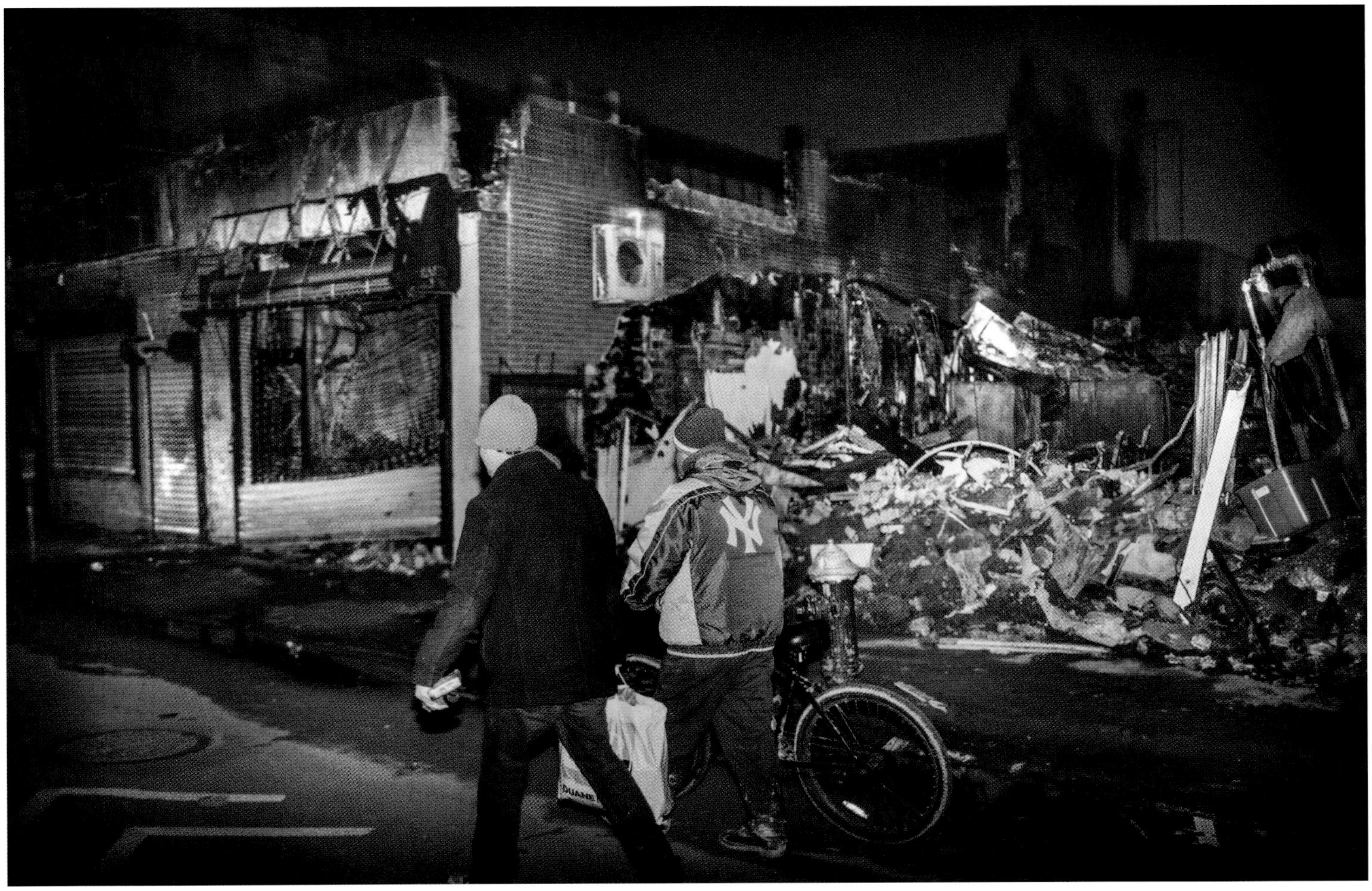
DUANE

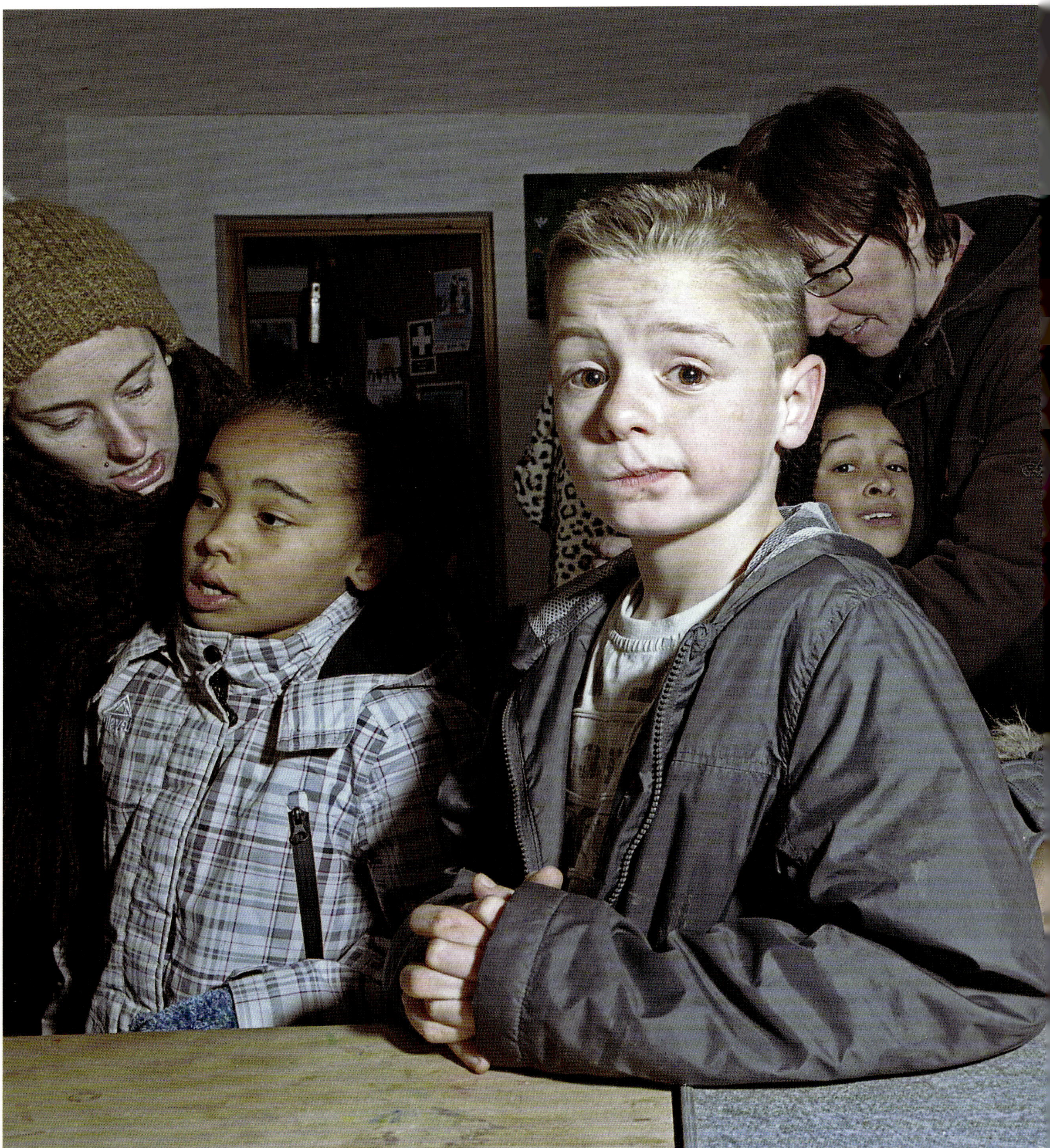

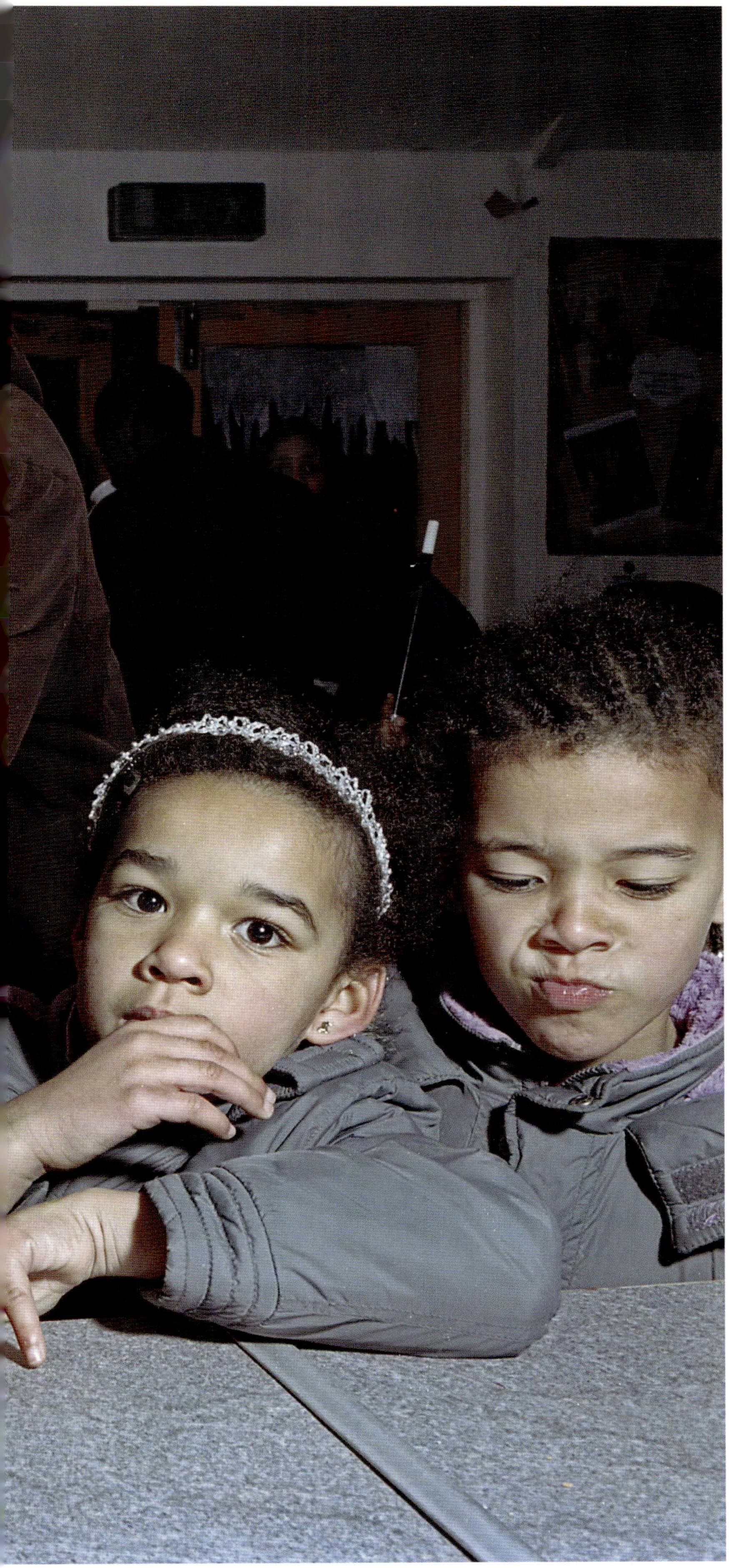

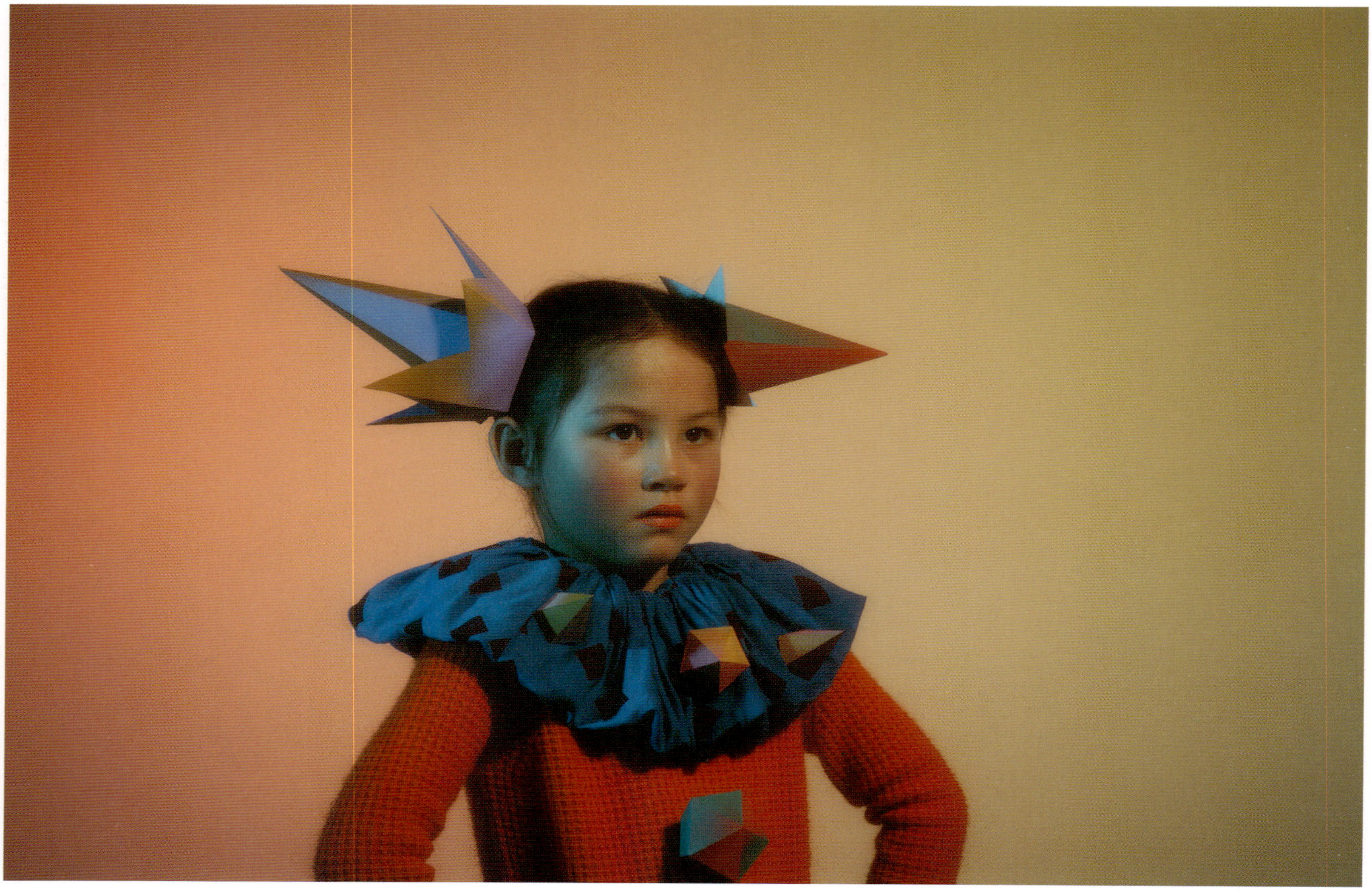

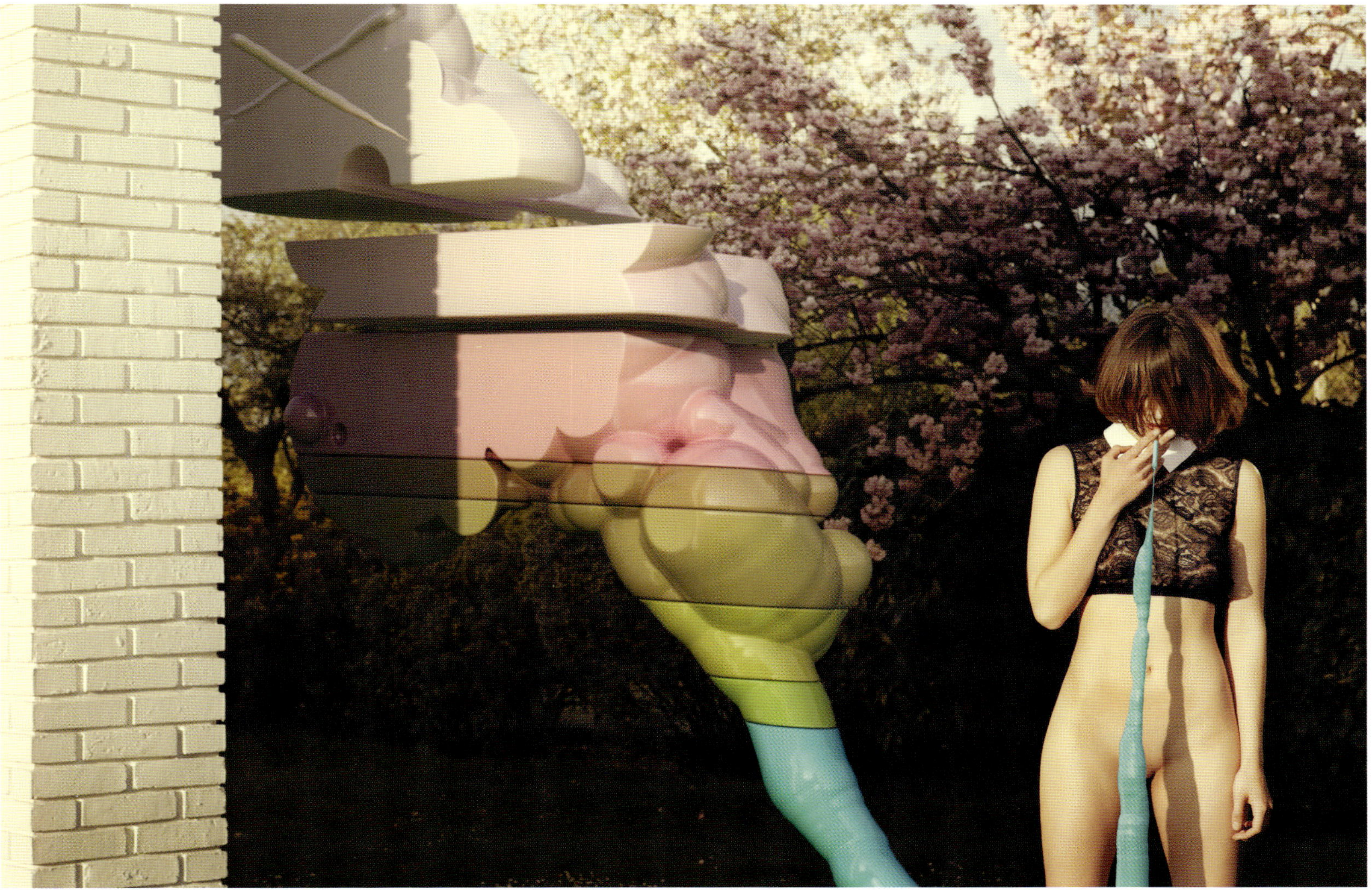

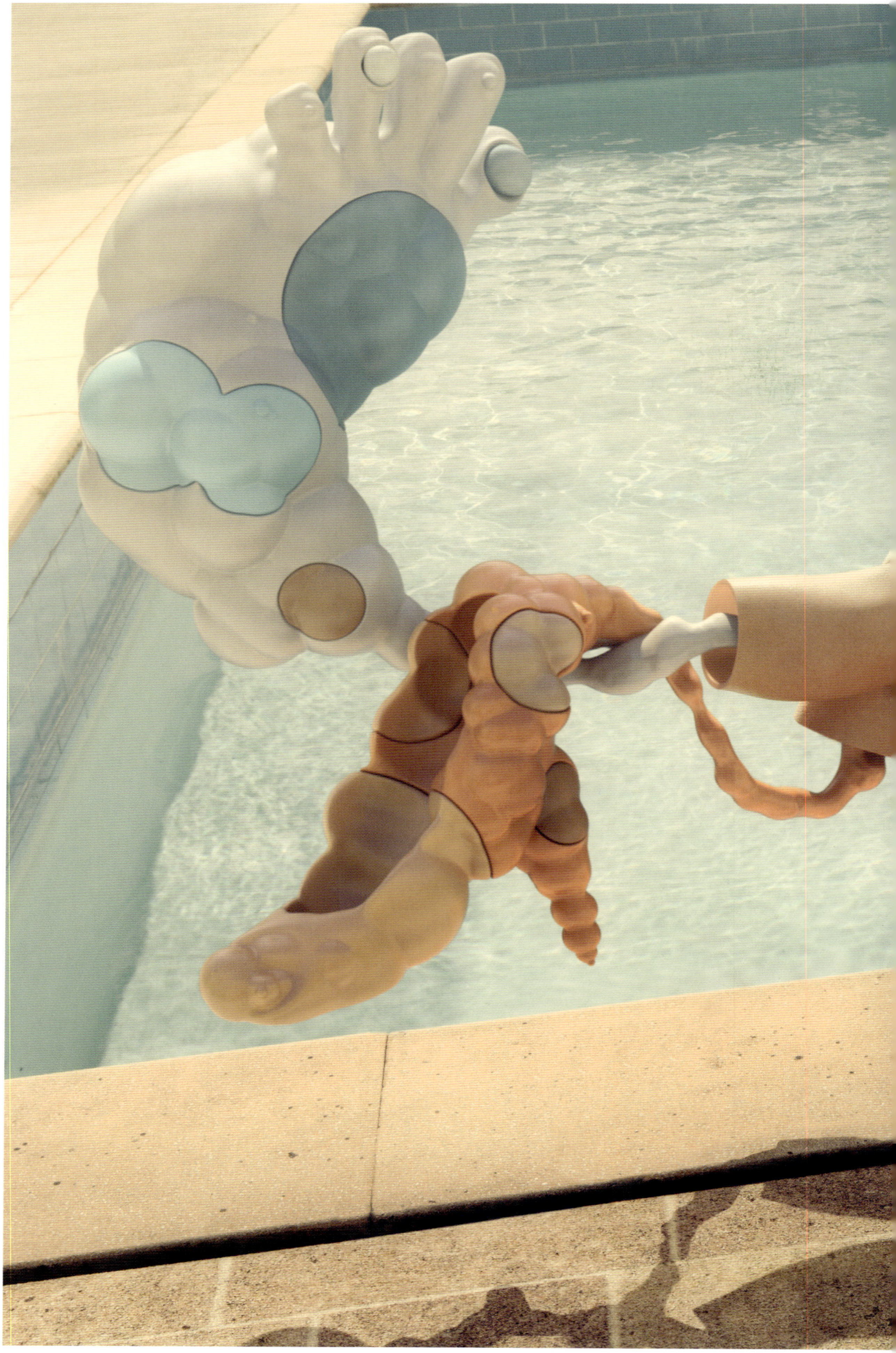

NICK & CHLOÉ
VS. ZEITGUISED

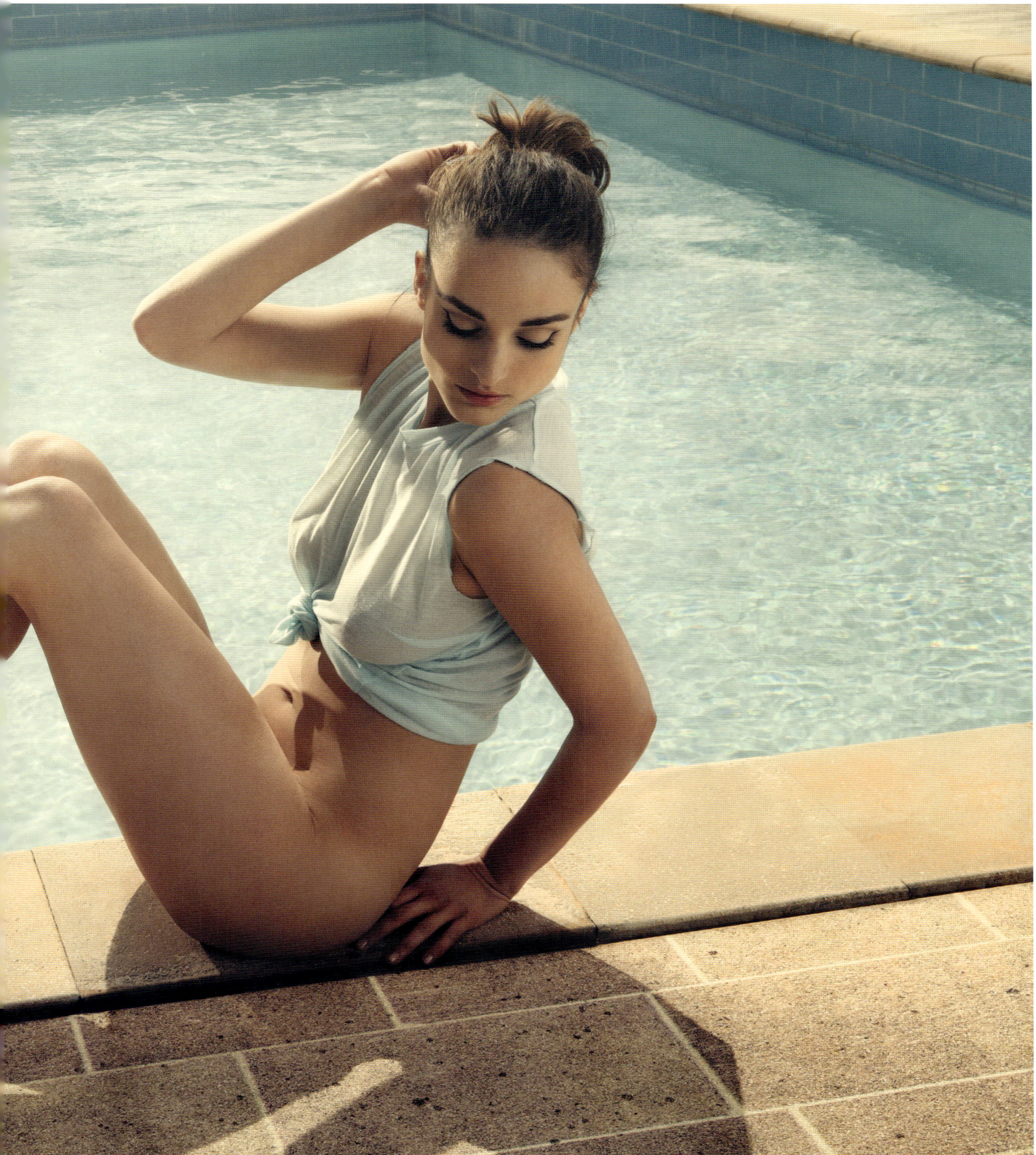

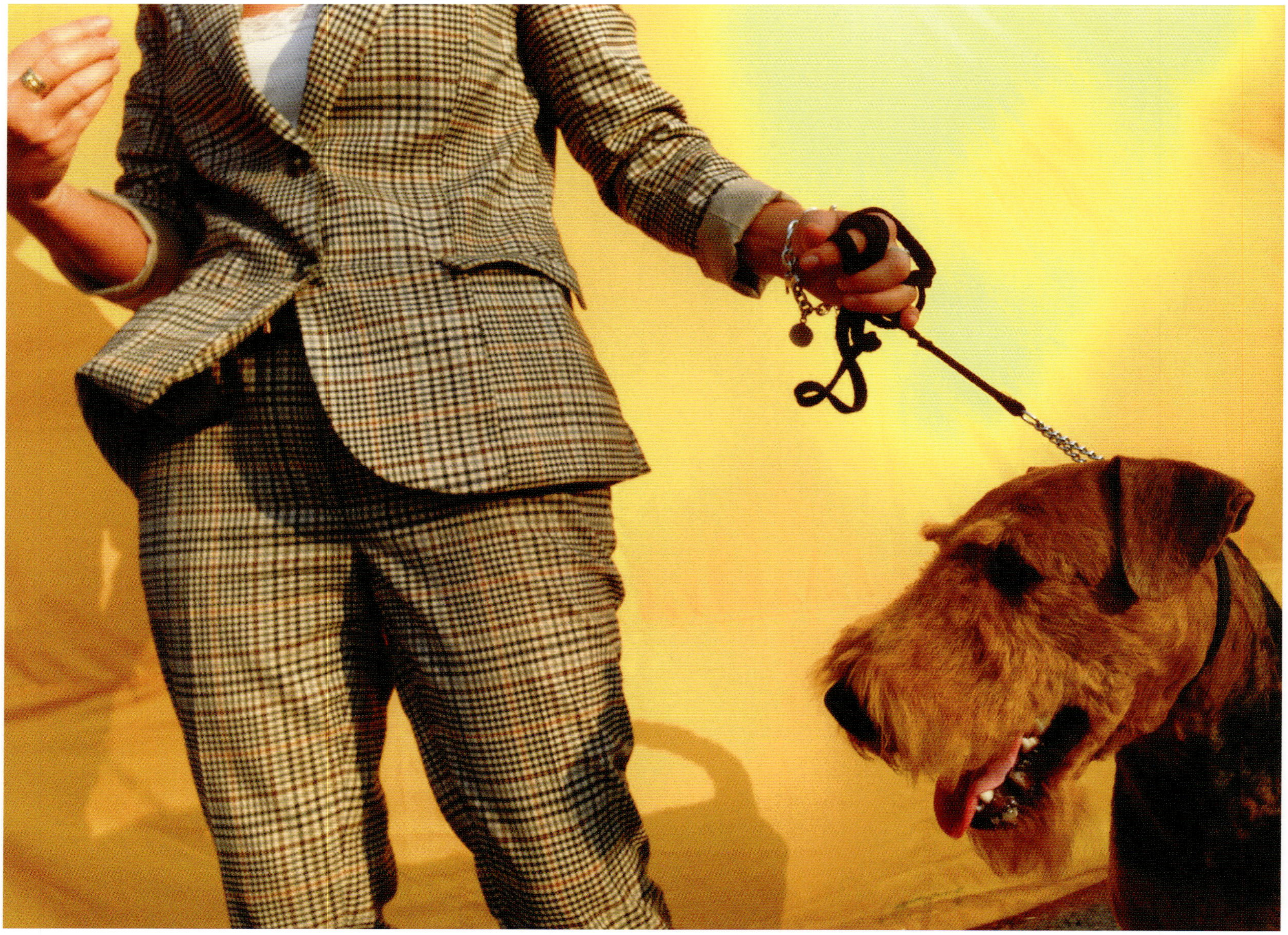

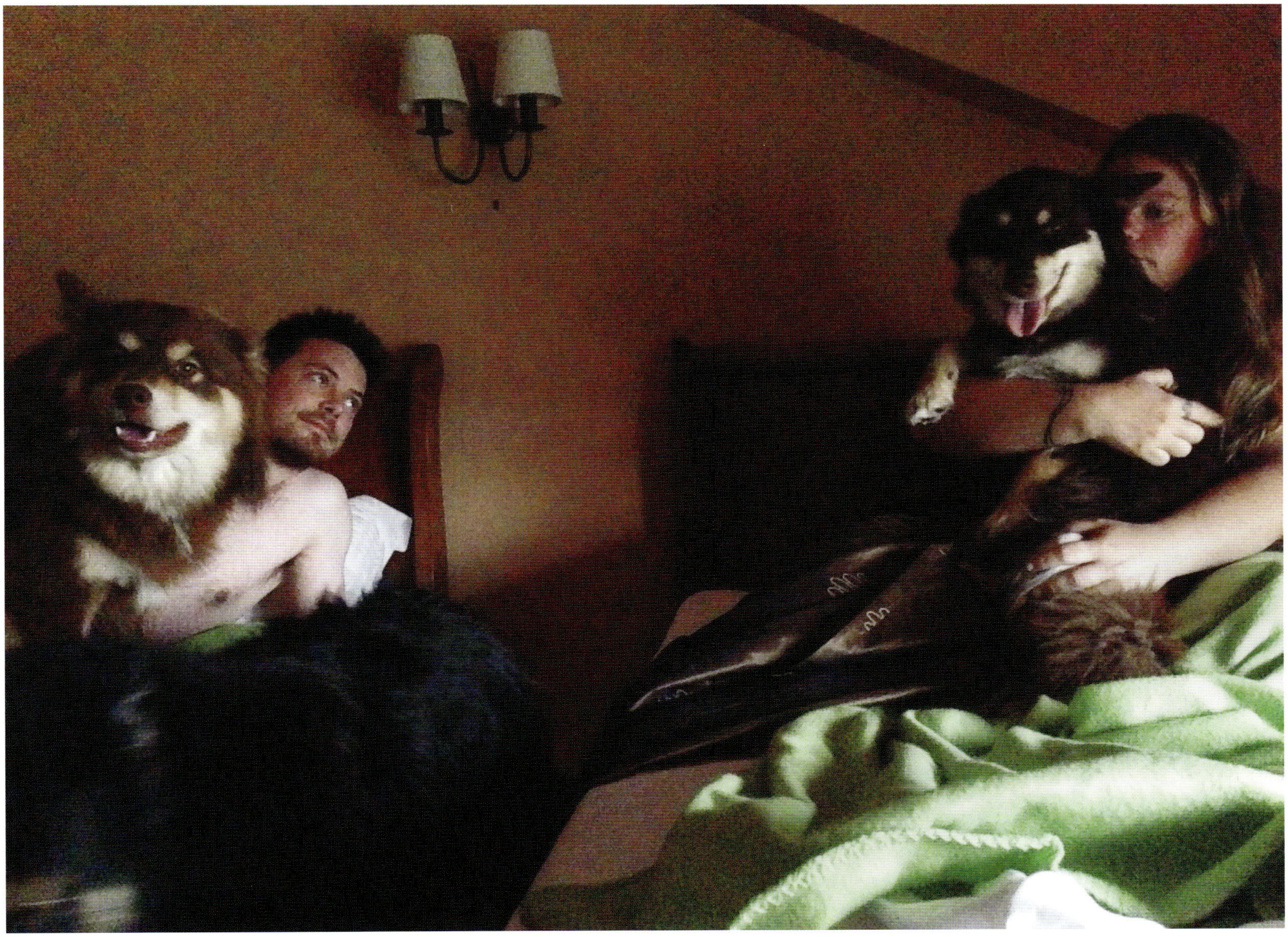

LANDON NORDEMAN

LANDON NORDEMAN

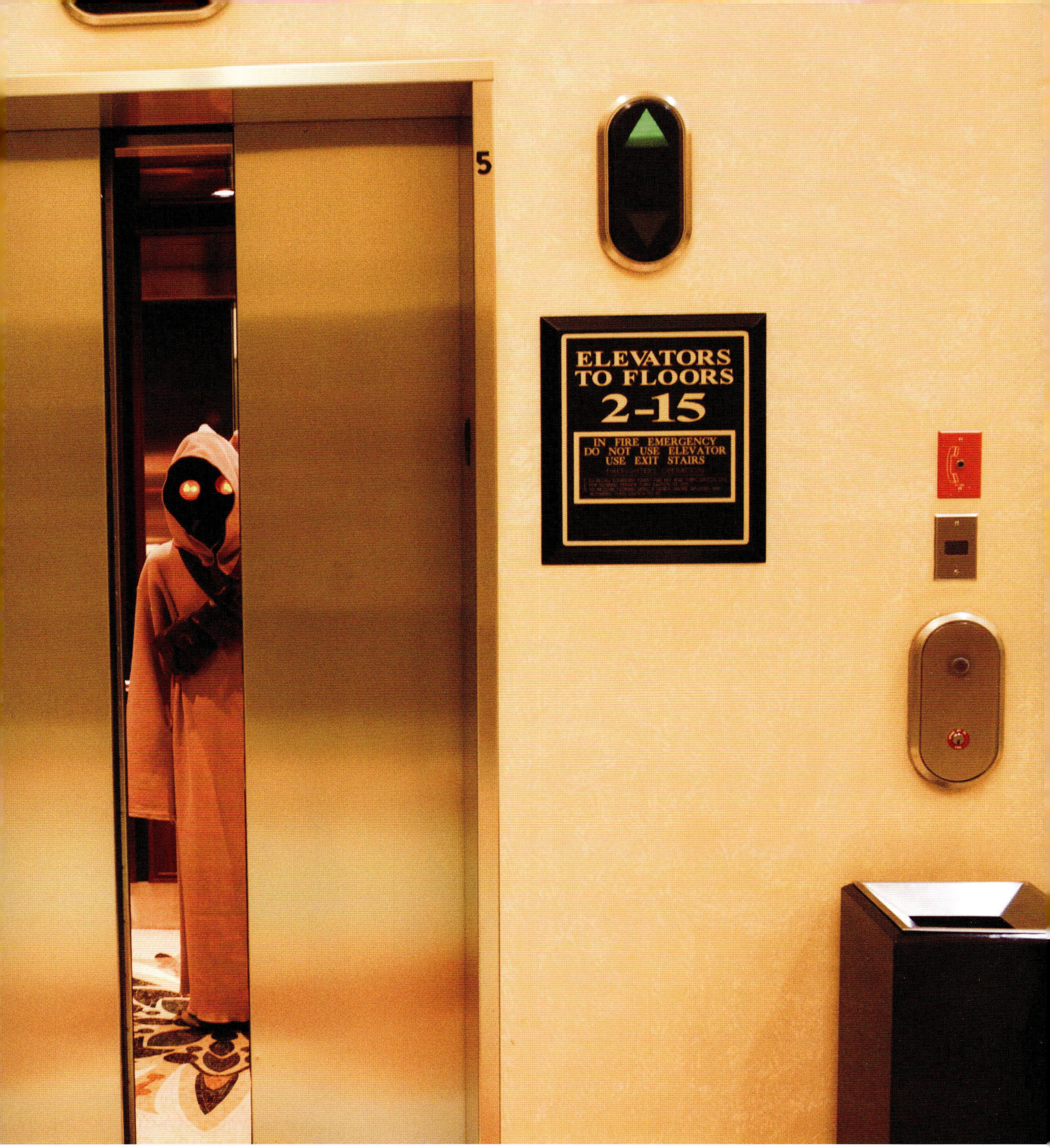
5
ELEVATORS
TO FLOORS
2-15
IN FIRE EMERGENCY
DO NOT USE ELEVATOR
USE EXIT STAIRS

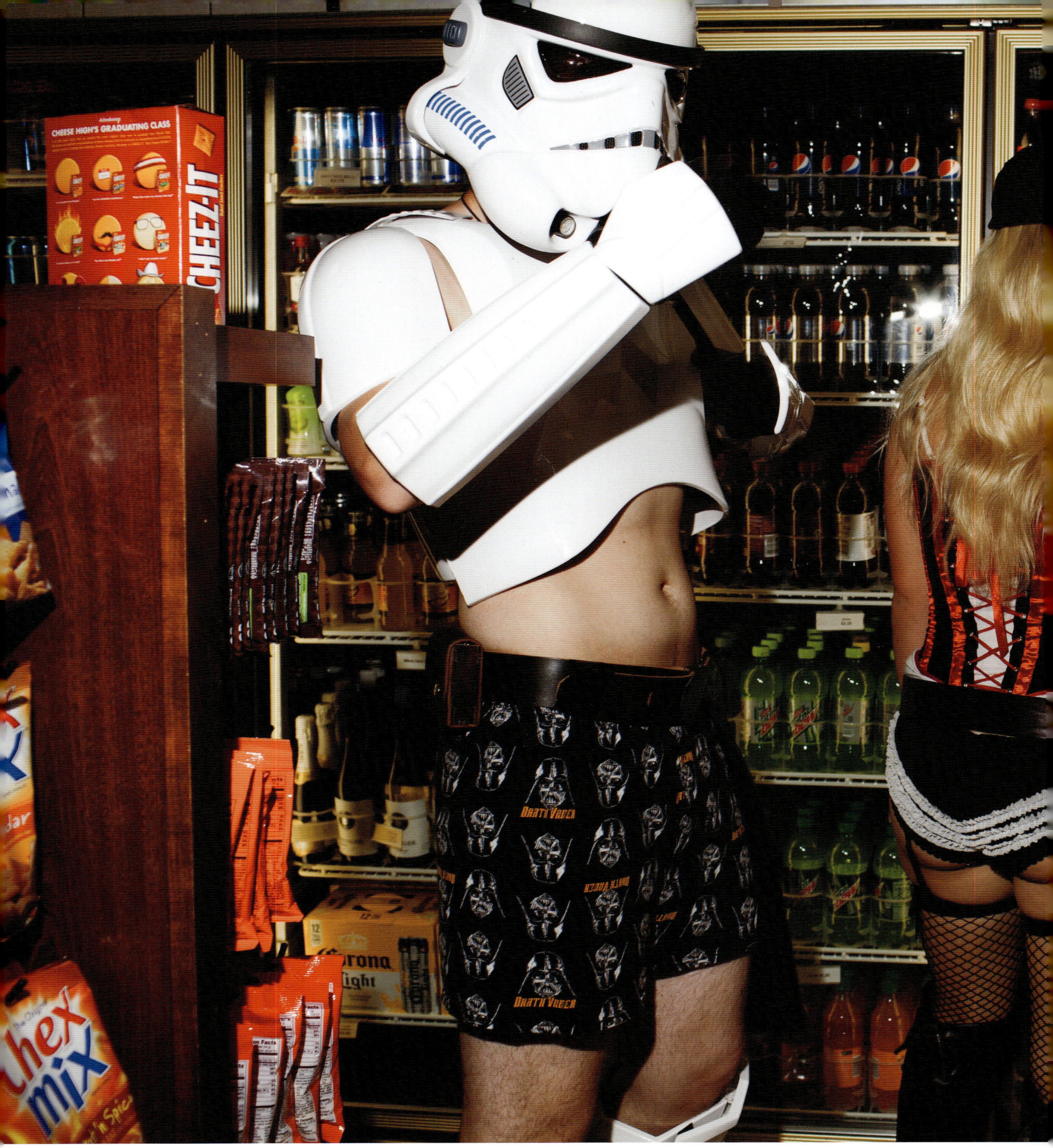
CHEESE HIGH'S GRADUATING CLASS
CHEEZ-IT
Corona Light
Chex mix

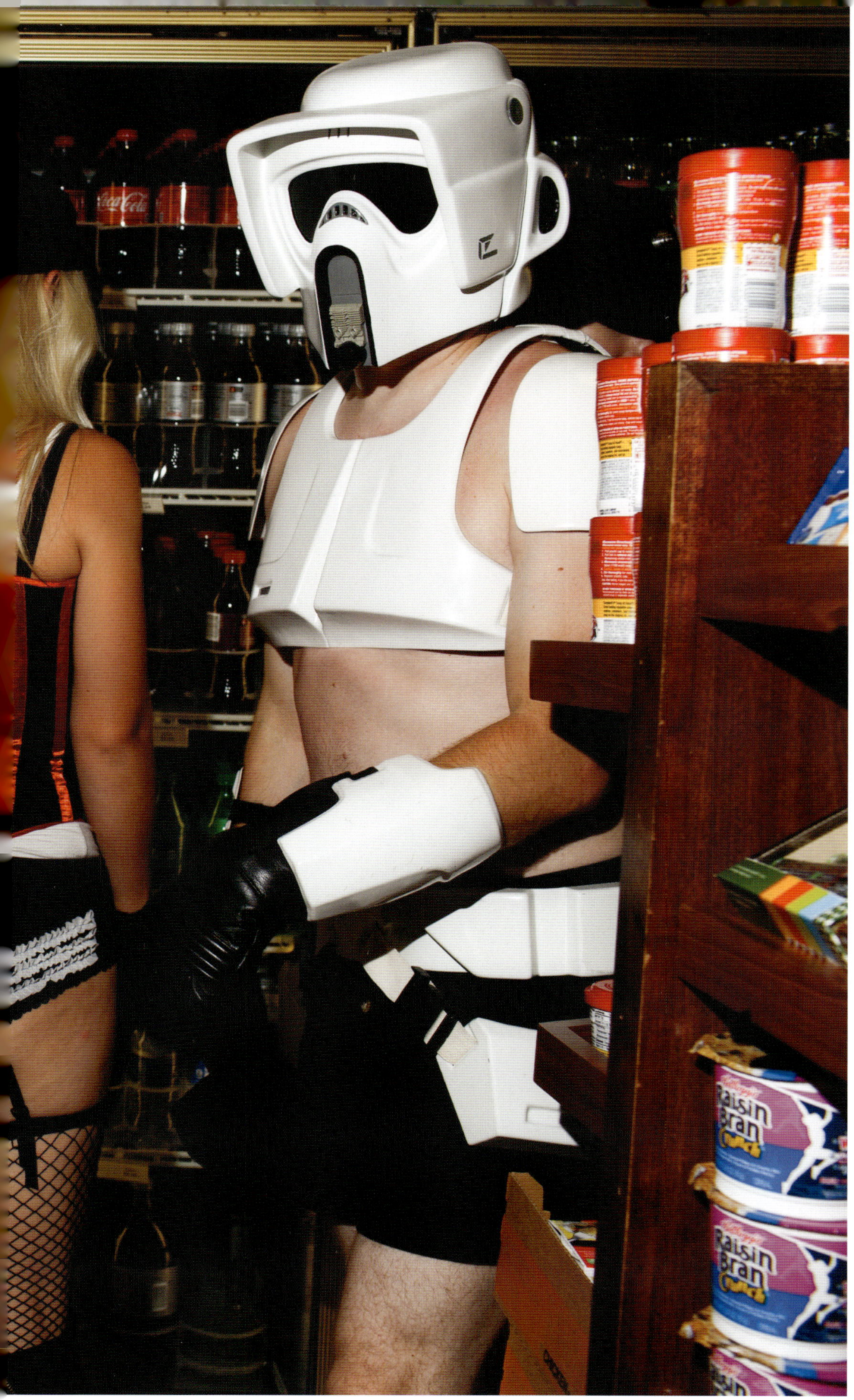

LANDON NORDEMAN

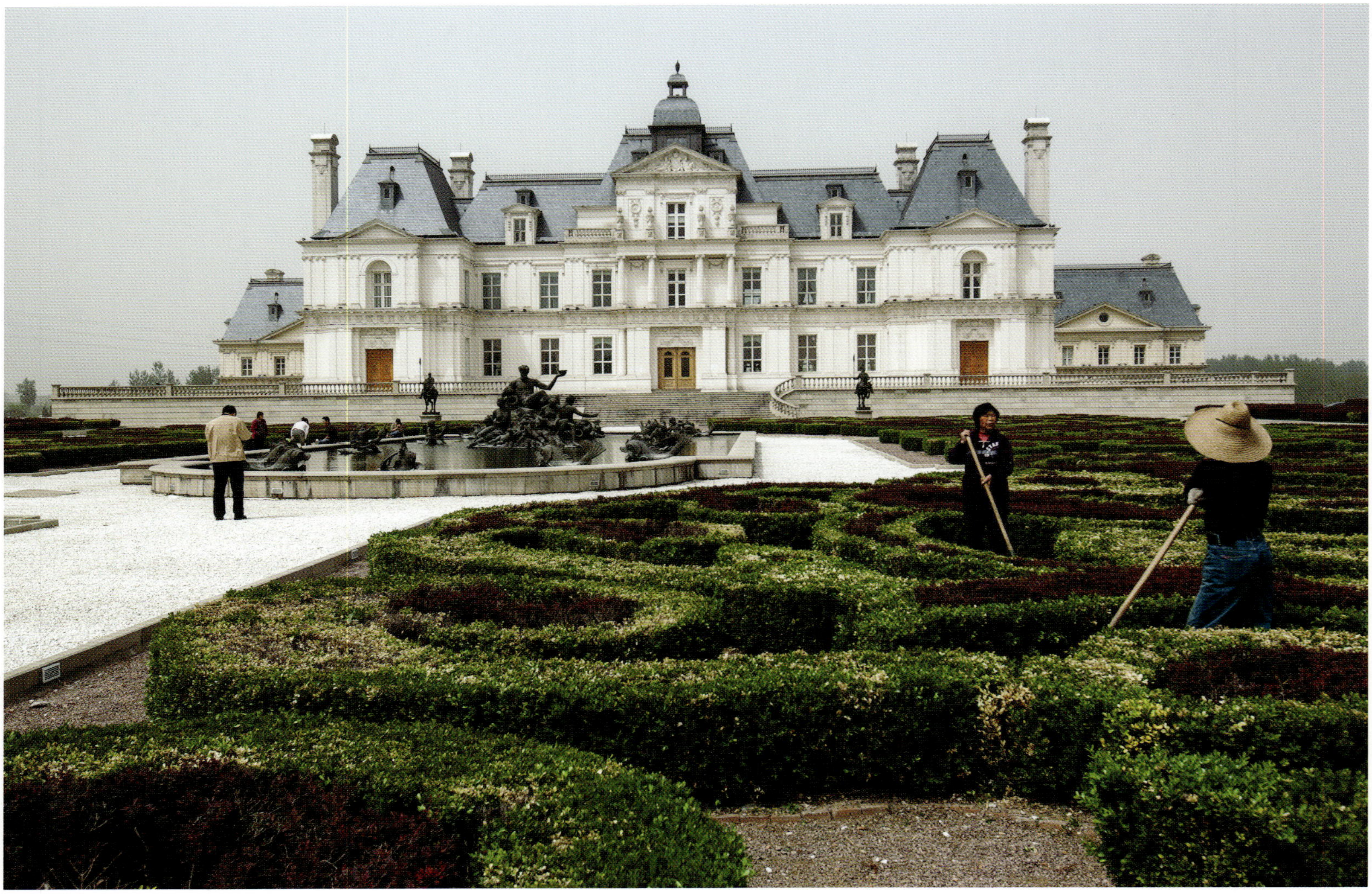

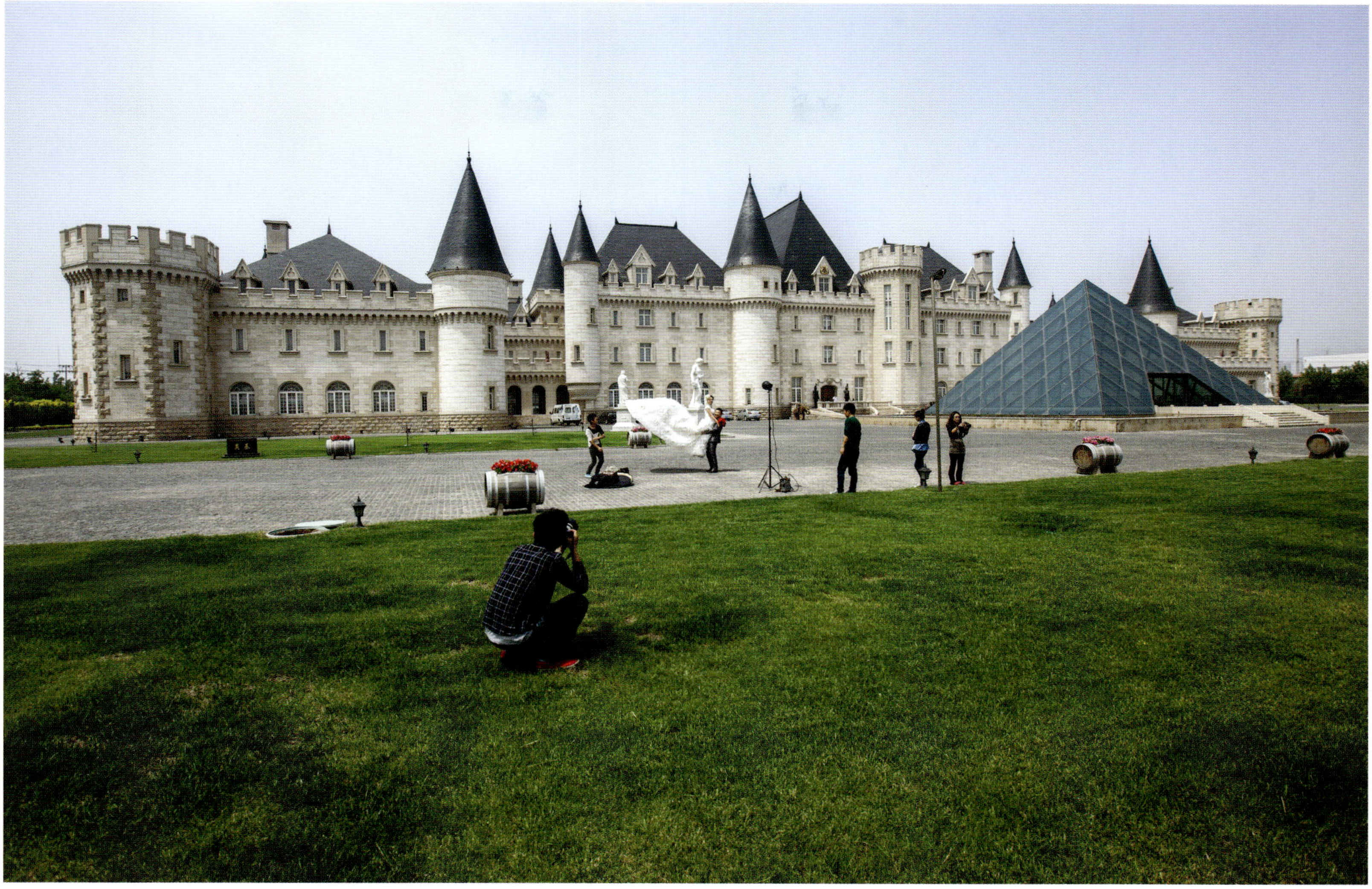

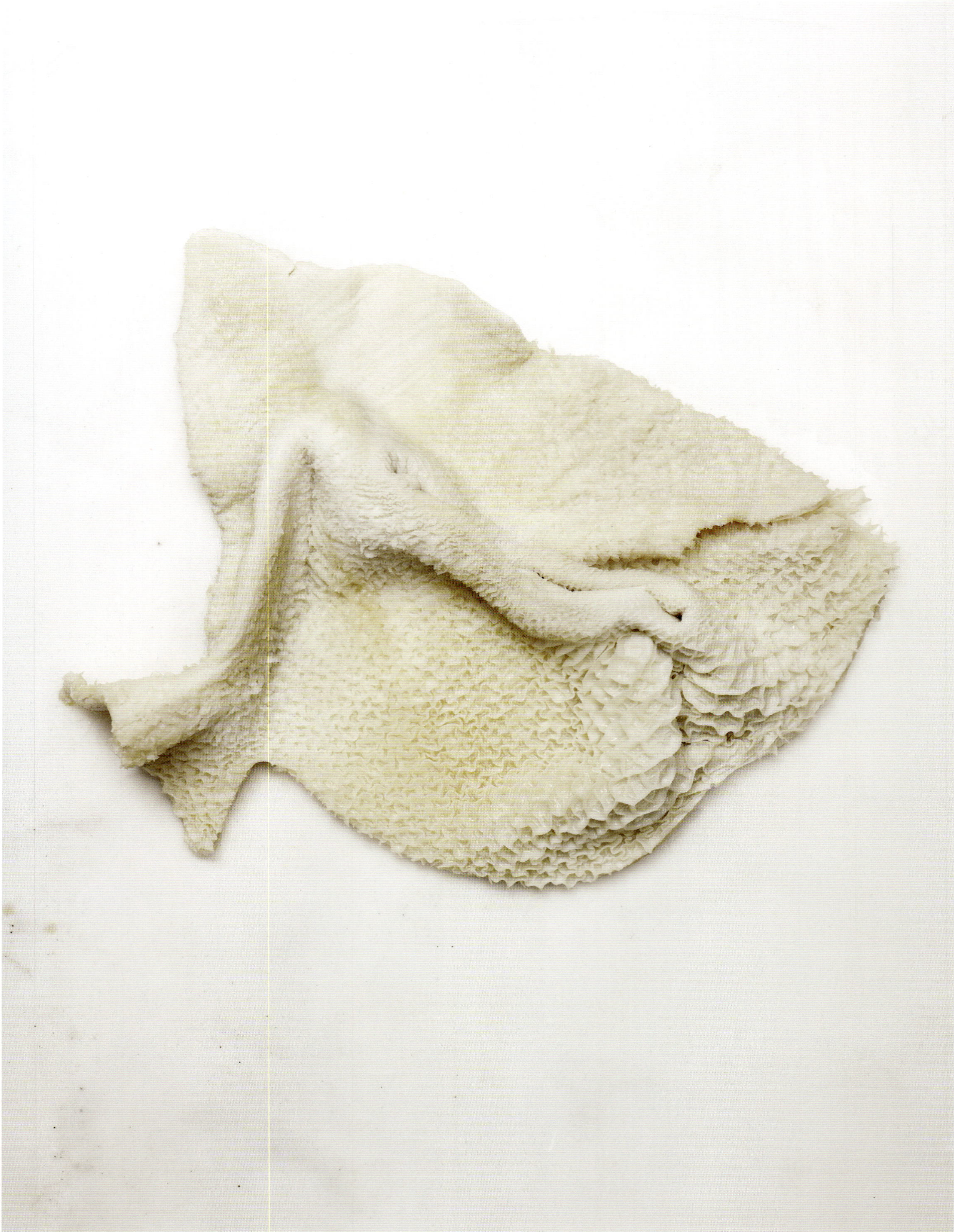

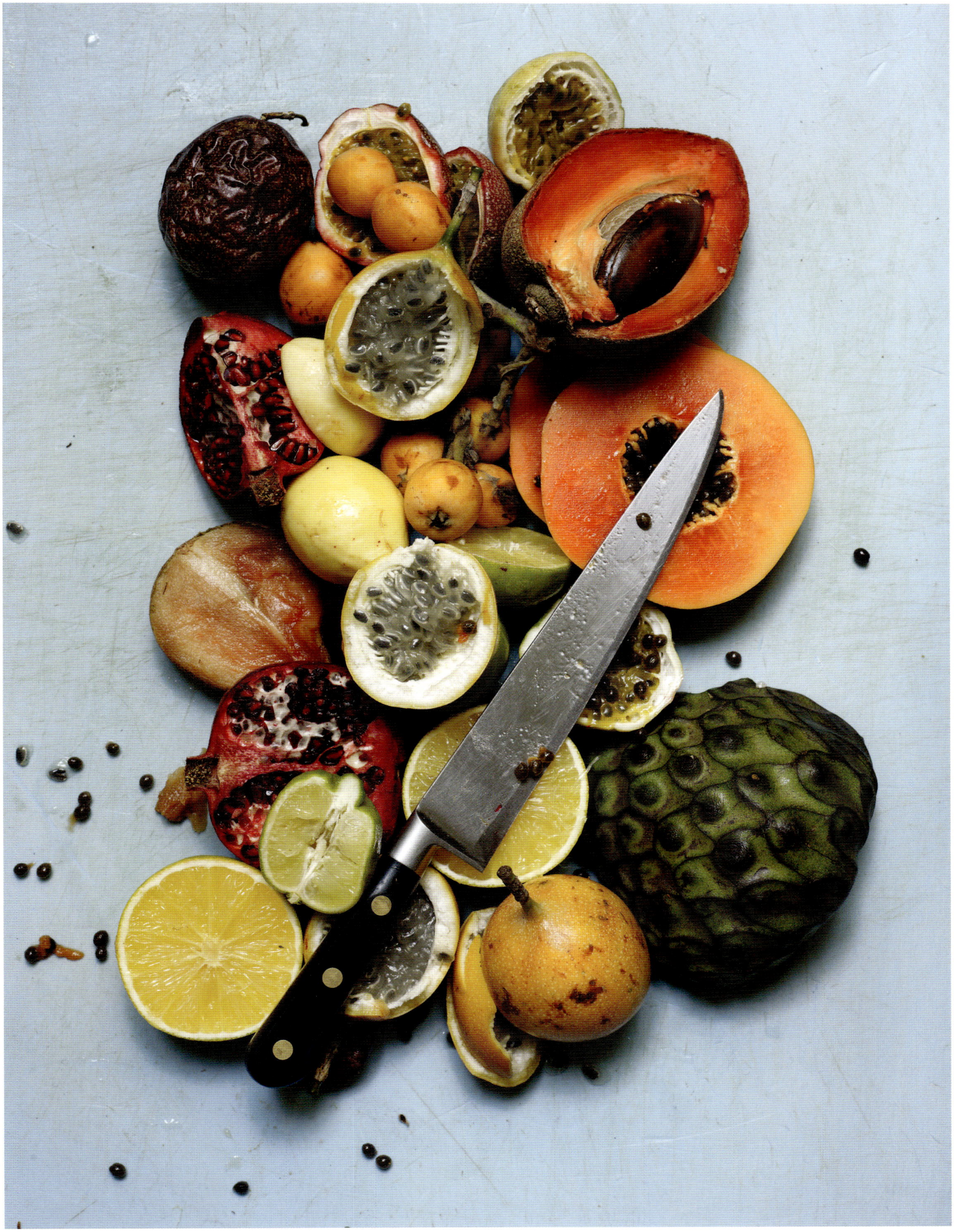

MARCUS NILSSON

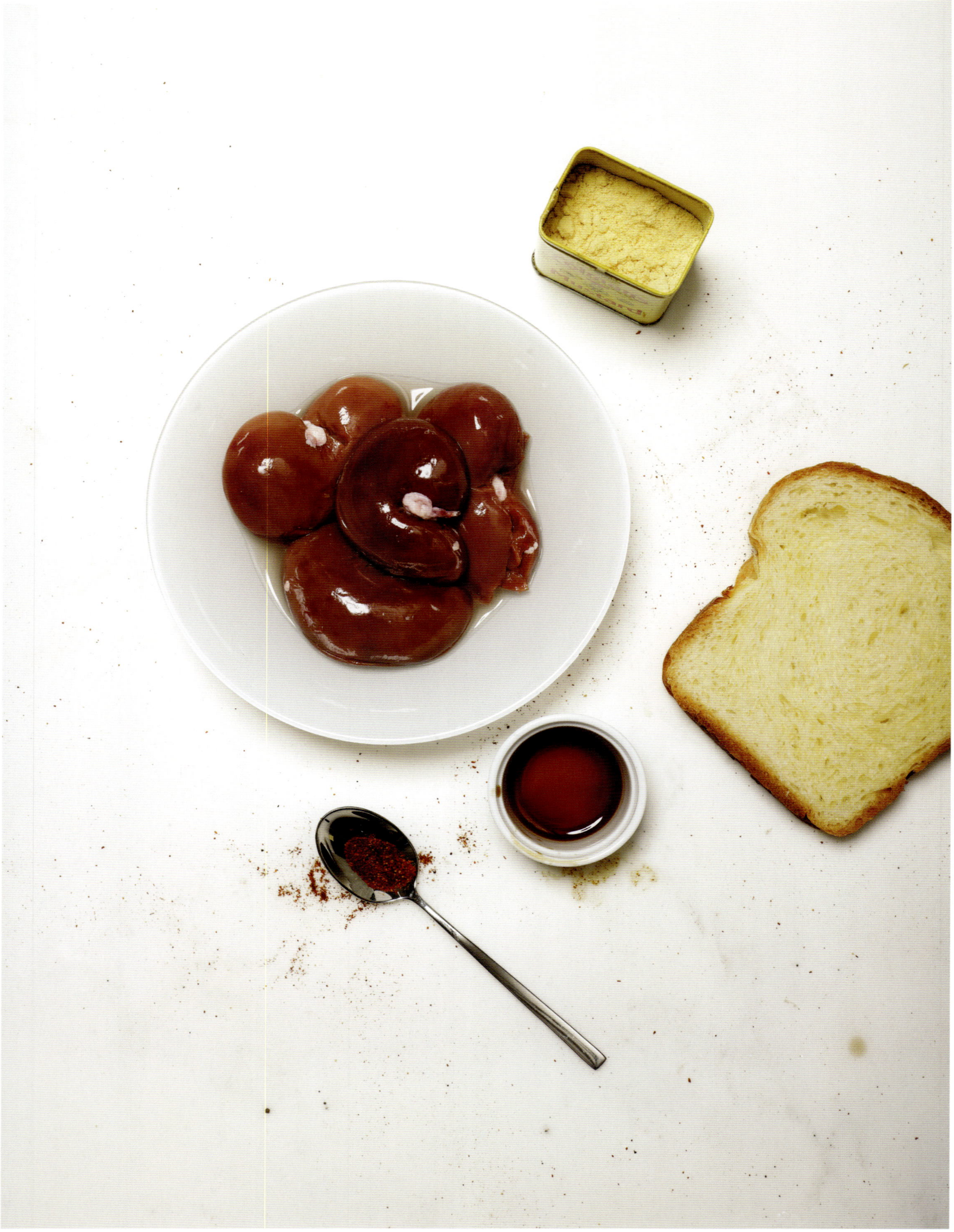

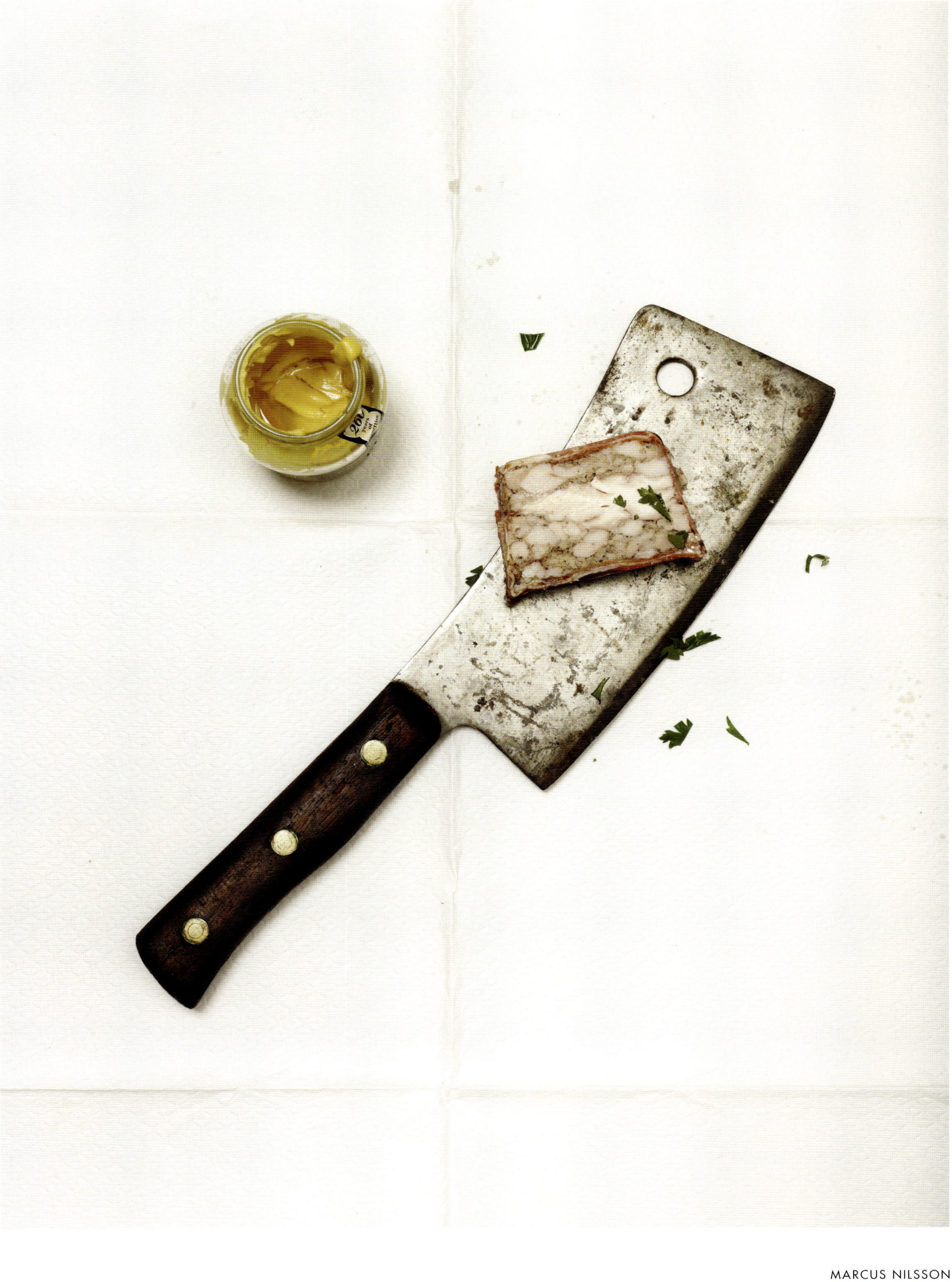

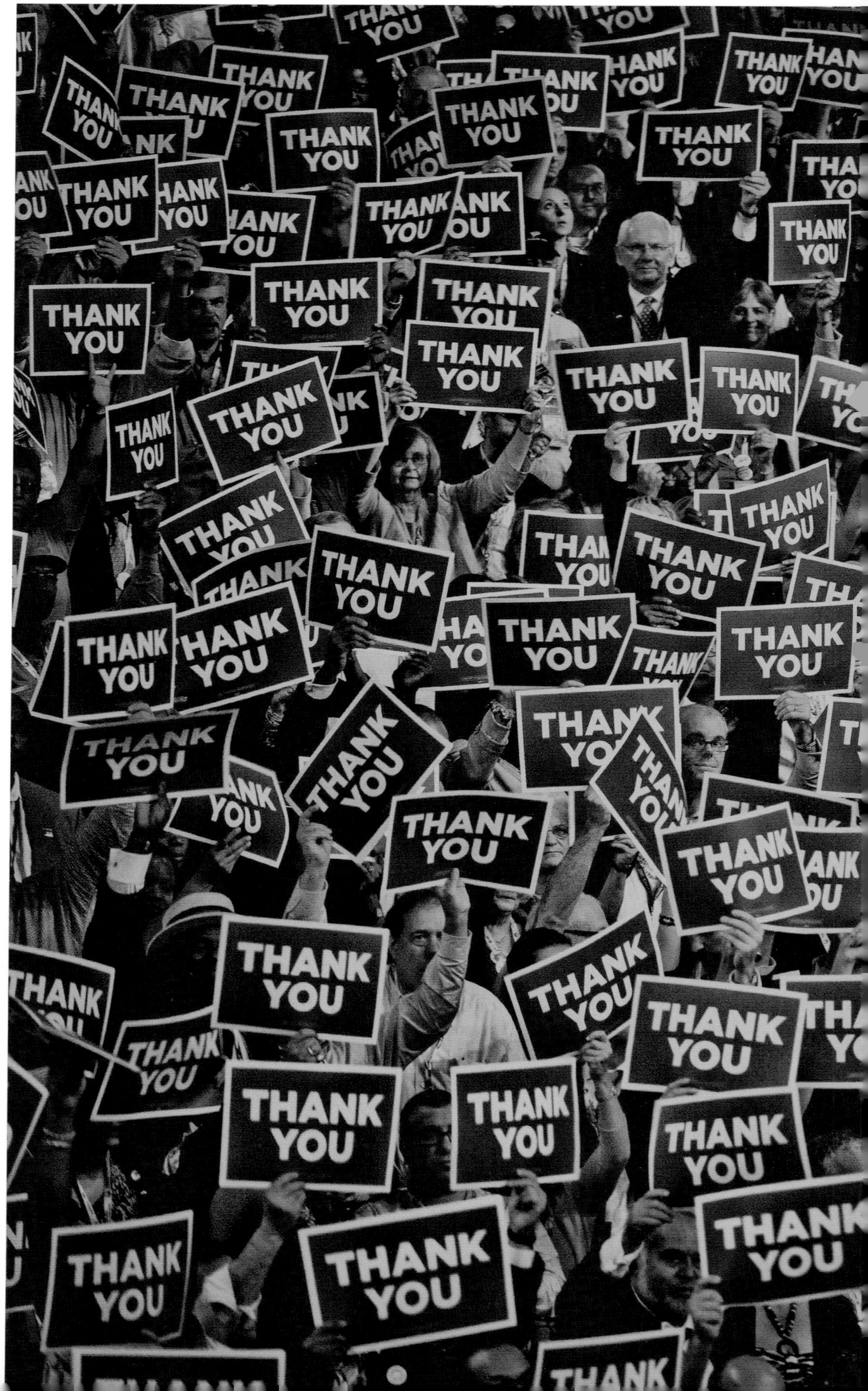
THANK YOU
THANK YOU
THANK YOU
THANK YOU
THANK YOU
THANK YOU
THANK YOU
THANK YOU
THANK YOU
THANK YOU
THANK YOU
THANK YOU
THANK YOU
THANK YOU
THANK YOU
THANK YOU
THANK YOU
THANK YOU
THANK YOU
THANK YOU

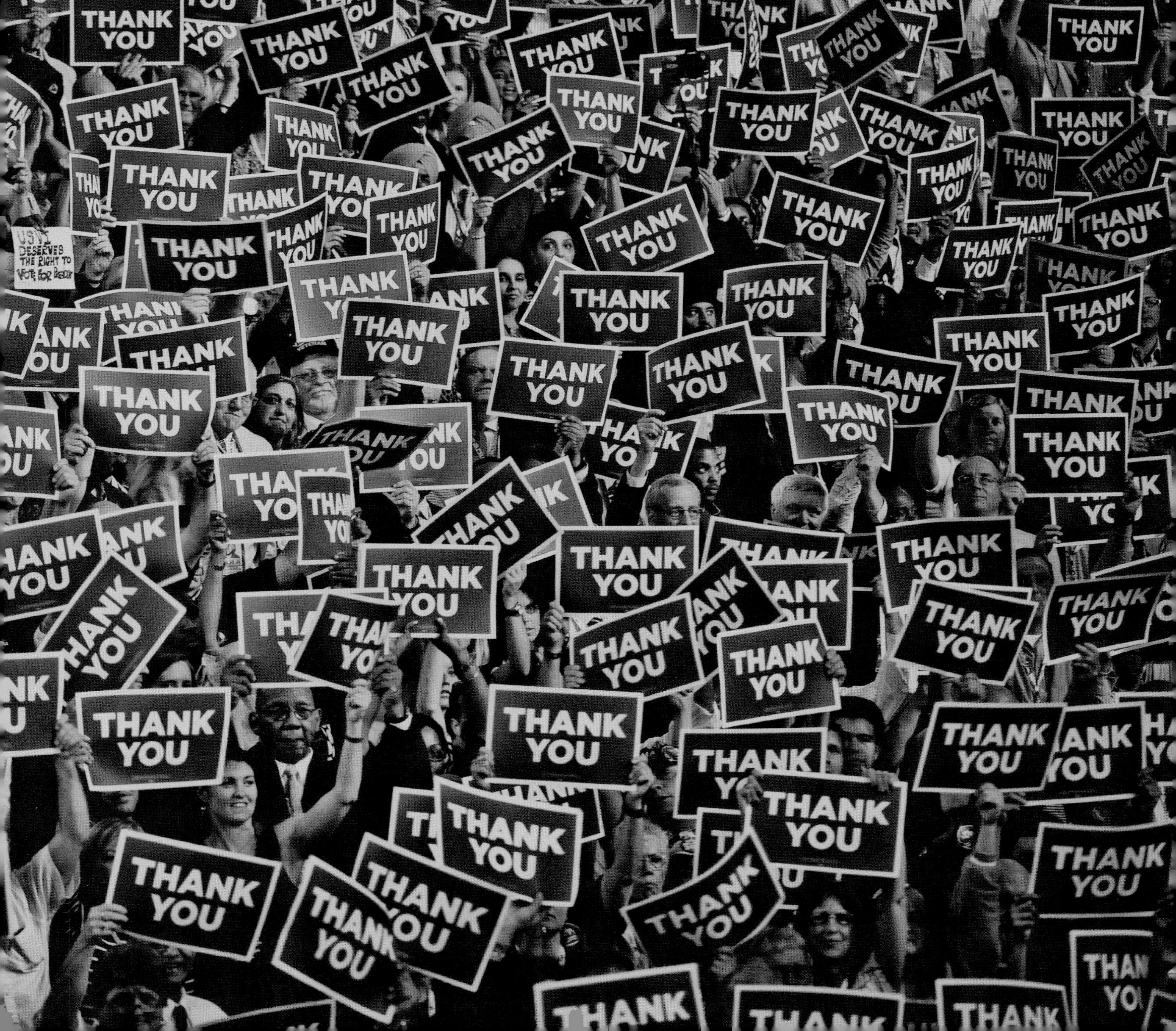
THANK YOU
DESERVES THE RIGHT TO

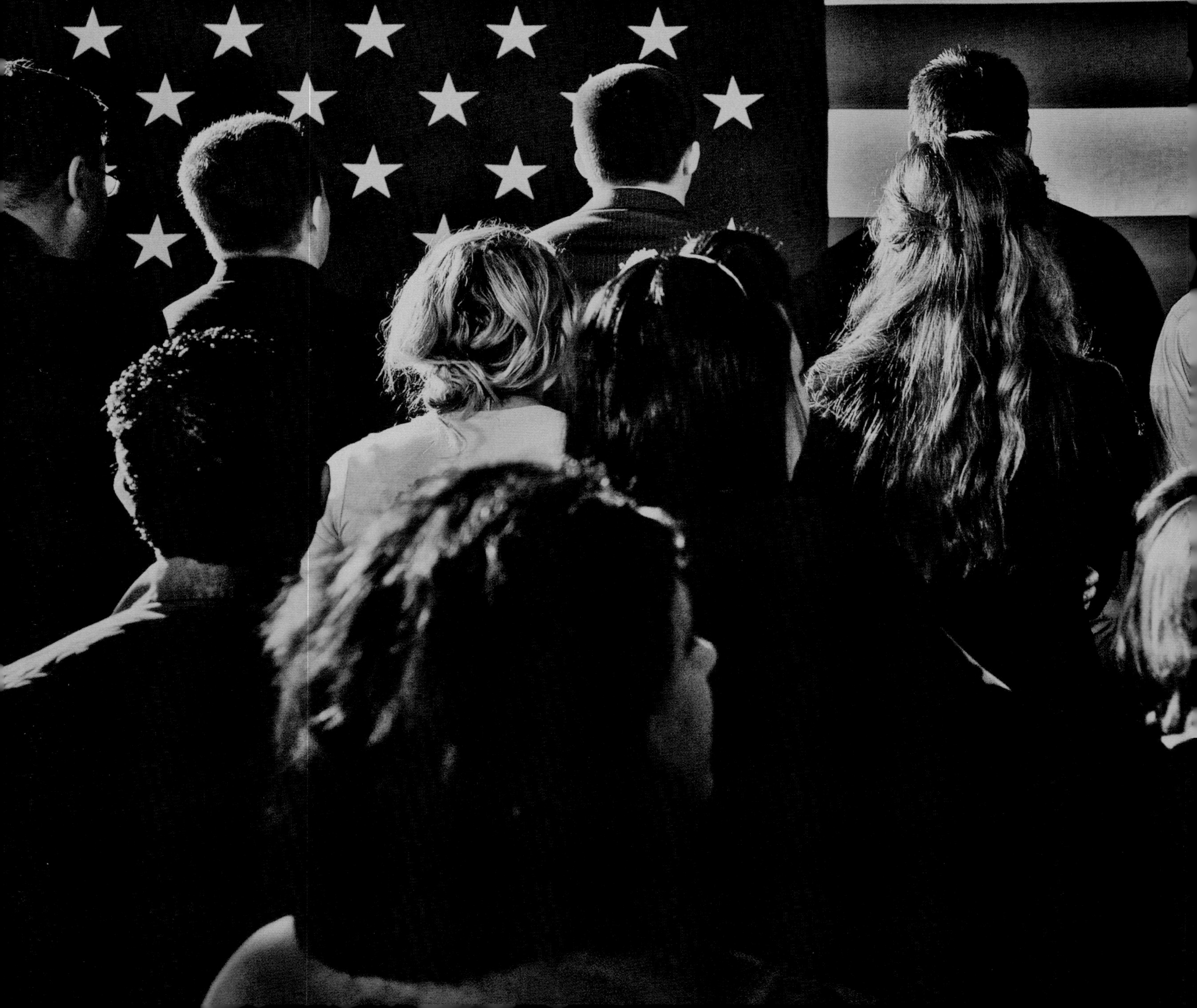

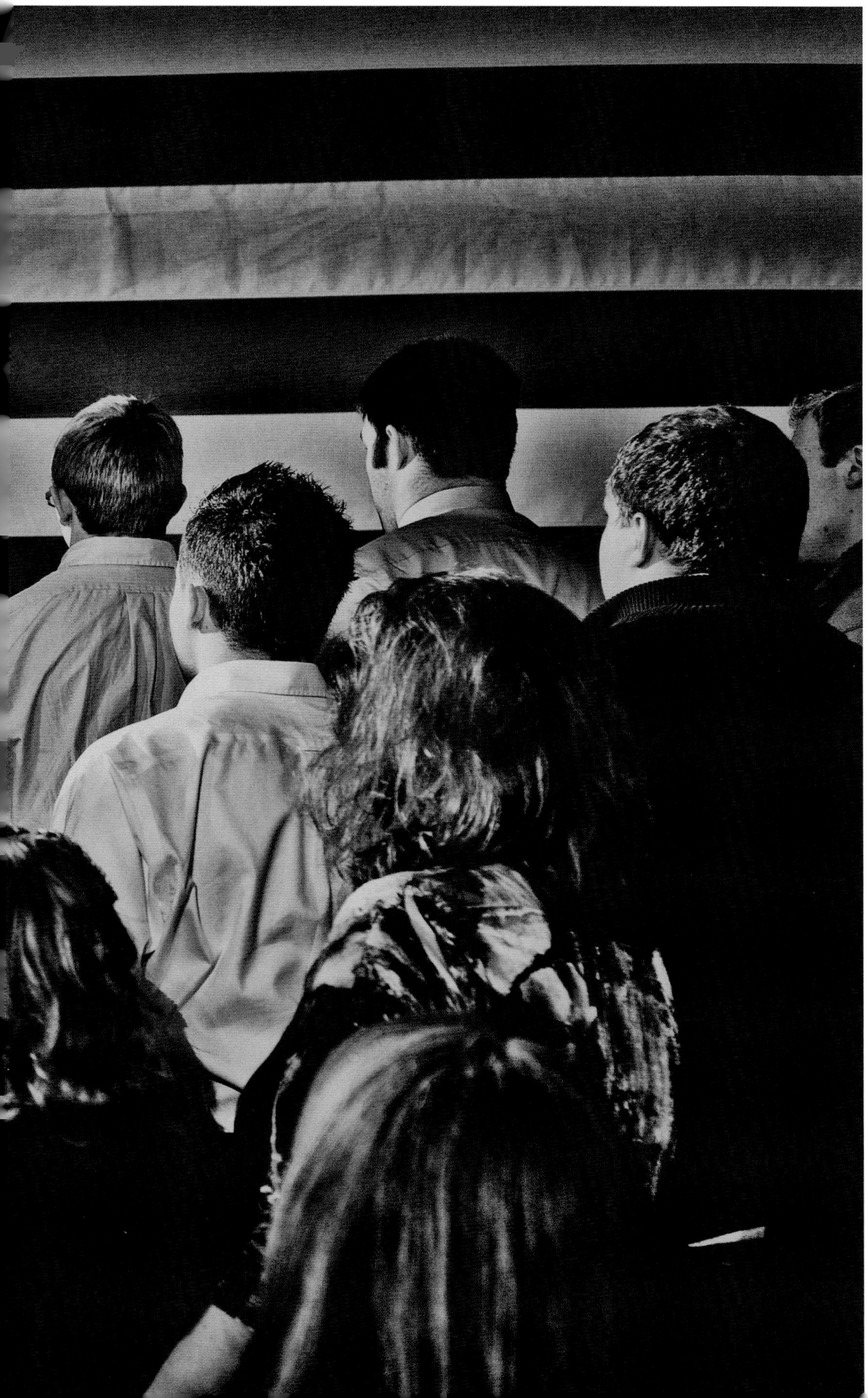

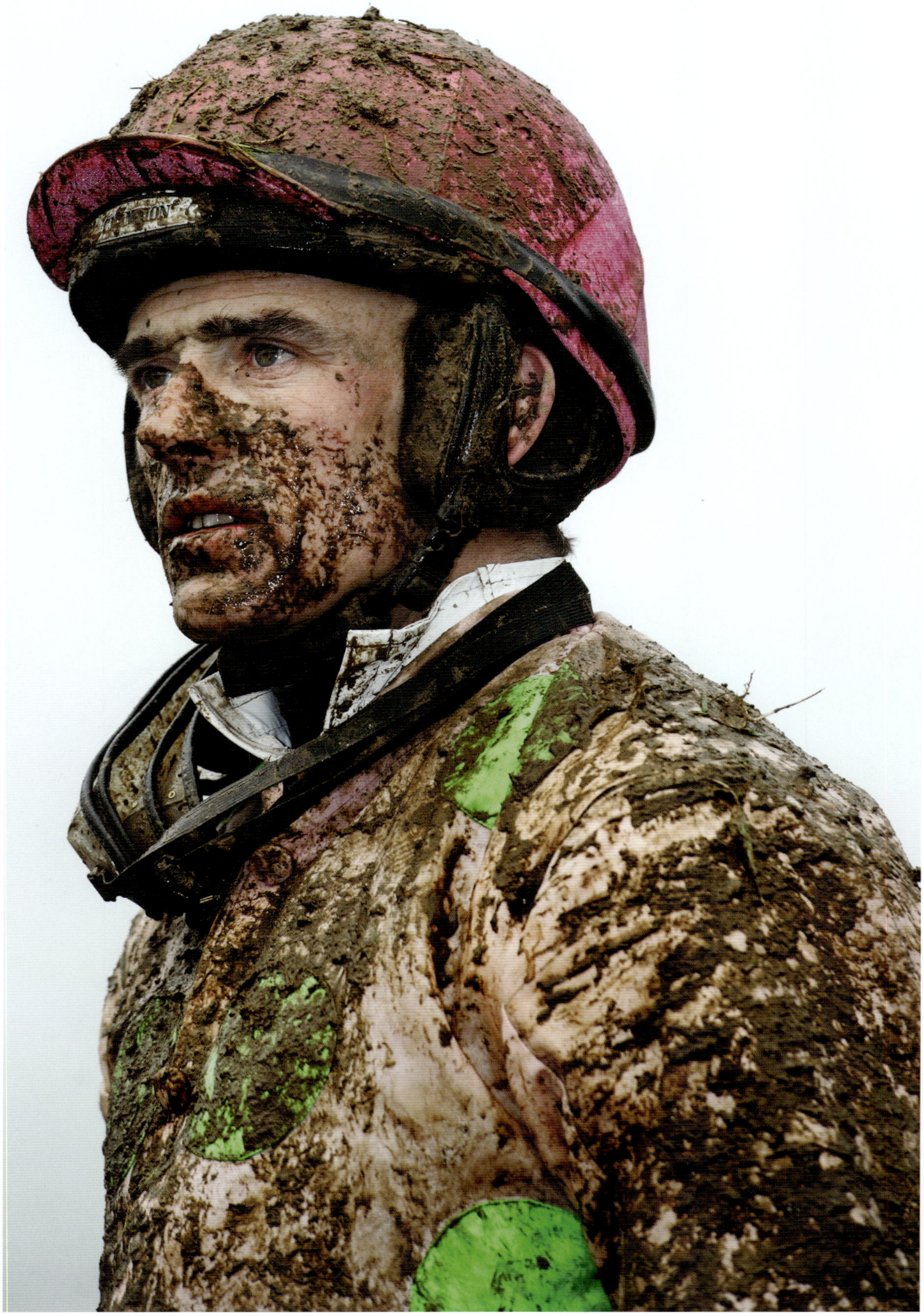

KENNETH O'HALLORAN

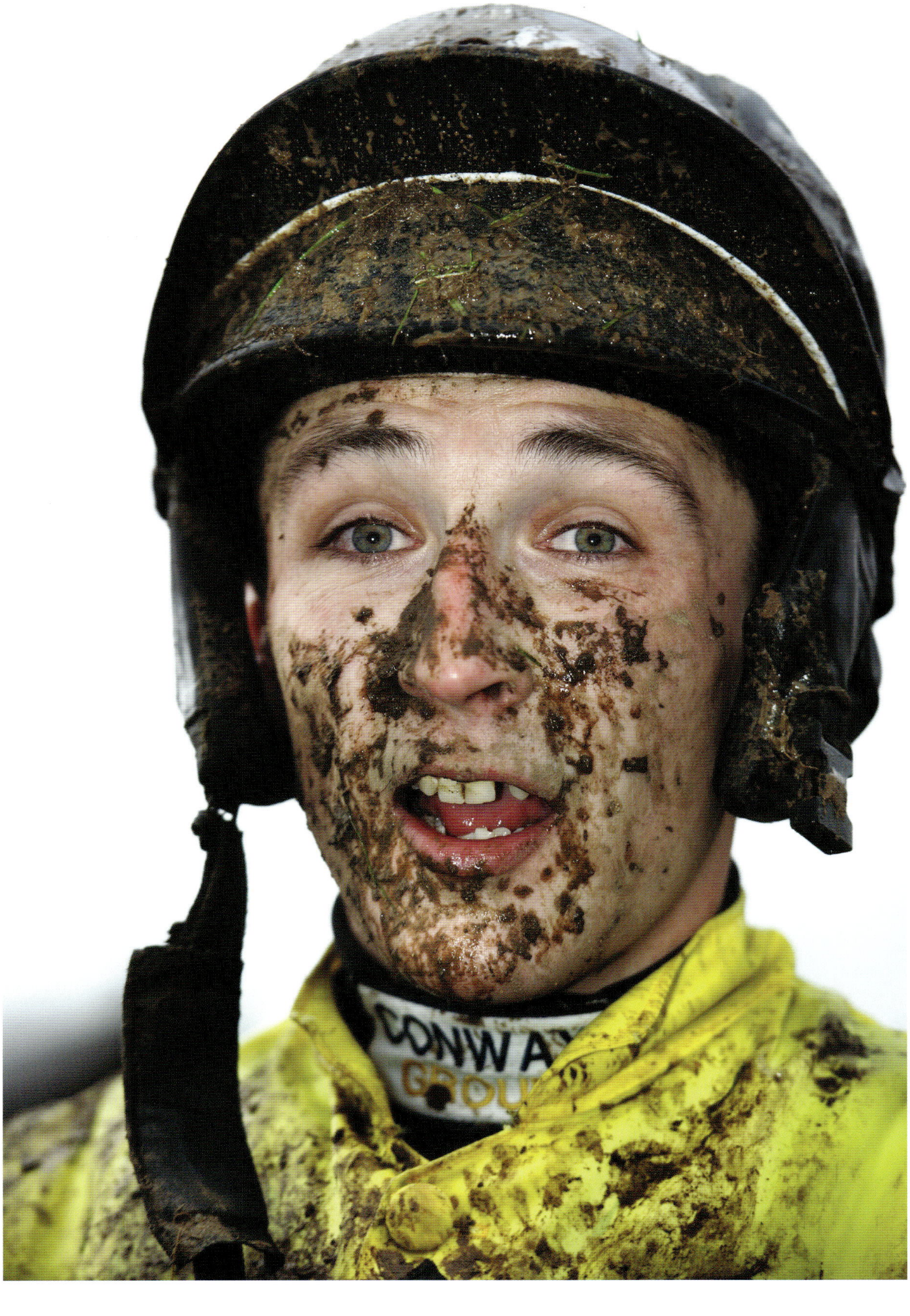

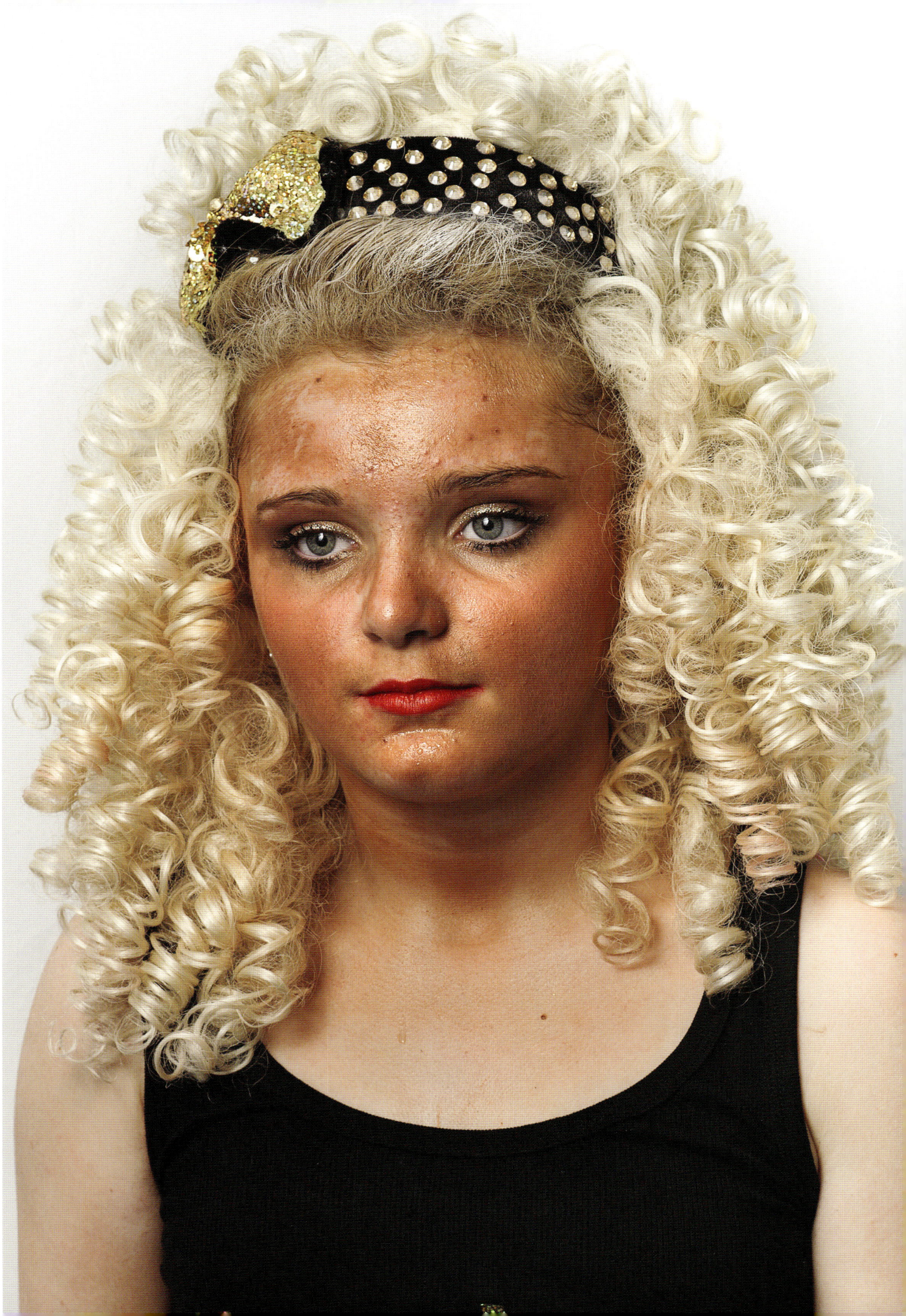

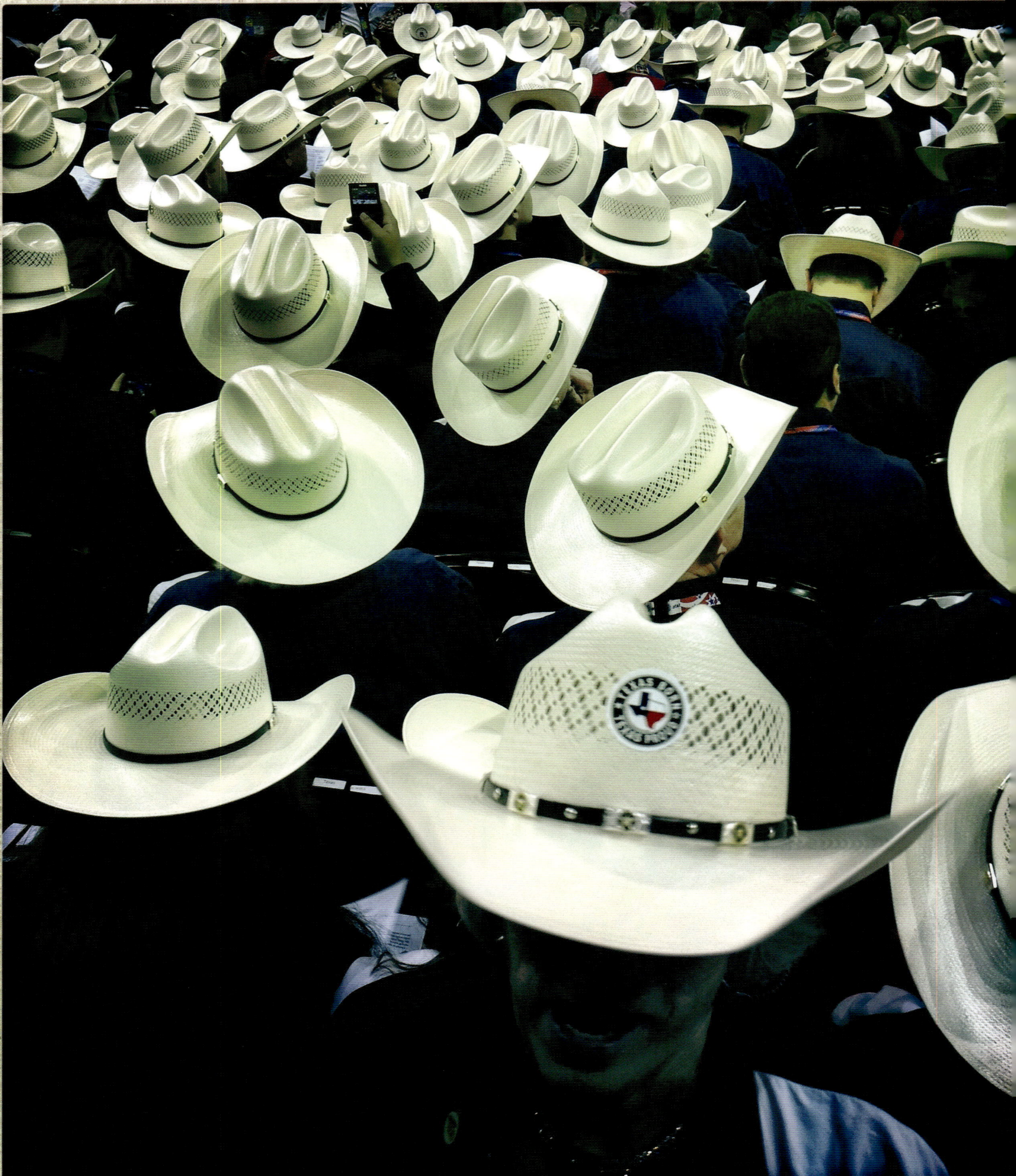

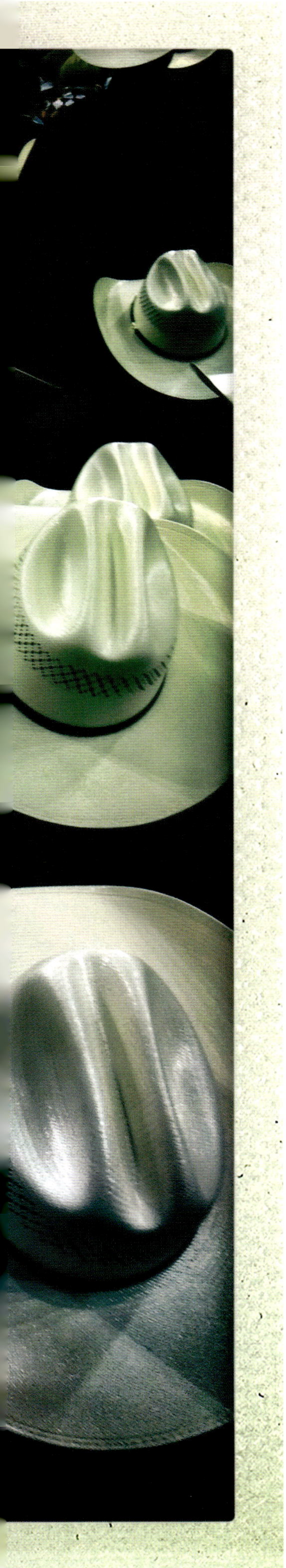

MARK PETERSON

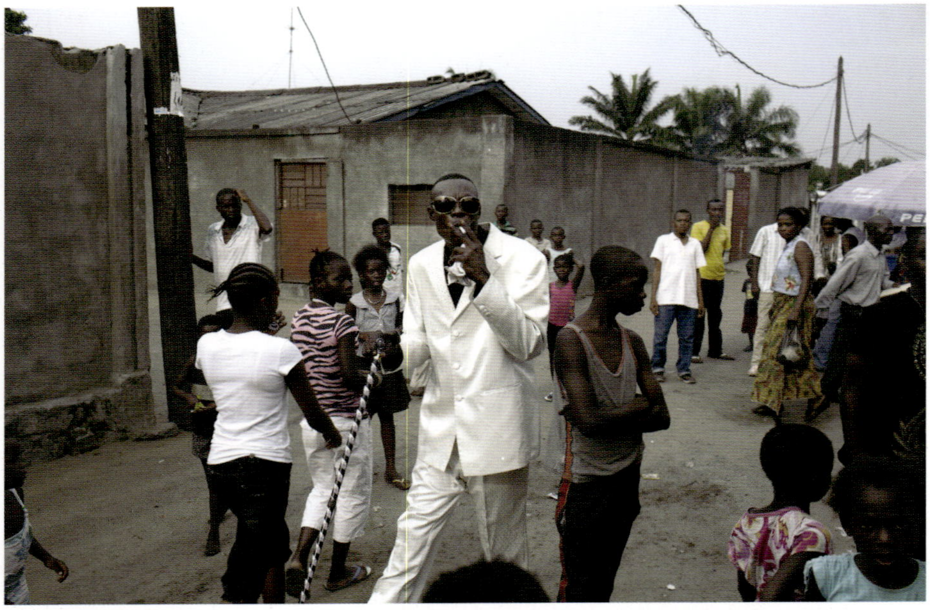

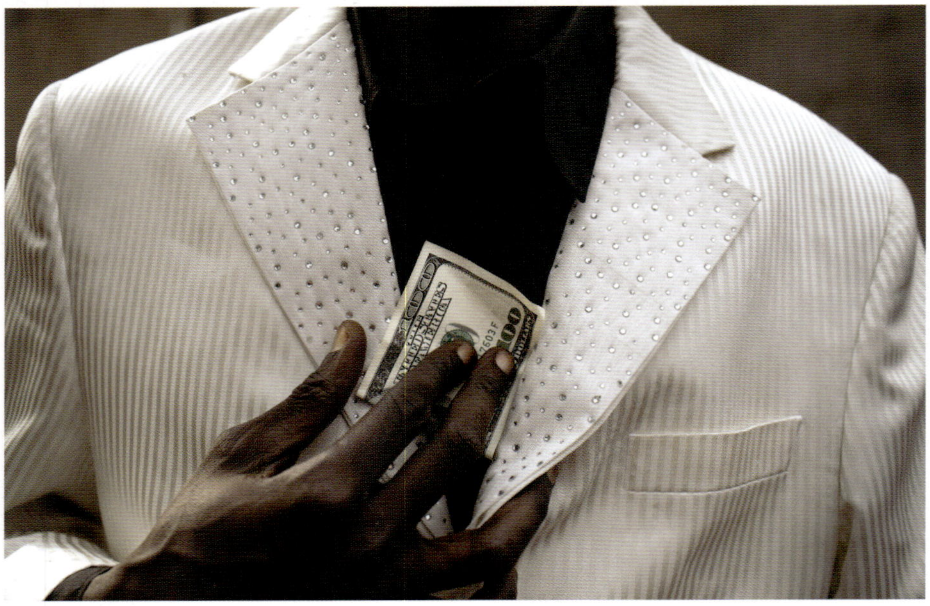

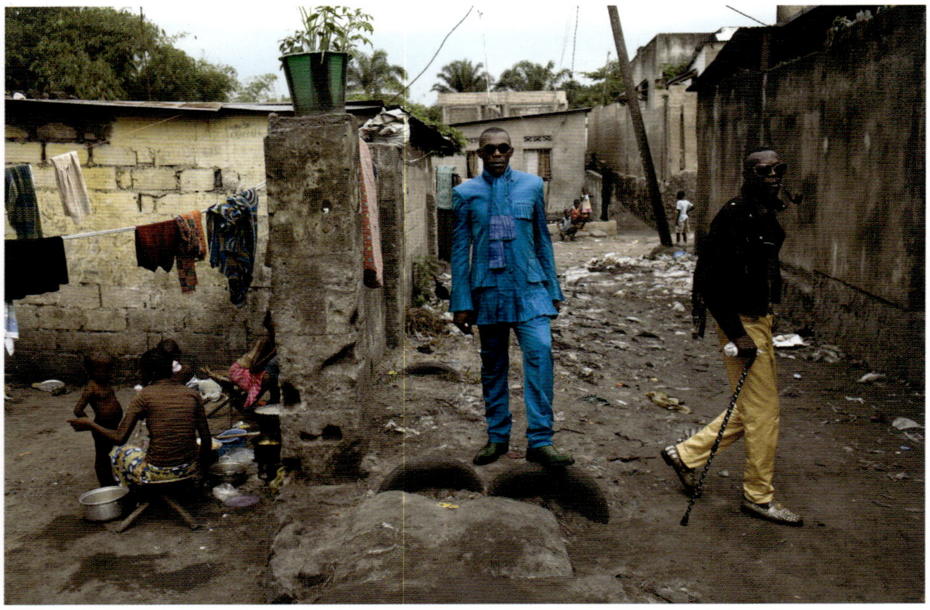

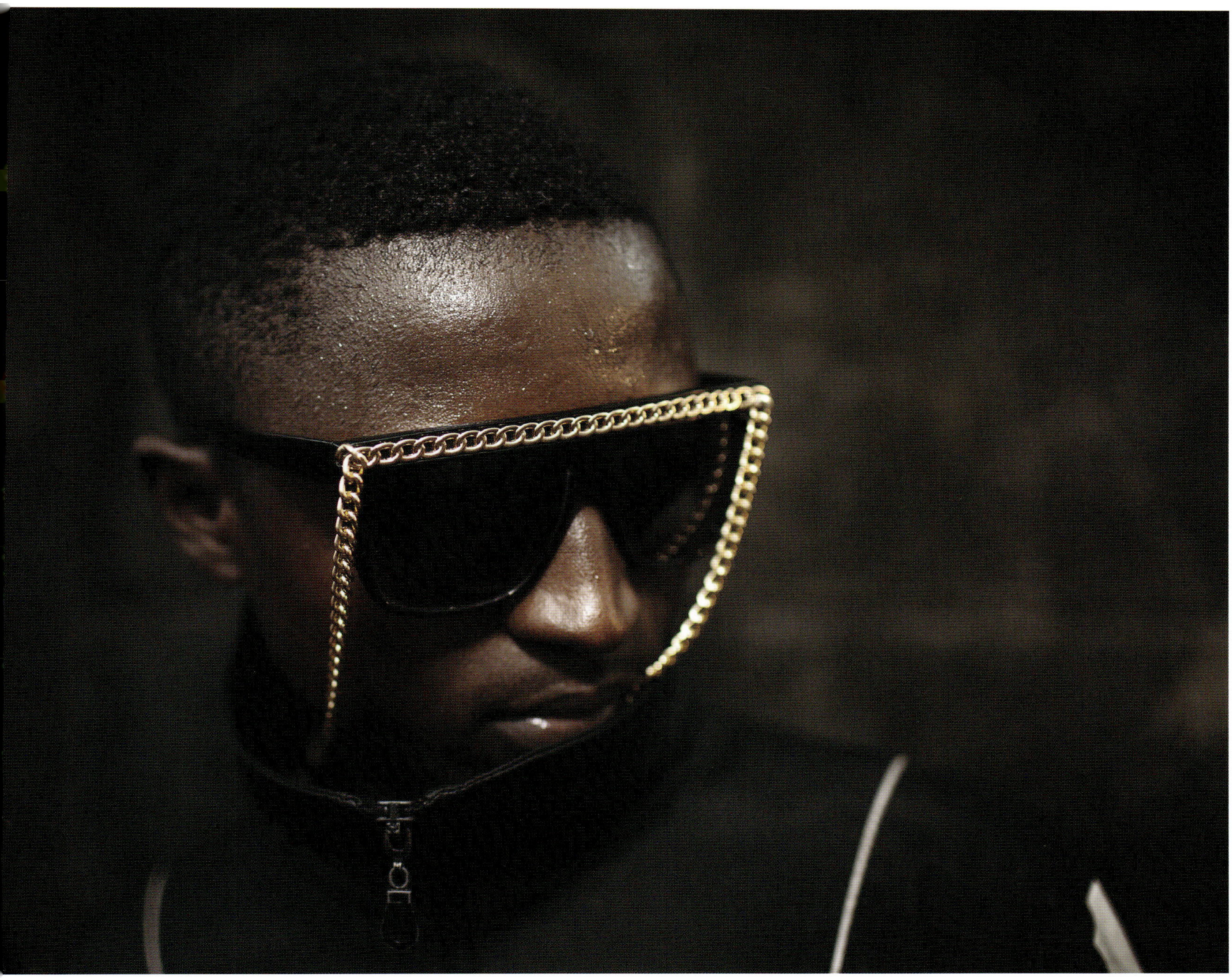

PER-ANDERS
PETTERSSON

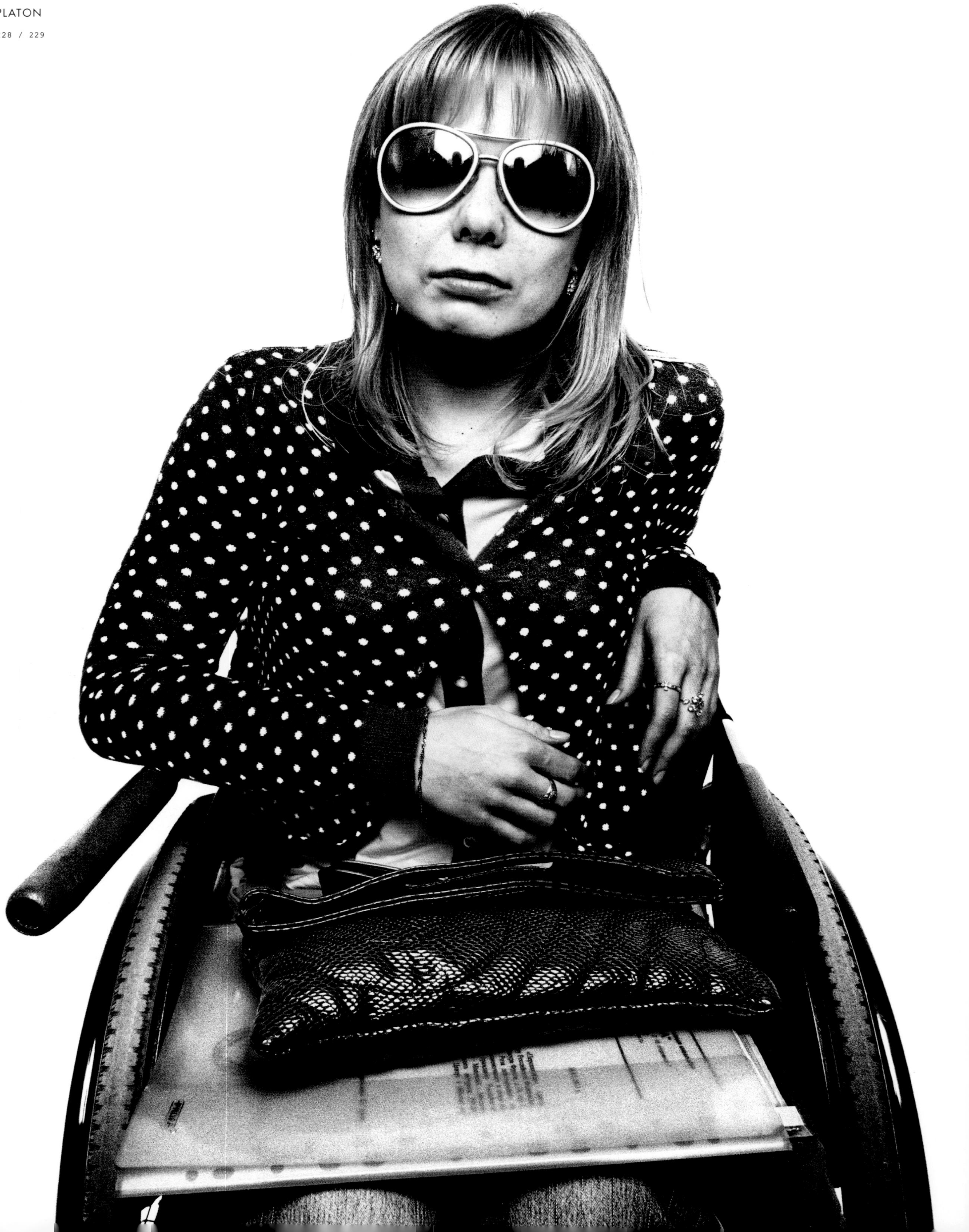

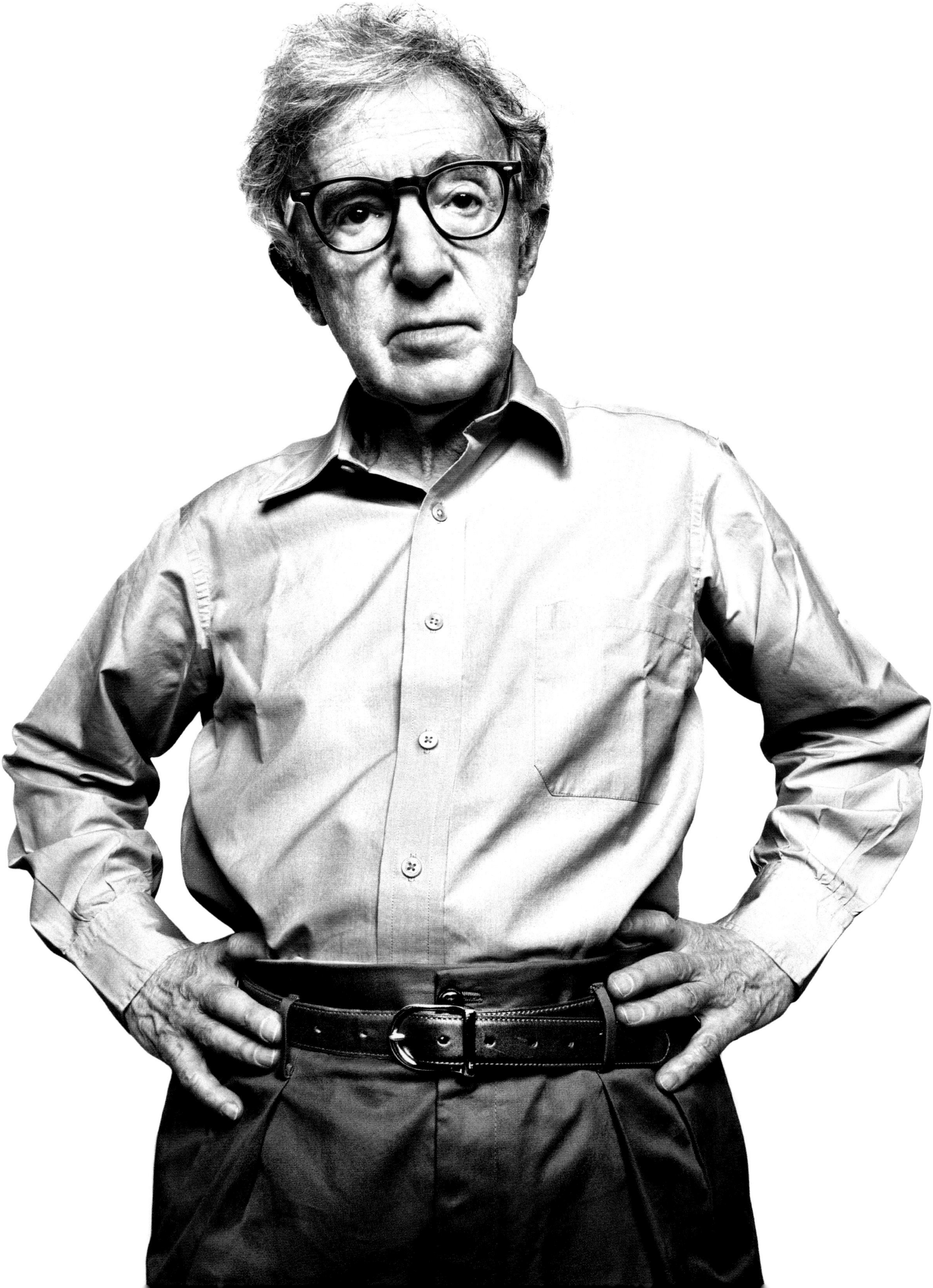

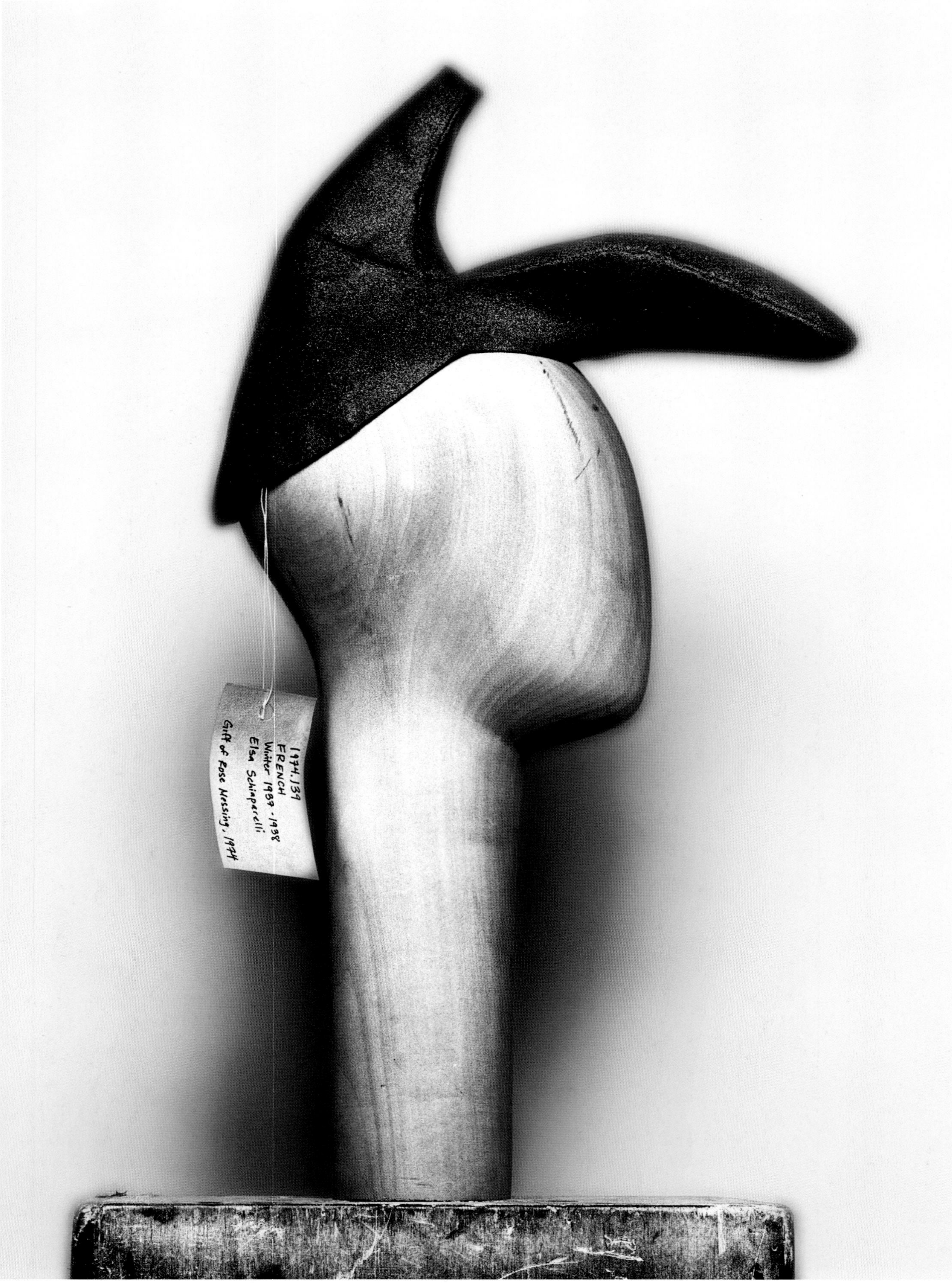
1974.139
FRENCH
Winter 1937-1938
Elsa Schiaparelli
Gift of Rose Messing, 1974

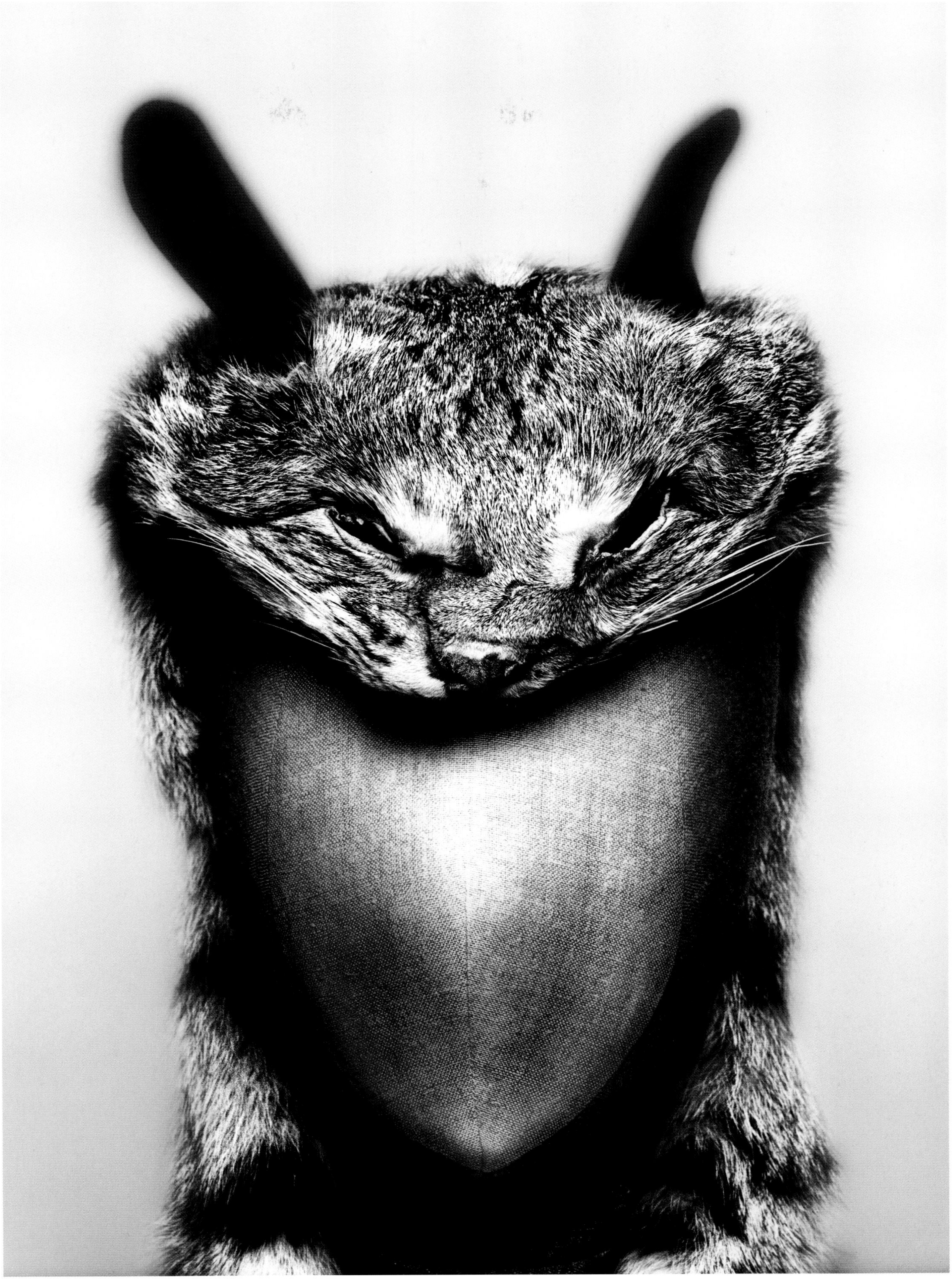

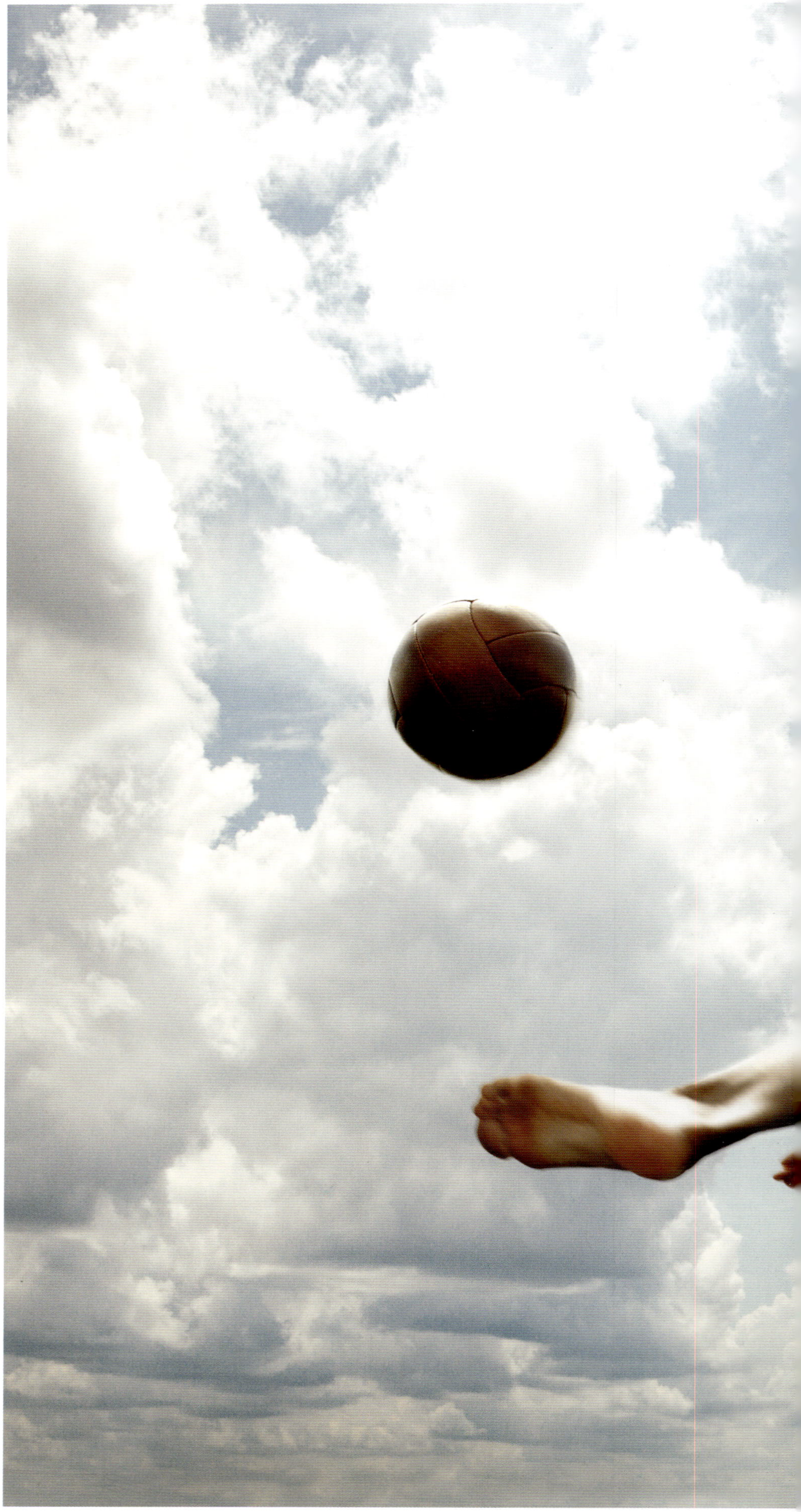

RICHARD PHIBBS

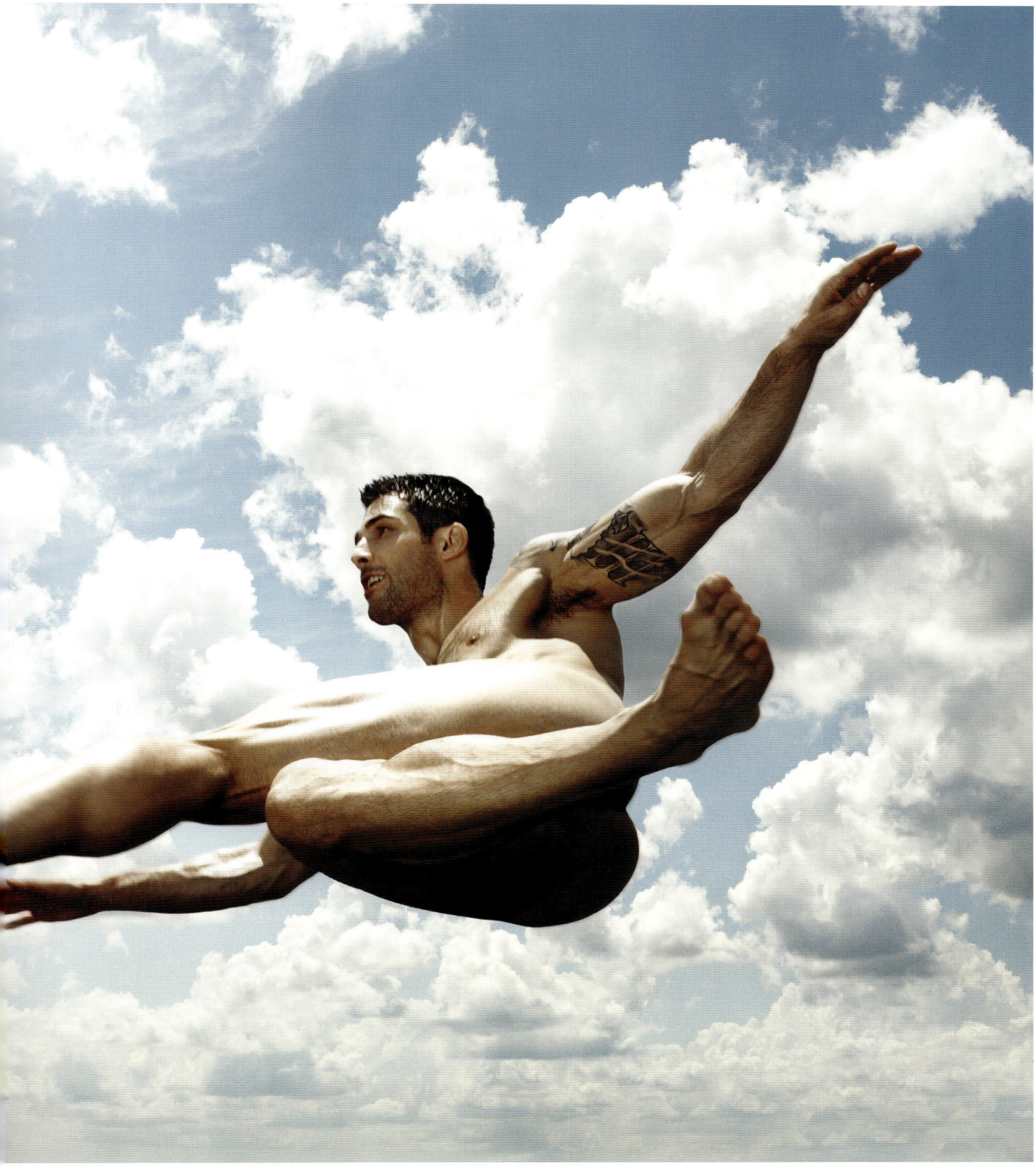

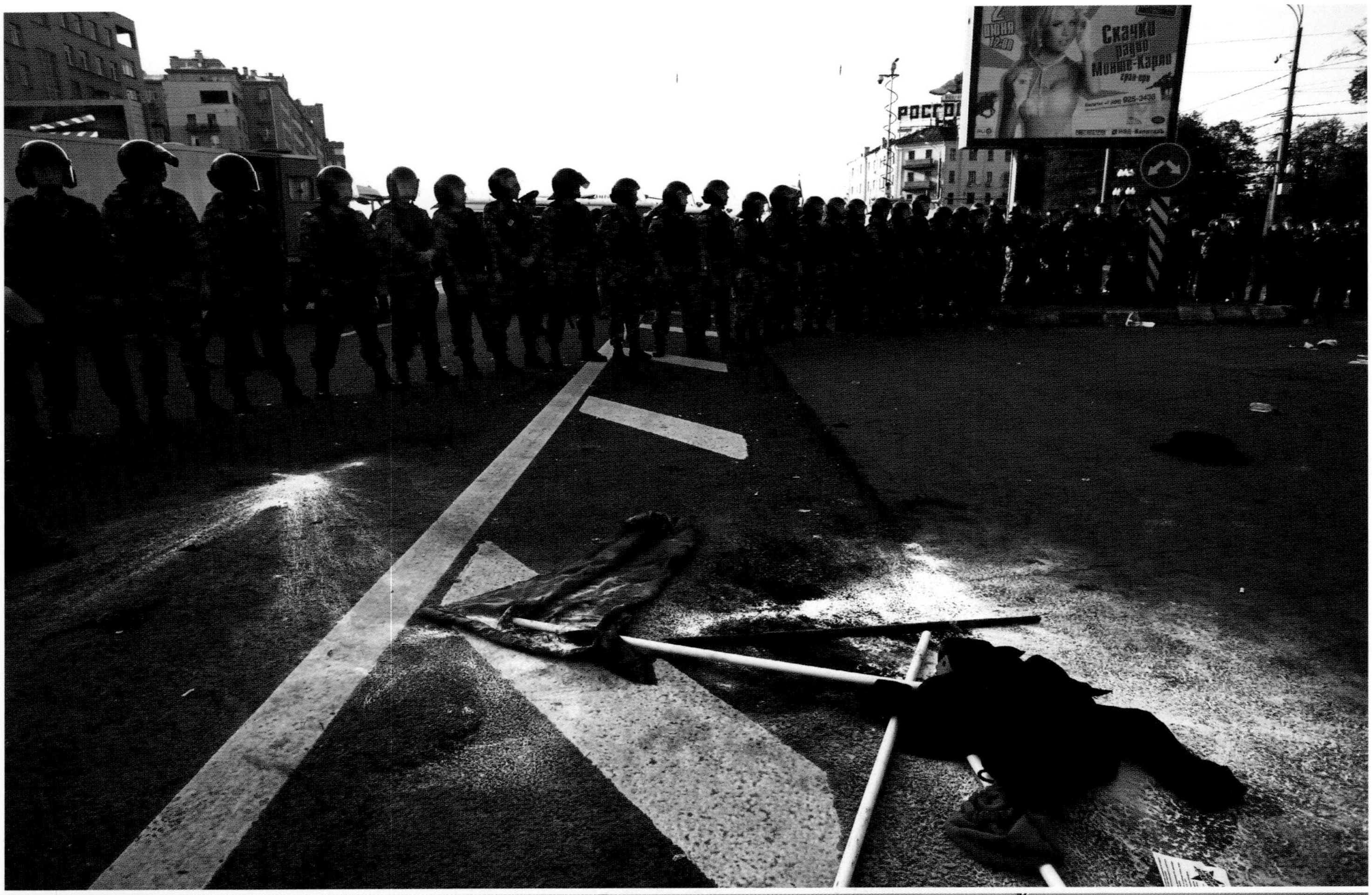
Скачки

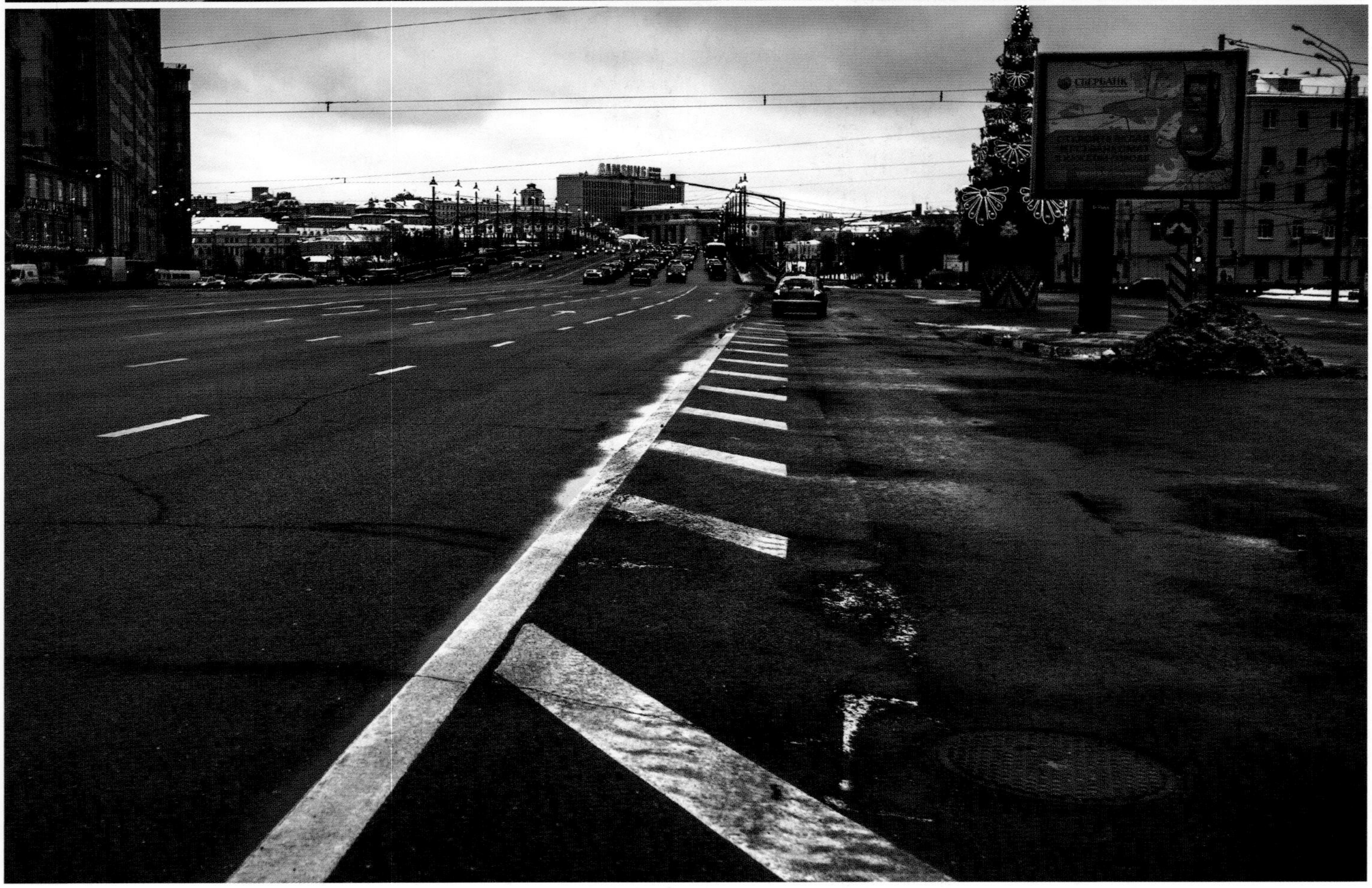
СБЕРБАНК

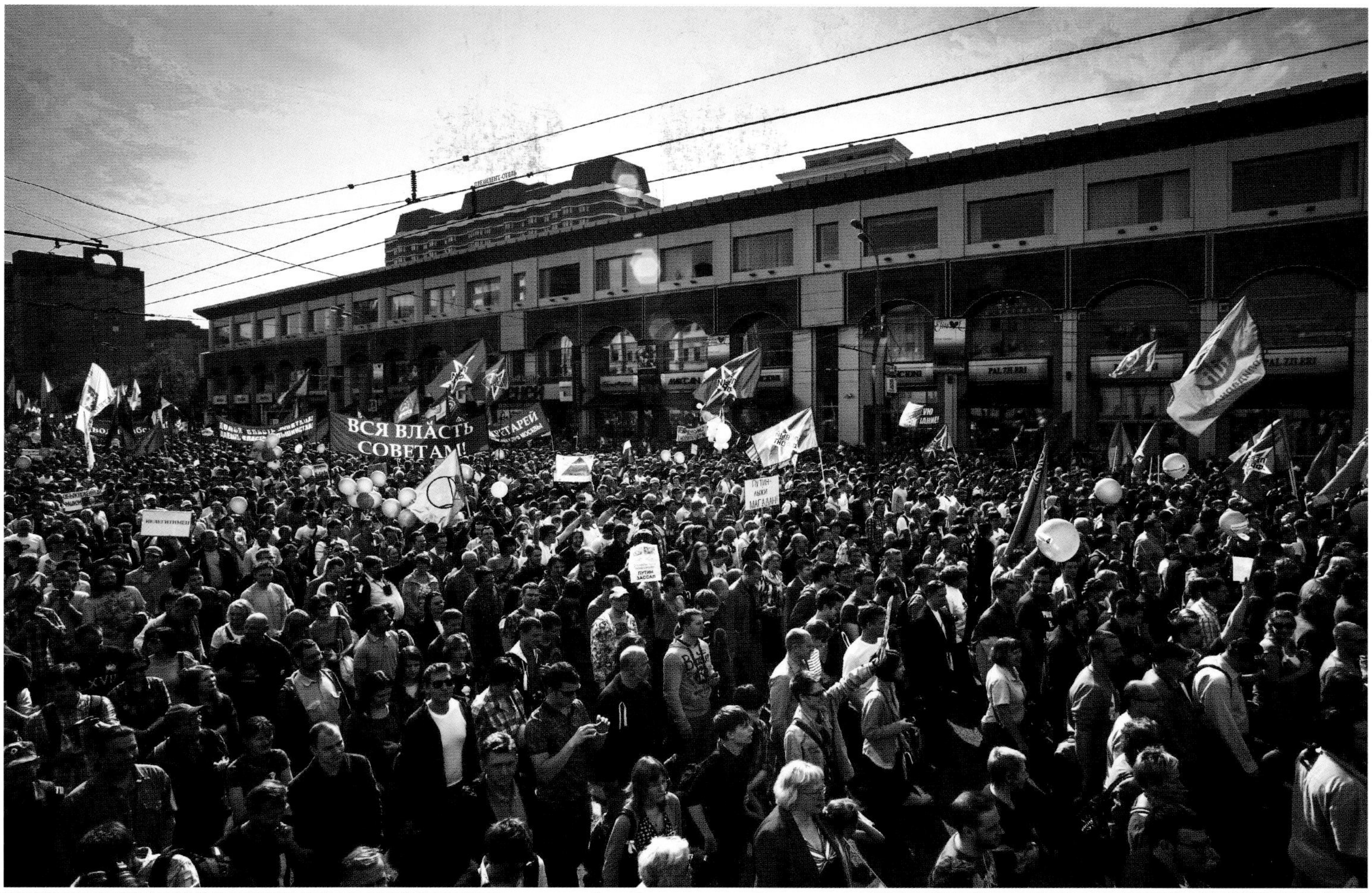
ВСЯ ВЛАСТЬ
СОВЕТАМ!

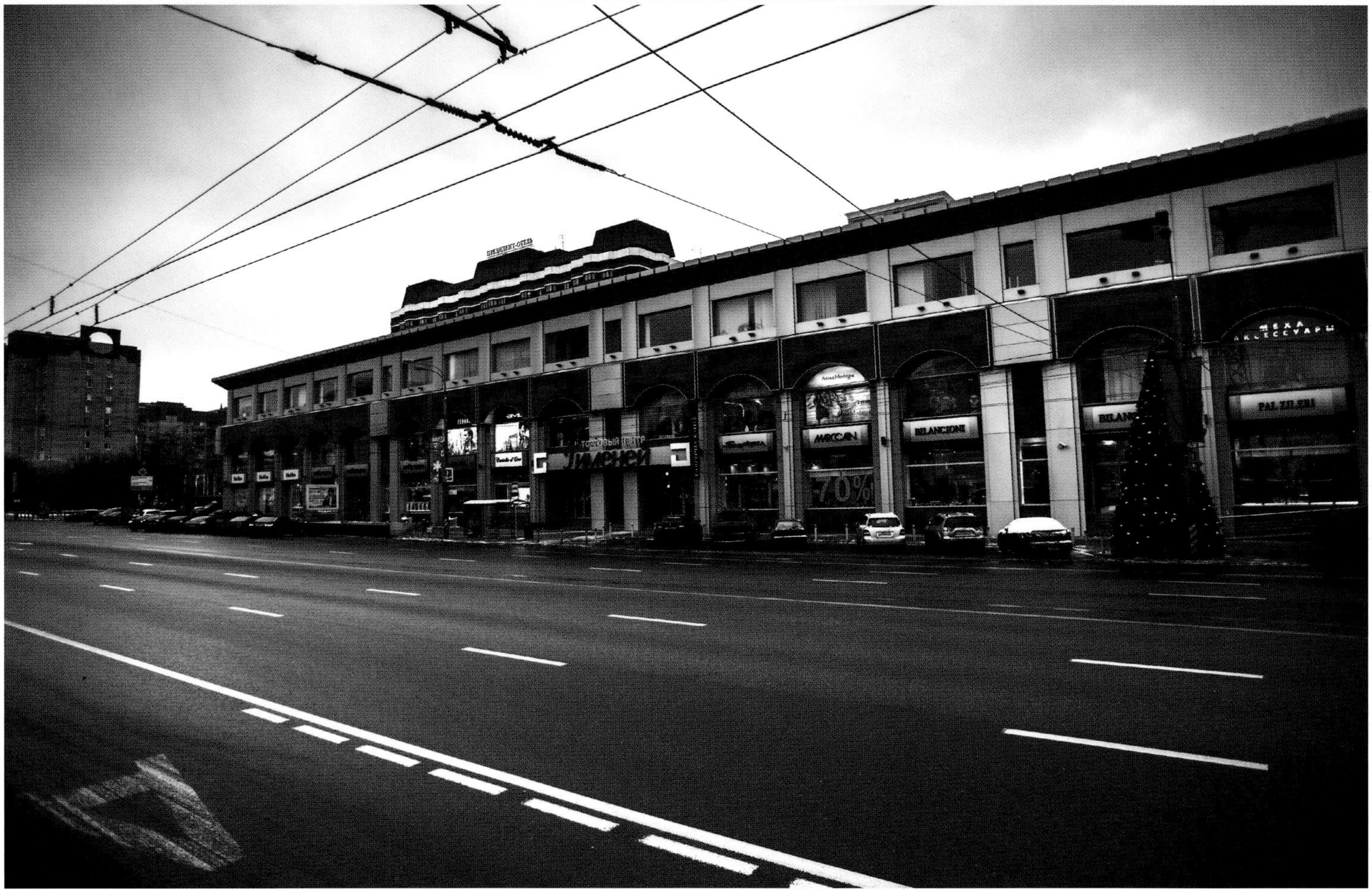
PAL ZILERI
70%

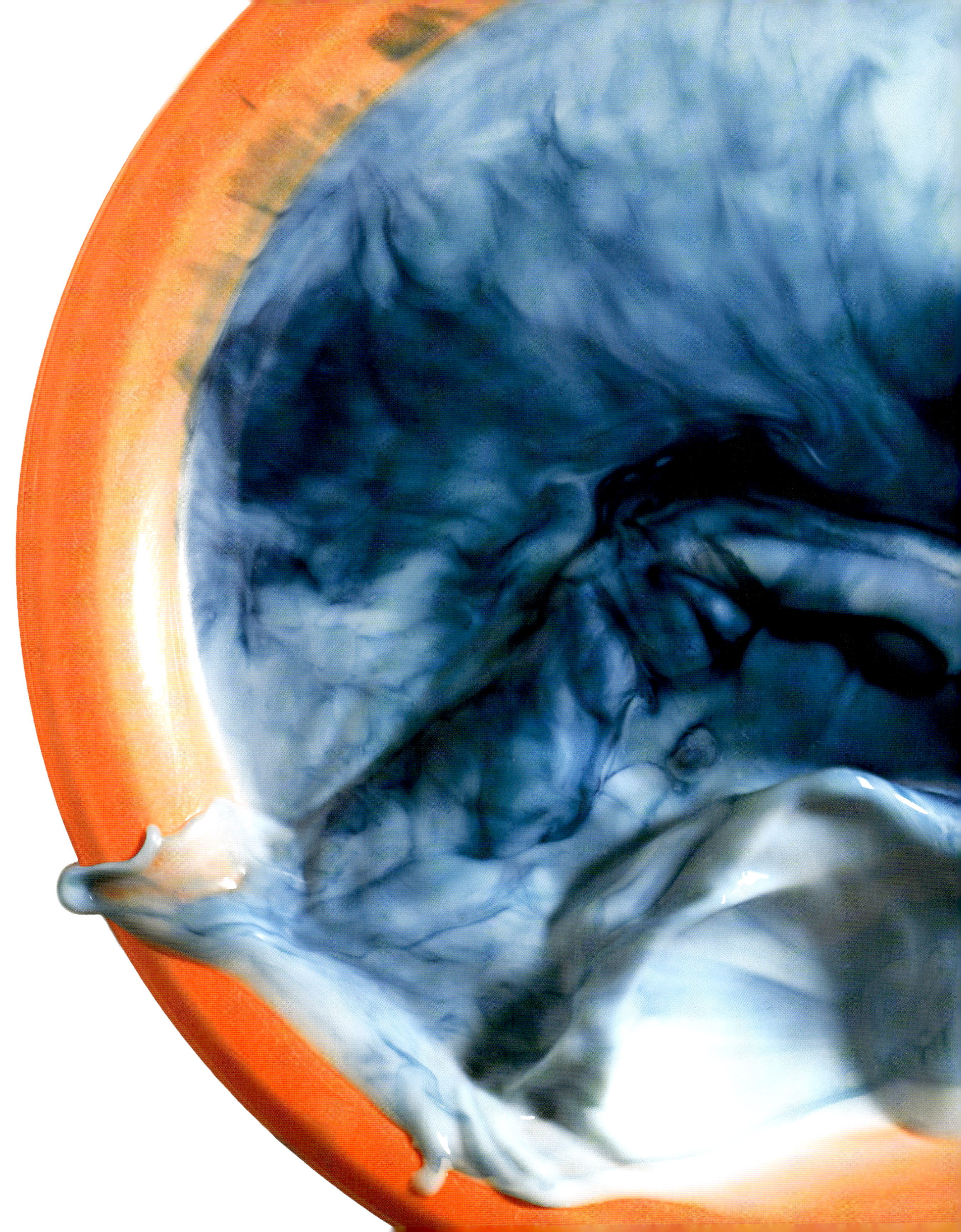

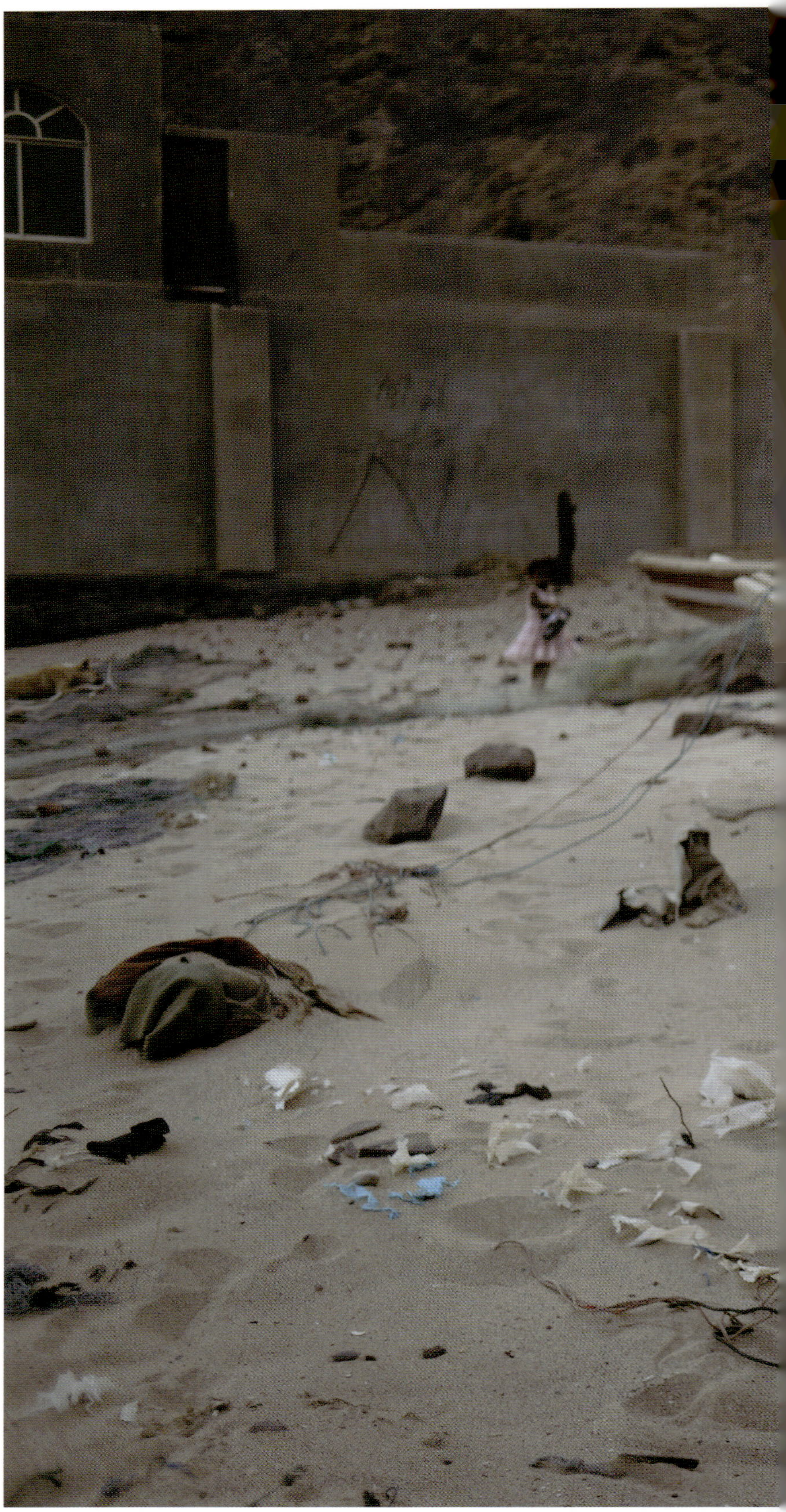

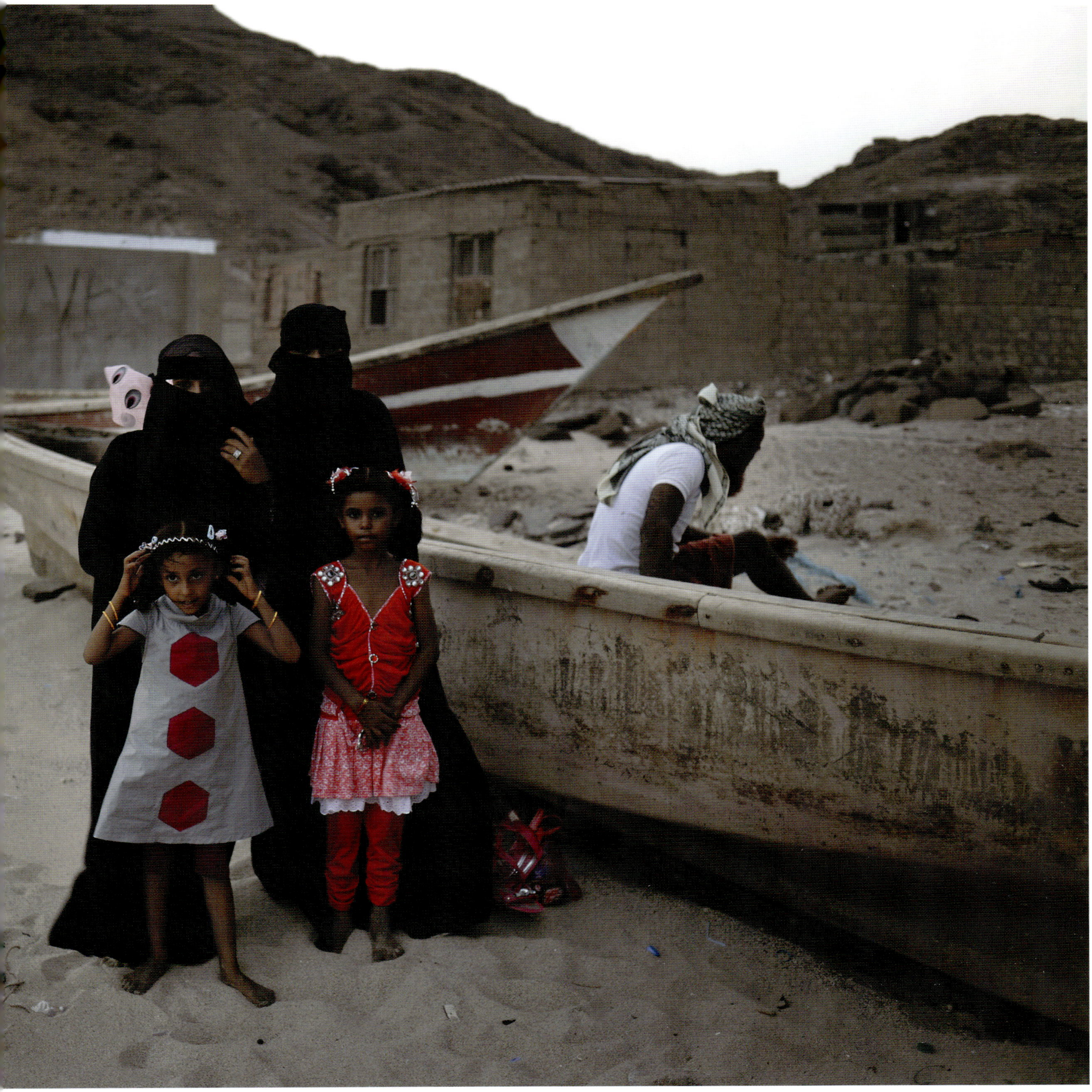

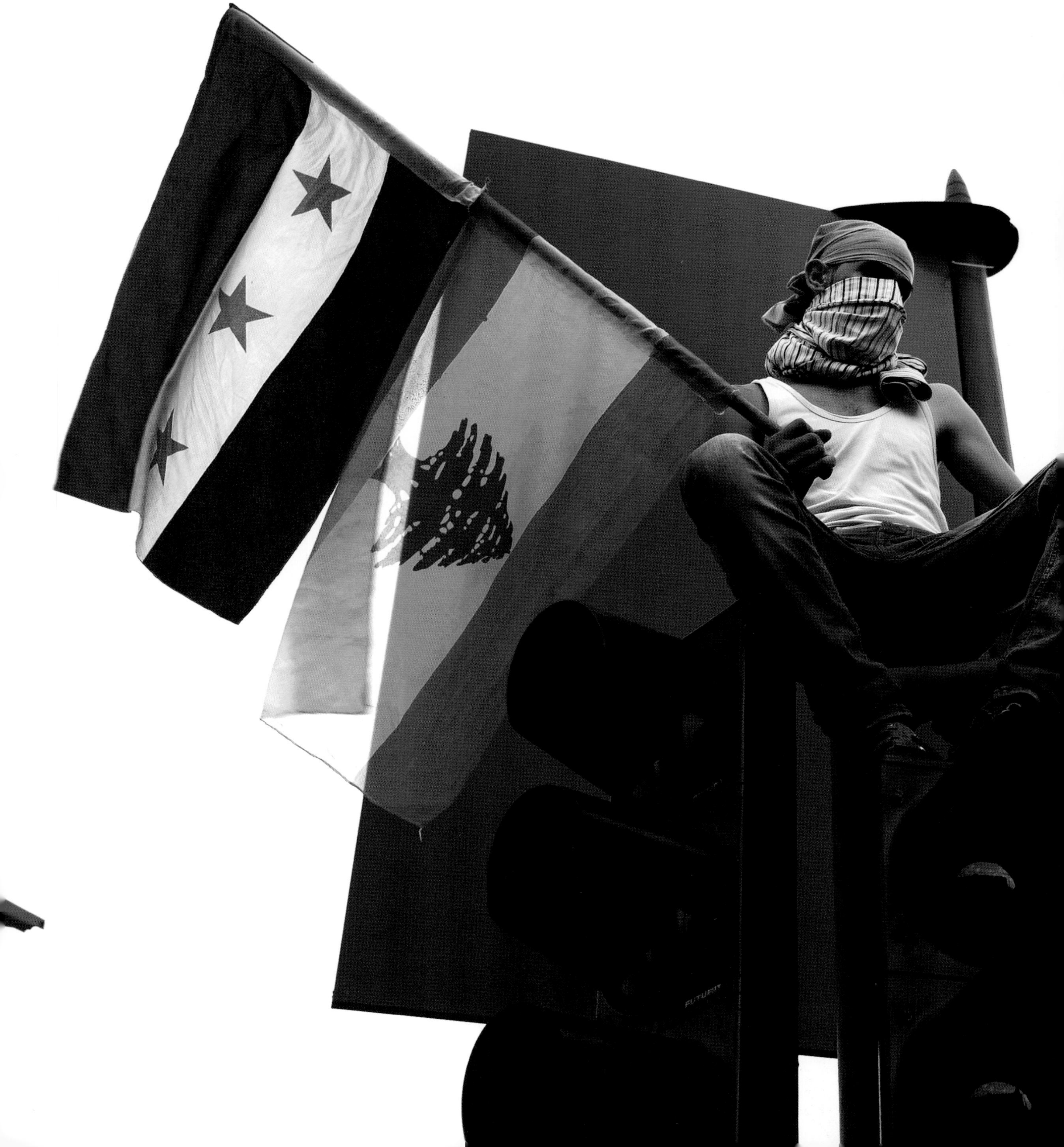

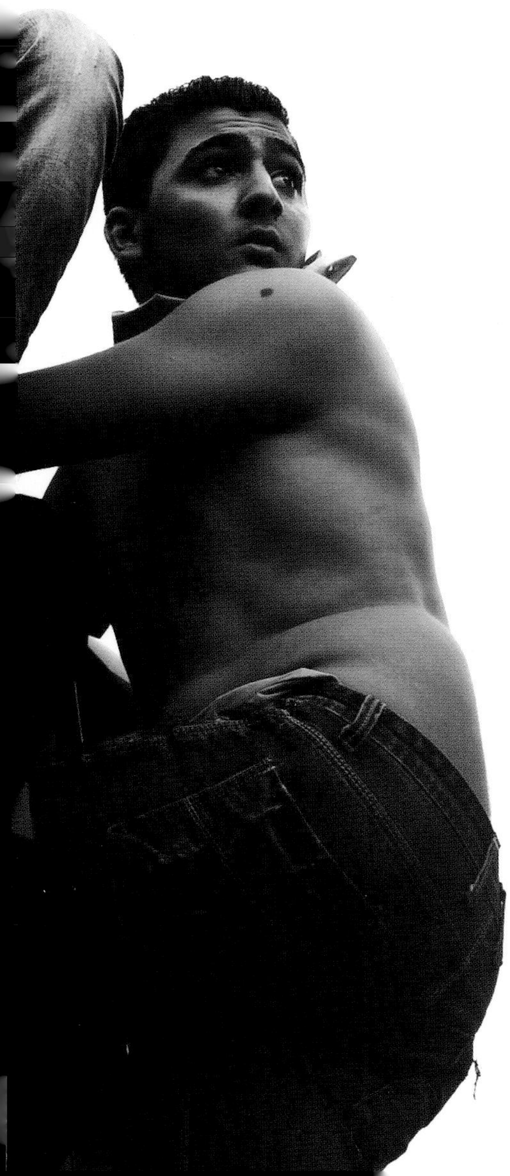

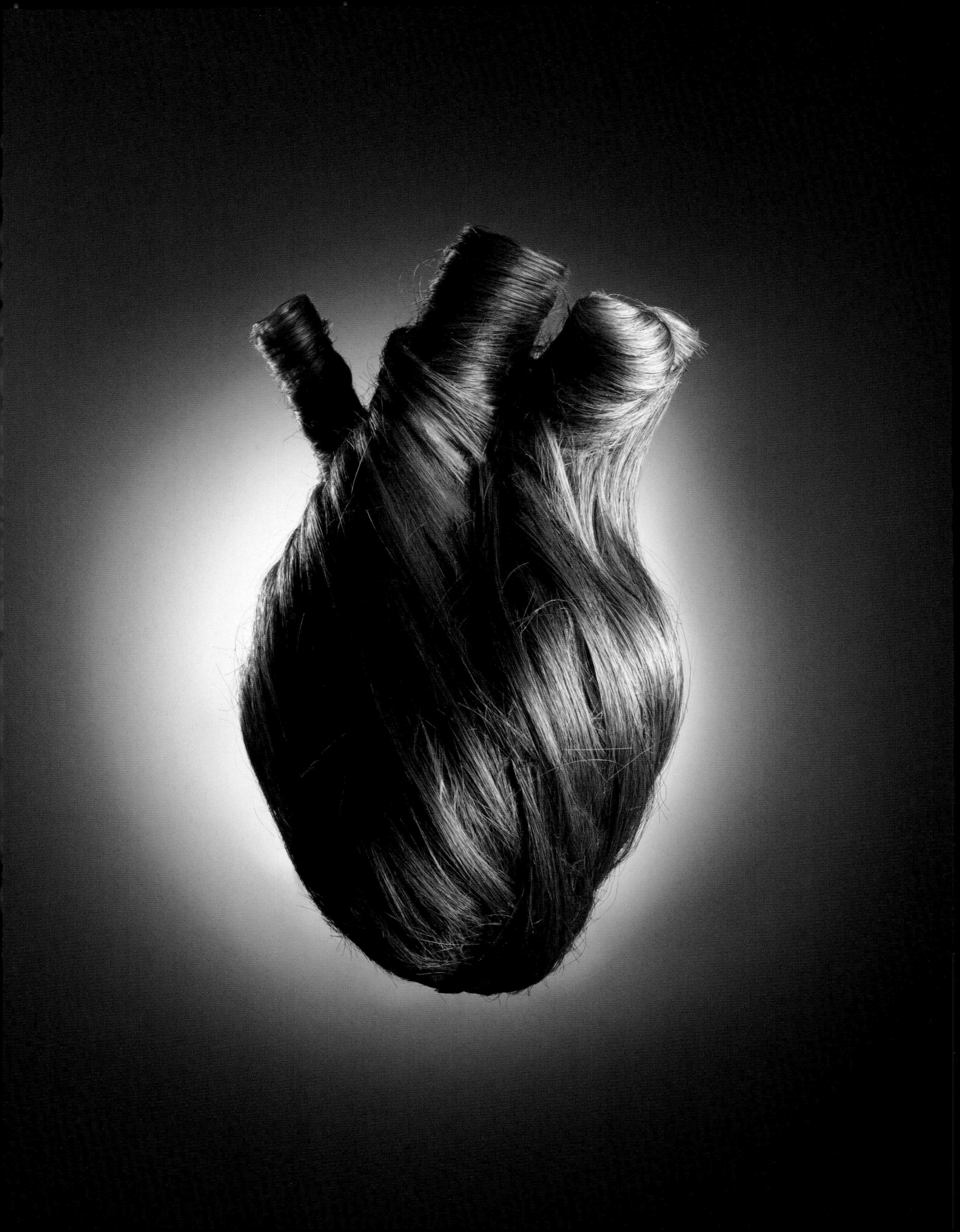

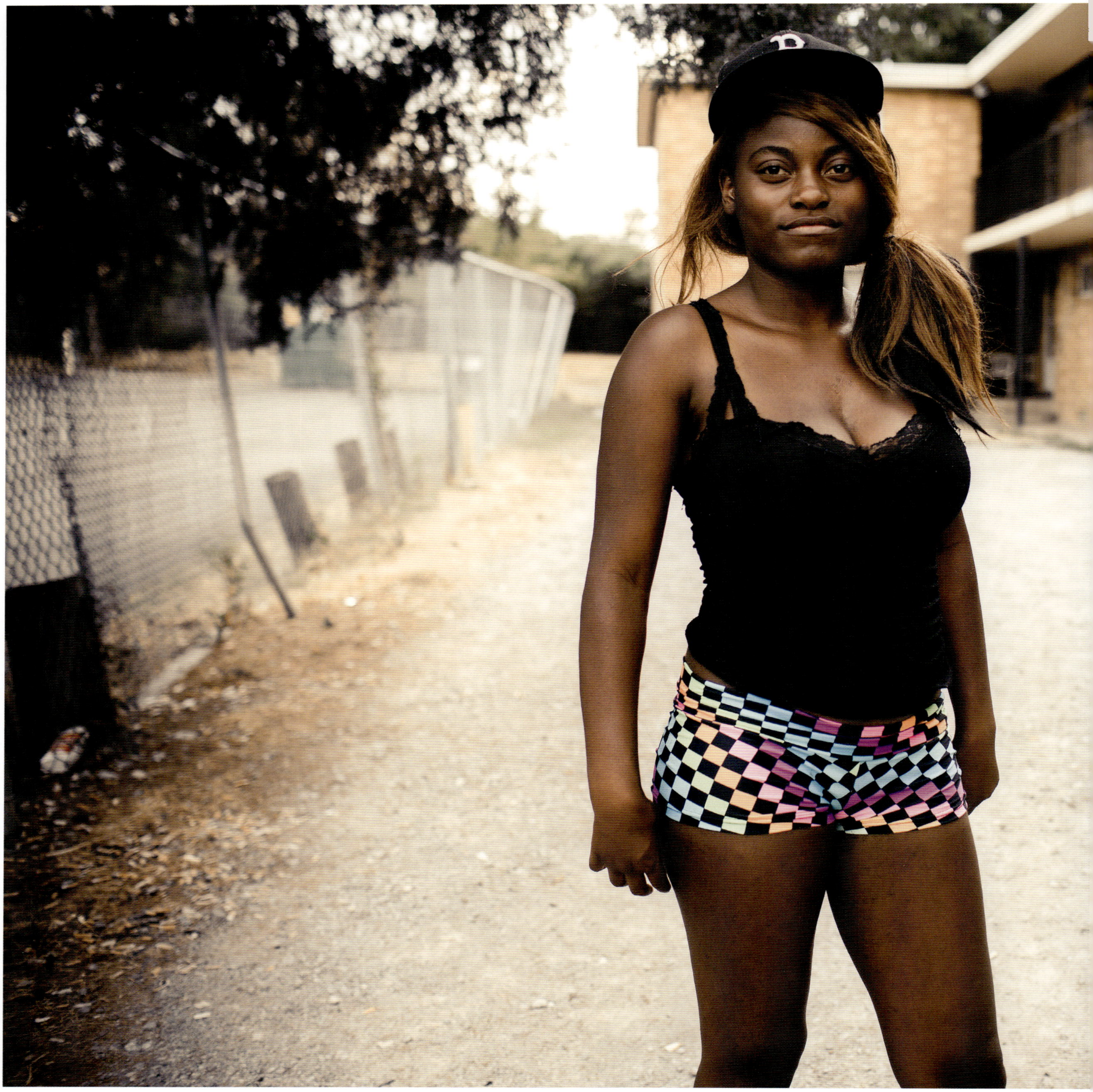

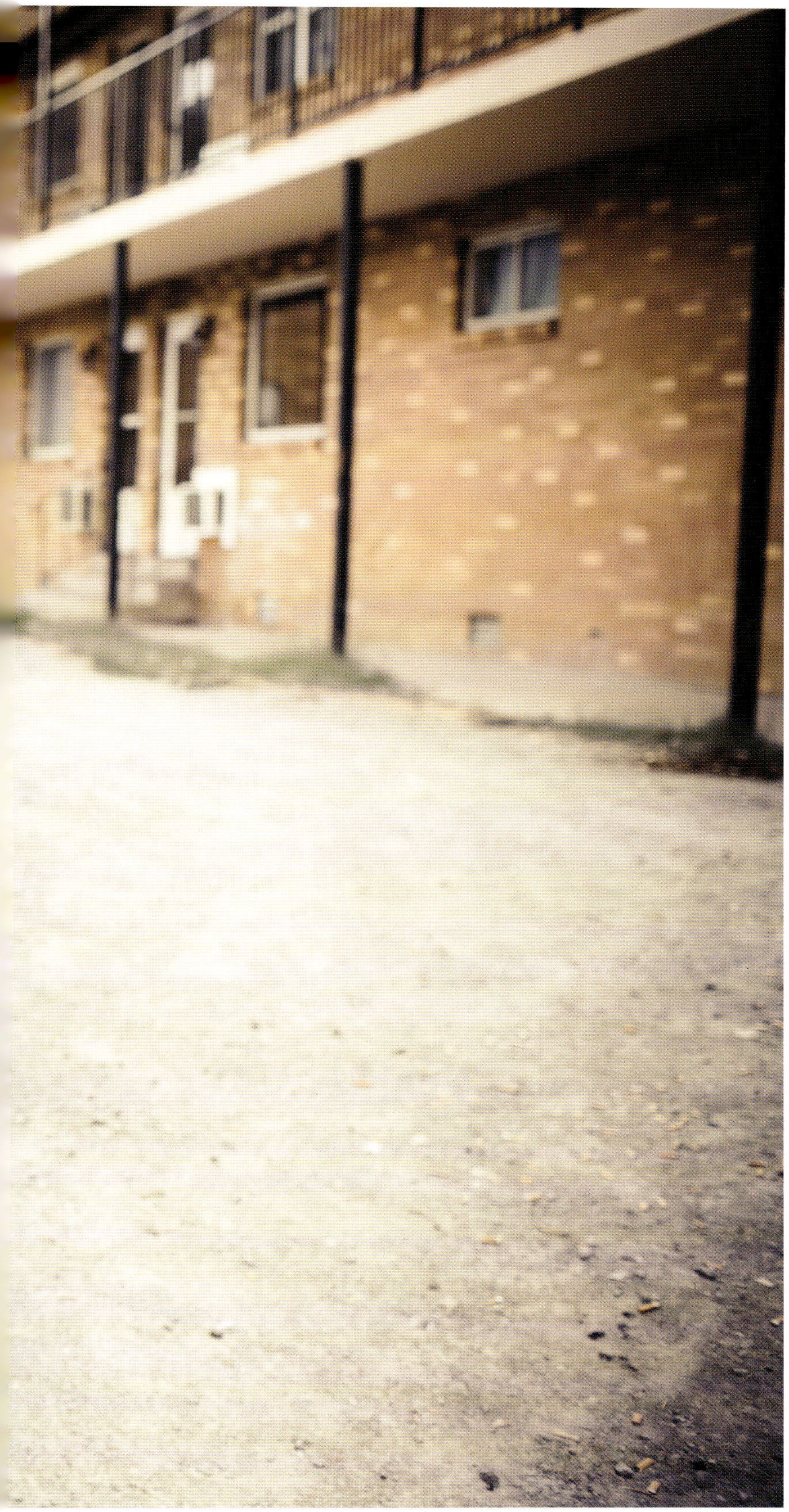

TAMARA REYNOLDS

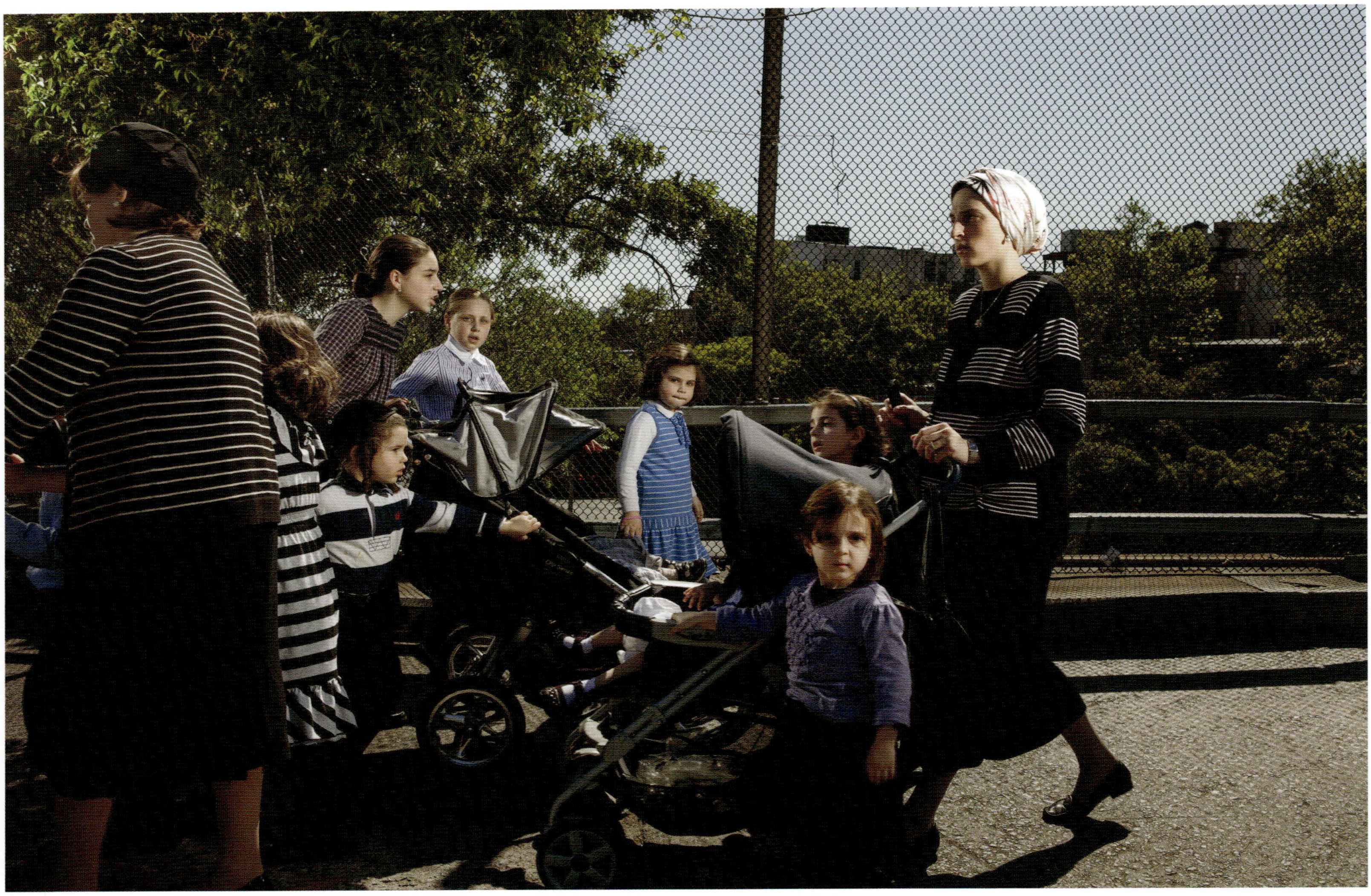

NICK RUECHEL

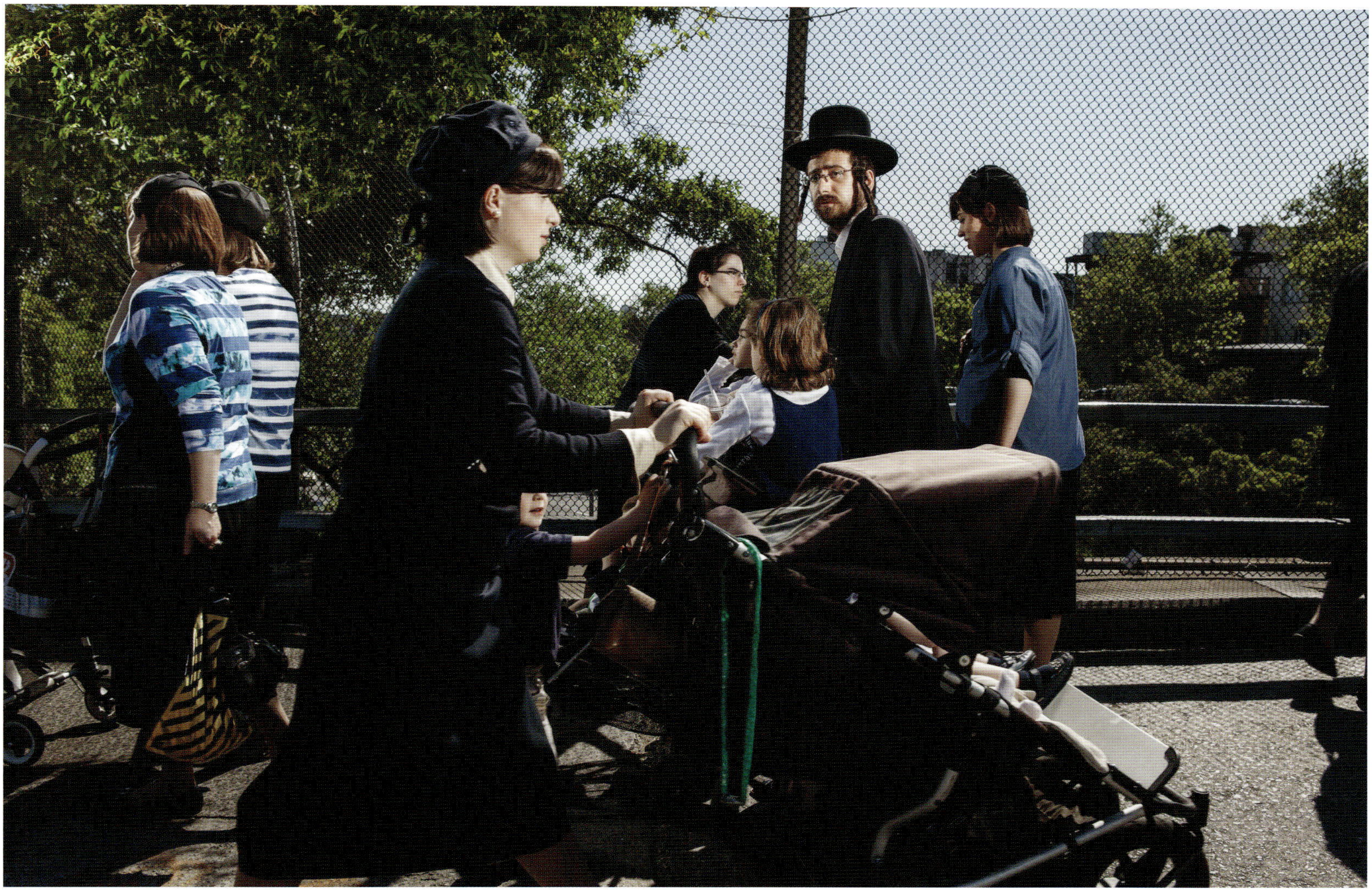

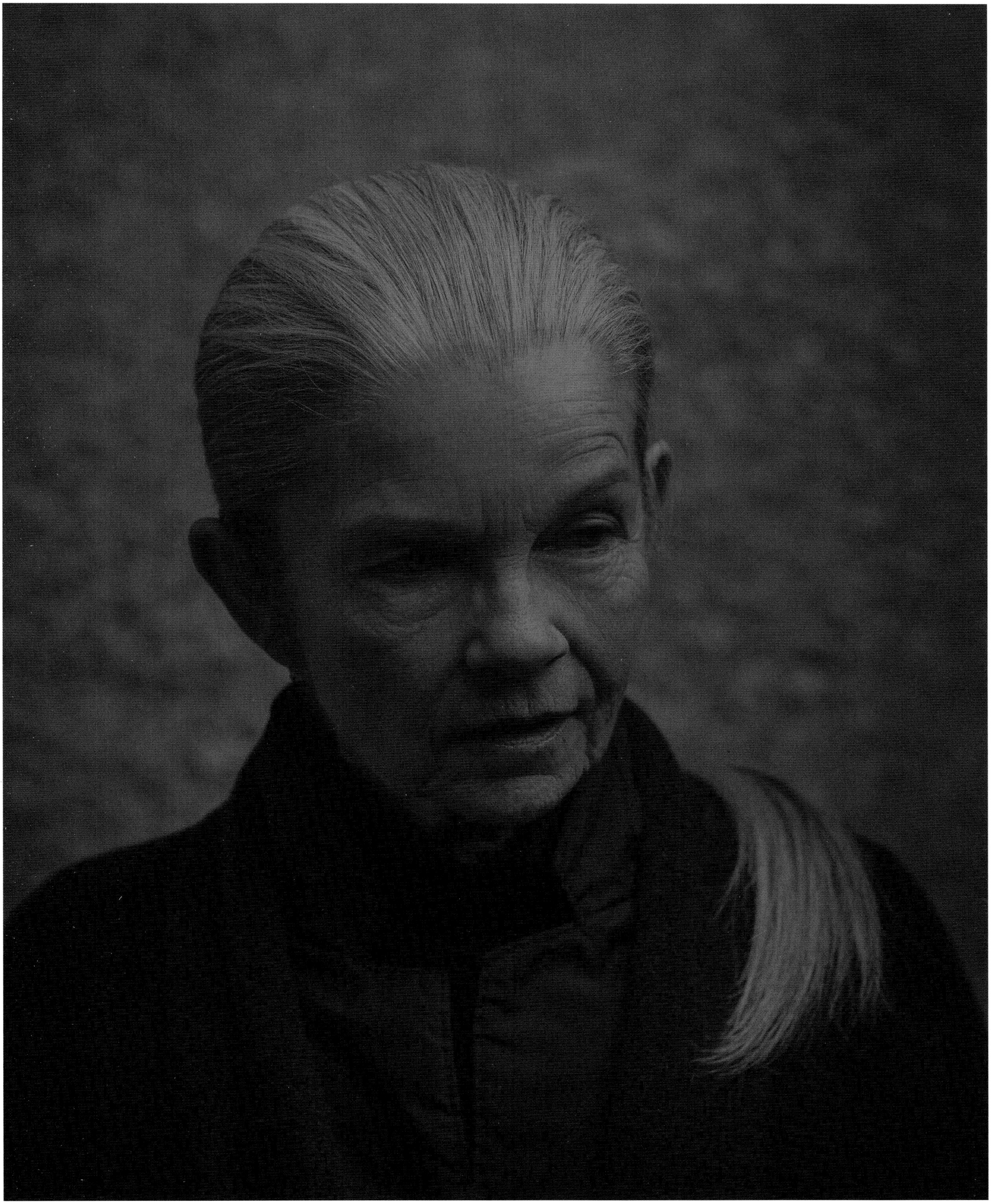

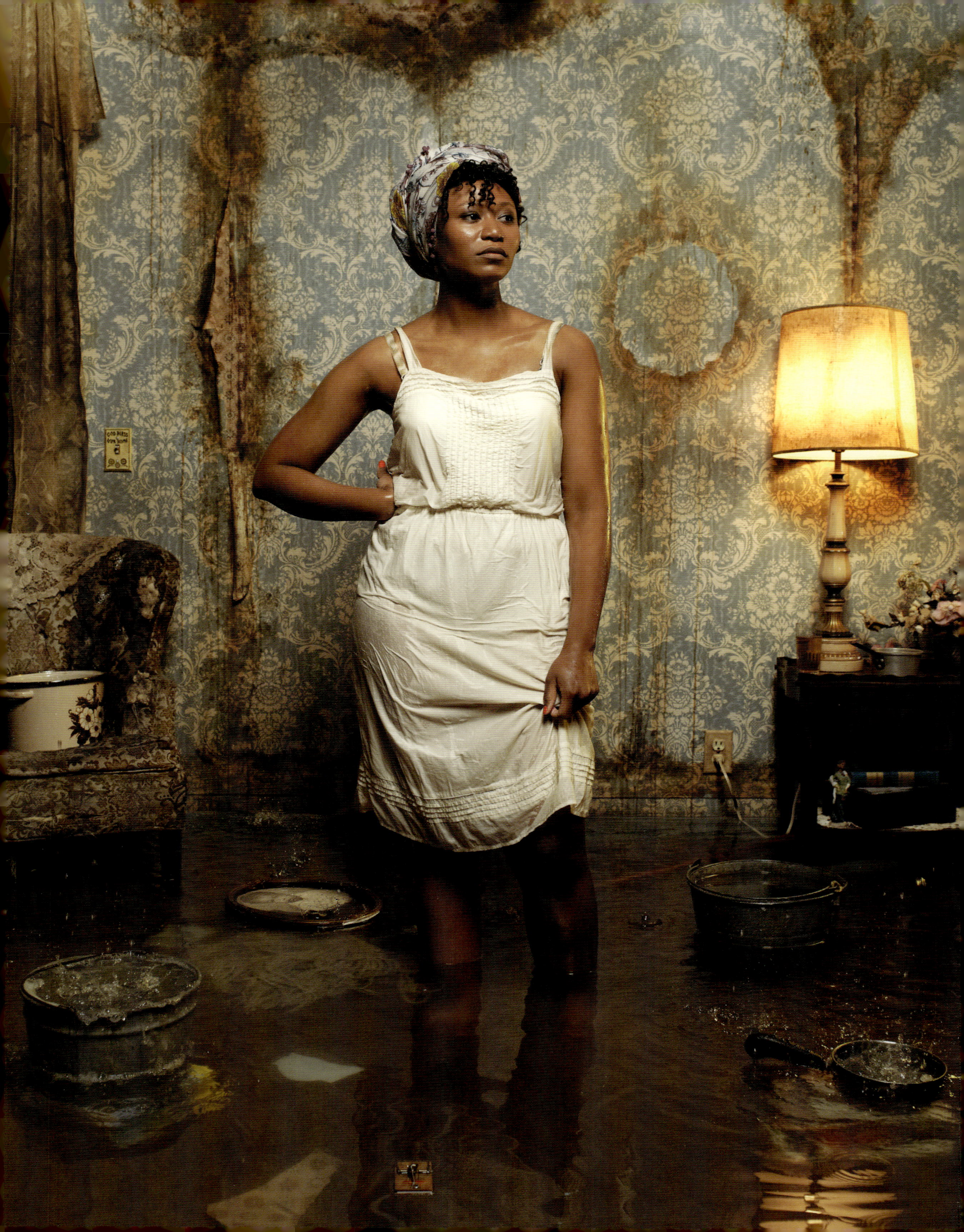

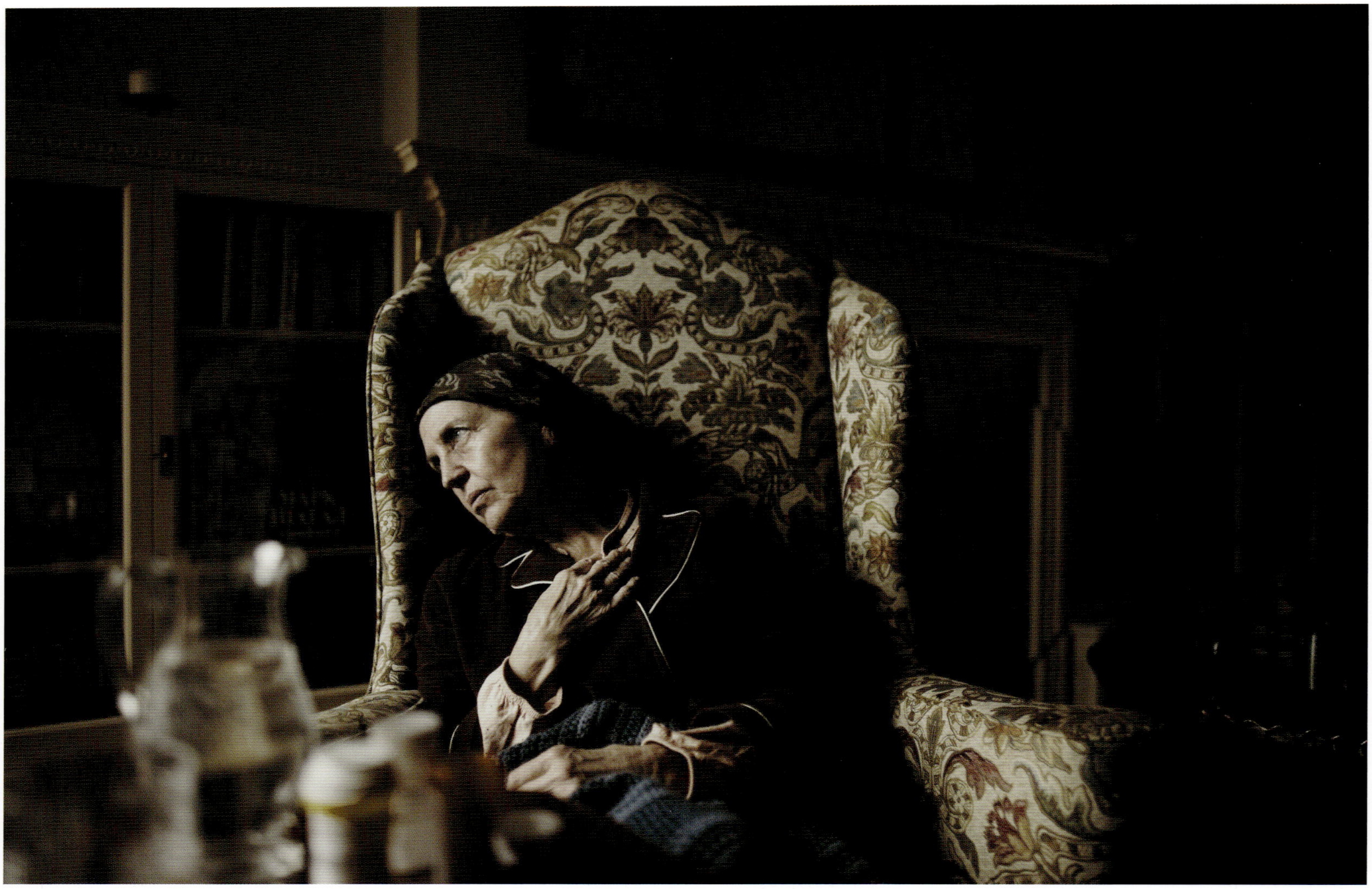

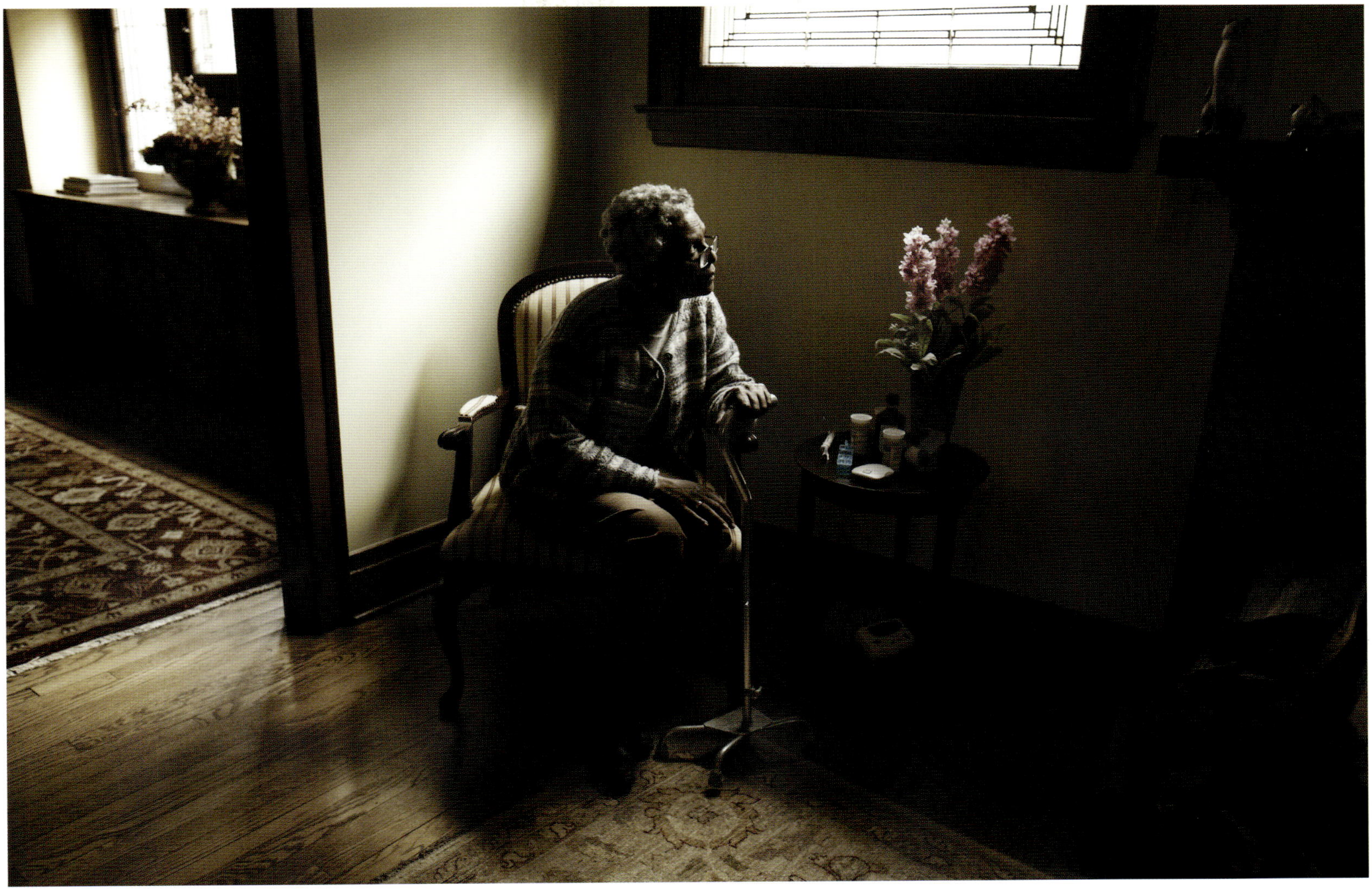

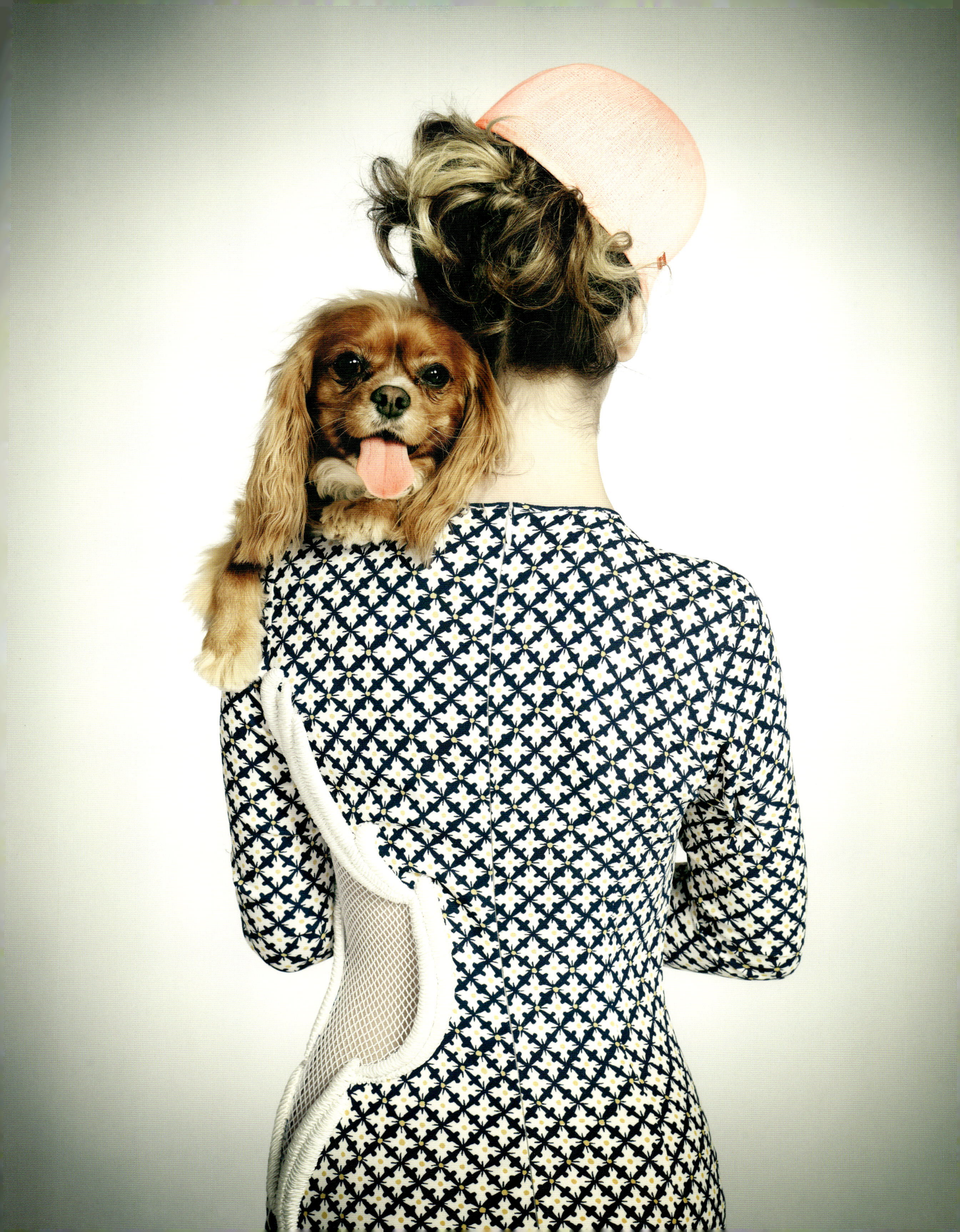

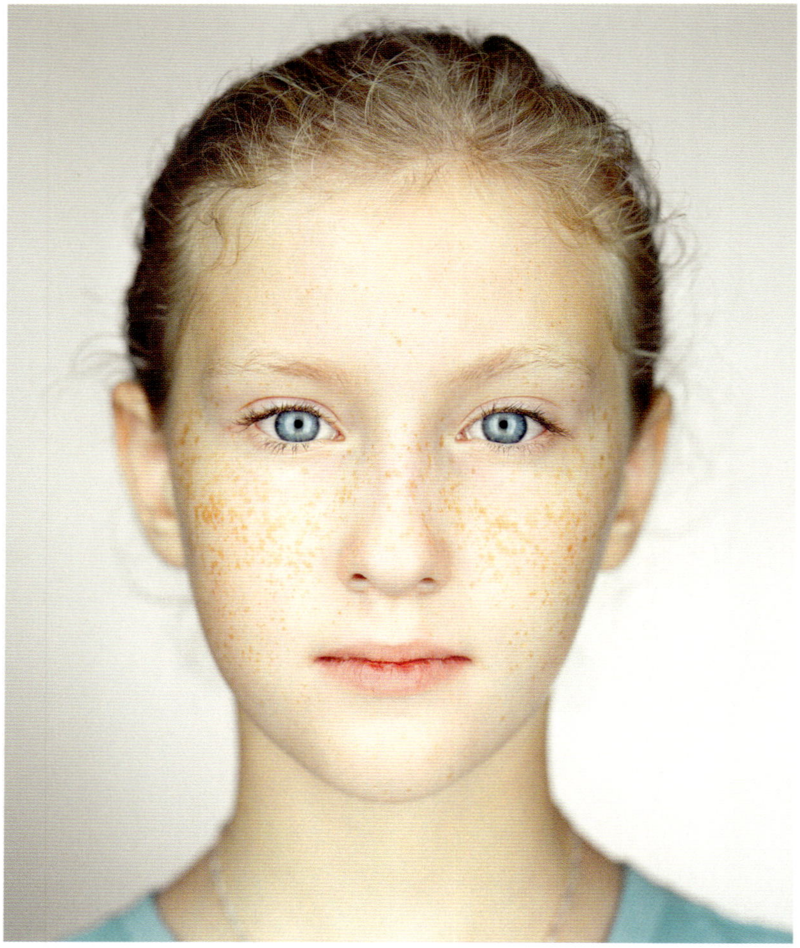
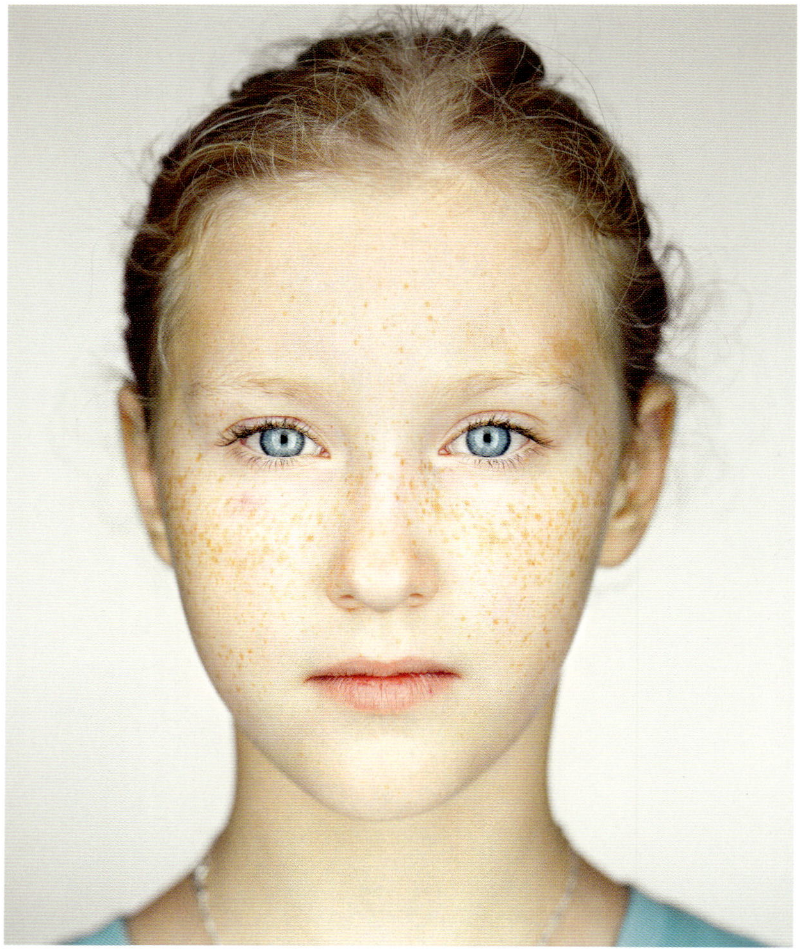
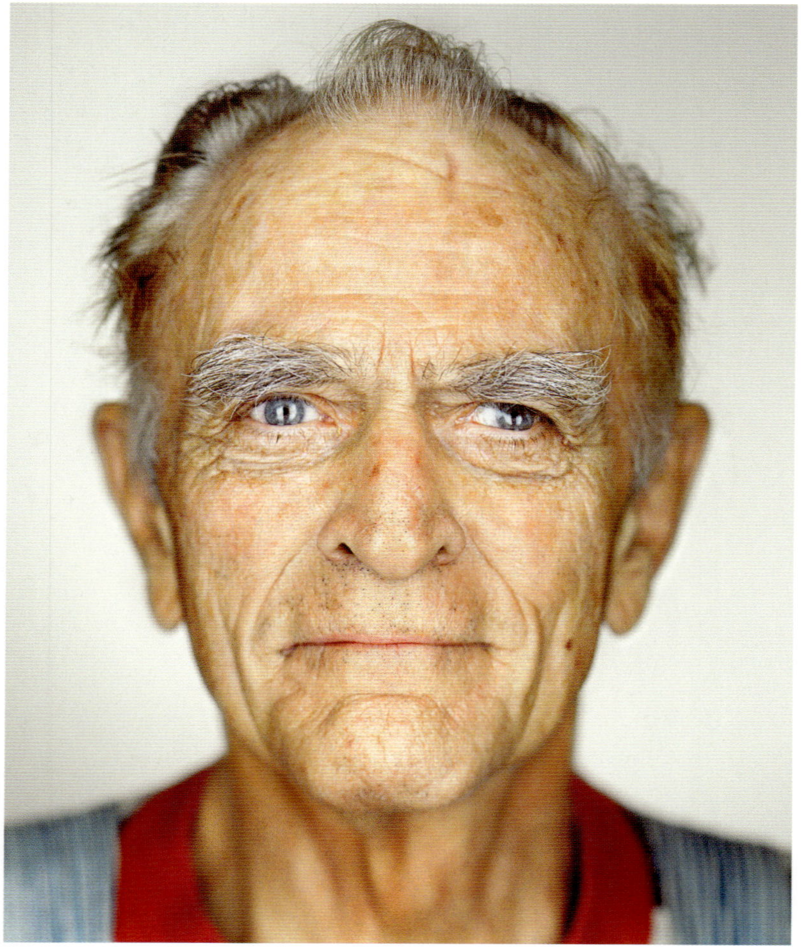
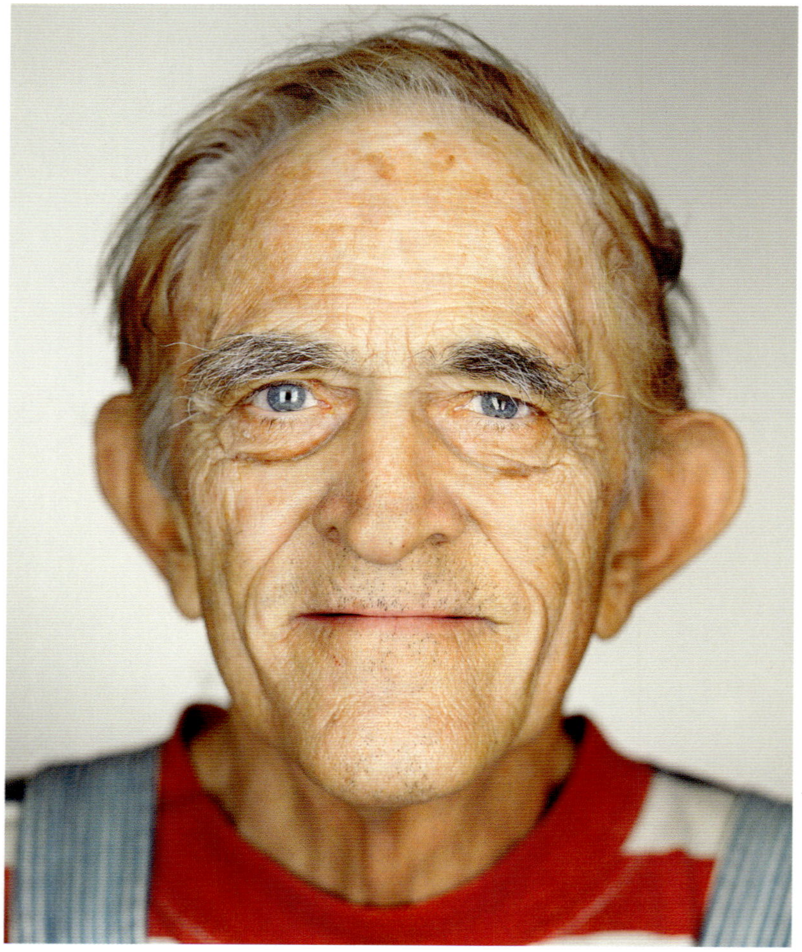

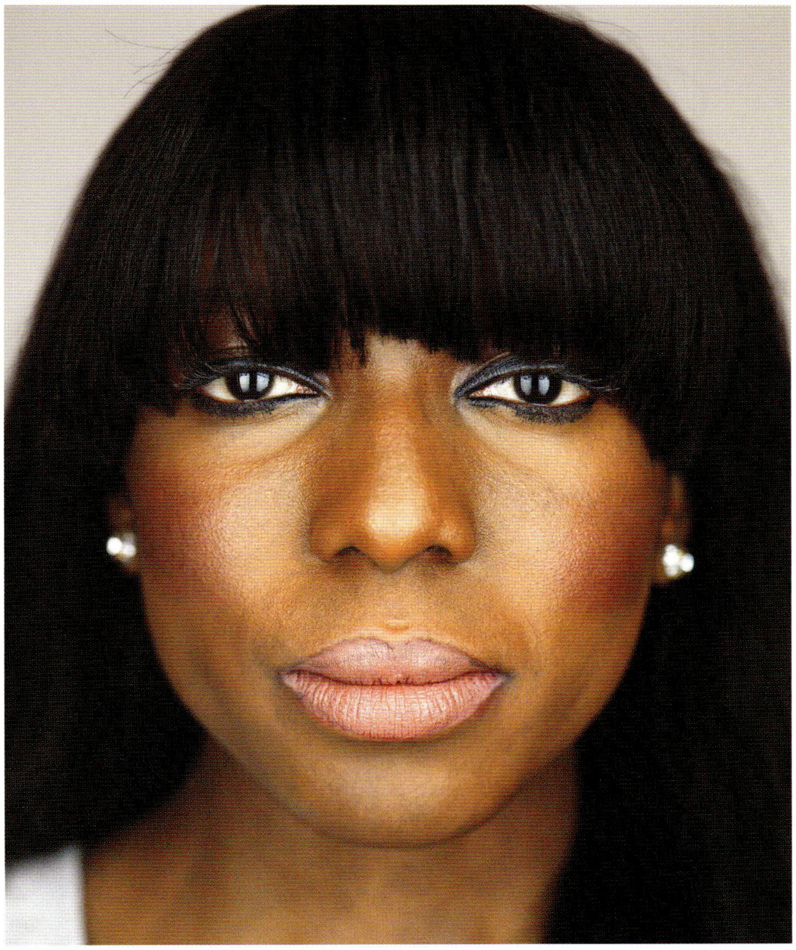
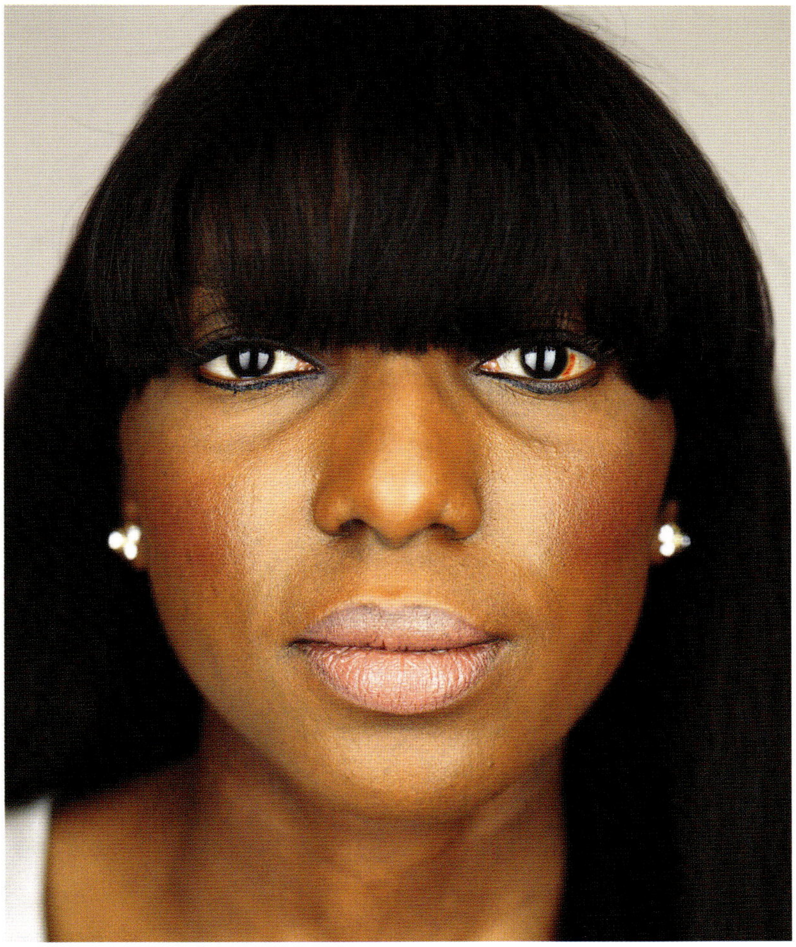
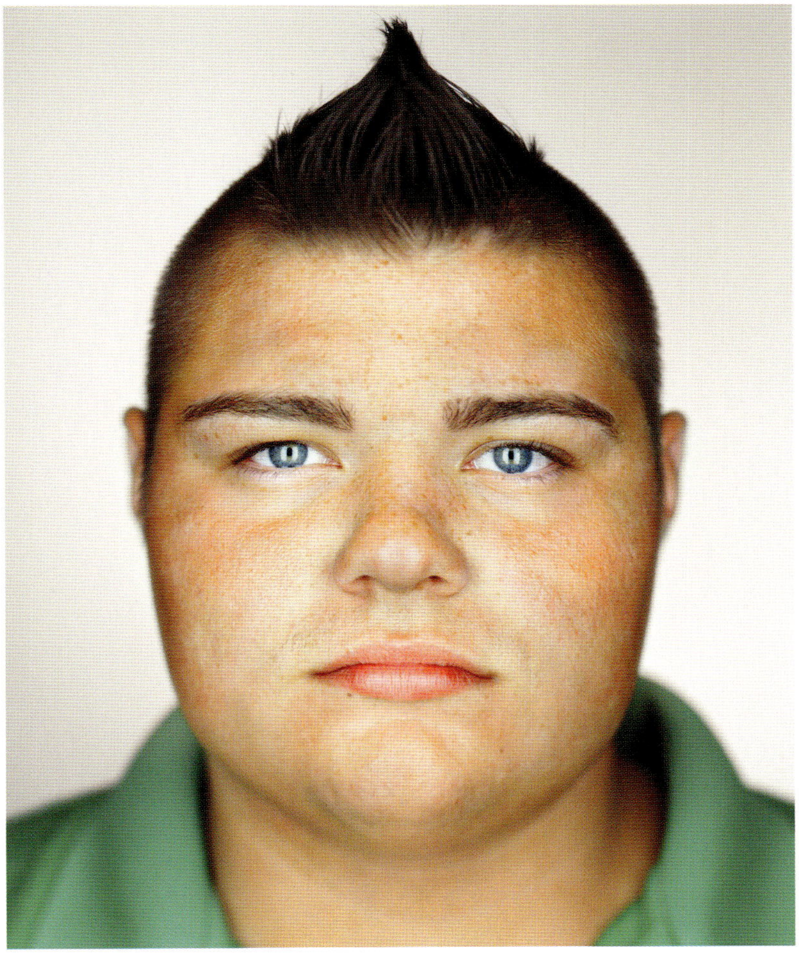
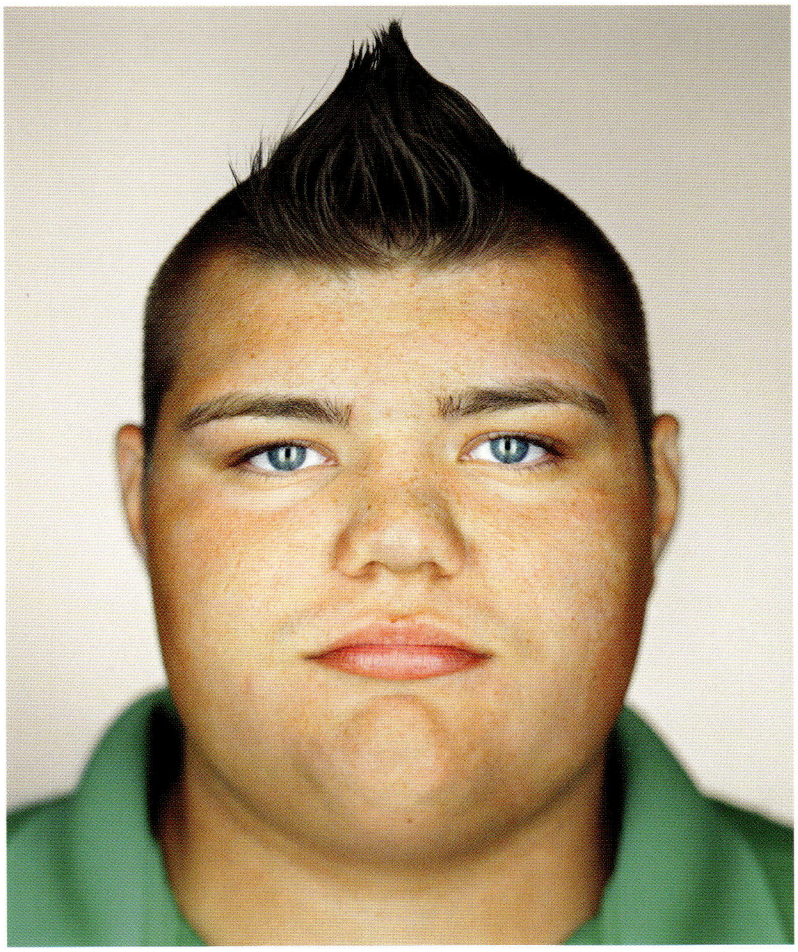

MARTIN SCHOELLER

247 / 248 / 249 / 250

FRANK SCHOTT

251 / 252

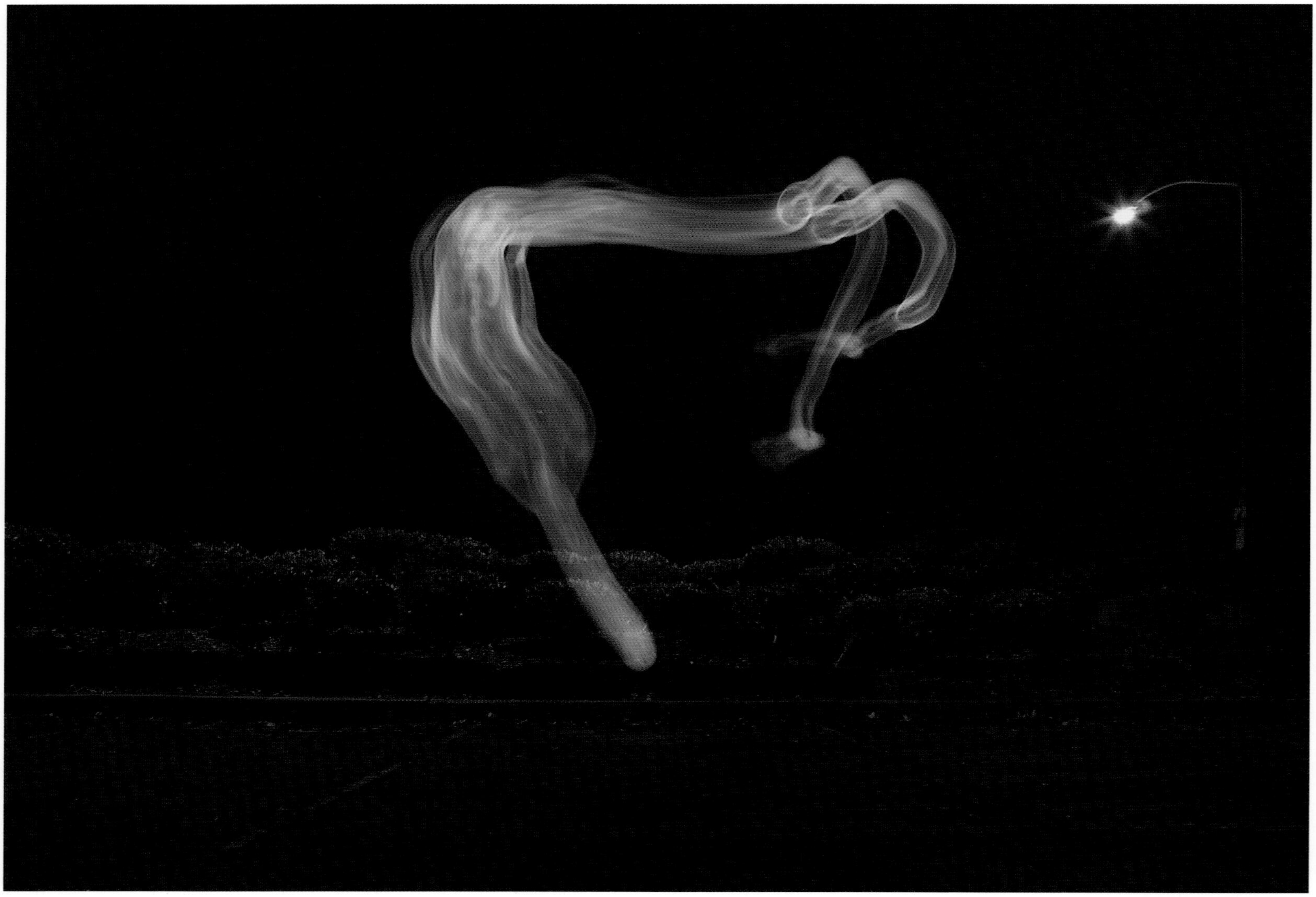

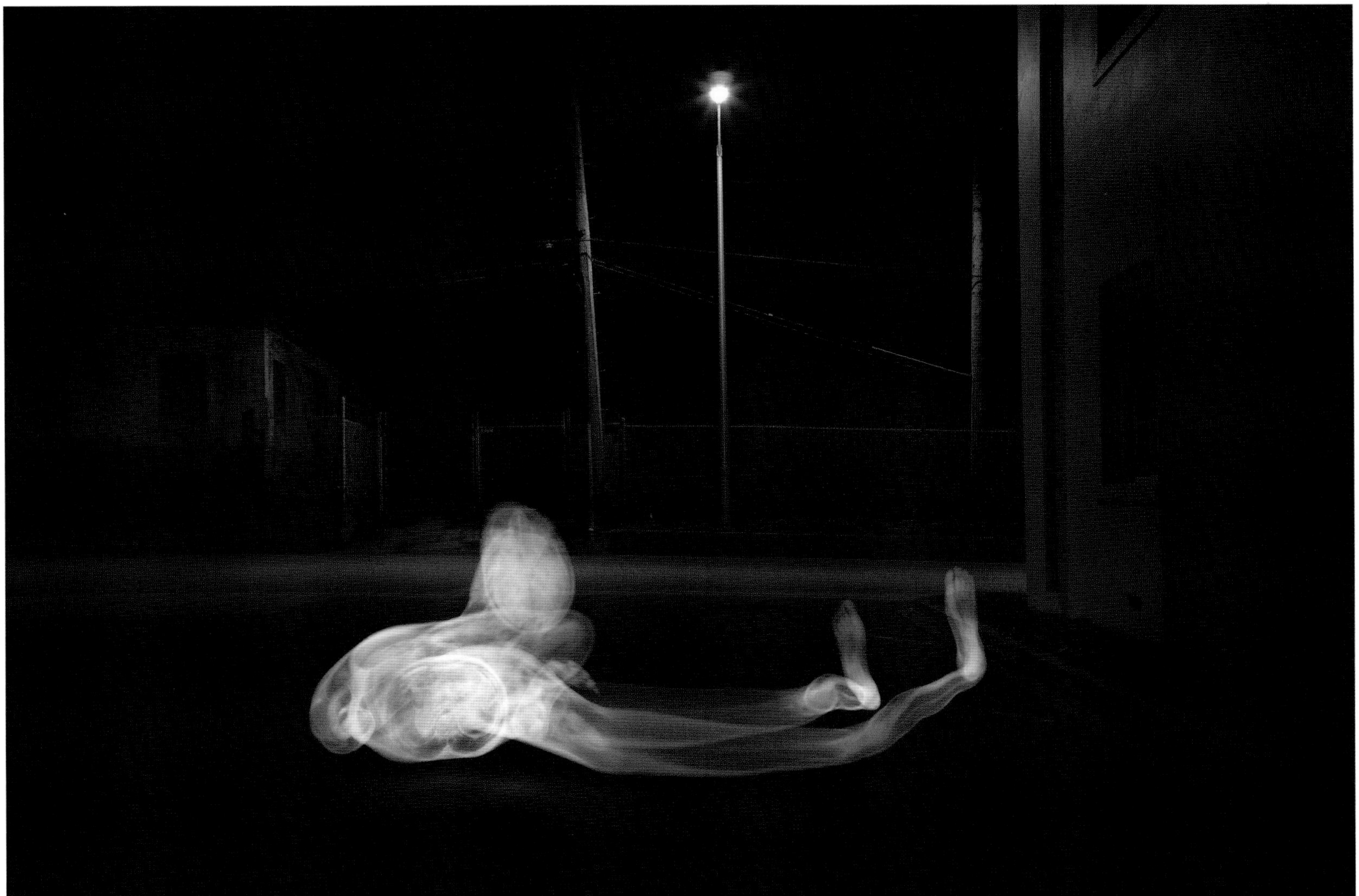

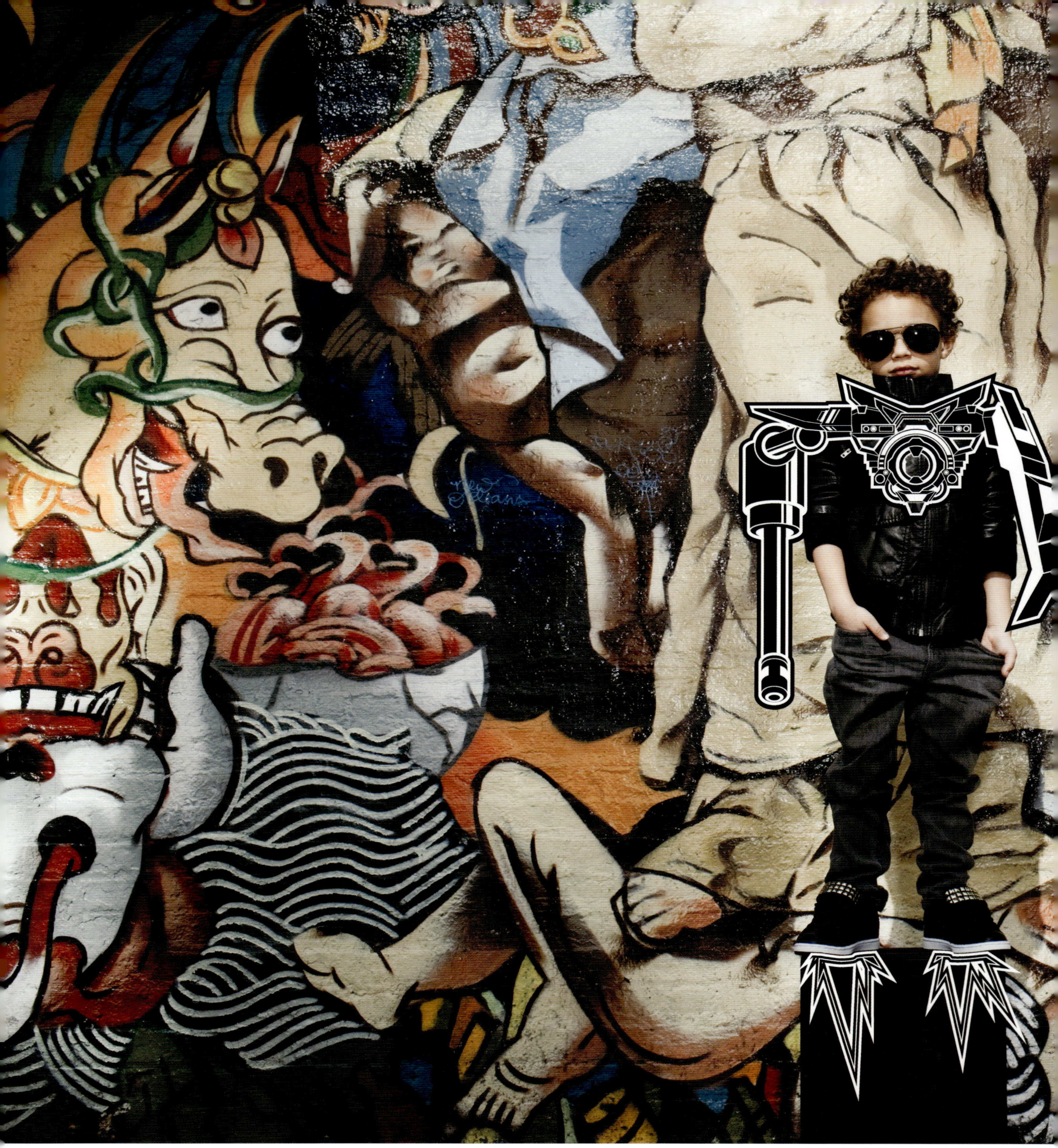

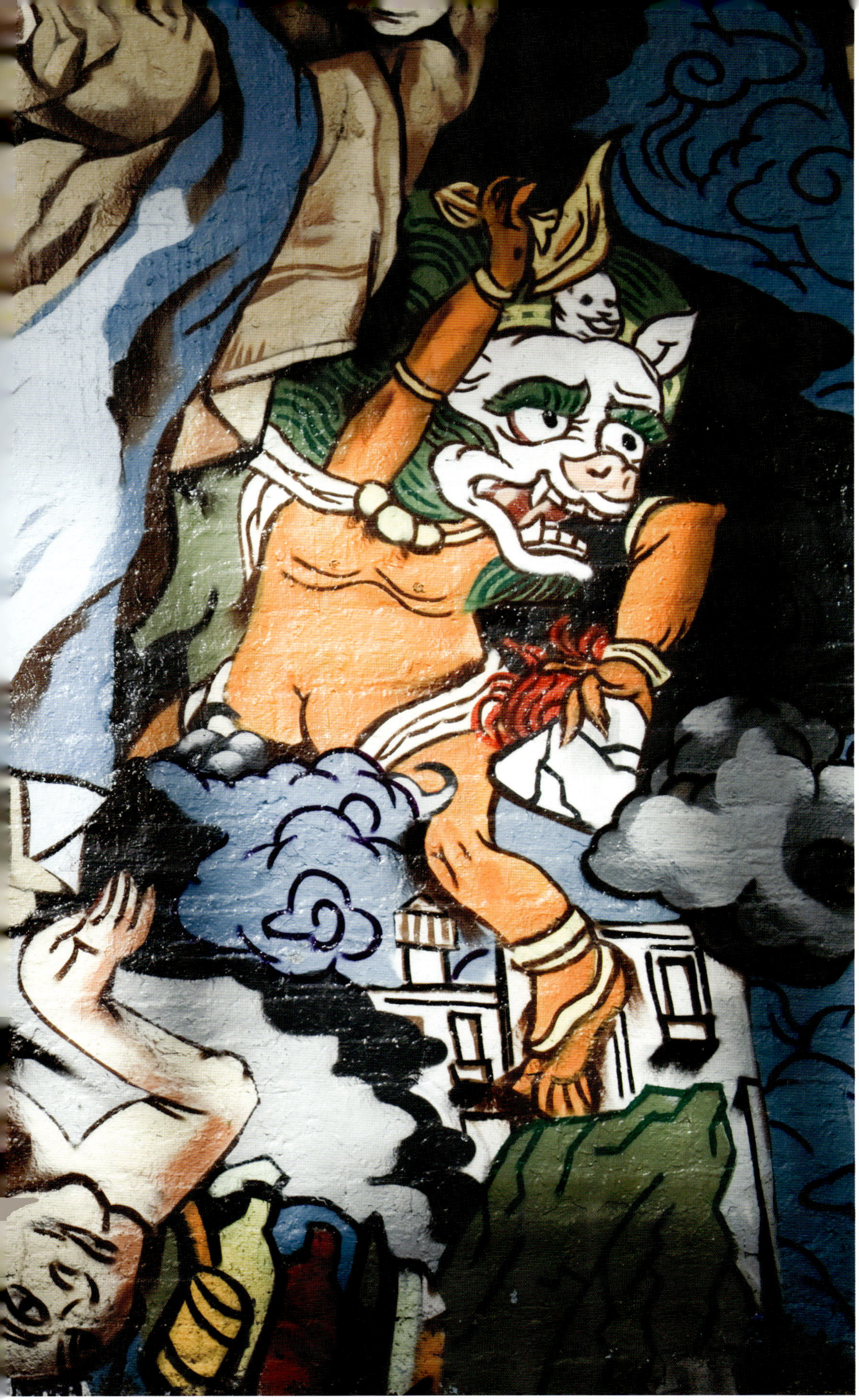

STOLTZE + STEFANIE

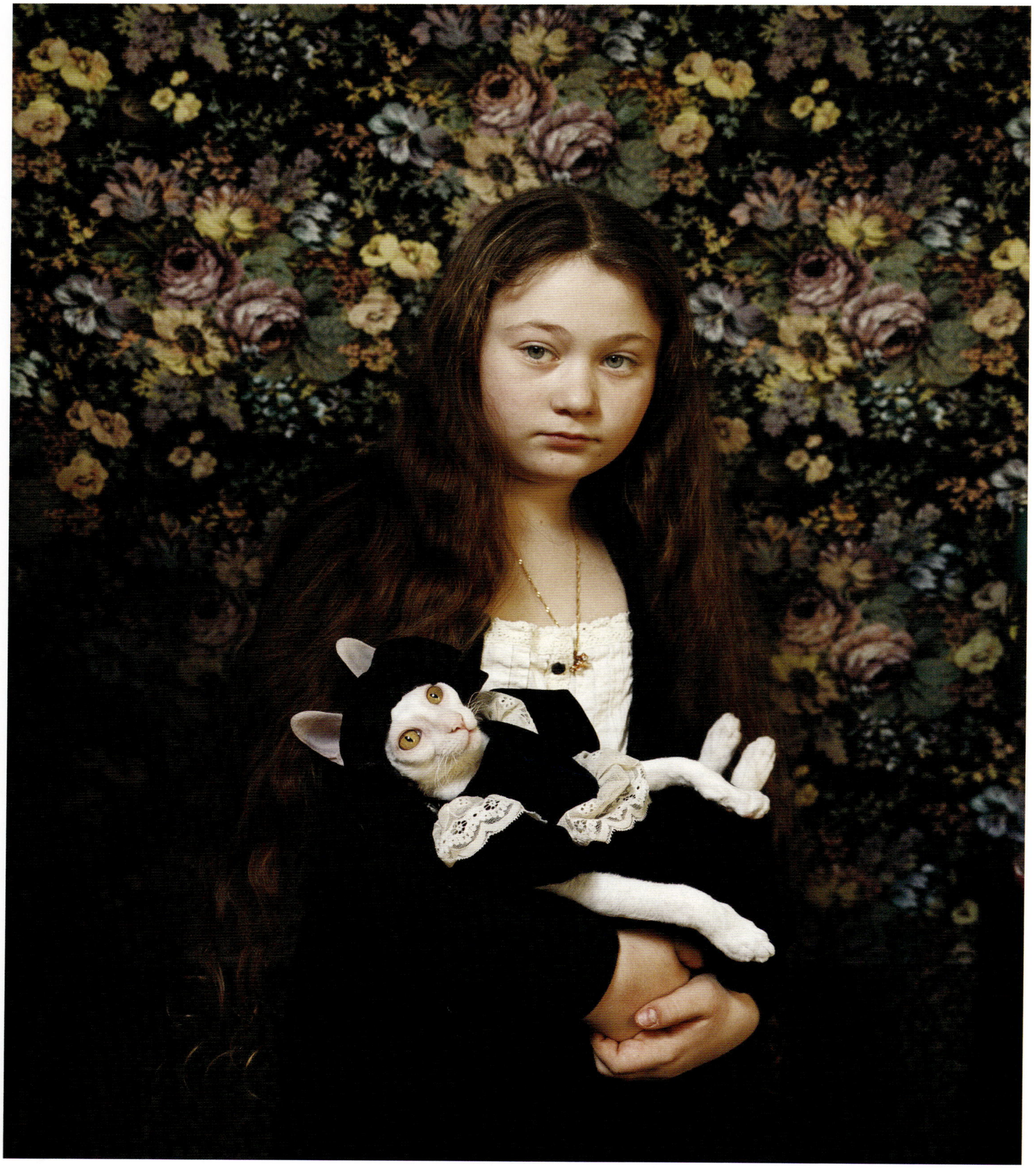

ROBIN SCHWARTZ

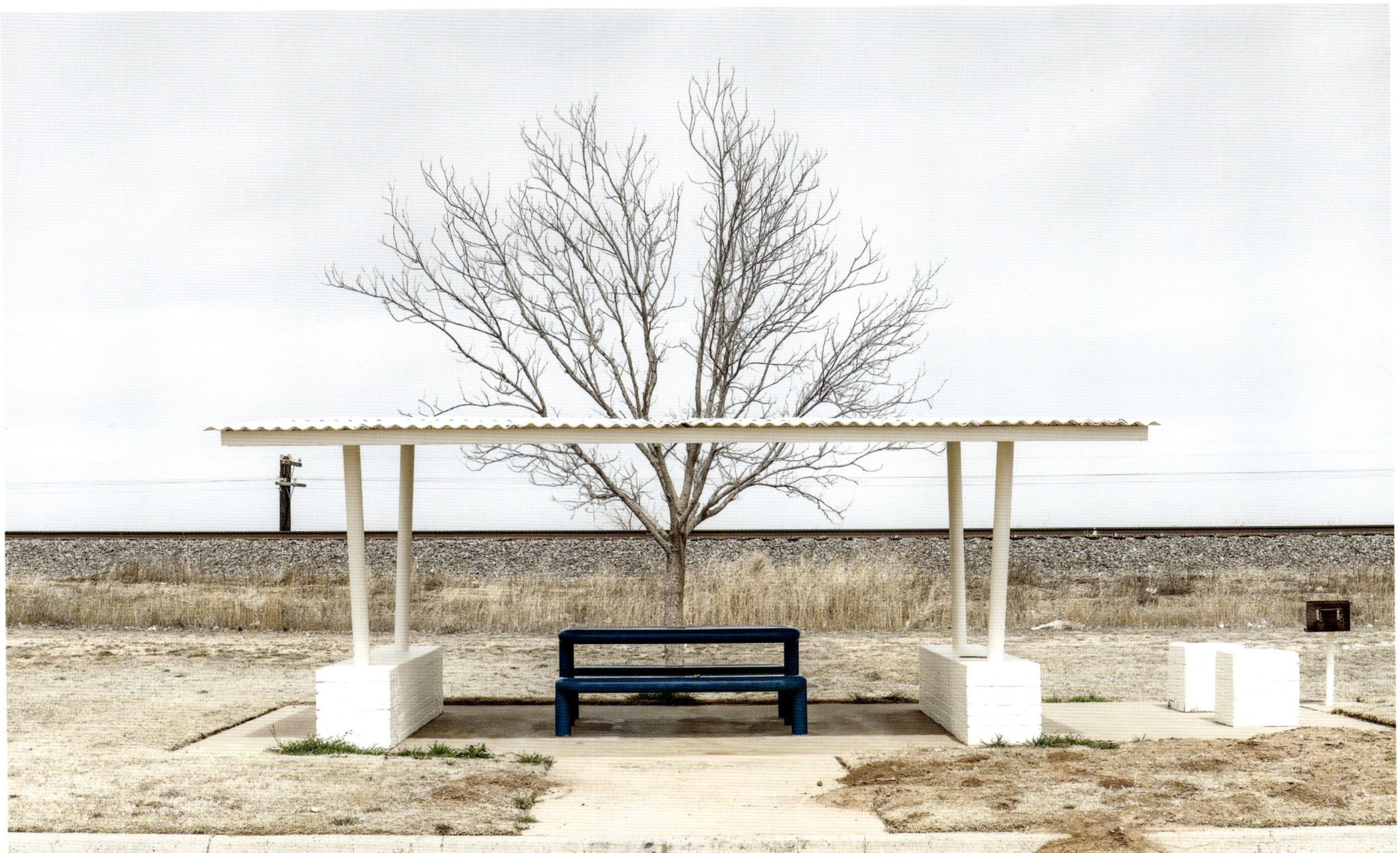

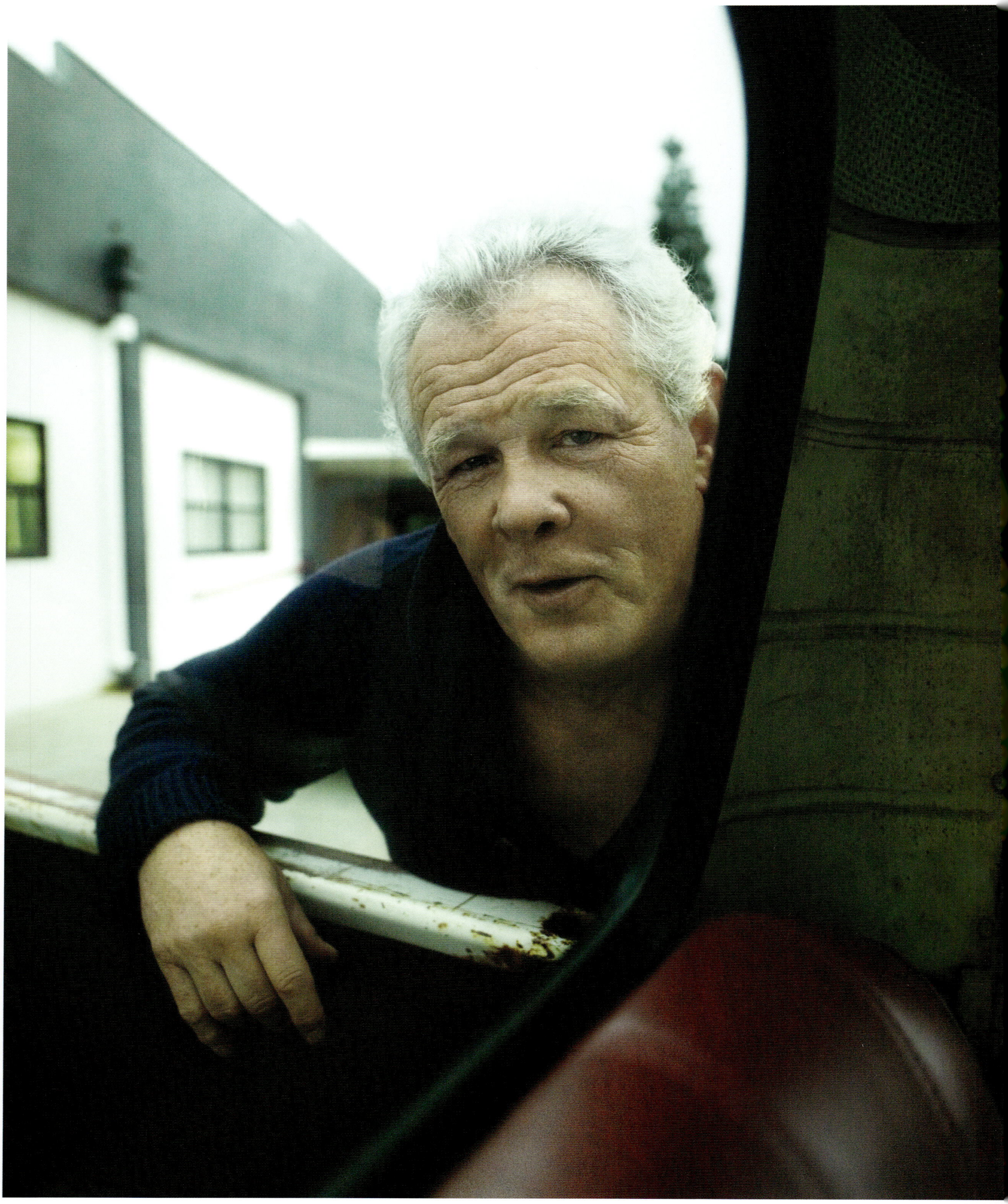

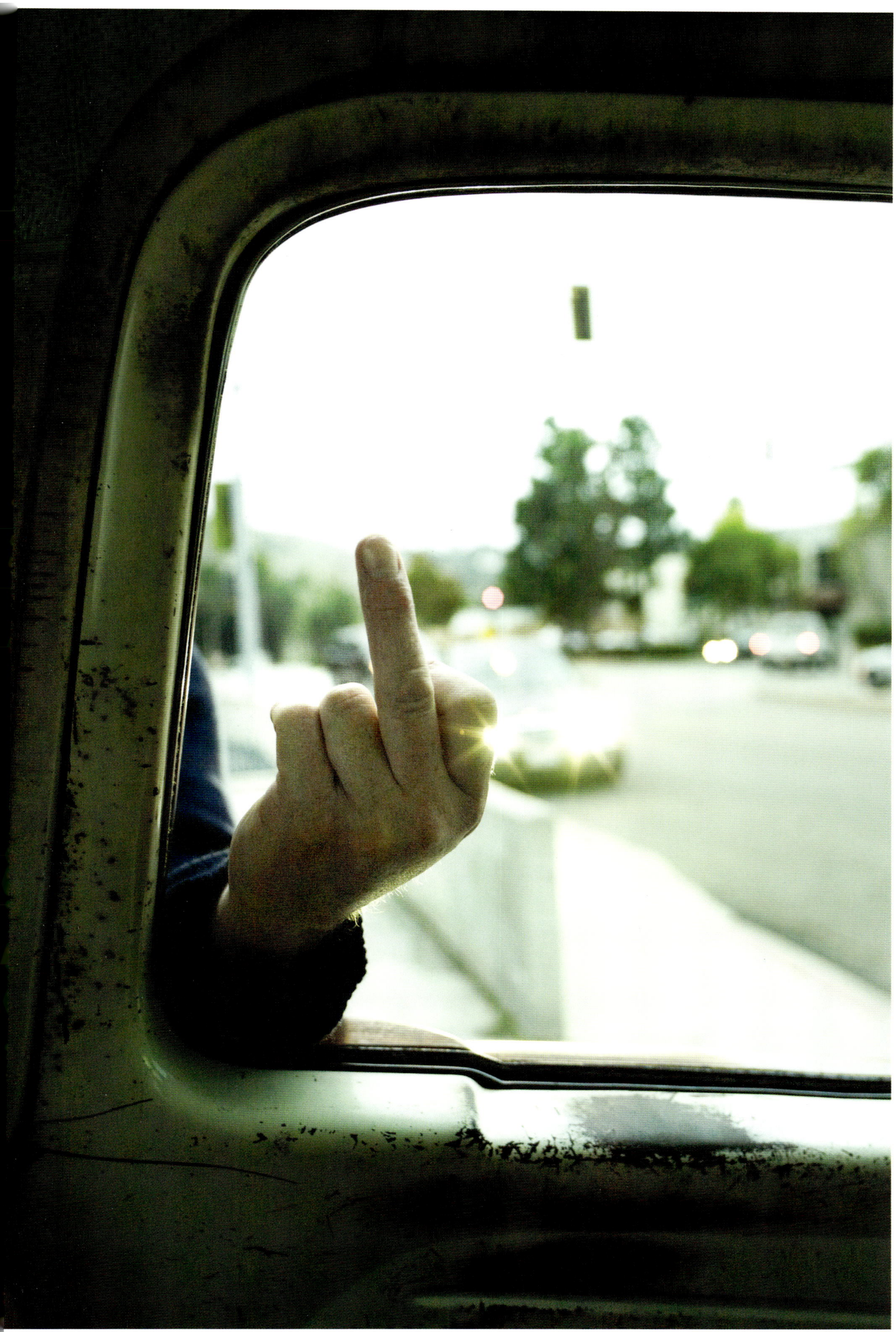

PEGGY SIROTA

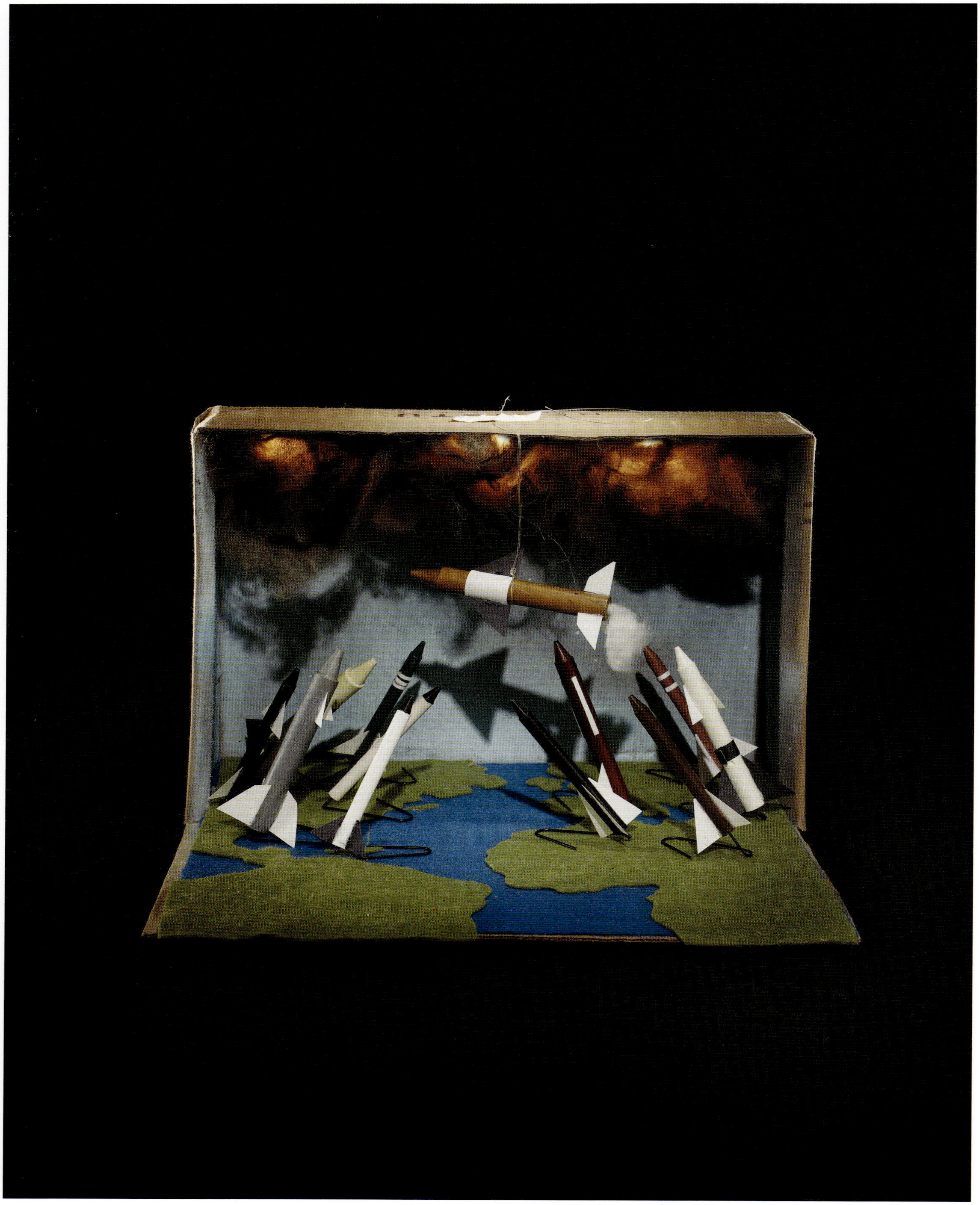

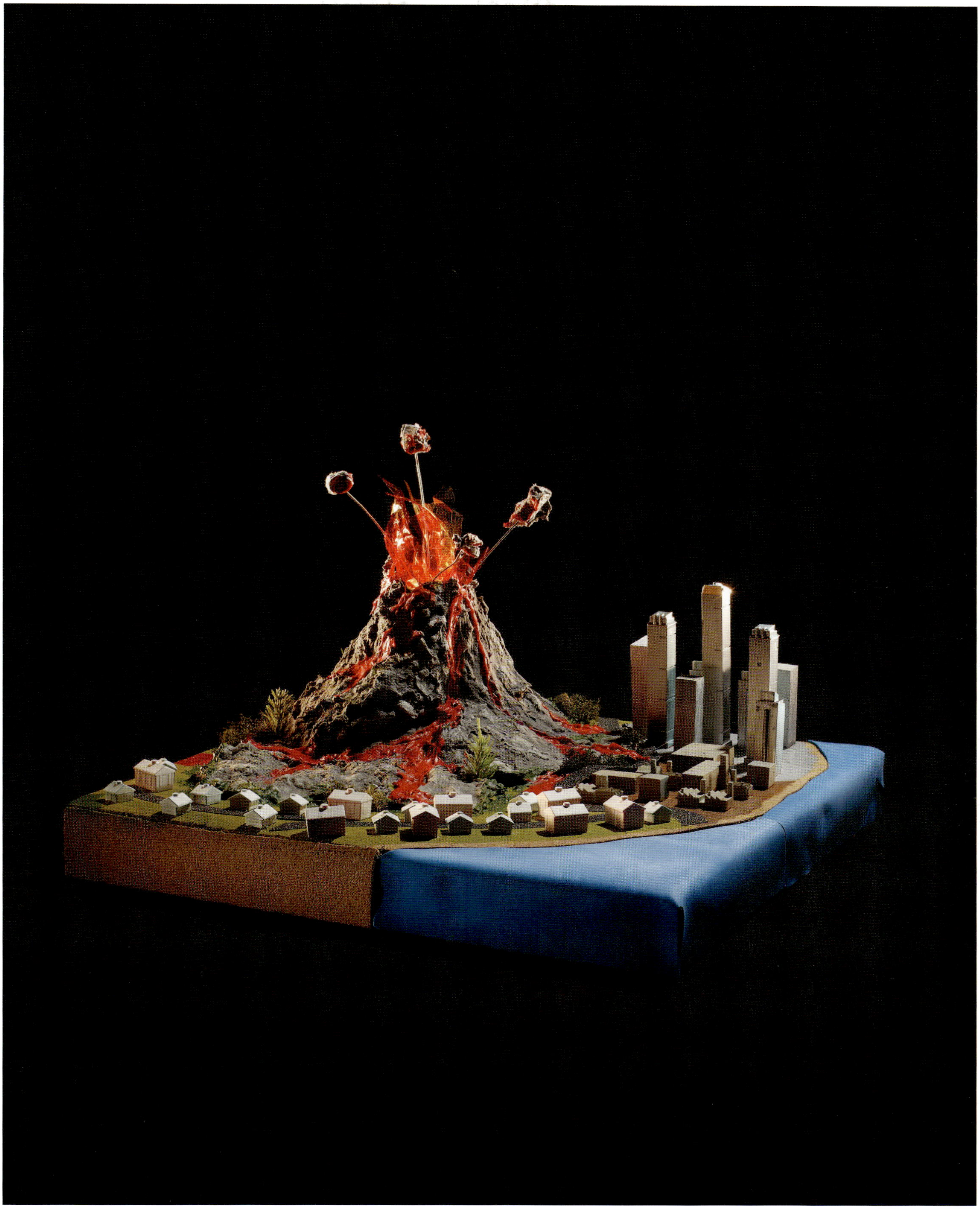

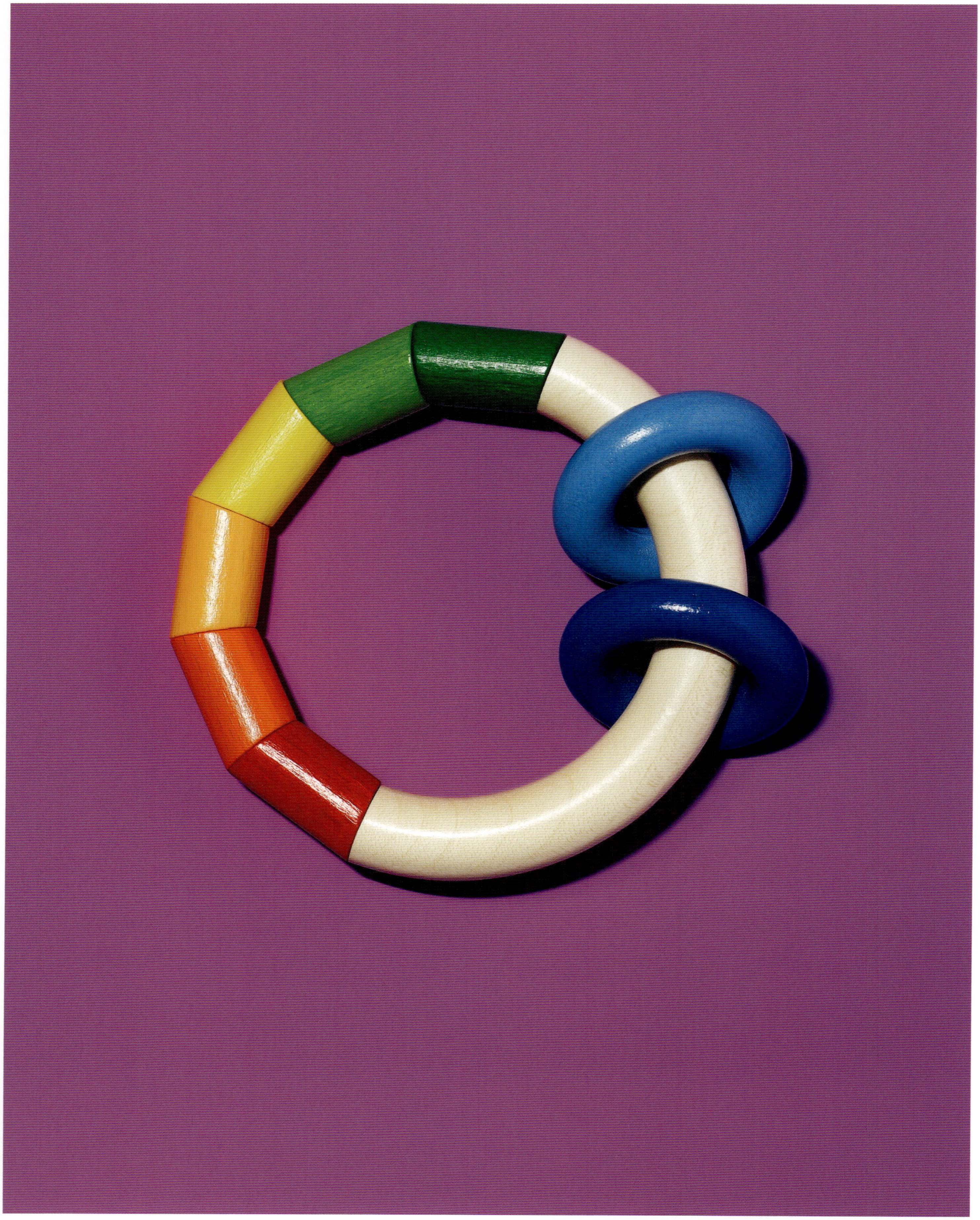

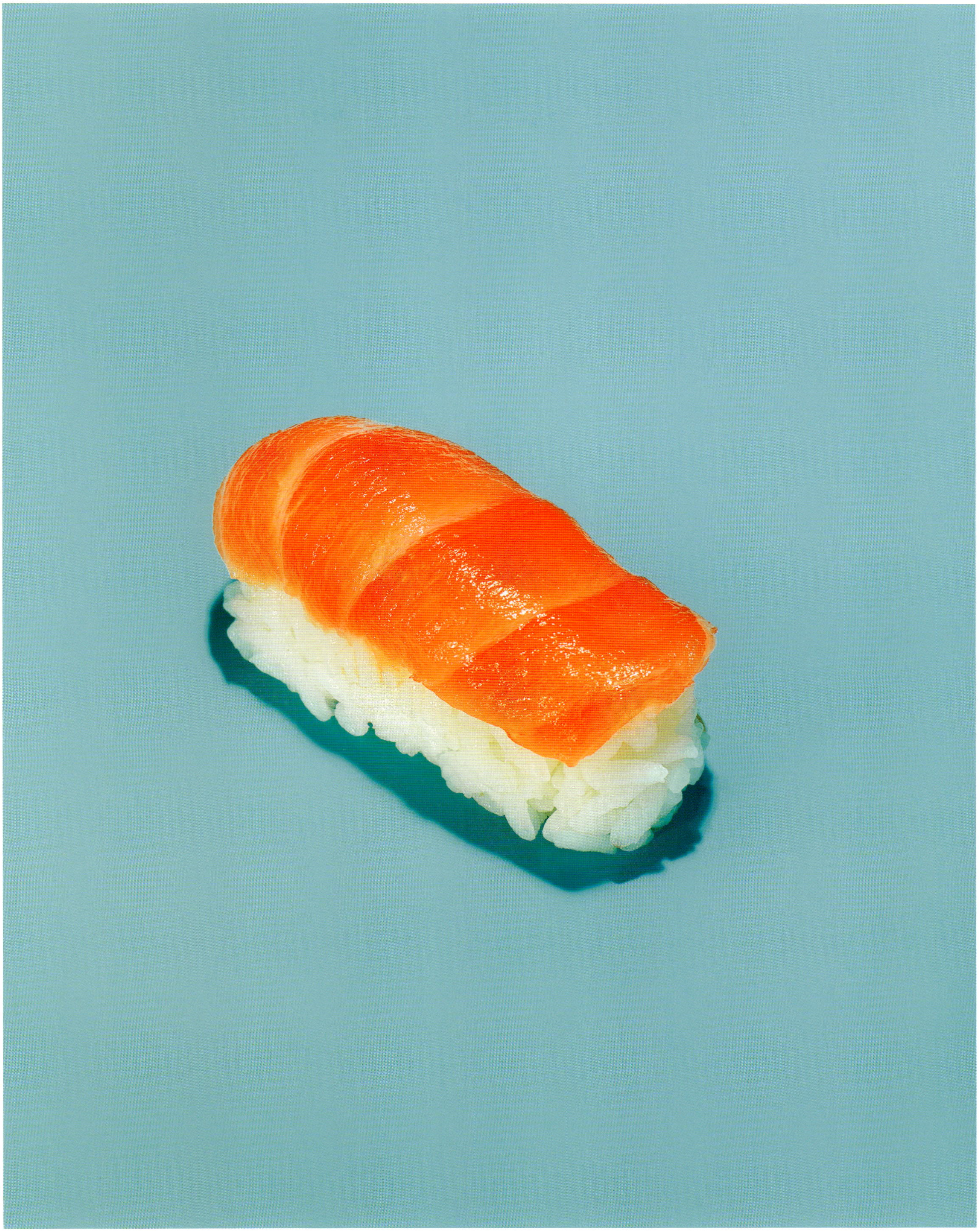

DAN SAELINGER

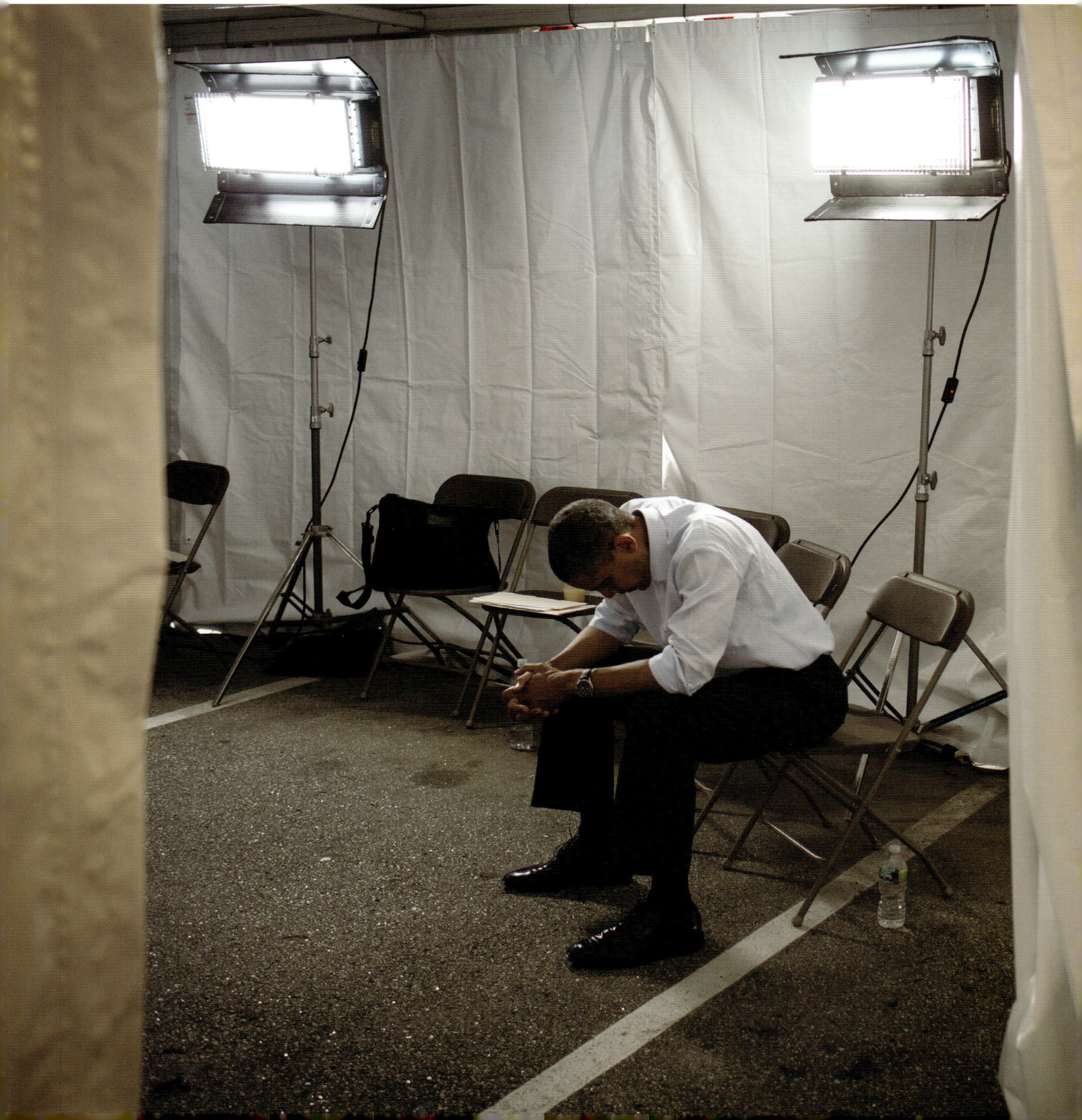

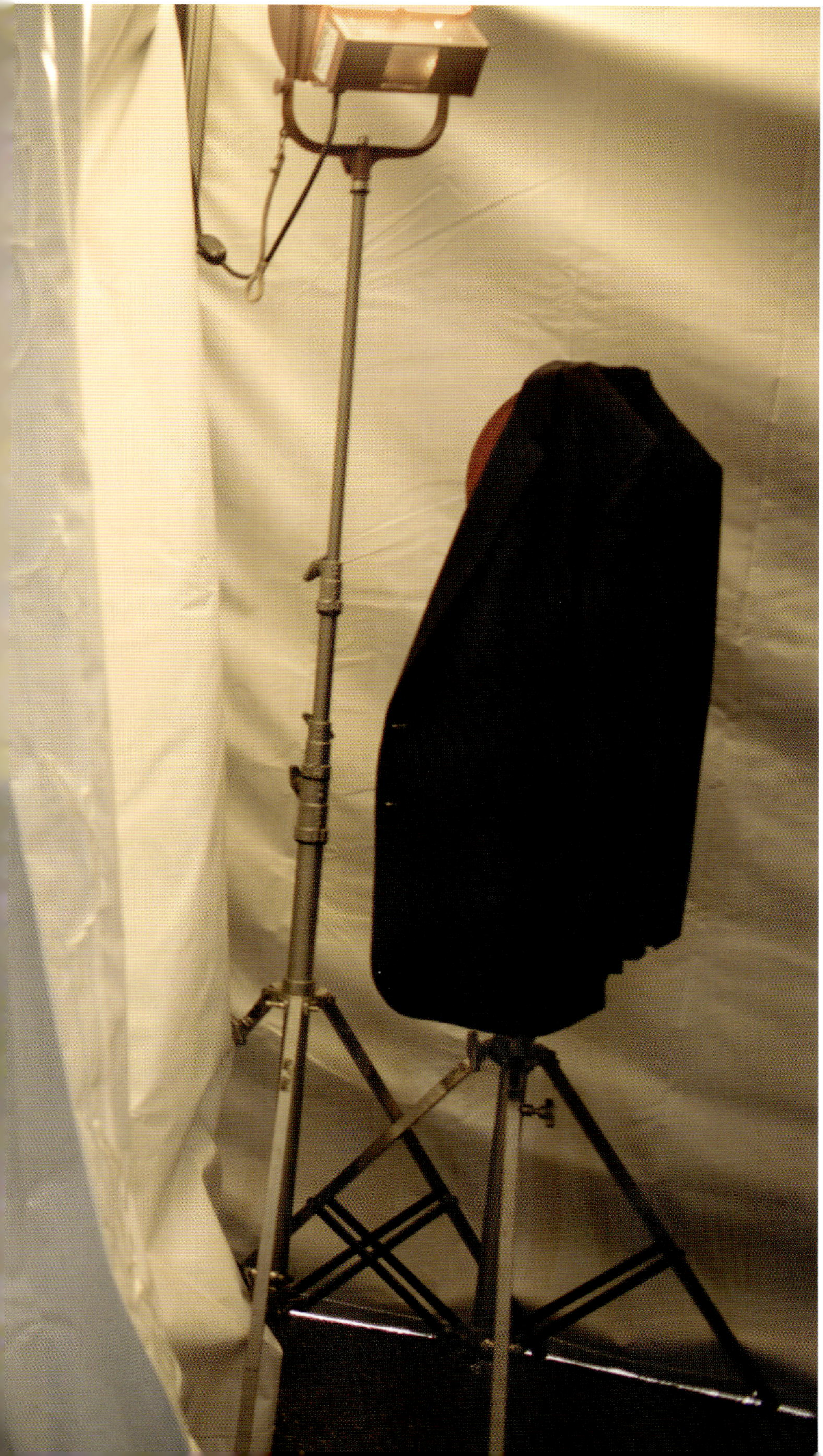

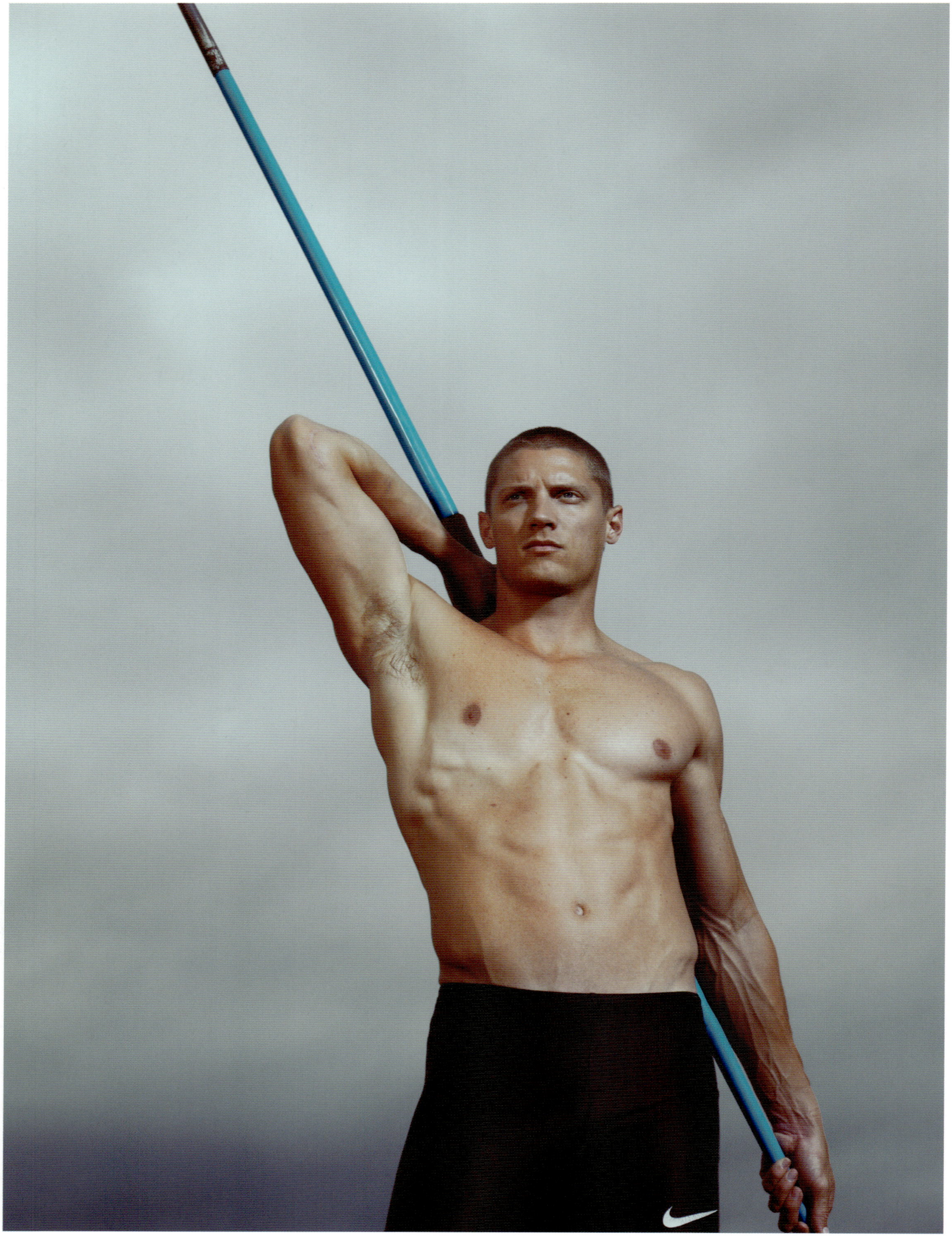

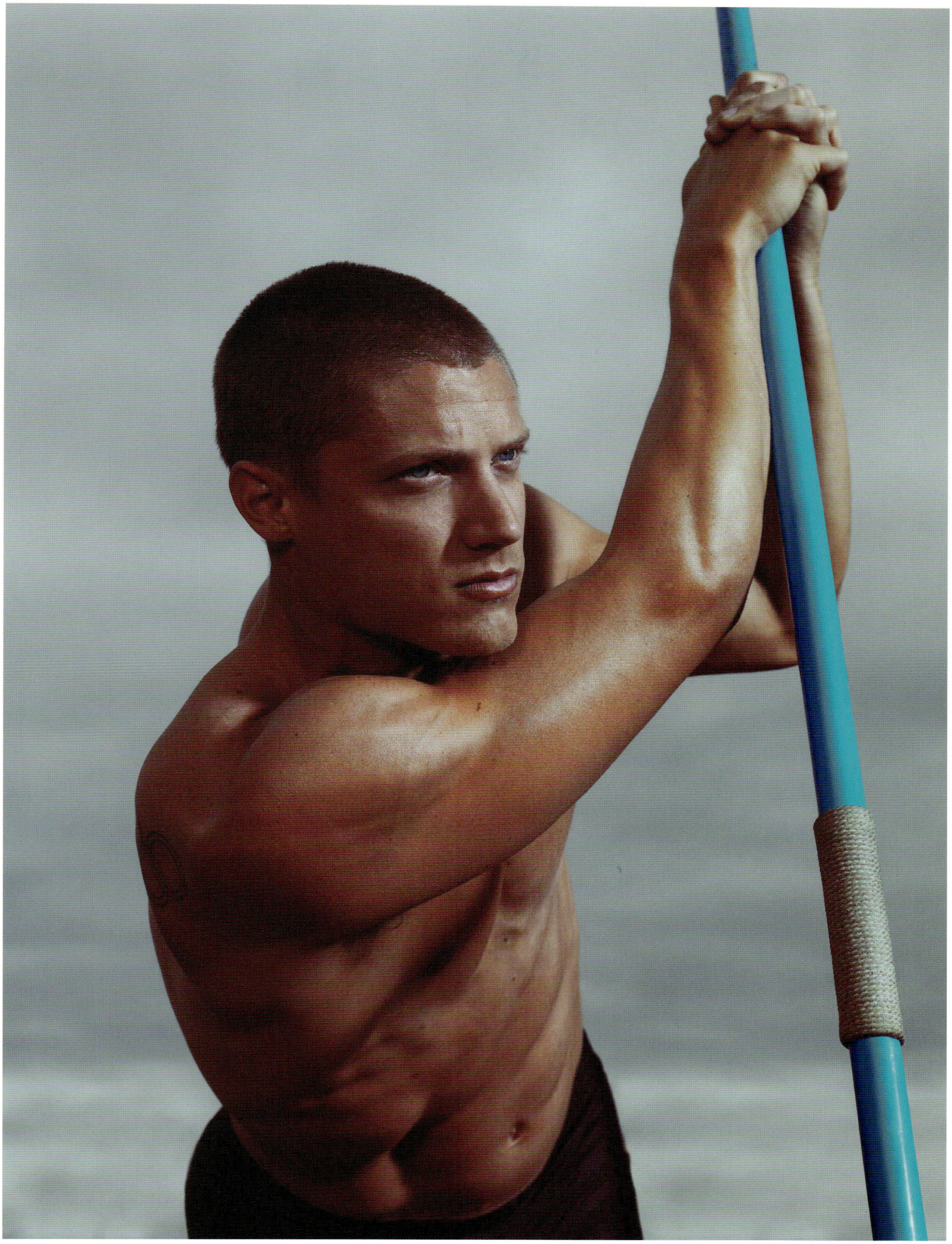

CARLOS SERRAO

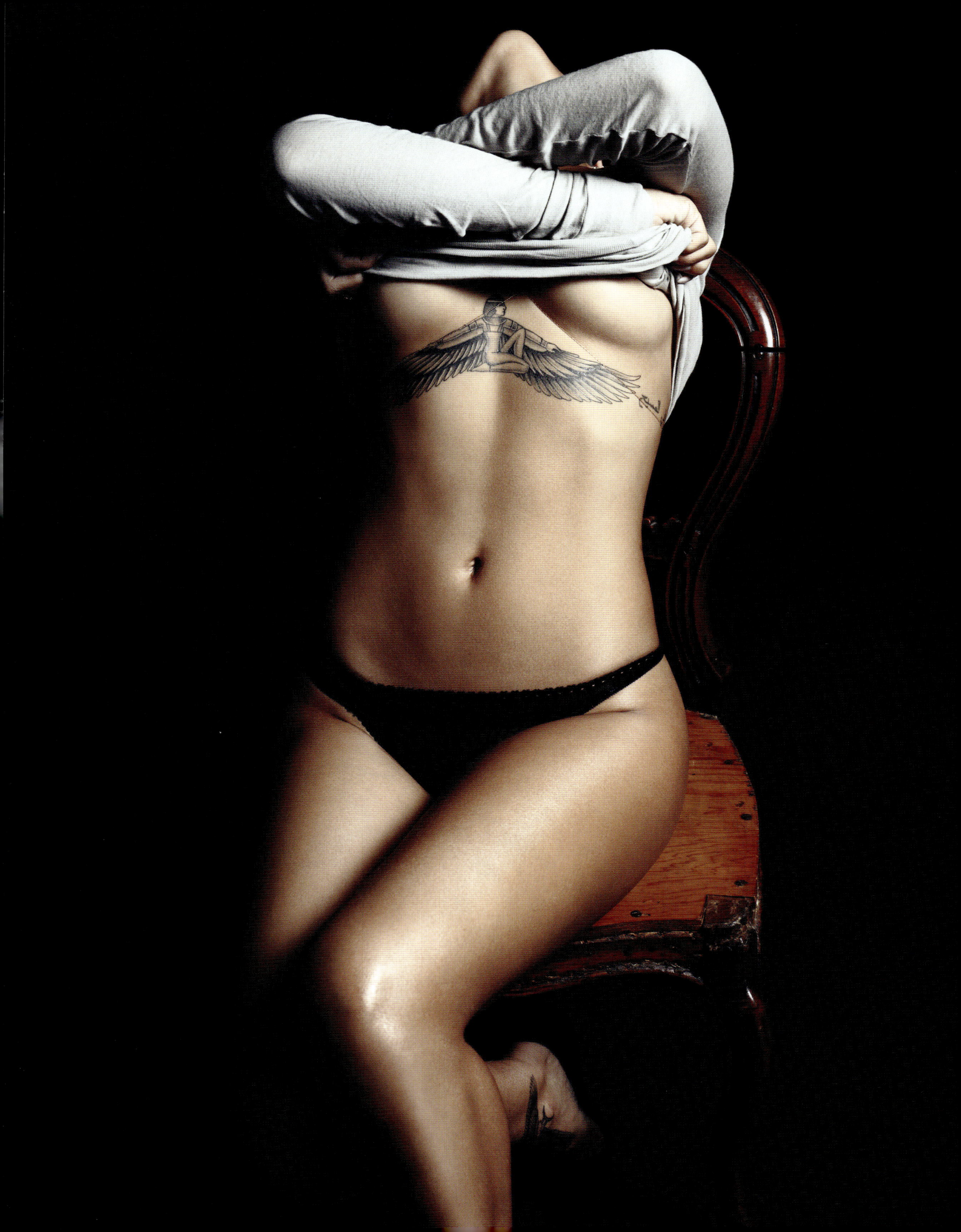

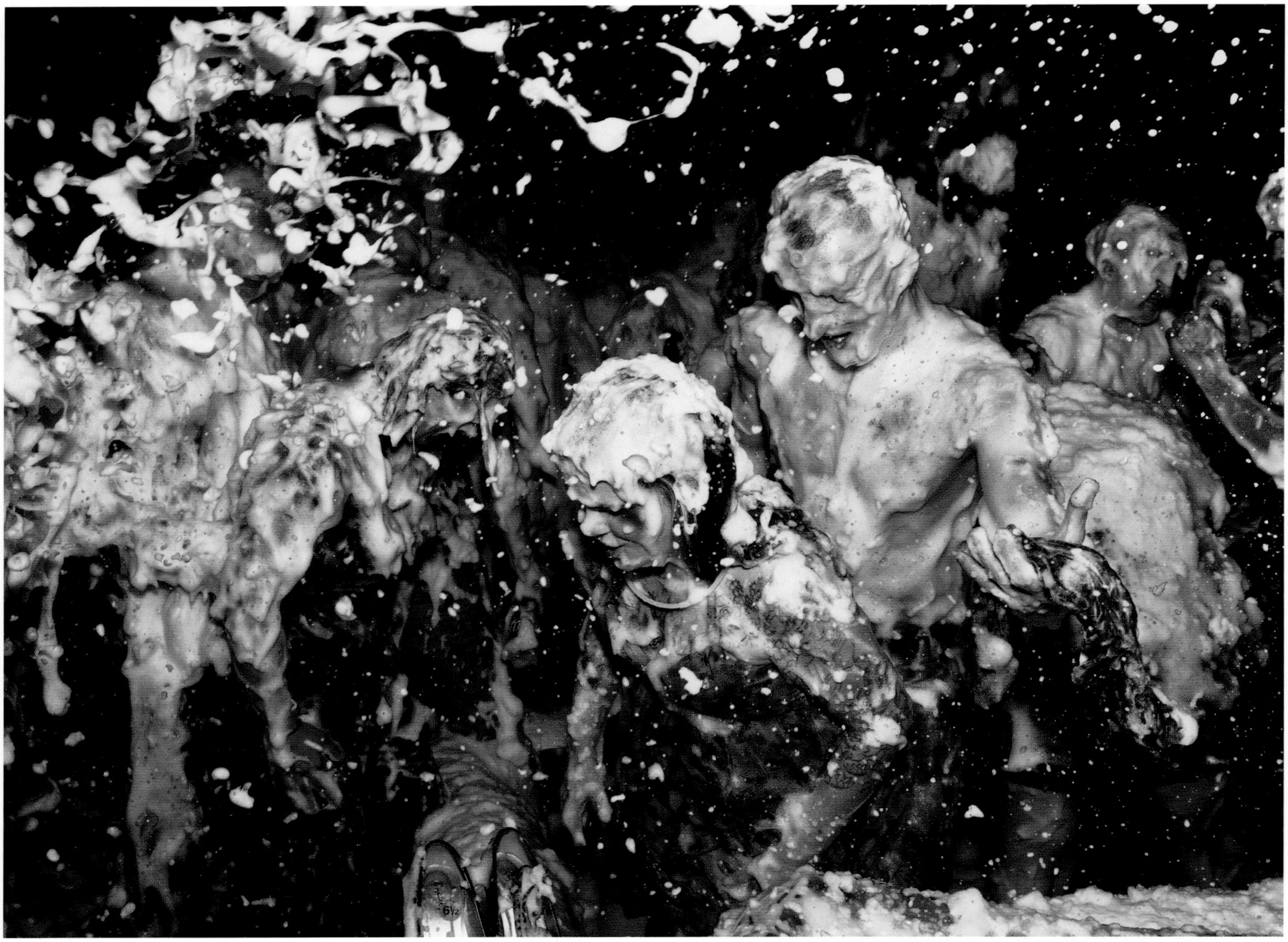

ALEC SOTH

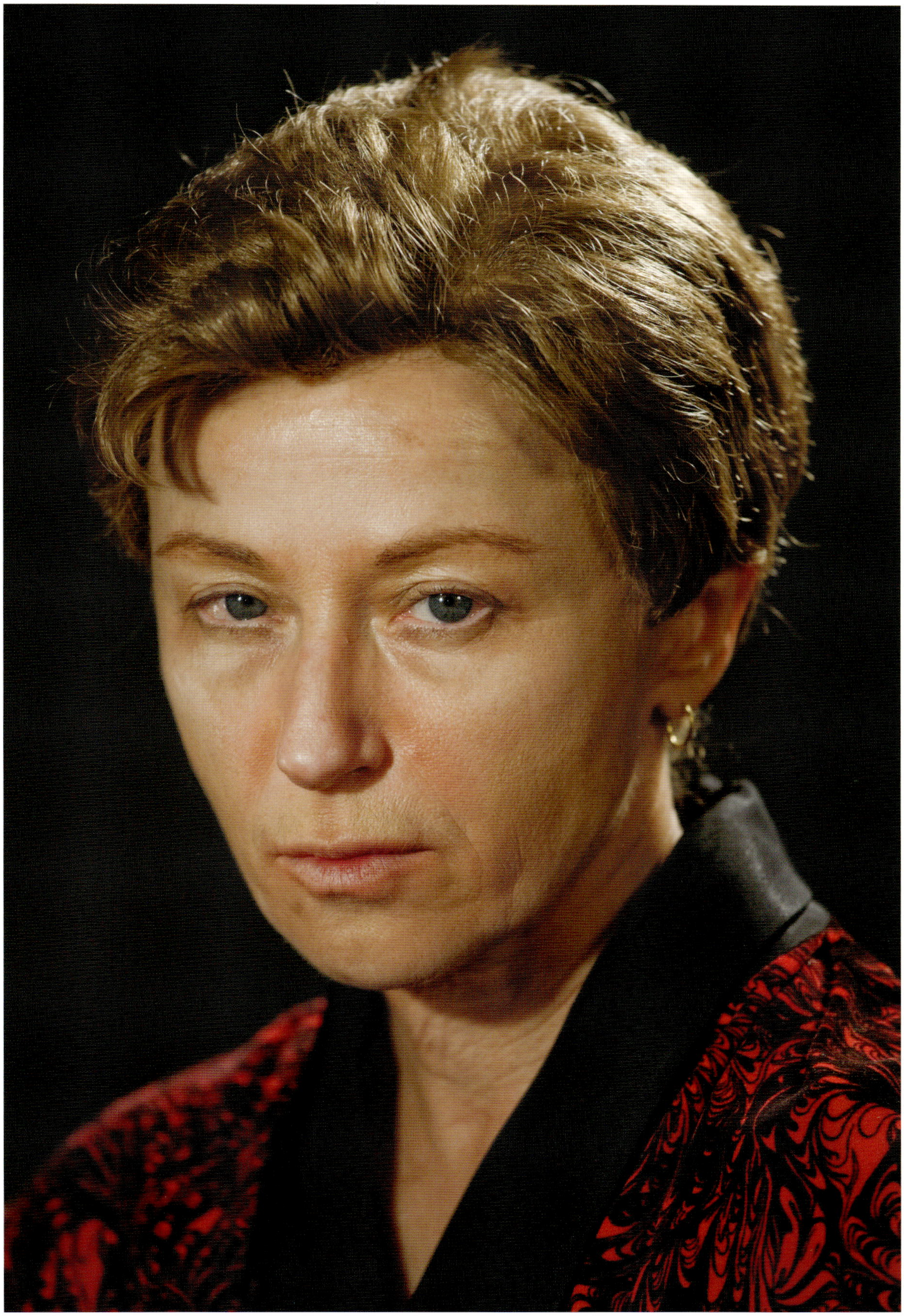

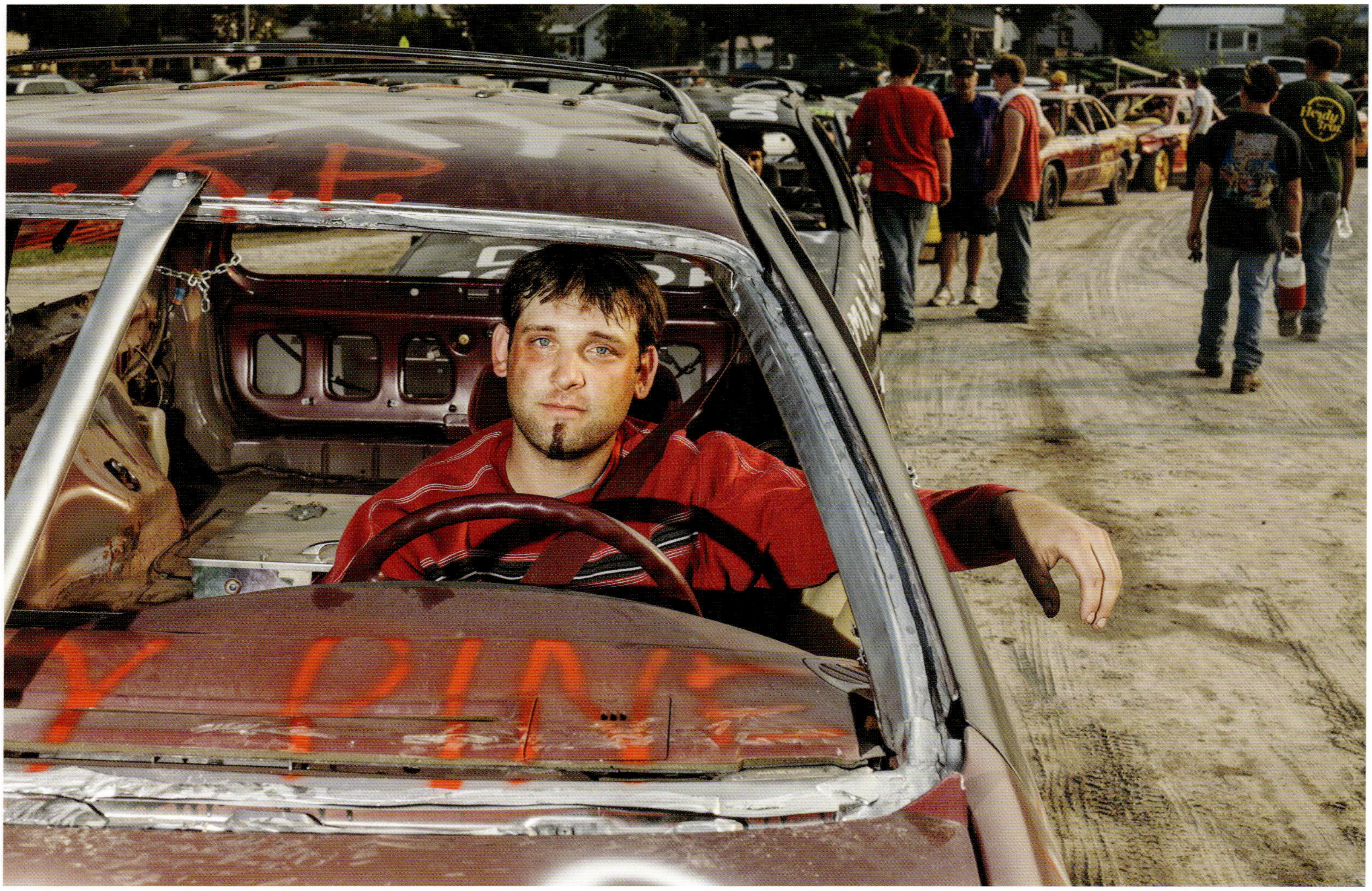

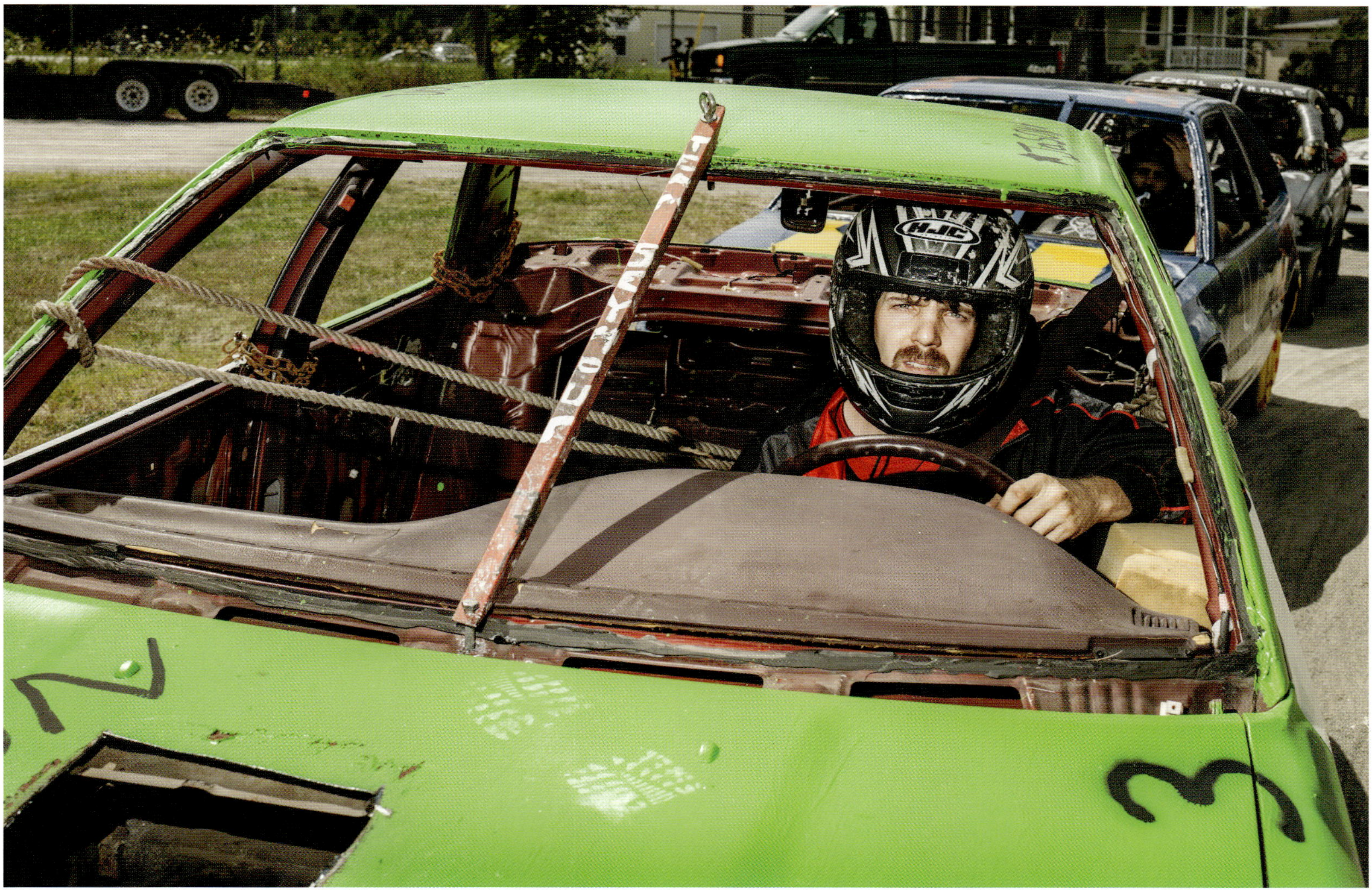

BEN STECHSCHULTE

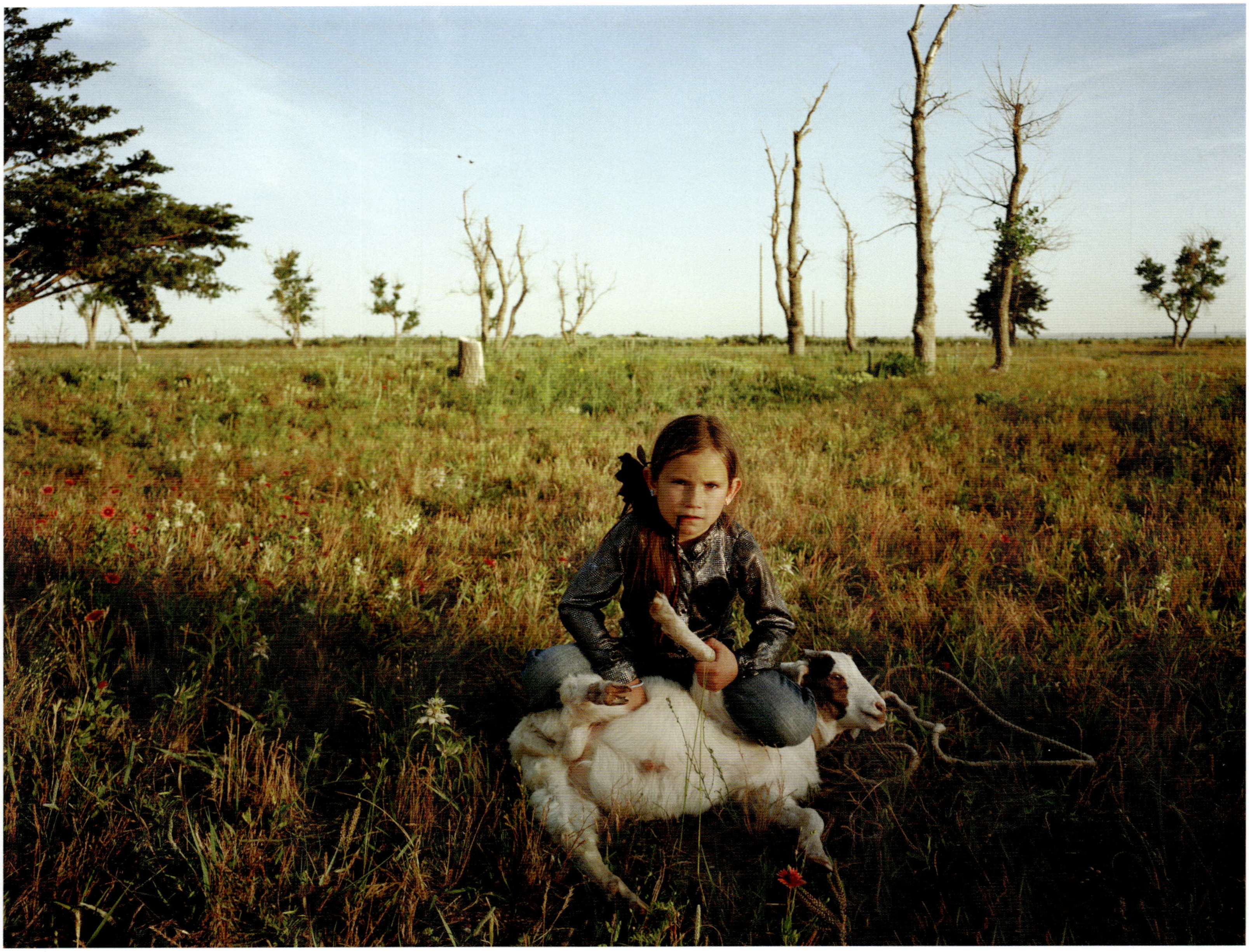

ILONA SZWARC

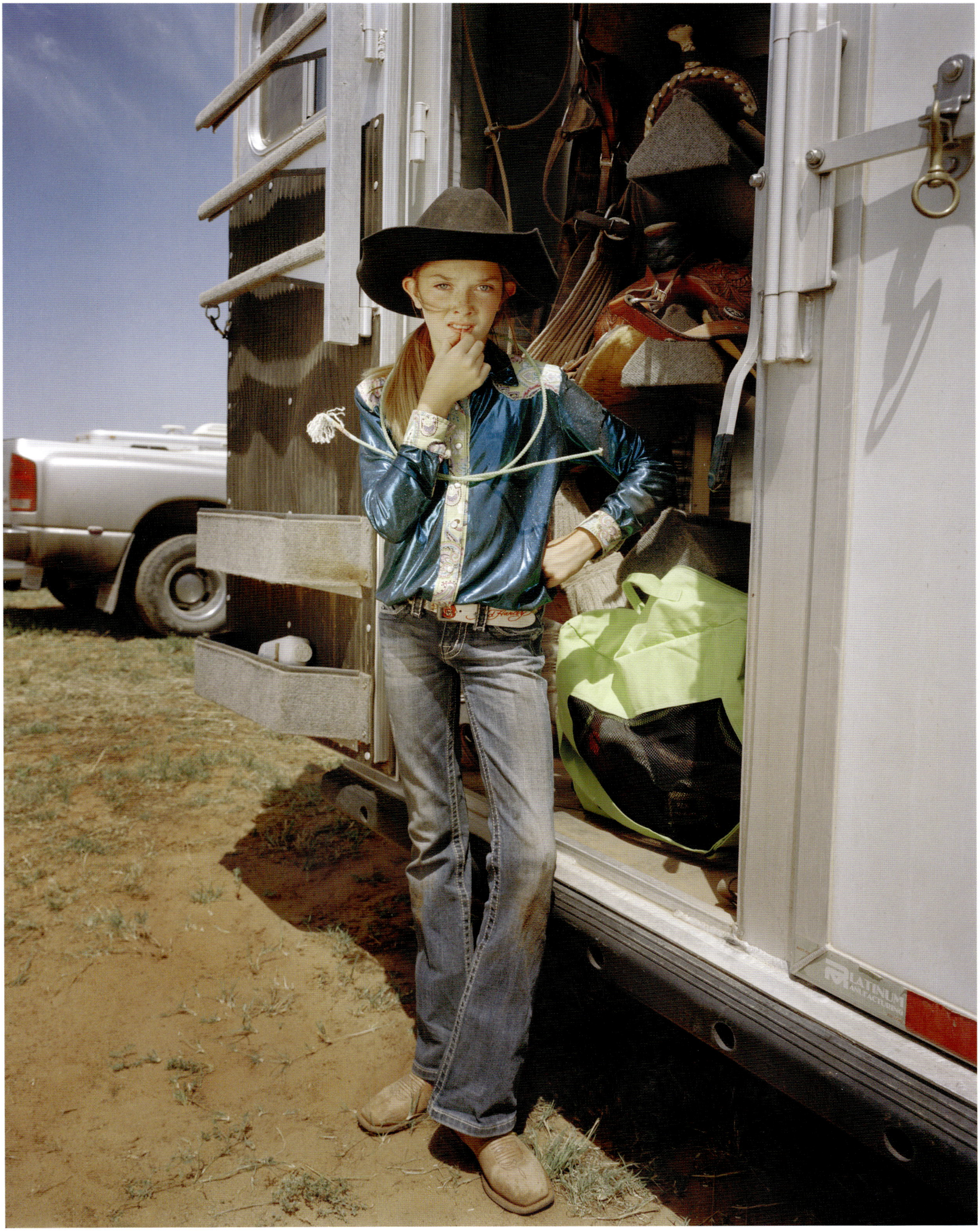

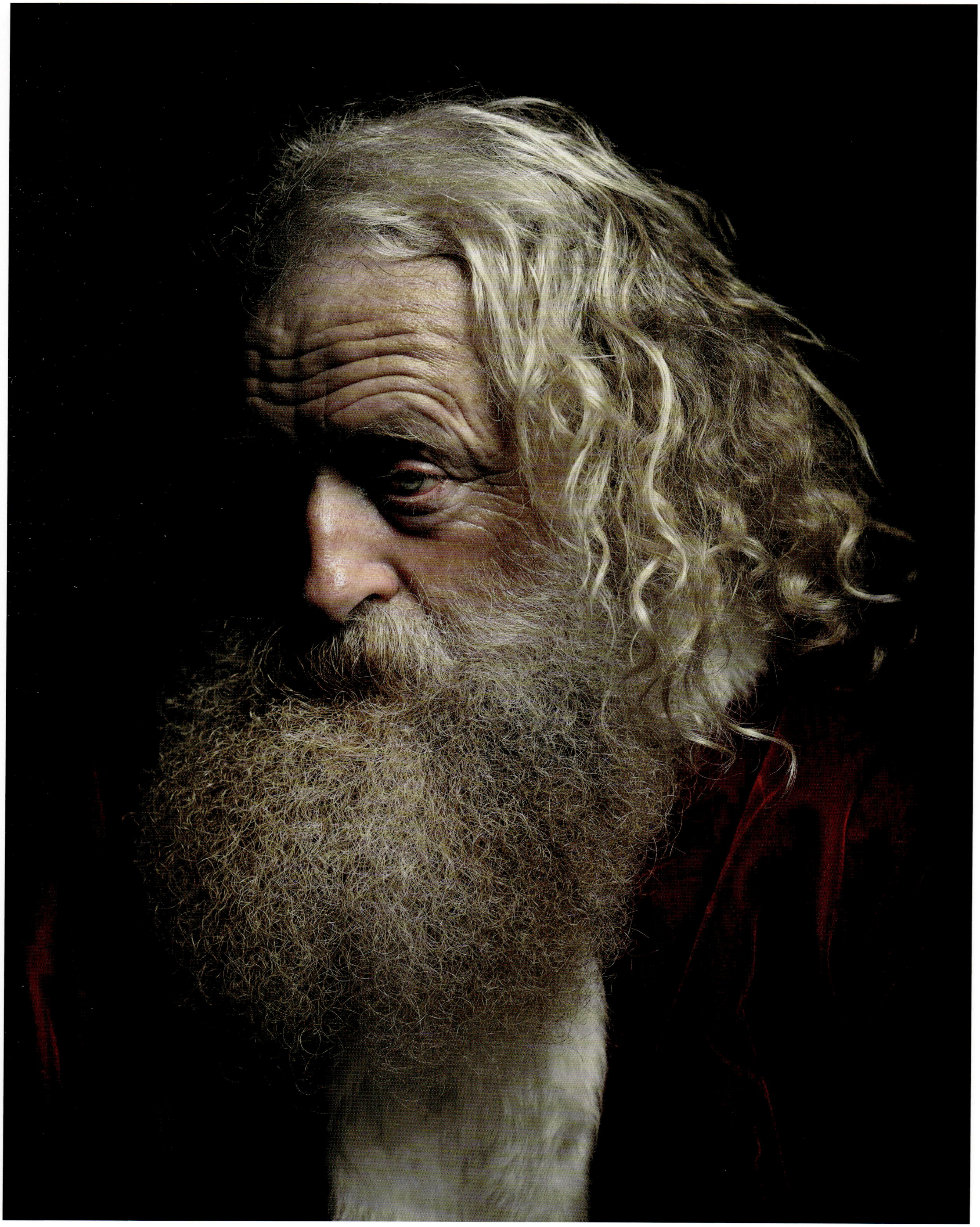

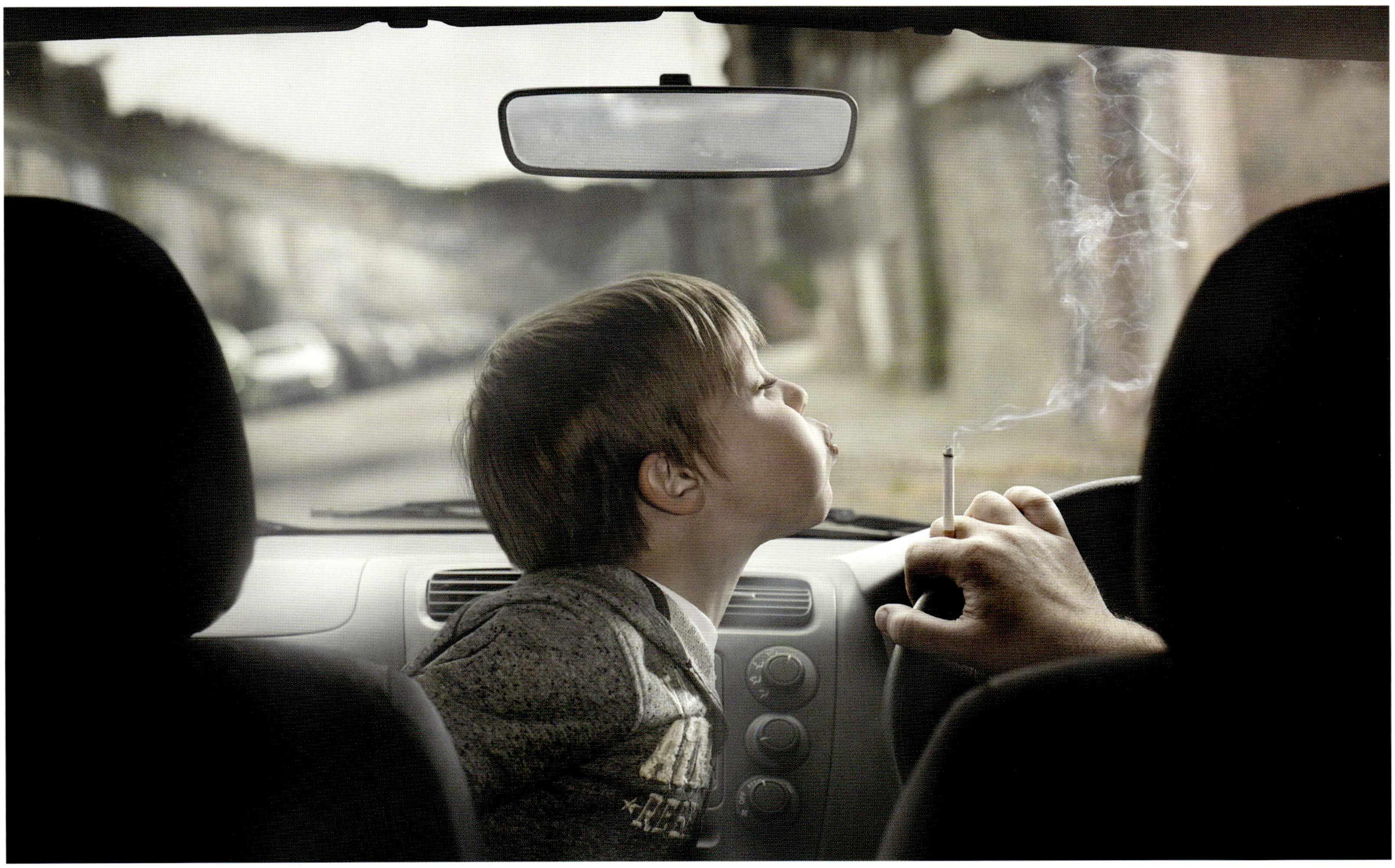

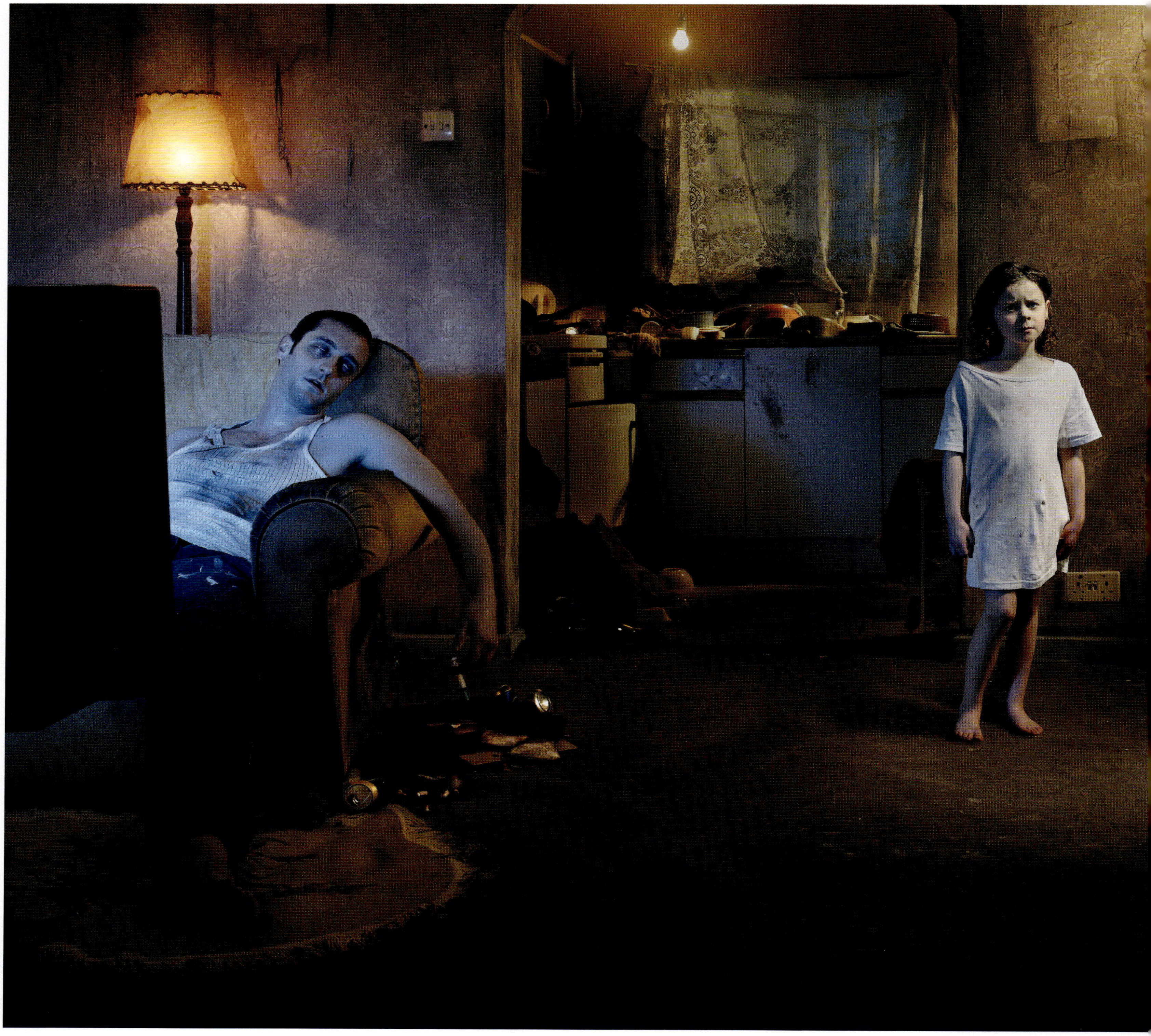

ALEX TELFER

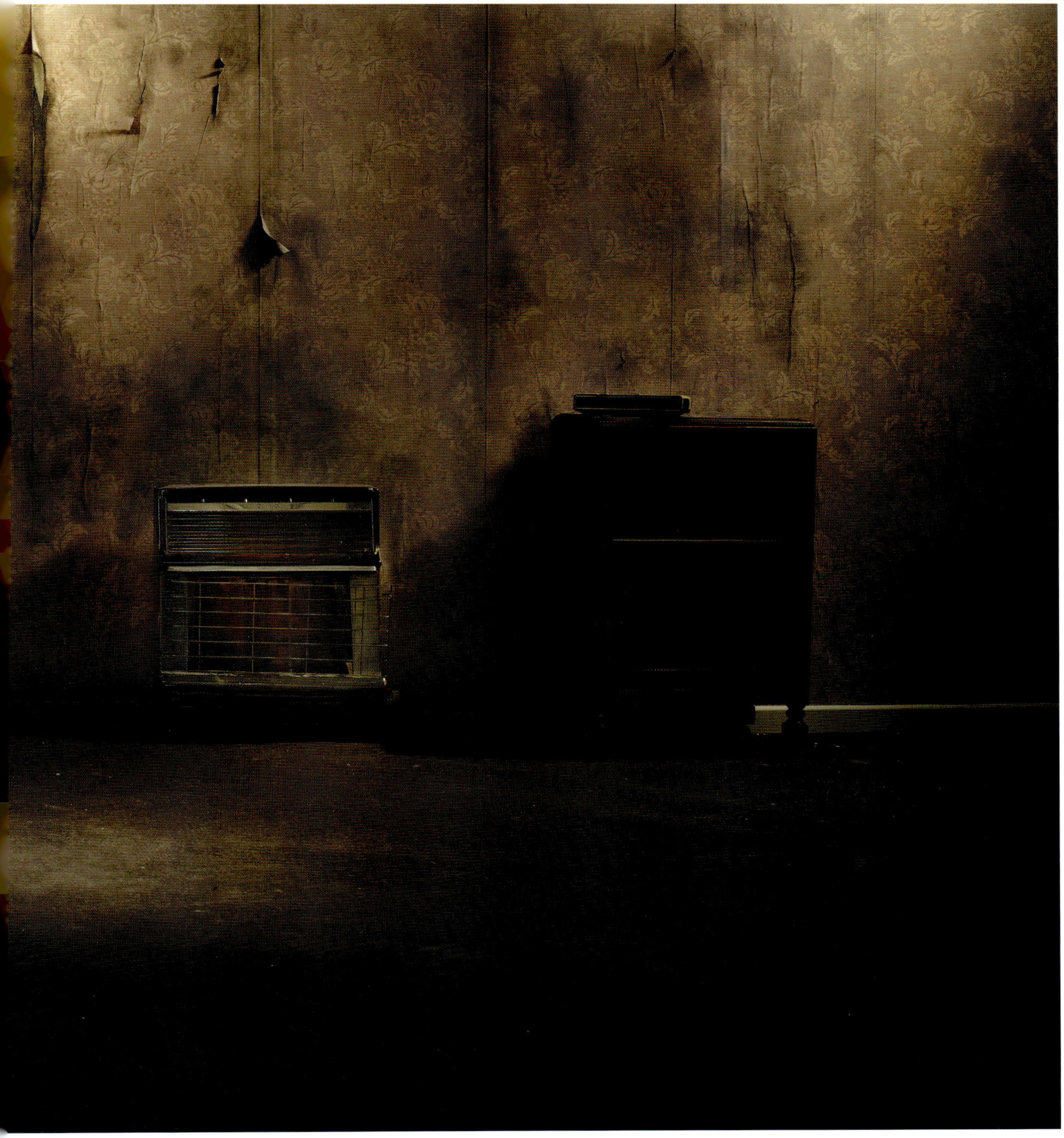

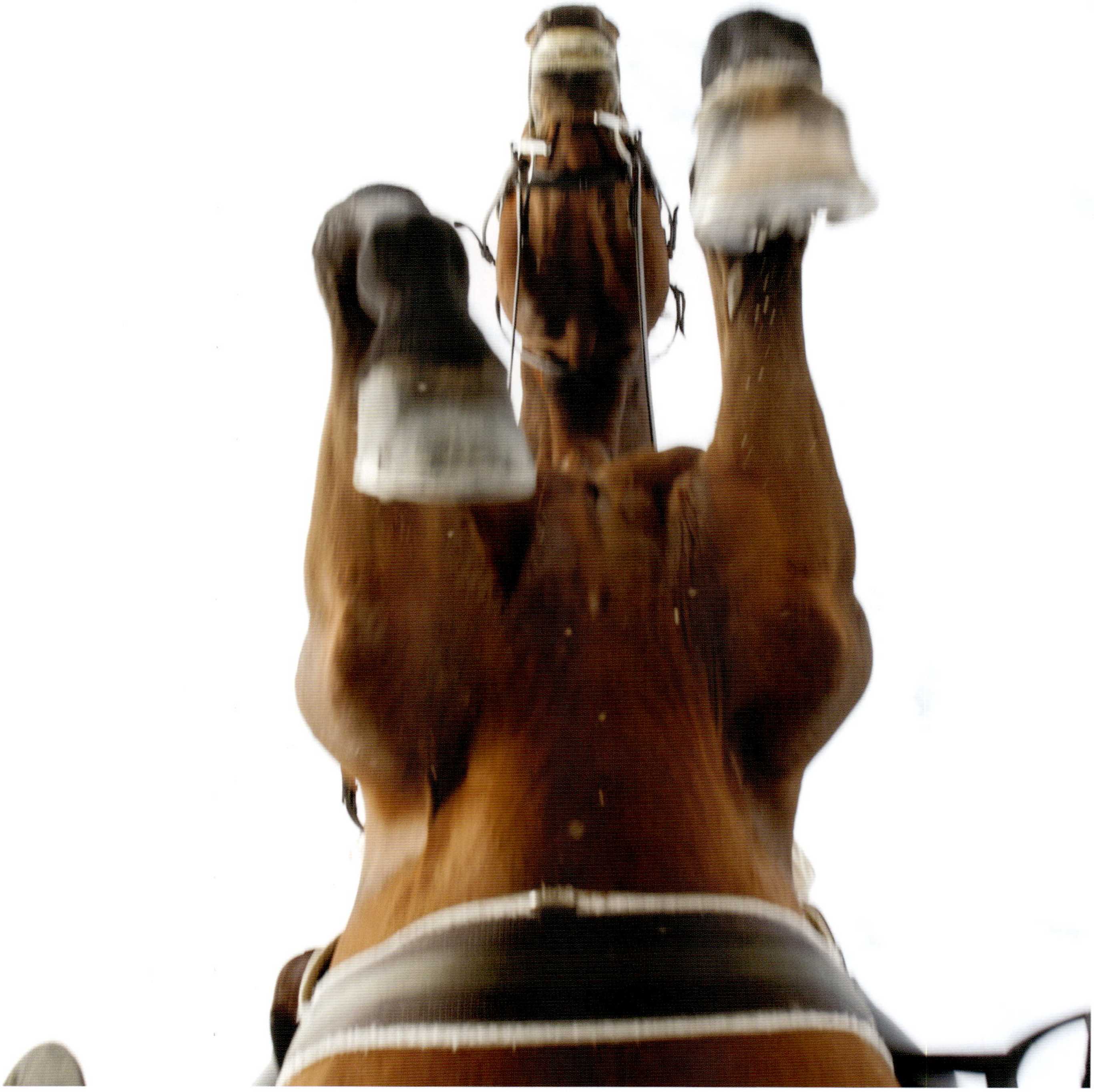

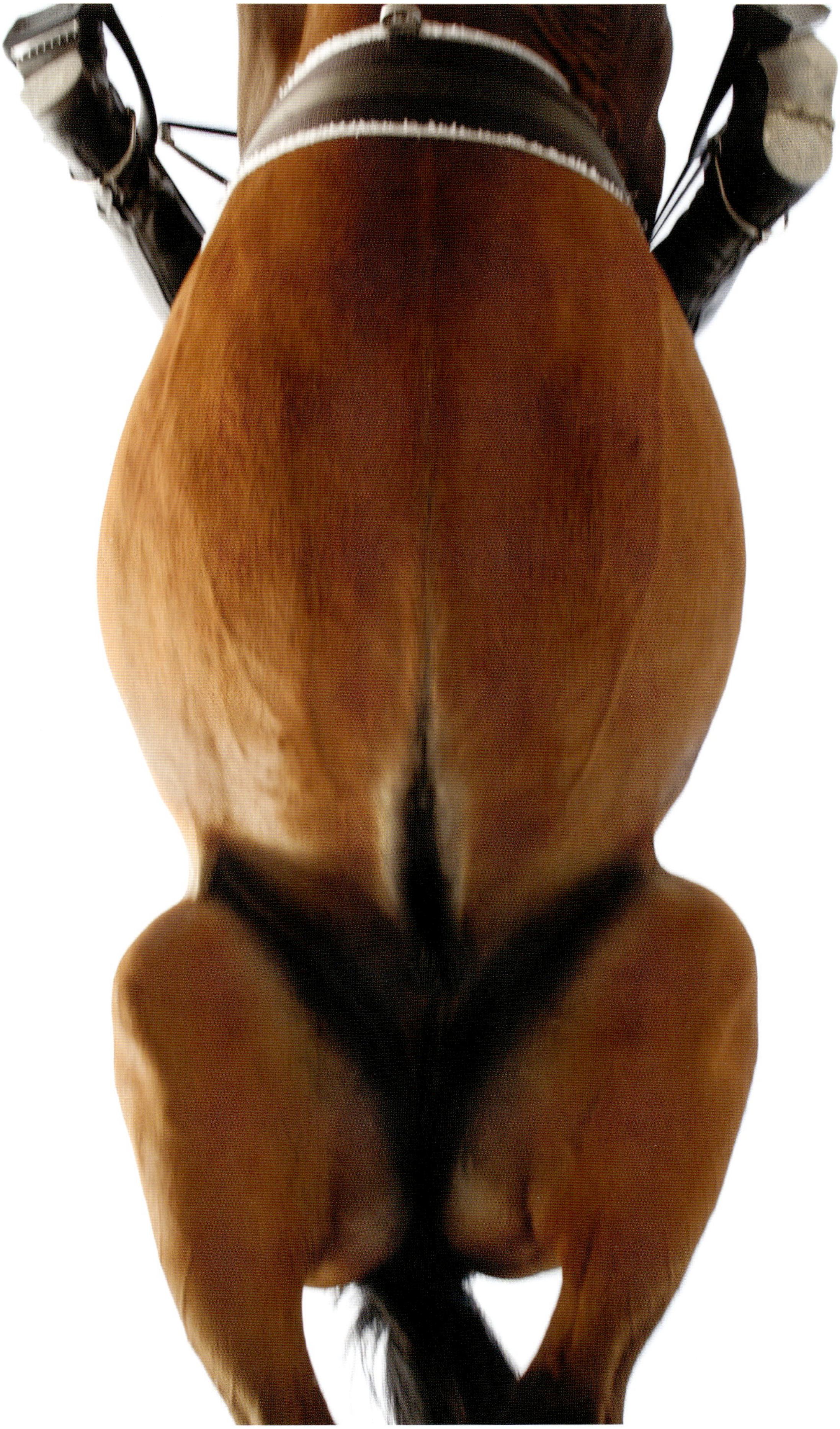

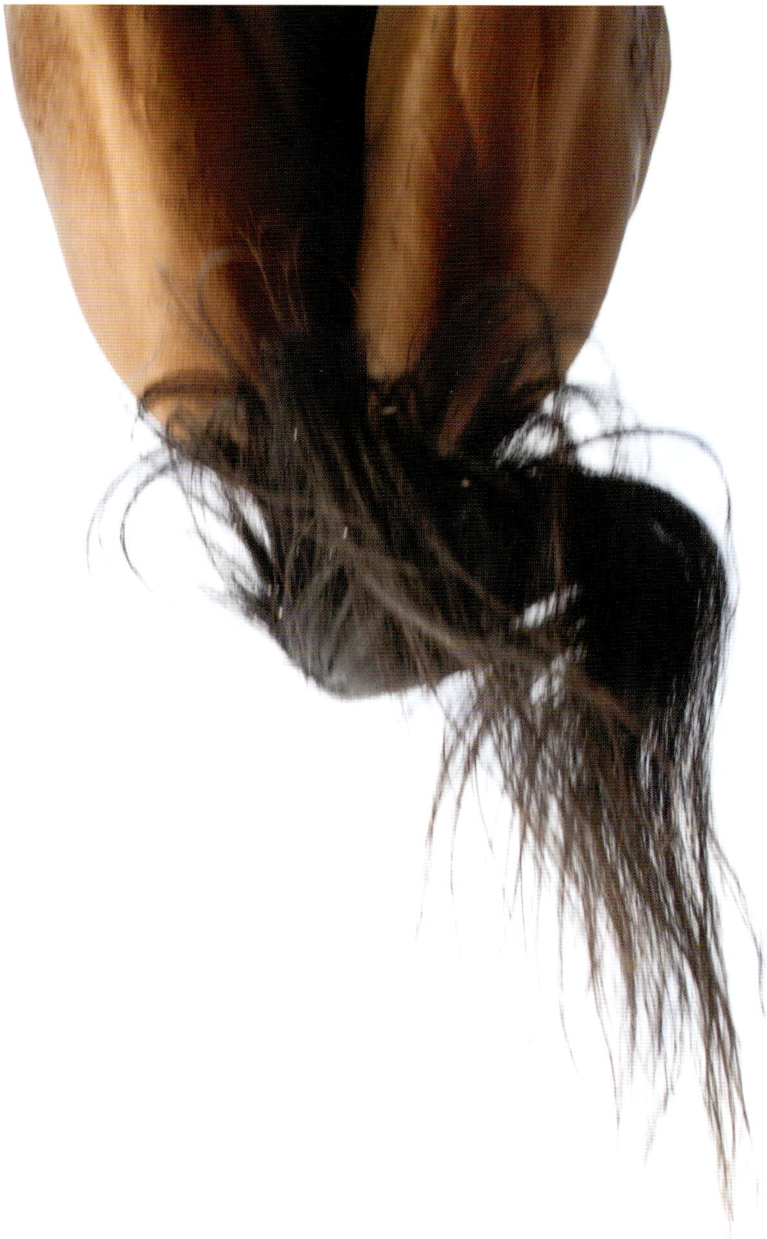

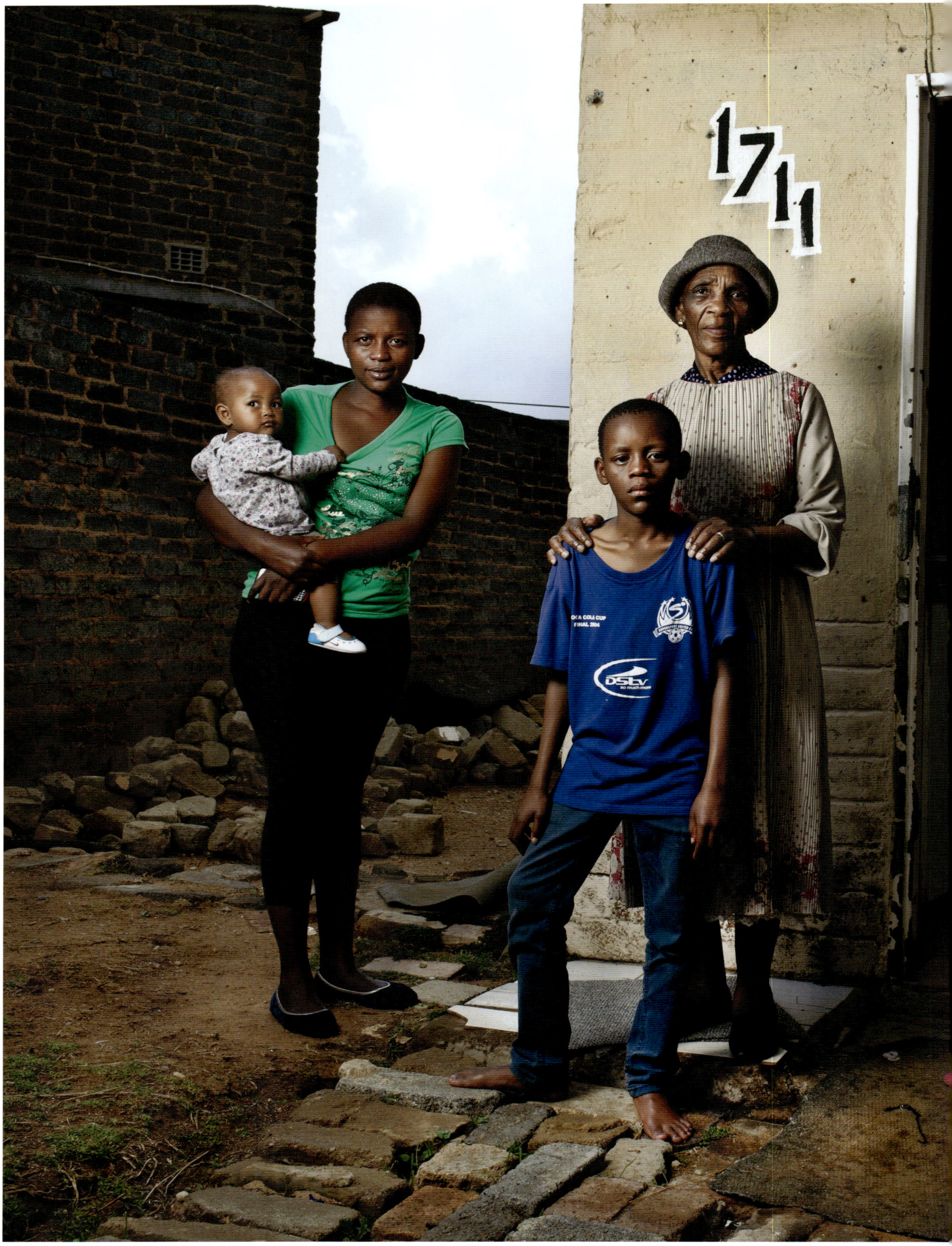
1711
DStv

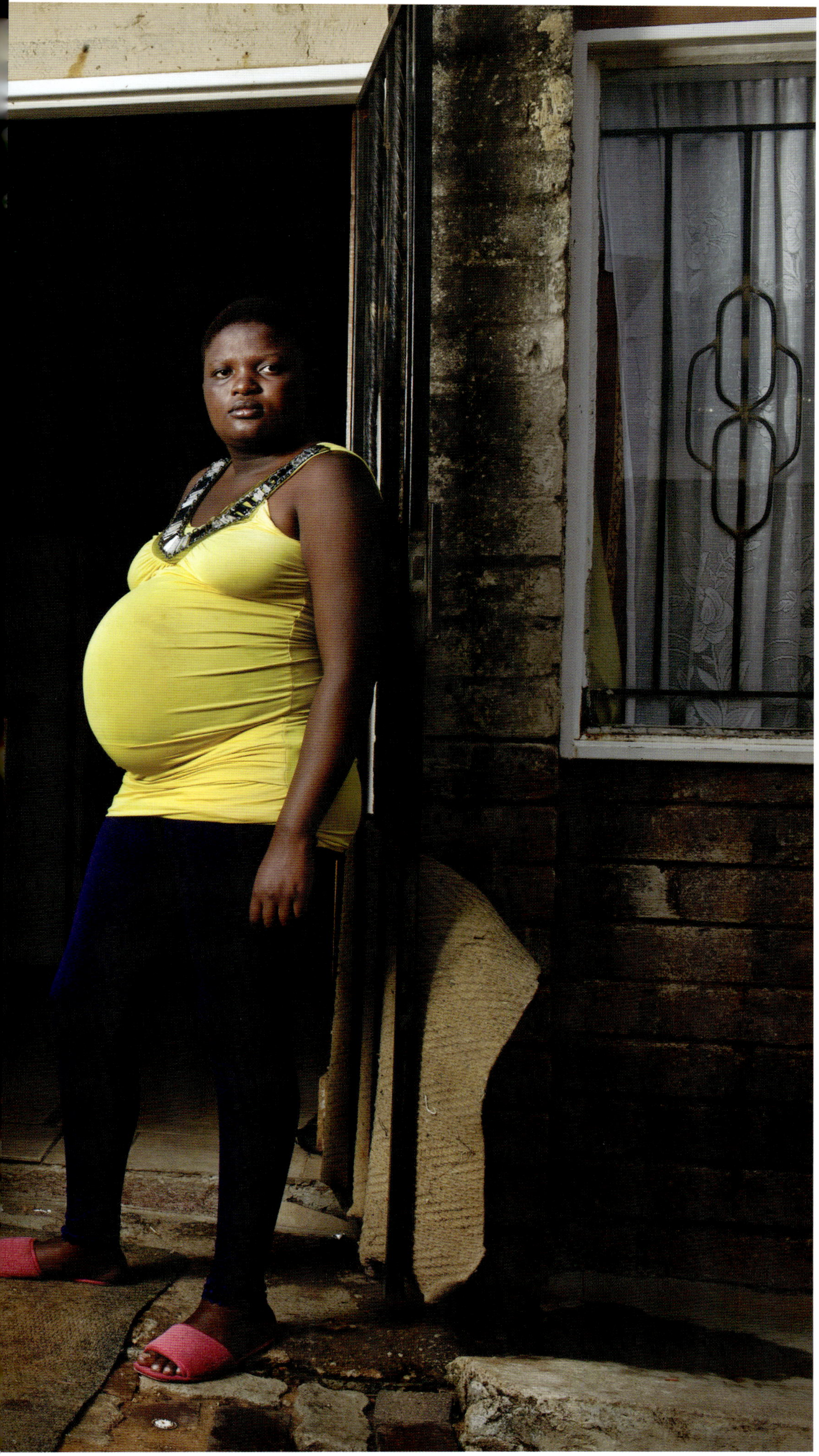

JONATHAN TORGOVNIK

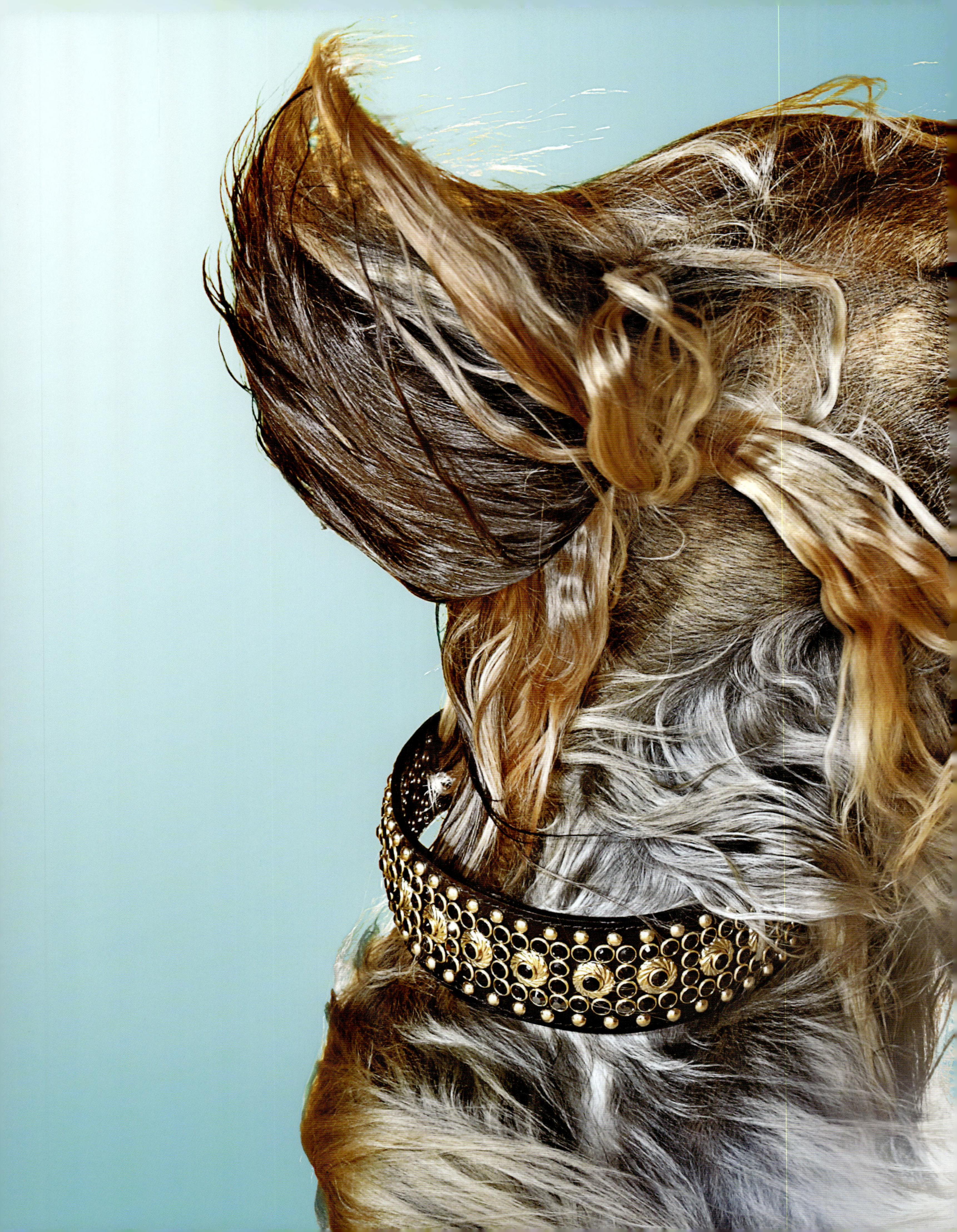

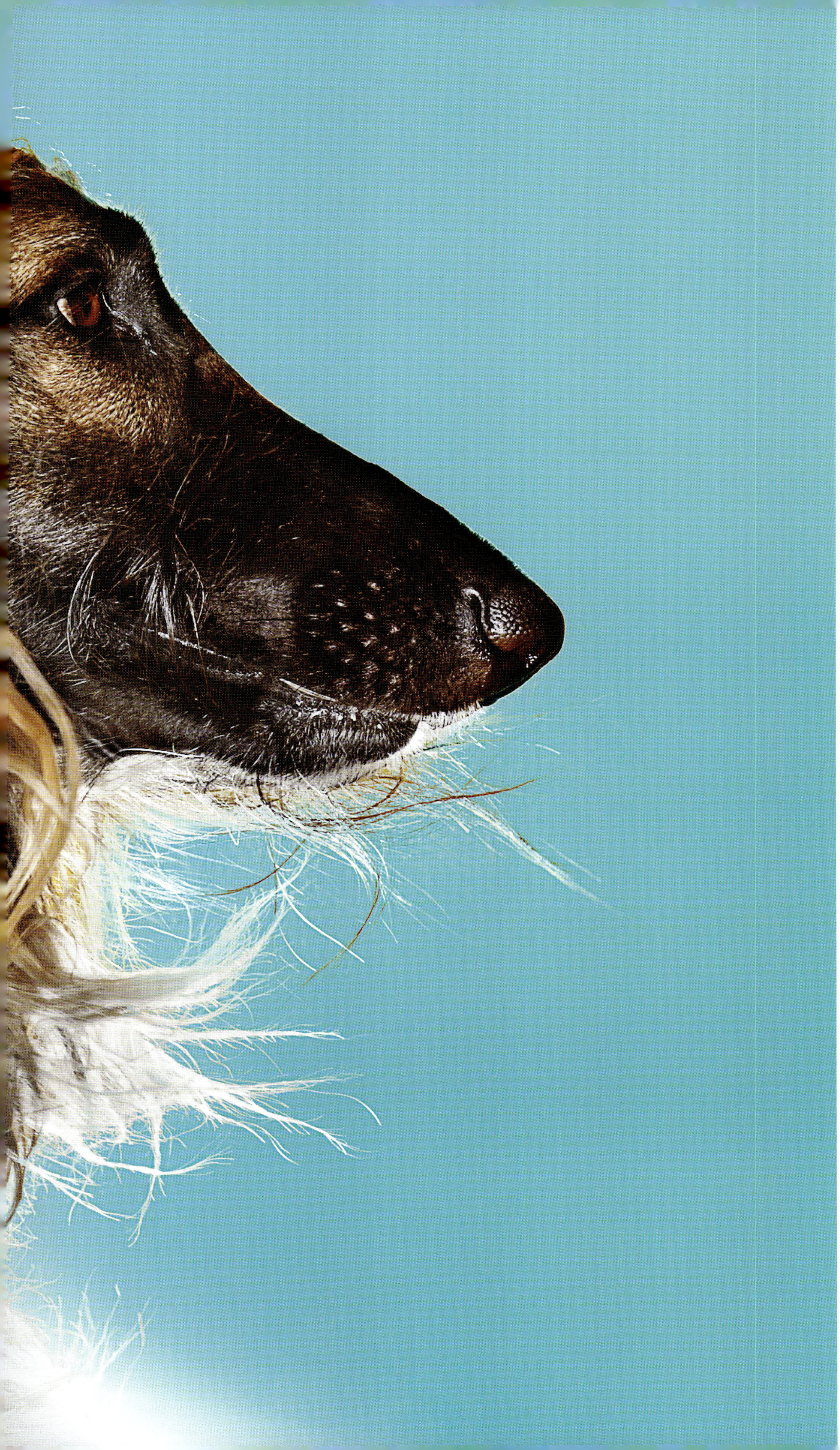

GANDEE VASAN

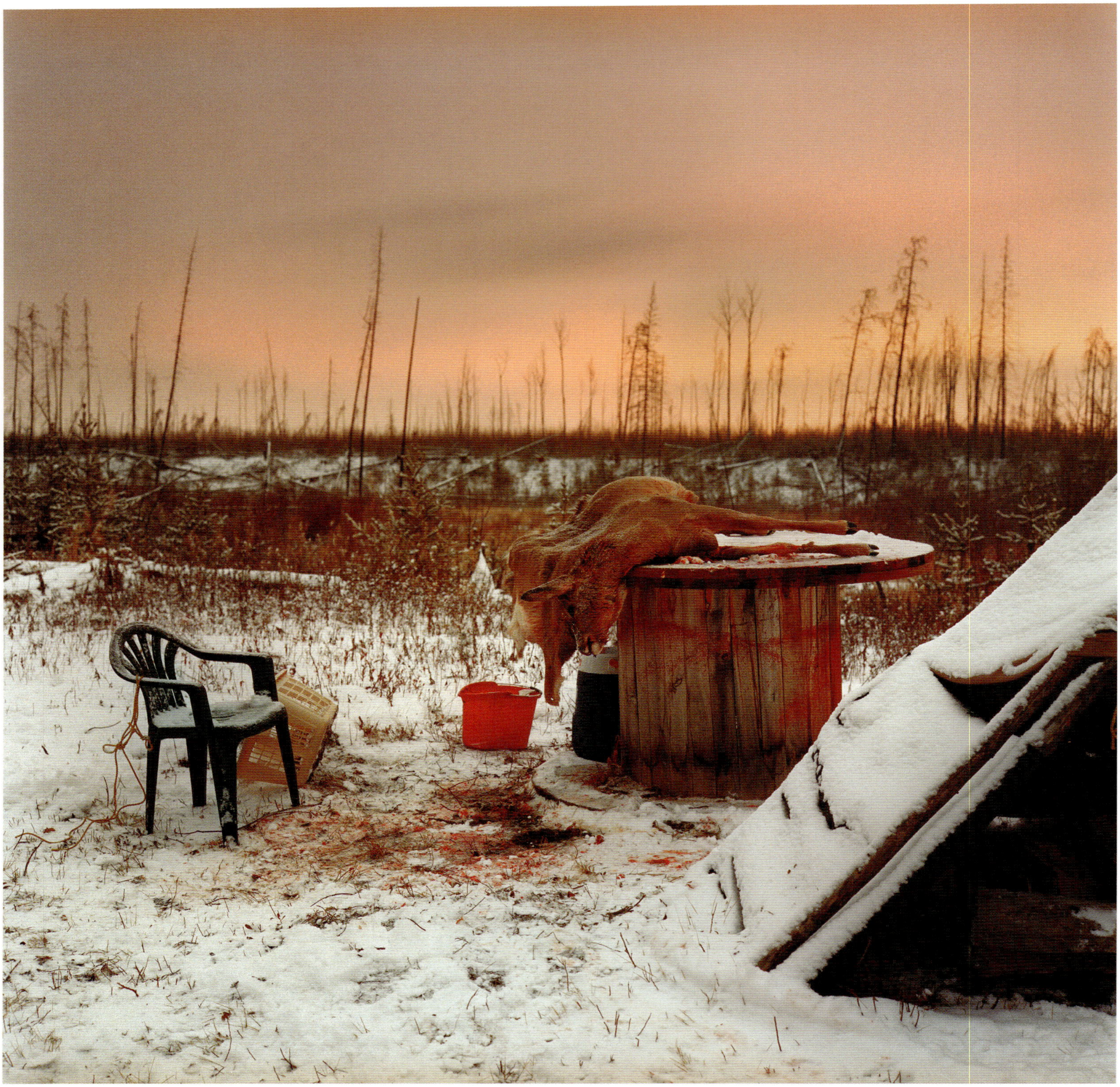

AARON VINCENT ELKAIM

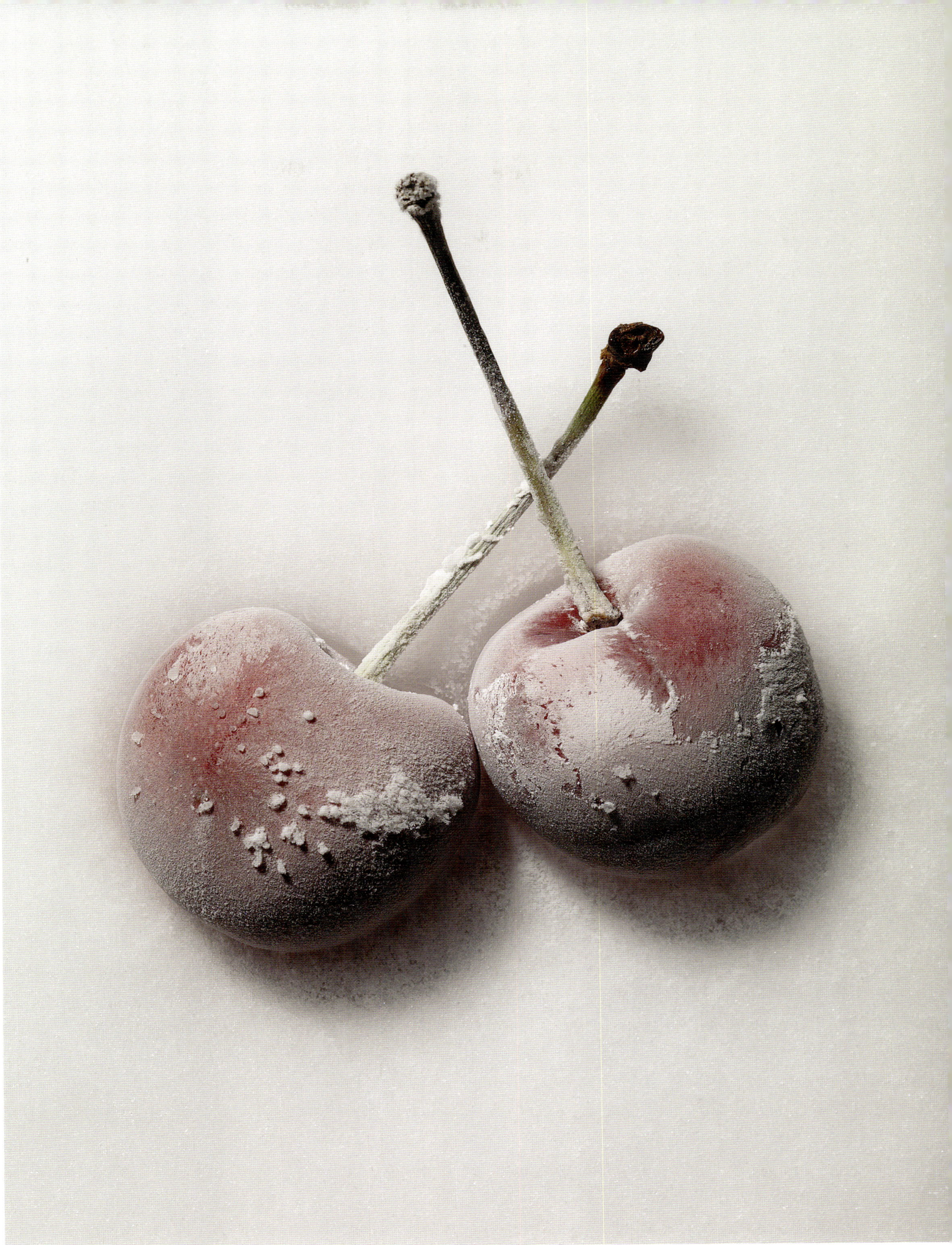

ADAM VOORHES

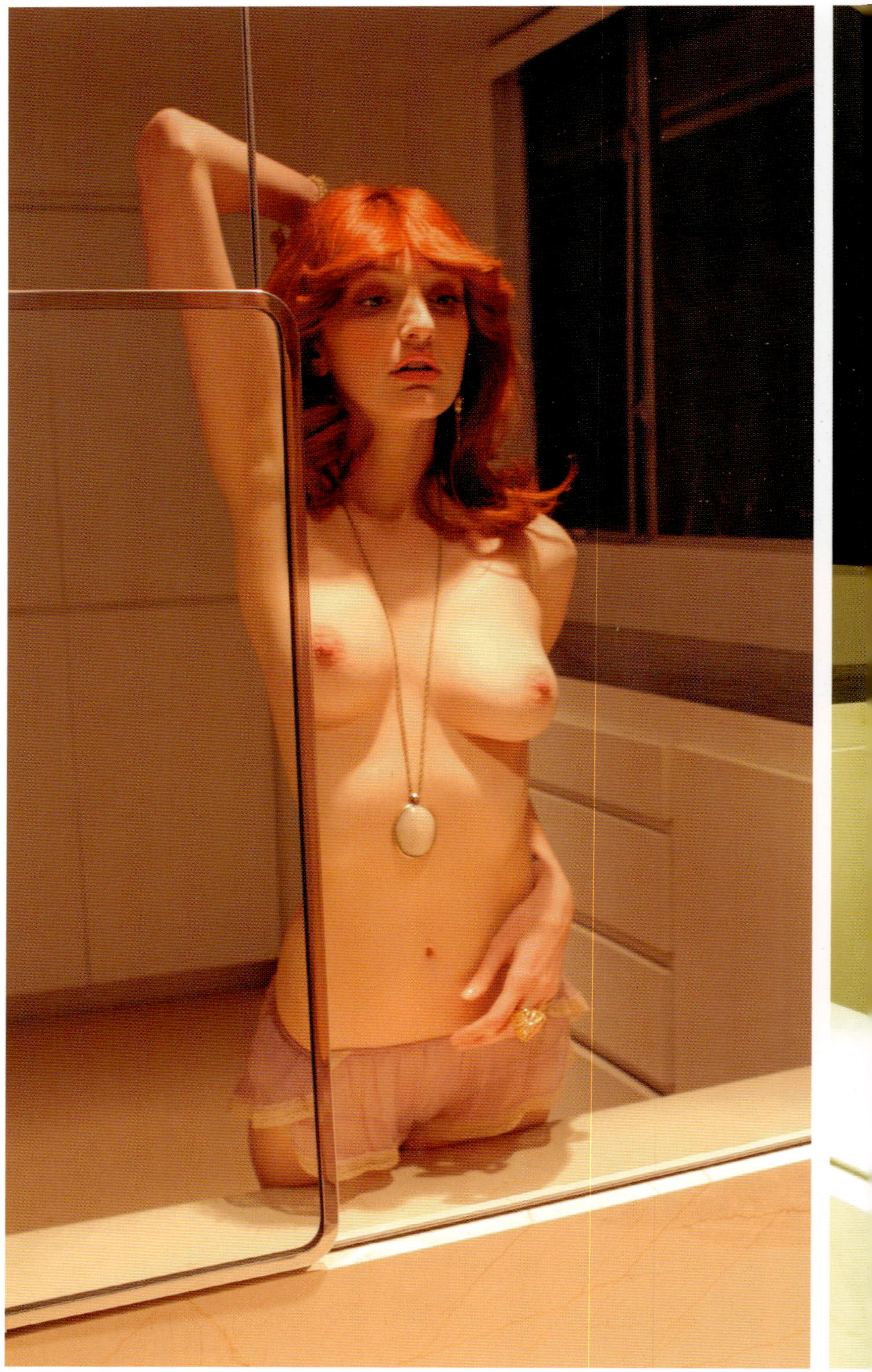

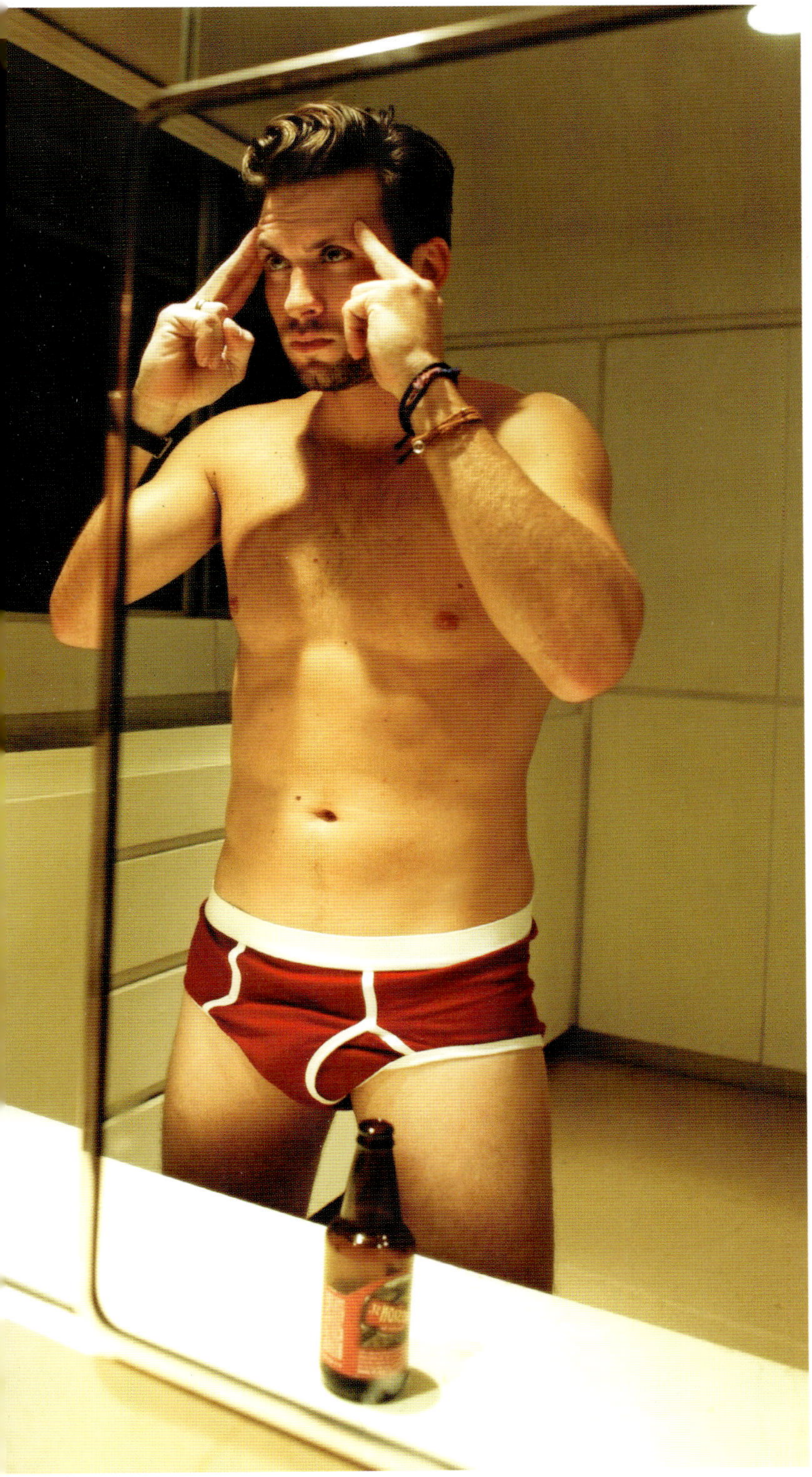

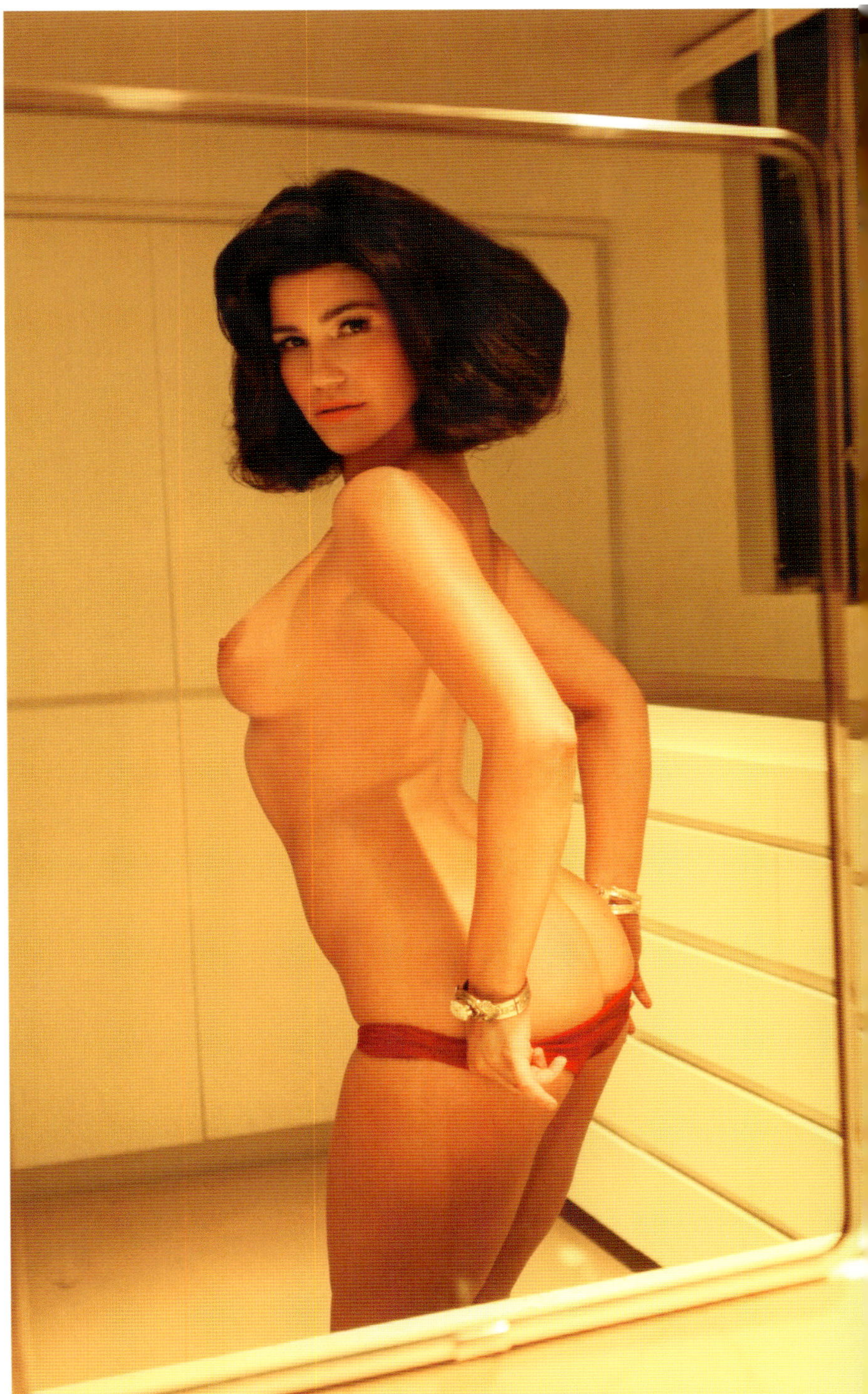

STEPHEN WILKES

282 / 283 / 284

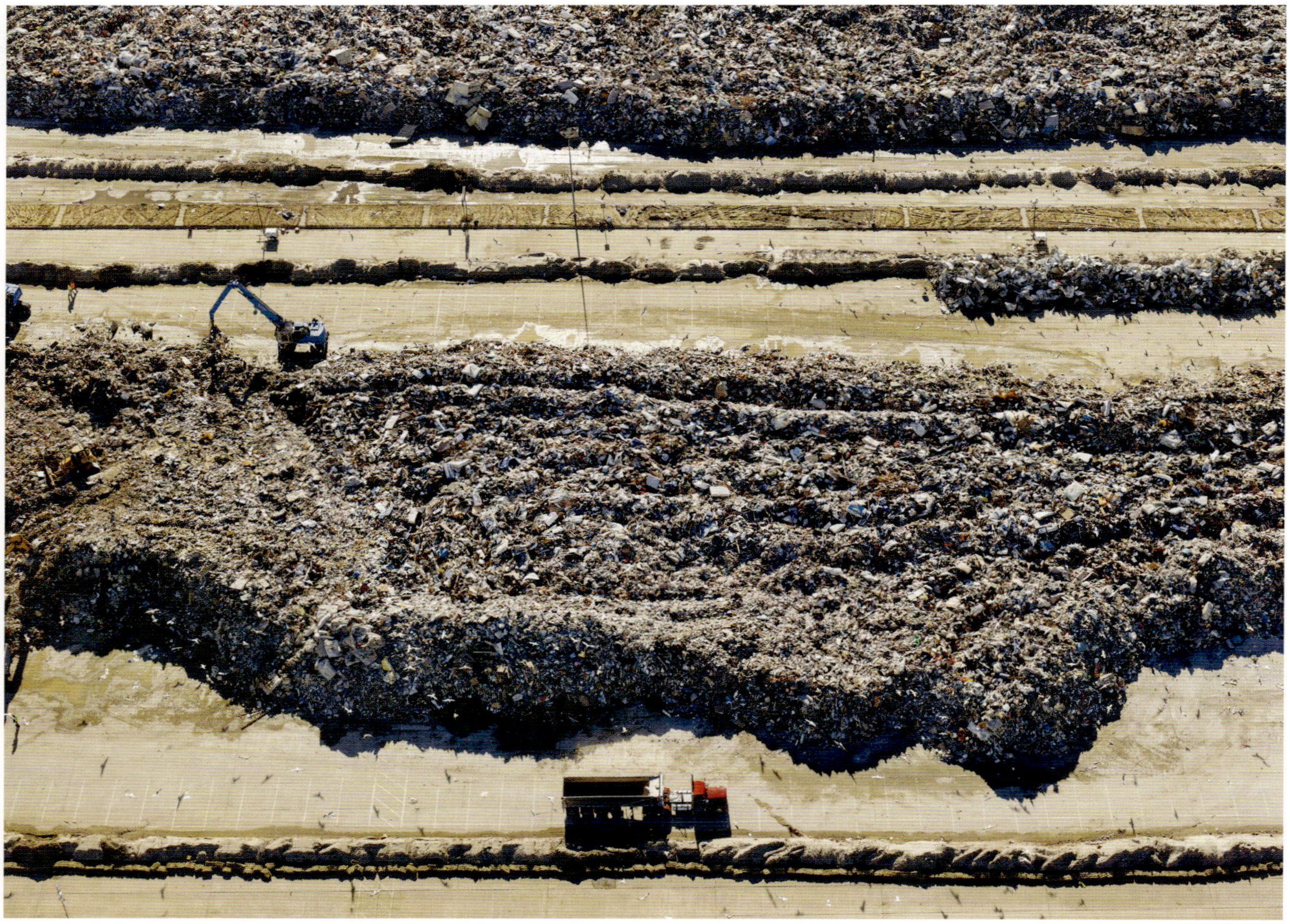

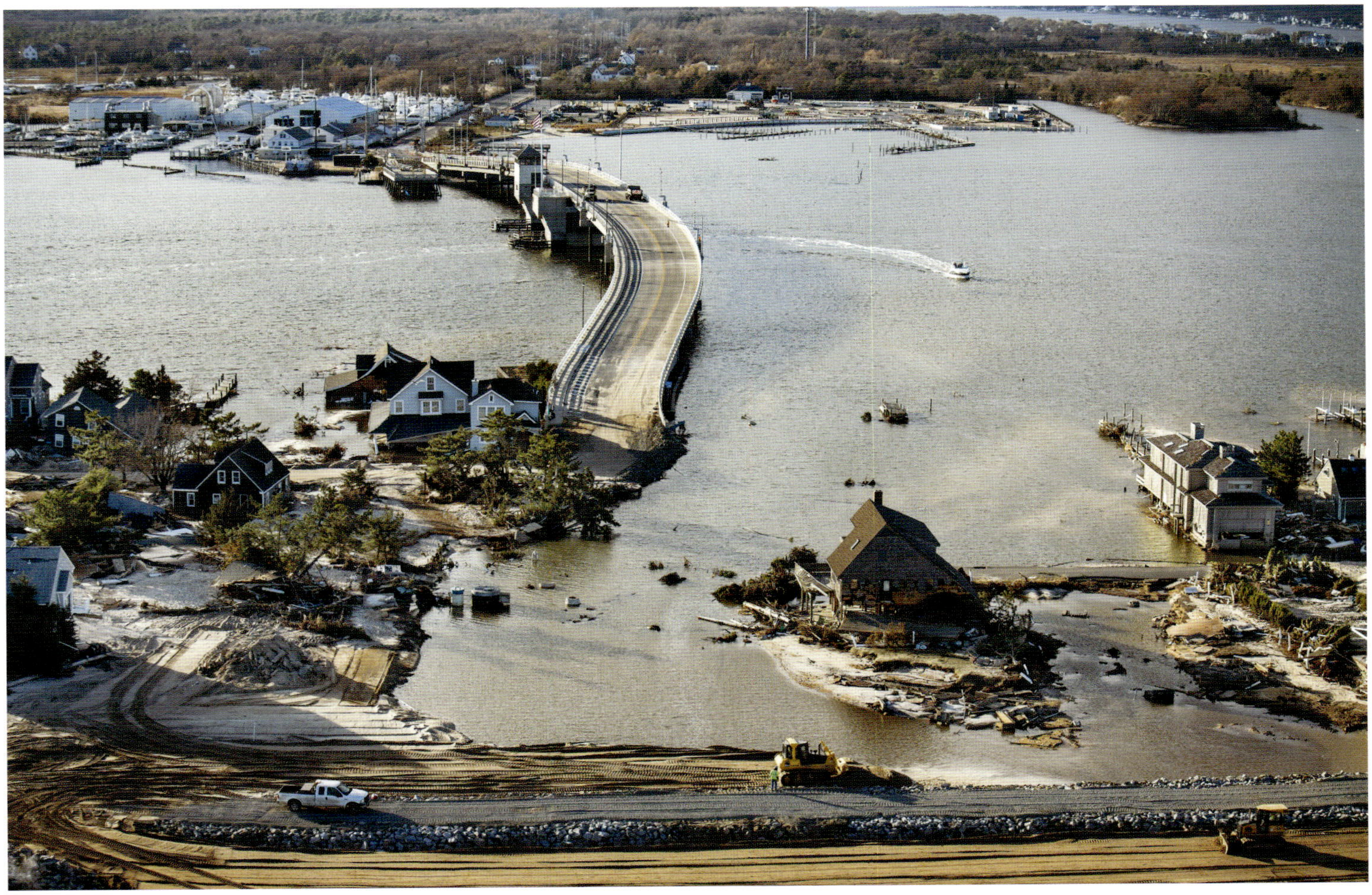

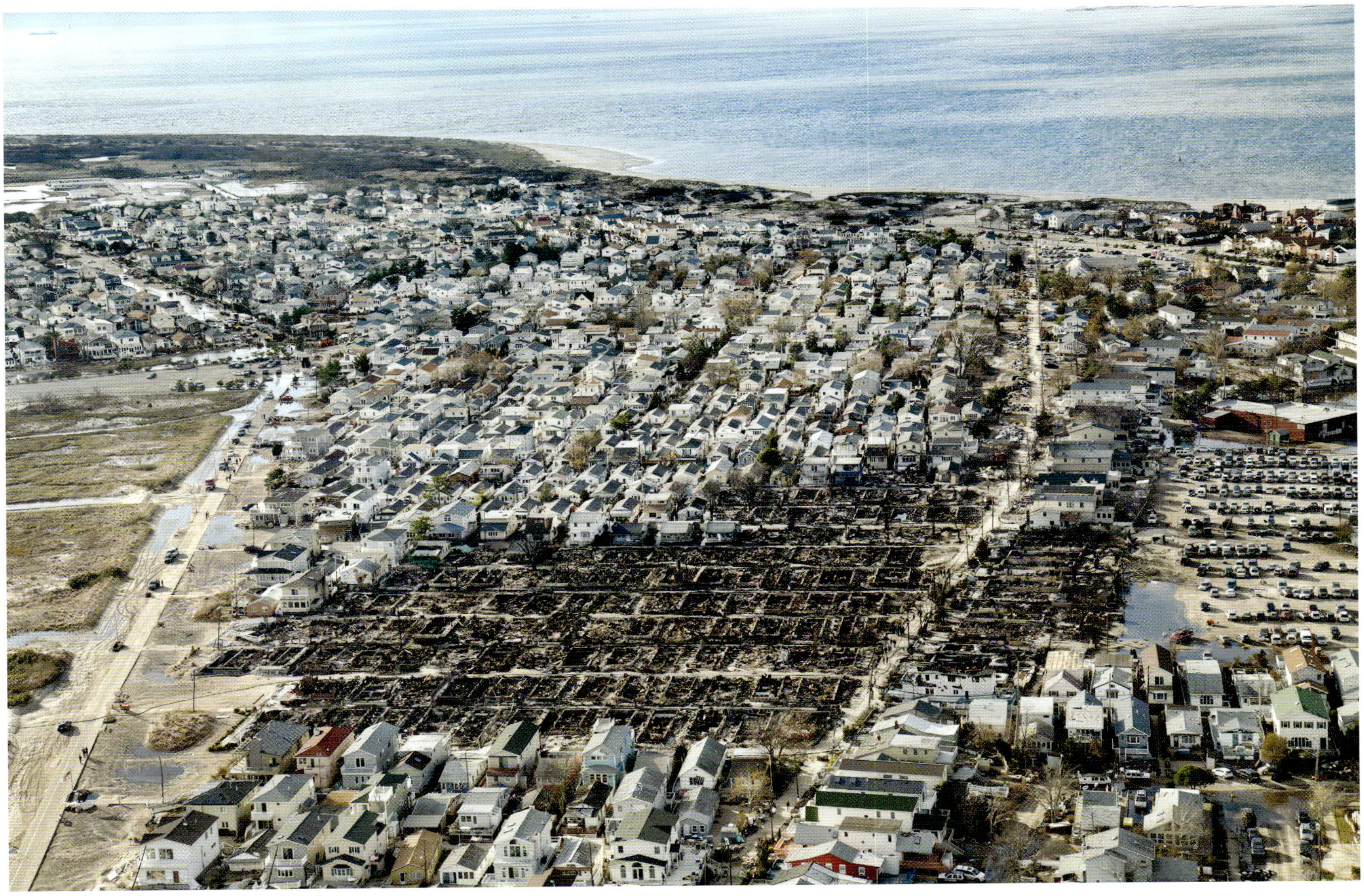

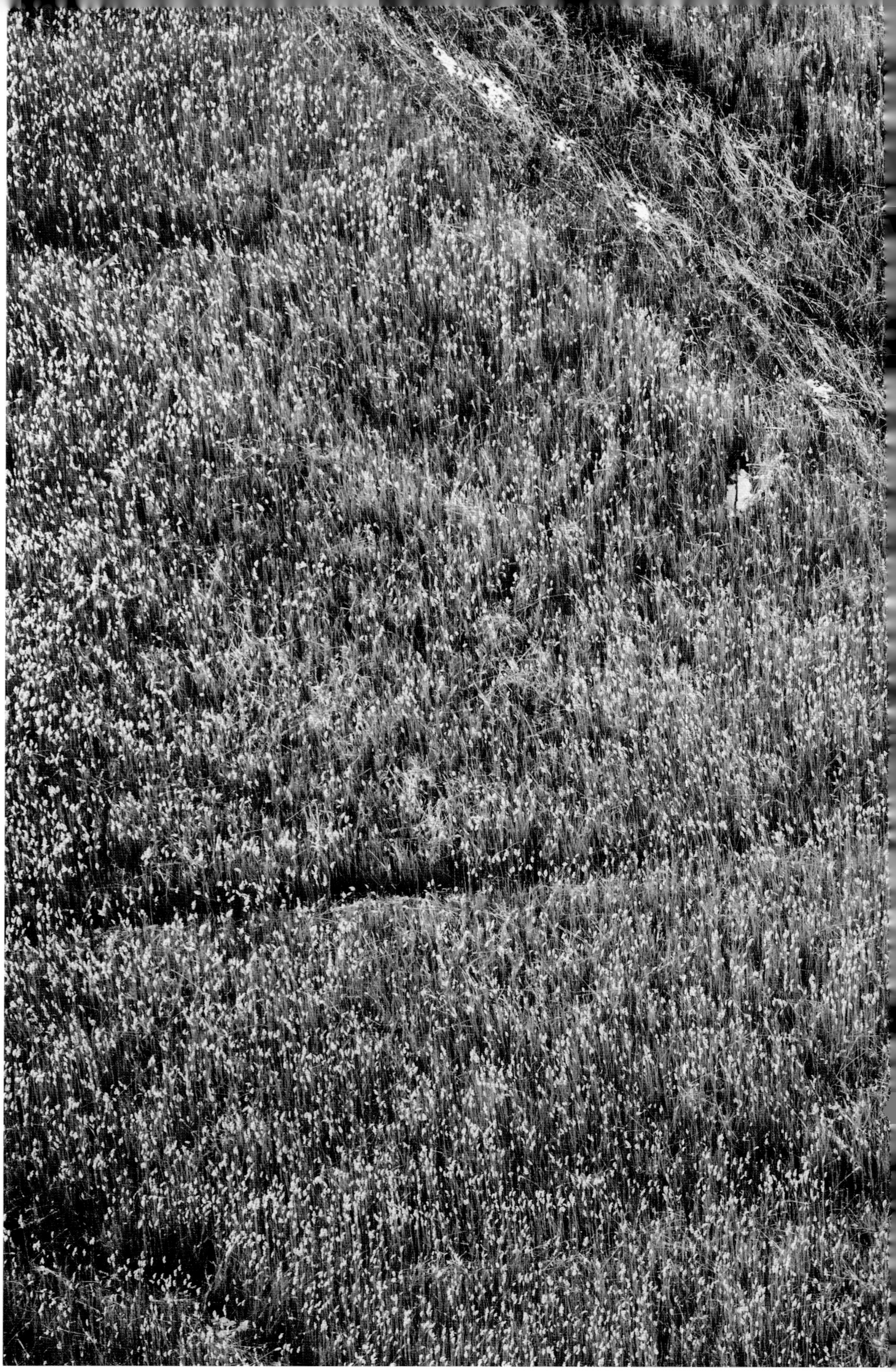

STEPHEN WILKES

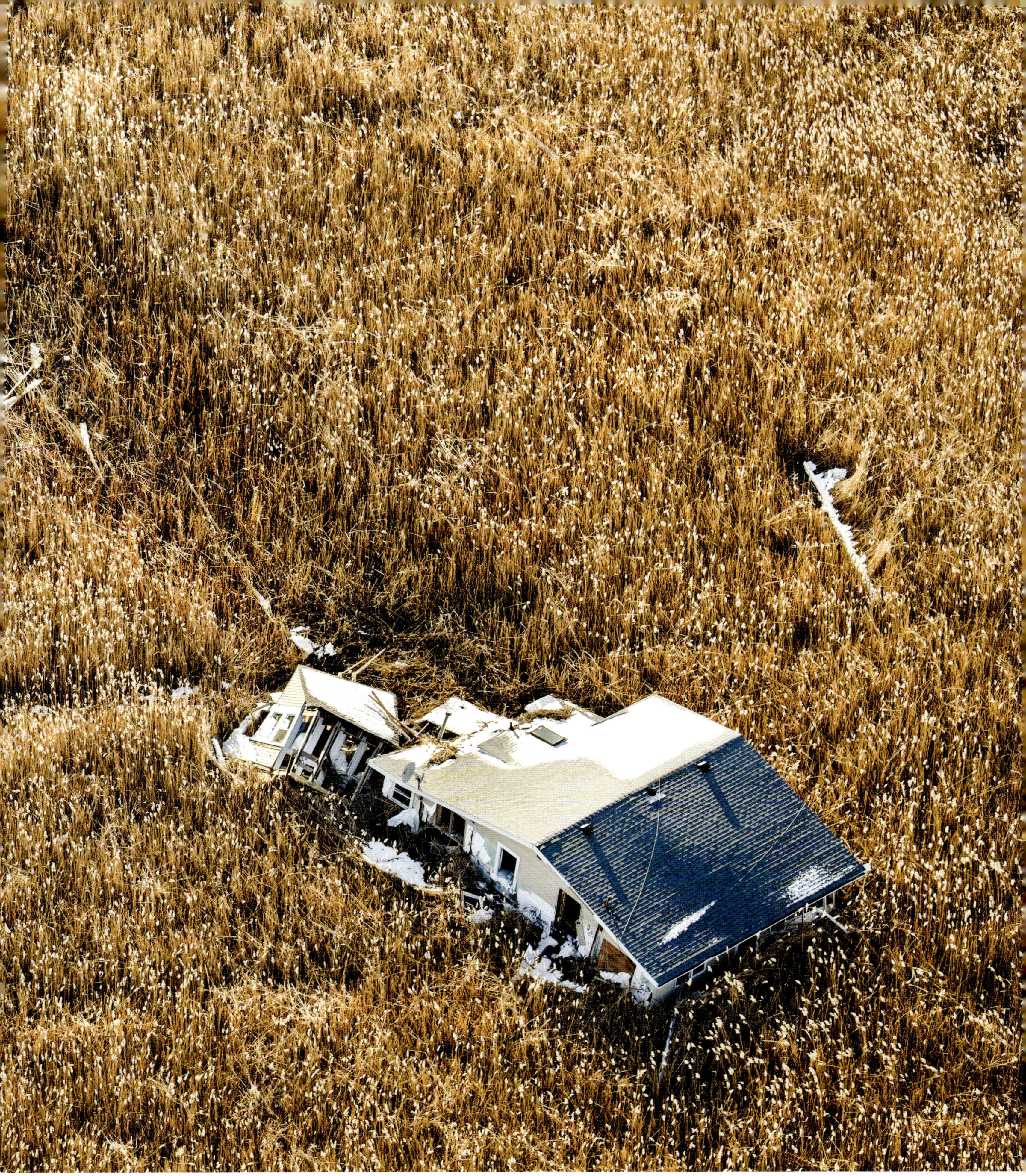

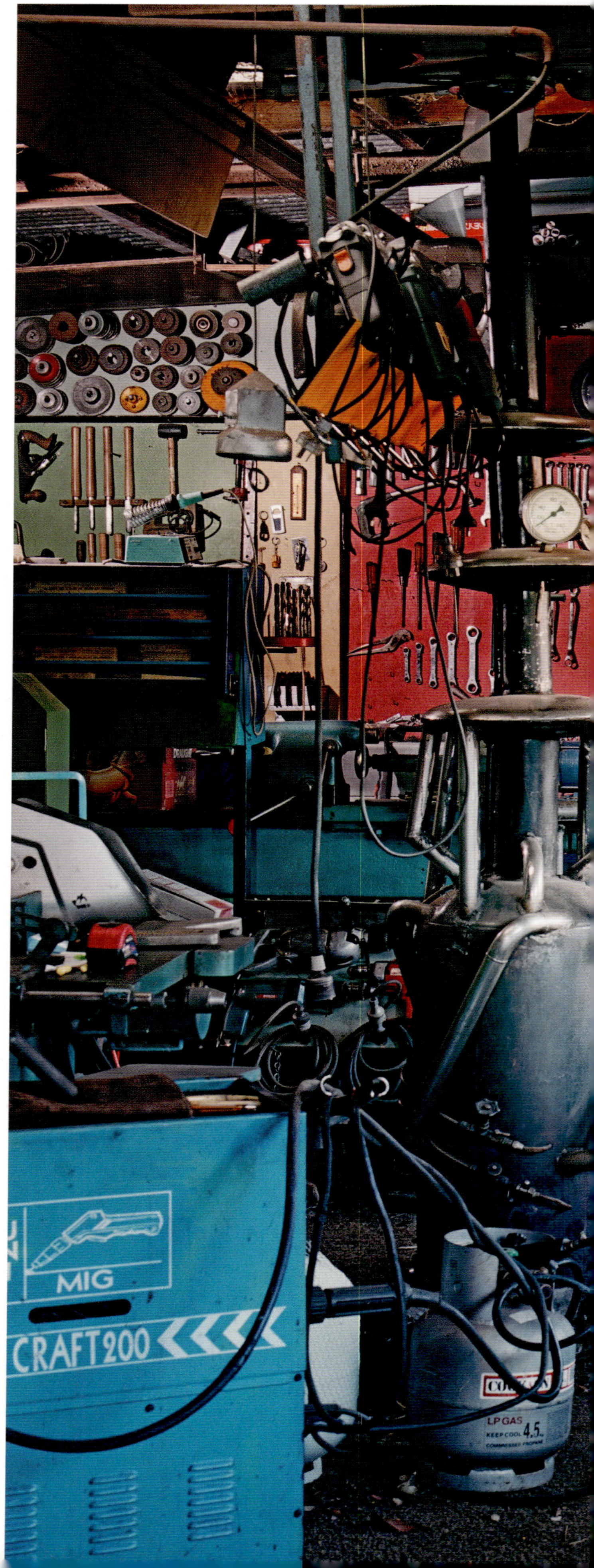
MIG
CRAFT200
LP GAS
KEEP COOL
4.5

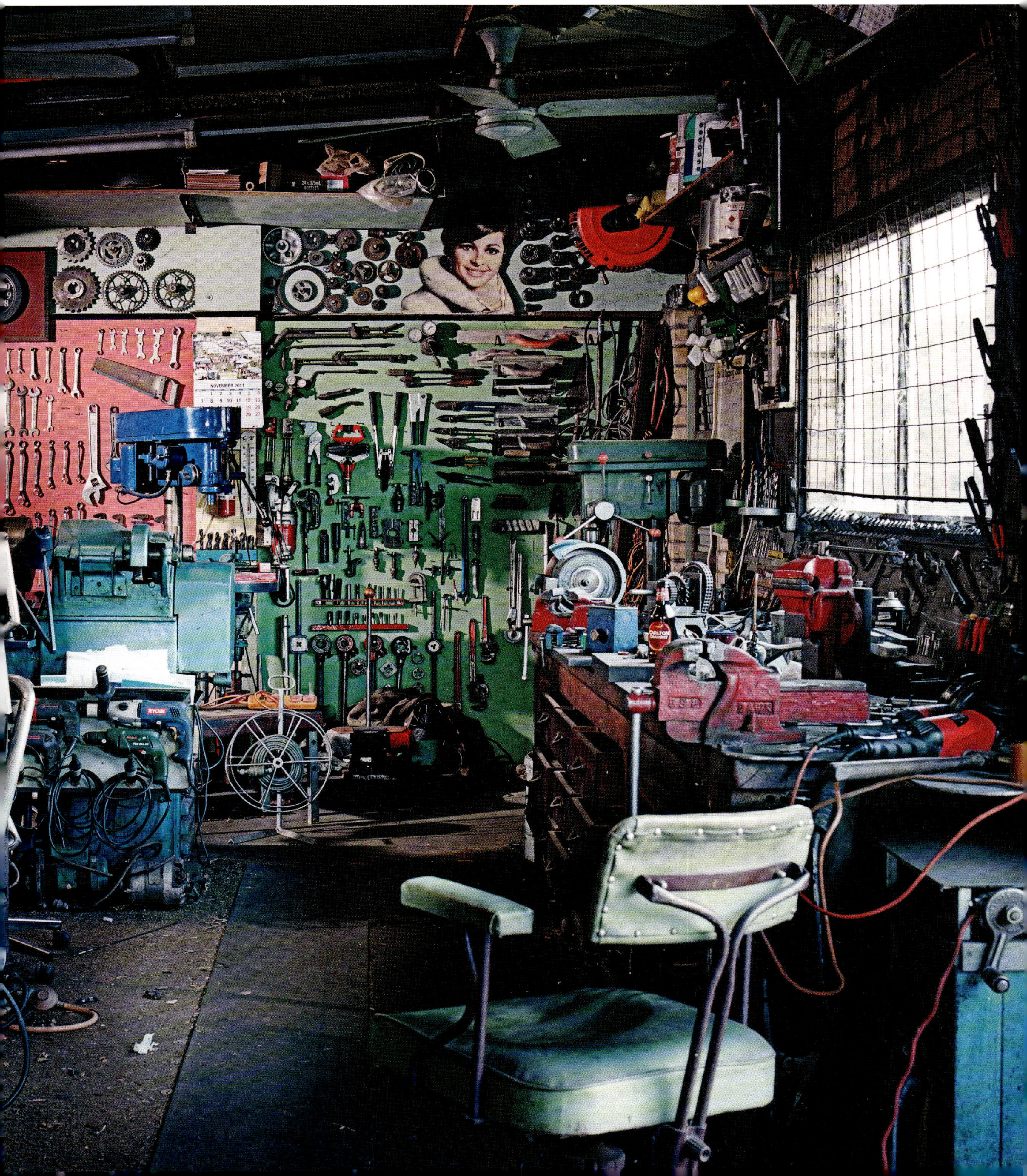
NOVEMBER 2011
RYOBI

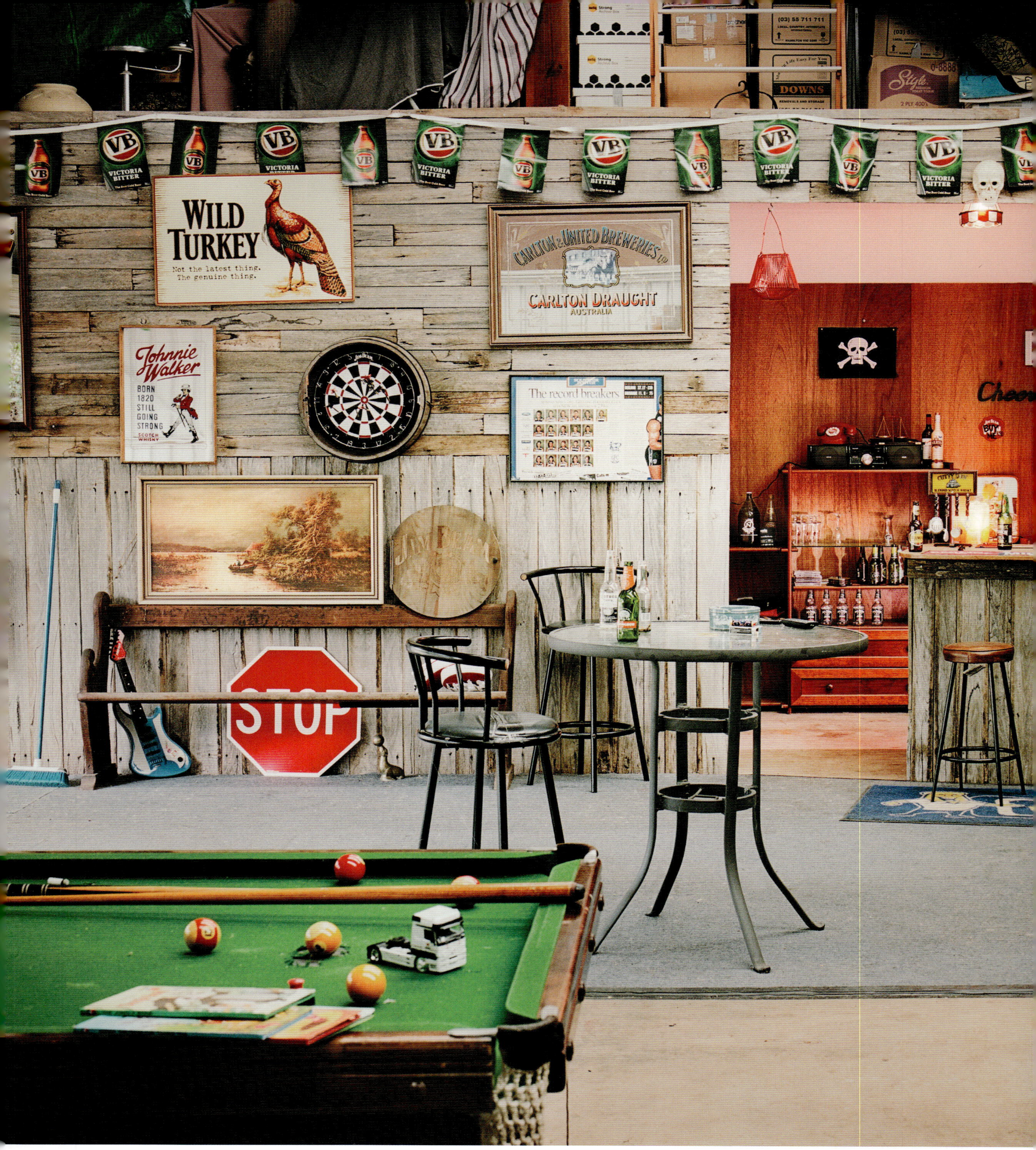
VB
VICTORIA BITTER
WILD TURKEY
Not the latest thing.
The genuine thing.
CARLTON & UNITED BREWERIES LTD
CARLTON DRAUGHT
AUSTRALIA
Johnnie Walker
BORN 1820 STILL GOING STRONG
SCOTCH WHISKY
The record breakers
STOP
DOWNS

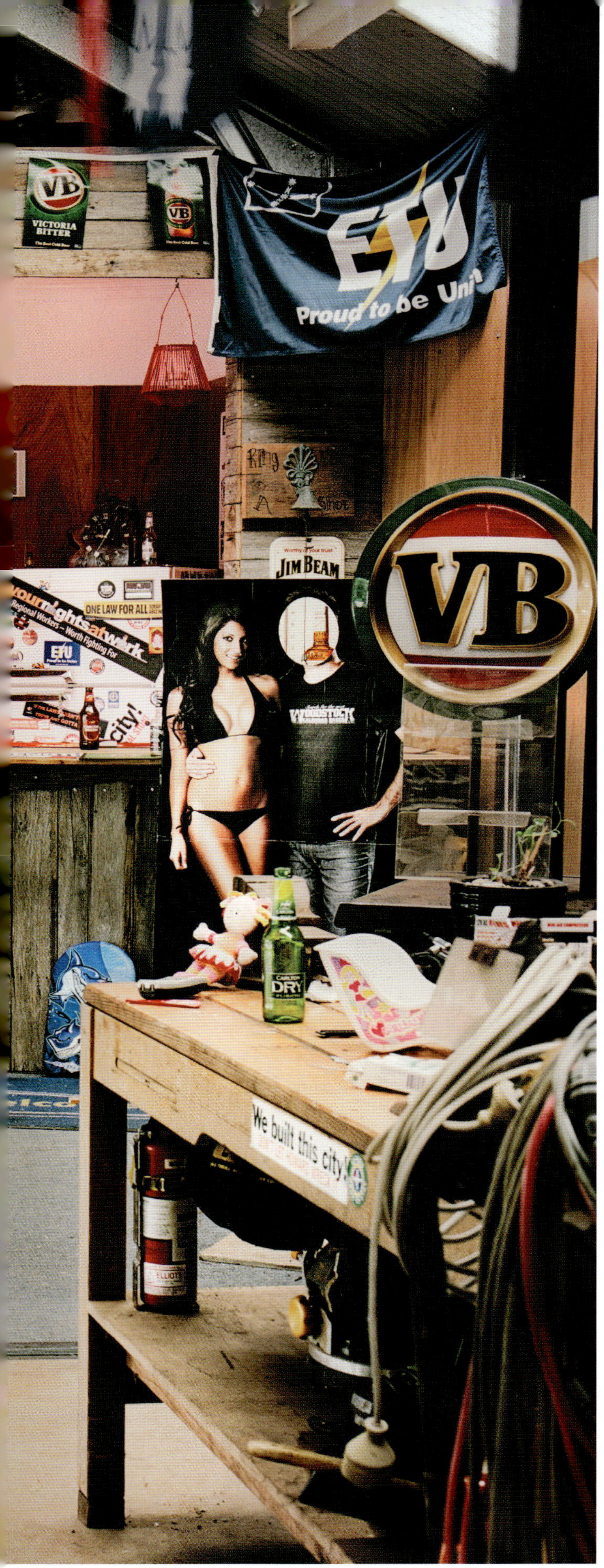
VICTORIA BITTER
ETU
VB
JIM BEAM
ONE LAW FOR ALL
We built this city!
DRY

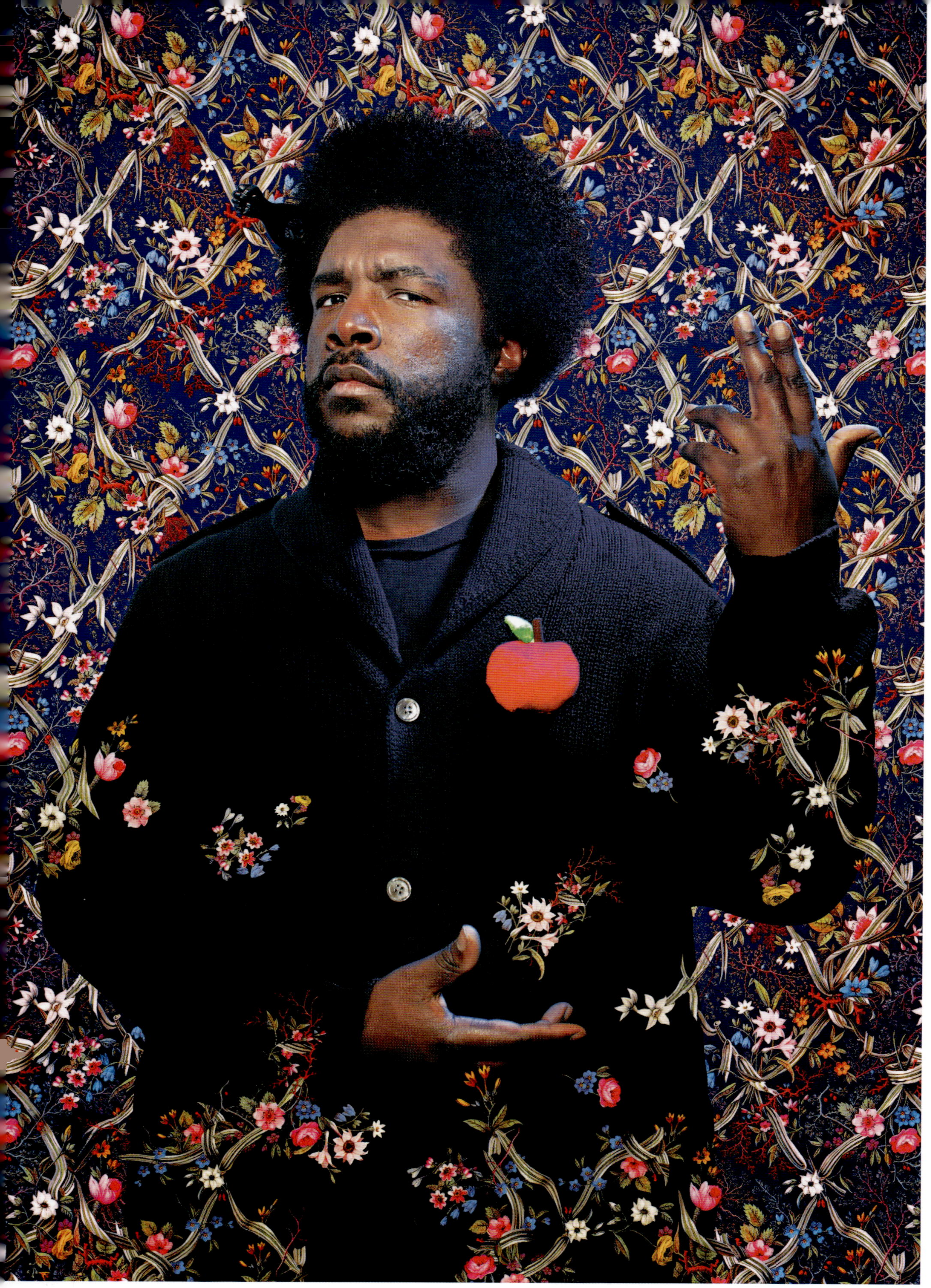

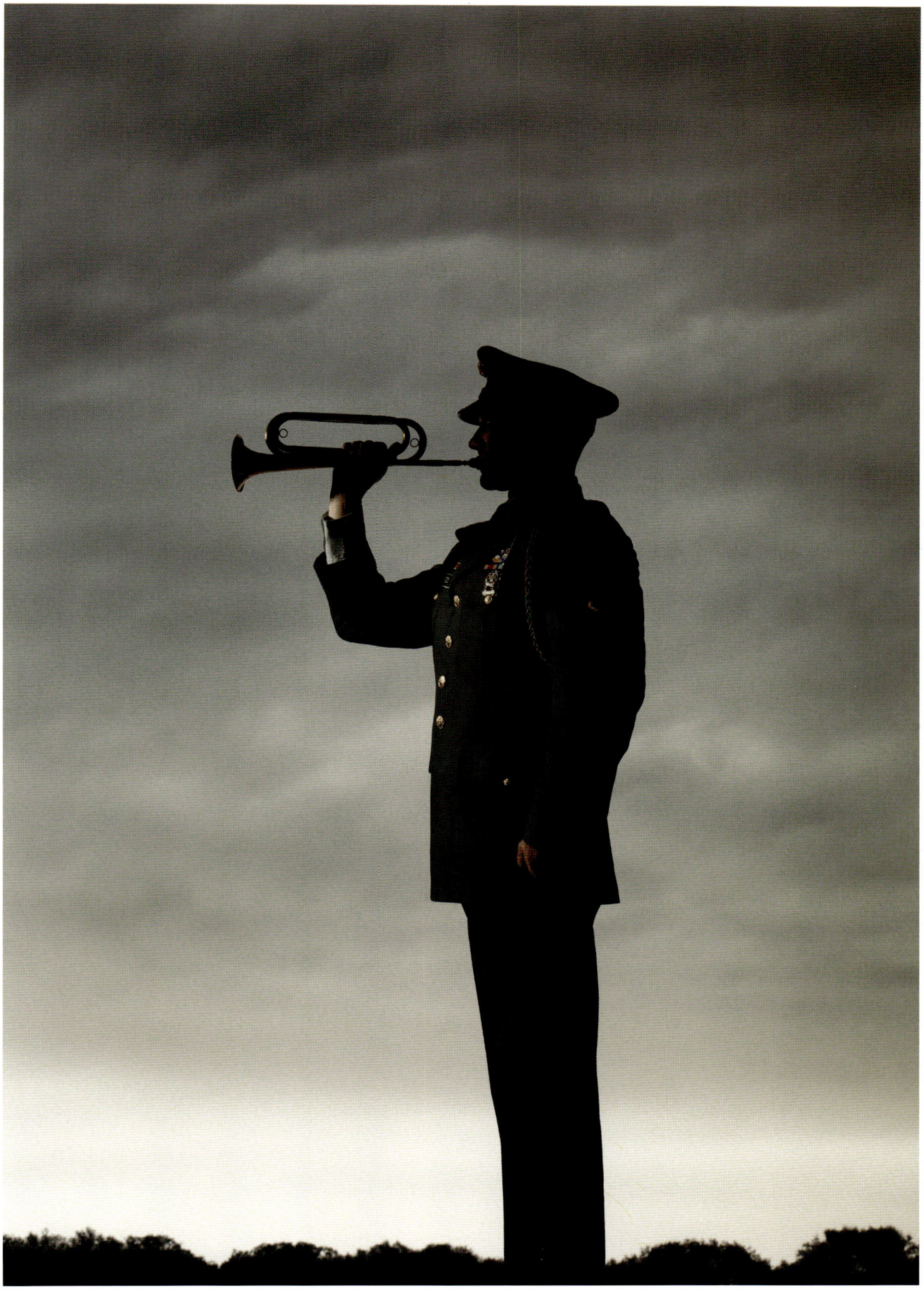

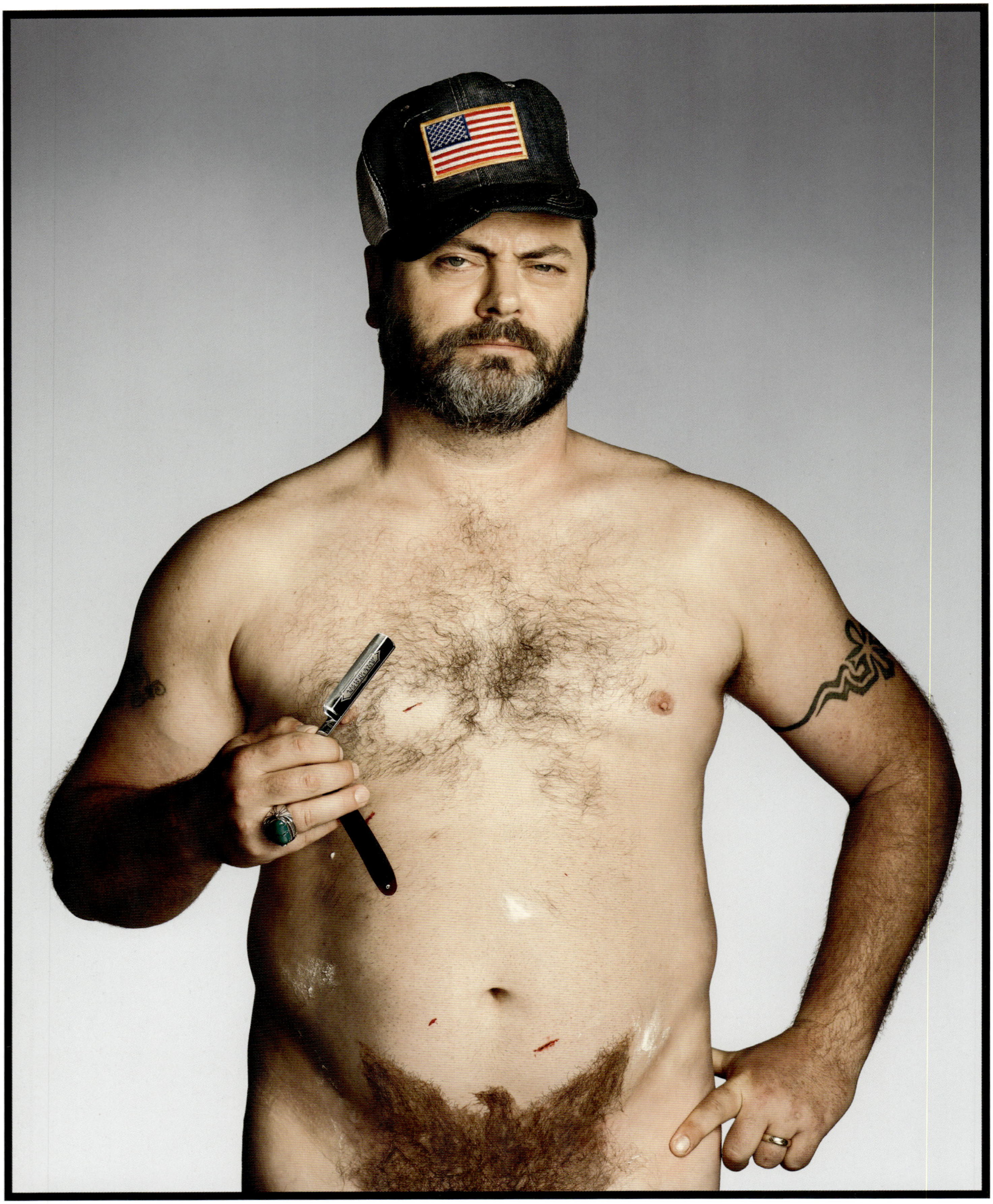

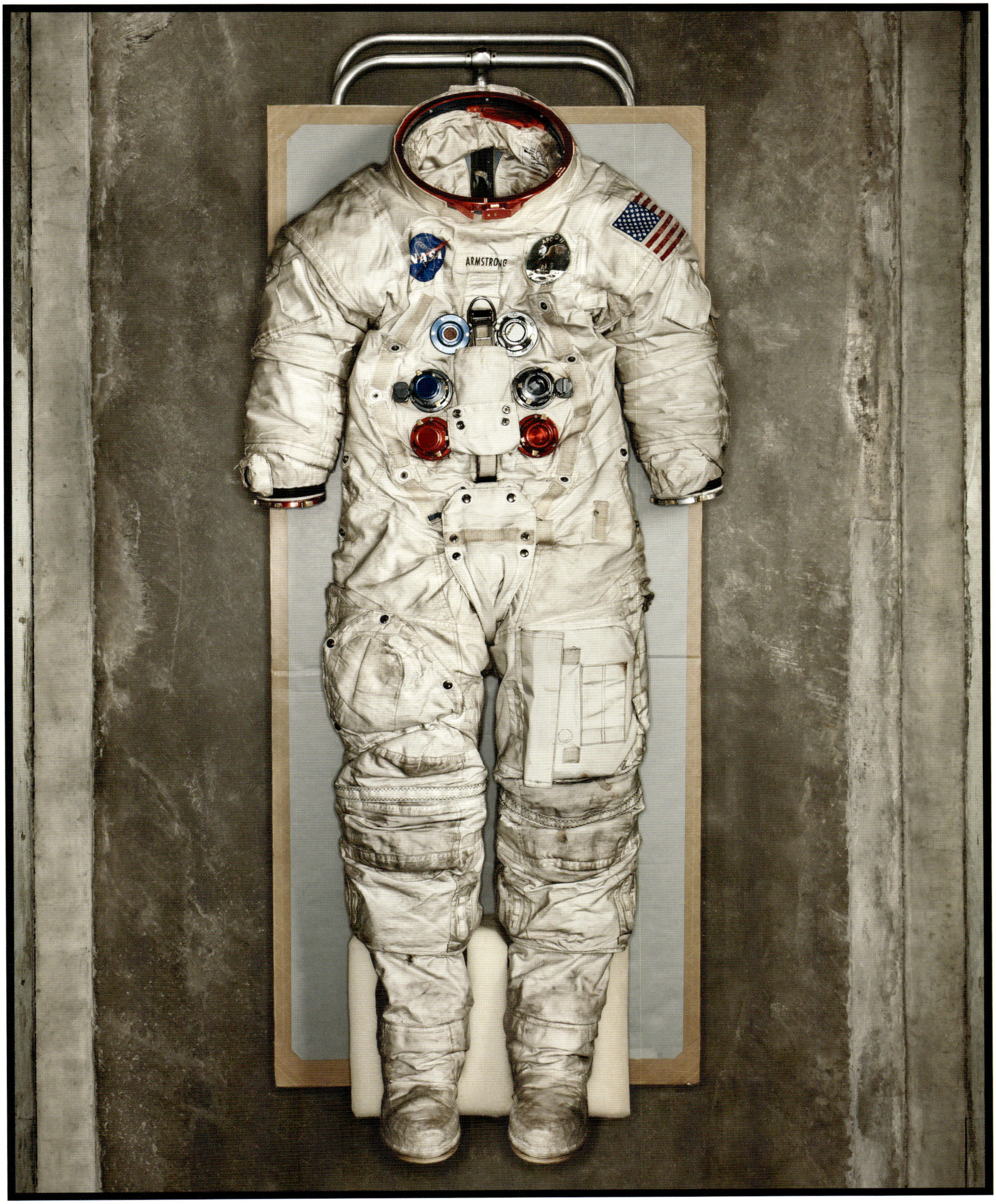

DAN WINTERS

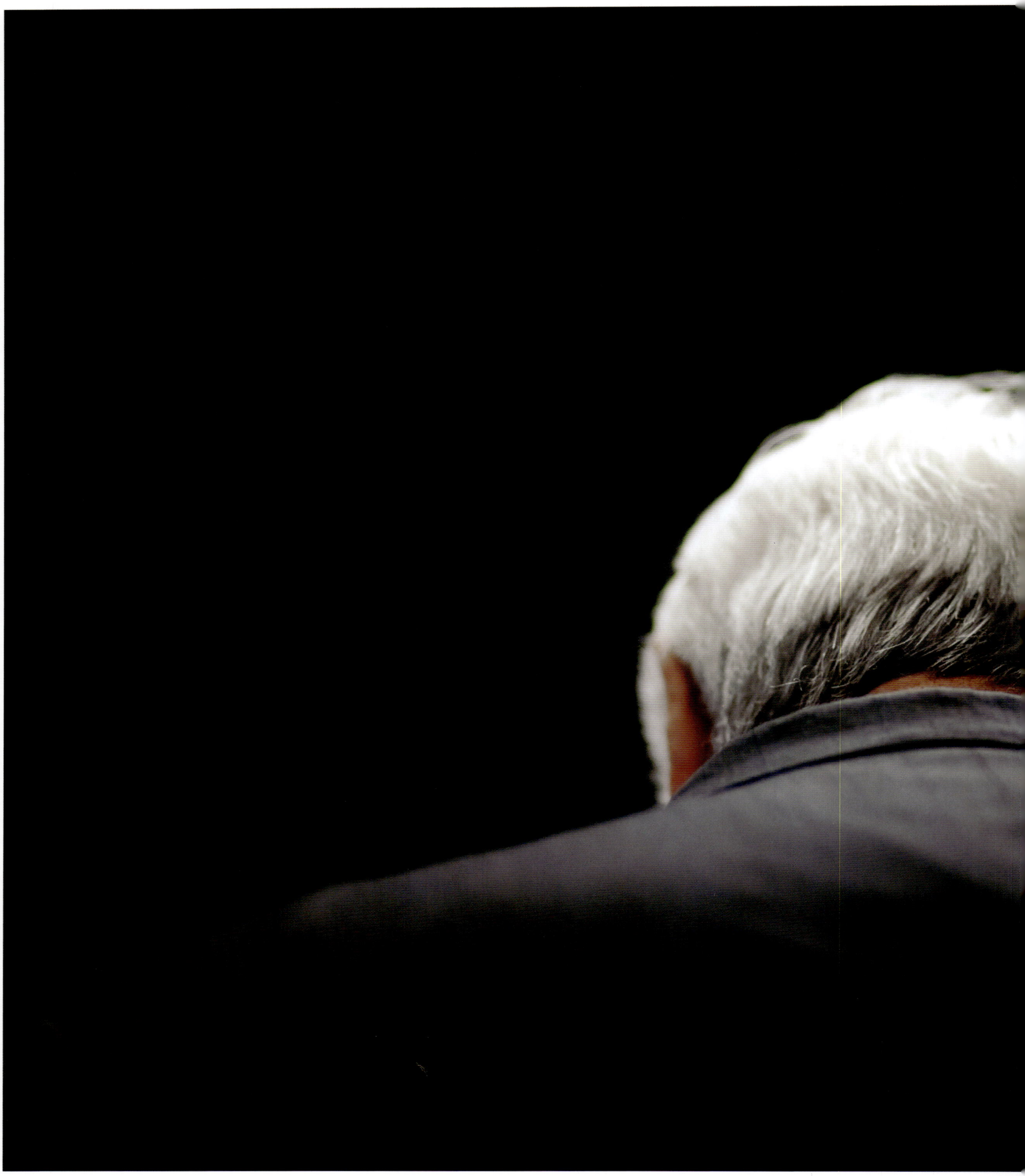

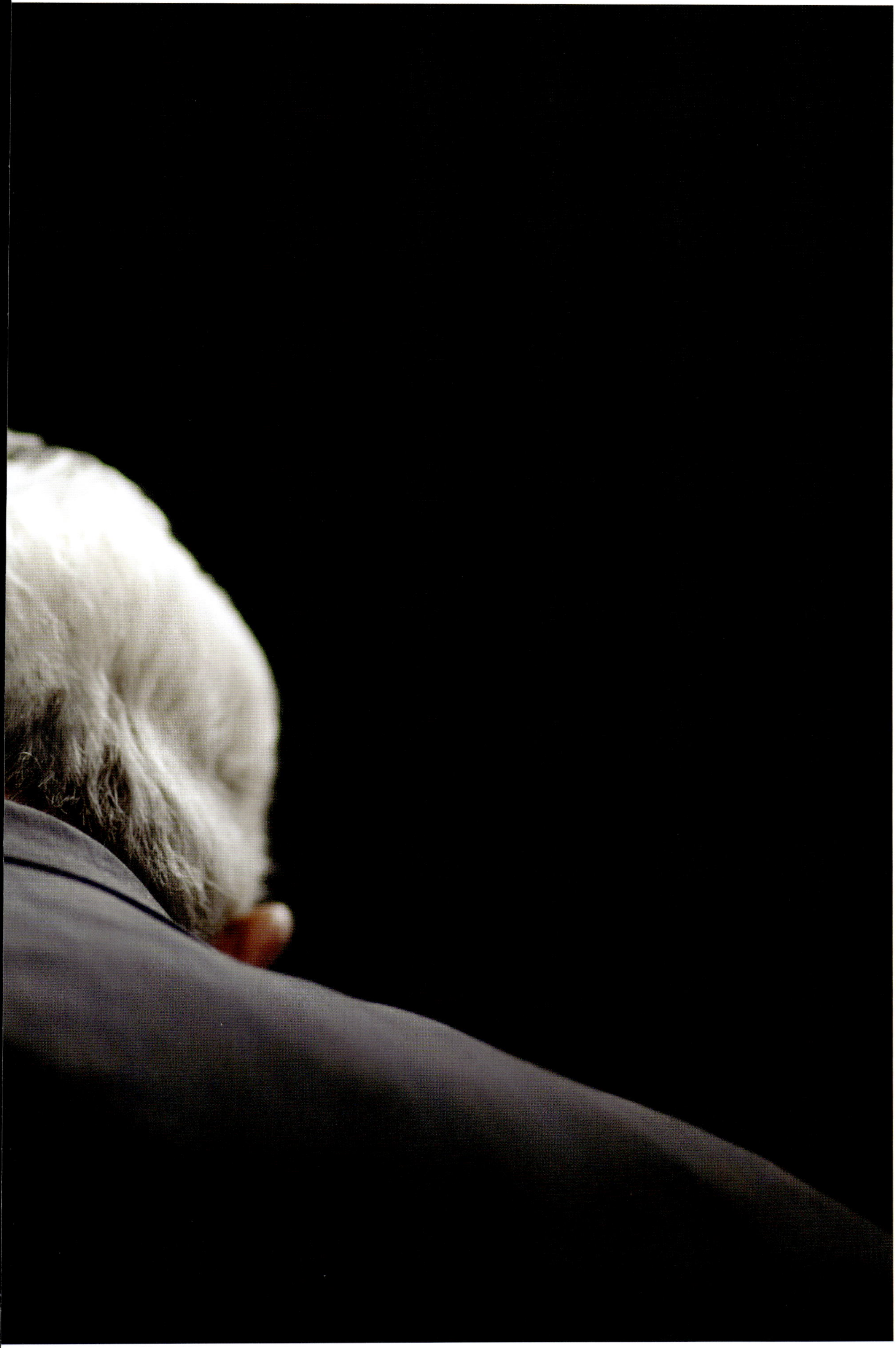

MARCUS YAM

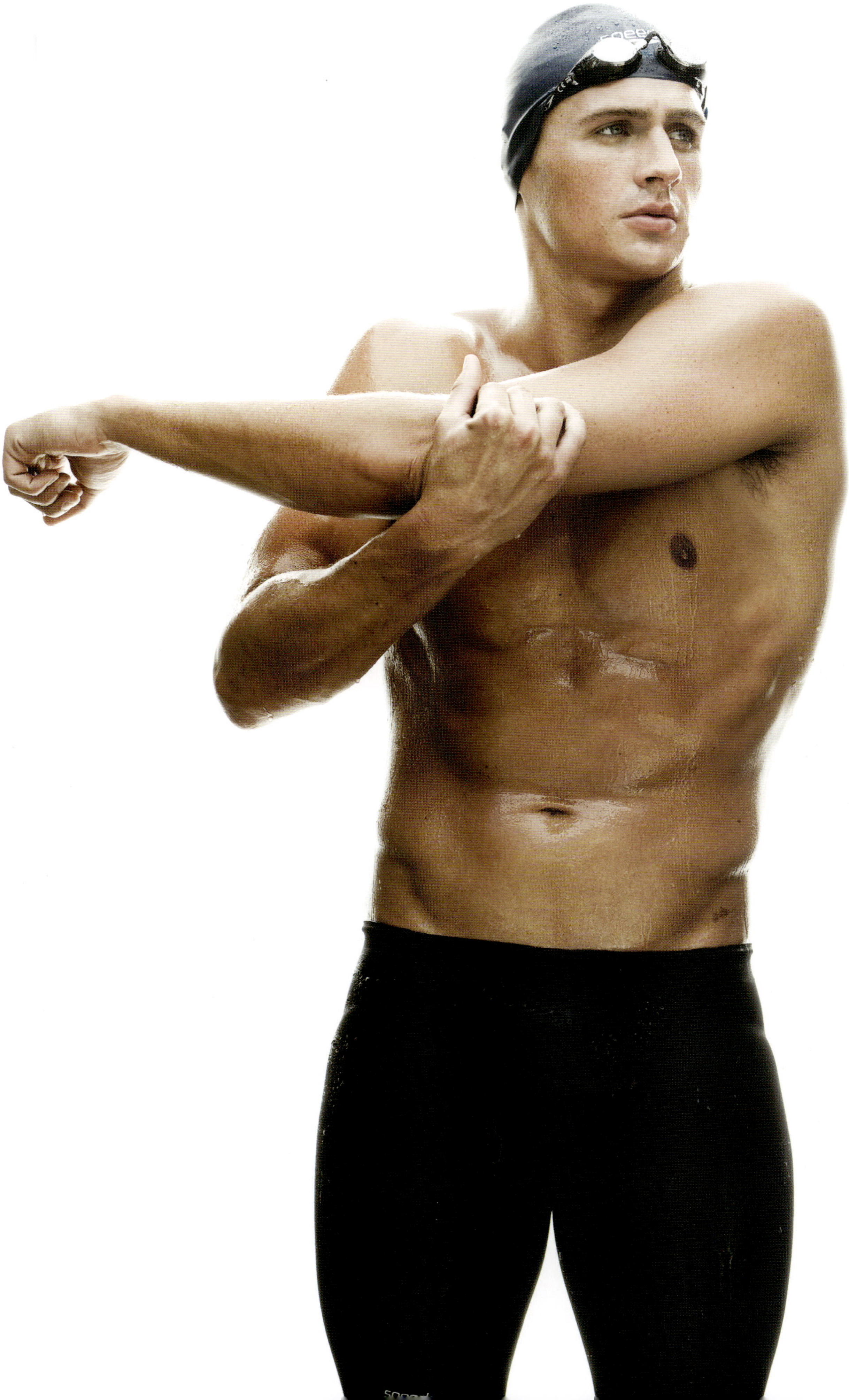

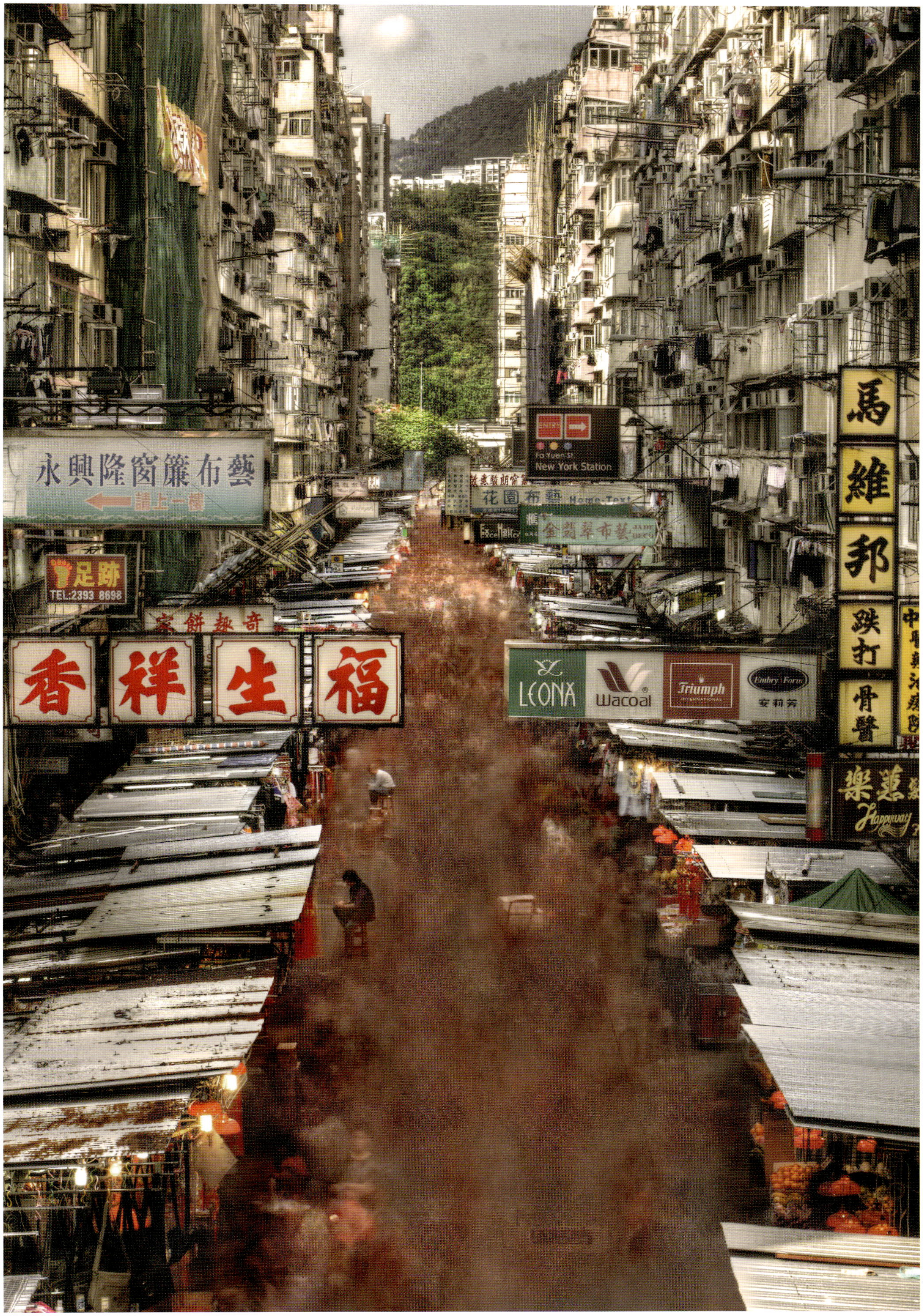
永興隆窗簾布藝
請上一樓
足跡
TEL:2393 8698
香 祥 生 福
ENTRY
Fa Yuen St.
New York Station
花園布藝
金翡翠布藝
LEONA
Wacoal
Triumph
Embry Form
安莉芳
馬維邦跌打骨醫
Happyway

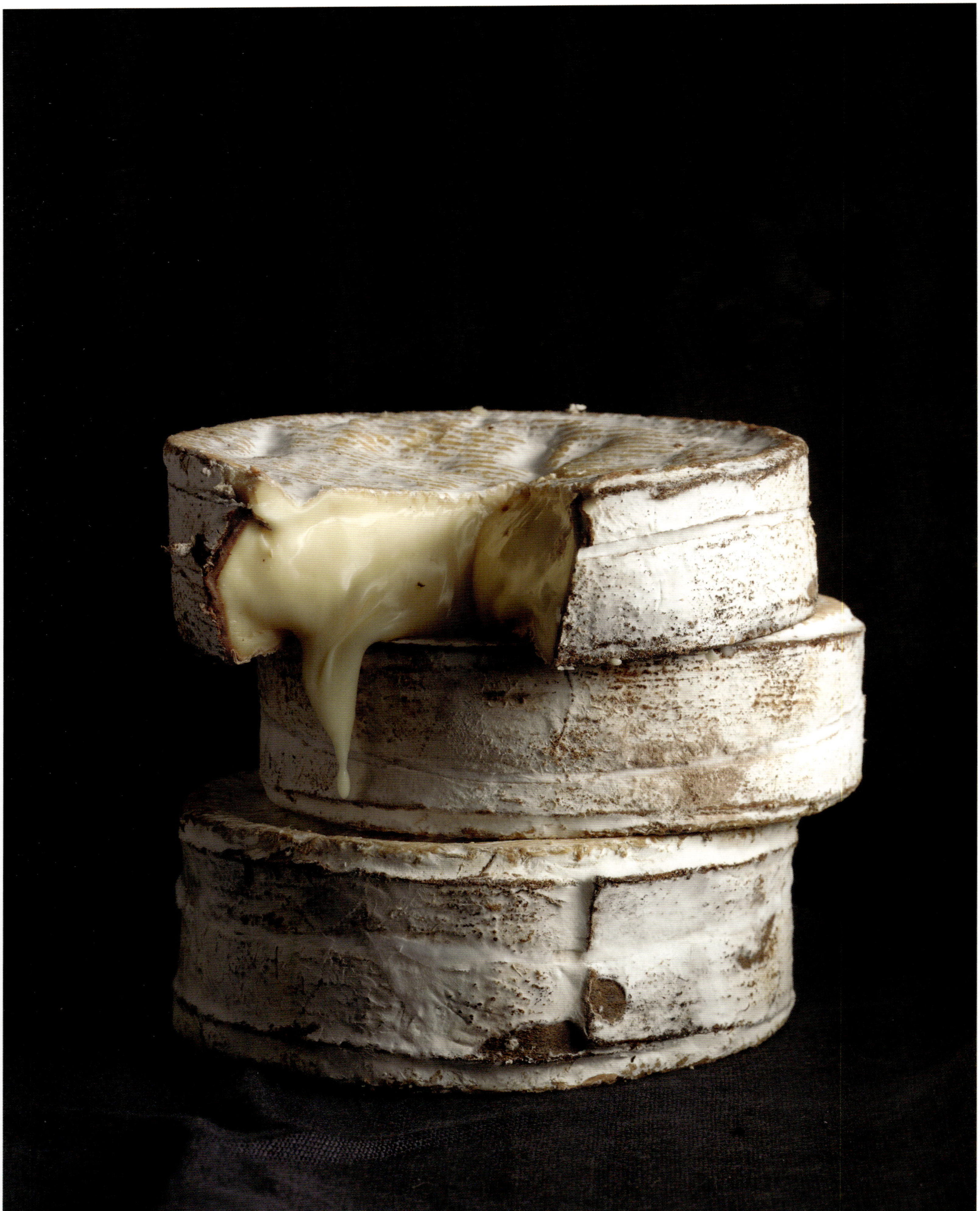

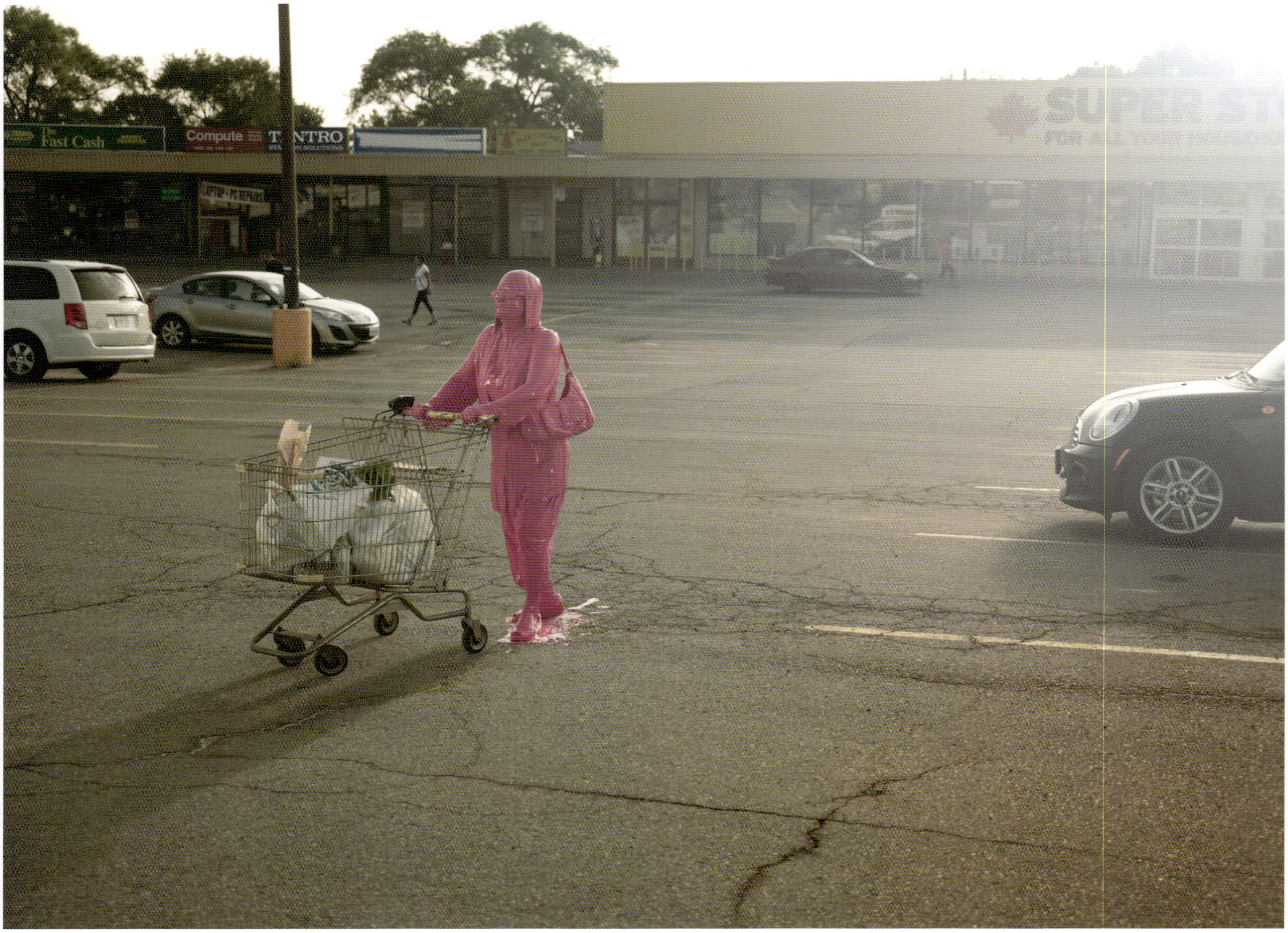
The
Fast Cash
Compute

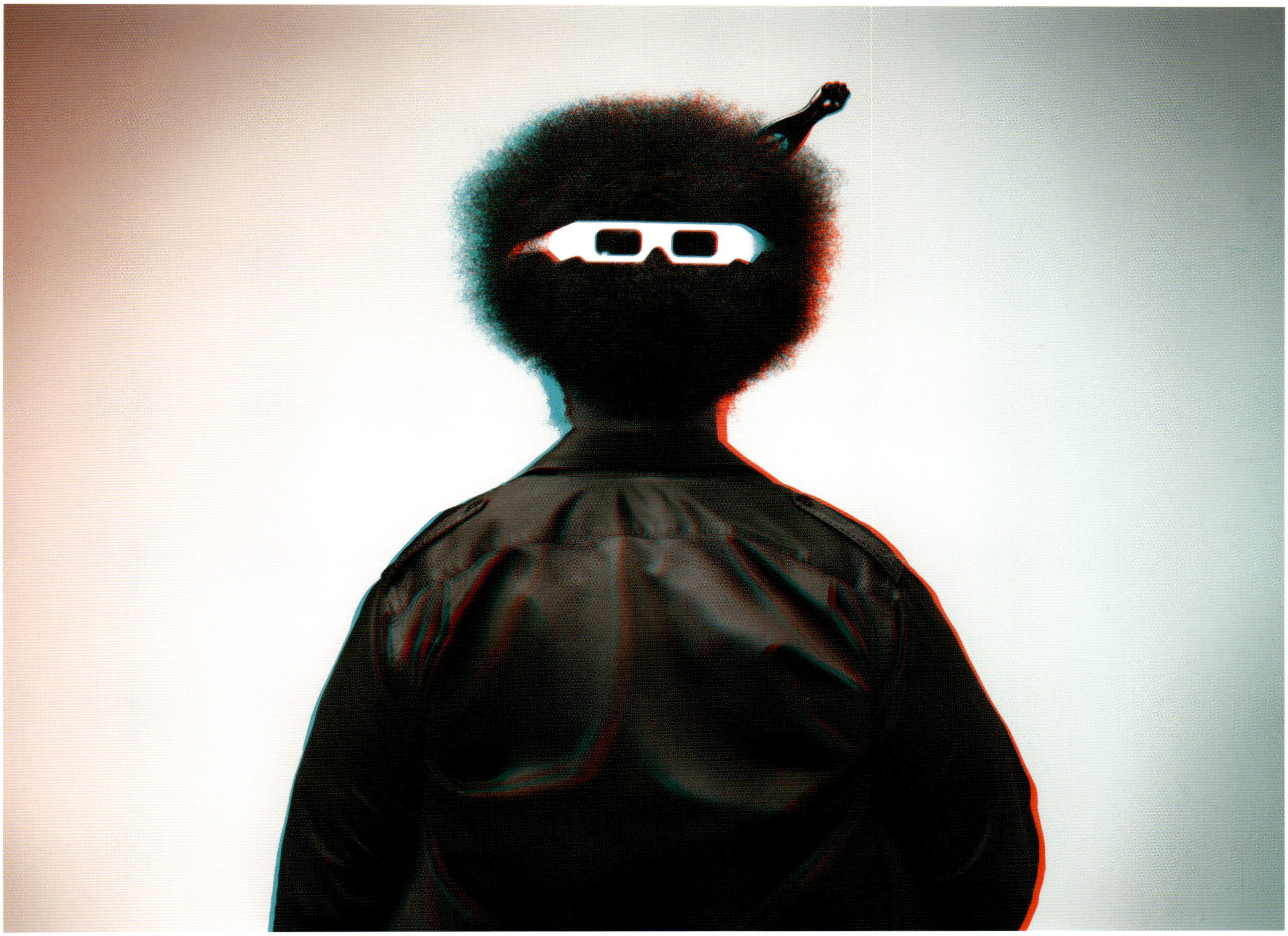

MARK ZIBERT

INDEX

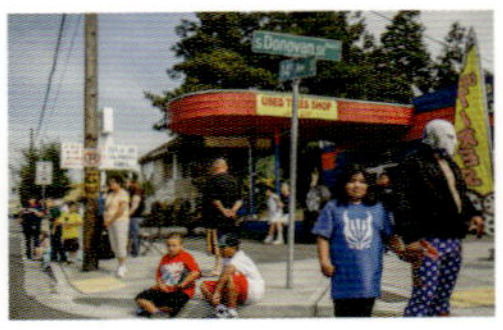
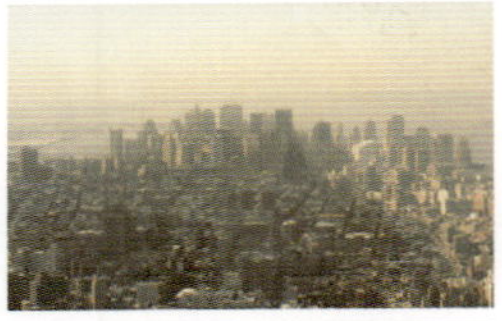
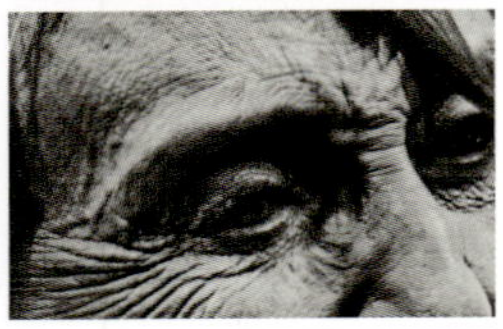
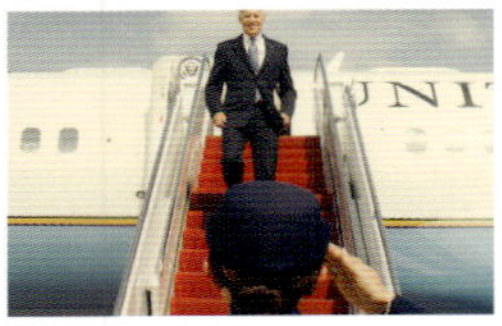
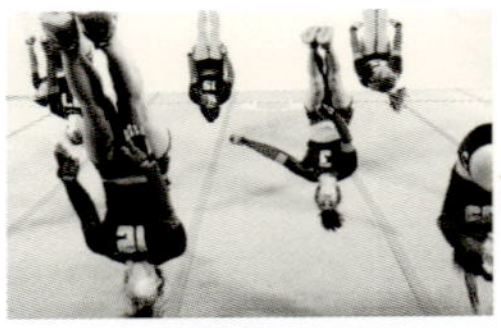
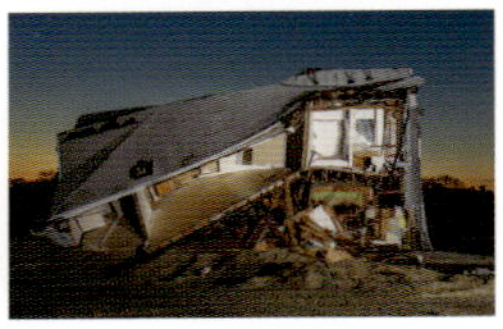
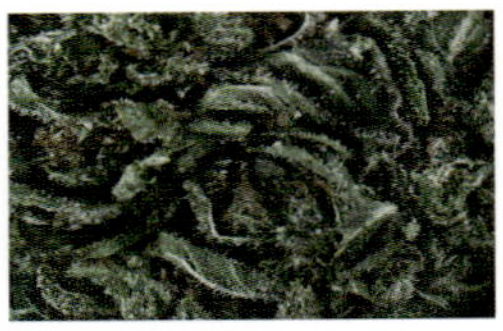
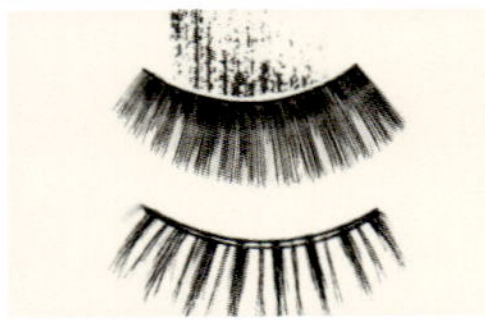
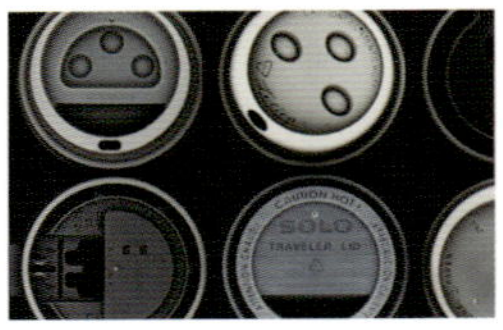
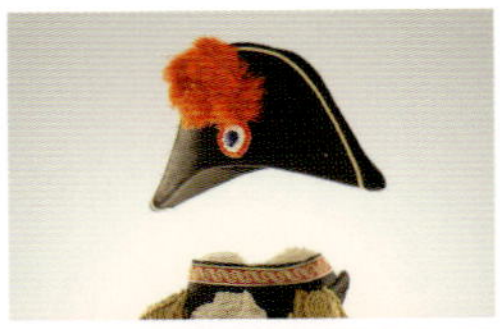
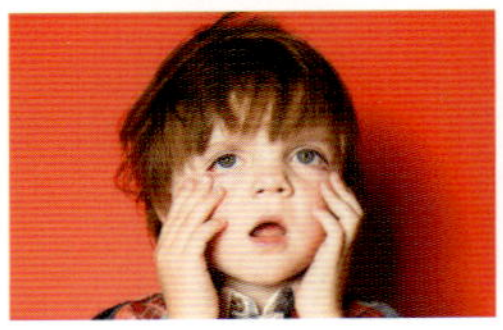
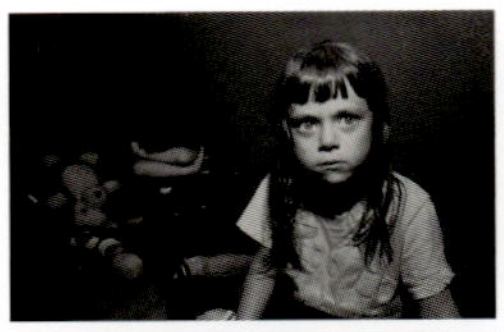
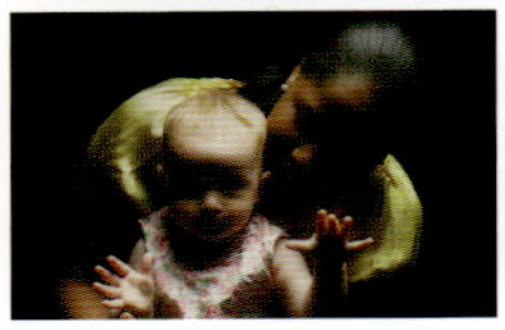
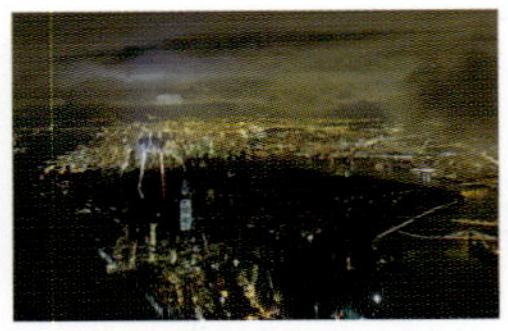
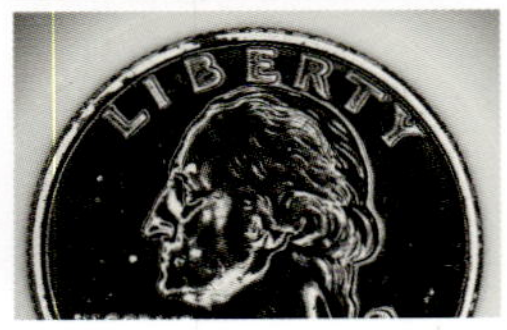

NICK ADAMS

<u>006</u> Fiestas Patrias, September 2012, a local parade in the small Seattle neighborhood community of South Park for the local news site The South Park News.

DAVID ALLEE

<u>001</u> One from the series Frame of View, exhibited at the Morgan Lehman gallery in New York.

—

GALLERY: Morgan Lehman

CHRISTOPHER ANDERSON

<u>002–003</u> Mitt Romney and Jan Brewer, two for "The Family Politic," October 10, 2012, a portfolio from the 2012 Presidential Campaign.

—

DIRECTOR OF PHOTOGRAPHY: Jody Quon
EDITOR-IN-CHIEF: Adam Moss
PHOTO EDITOR: Nadia Lachance
PHOTO EDITOR: Leonor Mamanna
PUBLICATION: New York

<u>004</u> Vice President Joe Biden, one from the feature "Joe Biden Isn't Finished," September 10, 2012, a story shot over three days through unprecedented access on Air Force 2.

—

DIRECTOR OF PHOTOGRAPHY: Jody Quon
EDITOR-IN-CHIEF: Adam Moss
PHOTO EDITOR: Leonor Mamanna
PUBLICATION: New York

HOLLY ANDRES

<u>007–008</u> Two from a series for the article "Cheer Factor," April 23, 2012. The Oregon acrobatics and tumbling team—a group that stresses the athletic ability of cheerleaders, not the rooting—practicing its moves at the University of Oregon in Eugene.

—

DESIGN DIRECTOR: DW Pine
DIRECTOR OF PHOTOGRAPHY: Kira Pollack
SENIOR ART DIRECTOR: Emily Crawford
ASSOCIATE PHOTO EDITOR: Natalie Matutschovsky
PUBLICATION: TIME

JASON ANDREW

<u>005</u> One for the article "Sandy Tears Through Region," November 5, 2012. The home of the former Mayor of Sea Bright, N.J., Jo-Ann Kalaka Adams, was destroyed after Hurricane Sandy tore through the region.

—

PUBLICATION: The Wall Street Journal

KENJI AOKI

Michael Ash Partners

<u>009–010</u> Two from a series for "The Truce on Drugs," December 2012, an article about the prohibition of drugs.

—

DESIGN DIRECTOR: Thomas Alberty
DIRECTOR OF PHOTOGRAPHY: Jody Quon
EDITOR-IN-CHIEF: Adam Moss
PHOTO EDITOR: Leonor Mamanna
PUBLICATION: New York

<u>011</u> One for the article "Big Beauty Try On," October 2012.

—

CREATIVE DIRECTOR: Debra Bishop
PHOTO DIRECTOR: Natasha Lunn
PUBLICATION: More

<u>012</u> One for a story about celebrity indulgences, September 2012.

—

CREATIVE DIRECTOR: Stephen Gan
PHOTO DIRECTOR: Sandra Kang
PHOTO EDITOR: Natalie Hazzout
PUBLICATION: V

TIMOTHY ARCHIBALD

Tidepool Reps

<u>013</u> Four in a series for "How The Chicken Conquered The World," a feature about the importance of the chicken as a compact and portable protein source in developing civilizations throughout history.

—

ART DIRECTOR: Maria Keehan
EDITOR-IN-CHIEF: Michael Caruso
DIRECTOR OF PHOTOGRAPHY: Molly Roberts
STYLIST: Shannon Amos
PUBLICATION: Smithsonian

MEIKO TAKECHI ARQUILLOS

Redeye Represents

<u>015–016</u> Two from a series for the article "How To De-Stress the Small Fry," August 2012, about children's stress and simple calming techniques that help them through tough times.

—

DIRECTOR OF PHOTOGRAPHY: Casey Tierney
PHOTO EDITOR: Lauren Epstein
SENIOR ART DIRECTOR: Abbey Kuster-Prokell
STYLIST: Shannon Ray
PUBLICATION: Real Simple Family

MARC ASNIN

Contrasto

<u>017–018</u> Two from the book Uncle Charlie, October 2012, a 30-year look at the photographer's uncle, his family and life of broken dreams and disappointment while having the resiliency to find slivers of happiness in an oppressed existence.

—

DESIGN FIRM: de.MO
DESIGNER: Giorgio Baravalle

MICHELE ASSELIN

<u>014</u> Nikki, 27, from Jamaica, one from a series for the article "The Other Mothers of Manhattan," July 15, 2012, a glimpse into the private world of nannies and the children they care for. Nikki has been a nanny for nearly 11 years.

—

DESIGN DIRECTOR: Arem Duplessis
DIRECTOR OF PHOTOGRAPHY: Kathy Ryan
ART DIRECTOR: Gail Bichler
ASSOCIATE ART DIRECTOR: Caleb Bennett
ASSOCIATE PHOTO EDITOR: Clinton Cargill
DEPUTY PICTURE EDITOR: Joanna Milter
DESIGNER: Drea Zlanabitnig
EDITOR-IN-CHIEF: Hugo Lindgren
PUBLICATION: The New York Times Magazine

IWAN BAAN

Reportage Getty Images

<u>028</u> Cover photograph for the Hurricane Sandy issue feature "The City and the Storm," November 12, 2012, capturing Manhattan from a helicopter in the aftermath and during the power outage that left the city half dark and half aglow.

—

DIRECTOR OF PHOTOGRAPHY: Jody Quon
SENIOR PHOTO EDITOR: Lea Golis
PHOTO EDITORS: Nadia Lachance, Leonor Mamanna
ASSISTANT PHOTO EDITOR: Jenny Westerhoff
ASSOCIATE PHOTO EDITOR: Roxanne Behr
EDITOR-IN-CHIEF: Adam Moss
PUBLICATION: New York

BART BABINSKI

<u>025</u> Lucre Nr.2, one from a personal, photographic study of the implicit interaction between currency and the human hand.

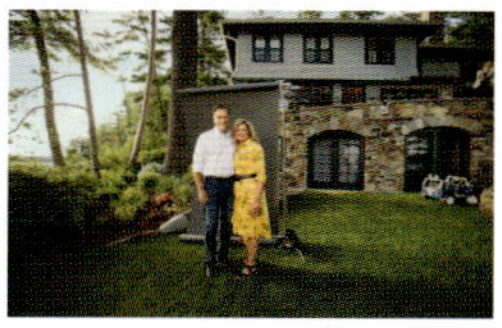
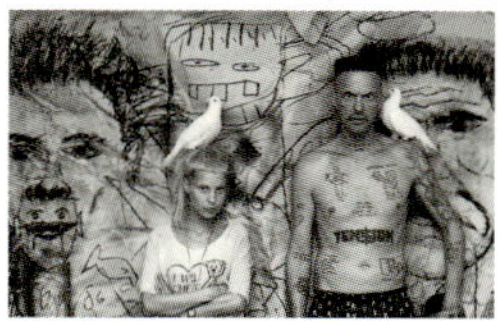
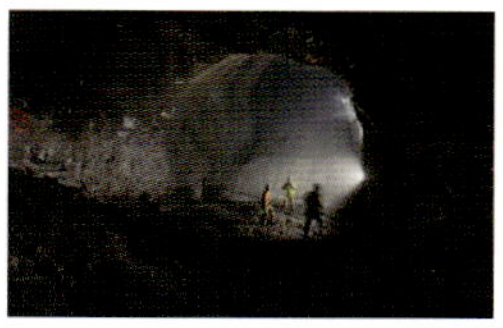
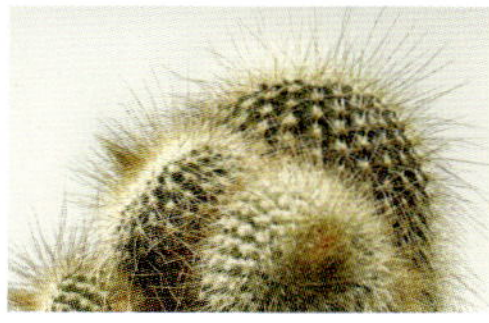
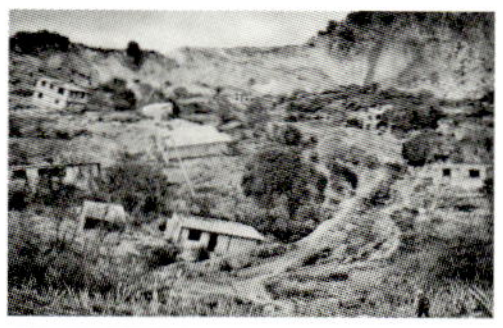
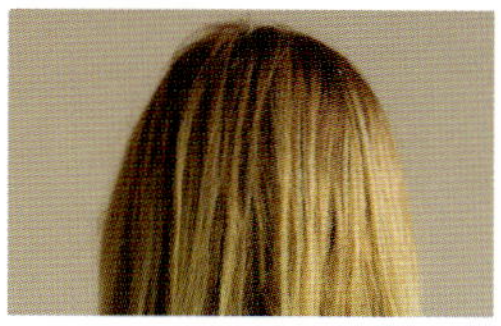
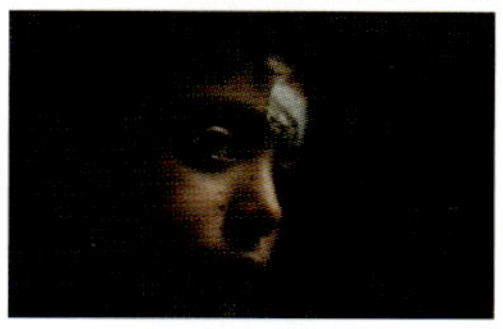
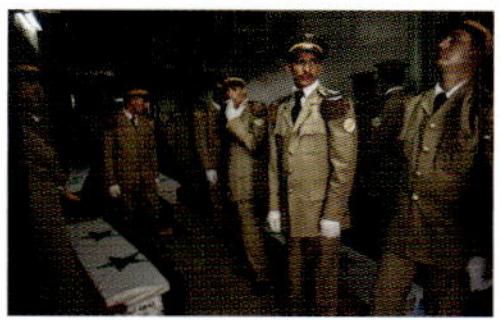
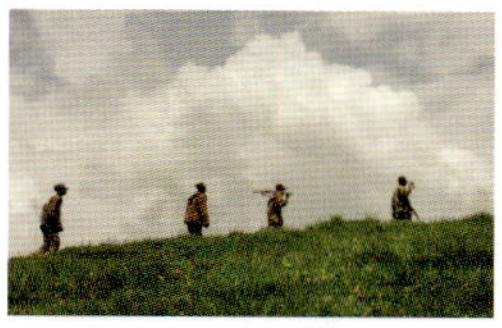
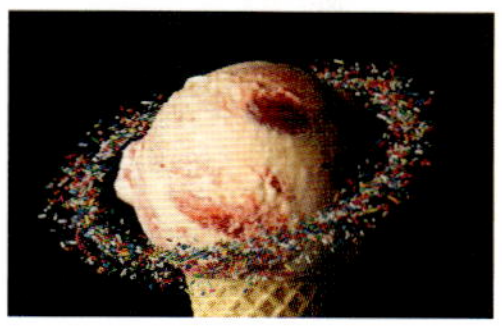
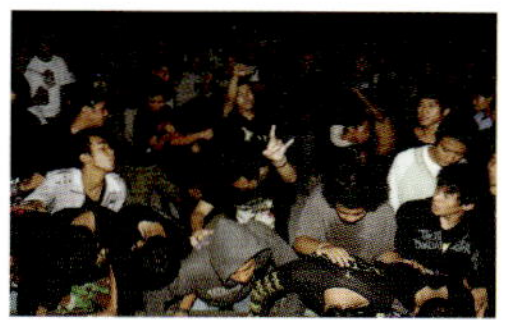
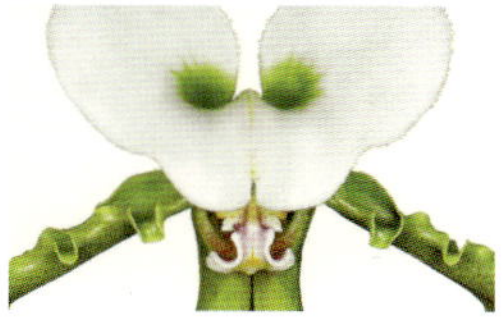
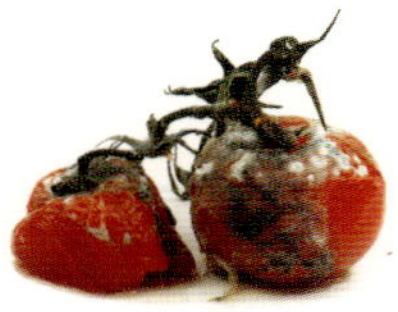
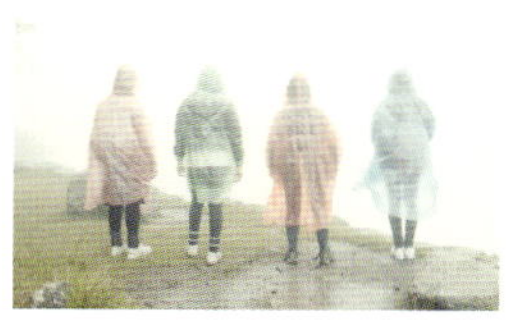

BEN BAKER
Redux Pictures

020 Republican presidential candidate Mitt Romney and his wife Ann at their New Hampshire home on Lake Winnipesaukee for a cover feature, July 2012.

—

CREATIVE DIRECTOR: Richard Baker
EDITOR-IN-CHIEF: Maggie Murphy
PHOTO DIRECTOR: Miriam White
PUBLICATION: Parade

ROGER BALLEN

024 Yo-Landi and Ninja (with doves) of the South African rap-rave group Die Antwoord, for the feature "The Brilliant Weirdness of Die Antwoord," January 29, 2012.

—

DESIGN DIRECTOR: Arem Duplessis
DIRECTOR OF PHOTOGRAPHY: Kathy Ryan
ART DIRECTOR: Gail Bichler
ASSOCIATE PHOTO EDITOR: Amy Kellner
DEPUTY ART DIRECTOR: Caleb Bennett
DEPUTY PHOTOGRAPHY DIRECTOR: Joanna Milter
DESIGNER: Chris Nosenzo
EDITOR-IN-CHIEF: Hugo Lindgren
PUBLICATION: The New York Times Magazine

RICHARD BARNES

022–023 Second Ave Subway, New York City, two from a series for the cover feature "Way Down in the Hole," August 5, 2012.

—

DESIGN DIRECTOR: Arem Duplessis
DIRECTOR OF PHOTOGRAPHY: Kathy Ryan
ART DIRECTOR: Gail Bichler
ASSISTANT PHOTO EDITOR: Amy Kellner
ASSOCIATE ART DIRECTOR: Caleb Bennett
DEPUTY PICTURE EDITOR: Joanna Milter
EDITOR-IN-CHIEF: Hugo Lindgren
PUBLICATION: The New York Times Magazine

CLAIRE BENOIST
Greenhouse Reps

021 One for the article "The Perfect Shave," January 2013.

—

CREATIVE DIRECTOR: Robert Festino
DIRECTOR OF PHOTOGRAPHY: Jeanne Graves
PHOTO EDITOR: Joe Rodriguez
PUBLICATION: Men's Health

MATT BLACK

029–032 Four from a series for the article "After the Fall," September 2012, about how rampant soil erosion has turned parts of southern Mexico into an ecological disaster zone.

—

EDITOR: Andrew D. Blechman
EDITOR-IN-CHIEF: H. Emerson Blake
PHOTO EDITOR: Jason Houston
PUBLICATION: Orion

TARA BOGART
Elizabeth Houston Hous Projects

026–027 A Modern Hair Study, January 2012, two from a personal series based on the archival photo Hair Study by Felix Nada at the National Library of France that depicts just a woman's back and her hair.

KATE BROOKS

035 Syrian Refugee Crisis, personal work, March 2012. A 9-year-old Syrian child named Shadi was injured by shrapnel from an unidentified explosion while crossing the border to Lebanon.

036 Damascus, Syria, funeral services at the Tishreen Military Hospital, one for the article "War Pierces Damascus' Bubble of Denial," June 23, 2012.

—

PICTURE EDITOR: David Furst
PUBLICATION: The New York Times

MICHAEL CHRISTOPHER BROWN

037–038 The Democratic Republic of Congo, two from a series for the article "Inside M23 and Congo's Rebel Uprising," December 2, 2012. A small legion of experienced fighters called the March 23 Movement (M23) are at the heart of a rebellion that's rocking the country to its core.

—

PHOTO EDITOR: Marion Durand
PUBLICATION: Newsweek

LEVI BROWN

033–034 Two from a series for the article "Conehead," August 2012, 31 facts about ice cream.

—

DESIGN DIRECTOR: Fred Woodward
DIRECTOR OF PHOTOGRAPHY: Dora Somosi
SENIOR PHOTO EDITOR: Krista Prestek
PHOTO EDITOR: Justin O'Neill
WRITER: Alan Richman
PUBLICATION: GQ

JÖRG BRÜGGEMANN
OSTKREUZ - Agentur der Fotografen

039 First Row, a concert of the Indonesian Death Metal band Death Vomit, Salatiga, Indonesia, February 2010, one from the book Metalheads - The Global Brotherhood, March 2012.

—

PUBLICATION: ZEIT Magazin, Metalheads - The Global Brotherhood

JG BRYCE

040–041 Tolumnia Maggie Khoo, Golden Sunset and Paphiopedilum Spicerianum, two from a series for "Orchid Olympics," a story about the World Orchid Conference in Singapore.

—

ART DIRECTOR: Maria Keehan
PHOTO EDITOR: Brendan McCabe
PUBLICATION: Smithsonian

JOE BUGLEWICZ

019 One for the article "Rotten," June 2012, exploring the global issue of food waste on a small level by photographing unintentionally spoiled items.

—

CREATIVE DIRECTOR: Florian Bachleda
PHOTO EDITOR: Leslie Dela Vega
PUBLICATION: Fast Company

JOAO CANZIANI

047 Outtake from "Fancy a Peruvian?" February 2012, a travel article concentrating on Lima, Cuzco, and Machu Picchu in Peru.

—

PICTURE EDITOR: Lucy Perceval
PUBLICATION: British Airways High Life Magazine

Full captions and contact information for the photographers is available online in The Archive at ai-ap.com/archive/AP

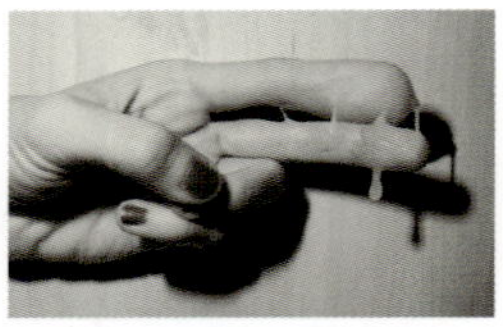
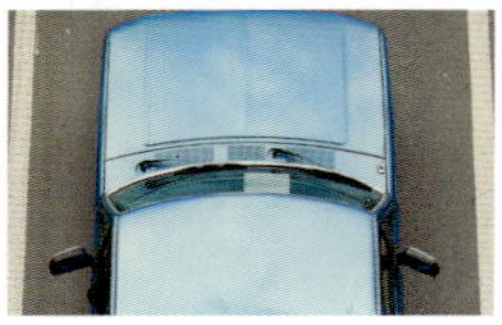
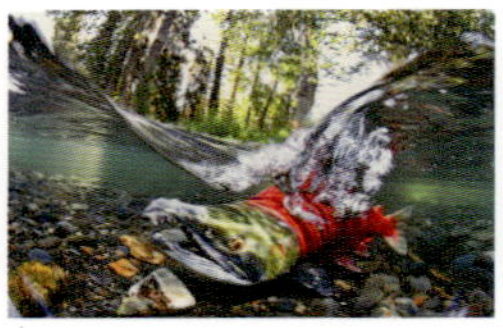
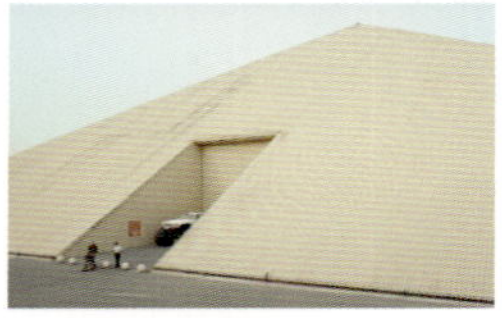
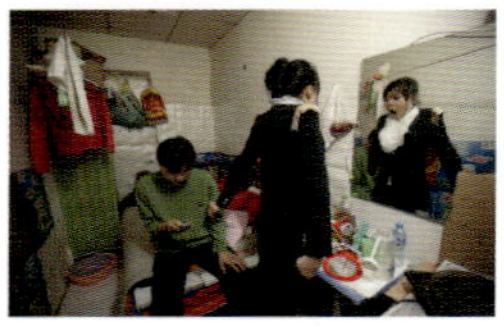
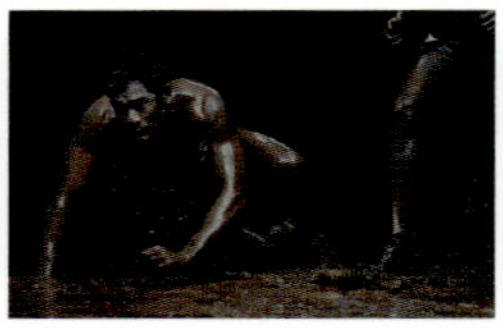
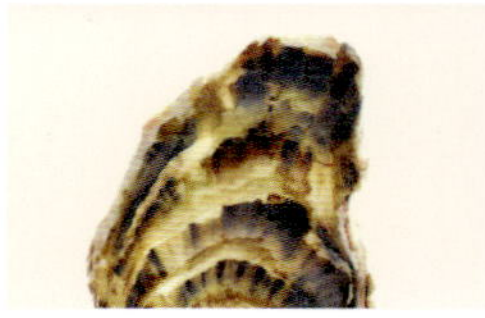
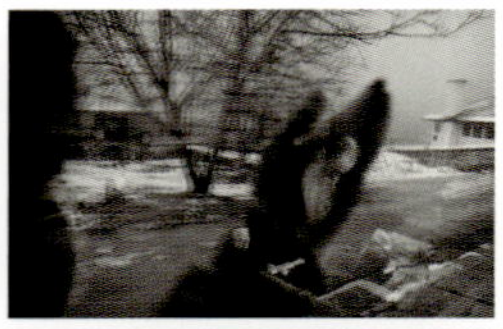
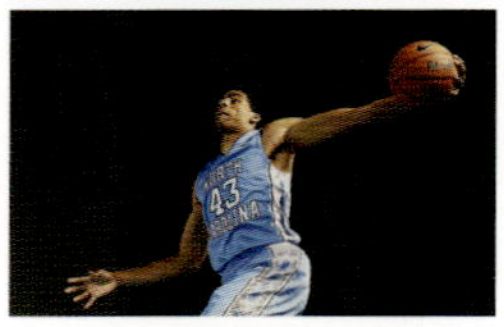
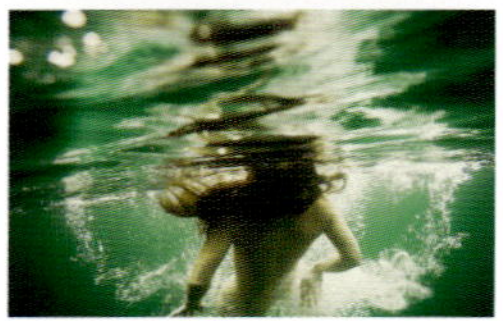
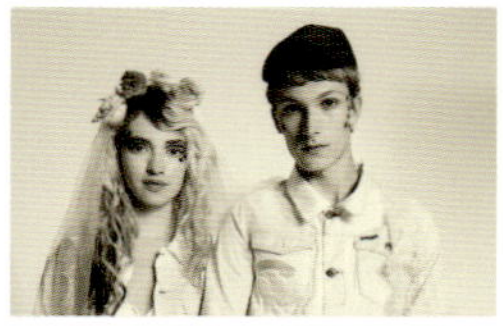
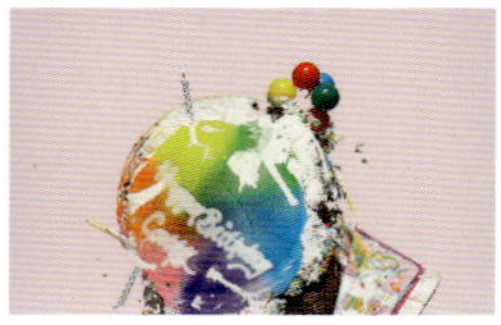
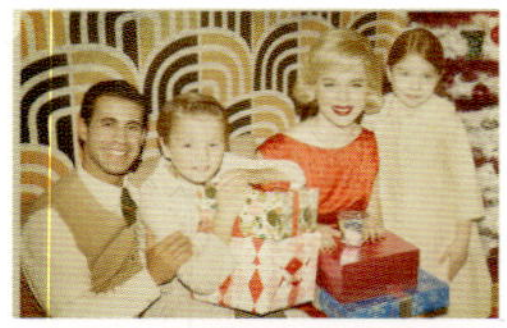
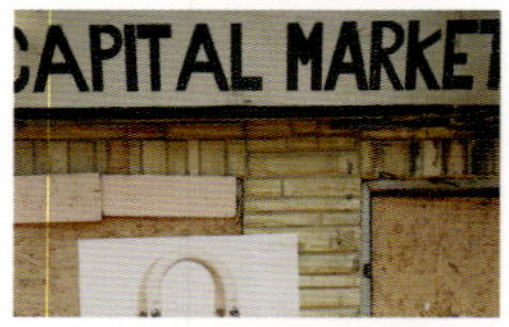

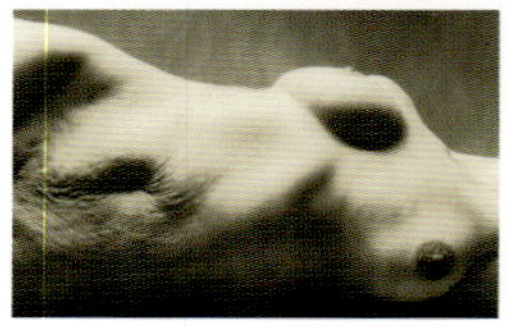

ASGER CARLSEN
Casey

044 One from the series Homemade, November 2012, which presents an illusion of pornography.

—

DIRECTOR OF DESIGN & DIGITAL MEDIA: Michael J. Walsh,
ASSOCIATE EDITOR: Sheilah Ledwidge
CREATIVE DIRECTOR: Anthony P. Rhodes
EDITOR-AT-LARGE: Mark Alice Durant
EDITOR-IN-CHIEF: Stephen Frailey
EDITORIAL ASSISTANT: Kimberlee Venable
FASHION EDITOR: Lindsay Hart Thompson
MANAGING EDITOR: Maria Dubon
PUBLICATION: Dear Dave, 12

ALEJANDRO CARTAGENA

048–049 Two from a series for the article "Labor Movement," April 2012. Shot from a morning-time perch above the southbound lanes of Highway 85 in Monterrey, Mexico, capturing people from the lower- or middle-class suburbs in the north on their way to work in the more affluent southern regions.

—

SENIOR PHOTO EDITOR: James Wellford
PUBLICATION: Newsweek

SETH CASTEEL

050 Sockeye salmon spawning in Alaska, one from the cover feature "One Fish, Two Fish, Dead Fish, New Fish," October 2012.

—

DESIGN DIRECTOR: Arem Duplessis
DIRECTOR OF PHOTOGRAPHY: Kathy Ryan
ART DIRECTOR: Gail Bichler
ASSOCIATE PHOTO EDITOR: Stacey Baker
DEPUTY ART DIRECTOR: Caleb Bennett
DEPUTY PICTURE EDITOR: Joanna Milter
DESIGNER: Tonya Douraghy
EDITOR-IN-CHIEF: Hugo Lindgren
PUBLICATION: The New York Times Magazine

PHILIP CHEUNG

054–055 The United Arab Emirates, two from a series for the feature "Desert Dreams: United Arab Emirates," July 2012.

—

PUBLICATION: VICE

SIM CHI YIN
VII Mentor Program

045–046 Portraits of migrants who live in Beijing's basements and air-raid shelters, two from a series for the article "Beijing's Basement Dwellers: China's Rat Tribe," July 2012.

—

SENIOR PHOTO EDITOR: James Wellford
PUBLICATION: Newsweek

JAMIE CHUNG
Bernstein & Andrulli

042 One for the feature "A Race to the Death," November 2012, about Tough Mudder, the hardcore 10 to 12 mile obstacle course designed by British Special Forces.

—

CREATIVE DIRECTOR: Robert Festino
DIRECTOR OF PHOTOGRAPHY: Jeanne Graves
PUBLICATION: Men's Health

043 Oyster, one for the article "The Ultimate Food-Storage Guide," April 2012. Food still-life illustrating a handbook with information about how to keep food in your refrigerator, freezer and pantry in peak condition.

—

CREATIVE DIRECTOR: Janet Froelich
DIRECTOR OF PHOTOGRAPHY: Casey Tierney
PUBLICATION: Real Simple

GIOVANNI COCCO

051–052 Visoki Decani Monastery, Kosovo - Cultural Genocide, December 2012, two from a series. After the war ended in the defeat of the Serbs in 1999, more than 100 Orthodox holy places were attacked and destroyed with the sole purpose of erasing their memory. The few monasteries that survived are closed enclaves and their existence and security depends on the presence of NATO.

DYLAN COULTER

058–059 Kyle Wiltjer and James Michael McAdoo, two for the article "College Hoops Tip-Off," November 2012, a series of action photographs and portraits of five college basketball players from the nation's top teams previewing the upcoming basketball season.

—

DIRECTOR OF PHOTOGRAPHY: Karen Frank
SENIOR PHOTO EDITOR: Kris LaManna
PUBLICATION: ESPN The Magazine

NEIL CRAVER

060–061 Phantasmic Cycle and Brilliantly Despairing, October 2012, two as part of an underwater photographic series and visual voyage of metamorphosis into the subconscious waters of the mind—the ultimate metaphysical quest into the undercurrent of consciousness.

CHRIS CRAYMER

056–057 Lohla & Craig and Steven & Magnus, two from a series for the article "Sposi Subito!" September 2012, part of a fashion and wedding story portfolio.

—

DIGITAL IMAGING: Alex Dow
RETOUCHING: Oznur Kuzu
STYLIST: Ye Young Kim
PUBLICATION: Italian Vanity Fair

MICHAEL CRICHTON
Lisa Bonnici (Canada)
Tim Mitchell (US)

053 A Series of Unfortunate Events, personal work, February 2012, part of an ongoing exploration of food portraits from the perspective of the floor.

—

CONCEIVED BY: Leigh MacMillan

H DATTU

067 One from a series celebrating captured and created Christmas moments and memories.

—

ART BUYER: Louise Degenais
ART DIRECTOR: Shira Kirsch
CREATIVE DIRECTORS: Nardia Ali, Matt Hassell
AGENCY: Ogilvy One Toronto

TIM DAVIS

065–066 Handbag, two from a series for "Post No Bills," November 2012, a fashion-accessories feature.

—

DIRECTOR OF PHOTOGRAPHY: Caroline Smith
PHOTO EDITOR: Lizzy Oppenheimer
SENIOR PHOTO EDITOR: Ashley Macknica
PUBLICATION: Marie Claire

SAMAN DEILAMANI

068 SOMA 32, part of a personal collection of photographs, April 2012, depicting segments of women's bodies, revealing the true nature of the flesh: awkward, elegant, sensual, sculptural and honest.

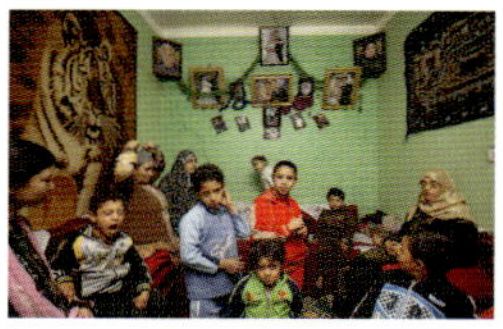
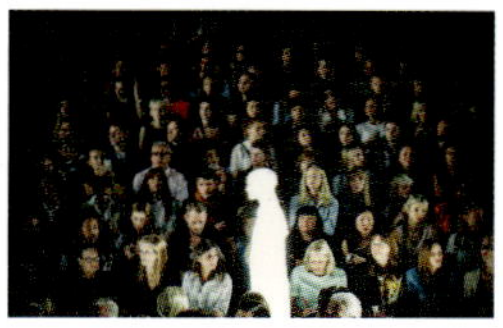
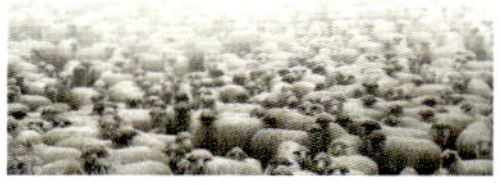
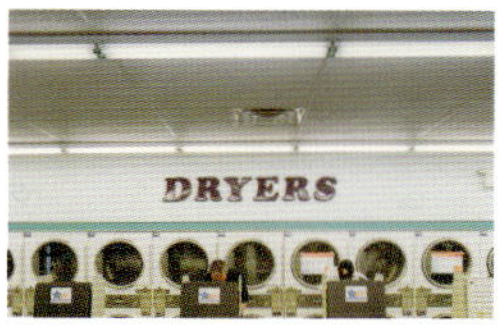

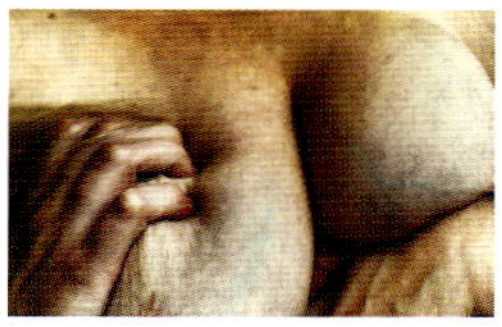
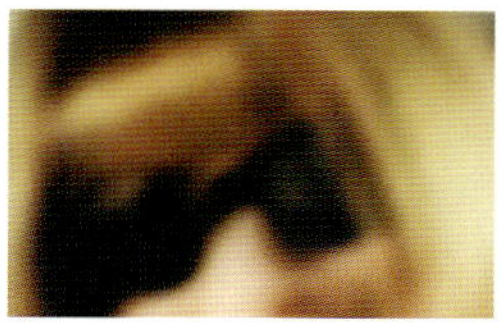
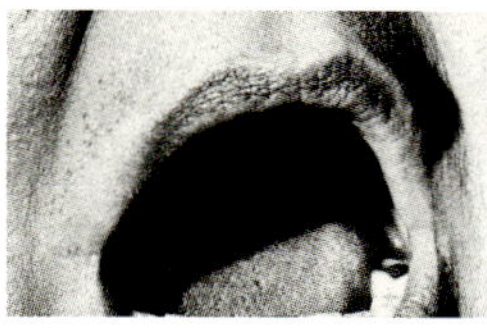
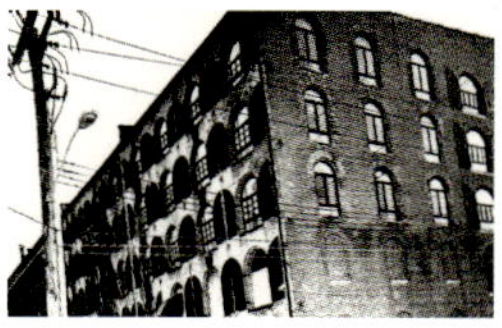
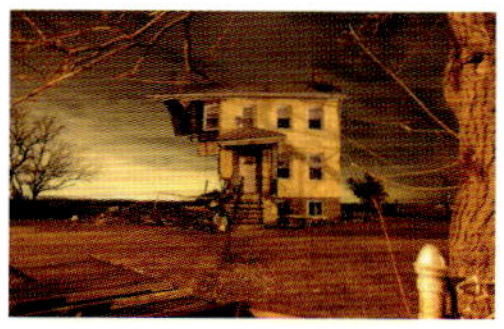
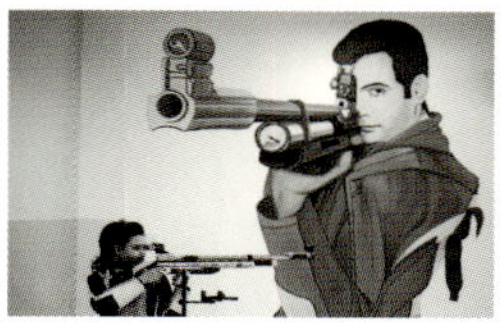
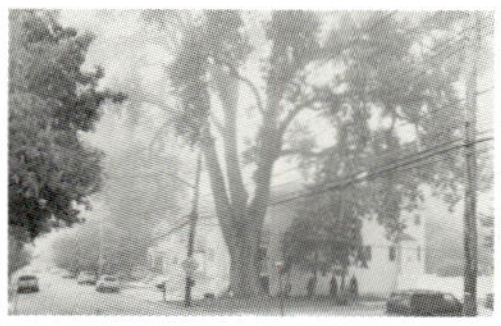
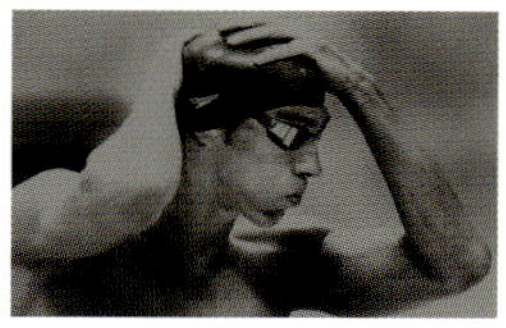
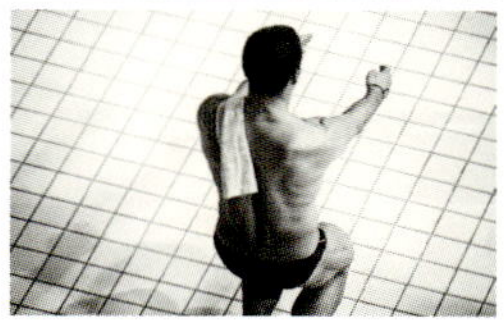
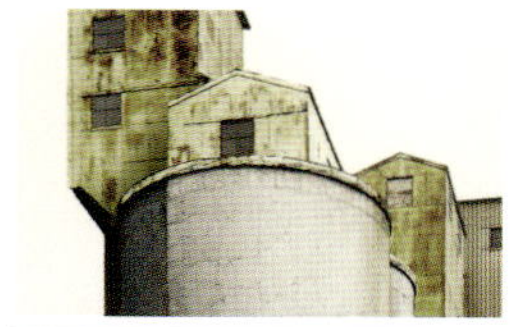
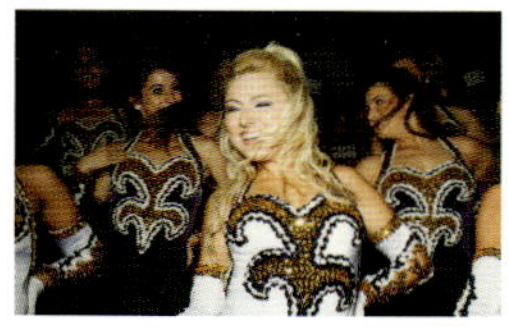
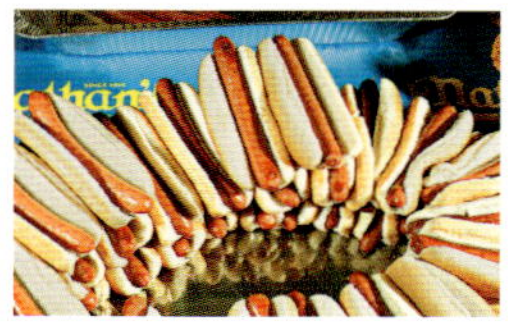

BIEKE DEPOORTER

069–070 Two from a series for the article "In Between - Cairo," December 26, 2012, an intimate look inside the private homes of families on nights during the Egyptian unrest in Cairo, capturing a time of great transformation in society parallel to that on the street outside the houses.

—

SENIOR PHOTO EDITOR: James Wellford
PUBLICATION: Newsweek

BRYAN DERBALLA

073 Ghosts of the Runway, Michael Kors, Lincoln Center, New York City, September 2012, part of the feature "Photos of The Moment New York Fashion Week Spring/Summer 2013."

—

PHOTO EDITOR: Rory Walsh
PUBLICATION: T: The New York Times Style Magazine

TAMAS DEZSO

Robert Koch Gallery

071–072 Sheep Farm, near Silvasu de Sus, West Romania and Choir, near Abrud, West Romania, February 2012, part of an ongoing book project about Romania and the transformation of a Balkan country surviving the region's hardest dictatorship.

—

AUTHOR: Eszter Szablyar

RYAN DONNELL

064 Su Nueva Lavenderia in Chicago, one for the article "Wash, Dry, Vote," October 2012, part of a personal project documenting the unique places where Americans vote.

—

ART DIRECTOR: Emily Kehe
DESIGNER: Chad McCabe
PHOTO DIRECTOR: Mia Diehl
PHOTO EDITOR: Michelle Wolfe
WRITER: Ryan Bradley
PUBLICAITON: Fortune

CHRISTOPHER LEE DONOVAN

074 Abby, Post Pregnancy Study VIII, January 2012, one from a personal series of photographs depicting changes in the body after pregnancy with the intent of contrasting images that are commonly taken before birth.

PARI DUKOVIC

062 Anna Wintour, part of a portfolio of images from the spring fashion shows February 22, 2012.

—

DIRECTOR OF PHOTOGRAPHY: Jody Quon
PHOTO EDITOR: Nadia Lachance
ASSOCIATE PHOTO EDITOR: Roxanne Behr
EDITOR-IN-CHIEF: Adam Moss
PUBLICATION: New York

063 Ambrogio Maestri as Dulcamara in L'Elisir d'Amore, one for a Culture section piece about the Metropolitan Opera's production, September 30, 2012.

—

DIRECTOR OF PHOTOGRAPHY: Jody Quon
ASSOCIATE PHOTO EDITOR: Roxanne Behr
EDITOR-IN-CHIEF: Adam Moss
PUBLICATION: New York

075–076 Red Hook, Brooklyn and south Williamsburg, two from the feature story "The City and the Storm," November 12, 2012—

—

DIRECTOR OF PHOTOGRAPHY: Jody Quon
SENIOR PHOTO EDITOR: Lea Golis
PHOTO EDITORS: Nadia Lachance, Leonor Mamanna
ASSISTANT PHOTO EDITOR: Jenny Westerhoff
ASSOCIATE PHOTO EDITOR: Roxanne Behr
EDITOR-IN-CHIEF: Adam Moss
PUBLICATION: New York

ARISTIDE ECONOMOPOULOS

077 The Princess Cottage at 705 Front Street in Union Beach, NJ, one for the article "Ghost Town Sandy: The Hurricane's Aftermath at Night," December 8, 2012. The images were all taken with long exposures, ranging from one to 30 seconds with only ambient light illuminating the subject.

—

DIRECTOR OF PHOTOGRAPHY: Chris Collins
PUBLICATION: The Star-Ledger

SARAH ELLIOTT

Getty Reportage

078–081 The Voice of Libyan Woman, four from the personal series Her Voice Counts, March 2012. When protests and uprisings broke out in Tunisia in January 2011, then quickly spread to Egypt and Libya, women were present on the frontline, standing side by side with men for the fight for freedom and democracy.

MITCH EPSTEIN

082 Eastern Cottonwood, Staten Island, 2011, one for the article "How to See a Tree," February 12, 2012, New York City, part of a series of arboreal landmarks.

—

DESIGN DIRECTOR: Arem Duplessis
DIRECTOR OF PHOTOGRAPHY: Kathy Ryan
ART DIRECTOR: Gail Bichler
DEPUTY ART DIRECTOR: Caleb Bennett
DEPUTY PICTURE EDITOR: Joanna Milter
EDITOR-IN-CHIEF: Hugo Lindgren
PUBLICATION: The New York Times Magazine

JASON EVANS

083, 086 Ukrainian swimmer Sergii Frolov and Michael Phelps before winning silver in the 200-meter butterfly, London Olympics, July 2012. Two from a series commissioned by the International Olympic Committee (IOC) for use by the Olympic Museum and the IOC magazine.

—

CREATIVE DIRECTOR: Mark Adams
DIRECTOR OF PHOTOGRAPHY: David Herren
PUBLICATION: Olympic Review
CLIENT: International Olympic Committee

084–085 Divers observe and mentally prepare during competition at the 2012 London Olympics, two from a series commissioned by the International Olympic Committee (IOC) for use by the Olympic Museum and the IOC magazine.

—

CREATIVE DIRECTOR: Mark Adams
DIRECTOR OF PHOTOGRAPHY: David Herren
PUBLICATION: Olympic Review
CLIENT: International Olympic Committee

COLIN FAULKNER

087–088 Graphic Architecture, Toronto, Canada, January 2012, two from an ongoing personal series about structures isolated from the surrounding environment to fully illustrate their graphic nature.

BRIAN FINKE

ClampArt

089–090 LSU vs. Alabama, two from a series for the article "One Day One Game," November 2012.

—

PHOTO DIRECTOR: Karen Frank
DEPUTY DIRECTOR OF PHOTOGRAPHY: Jim Surber
SENIOR PHOTO EDITOR: Nancy Weisman
PUBLICATION: ESPN The Magazine

091–092 Takeru Kobayashi at Nathan's Annual Hot Dog Eating Contest, two from a series for the article "Clear Eyes, Full Plates, Can't Puke," November 2012.

—

DESIGN DIRECTOR: Fred Woodward
DIRECTOR OF PHOTOGRAPHY: Dora Somosi
PHOTO EDITOR: Justin O'Neill
WRITER: Jon Ronson
PUBLICATION: GQ

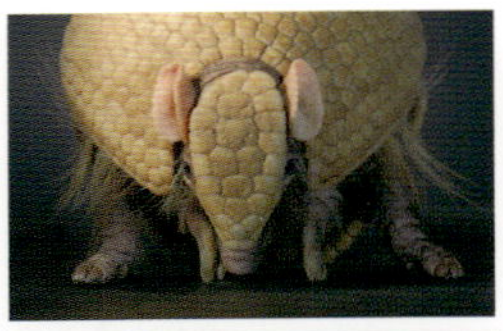
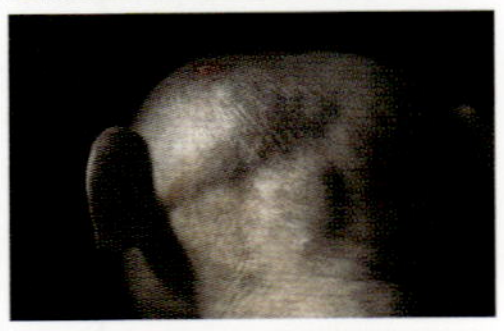
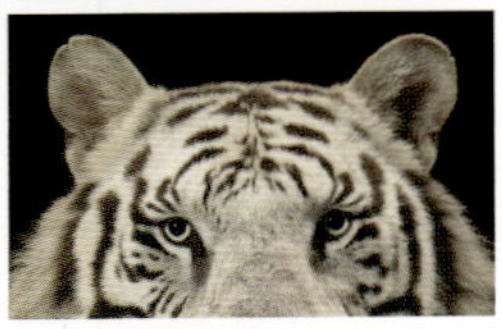
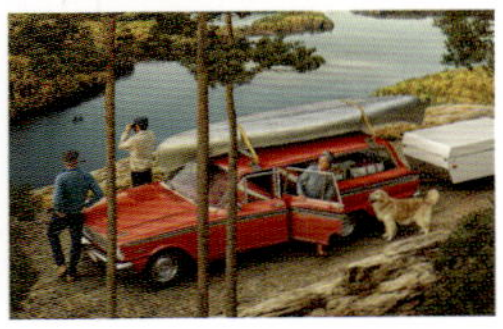
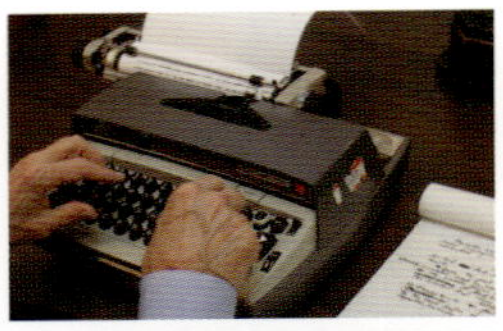
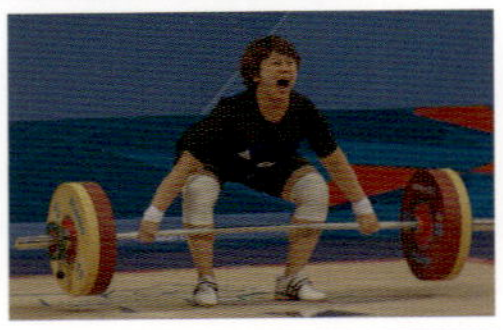
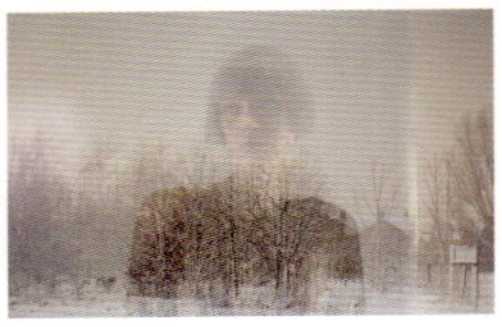
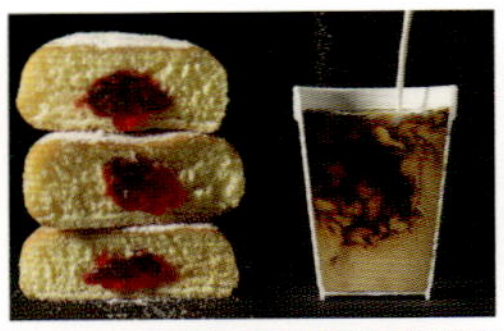
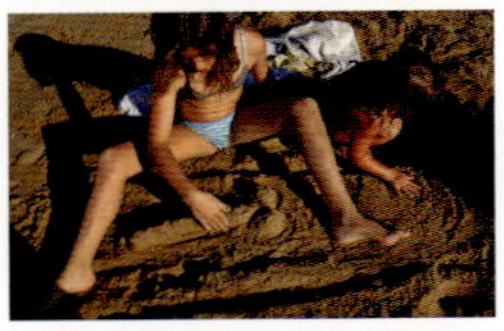
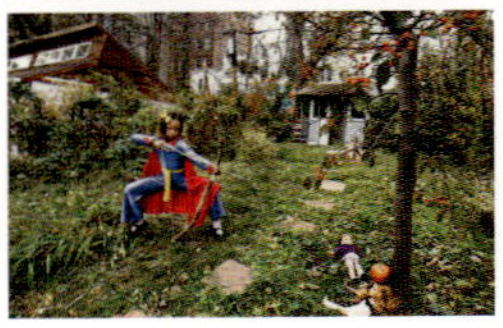
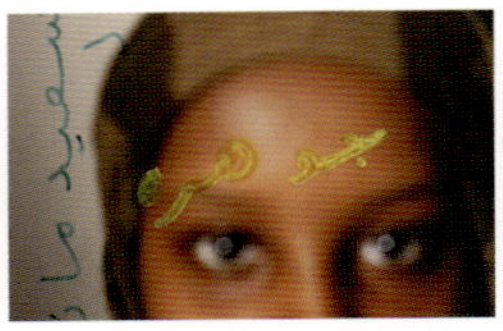
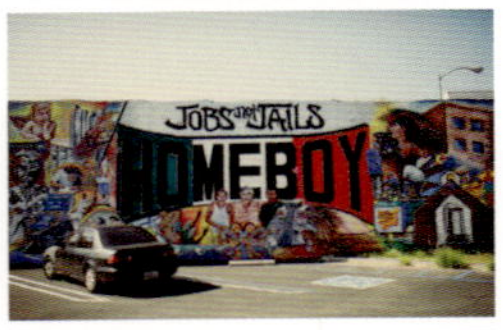

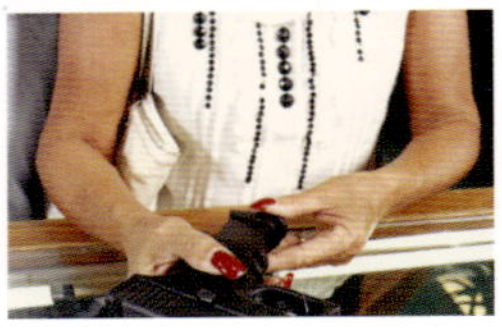
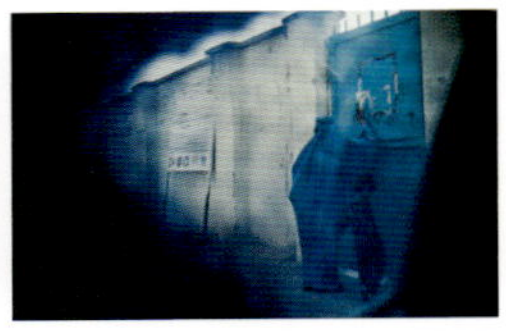
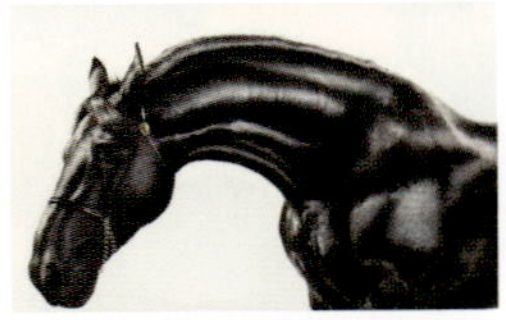
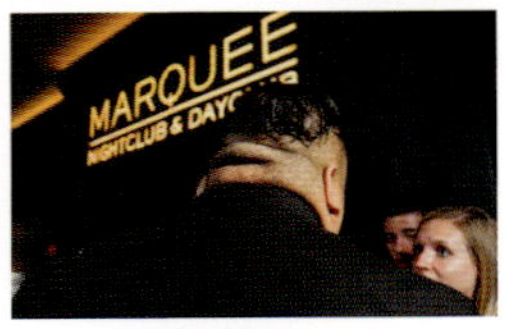

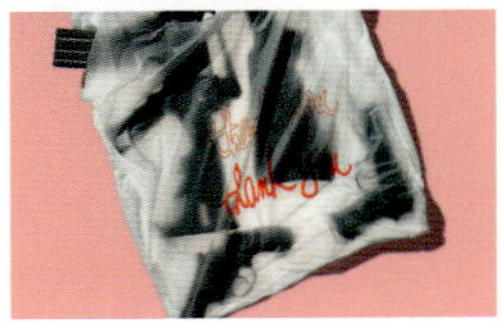
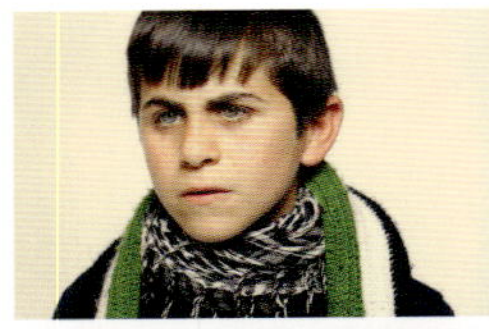
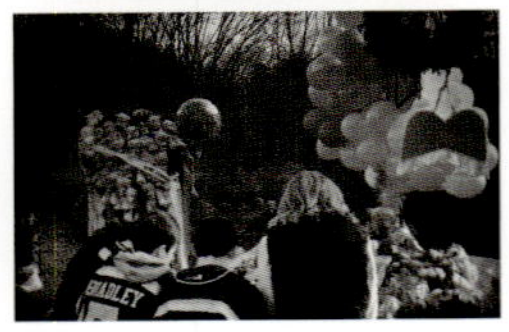

TIM FLACH

093–094 Southern three-banded Armadillo, one from the book More Than Human, October 2012, a photographic exploration of species ranging from mammals to marine creatures to insects.

—

ART DIRECTOR: Lewis Blackwell
CREATIVE DIRECTORS: Geoff Blackwell, Cameron Gibb
PRODUCTION COMPANY: PQ Blackwell Limited
PUBLICATION: More Than Human

095 Jambo, a resident of the World Primate Centre, Twycross Zoo, October 2012, who suffers from total alopecia, a complete loss of hair.

096–097 Two from Tiger Breeding Series - Royal White Tiger, September 2012. An overwhelming majority of the captive tiger population has been bred without regulation and used to produce hybrids as attractions which would never naturally occur in the wild.

RANDAL FORD

Greenhouse Reps NY

098 Acadia National Park, Me., part of a series created for LL Bean's 100th anniversary, reinterpreting paintings LL Bean commissioned for its covers from 1920 to 1960.

—

CREATIVE DIRECTOR: Marcia Minter
ART DIRECTOR/DESIGNER: Kindra Predmore-Thompson
CLIENT: LL Bean
COMPUTER ENHANCEMENT: Small Dog Imageworks
PRODUCTION COMPANY: Lockbox Productions

MARTINE FOUGERON

099–100 Robert Caro, in his office near Columbus Circle, Smith Corona Electra 210, two from a series for the article "Robert Caro's Big Dig," April 15, 2012, as The Passage of Power, his latest in a series of biographies about President Lyndon B. Johnson was published.

—

DESIGN DIRECTOR: Arem Duplessis
DIRECTOR OF PHOTOGRAPHY: Kathy Ryan
PHOTO EDITOR: Joanna Milter
WRITER: Charles McGrath
PUBLICATION: The New York Times Magazine

JASON FULFORD

101–102 Two for the article "A Brief Period of Rejoicing," November 2012, a series of photographs from the 2012 London Olympics.

—

ART DIRECTOR: Stacey D. Clarkson
ASSISTANT ART DIRECTOR: Sam Finn Cate-Gumpert
PUBLICATION: Harper's

JULIA FULLERTON-BATTEN

Vaughan Hannigan, NY

103 One from a series for The Renaissance Photography Prize, an international photography competition that raises money to support younger women with breast cancer.

—

CREATIVE DIRECTOR: Justin Tindall
ART BUYER: Simon Pedersen
ART DIRECTORS: Will Thacker, Blake Waters
CLIENT: The Renaissance Photography Prize

BETH GALTON

True Management

104 Donuts & Coffee, April I, 2012, part of a series of cut food inspired by an assignment in which the client asked to cut a burrito in half as a cross section as opposed to shooting the surface or taking a bite or piece out.

—

STYLIST: Charlotte Omnès

PRESTON GANNAWAY

105 Anatomy of Sand, December 2012, one from the series Between the Devil and the Deep Blue Sea, an ongoing documentary project about the changing character of a working-class seaside community.

—

PHOTO EDITOR: Nicole Fruge

TIERNEY GEARON

Trish South

106 Quvenzhané Wallis of Beasts of the Southern Wild, one from a series for the article "Wide Awake," December 9, 2012, featuring 13 actresses whose performances defined the year in film.

—

DESIGN DIRECTOR: Arem Duplessis
DIRECTOR OF PHOTOGRAPHY: Kathy Ryan
ART DIRECTOR: Gail Bichler
ASSOCIATE ART DIRECTOR: Caleb Bennett
DEPUTY PICTURE EDITOR: Joanna Milter
EDITOR-IN-CHIEF: Hugo Lindgren
PUBLICATION: The New York Times Magazine

JIM GOLDBERG

107–110 Four from a series for "Open See," June 2012, Athens Greece, 2004, a story about Somali refugees escaping to Greece.

—

DIRECTOR OF DESIGN & DIGITAL MEDIA: Michael J. Walsh
ASSOCIATE EDITOR: Sheilah Ledwidge
EXECUTIVE VICE PRESIDENT: Anthony P. Rhodes
EDITOR-AT-LARGE: Mark Alice Durant
EDITOR-IN-CHIEF: Stephen Frailey
EDITORIAL ASSISTANT: Kimberlee Venable
FASHION EDITOR: Lindsay Hart Thompson
MANAGING EDITOR: Eleanor Oakes,
PUBLICATION: Dear Dave, 11

MELISSA GOLDEN

111 Homeboy Industries, one from a series for the article "House of Second Chances," April 2012.

—

CREATIVE DIRECTOR: Florian Bachleda
PHOTO EDITOR: Leslie Dela Vega
PUBLICATION: Fast Company

DAVID GRAHAM

112–115 Sprague's Sports in Yuma, AZ, four from a series for the article "Guns 'R Us," September 2012, about a mega-shop that specializes in Glocks and AK-47s.

—

DESIGN DIRECTOR: Fred Woodward
DIRECTOR OF PHOTOGRAPHY: Dora Somosi
PHOTO EDITOR: Krista Prestek
WRITER: Jeanne Marie Laskas
PUBLICATION: GQ

TONI GREAVES

116–117 Traveling by Burqa, Afghanistan, March 2012, two from a series showing daily life as viewed through a Burqa, Helmand Province, Afghanistan.

—

CLIENT: Mercy Corps

JILL GREENBERG

Jason Eason at Angela De Bona

118–119 Two from a photography-based series of horses in-studio and on-location for a book project, October 2012.

LAUREN GREENFIELD

INSTITUTE

120 One for the article "The Best Night $500,000 Can Buy," September 2012, a security guard at the Marquee Las Vegas protects the entrance of the highest grossing nightclub in America.

—

DESIGN DIRECTOR: Fred Woodward
DIRECTOR OF PHOTOGRAPHY: Dora Somosi
ASSISTANT PHOTO EDITOR: Michael Allin
PRODUCER: Rebecca Black
PUBLICATION: GQ

CHRISTOPHER GRIFFITH

121 One for the article "Battleground America," April 23, 2012, about U.S. gun control.

—

CREATIVE DIRECTOR: Wyatt Mitchell
DIRECTOR OF PHOTOGRAPHY: Whitney Johnson
PHOTO EDITORS: Elissa Curtis, Maria Lokke, James Pomerantz, Jessie Wender
PUBLICATION: The New Yorker

PETER HAPAK

122–123 Two from a series of portraits for the article "Flight Of The Syrians," April 23, 2012, Syrian citizens at the Reyhanli refugee camp in southern Turkey, April 9, 2012.

—

DESIGN DIRECTOR: DW Pine
DIRECTOR OF PHOTOGRAPHY: Kira Pollack
INTERNATIONAL PHOTO EDITOR: Patrick Witty
SENIOR ART DIRECTOR: Emily Crawford
WRITER: Rania Abouzeid
PUBLICATION: TIME

RON HAVIV

VII Photo Agency

125–128 Four from a series for the article "Remnants Of An American Tragedy," December 15, 2012, about Newtown, Conn. in the hours following the shooting at Sandy Hook Elementary.

—

DEPUTY PICTURE EDITOR: Debbe Edelstein
DIRECTOR OF PHOTOGRAPHY: Chris Dougherty
PUBLICATION: People

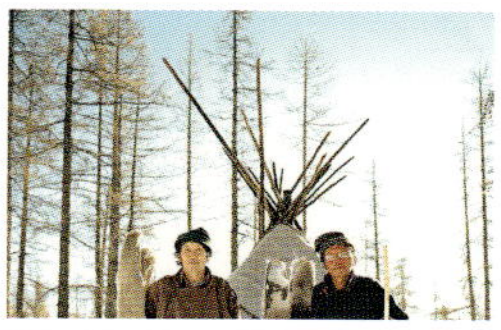
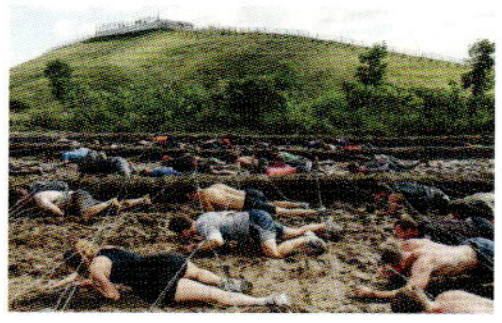
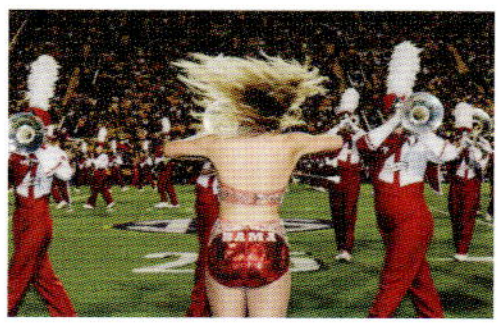
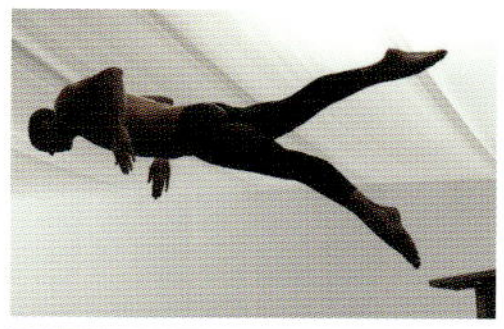
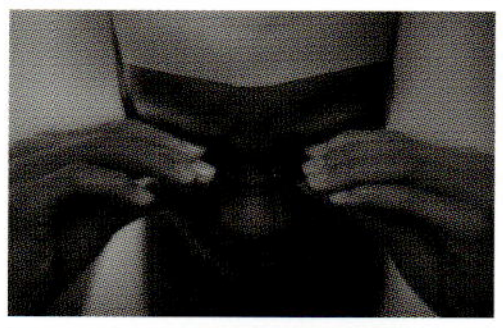
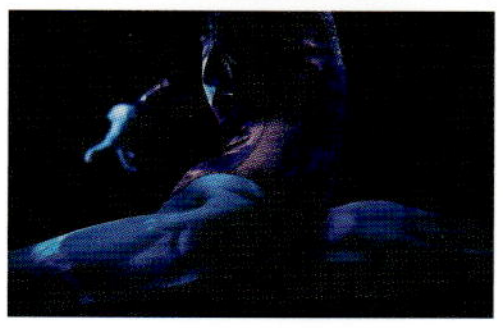
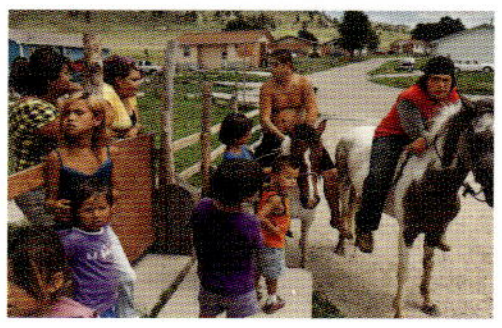
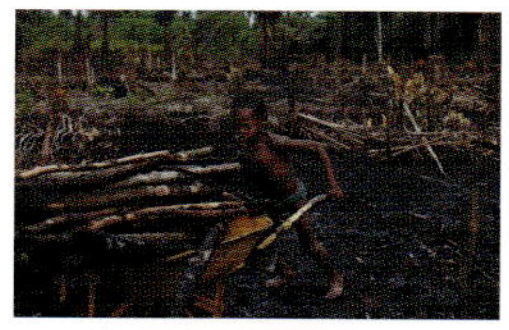
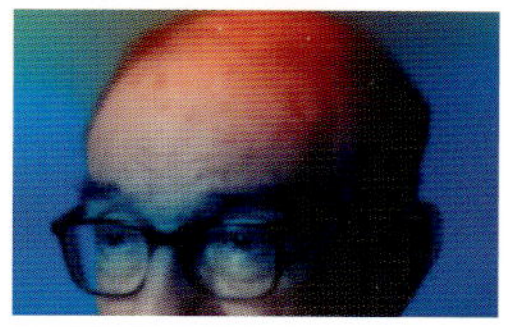
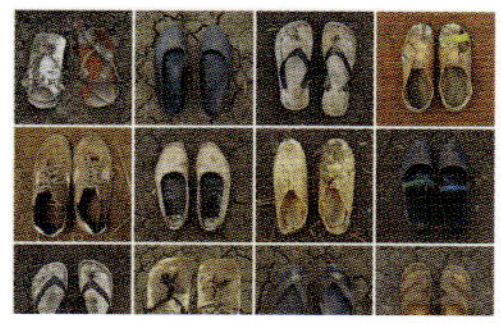
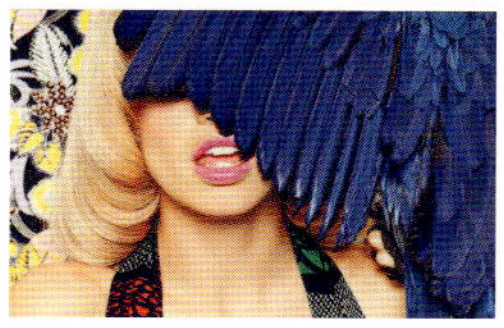
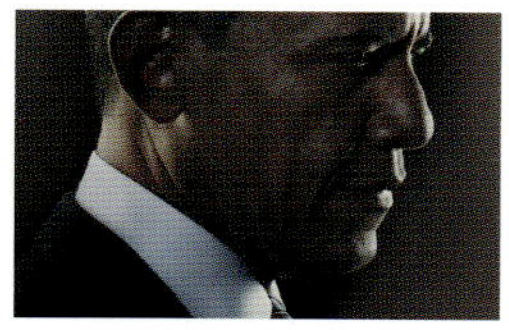
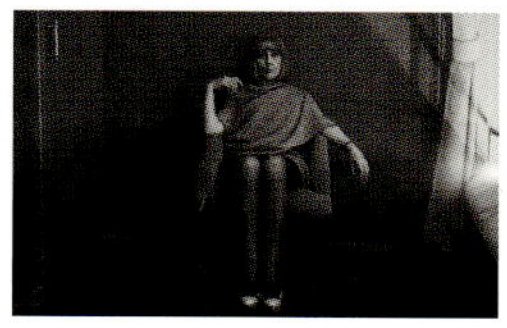
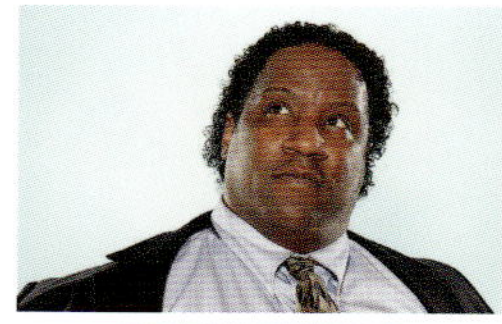
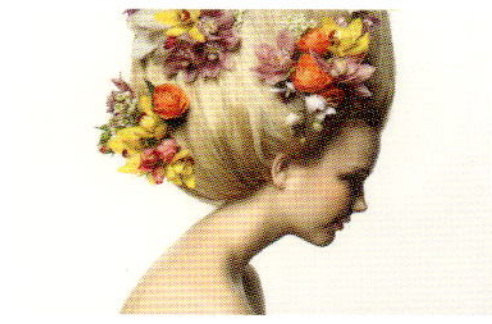
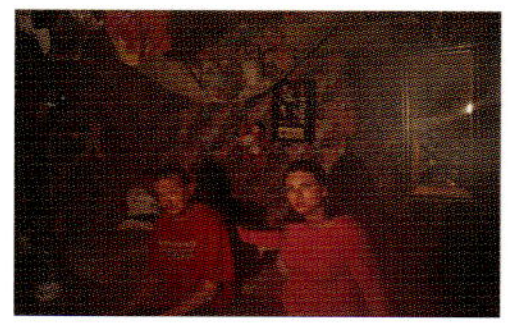

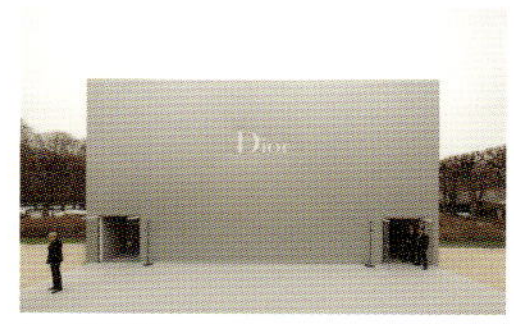
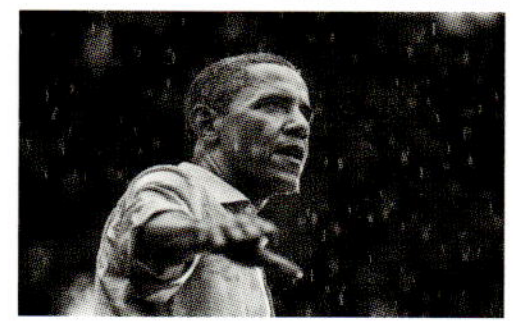

ILJA HERB
124 Ganbat and Uvedorj of the Tsaatan people, Mongolia, one from a series for the article "Into the Nines," December 2012.
—
CREATIVE DIRECTOR: Eleanor Williamson
DIRECTOR OF PHOTOGRAPHY: Keri Bascetta
EDITOR: Kimberly Beekman
EDITOR-IN-CHIEF: Sam Bass
WRITER: Evelyn Spence
PUBLICATION: Skiing

ANDREW HETHERINGTON
Julian Richards

129 One from a series for the article "Playing Dirty," November 2012, investigating the Tough Mudder Toronto event.
—
CREATIVE DIRECTOR: Hannah McCaughey
PHOTO EDITOR: Amy Silverman
PUBLICATION: Outside

130 Half time show during LSU V Alabama football game, one for the special issue "One Day One Game LSU V Alabama," November 2012.
—
CREATIVE DIRECTOR: John Korpics
PHOTO EDITORS: Nick Galac, Jim Surber, Stephanie Weed, Nancy Weisman
DIRECTOR OF PHOTOGRAPHY: Karen Frank
PUBLICATION: ESPN The Magazine

JOHN HUET
Marilyn Cadenbach

134 Michael Phelps, January 2012, for a print campaign for Mazda in China.
—
CLIENT: Mazda

135 Part of a broadcast and print campaign for Playtex, January 2012.
—
ART DIRECTOR: Shardae Mendes-DeJesus
CREATIVE DIRECTORS: Elaine McCormick, Fran Sheff-Mauer
DIRECTOR: John Huet
PRODUCTION COMPANY: Element
CLIENT: Playtex

136–137 Gymnast Gabrielle Douglas at the 2012 London Olympic Games, two from a series, August 2012.
—
CREATIVE DIRECTOR: Mard Adams
DIRECTOR OF PHOTOGRAPHY: David Herren
CLIENT: International Olympic Committee

AARON HUEY
131–133 Pine Ridge Indian Reservation, South Dakota, three for the cover story "In The Shadow of Wounded Knee," August 2012.
—
PHOTO EDITOR: Sarah Leen
PUBLICATION: National Geographic

SAMUEL JAMES
139–142 Four from a series for the article "The Water of My Land," September 2012. Fires from hundreds of illicit fuel refineries burn every night throughout the Niger Delta.
—
ART DIRECTOR: Stacey D. Clarkson
ASSISTANT ART DIRECTOR: Sam Finn Cate-Gumpert
PUBLICATION: Harper's

MACIEK JASIK
138 Portrait of Alan Greenspan, former Fed chairman, one for the annual Interview Issue, August 2012.
—
DIRECTOR OF PHOTOGRAPHY: David Carthas
PHOTO EDITOR: Meagan Ziegler-Haynes
PUBLICATION: Bloomberg Businessweek

SHANNON JENSEN
145 One from a series for the article "A Long Walk," September 3, 2012, representing a journey of thirty-thousand in one image.
—
SENIOR PHOTO EDITOR: James Wellford
PUBLICATION: Newsweek

JUCO PHOTO
143–144 Macaw 1 and Girl and Hyacinth, two for "Flight Patterns," March 2012, a Spring 2012 editorial studio shot in Los Angeles.

NADAV KANDER
Stockland Martel

146 U.S. President Barack Obama, TIME's 2012 Person Of The Year, cover portrait photographed on December 12, 2012 in the Diplomatic Room of the White House.
—
DESIGN DIRECTOR: DW Pine
DIRECTOR OF PHOTOGRAPHY: Kira Pollack
ASSISTANT ART DIRECTOR: Ryan Moore
DEPUTY PICTURE EDITOR: Paul Moakley
PUBLICATION: TIME

147–148 Actor Daniel Kaluuya, 22, and London theater actress Eileen Atkins, 78, two from a series for the article "Titans of the Stage," March 4, 2012.
—
DESIGN DIRECTOR: Arem Duplessis
DIRECTOR OF PHOTOGRAPHY: Kathy Ryan
ASSOCIATE PHOTO EDITOR: Clinton Cargill
DEPUTY ART DIRECTOR: Caleb Bennett
DEPUTY PICTURE EDITOR: Joanna Milter
DESIGN DIRECTOR: Gail Bichler
EDITOR-IN-CHIEF: Hugo Lindgren
PUBLICATION: The New York Times Magazine

ELI MEIR KAPLAN
151–152 CeeCee Leone and Mona Lotts, two from a series for the article "Fabulous!" March 2012, portraits of Washington-area drag queens, in and out of drag.
—
CREATIVE DIRECTOR: Michael Goesele
PHOTO EDITOR: David Hicks
PUBLICATION: Washingtonian

GEOF KERN
Friend + Johnson

157 One for the article "Summer Hair Guide For Grownups," June 2012.
—
CREATIVE DIRECTOR: Debra Bishop
DIRECTOR OF PHOTOGRAPHY: Natasha Lunn
PUBLICATION: More

NATALIE KEYSSAR
153–154 Two from a series for the article "Just For Now: A Year In Tent City," November 22, 2012, about a 7-year-old community of about 100 homeless people living in tents and shacks in a publicly owned patch of woods in suburban Lakewood, NJ.
—
PHOTO EDITOR: Tracy Armstead
PUBLICATION: The Wall Street Journal

IDRIS KHAN
149–150 Photo illustrations using found images of London's landmarks, two from a series for "The London Issue," March 4, 2012.
—
DESIGN DIRECTOR: Arem Duplessis
DIRECTOR OF PHOTOGRAPHY: Kathy Ryan
ART DIRECTOR: Gail Bichler
ASSOCIATE PICTURE EDITOR: Stacey Baker
DEPUTY ART DIRECTOR: Caleb Bennett
DEPUTY PICTURE EDITOR: Joanna Milter
EDITOR-IN-CHIEF: Hugo Lindgren
PUBLICATION: The New York Times Magazine

NIKOLAS KOENIG
158 Dior fashion show at the Rodin Museum, Paris, one for the article "Big Show," March 2012.
—
CREATIVE DIRECTOR: Marcelo Junemann
PUBLICATION: Big Magazine

BROOKS KRAFT
Corbis

159–160 President Barack Obama and Bill Clinton at two campaign events, two for the article "For Obama, Survival Is the New Winning," November 19, 2012.
—
DESIGN DIRECTOR: DW Pine
DIRECTOR OF PHOTOGRAPHY: Kira Pollack
DEPUTY ART DIRECTOR: Chrissy Dunleavy
DEPUTY PICTURE EDITOR: Paul Moakley
PUBLICATION: TIME

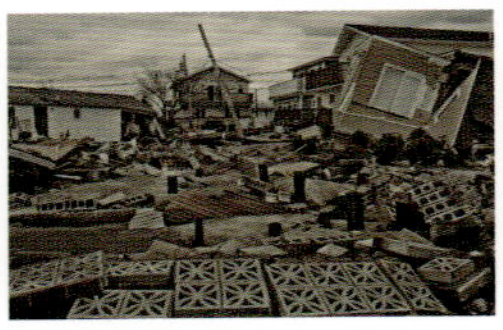

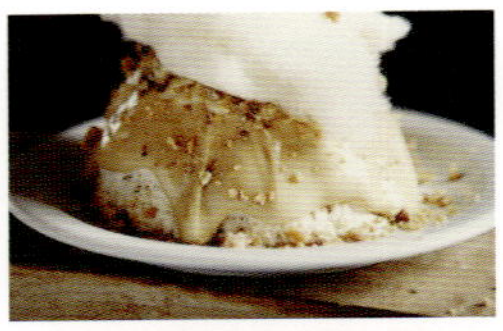

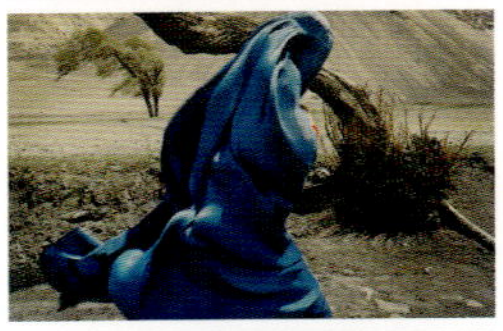

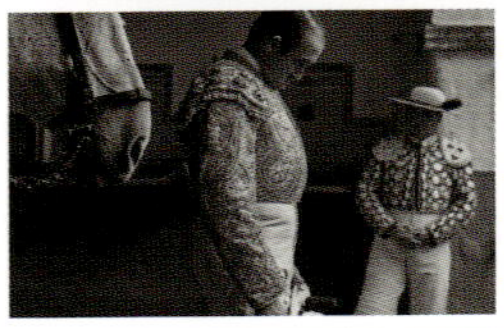

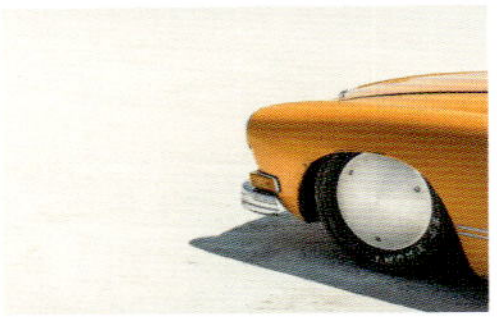

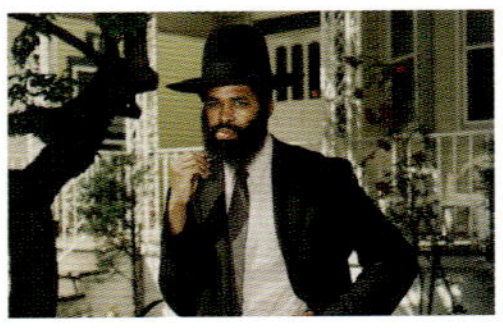

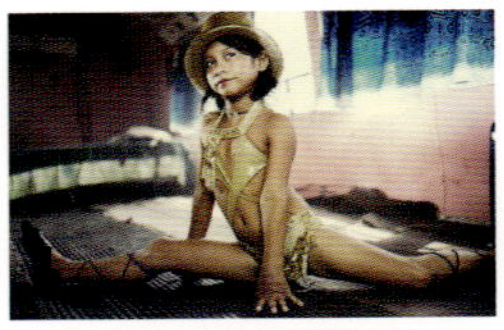

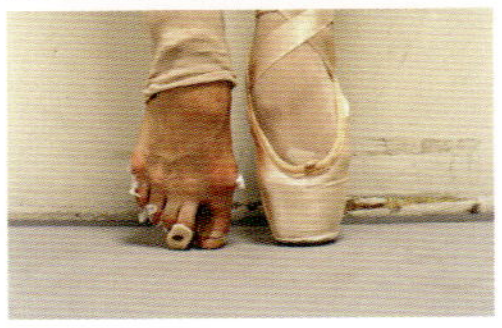

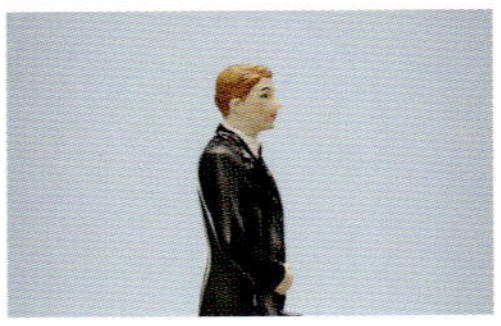

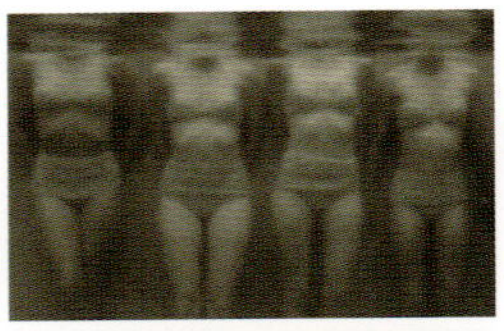

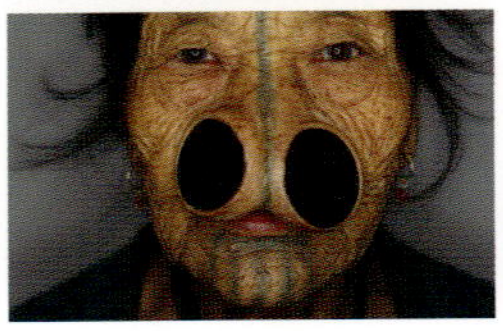

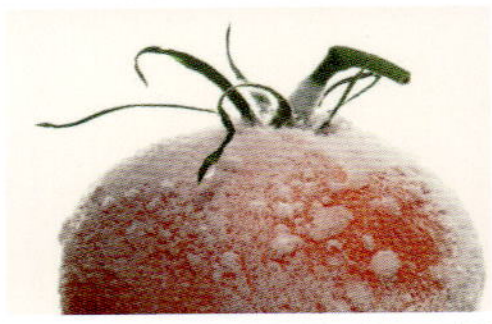

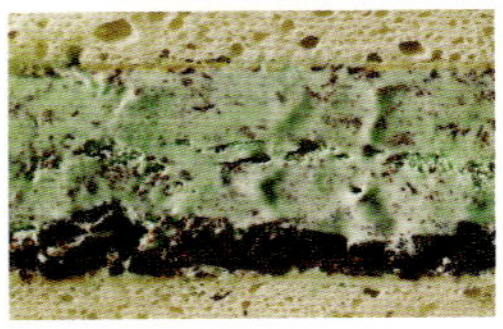

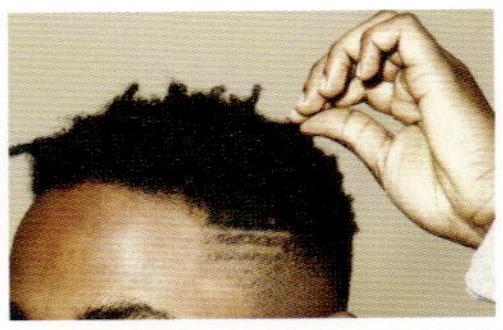

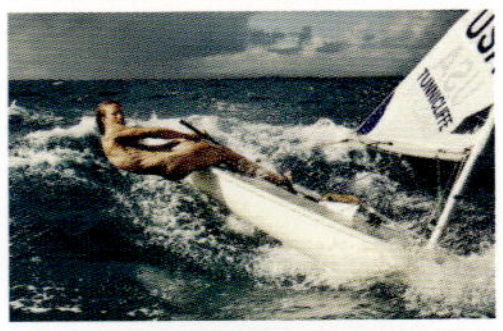

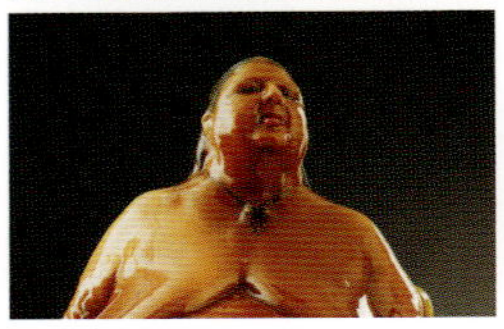

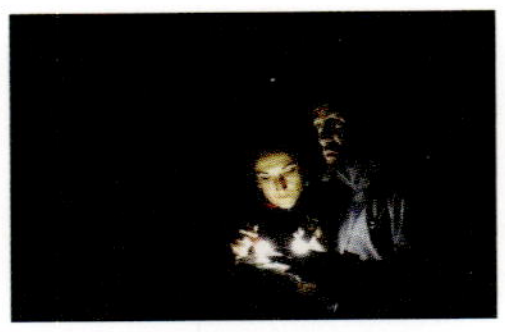

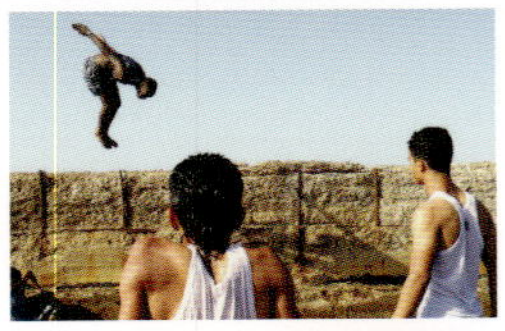

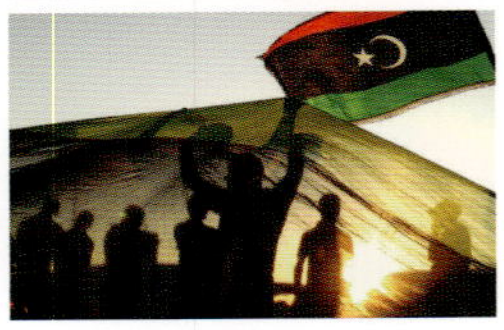

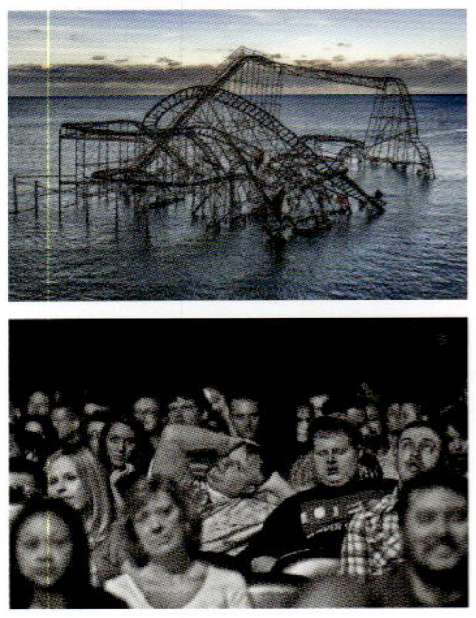

TERU KUWAYAMA

155–156 Aftermath of Hurricane Sandy, Breezy Point, NY, October 31, 2012, two for an article about the Hurricane that hit the East Coast, November 12, 2012.

—

SENIOR PHOTO EDITOR: James Wellford
PUBLICATION: Newsweek

DOMINIQUE LAFOND

161 Frozen Nougat with Maple Cotton Candy from Au Pied de Cochon, one for the article "Sweet Spot," January 2012.

—

CREATIVE DIRECTOR: Alex Grossman
PHOTO DIRECTOR: Alex Pollack
PHOTO EDITOR: Susan Getzendanner
PUBLICATION: Bon Appetit

FREDERIC LAGRANGE

162 Sunni woman walking along The Wakhan Corridor, Afghanistan, personal work, March 2012.

AITOR LARA

165–168 Four from a series of bullfights televised again in Spain after a six-year hiatus, for the article "To The Death," October 29, 2012.

—

SENIOR PHOTO EDITOR: James Wellford
PUBLICATION: Newsweek

DAVE LAURIDSEN

Julian Richards

164 One from a personal series shot at the Bonneville Land Speed Races, August 2012, Bonneville, Utah.

WAYNE LAWRENCE

INSTITUTE

163 Nechemyah Davis, Borough Park, one from a series for the article "The Black Orthodox," December 31, 2012.

—

DIRECTOR OF PHOTOGRAPHY: Jody Quon
EDITOR-IN-CHIEF: Adam Moss
PUBLICATION: New York

STEVEN LAXTON

171–172 Contortionist girl and clown applying makeup, two for the article "Life on a Tight Rope," October 2012, a series on the lives of nomadic circus families of El Salvador.

—

DIRECTOR OF PHOTOGRAPHY: Lisa Vosper
ASSOCIATE PHOTO EDITOR: Natalie Gialluca
PUBLICATION: Latina

HENRY LEUTWYLER

174 Dancer Megan LeCrone, one for the book Ballet, December 2012, a collection of photographs of the New York City Ballet.

—

DESIGN FIRM: Water
DESIGNERS: Ruba Abu-Nimah, Kevin Ley, Eleanor Rogers
PUBLICATION: Ballet

ADAM LEVEY

173 One from a series for the article "The 35 Truths About Marriage," May 2012.

—

DESIGN DIRECTOR: Fred Woodward
DIRECTOR OF PHOTOGRAPHY: Dora Somosi
SENIOR PHOTO EDITOR: Krista Prestek
PHOTO EDITOR: Justin O'Neill
PUBLICATION: GQ

TAMAR LEVINE

175 One from a series The Swimmers, February 2012.

—

ASSISTANT: Samantha Zachrich
EDITOR: Diane Wallace
STYLISTS: Marybeth Bagonghasa, Tashina Hunter, Jane Phu
PUBLICATION: Litrof

BRENT LEWIN

Redux Pictures

176–177 Ngilyang Empu and Tailyang Yaming of the Apatani tribe pose for a portrait in Ziro, India, two from the series Stealing Beauty - The Apatani, February 2012.

STEPHEN LEWIS

Art & Commerce

169 Frozen tomato, one for the article "How To Fix Dinner," January 2012, a conceptual still life illustrating 17 all-too-common cooking mistakes.

—

CREATIVE DIRECTOR: Janet Froelich
DESIGN DIRECTOR: Cybele Grandjean
DIRECTOR OF PHOTOGRAPHY: Casey Tierney
PHOTO EDITOR: Lauren Reichbach Epstein
PUBLICATION: Real Simple

170 Mint Chip Ice Cream Cake, one for "Layer It On," October 2012.

—

CREATIVE DIRECTOR: Alex Grossman
PHOTO DIRECTOR: Alex Pollack
PHOTO EDITOR: Susan Getzendanner
PUBLICATION: Bon Appetit

TURE LILLEGRAVEN

178–179 Schoolboy Q, Kenrick Lamar, Jay Rock and Ab-Soul, two for a feature about the hip-hop collective Black Hippy, March 2012.

—

PHOTO DIRECTOR: Michelle Egiziano
PHOTO EDITOR: Jennifer Edmondson
PUBLICATION: Spin

STEVEN LIPPMAN

Stockland Martel

181 Anna Tunnecliffe sailing over rough seas in Ft. Lauderdale, FL, one for the annual Bodies We Want photo portfolio of nude athletes, July 2012.

—

SENIOR PHOTO EDITOR: Nancy Weisman
PUBLICATION: ESPN The Magazine

BLAKE LITTLE

180 Catherine, one from an ongoing, personal project The Preservation Photographs, December 2012.

BENJAMIN LOWY

Reportage by Getty Images

182 French tourists Virginia and David use a cellphone to light a map while navigating the darkened streets of downtown New York during the Hurricane Sandy blackout, October 31, 2012.

183 Young Libyans swim on a rubble-strewn stone cornish during a hot summer day on July 3, 2012 in Tripoli.

184 Libyans rejoice with song and dance along the boardwalk of Benghazi after a vote for the first time in more than 40 years on July 7, 2012 in Benghazi.

185 Boardwalk promenade, Seaside Heights, NJ, one for the article "Superstorm Sandy: Heroes of the Storm," November 2012.

—

DESIGN DIRECTOR: Andrea Dunham
DIRECTOR OF PHOTOGRAPHY: Chris Dougherty
PHOTO EDITOR: Debbe Edelstein
PUBLICATION: People

186 Fans watching an Ultimate Fighing Club (UFC) match, one from a series for the article "UFC Tries to Prove It's Capable of a Knockout," November 2012.

—

CREATIVE DIRECTOR: Florian Bachleda
PHOTO EDITOR: Leslie Dela Vega
PUBLICATION: Fast Company

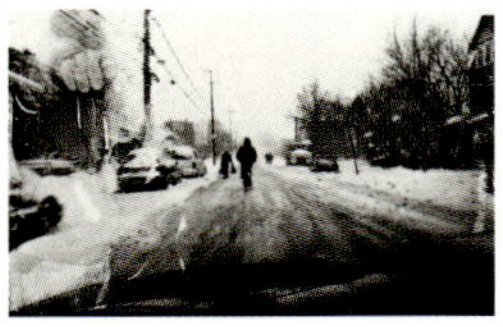
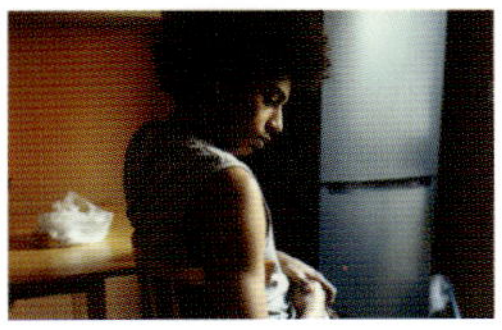
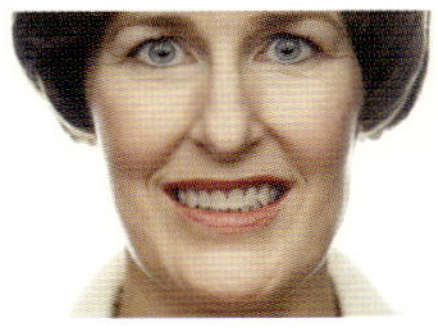
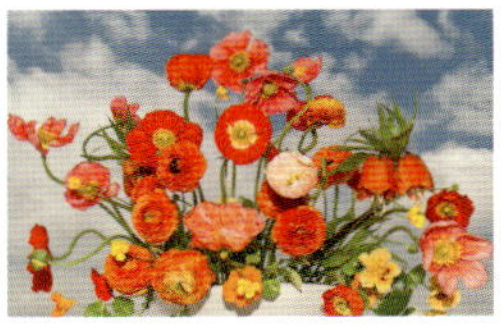
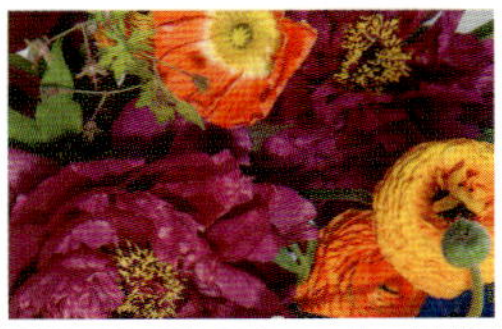
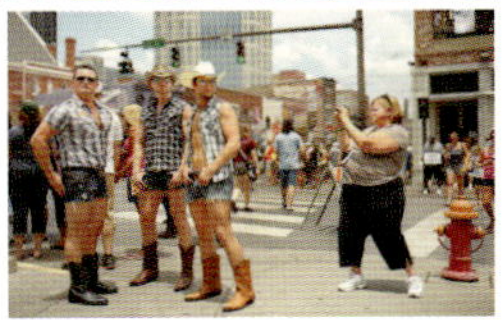
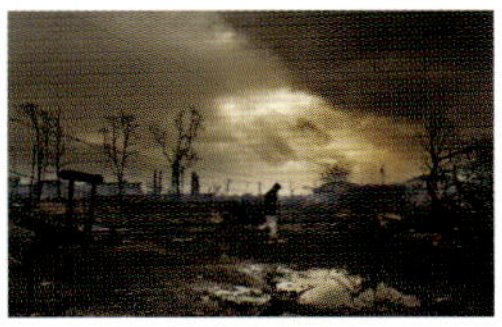
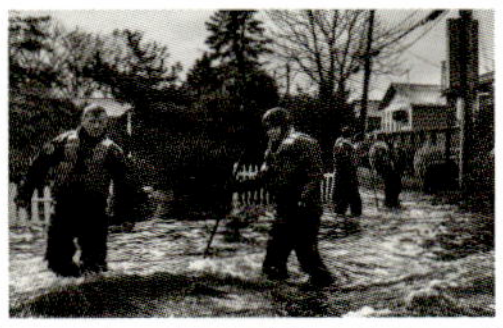
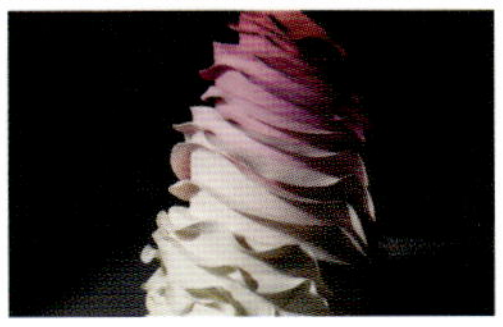
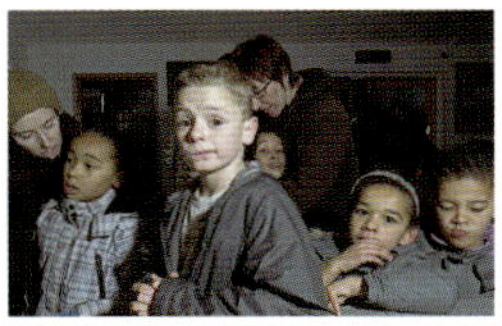
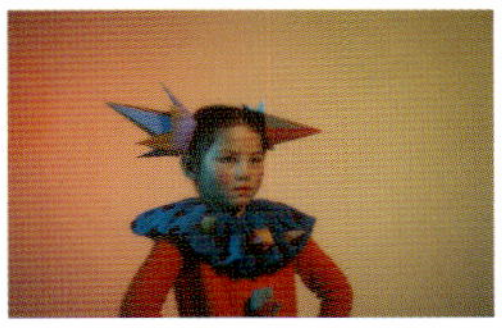
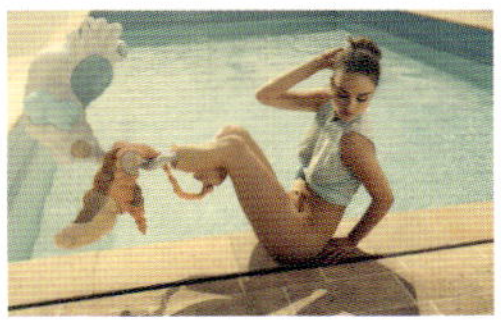
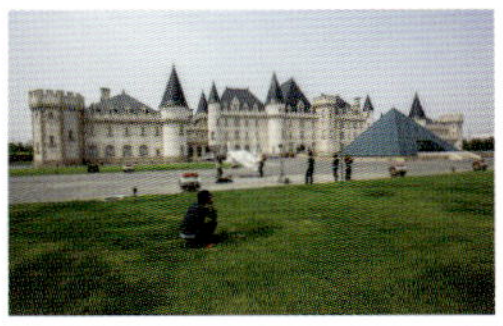
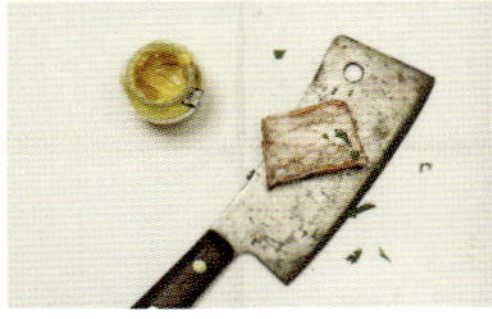
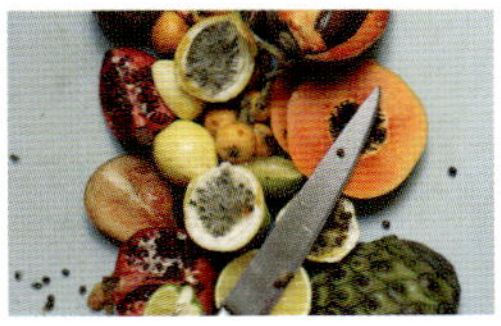
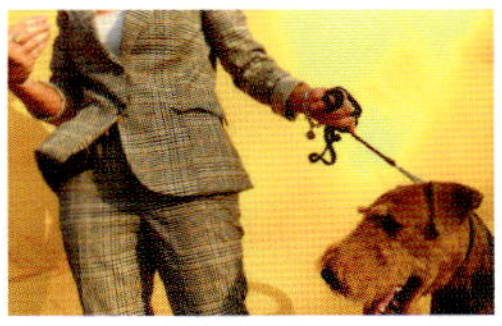
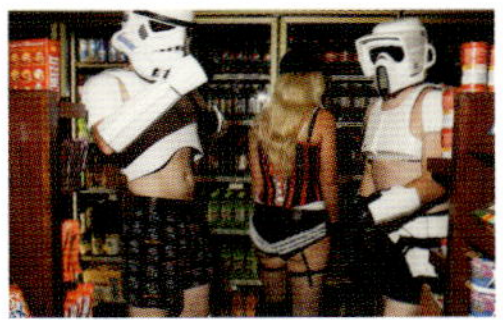

JUSTIN MAXON

187–190 Four from the project When The Spirit Moves, December 2012, documenting the many issues that plague the inner-city community of Chester, PA. Located on the Delaware River, the city experienced an industrial collapse in the 1960s and subsequent economic meltdown.

GARETH MCCONNELL

191–192 Ysham Avdulahi, 20, from France, and Akoul de Mabior, 23, from Sudan model in London, two from a series for "Migratory Models," March 4, 2012.

—

DESIGN DIRECTOR: Arem Duplessis
DIRECTOR OF PHOTOGRAPHY: Kathy Ryan
ART DIRECTOR: Gail Bichler
ASSISTANT PHOTO EDITOR: Gabrielle Plucknette
DEPUTY ART DIRECTOR: Caleb Bennett
DEPUTY PICTURE EDITOR: Joanna Milter
DESIGNER: Drea Zlanabitnig
EDITOR-IN-CHIEF: Hugo Lindgren
PUBLICATION: The New York Times Magazine

MIKE MCGREGOR

Julian Richards

193–194 Ray Persons and Anne Rea, two from a series for the article "American Lawyer's Litigators of the Year," January 2012, a portrait series of the most powerful litigators in America.

—

DESIGN DIRECTOR: Joan Ferrell
PHOTO EDITOR: Maggie Soladay
PUBLICATION: The AmericanLawyer

TONY MENDOZA

195 One for "On The Wild Side," August 2012, an article about wedding centerpieces.

—

CREATIVE DIRECTOR: Cybele Grandjean
DIRECTOR OF PHOTOGRAPHY: Mary Clare Cahill
ASSOCIATE PHOTO EDITOR: Amelia Hoffman
DEPUTY ART DIRECTOR: Jennifer McManus
PUBLICATION: Brides

196 Frontis, August 2012, opener for a story.

—

CREATIVE DIRECTOR: Cybele Grandjean
DIRECTOR OF PHOTOGRAPHY: Mary Clare Cahill
ASSOCIATE PHOTO EDITOR: Amelia Hoffman
DEPUTY ART DIRECTOR: Jennifer McManus
PUBLICATION: Brides

GREG MILLER

198 Fan Fair in Nashville,part of the 2012 Country Music Awards Music Fest, June 2012, one for the article "When The Fans Come To Nashville," October 2012.

—

DESIGN DIRECTOR: Andrea Dunham
DIRECTOR OF PHOTOGRAPHY: Chris Dougherty
DESIGNER: Jaclyn Steinberg
PHOTO EDITOR: Christine Ramage
PUBLICATION: People Country

PHILIP MONTGOMERY

199 Residents of the Rockaways, hard-hit by Superstorm Sandy, remained without power, many in dilapidated structures for weeks after the storm made landfall in New York City.

—

PHOTO EDITOR: Jon Protas
PUBLICATION: The Wall Street Journal

200–203 Four for the article "After Blaze, Breezy Point Bands Together," October 30, 2012, about Superstorm Sandy that hit New York City on October 29, 2012 where 100 homes were leveled by fire in the beach-front Queens community.

—

PHOTO EDITOR: Tracy Armstead
PUBLICATION: The Wall Street Journal

ANGELA MOORE

197 One from a series for the article "A Dash of Fashion," September 2012, a story about wedding cakes inspired by the runway.

—

CREATIVE DIRECTOR: Cybele Grandjean
DIRECTOR OF PHOTOGRAPHY: Mary Clare Cahill
ART DIRECTOR: Jaspal Riyait
ASSOCIATE PHOTO EDITOR: Amelia Hoffman
PUBLICATION: Brides

MARK NEVILLE

204 One for the article "Here is London," March 4, 2012, part of an ongoing series shot around London that captured diverse portraits ranging from nightlife to banking, education to community organizing, and the ways these worlds intersect.

—

DESIGN DIRECTOR: Arem Duplessis
DIRECTOR OF PHOTOGRAPHY: Kathy Ryan
ART DIRECTOR: Gail Bichler
ASSOCIATE PHOTO EDITOR: Stacey Baker
DEPUTY ART DIRECTOR: Caleb Bennett
DEPUTY PICTURE EDITOR:: Joanna Milter
EDITOR-IN-CHIEF: Hugo Lindgren
PUBLICATION: The New York Times Magazine

NICK & CHLOÉ

Bernstein & Andriulli

205 Moon, one for a fashion editorial inspired by the commedia dell'arte characters Pierrot and the Harlequin encountering a bewildering blue moon, September 2012.

—

FASHION EDITOR: Julie Vianey
PUBLICATION: Papier Maché

206–207 Two from Are We Hard Yet? April 2012, a collaborative project by Nick & Chloé vs. Zeitguised, that deconstructs hierarchies of photographic elements, creating new meanings by playfully twisting the language of erotic imagery into absurdity without collapsing the celebration of the senses.

—

CONCEIVED BY: Nick & Chloé vs Zeitguised
FASHION EDITOR: Yoko Miyake

MATTHEW NIEDERHAUSER

INSTITUTE

212–213 Chateau Zhang Laffite, Beijing, the oriental twin of France's Château Maisons Laffitte Chateau Dynasty, Tianjin, a vineyard designed in a similar style to that of Montaigne's castle in France.Two from a series for "Counterfeit Paradises," July 2012, an article that explores the cracks between the cities developing across China.

MARCUS NILSSON

JMI

214, 216, 217 Tripe, Lamb's Brain Terrine and Deviled Lamb's Kidneys, three from a series for "Guts of the Beast," October 2012, about English chef Fergus Henderson.

—

ART DIRECTOR: Alexander Spacher
CLIENT: Black Ink/American Express
STYLISTS: Angharad Bailey, Victoria Granof

215 Fruit from the Central de Abasto wholesale market in Mexico City, one for the article "Strange Fruit," January 2013.

—

ART DIRECTOR: James Casey
PUBLICATION: Swallow

LANDON NORDEMAN

208–209 Two from a series for the article "Canine Kingdom," October 2, 2012, iPhone photographs for the magazine's Instagram feed covering four dog shows in Romania.

—

DIRECTOR OF PHOTOGRAPHY: Whitney Johnson
PHOTO EDITOR: Maria Lokke
PUBLICATION: The New Yorker

210–211 Two from a series for the article "The Force is Strong," December 2012, about the biannual Star Wars celebration in Orlando, Florida.

—

DIRECTOR OF PHOTOGRAPHY: Mia Diehl
PHOTO EDITOR: Michelle Wolfe
PUBLICATION: Fortune

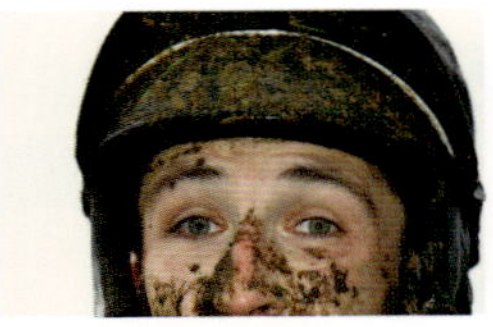
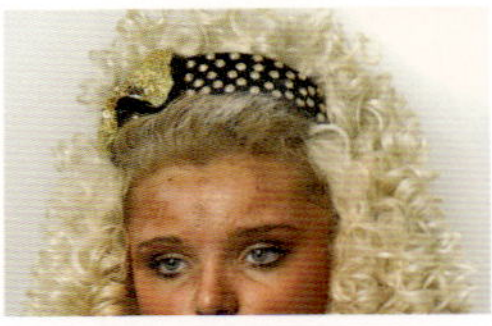
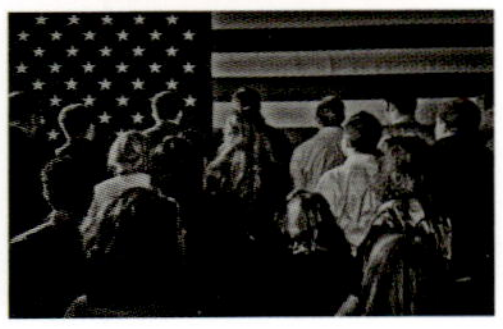
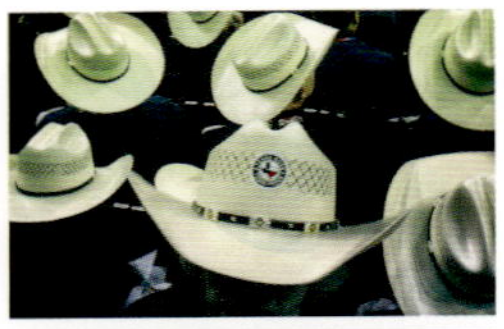
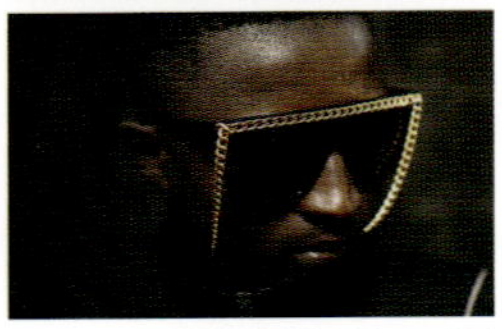
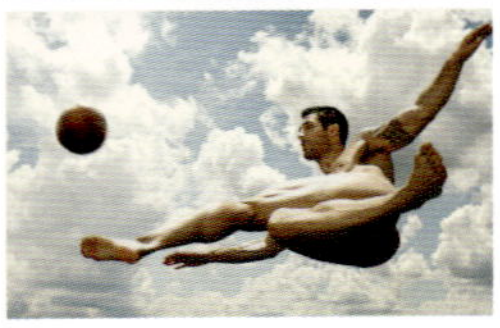
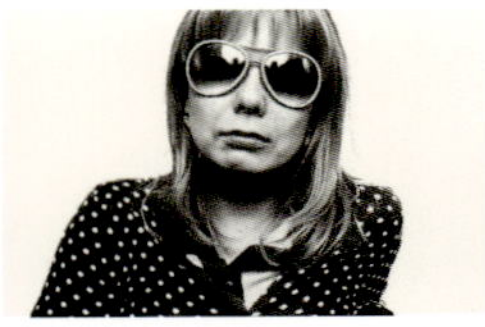
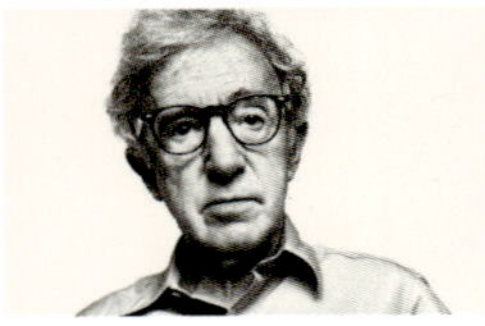
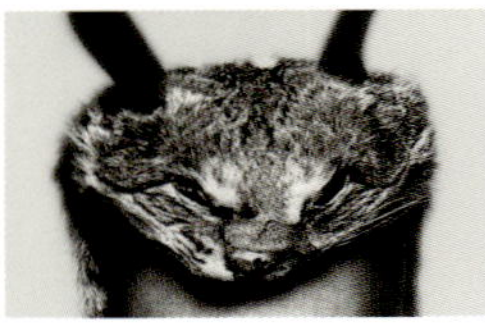
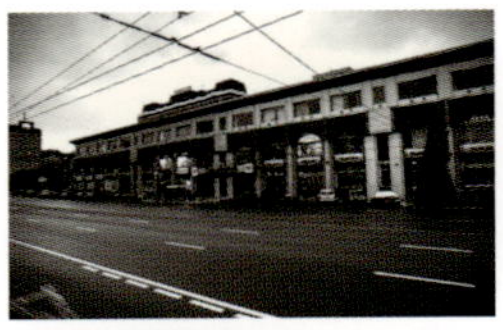
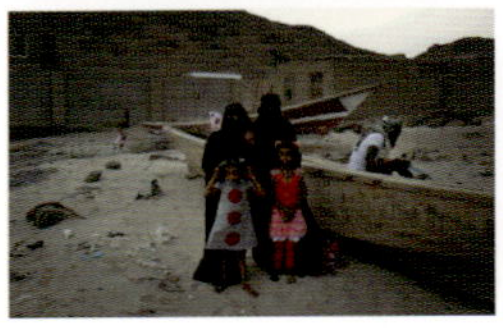
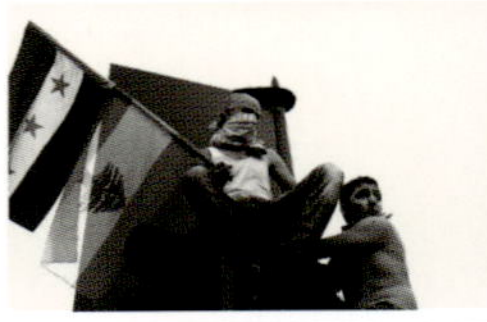
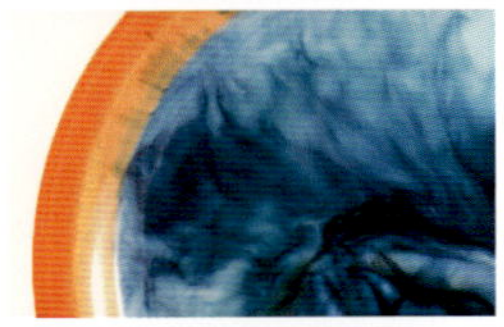
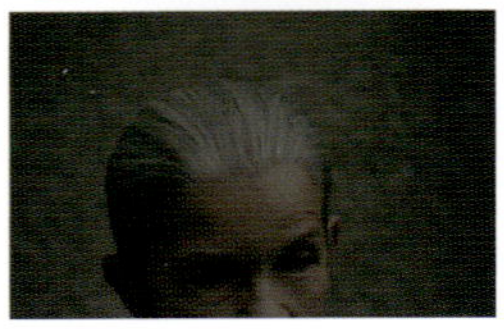
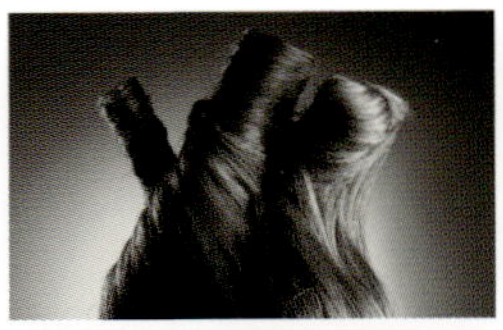
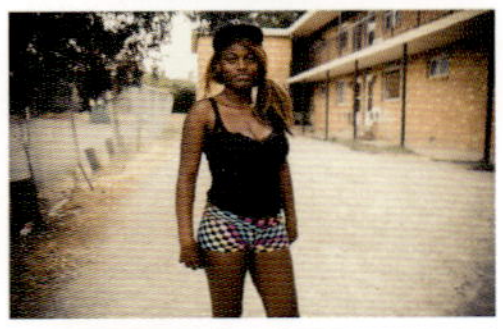
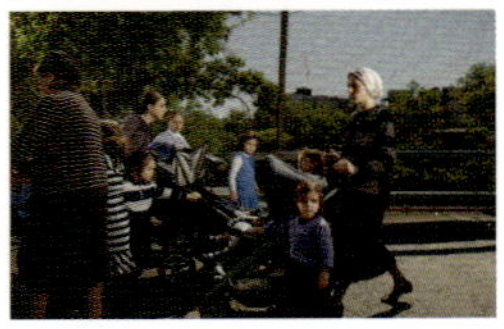
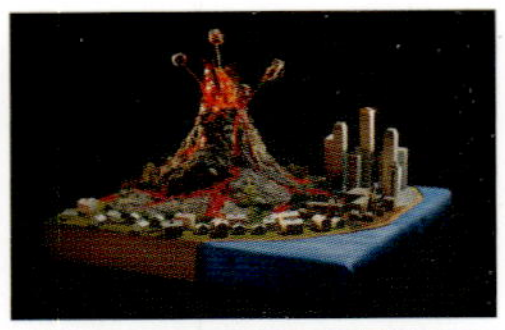
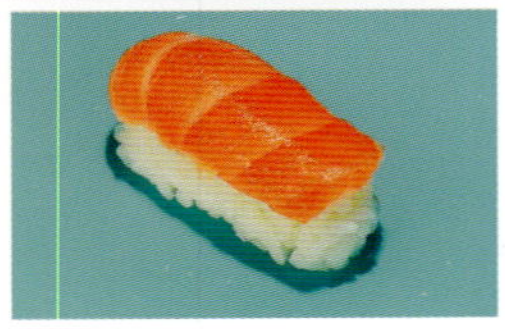

KENNETH O'HALLORAN

220–221 Eddie O'Connell and Ruby Walsh, Jockeys, two portraits from a series for the article "Muddy Business," November 11, 2012.

222 Karajane Hesford, 12, of Glasgow, from the nine-day World Irish Dancing Championships in Belfast, one for the article "The Jig in On," June 17, 2012.

—

DESIGN DIRECTOR: Arem Duplessis
DIRECTOR OF PHOTOGRAPHY: Kathy Ryan
ART DIRECTOR: Gail Bichler
ASSOCIATE ART DIRECTOR: Caleb Bennett
ASSOCIATE PHOTO EDITOR: Stacey Baker
DEPUTY PICTURE EDITOR: Joanna Milter
DESIGNER: Drea Zlanabitnig
EDITOR-IN-CHIEF: Hugo Lindgren
PUBLICATION: The New York Times Magazine

CHARLES OMMANNEY
Reportage by Getty Images

218–219 Two from a story that documents the candidates, voters and events surrounding the 2012 U.S. presidential election.

—

PHOTO EDITOR: Elizabeth Johnson

MARK PETERSON
Redux Pictures

223 The Texas delegation at the Republican National Convention in Tampa, Fl. on August 28, 2012, for the online article "Sea of Hats," August 2012.

—

DIRECTOR OF PHOTOGRAPHY: Dora Somosi
PUBLICATION: GQ.com

PER-ANDERS PETTERSSON
Works Artists, New York

224–227 Four from a series about the Sapeur movement in Kinshasa, Congo, DRC, men who dress up in European and Japanese fashion labels and compete and perform in street and corporate events.

RICHARD PHIBBS
Art Department

232 U.S. Men's National Soccer Team defender Carlos Bocanegra flying through the clouds for the annual "Bodies We Want" photo portfolio of nude athletes, July 2012.

—

DIRECTOR OF PHOTOGRAPHY: Karen Frank
PHOTO EDITOR: Freyda Tavin
PUBLICATION: ESPN The Magazine

PLATON

228 Yulia Simonova leads the Perspektiva, a Russian organization that works toward a better quality of life for people with disabilities, for the article "A Russia For All Russians," October 8, 2012.

—

PHOTO EDITOR: Marion Durand
PUBLICATION: Newsweek

229 Woody Allen photographed at his office in New York, one for the article "Woody Allen's Black Magic," June 25, 2012.

—

SENIOR PHOTO EDITOR: Carolyn Rauch
PUBLICATION: Newsweek

230–231 Two for Portfolio By Platon, March 26, 2012, a series of photographs of designs by Elsa Schiaparelli and Miuccia Prada.

—

CREATIVE DIRECTOR: Wyatt Mitchell
DIRECTOR OF PHOTOGRAPHY: Whitney Johnson
PHOTO EDITORS: Elissa Curtis, Maria Lokke, James Pomerantz, Jessie Wender
PUBLICATION: The New Yorker

MARIA PLESHKOVA

233–234 Two from Landscapes of Protest, May 6, 2012, an ongoing personal series of diptychs that show a location during a protest and afterward in Moscow.

ALEX POTTER
Polaris Images

236 Mohammad sits with his family in their village of Kupbagan, outside Aden, Yemen, For My Family, August 2012, student work.

—

SCHOOL: American University of Beirut

237 Young people attacked the Grand Serail in Beirut, Lebanon following the funeral of Wissam al Hassan, After the Funeral, October 2012, student work.

—

SCHOOL: American University of Beirut

MELISSA PUNCH
Big Leo

235 Blue Splash, January 2013, part of a personal project mixing milk and ink. Inspired by liquid, air and finding movement in still objects.

RAINA+WILSON
Kith and Kin

242 Actress Genevieve Bujold, for a story, January 2013.

—

ART DIRECTOR: Patrice Larose
CREATIVE DIRECTOR: Chantal Levesque
PUBLICATION: Reader's Digest

TRAVIS RATHBONE
Apostrophe Reps

238 Still life for the Bulletins section opener "Comb For Clues," October 2012.

—

CREATIVE DIRECTOR: Robert Festino
DIRECTOR OF PHOTOGRAPHY: Jeanne Graves
SENIOR PHOTO EDITOR: Michelle Stark
PUBLICATION: Men's Health

TAMARA REYNOLDS
RepGirl.com

239 Jefferson St, one from Southern Route, an ongoing, personal series about the South, for exhibition and publication.

NICK RUECHEL

240–241 Satmar Hasidim, Brooklyn, NY, 2012, two as part of the personal project Hasidim, a series of unpublished photographs of Hasidic Jews in Brooklyn, NY.

DAN SAELINGER
Apostrophe

257–258 A 12-year-old boy interprets superstitions about how the world will end, two from a series for the article "That's All Folks," February 2012.

—

DIRECTOR OF PHOTOGRAPHY: Allyson Torrisi
MODEL MAKER: Megan Caponetto
PUBLICATION: Popular Mechanics

259–260 Two as part of a campaign of tongue-in-cheek photo diptychs of objects for moms and their kids for the launch of Nickelodeon's new network Nick Mom, October 2012.

—

CREATIVE DIRECTOR: Keira Alexandra
AGENCY: Employee 1
CLIENT: Nickelodeon

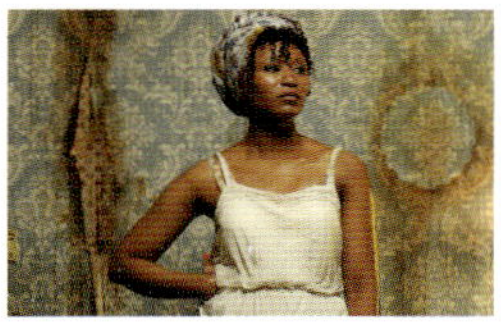
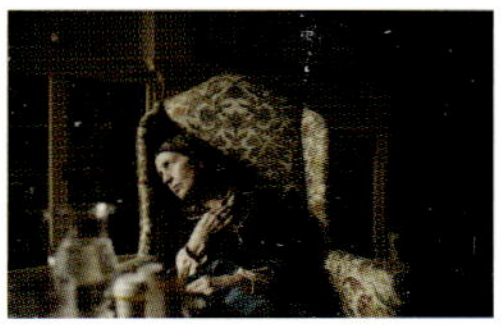
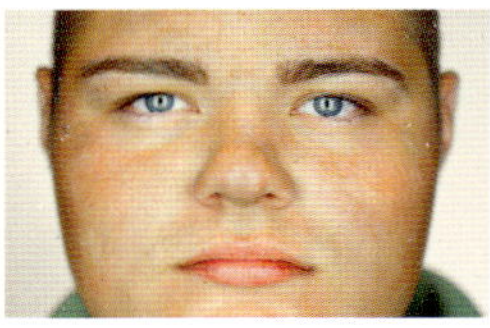
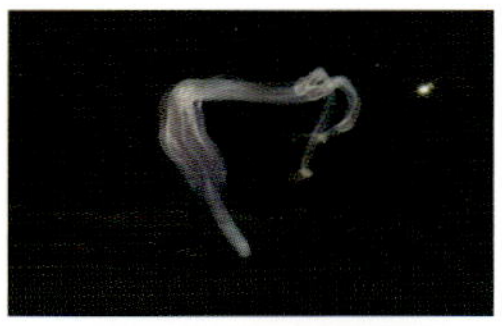
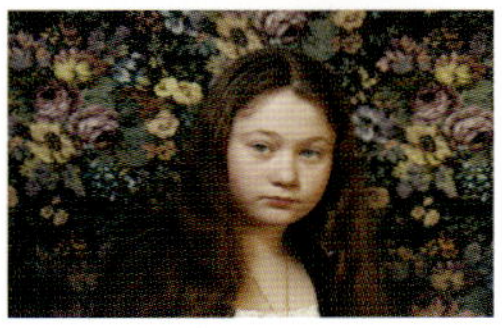
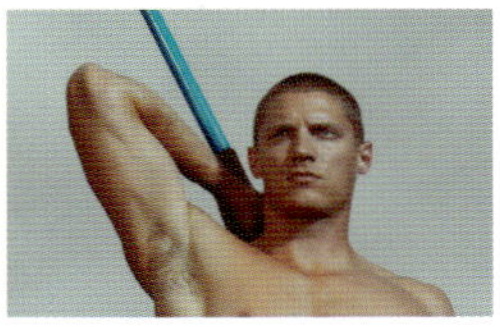
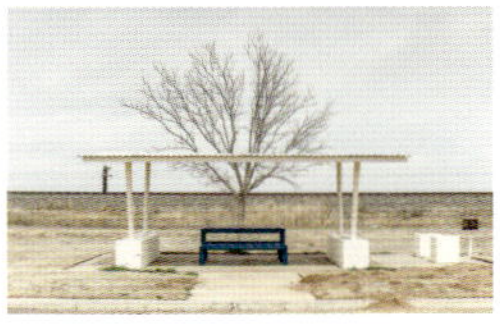
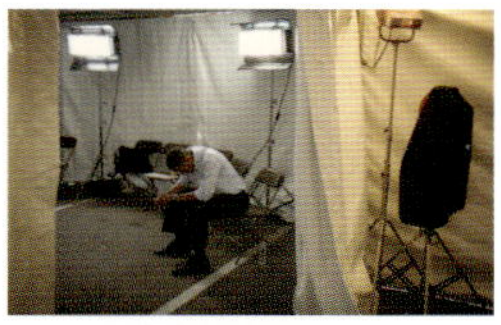
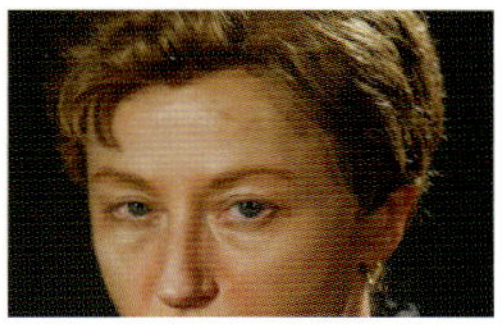
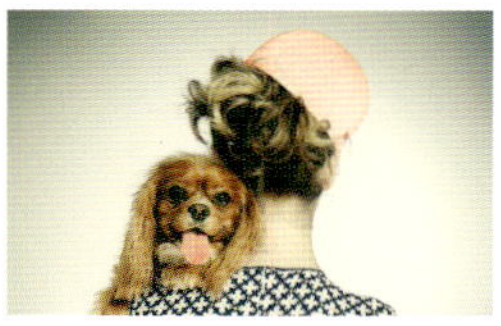
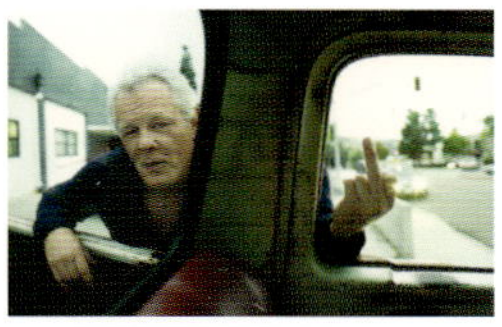
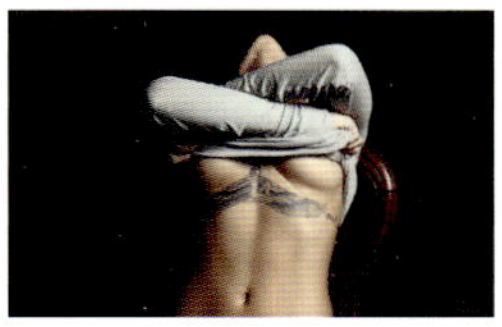
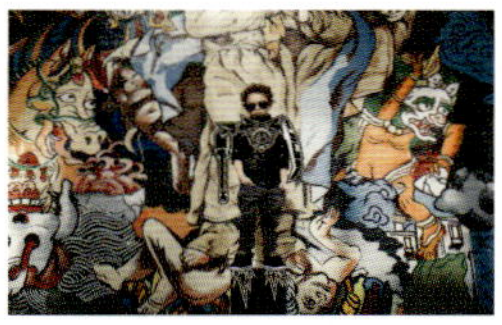
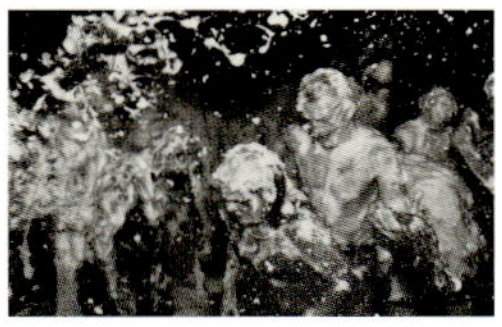
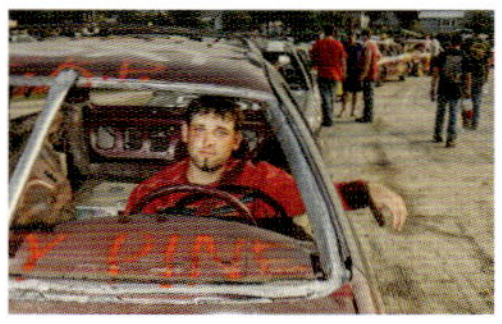
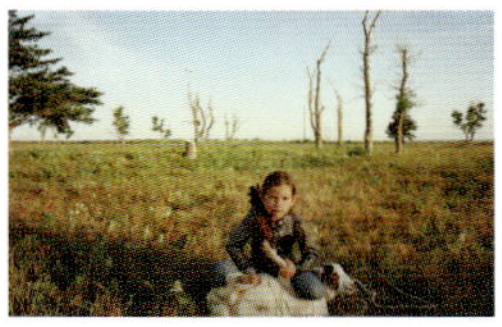

SANDRO
Patti Schumann

243 Image created for the playbill and advertising for the Steppenwolf Theatre production of Head of Passes, June 2012.
—
CREATIVE DIRECTORS: Joe Sciarrotta, Gabriel Chu Usadel
DESIGNER: Rod Hunting
AGENCY: Ogilvy & Mather, Chicago
CLIENT: Steppenwolf Theatre

244–245 Two from a series for Xgeva Global Disease State Awareness Campaign, March 2012, created for the drug Xgeva, used to prevent bone fractures and other skeletal conditions in people with tumors that have spread to the bone.
—
CREATIVE DIRECTOR: Glenn Batkin
ART DIRECTORS: Jenn Ng, Matt Shih
COPY WRITERS: Joen Moen, Adam Siers
AGENCY: CDM
CLIENT: Amgen

MARTIN SCHOELLER
Vaughan Hannigan

247–250 Four from a series for the book Identical: Portraits of Twins, December 2012, a landmark photographic study of twins and multiples using distinctive close-up portrait style, capturing every subtle aspect of their facial structure, myriad similarities and seemingly miniscule—yet significant—differences.
—
PUBLICATION: Identical: Portraits of Twins

FRANK SCHOTT
251–252 Project 12:31, January 2012, two from a series of motion-video light drawings created with data from the Visible Human Project.
—
ART DIRECTOR: Croix Gagnon

ROBIN SCHWARTZ
ClampArt Gallery

254 One from Amelia's World Project, January 2012. The photographer and her daughter share an affinity with the animal kingdom, playing out fantasies and exploring eccentricities by creating fables where animals coexist and interact as full partners in their invented world.

CARLOS SERRAO
Beauty & Photo

262–263 Trey Hardee, Silver medalist decathlete in the London 2012 Olympics, cover and inside portraits for "Notes from an Alchemist," July 2012, a feature about athleticism and physicality.
—
CREATIVE DIRECTOR: Hannah McCaughey
PHOTO EDITOR: Amy Silverman
PUBLICATION: Outside

NICOLÒ SERTORIO
SmartMagna

255 33°44′32″ N 102°3′36″ W, one from a personal project about U.S. interstate rest-areas, January 2013. Safety rest areas, part of the U.S. interstate road system since the early '60s, are managed by individual state departments of transportation; hence the disparate philosophies, designs and conditions.

CALLIE SHELL
Aurora

261 After a long day, U.S. President Obama waits in a tent before a rally at the Rochester Commons, August 18, 2012, one for the article "Obama Plays Hard Ball," September 10, 2012.
—
DESIGN DIRECTOR: DW Pine
DIRECTOR OF PHOTOGRAPHY: Kira Pollack
DEPUTY ART DIRECTOR: Chrissy Dunleavy
DEPUTY PICTURE EDITOR: Paul Moakley
PUBLICATION: TIME

CINDY SHERMAN
266 Self-portrait by Cindy Sherman for the Spring Fashion issue, in conjunction with her upcoming retrospective at the Museum of Modern Art, February 22, 2012.
—
DIRECTOR OF PHOTOGRAPHY: Jody Quon
EDITOR-IN-CHIEF: Adam Moss
PUBLICATION: New York

EMILY SHUR
246 Drake with model, Los Angeles, one from a series for the fashion story "Dog Days," February 2012.
—
PHOTO EDITOR: Mickey Boardman
PUBLICATION: Paper

PEGGY SIROTA
Elyse Connolly

256 Nick Nolte, one for the article "The Madman of Malibu," January 2012. People's Sexiest Man Alive 20 years ago is now better known for a mug shot that he's oddly proud of.
—
DESIGN DIRECTOR: Fred Woodward
DIRECTOR OF PHOTOGRAPHY: Dora Somosi
SENIOR PHOTO EDITOR: Krista Prestek
PUBLICATION: GQ

MARIO SORRENTI
Art Partner

264 Rihanna, one for the feature "Obsession of the Year," December 2012, about how she drove men wild even before she released the sexiest and most outrageous album of the year.
—
DESIGN DIRECTOR: Fred Woodward
DIRECTOR OF PHOTOGRAPHY: Dora Somosi
SENIOR PHOTO EDITOR: Krista Prestek
PUBLICATION: GQ

STOLTZE & STEFANIE
253 One for "Imaginary Superheros," January 2012, part of a series for a luxury European kids magazine. Shot in scouted locations throughout lower Manhattan, the concept to reimagine a child's perspective of being a superhero was translated into illustration and placed in post-production.
—
CREATIVE DIRECTOR: Stefanie Djie
ASSISTANT: Katherine Bayard
ILLUSTRATOR: Christopher Chai
STYLIST: Mambi
PUBLICATION: Kikimora

ALEC SOTH
265 A foam party at Crazy Legs Saloon, in Watertown, NY, one from a series for the article "There Will Be Foam," November 18, 2012.
—
DESIGN DIRECTOR: Arem Duplessis
DIRECTOR OF PHOTOGRAPHY: Kathy Ryan
ART DIRECTOR: Gail Bichler
ASSOCIATE PHOTO EDITOR: Stacey Baker
DEPUTY ART DIRECTOR: Caleb Bennett
DEPUTY PICTURE EDITOR: Joanna Milter
DESIGNER: Drea Zlanabitnig
EDITOR-IN-CHIEF: Hugo Lindgren
PUBLICATION: The New York Times Magazine

BEN STECHSCHULTE
Redux Pictures

267–268 Two from a series for the article "Dude, Where's My Windshield?" August 5, 2012, about demolition derby participants at the Essex County Fair in Westport, NY.
—
DESIGN DIRECTOR: Arem Duplessis
DIRECTOR OF PHOTOGRAPHY: Kathy Ryan
ART DIRECTOR: Gail Bichler
ASSOCIATE PHOTO EDITOR: Stacey Baker
DEPUTY ART DIRECTOR: Caleb Bennett
ASSOCIATE PHOTO EDITOR: Clinton Cargill
DEPUTY PICTURE EDITOR: Joanna Milter
DESIGNER: Sara Cwynar
EDITOR-IN-CHIEF: Hugo Lindgren
PUBLICATION: The New York Times Magazine

ILONA SZWARC
269–270 Rodeo Girls, March 2012, two from an ongoing personal project about young girls from Texas who compete in rodeos and their fundamentally different ideas about femininity and contrasting attitudes toward gender roles, student work.
—
SCHOOL: School of Visual Arts

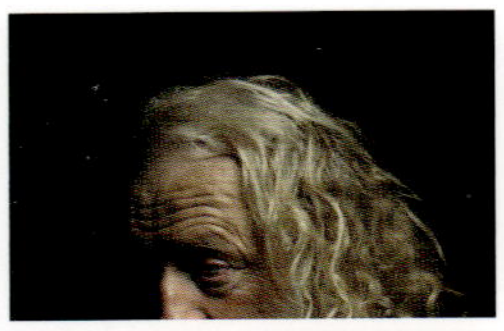
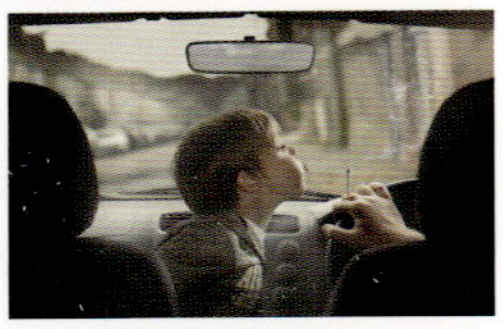
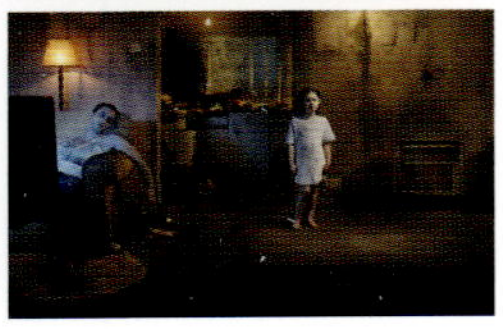
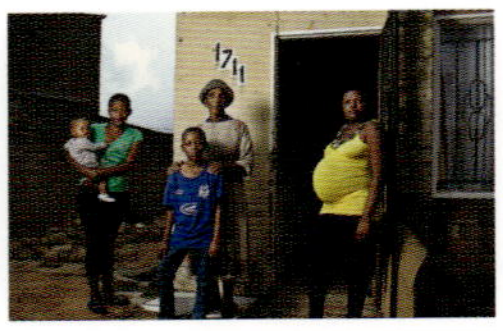
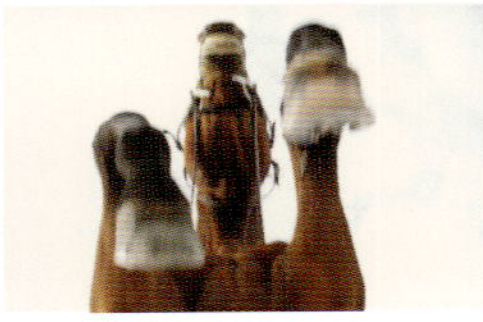
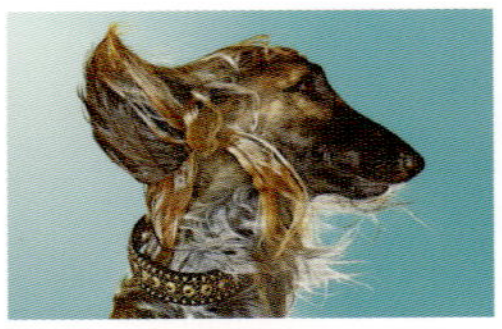
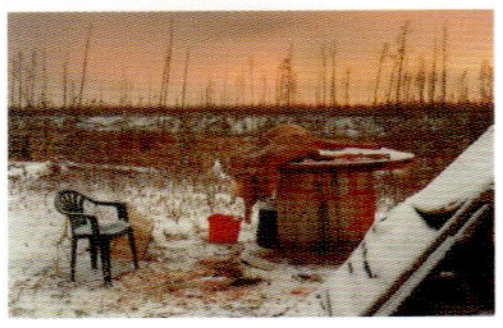
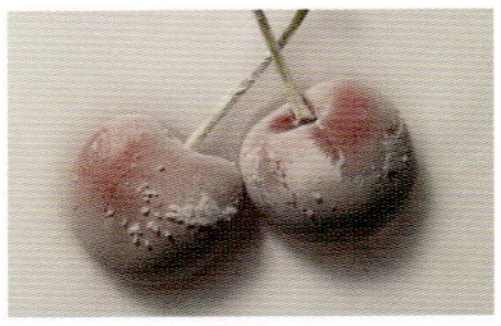
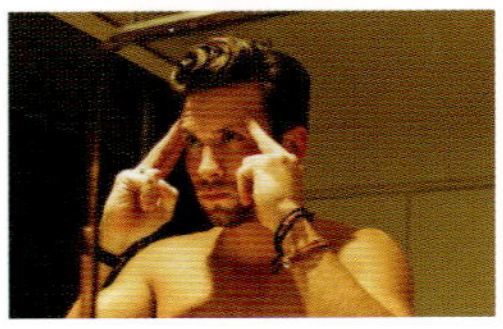
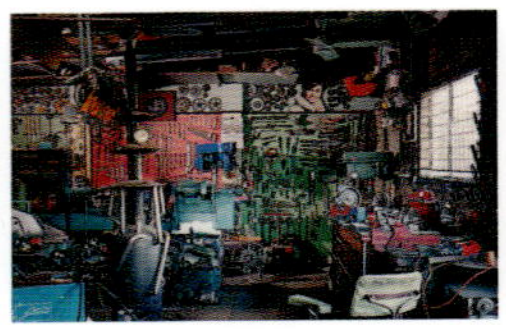
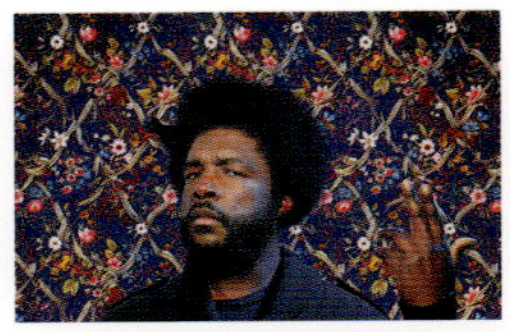
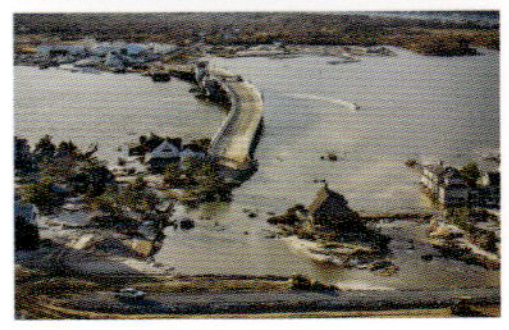
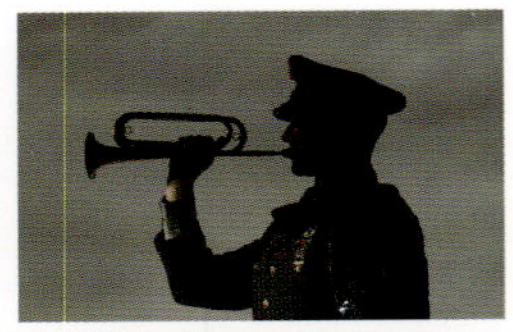
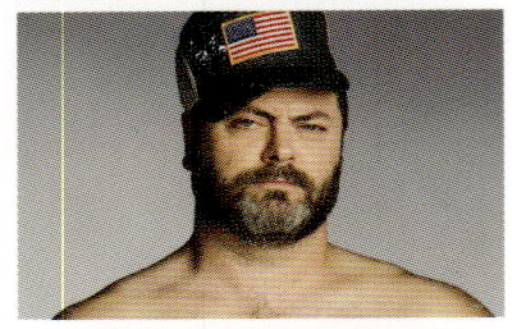
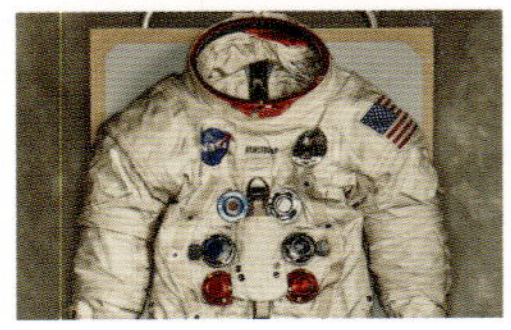

▼

ALEX TELFER

271 Santa Claus, December 2012, one for The Irish Society for the Prevention of Cruelty to Children (ISPCC), an Irish charity that advocates children's rights and provides services for children in need.

—

AGENCY: Laurence O'Byrne - Ogilvy Ireland
CLIENT: The Irish Society for the Prevention of Cruelty to Children

272 One for an anti-smoking campaign showing how children wish their smoking parents would quit, June 2012.

—

ART DIRECTOR: Dave Abbott
AGENCY: Golley Slater

273 One for a campaign for The Children's Panel, an organization that makes vital decisions about vulnerable children in need of care, including those who need legal representation at hearings.

—

ART DIRECTOR: Rufus Wedderburn
AGENCY: Newhaven

JONATHAN TORGOVNIK

Reportage by Getty Images

277 Alexandra Township, South Africa, one from a series for the article "A Generation Lost - Grannies and AIDS Orphans," December 2012.

DIRECTOR OF PHOTOGRAPHY: Kira Pollack
DEPUTY PHOTO EDITOR: Paul Moakley
PUBLICATION: TIME

MICHAEL TUREK

Bernstein & Andriulli

274–276 Horse Jump, March 2012, series of three for a feature about the Savannah College of Art and Design.

—

PUBLICATION: Departures

▼

GANDEE VASAN

Watson + Spierman Productions

278 Cartier, Afghan Hound, one from a series for "Dog's Rock," July 2012, a project that portrays dogs as rock stars!

—

ART BUYER: Clair DelaFons
ART DIRECTORS: Phoebe Coulton, Nicholas Tasker
AGENCY: TBWA London

AARON VINCENT ELKAIM

Boreal Collective

279 Fort McKay Trapline, Alberta, Canada, one from Sleeping with the Devil, July 2012, about the people of The First Nation Reserve in Northern Alberta's Boreal forest who prosper from a partnership in The Athabasca Oil Sands that surround them, but suffer health problems, pollution and lost wild life.

ADAM VOORHES

280 One for the article "Cherries on Ice," February 2012, a series of abstract images illustrating chilled cherries for the summer months.

—

PHOTO EDITOR: Susan Getzendanner
STYLIST: Robin Finlay
PUBLICATION: Bon Appetit

STEPHANIE VOVAS

Nest Artists

281 One from a series for the story "Diora's Key," April 2012, a triptych from a series inspired by Ang Lee's movie, The Ice Storm, in which married couples switched partners for the night.

—

PHOTO EDITOR: Rebecca Black
PUBLICATION: Treats!

▼

JASPER WHITE

Trayler & Trayler

286–287 Two from a personal project, November 2012, shot in various locations throughout Australia, revealing the private world of working men's sheds, each filled with the various ephemera of their lives and interests.

—

GALLERY: gallerynine5
ASSISTANTS: Arancha Chia, Lauren Trompp

KEHINDE WILEY

288 Portrait of musician Quest Love for the article "The Rhythm In Everything," November 12, 2012.

—

CREATIVE DIRECTOR: Wyatt Mitchell
DIRECTOR OF PHOTOGRAPHY: Whitney Johnson
PHOTO EDITORS: Elissa Curtis, Maria Lokke, James Pomerantz, Jessie Wender
PUBLICATION: The New Yorker

STEPHEN WILKES

Bernstein & Andriulli

282–285 Four from a series for the article "Flooded, Uprooted, Burned: The Tracks of Hurricane Sandy," November 26, 2012. Scenes from Jacob Riis Park, Queens, NY; Mantoloking, NJ; Breezy Point, Queens, NY; Oakwood, Staten Island, NY.

—

DESIGN DIRECTOR: DW Pine
DIRECTOR OF PHOTOGRAPHY: Kira Pollack
SENIOR ART DIRECTOR: Emily Crawford
ASSOCIATE PHOTO EDITOR: Bridget Harris
PUBLICATION: TIME

DAN WINTERS

289 U.S. soldier, cover photograph for "One A Day - The War On Suicide?" July 23, 2012, an article about soldiers and suicide in the U.S. military.

—

DESIGN DIRECTOR: DW Pine
DIRECTOR OF PHOTOGRAPHY: Kira Pollack
PUBLICATION: TIME

290 Actor Nick Offerman for the "Proud List of the 25 Most American Things You Can Do Today (That You Can't Do in Socialist Europe or Some Other Backwater)," July 2012.

—

DESIGN DIRECTOR: Fred Woodward
DIRECTOR OF PHOTOGRAPHY: Dora Somosi
SENIOR PHOTO EDITOR: Krista Prestek
PUBLICATION: GQ

291 Neil Armstrong's Spacesuit at the Smithsonian Air and Space Museum, July 2012.

—

PHOTO EDITOR: Molly Roberts
PUBLICATION: Smithsonian

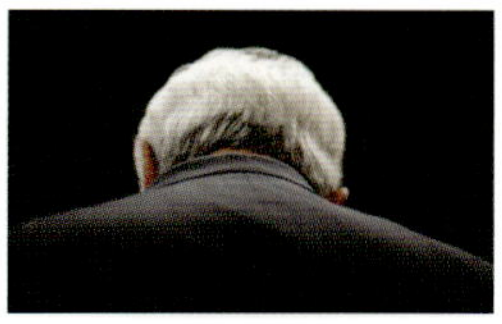
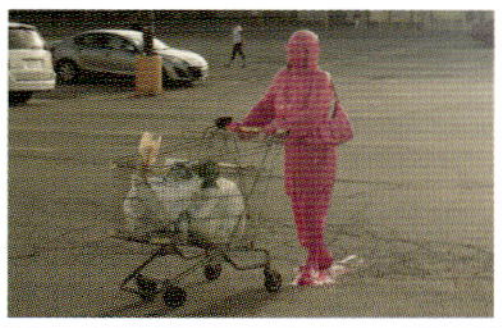
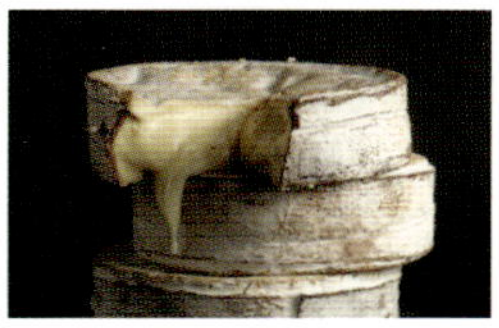
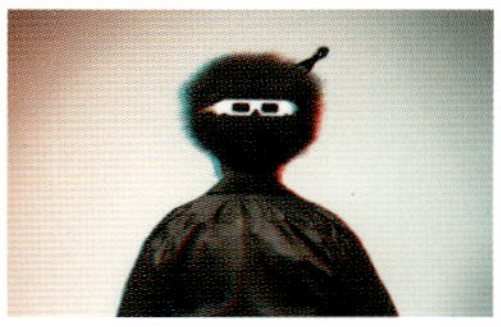
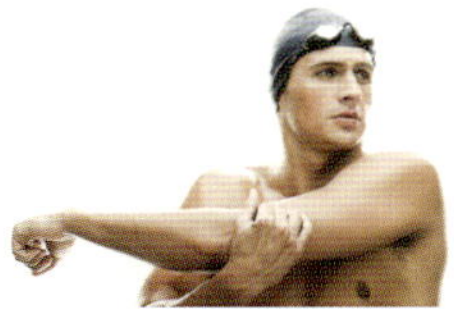
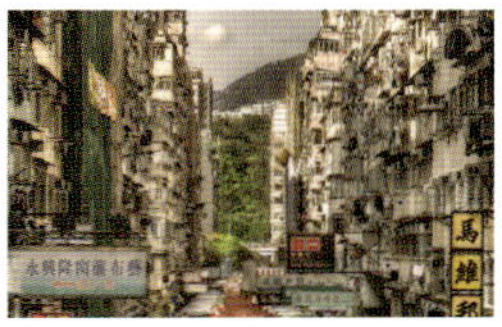

MARCUS YAM
292 Former Speaker of the House Newt Gingrich campaigns during the New Hampshire Primary in Manchester, NH, January 2012.

ROMULO YANES
295 Rush Creek Reserve from Uplands Cheese Company, one for the feature "2012 Tastemakers," March 2012.

—

CREATIVE DIRECTOR: Alex Grossman
DIRECTOR OF PHOTOGRAPHY: Alex Pollack
PHOTO EDITOR: Susan Getzendanner
PUBLICATION: Bon Appetit

PETER YANG
293 Olympic swimmer Ryan Lochte, one for the 2012 Olympic Preview Table of Contents page, July 2012.

—

CREATIVE DIRECTOR: Robert Festino
DIRECTOR OF PHOTOGRAPHY: Brenda Milis
PHOTO EDITOR: Mark Haddad
PUBLICATION: Men's Health

BRIAN YEN
294 Mongkok, Hong Kong, part of the personal series Ebb and Flow, depicting the flow of humanity from morning to night, from their beds to the city's streets as a growing mass.

MARK ZIBERT
296 Campaign for the Museum of Contemporary Canadian Art, October 2012. Tagline: Get Contemporary.

—

CLIENT: Museum of Contemporary Canadian Art

297 Questlove, portrait for a campaign for ADCOLOR, a nonprofit organization that promotes diversity in advertising, October 2012.

—

CLIENT: ADCOLOR

AGENCIES/CLIENTS/ DESIGN FIRMS/GALLERIES

ART/CREATIVE/ DESIGN DIRECTORS

DESIGNERS

PHOTO EDITORS

PUBLICATIONS

REPRESENTATIVES

SCHOOLS

STYLISTS

AMERICAN PHOTOGRAPHY 29 CHOSEN

We congratulate the following 130 photographers for receiving at least two votes from our jury. Participating chosen photographer's work can be found online in The Archive at ai-ap.com with complete contact info, captions and credits in a searchable collection that also includes the selected images in this book.

Lamia Maria Abillama
Erik Almass
Jason Andrew
Zachary Bako
Ball & Albanese
Emily Berl
Brett Beyer
Jerome Bonnet
Mathias Braschler & Monika Fischer
Robin Broadbent
Jean-Marc Caimi
Gregory Costanzo
Cameron Davidson
Gregg Delman
Yongshen Deng
Stephanie Diani
Dirk Anschutz Dirk
Nicholas Duers
Bryce Duffy
Michael Duva
Paul Edmondson
Matt Eich
Dwight Eschliman
Mitchell Feinberg
Philip Ficks
Ryan Field
Sarina Finkelstein
Laurie Frankel
Andrea Frazzetta
Matt Furman
Nick Gaetano
Massimo Gammacurta
William Garrett
Danny Ghitis
Glenn Glasser
Melissa Golden
Jim Golden
Andy Goodwin
Rebecca Harlan
David Harvey
Aaron Hewitt
Brendan Hoffman
Andrew Holbrooke
Bill Hornstein
Rainer Hosch
Sandy Huffaker
Kathryn Allen Hurni
Vance Jacobs
Janet Jarman
Greg Kahn
Jonathon Kambouris
Sam Kaplan
Ed Kashi
Amelia Katz
Ingvar Kenne
T.J. Kirkpatrick
Jamie Kripke
John Kuczala
Gaston Lacombe
Frederic Lafargue
Nick Laham
Jeremy M. Lange
Gillian Laub
Catherine Ledner
Thomas Lee
Mark Leong
Gina LeVay
David Leventi
Michael Limbert
Amy Lombard
John Loomis
Megan Maloy
Vittoria Mentasti
Greg Miller
Jeff Minton
Logan Mock-Bunting
Danielle Moir
Montalbetti+Campbell
Geoff Moore
RJ Muna
Mark Murrmann
Wynn Myers
Andrew B. Myers
Raphael Ouellet
Rachel Papo
Kate T. Parker
Peden+Munk
Christopher Peters
Ethan Pines
Dan Poyourow
Joe Pugliese
Dirk Rees
Tamara Reynolds
Jessica Sample
Aaron Joel Santos
Deniz Saylan
Kevin Scanlon
Michael Schnabel
Ryan Schude
Gregg Segal
Chris Sembrot
Derek Shapton
Kevin Shea Adams
Erica Shires
Phillip Simpson
Ben Sklar
Matt Slaby
Ali Smith
Andrew Spear
Sean Sprague
Kevin Steele
Justin Steele
Rob Stephenson
Simon Stock
Art Streiber
Braden Summers
Chris Thomaidis
Bryan Thomas
Robert Trachtenberg
Alina Tsvietkova
Richard Tuschman
Terry Vine
David Vintiner
Stephen Voss
Sandra Chen Weinstein
Matthew Welch
Lisa Wiltse
Winni Wintermeyer
James Worrell
Ji Yeo

American Photography 29 presents the winning images from our annual competition held in February 2013 in New York City. From 9,075 images submitted by 875 photographers, magazines, agencies, publishers and schools only 299 were Selected by a majority vote or better to appear in the book, representing the best images from 2012 (295 professional, 4 student). Another 185 images were then Chosen with at least two votes to appear on our website (177 professional, 8 student).

American Photography 29 was launched November 6-7th, 2013 at The Party, our annual event held at the Angel Orensanz Foundation on New York City's Lower East Side. The book launch was held in conjunction with our BIG TALK symposium.

All winning images with contact for the photographers are included on The Archive, AI-AP's online juried collection at ai-ap.com, searchable by volume, photographer, creative, publication, client, school, instructor and subject.

American Photography 29, designed by Robert Festino, creative director of Men's Health magazine, was produced with a slipcase cover that includes a photograph by Tamas Dezso printed on foil paper. The two-piece, hardcover book includes a photograph by Christopher Griffith that was originally commissioned by The New Yorker. AP29 is 384 pages, printed 4-color throughout on 150gsm matt art paper with spot varnish and uses Courier and Futura typefaces.

The Selected photographs are presented in alphabetical order, one-image-per-page with a special back of the book image index that lists the image captions and complete creative credits along with a creative index that lists all personnel, publications, clients, representatives, galleries, and schools involved in the creation and utilization of the winning images. A complete list of the Chosen photographers whose work appears online can be found in the back of this book.

If you are a photographer, art director, designer, publisher, artist representative, student or educator, or anyone who commissions photography and would like to submit work to the next annual competition, join our mailing list at: ai-ap.com/register

American Photography
15 East 32nd Street, 7th Floor
New York, NY 10016
917-408-9944
info@ai-ap.com
ai-ap.com

Deadline to the next American Photography 30 Call For Entries will be in January 2014.

Additional features on the winning photographers along with related articles about the global creative community can be found on DART: Design Arts Daily, Pro Photo Daily, Motion Arts Pro and Dispatches from Latin America. To subscribe for free, go to: ai-ap.com/register.

Distributor to North America and the World:

D.A.P./Distributed Art Publishers
155 Sixth Avenue, 2nd Floor,
New York, NY 10013
Telephone: 212-627-1999
Fax: 212-627-9484
Orders to the Trade:
800-338-2665

Direct Mail /
Discount Subscription Orders:

Amilus Inc.
15 East 32nd Street, 7th Floor
New York, NY 10016
917-408-9944

info@ai-ap.com or order online at: ai-ap.com

ISBN 10: 1-886212-40-6
ISBN 13: 978-1-886212-40-4

Printed and bound by Prolong Press Limited, CHINA